Encyclopedia of Local History

About the Series
The American Association for State and Local History Book Series publishes technical and professional information for those who practice and support history, and addresses issues critical to the field of state and local history. To submit a proposal or manuscript to the series, please request proposal guidelines from AASLH headquarters: AASLH Book Series, 1717 Church St., Nashville, Tennessee 37203. Telephone: (615) 320-3203. Fax: (615) 327-9013. Web site: <www.aaslh.org>.

About the Organization
The American Association for State and Local History (AASLH) is a nonprofit educational organization dedicated to advancing knowledge, understanding, and appreciation of local history in the United States and Canada. In addition to sponsorship of this book series, the Association publishes the periodical *History News*, a newsletter, technical leaflets and reports, and other materials; confers prizes and awards in recognition of outstanding achievement in the field; and supports a broad educational program and other activities designed to help members work more effectively. To join the organization, contact: Membership Director, AASLH, 1717 Church St., Nashville, Tennessee 37203.

Encyclopedia
of
Local History

CAROL KAMMEN
and
NORMA PRENDERGAST

A Division of
ROWMAN & LITTLEFIELD PUBLISHERS, INC.
Walnut Creek • Lanham • New York • Oxford

ALTAMIRA PRESS
A Division of Rowman & Littlefield Publishers, Inc.
1630 North Main Street, Suite 367
Walnut Creek, CA 94596
http://www.altamirapress.com

Rowman & Littlefield Publishers, Inc.
4720 Boston Way
Lanham, Maryland 20706

12 Hid's Copse Road
Cumnor Hill, Oxford OX2 9JJ, England

British Library Cataloguing in Publication Information Available

Library of Congress Cataloging-in-Publication Data
Kammen, Carol, 1937–
    Encyclopedia of local history / Carol Kammen and Norma Prendergast.
        p. cm. — (American Association for State and Local History book series)
    Includes bibliographical references.
    ISBN 0-7425-0399-2 (cloth : alk. paper)
    1. United States—History, Local—Research—Encyclopedias. 2. United
States—Historiography—Encyclopedias. I. Prendergast, Norma. II. Title.
III. Series.
    E180 .K25 2000
    973'.07'2—dc21   00-060560

Printed in the United States of America

for
MICHAEL *and* **OLIVER**

CONTENTS

A NOTE ABOUT THIS BOOK

It is easier to define this book by stating what it is not: this encyclopedia is not about the history of a specific place; it is not an encyclopedia of American or even North American history. It is, rather, a companion to aid local and regional historians, and many others interested in the history of place, to think about and research that history. This book presents ideas to consider, sources to use, and historical fields and trends to explore, and it provides commentary—useful, whimsical, and otherwise—on a number of subjects that local historians encounter every day.

One of our goals is to encourage local researchers to think about the context of local events and institutions, to move beyond the records in a locality in order to understand an event or institution in a broader regional or national context. The book helps by providing information about how fields of history developed and which classic works might be consulted for the information contained, the methodology used, or the bibliographic references.

Another topic considered here is how local history is thought about and "done" elsewhere. (See the essays about local history in England, Scotland, New Zealand, Germany, Nigeria, and Canada among the countries represented.) Not every country is included, but a number are here to provide ideas about what others are doing.

The topics in this book evolved. Some we included because we thought they would be helpful; others we thought would be explanatory or that we simply found interesting ourselves. Some entries are included because they extend an individual's way of thinking about or "doing" local history. We accepted the advice of a number of people who suggested additions to the book or who took a topic and shaped it as he or she saw fit. We encouraged writers to speak directly to the reader, and not attempt what is often called an "encyclopedic tone."

Some topics included in this book will be those researchers will look for: Sanborn maps, for example, or Indian history, or ethics. But much of what is included might not be expected, so some entries—such as the delightful essay on virtual shopping or the commentaries on slang—we suspect readers will come upon serendipitously. We hope that both approaches will lead readers forward. We have provided a number of references that link topics together.

We happen to live near a marvelous research library, but not everyone does. The references in most entries, however, assume that everyone has access to interlibrary loan. If you have not used this service in the past, we trust you will meet and get to know the interlibrary loan librarian in your community, for this service can link you to all or most of the books listed here.

There are some inconsistencies: some because of the interests of the people we talked to, some because we were limited in our author search to people we knew and were requested to contribute, or those we found or found us. All but two of our authors are linked to us by e-mail, and, because of our dependence upon that means of communication, we might have missed others who would have been equally generous and helpful. The readers of H-Local responded enthusiastically to our requests for aid, and we are grateful to them and to Randy Patton, Tom Costa, and Mary Mannix—the H-Local editors—for their aid.

How We Worked/What We Did

When we signed on to compile this book, Norma and I worked closely together to create an entry list. Our first attempt covered 20 or more pages and contained about 982 items. Seeing that list allowed us to realize what this book was not. So we started over again. What appears is partially here by design, partially by the interests and specialties of the authors, and partially by some sort of Clio-inspired luck.

Local history lends itself to a particular sort of encyclopedia, one that stresses the process of doing local history—the thinking about it, thinking about the particular public interested in local history, considering the role of local history in our various communities. So in the end, our entry list reflected thinking about local history rather than specific history topics, such as the Compromise of 1850—which you will not find here.

Once the entry list seemed reasonable, we divided the work: I contacted just about everyone I have ever known, heard of, or was put in touch with to write essays. The three common traits these authors had were that they were experts and willing to help us out and that they were, with two exceptions, on e-mail. This book would not exist without their generosity. What I learned in this process, which went on right up to the deadline, was that those I contacted were gracious and interested in aiding us.

As I gathered essays, I also began writing some; so did Norma, who handled the administrative side of the project: gathering the letters of permission required by the publisher, keeping records as to who had agreed to write what, and when those essays were due. As the essays began to come in (and some came immediately—one even arrived the day I requested it, breaking all sorts of records!) I read them, entered them in the main entry disc, and then Norma took them through the critical editing phase, setting editorial standards, and catching the little gremlins that sometimes appeared.

In May 1999 I began printing out chunks of the book, by letter groups. After that, we spent our days checking the entries, finding new essays that were needed, and responding to the suggestions of a number of people who wondered if we would be interested in a particular topic or if they could add something to the stew. We found all suggestions helpful and responded as quickly as we could to each of them. Most of these suggestions made their way into the book.

What we learned along the way is that we had more of a sense of what this book was all about *before* we started, than we did when we were in the middle of the process, and I am not sure yet that we have a sense of the whole. We realized quickly that this book is not really an encyclopedia—that is, an alphabetic listing of everything. That can't be done. This book is more a companion, a helpful friend, a nudging accomplice, a way of looking and of thinking about researching and presenting local history. We have left all the business about organizations and museums to other books; we felt we had enough to cover just managing the topics presented here.

We learned that people, given range to answer the most frequently asked questions about their area of expertise, as well as the questions novices and others don't necessarily know to ask, wrote sprightly and interesting essays. We learned also that the field of local history is, as we knew at the start, the grandest way of attempting to write history for, while the geographic area might be limited, the ways of looking at it and thinking about it present vast opportunities.

It has been a privilege to be the midwives of this book, and for me it has been a wonderful comfort to work with Norma Prendergast, who has brought to the work her keen sense of language, her wit, her picky ability to get things right, her inquiring mind always asking "whatever does this mean?" and her ability to find just the right way of tweaking an essay to help all of us communicate better.

We hope this book is, in the last word, useful. We don't think it is perfect, and those of you with suggestions about improvements, additions, or corrections for a future edition are encouraged to write to the publisher or e-mail me at <ckk6 @cornell.edu>. We had some problems: the major one was that we could not find authors for some of the essays we thought should be included. Even requests through H-Local, where the members were extraordinarily generous in helping us out, sometimes didn't end with positive results.

We wanted to call this book "a compendium of useful information, interesting scholarship, and other good stuff." Although to us that title seemed to be just right, others thought it a too casual and messy way of describing our volume. *Encyclopedia of Local History*, after all, sounds ever so much more sophisticated. But you will find this to be just what we said: a compendium of useful information, interesting scholarship, and other good stuff. Enjoy!

Carol Kammen

HOW TO USE THIS BOOK

We recommend that you look up topics that interest you: fields of history, sources for local history, questions you might have about ethics, historical truth, or copyrights. We hope that in doing so, an adjacent article will tempt you to see what it is all about.

We have also included a good deal of information about the Internet. This book provides an abundance of Internet addresses in which to further pursue local history topics. See databases for local history.

Throughout, there are "*"s that indicate cross-references from the essay you are reading to another with the asterisked title. Frequently, at the end of an essay there will be a "See" directing you to other essays that might be of interest. In this way a great many of the essays in the book are tied together.

The contributor or contributors is/are listed at the end of essay, except for some topics that were done "in house." To find out more about the contributor(s), you can refer to the "About the Contributors" section, which begins on page 527.

There are four appendices. The first one (Appendix A) alphabetically lists ethnic groups found in North America; the second one (Appendix B) lists religious organizations. In each of these a short current bibliography is provided. We refer readers back to the general essays in the book on "ethnic history" and "religious history." Everything else, we trust, is straightforward. Appendix C provides the names and addresses of major state historical organizations; and Appendix D does the same for National Archives and Records Administration (NARA) regional facilities.

C.K. & N.P.

ACKNOWLEDGMENTS

This book has been created by a number of people and we are pleased to be able to acknowledge their help and to offer them our thanks and friendship.

First, we recognize Barbara Howe, Hartman Lomawaima, Philip Scarpino, and Raymond Starr, who served as an advisory board for this book.

We owe a great debt to our husbands: Oliver French cheerfully solved all sorts of technical problems for us, and Michael Kammen listened endlessly to questions and worries and wrote a number of essays that appear here. We could not have had better partners for this enterprise, and in life itself.

A number of others have been extraordinarily gracious. We thank especially Ken Atkin, Judith Austin, Jere Daniell, Christopher Densmore, Jim Nasson, John Pearce, Alan Rogers, Jim Summerville, and Robert Tabak. Also, Terry Davis and her staff at AASLH.

Steven Kaplan, professor of French history at Cornell University, came to our rescue by locating a scholar to write the essay on French local history, as did Sherman Cochran, who suggested the author for Chinese local history, and I. V. Hull, who found a writer for the essay on German local history.

Jackie Hubble, of Cornell's Department of History aided us time and again when I could not get an attachment to open or thought I could do something on the computer but couldn't manage to figure out how.

The clever cartoon regarding family relationships that appears on page 181 was created by Tammy Ohr-Campbell, Norma's daughter-in-law. Her son is also among the authors.

The staff at Olin Library at Cornell University has been exceedingly helpful. The informative essay on the census was written by Robert Kibbee, and those on databases and vital statistics by Martha Hsu, both librarians at Cornell. Ann Sullivan of the Tompkins Cortland Community College contributed the essay on special websites. Other librarians have answered our questions, led us to works of reference, and gotten us out of snarls of others' or of our own creation.

Mitch Allen and Pam Winding of AltaMira Press have been supportive, as has been Dorothy Bradley of Rowman & Littlefield Publishing Group. Bob Kowkabany of Doric Lay Publishers has responded to our desire to have this book look as handsome as it is. We are indebted to Christopher Genevese and to Tina Thomas of the Sanborn Mapping Company for permission to use Sanborn designs.

While I do not think of myself as a technological person, this book would not happened without two recent innovations. We have both worked on computers, which have made the editorial process much easier than it would have been for people doing this sort of book 30 or 40 years ago. As the manuscript grew, the computer took care of the adjustments that would otherwise have mired us in typing and retyping. In addition, e-mail allowed me to "talk" to people across this country and all over the world, to gather information and essays, and to learn of others who were willing to aid this enterprise.

Creating the *Encyclopedia of Local History* has been a joint effort, between the two of us and the many people who appear here as contributors and those others who give us advice, led us to just the right person to write an essay, or were patient listeners when we had problems to talk out. We have found friends all over the country whose interest is how to do the local history of place and we trust this book will further that effort for all of us.

C.K. & N.P.

among whites, but an increasingly vocal movement played a crucial role in U.S. society after the 1830s. While a small number of sympathetic whites provided an essential biracial component to abolitionism, free Northern African Americans—many of them escaped slaves—remained the driving force behind the movement to abolish slavery and to attain full citizenship rights. One might say that the first African American civil rights movement took shape during the early 1800s.

That movement appeared to have achieved its goals during the Civil War era. Between 1865 and 1870 slavery was abolished, African Americans' citizenship rights were protected under the constitution, and black males were guaranteed the right to vote. By 1880, however, white-supremacist governments had reclaimed power in the South, and through violence, economic coercion, and legal trickery, quickly stripped Southern blacks of their rights and imposed the system of Jim Crow segregation that defined southern race relations up to the 1960s.

This erosion of black rights in the South was all the more important because, even as late as 1900, 90 percent of African Americans lived in that section. Under the system of sharecropping, blacks with little educational opportunity and few rights or options continued to provide the labor that supported the southern agricultural economy. The major political parties showed little interest in protecting African Americans' rights, so black activists worked for their economic, political, and civil rights largely through their own organizations.

The twentieth century brought both dramatic changes and disturbing continuities in the experiences of African Americans. One of the most striking developments has been the "Great Migration." In 1900, 90 percent of African Americans lived in the rural South. By 1960, over half of all African Americans lived in urban areas outside the South. While blacks in non-Southern cities generally found greater educational and employment opportunities and greater protections of their citizenship rights, they also found continued discrimination in housing, where restrictive policies limited most blacks to racially defined ghettos. In many respects the ghetto helped stimulate thriving community institutions and a growing black middle class. Urban African American writers, artists, and performers also began having a larger impact on American popular culture than ever before. But the limited opportunities of the ghetto helped to create problems in underemployment, crime, and poverty that continue to plague inner cities.

In the South, sharecropping, segregation, and white supremacy enforced by violence continued to define the experiences of most African Americans through World War II. After the war, mechanized agriculture displaced many black sharecroppers who increasingly moved to Northern, Western, and Southern cities to find employment. In addition, the modern civil rights movement began to challenge the racial order that had been in place since Reconstruction. By the mid-1960s the federal government finally began using its authority, through Supreme Court decisions and congressional legislation, to protect African Americans' constitutional rights. The system of legal segregation was gradually dismantled and black voting rights expanded markedly.

The gains of the civil rights movement in the South, however, were counterbalanced by the continued oppression of blacks in Northern and Western ghettos. Police brutality, discrimination in housing and education, and unemployment gave rise to a series of urban riots during the mid-1960s, illustrating blacks' frustration. The cry of "Black Power" swept out of the South, giving rise to movements for greater solidarity and community control among urban blacks. An emphasis on the distinctive elements of black American culture expressed itself in hairstyles, clothing, arts, and political activism, primarily geared toward the full empowerment of black Americans, both in their own communities and in American society as a whole.

There have been mixed results from the turmoil of the 1960s. Federal government protections have allowed an unprecedented degree of African American participation in politics, and educational and employment opportunities have expanded. But these advances have been uneven. While the black middle class has grown dramatically, a black underclass rooted in urban ghettos has also grown since the 1970s. Employment and educational opportunities are limited, and patterns of segregation in housing have changed little since the 1970s. America remains a racially divided nation, and African Americans, perhaps more than ever before, are divided internally along class lines. This situation has caused some analysts to suggest that black Americans in the 1990s faced their most severe crisis since the end of slavery.

The first generation of historians interested in African American history was comprised of free blacks in the Northern states between the 1840s and 1870s. Their early works called attention to the long history of African Americans' contributions to American society, and emphasized their rights to full citizenship. Black men's patriotic military service in the Revolution and the Civil War was especially accentuated. This project took on great importance since popular white-authored histories excluded any mention of African Americans and, even after blacks' rights were protected by constitutional amendments during Reconstruction, racial discrimination and violence continued to restrict black opportunities in education, employment, political participation, and all realms of public life. Key works from this period include William C. Nell, *The Colored Patriots of the Revolution* ([1855] Boston, 1968); William Wells Brown, *The Black Man* ([1863] N.Y., 1968) and *The Negro in the American Rebellion* ([1867] N.Y., 1968); and William Still, *The Underground Railroad* ([1872] N.Y., 1968).

Between the 1880s and the 1910s African American historians expanded and professionalized their work. George Washington Williams' two-volume *History of the Negro Race in America from 1619 to 1880* ([1882] N.Y., 1968) was the first comprehensive scholarly treatment of the African-American past. By the early twentieth century, organizations like Philadelphia's American Negro Historical Society (1897) and New York's Negro Society for Historical Research (1911) were systematically collecting documents and artifacts related to black history. W. E. B. Du Bois became the first African American to receive a Ph.D. in history (Harvard, 1895), and numerous works were written attempting to describe African Americans' role in the nation.

A real turning point came in 1915 with Du Bois's publication of his ambitious study, *The Negro* ([1915] Millwood, N.Y., 1975). But it was Carter G. Woodson, another Harvard Ph.D., who became the dominant force in black history for the first half of the century. Beginning with his founding of the Association for the Study of Negro History and Life (1915) and *Journal of Negro History* (1916), Woodson and his many protégés began a thorough scholarly exploration of the historical experiences of black Americans. Woodson's *The Negro in Our History* ([1922] Washington, D.C., 1972) and *The Mis-Education of the Negro* ([1933] N.Y., 1977) were important critiques of the exclusion or distortion of black history in mainstream works by white historians. Woodson's followers made outstanding contributions that slowly began to awaken the historical profession to the legitimacy of studying the African American past. Works by Lorenzo Greene, A. A. Taylor, Charles H. Wesley, and Rayford Logan investigated various aspects of the black past with academic rigor that white historians had to respect. Greene's *The Negro in Colonial New England, 1620–1776* ([1942] N.Y., 1968), for example, is still considered by many the best single volume work on

that topic. Another key work from this period was Du Bois's *Black Reconstruction in America, 1863–1880* ([1935] Cleveland, 1969), which challenged the existing racist scholarship on that subject. Du Bois's interpretations are now considered far more accurate than those of the white supremacists whose interpretations held sway through the 1950s.

While African Americans had been producing important studies of the African American past since the mid-nineteenth century, the mainstream historical profession has only begun a systematic exploration of the field since World War II. Before that time white historians considered African American history a marginal and unimportant subject about which there was little of value to say and nothing that would add to the understanding of United States history. The "Woodson school" was beginning to turn some heads, but it was two black scholars not closely associated with Woodson who had the greatest impact on the mainstream profession.

John Hope Franklin (Harvard Ph.D., 1941) and Benjamin Quarles (Wisconsin Ph.D., 1940) departed from previous black historians by emphasizing the integration of African American history with broader patterns of the American past. Franklin's *From Slavery to Freedom: A History of Negro Americans* (N.Y., 1947) was immediately recognized as a thorough and objective survey of African American history, and influenced many scholars to take the subject seriously as an important aspect of the American past. The book is now in its seventh edition (1994) and remains the standard textbook for college-level survey courses. Quarles, like Franklin, devoted much of his career to advancing the idea that African American history is an integral part of American history. This objective is reflected in the title of his best-known book, *The Negro in the Making of America* ([1964] N.Y., 1987). Quarles and Franklin were instrumental in opening the mainstream historical profession to black scholars. Franklin, in particular, compiled an impressive list of "firsts" in publishing, presenting papers, joining and chairing university departments, and leading major historical associations.

During the 1950s and 1960s, white historians, stimulated in part by World War II's assault on racism in Europe and by a reinvigorated civil rights movement, joined black scholars in reevaluating American slavery, studying the development of black urban ghettos and the system of racial segregation, and generally assessing the important role African Americans have played in United States history. Two books, Kenneth Stammp's *The Peculiar Institution* (N.Y., 1956) and Stanley Elkins's *Slavery* (Chicago, 1959), represent early examples of white scholars' attempts to challenge the racist interpretations of slavery that had dominated the field. Other important works include C. Vann Woodward's *The Strange Career of Jim Crow* (N.Y., 1955), which examined the emergence of legal segregation in the post–Civil War South; Gilbert Osofsky's *Harlem: The Making of a Ghetto* (N.Y., 1966), which dealt with urbanization as a major aspect of Northern blacks' experiences; and Winthrop Jordan's *White Over Black* (Chapel Hill, N.C., 1968), which ex-

plored the history of racism and race relations during the colonial era. While this acceptance of African American history by the profession is important, most works from this period portrayed blacks as the passive victims of white racism, and their conclusions have been revised by more recent studies.

During the 1970s, in the wake of the civil rights and black power movements, both university history departments and major publishing houses began to devote more attention to black history. An explosion of works were published by white and black historians, black studies departments were formed in many universities, and history departments began to offer courses in African American history. Much attention was devoted to treating blacks as active creators of their history rather than as passive victims of whites. This became a special focus for scholars interested in slavery and blacks' resistance to their enslavement. Much of this scholarship focused on enslaved blacks' worldview and culture, arguing that even under slavery black Americans developed their own institutions and were not completely controlled by white slaveholders. John Blassingame's *The Slave Community* (N.Y., 1972) departed from earlier studies by using the recollections of former slaves in order to describe slave culture, and Albert Raboteau probed the distinctive spiritual lives of enslaved African Americans in his *Slave Religion* (N.Y., 1978). Perhaps the most ambitious, and controversial, reassessment of slavery during this era was Eugene Genovese's *Roll, Jordan, Roll* (N.Y., 1974), which argued that slavery involved a compromise between the needs and demands of both the slaveholders and the enslaved. Lawrence Levine's influential *Black Culture and Black Consciousness* (N.Y., 1977) extended the community/culture analysis into the twentieth century, examining black folk culture in order to understand the attitudes and actions of the black masses in slavery and in freedom.

Since the 1970s, scholarship on African American history has continued to accelerate, giving us unprecedented opportunities for appreciating the role black Americans, their culture, and their institutions have played in the nation and in local communities. The vast complexities and varieties of African Americans' historical experiences make African American history one of the most exciting and active areas of historical study. The following recent general works provide both a starting point for understanding the major themes in the black American experience and an overview of the study of African American history. Most of these works contain bibliographies or footnotes indicating sources on more specialized topics. In addition, a growing number of monographs, often produced by smaller presses and historical societies, explore the African American experience in local communities, large and small.

Some to note are: James Oliver Horton and Lois E. Horton, eds., *A History of the African American People: The History, Traditions, and Culture of African Americans* (Detroit, 1997); Robert L. Harris, Jr., *Teaching African American History* (Washington, D.C., 1992); John Hope Franklin and Alfred A. Moss, *From Slavery to Freedom: A History of African Americans*, 7th ed. (N.Y., 1994); Peter Kolchin, *American Slavery, 1619–1877* (N.Y., 1993); Alton Hornsby, *Chronology of African American History: Significant Events and People from 1619 to the Present* (Detroit, 1991); Darlene Clark Hine, ed., *The State of African American History: Past, Present, and Future* (Baton Rouge, 1986); August Meier and Elliott Rudwick, *Black History and the Historical Profession, 1915–1980* (Urbana, 1986).

Basic encyclopedias of the African American experience include Jack Salzman, David Lionel Smith, and Cornell West, eds., *Encyclopedia of African American Culture and History*, 5 vols. (N.Y., 1996); Rayford W. Logan and Michael R. Winston, eds., *Dictionary of American Negro Biography* (N.Y., 1982); Jessie Carney Smith and Carrell Horton, eds., *Historical Statistics of Black America*, 2 vols. (N.Y., 1995); Darlene Clark Hine, Elsa Barkley Brown, and Rosalyn Terborg-Penn, eds., *Black Women in America: An Historical Encyclopedia*, 2 vols. (Brooklyn, 1993).

In some areas of the country, especially near large cities, one can find important repositories of documents relating to African American history. Some of the most extensive collections are found at include the *Schomburg Center for Research in Black Culture in New York, the *Amistad Research Center at Tulane University in New Orleans, the *Moorland-Spingarn Research Center at Howard University in Washington, D.C., and the Charles L. *Blockson Afro-American Historical Collection at Temple University in Philadelphia.

In addition, there are numerous Internet resources relating to the study of

African American history. One must always use caution in relying on Internet information, as there is no control over the reliability of these sources. Generally speaking, sites related to universities are the most reliable for scholarly information. A few useful sites, all of which provide links to other Internet sources on black history, include the Black Studies site from the University of California at Santa Barbara <www.library.ucsb.edu/subj/black.html>, which provides many links in categories including archives, politics, news, literature, and religion. Another site with an extensive annotated directory of Internet resources on a wide range of black history topics can be found at <http://academicinfo.net/africanam.html>. Finally, for those interested especially in genealogy, the African American Genealogy Ring<www.geocities.com/Heartland/Prairie/6288/afamgenring.html> links to numerous sites pertaining to African American family histories.

Communities with significant African American populations often have resources related to local black history. Local or regional African American newspapers began appearing in large numbers after the Civil War. Many contain a wealth of information on political debates, meetings of organizations and clubs, marriages and social events, church activities, black businesses, and more. Even the advertisements and classified sections can illuminate aspects of black community life that may not be readily apparent from other sources. These papers are often available on microfilm at university libraries and at local or state historical societies.

Census and city directory data can also suggest patterns of black population change in a community. Before the 1920s or so, many city directories noted race in their entries, which can help develop a sense of racially defined residence patterns. Property deeds can also be useful in this regard. General county or local histories, especially those published before the 1960s, rarely contain much information on African Americans, but they can provide at least a few names or events as a starting point for an investigation of other sources. Many states were included in government-sponsored WPA writing projects during the 1930s, and at times produced volumes giving brief but useful overviews of the black presence in the state. Also, theses and dissertations from nearby colleges can be important sources for understanding historical patterns in local African American communities. Churches, fraternal orders, community centers, NAACP branches, and other black community institutions might have records they would be willing to share. And, of course, *oral history is crucial. Black history has long been transmitted through stories passed from generation to generation, and the memories of older local residents are irreplaceable sources for understanding patterns of everyday life in a community. If trust is established, individuals might be willing to share both their stories and the miscellaneous information (photos, clippings, programs, etc.) contained in scrapbooks or shoeboxes in the attic.

Researchers of black communities must always keep in mind the diversity of people's experiences, even in a small town. Also, it is necessary to make connections between local events and developments and the broader patterns of African American history in order to understand the way a particular community reflects changes and continuities in American and African American society.

MITCHELL A. KACHUN

African Methodist Episcopal Church. See Appendix B.

African Methodist Episcopal Zion Church. See Appendix B.

agricultural and mechanical colleges. The Morrill Land Grant Act of 1862 created landgrant institutions to teach agriculture, engineering, and military science. Some money went to existing schools, but the measure is known for having created a number of state universities. Congress passed a second Morrill Land Grant Act in 1890 that brought into existence a number of Southern colleges primarily for African American students.

See Robert L. Williams, *The Origins of Federal Support for Higher Education: George W. Atherton and the Land-Grant College Movement* (University Park, Pa., 1991) and Laurence R. Veysey, *The Emergence of the American University* (Chicago, 1965).

agricultural history. The United States is an unparalleled agricultural resource consisting of one billion acres of farm land favored by climates suited to wheat, corn, soybeans, cotton, apples, oranges, grapes, potatoes, tomatoes, and an enormous variety of fruits and vegetables. Highly productive land provides Americans with relatively inexpensive food that many have come to take for granted, and food and natural fiber from the United States contributes to the vitality of the U.S. economy while sustaining life for many foreign people.

But agricultural abundance and the people who are fed and clothed may be a continent or an ocean apart. After inadequate transportation for a basic commodity—corn—precipitated the so-called Whiskey Rebellion in 1786, it was understood that agriculture and transportation were intertwined. In the nineteenth century, America was primarily a nation of farmers, and improving roads, canals, and railroads in order to move farm goods to market was atop the national agenda. Now an international network links America's farms with worldwide markets.

Until the latter part of the twentieth century, most farms produced both crops and livestock. Corn and hay usually went to market in the form of beef, pork, milk, chickens, eggs, mutton and wool. Vast amounts of hay and oats were consumed by horses that powered American farms until tractors replaced them in the 1930s. After World War II, farming became specialized; mixed farming gave way to producing the most profitable crops a particular area could support such as corn and soybeans in the Midwest. Animals were increasingly raised in feed lots on rations purchased from other producers. In the United States, we had meat, milk, and other animal products approximate corn, wheat, soybeans, and other field crops in value; each category generated about 80 billion dollars in 1997, while fruit and vegetables added 30 billion and cotton, 6 billion dollars.

Since the Colonial period, family-owned and operated farms have competed with farms operated by tenants or slave labor. After the Civil War eliminated slavery, the federal government encouraged families to convert a large part of the middle of the country from grazing land to farm land by granting homesteads from the public domain, which were initially 160 acres.

Family production has continued to characterize farming in the United States. The composition of the family in number of people and mix of gender and ages is well adapted to performing the diverse tasks associated with creating commodities that have lifecycles. During planting and harvesting, farming's critical periods, men, women, and children who have overlapping skills and a stake in the success of the business, make every moment of favorable weather productive. At other times, they respond with remarkable flexibility to what needs to be done as weather, season, and market opportunities intersect with plant and animal life cycles. This capacity allied with self-reproduction has kept family farms from being taken over by other organizations. The birth of children and the apprenticeship of working a family farm enables farm people to participate in the business at an early age. Beginning with simple tasks, they progress to operating machinery and eventually to running the farm.

Although farmers have adopted machines and industrial techniques along with the rest of the U.S. economy during the twentieth century, after extensive consolidation in other sectors of the nation's economy—automobiles, airplane manufacture, newspapers, retail stores—the United States is entering the second millennium with nearly two million farms, a third of the number that existed when the century began. Farms average 450 acres, but in the United States, farm size varies with farm products. For example, in Massachusetts, where fruit and vegetables predominate, the average is under 100 acres; while in Arizona, where cotton is king, the average exceeds 4,000 acres.

Two centuries ago, farming and agriculture were synonymous; everything farmers used while raising crops and animals was made on the farm or in the community. Farm products reached consumers in the form they left the farm. A century ago farming had become part of agriculture, and while it was the largest part in terms of number of people employed and product value, the manufacturing part of agriculture was expanding rapidly. Farmers purchased plows, mowers, reapers, cultivators and other labor-saving devices from McCormick, Deering, John Deere, J. I. Case and other, less well-known companies. Horse-powered machines, wire fencing, and other labor-saving technology reduced the labor component of a bushel of corn or quart of milk. Then between 1920 and 1940, petroleum fueled powerful tractors, replacing horsepower. After World War II, tractors and other machines with rubber tires and hydraulically controlled attachments further expanded what a farmer could accomplish in an hour.

The nonfarm part of agriculture, commonly known as agribusiness, continued to expand in the latter part of the twentieth century by supplying farmers with nitrogen, potash, and potassium to fertilize crops and herbicides and insecticides to control unwanted organisms. Production per acre increased as dramatically as production per hour of labor had increased earlier, so that during the century productivity increased fourfold. Corn yielded 30 bushes an acre in 1900—130 today; wheat increased from 12 to 40 bushels an acre; and milk per cow increased from 4,000 pounds to 16,000 pounds.

But increased productivity had undesired side effects. When fertilizers were overused or applied in adverse conditions, nutrient runoff polluted nearby wells, ponds, and streams; herbicides and insecticides killed desirable plants and animals along with the undesirable; and heavy machines reduced yields by compacting soil. During the 1980s, widespread evidence of environmental damage led to government action to prevent soil erosion, prevent chemical damage to soil and water, and to protect the health of people who apply toxic agricultural chemicals. And farmers have become more committed to sustaining soil and water resources. As the United States enters the second millennium, they are also reducing soil compaction by increasing the number of wheels on heavy equipment. Machines are now planting crops without prior tillage, thereby improving soil tilth and decreasing soil erosion. Global-positioning technology is coming into use that will enable farmers to adjust the application of fertilizer and other chemicals to varying field and crop conditions with far greater precision.

Agribusiness has changed farming's output as well. When the twentieth century opened, consumers were already buying flour instead of grain, and cuts of meat rather than the entire carcass. However, during the century industrial food processing has largely replaced preparing food at home ingredient by ingredient. Shredded Wheat and other commercial cereals propelled the transition. Television's advent created a demand for portable, ready-to-eat meals and a great variety of snack foods. By the 1990s these bland concoctions had been joined by a variety of ethnically influenced, microwave-ready meals and a great variety of snack foods.

Farming and industry are no longer as different as they were before farmers acquired expensive machinery and employed chemicals extensively, and some aspects of farming have become indistinguishable from industry. Chickens and eggs have become industrial products created by mass-production-techniques, and during the 1990s hog producers adopted many of these techniques. Milk producers with large herds are not far behind. Yet farming remains a family business. In an occupation that is renewed by another generation of the family taking over its businesses, incorporating the business can reduce estate taxes and inheritance problems. Over 90 percent of corporations engaged in farming are family businesses. Recent technology, in conjunction with a societal push toward gender equality, is making farming an equal-opportunity occupation for men and women. Heavy lifting has been virtually eliminated, paternalism has gone out of style, and women can use computers as effectively as men. Farming remains a highly competitive occupation and many businesses are surviving only because families have been combining it with other sources of income. For the past four decades, farm families have obtained more income from off-farm jobs and investments than from raising and marketing crops and animals.

The most realistic accounts of agriculture are found in novels. Ole Rolvaag's *Giants in the Earth* (N.Y., 1929) describes farm-making in the upper *Midwest; John Steinbeck's *The Grapes of Wrath* (N.Y., 1939) chronicles the migration to California of farm people from the lower midwest during the thirties' drought and economic depression. In a modern setting, Jane Smiley's *A Thousand Acres* (N.Y., 1991) reveals how family instability can destroy a farm business. Books by Laura Ingalls Wilder, Willa Cather, Marie Sandoz, John Steinbeck, and Upton Sinclair are excellent sources. Farm implements and other supplies are illustrated and described in annual Sears and Roebuck catalogs, many of which have been republished, as well as in regional farm publications. Books about agriculture by historians are far from comprehensive, but for the nineteenth century, Paul W. Gates, *The Farmers' Age: Agriculture, 1815 to 1860* (White Plains, N.Y., 1960) and Fred Shannon's *The Farmers' Last Frontier, Agriculture 1860–1897* (N.Y. and Toronto, 1945) are useful. Wayne Rasmussen's four-volume, *Agriculture in the United States: A Documentary History* (N.Y., 1974–75) is also of use. The journal *Agricultural History* has been published by the Agricultural History Society in Chicago since January 1927.

GOULD P. COLEMAN

ague. This was a term used for fever and sickness, often malarial in nature, associated with low-lying areas. Ague is often mentioned in the mid-nineteenth century as a factor in families leaving the Mississippi Valley area for the West.

Albanian immigrants. See Appendix A.

almanacs. The most famous of these annually issued books is *The Farmer's Almanack*, which contains a calendar of days, weeks, and months; astronomical data such as the phases of the moon; and various statistics. The first book of this sort was *An Almanac for New England for the Year 1639*, compiled by William Pierce and printed under the supervision of Harvard College. Many people associate Benjamin Franklin with the origins of almanacs because of the popularity of *Poor Richard's Almanac*, which he first issued in 1732. In the nineteenth century there were approximately 2,000 almanacs printed yearly. Those published locally often contain somewhat eccentric information, but there is usually an interesting section of local advertising, announcements of local manufacturers, and other eclectic data. See Robert K. Dodge, *A Topical Index of Early United States Almanacs, 1776–1800* (Westport, Conn., 1997).

See also herbal.

aliens. The number of aliens, that is, resident noncitizens, is listed in the first Federal Census (1790) and appears thereafter.

AltaMira Press. AltaMira Press, a division of Rowman & Littlefield Publishers, is a leading publisher of local history. It was founded in 1995 as a division of Sage Publications, a well-known scholarly press. AltaMira entered into a publishing partnership that same year with the American Association for State and Local History (AASLH). The AASLH–AltaMira book series currently contains about forty new and backlist books—including this encyclopedia—and a museum software program. AltaMira also publishes scholarly and professional works on museums, cultural resources management, history, anthropology, archaeology, ethnic studies, religion, cultural studies, and other humanities fields. The press is located at 1630 North Main Street, Suite 367, Walnut Creek, CA 94596; (510) 938-7243; fax (510) 933-9720; <explore@altamire.sagepub.com>.

MITCH ALLEN

alumni records. Many colleges and universities and some private secondary schools keep records about a student's admission, progress through the college, and events in later life including awards, honors, jobs, and participation in alumni events. Sometimes there will be pictures or letters. These can be very helpful to the local historian, but are infrequently consulted. Expect restrictions for persons who are still alive; by and large grades will not be available for view without special permission. Write to the alumni office or to the university archives and request by name, class, and date of death.

For some essays about alumni, see Clifford K. Shipton, ed., *New England Life in the 18th Century: Representative Biographies from Sibley's Harvard Graduates* (Cambridge, 1963).

amateur. From the Latin, amateur means "lover of," an amateur historian is regarded as a lover of the history of a place. The rise of the professional historian, dating from 1884 with the creation of the American Historical Association, led to a devaluation of the works of amateurs, and there has been some recent discomfort with the word as amateur came to mean the opposite of "professional" or "academic." The premise that amateur works of local history could be as good as any other is the focus of the *Nearby History series.

See Carol Kammen, *On Doing Local History: What Local Historians Do, Why and What it Means* ([1986] Walnut Creek, Calif., 1997); and *Pursuit of Local History: Readings on Theory and Practice* (Walnut Creek, Calif., 1996).

Amateur Historian. This was the original name of the journal published by the Standing Conference for Local History in Great Britain, from 1952 until 1968, when its name was changed to *The Local Historian.

American. Until the outbreak of the Revolutionary War, we were English and colonials. Afterwards, we were Americans. The use of the term "American" to denote only citizens of the United States is misleading, since Canadians and residents of Central and South America also refer to themselves as Americans.

American Antiquarian Society. The AAS is a learned society founded in 1812 in Worcester, Mass. It is the third-oldest historical society in the United States and maintains the single largest collection of printed source material of American history and culture in the United States. Its holdings include over three million books, papers, manuscripts, maps, newspapers, and other printed material. It is particularly rich in material from the beginning of the American period to 1877. The American Antiquarian Society publishes scholarly books and a journal, *Proceedings of the American Antiquarian Society*. 185 Salisbury St., Worcester, MA, 01609-1634; (508) 755-5221; fax (508) 753-3311; <www.rlg.org/sharesoag/oagmaar.utml>.

American Association for State and Local History. The American Association for State and Local History (AASLH) began as the Conference of State and Local Historical Societies, organized in 1904 in Chicago during the annual meeting of the American Historical Association. The Conference continued as a part of the AHA for several years, its members consisting of organizations, such as state historical societies, academic history departments, archives, and libraries. With the development of the Organization of American Historians in 1907 (then called the Mississippi Valley Historical Association), the Conference began to wane, and eventually became a two-hour session at the AHA annual meeting.

At the 1939, thirty-fifth annual Conference in Washington, D.C., it was proposed that membership be expanded to include individuals, for which a separate board was established. Then president, Dr. Christopher C. Crittenden, secretary of the North Carolina Historical Commission, provided leadership for a plan that the Conference include a publishing program, and a place for the field to talk about new ideas, opportunities, and solutions. On December 27, 1940, the Conference disbanded and established a new organization: The American Association for State and Local History.

In 1956, incoming president Clifford L. Lord of the State Historical Society of Wisconsin hired AASLH's first staff member. Clement M. Silvestro became a part-time administrative assistant. In 1957 Silvestro's position was increased to full time, and he was named editor of *History News*, and subsequently director of AASLH. In 1964, William T. Alderson from the Tennessee State Library and Archives took over the position, and Dr. Alderson remained the driving force behind the growth of AASLH for fourteen years.

Since 1940, AASLH has continued to maintain a thriving publishing program. And, just as Dr. Crittenden and his colleagues imagined, the Association remains a forum for both organizations and institutions who work in the field of state and local history—a place to share models of programs that work, and develop solutions for persistent challenges. From its national headquarters in Nashville, Tennessee, AASLH enjoys a following of long-time AASLH members who literally grew up in AASLH— through professional development workshops, annual meetings, technical leaflets and books, *History News* magazine and *Dispatch* newsletter. Professional training and advancement for the field remain the mainstay for AASLH. AASLH is located at 1717 Church Street, Nashville, TN 37203-2991; (615)

320-2303; fax (615) 327-9013; <www.aaslh.org>.

TERRY DAVIS

American Association of Museums. An organization for museums of all types from art museums to historic sites and botanical gardens. The organization provides an assessment program to assist museum staff in issues of museum management, curatorship, and marketing. It also offers a professional accreditation program and provides various types of technical assistance. The Association publishes *Museum News*, a bimonthly magazine, and *Aviso*, a monthly newsletter; both are addressed to museum professionals and volunteers. The headquarters is at 1575 Eye St., NW, Suite 400, Washington DC, 20005; (202) 289-1818; fax (202) 289-6578; <www.aam-us.org.>.

American exceptionalism. This phrase, widely used and much abused, actually has two meanings. The first, which is as old as the nation itself, expresses the belief that the United States is not only unique compared with all other nations and cultures, but morally and socially superior in its distinctiveness. Advocates of American exceptionalism in that sense would point to the virtue of the American yeoman farmer and the remarkably high standard of living achieved in the United States. Some people even called attention to the notion of Americans enjoying a special covenant with the Almighty, thereby achieving the status of a chosen people.

The second, and much more recent usage, commonly found in current scholarship and supported by numerous comparative studies (e.g., of slavery and race relations, of industrialization, and of modes of commemoration) simply contends that *every* nation-state is distinctive in significant ways and seeks to determine the nature (or configuration) of qualities that make the United States different from other societies. The latter definition continues to have its critics, especially those who believe that industrialization and modernization have increased international (and also national) similarities; but almost no one who subscribes to it insists that America is *better*, only that it is *different*. They would readily acknowledge the same for France, Russia, Brazil, and Japan.

MICHAEL KAMMEN

American Heritage Magazine. In 1946, members of *AASLH's committee for local history in the schools proposed a new publication dedicated to the techniques of teaching local history. After approval by the Council, Mary E. Cunningham of the New York State Historical Association began editing *American Heritage* magazine, which found strong success with schools and libraries. In 1949, the magazine was revamped into a larger quarterly, *American Heritage: New Series*, with numerous illustrations and popularly written articles. The increased popularity of the magazine attracted the attention of James Parton, a former executive with the Time-Life organization. His proposal to take over publication was accepted. In exchange for being the publication's sponsor, AASLH received regular royalty checks. Those checks allowed AASLH to hire a part-time director and launch a new, expanded phase of development. AASLH later sold its role in *American Heritage* magazine to Forbes, Inc. The address for *American Heritage* is 60 Fifth Ave., New York, NY 10011; (800) 777-1212; <http.//www.americanheritage.com>.

American Historical Association.

AHA is a nonprofit membership organization founded in 1884 and incorporated by Congress in 1889. Its purpose is to promote historical studies, collect and preserve historical documents and artifacts, and to disseminate research information. It is the largest historical organization in the United States. It publishes *Perspectives* and the *American Historical Review* as well as annual directories, bibliographies, resource guides, individual booklets and a series of short, scholarly pamphlets that provide overviews of specific historical topics. The address of the AHA is 400 A St., SE, Washington, DC 20003-3889; (202) 544-2422; fax (202) 544-8307; <www.http://chnm.gmu.edu/aha/index.html; aha@theaha.org>.

American Indian history. Until recently, someone browsing through the literatures on local and American Indian histories could reasonably have concluded that American Indian history is not a history of communities and that the history of American communities does not include American Indians. Assumptions about both the nature of Indian life—tribal, nomadic, primitive—and the options open to Indians confronted by Euro-American expansion—retreat, removal, reservations—

precluded serious discussion of either Indian towns or Indians' places within American communities. The situation, however, has begun to change. A more nuanced understanding of Indian societies and a deeper appreciation for the possibilities inherent in culture contact and territorial expansion have led scholars to re-evaluate old assumptions about the American past. For local historians, these developments offer a variety of challenges and opportunities. Scholars focused on the history of a particular area will increasingly be encouraged to include Indian communities within their research projects. At the same time, these scholars will face mounting pressure to acknowledge—and account for—American Indians within both their own communities and their models of local development.

As European explorers fanned out across what was to them "the New World," they encountered peoples so diverse that their very dissimilarity—hundreds of mutually unintelligible languages, tens of thousands of distinct communities—bespoke this world's antiquity. In North America alone, Native communities ranged from the *Southwest's nucleated pueblos to mobile bands inhabiting the far north and the deserts; from sedentary villages on the Pacific coast to seasonally occupied towns bordering the Plains; from Mississippians living in hierarchically-ranked towns to eastern villages whose people combined sedentism and mobility. Local historians seeking to incorporate the realities of this world into their narratives must acquaint themselves with the general outline of their region's pre-Columbian cultures. Then, archaeological evidence, native traditions, and ethnographic analogy can provide more detail on a specific community.

The arrival of literate Europeans, of course, opens up new vistas for local history. Although European documents must be approached with caution, they allow scholars to investigate aspects of American Indian communities that other sorts of evidence rarely address; when combined with archaeology and oral traditions, local historians will find that some Indian communities have surprisingly accessible pasts. That said, however, post-contact Indian history presents local history with conceptual and methodological challenges.

In the first place, the presence of Europeans did not transform North America's native tribes into a culturally homogenous people; in fact, contact with Europeans only encouraged American Indian diversity. For example, some tribes, responding to opportunities offered by the newcomers, relocated their villages or re-configured their seasonal activities; while others, reeling from the impact of foreign diseases and European-induced wars, came together in multiethnic communities. Even indirect contact with the newcomers encouraged cultural experimentation and elaboration; the buffalo-hunting, nomadic, Plains peoples—the archetypal image of the American Indian—had been agriculturalists prior to obtaining European horses. For local historians interested in their area's Indian communities, then, the onset of the "historic" era necessitates a heightened awareness of both the distinctiveness of local Indian culture and the fluid nature of post-contact sociocultural patterns.

Moreover, for generations following the Europeans' arrival, the vast majority of Indian communities were, if not free from Euro-American influence, certainly independent of Euro-American control. Local historians studying these communities must, therefore, come to grips with unfamiliar models of social organization and community process. Modern understandings of the nature and scope of "local" and "community" frequently differ profoundly from those of colonial-era Indians. To begin with, "community" could depend as much upon social relations as upon contiguity; an eighteenth-century Creek town, for example, consisted of people who looked to a common square ground for sociospiritual renewal, no matter how far apart they lived. In addition, the "local" area visited by Indian townspeople on a regular basis could cover hundreds of miles; thus, many New England Indians left settled agricultural villages for yearly expeditions to hunting grounds or seacoasts. Finally, many Indians valued what one historian calls "spiritual community," affective bonds transcending vertical (upper and lower worlds) and horizontal (plants and animals) boundaries. Local Indian history, therefore, encourages an expansive notion of the local.

These challenges notwithstanding, the good news for local historians is that the study of Indian communities prior to the reservation period is wide open. Academic historians have acknowledged the importance of examining this level of Indian life, but studies of towns in "Indian Country" are few and far between. Local historians, with their knowledge of their areas' history and natural characteristics, have a great deal to contribute to the study of these communities. To do so, they must examine the (often published) papers of the colonists who oversaw diplomacy and trade, as well as newspapers, traders' records, and travellers' accounts. They must also resign themselves to the fact that Euro-American concerns pervade the documents. Thus, the fur trade receives more play than agriculture, and international diplomacy overshadows intratown relations. The creative use of material culture and oral history can offset the documents' weaknesses and enhance their strengths, as can carefully controlled comparisons to neighboring Indian communities.

Of course, as Euro-American expansion picked up speed, fewer and fewer Indian communities enjoyed the degree of autonomy experienced by their contemporaries in Indian Country. New types of Indian communities, with varying degrees of Euro-American supervision, appeared in areas controlled by non-Natives. The Spanish founded mission towns for Indians in the sixteenth century, and French and English versions appeared less than a century later. Reservations, under various guises, date back almost as far, although they became the cornerstone of U.S. Indian policy only in the mid-nineteenth century. Local historians interested in investigating these manifestations of Indian community history will find that the Euro-Americans' focus on converting and "civilizing" the Indian inhabitants translated into a concern with all aspects of Indian life. As a result, even the older missions may have

archival resources well beyond those available for an Indian community in Indian Country, and the quality of data available for reservation peoples has led two historians to describe these American Indians as "among the best documented populations in the world."

Local historians who focus on such a community—for example, a mission in the area, or the current reservation of a people who once lived nearby—should be aware that historians and anthropologists have abandoned assumptions about the inevitability of Indian assimilation and deculturation. Recent scholarship—on subjects including Cherokee basketry, Crow settlement patterns, California mission leadership styles, and Comanche sociality—demonstrates that U.S. Indians have succeeded in articulating distinctive values and identities while simultaneously participating in American culture. Local historians focused on mission and reservation communities will need both to consider the tremendous changes in Indian lifeways and to acknowledge the continuity in crucial aspects of personal and corporate identity and behavior.

Local historians who wish to make sense of the complexities apparent in these Indian communities—to understand, in the words of one historian, "the human decisions that shape the meanings embedded in a census report"—should avail themselves of the knowledge preserved in the Indians' own historical traditions. A number of tribes have developed programs for preserving and disseminating this information. These archives, research projects, speakers, and publications will be quite useful to local historians.

Moreover, many Indian cultures have made the collection and transmission of historical knowledge the province of elders trained in techniques of memorization and exposition. Although these men and women can be of tremendous help to historians, non-Indians must be aware that generations of scholarly misappropriation has made Indians leery of sharing their knowledge with outsiders. Interested parties should contact tribal officials to find out the appropriate method for inquiring into that people's oral traditions. Be prepared to explain your project's relevance to the Indian community; to treat interviewees as collaborators, not sources; to respect both their traditions and their silences.

It would be a mistake, however, for local historians to assume that studying American Indians will necessarily take them outside of their own area. Our national narrative of an onrushing frontier that pushed Indians away from Euro-American settlements has been challenged by scholars stressing the fluid nature of frontier regions, the mosaic-like quality of settlement patterns, and the possibilities for social coexistence, cultural interpenetration, and ethnic persistence long after "the frontier . . . passed by." Historians working in the southeast, New England, and the Mississippi Valley have demonstrated that American Indians found a variety of ways to integrate themselves into U.S. communities while maintaining distinct cultural practices, social networks, and group identities; Mestizo communities in the Southwest and Metis communities in the upper Midwest offer additional evidence of the cultural and biological fluidity of American life. The titles from recent works focusing on Indians in nineteenth-century New England attest to the emergence of a new narrative: "Unseen Neighbors"; "They Were Here All Along"; "Presence and Persistence"; "Enduring Traditions"; "Behind the Frontier."

When viewed in this light, local history's long-standing tendency to refer to Indians in post-frontier communities as either colorful primitives or as people "who were here but now are gone" obviously requires rethinking. To exclude Indians from local histories that might reasonably include them results in two disturbing problems. To begin with, an approach that denies Indian peoples their rightful place in our collective past inevitably produces bad local history; inaccurate and exclusionary assumptions produce misleading and partial narratives. Of equal importance, the absence of Indians in local history allows the general public to dismiss Indians who share our modern communities as fakes and opportunists; "real" Indians, people assume, live elsewhere.

Local historians who seek to remedy this situation must recall that, for much of the last two hundred years, this country was dominated by a bipartite racial system that had little room for Indians. Moreover, Euro-Americans often had economic and political reasons for insisting that Indians no longer lived in their area. Indians, in consequence, frequently disappeared (for official purposes) into the "colored" category. Yet many of these people continued to view themselves as Indians, and researchers have been remarkably successful in mining the archives for hints about their lives. Investigations often begin with a stray reference, one clue to a person's identity or a place's use that can lead to an ever-widening search for the networks and behaviors that allowed individuals to live as Indians in U.S. towns.

In investigating the place of Indians in an area's history, local historians have the opportunity to address a number of important issues. Most obviously, local Indian history offers new perspectives on changing racial and ethnic relations, as well as on debates about resource ownership and utilization. Perhaps more fundamentally, however, local Indian history allows scholars to consider the relationship between the Indians' presence, beliefs, and actions, on the one hand, and the larger community's articulation of social boundaries, behavioral standards, and local self-image, on the other.

Different, but equally exciting, opportunities await local historians who focus on a single Indian community. Historians who study communities in Indian Country come face-to-face with our nation's diverse past. Such investigations challenge local historians to rethink cherished notions about community boundaries and processes, while providing researchers with a greater understanding of the situation confronting the initial generations of Euro-Americans in the area. Likewise, reservation and mission communities offer local historians the chance to delve into unfamiliar aspects of their area's distant and/or recent past. Moreover, Indian experiences on reservations and in mis-

sions challenge all historians to reconsider their understanding of cross- cultural interaction, identity formation, and community development. Whichever area of Indian life local historians elect to investigate, however, they can be confident that their efforts will contribute to the ultimate goal of local history. to describe a locality's distinctive aspects while discussing its connections to more broad-reaching developments.

JOSH PIKER

American Revolution celebrations.
The two national celebrations of the American Revolution have been especially important to local historians. The Centennial, held in 1876 in Philadelphia, was ushered in by President Ulysses S. Grant who signed a proclamation on May 25, 1876 in which he "recommended . . . to the people of the several states that they assemble in their counties or towns on the approaching centennial anniversary of our national independence and that they cause to have delivered on such day an historical sketch of said county or town from its formation, and that a copy of said sketch may be filed, in print or manuscript, in the clerk's office of said county, and an additional copy, in print or manuscript, to be filed in the office of the Librarian of Congress to the intent that a complete record may thus be obtained of the progress of our institutions during the first centennial of their existence." Americans, of course, did just that. The result was an immense outpouring of local history over the next 25 years.

The literary response to the era was a blossoming of *local color literature, not self-consciously linked to the Centennial, but a response, nonetheless to an interest and celebration of the local. So George Washington Cable and Bret Harte, Marietta Holley and Sarah Orne Jewett, Elizabeth Whitcher and countless others began to write stories reflective of a locality, often using dialect, creating local characters with care and love and a critical eye.

The celebration of the Bicentennial of the American Revolution in 1976 was equally challenging to local historians. While national interest focused upon events such as the arrival of the "Tall Ships," localities everywhere looked for appropriate ways to commemorate the founding of the country. In many cases, older histories were reprinted, and some new histories were written. There was a focus also, at the time, upon our home town architectural treasures and on Main Street, U.S.A.

The charge heard across the country, to which a great number of people responded, was the challenge posed by Alex Haley's book *Roots (N.Y., 1976) and the television miniseries based on it. Haley presented the history of his family, from their African origins to slavery in the New World, and on into freedom, in a dramatic fashion that empowered others to look at their own family history. Since 1976 there have been a great many genealogies created by people who earlier might not have regarded *genealogy as something appropriate or even possible for their own family experience. A great many books appeared offering to show how to research a family's past. *Finding Your Hispanic Roots* (N.Y., 1997) and *A Sourcebook for Jewish Genealogies and Family*

Histories by David Zubatsky (Teaneck, N.J., 1996) are but two examples. The popularity of the Internet has expanded this growing field with websites devoted to particular families and ethnicities and with programs offered for the amateur and even for the more experienced genealogist.

This democratization of genealogy is significant as much of the research necessarily occurs in local historical societies and many of the training sessions offered have been sponsored by local agencies. This trend presents an opportunity for local historical societies to help individuals see themselves in history, in time, and in place. The literary component of this late nineteenth century interest in family has been an outpouring of literary *memoirs.

See memoirs.

Amish. See Appendix B.

Amistad Research Center. This research library, located at Tulane University, was founded in 1966 and features collections of manuscript materials and a library focused on ethnic minorities in America, on African American history and culture, on civil rights, on Africa and abolitionism. There is also a collection on the Church of Christ. The Center has several substantial art collections; issues newsletters, and a magazine, the *Amistad Log*; and is open to the public. The address is 16823 St. Charles St., New Orleans, LA 70118; (504) 865-5535 <www.arc.tulane.edu> or <amistad @mailhost.tsc.tulane.edu>.

Anabaptist. The name given to Protestant sects in Europe, many of whom, beginning in the seventeenth century, emigrated to the United States and Canada. Anabaptists believe the church is a society of adult believers and oppose infant baptism. They are known today by various names, including Amish, Mennonites, and Hutterites, each having evolved independently and with separate identities in the New World despite many common concerns.

Anglicans. See Appendix B.

Annales School. The Annales School is the name given to one of the most influential approaches to historical inquiry developed in the twentieth century. Its founders during the 1920s, Lucien Febvre (1878–1956) and Marc Bloch (1886–1944), along with their most prominent disciple, Fernand Braudel (1902–1985), emphasized social and economic forces as being more consequential than political and diplomatic events, whose mere chronology seemed a superficial approach to understanding the past and its legacy for the present.

These French Annalistes also highlighted the importance of geographical and climatic influences. They insisted upon the need for *histoire totale*, a multidimensional approach to history, by probing unconventional sources in depth and using quantitative methods wherever possible in order to be more precise. In recent decades (since the 1970s), members of the Annales school have also been receptive to new ways of thinking about cultural history, such as the development of literacy and numeracy.

Work done by the Annalistes is im-portant for local historians because its members have created some masterpieces of microhistory as a new, subtle genre, combining neglected primary sources, complex and multifaceted analysis, and engaging narrative. They commonly use a historical crisis or episode as the point of departure for recreating historical context and implications in astonishing depth. Prime examples include Bloch's *The Ile de France: The Country around Paris* ([1913] Ithaca, N.Y., 1971), and two books by Emmanuel LeRoy Ladurie, *Montaillou: The Promised Land of Error* (N.Y., 1978) and *Carnival in Romans* (N.Y., 1979).

MICHAEL KAMMEN

annuity. An annual payment from an investment or as the result of an agreement. For example, the Iroquois were paid an annuity by the state of New York in exchange for their removal from the land.

anthropology and local history. See ethnography.

antiquarian. Antiquarian pertains to antiquaries or to one interested in antiquaries. J. D. Marshall, in his book *The Tyranny of the Discrete* (Aldershot, Hants., Eng., 1997), cautions against the dangers of antiquarianism in local history. He offers the following: antiquarianism is "an historical heresy," or "an inability to distinguish what features of the past are historically significant; an indiscriminately romantic attitude to the past" (p. 46).

Appalachia. Defining Appalachia may, at first glance, seem a rather simple proposition. The Appalachian mountains sweep from Canada southwestward to Texas. Crafting boundaries that accommodate the cultural variations inherent in such a wide swath of territory has, however, bedeviled even the region's closest and most astute observers. The difficulty in precisely mapping the region's boundaries has not prevented a host of attempts. Most frequently, Appalachia has been defined as encompassing the mountainous territory from northeastern Alabama to the southern half of New York. Precisely which counties within which states are included in this definition has been a source of disagreement. In his 1921 study, for example, the sociologist John C. Campbell included 254 counties, but no states north of Maryland. Forty-one years later a Ford Foundation study pared the number of counties down to 190, ended the region at Maryland's northern border, and reversed Campbell's inclusion of South Carolina and Maryland. In a 1965 survey for a newly formed federal agency, the Appalachian Regional Commission, the number of counties ballooned to 360, and the northern border extended into New York; political pressures by 1967 had increased the number of counties to 397.

Even the narrowest definition still covers 80,000 square miles, so many scholars have attempted to isolate distinct subregions such as the Blue Ridge, the Cumberland Plateau, and so on. Most of these definitions attempt to combine physical geography with social and cultural factors, such as income level, dialect, folk traditions, and religious affiliation. Until recently, the residents themselves were not asked whether they considered themselves Appalachian. In large part, the problem of defining the area arises from deciding which criteria are essential to fixing *regional identity. Consequently, the researcher should use the term "Appalachia" with caution, and should fully examine how and why the term is relevant and useful to their study.

In the popular imagination the region is, at best, the home of quaintly old-fashioned inhabitants ("yesterday's people") and, at worst, a hillbilly haven. The people are considered uniformly poor, white, and intensely rural. However, these generalizations do not withstand close scrutiny. Unquestionably the region has significant pockets of poverty, racial and ethnic homogeneity, and deep isolation. At the same time, Appalachia has always supported a large and prosperous class of people, had a significant nonwhite population, and been home to important cities. In the period before the Civil War many landowners, like their lowland kin, reaped hefty profits from plantation agriculture, and had significant contacts with cultural and political trends outside the region. Their use of slave labor introduced a sizeable group of African Americans into the region, whose numbers were augmented in the post–Civil War period by black migrants searching for work in lumber camps, mines, and on railroad construction crews. The significant presence of Native Americans, particularly the Cherokee in western North Carolina, further complicates the portrait of homogenous whiteness. Nor have the Appalachian people lived solely in remote mountain coves. Major urban centers like Asheville, North Carolina; Knoxville, Tennessee; and Charleston, West Virginia, were and remain important cities. In short, it is very hard to make useful generalizations about Appalachia. In fact, the difficulty in arriving at a unified portrait has prompted one of the region's most thoughtful scholars to argue that "it is futile to look for a 'correct' definition of the region" (David E. Whisnant, *Modernizing the Mountaineer: People, Power, and Planning in Appalachia*, 2d ed., rev. [Knoxville, Tenn., 1994], 134).

Those interested in learning more about the region should consult John C. Campbell's dated, but still valuable book *The Southern Highlander and his Homeland* ([1921] Spartanburg, S.C., 1973) as well as the links on the Appalachian Studies website maintained by Appalachian State University in Boone, N.C. <www.appstudies.appstate.edu/appandweb.html>.

GAVIN JAMES CAMPBELL

Arab Americans. See Appendix A.

Archaeological Institute of America. A nonprofit cultural and educational organization chartered by the U.S. Congress. It is the oldest and largest archaeological organization in North America with more than 11,000 members. AIA publishes *Archaeology*, a magazine written by professionals for the general public, *The American Journal of Archaeology*, a publication addressed to scholars, as well as a number of monographs. The Institute is located at 656 Beacon St., Boston, MA 02215-2010 <www.archaeological.org>.

The Archaeological Institute of America/Institut Archeologique d'Amerique. Formed in 1994 as an independent Canadian affiliate. The address is #T6093, P.O. Box 6100, Postal Station F, Toronto, Ontario, M4Y2Z2, Canada.

archaeology.

In sum, if we wish to have a future with greater meaning, we must concern ourselves not only with the historic highlights, but we must be concerned with the total heritage of the nation and all that is worth preserving from our past as a living part of the present.

With Heritage So Rich (N.Y., 1966)

Archaeological resources are an important part of the local history record for every community. The significance of these resources to our communities is explicitly stated in the preamble to the Historic Preservation Act of 1966, which encourages their preservation as a "living part of our community life in order to give a sense of orientation to the American people" (Public Law 89-665; 16 USC 470). We often underestimate the value of the past in our "backyard" or are put off by difficulties in finding resources that would help define and protect archaeological sites and properties that are important to our communities.

Archaeology is sometimes thought of in terms of either grand discoveries of a pharaoh's tomb or a fictional "Indiana Jones"–style caricature. These depictions of the field of study have a tendency to make archaeological inquiry appear both remote and adventurous. In order to better place archaeology within a local history context it is better to view archaeology as a more democratic study of past ways of life (Stuart and Mc-Manamon, *Archaeology and You*, p. 1). Christopher R. DeCorse provides a good introduction to the field of archaeology in *The Record of the Past*. In this volume he notes that through archaeological study "we learn about the culture of those societies, the shared way of life of a group of people that includes their values, beliefs, and norms" (DeCorse, p. 5). Archaeological sites include a full suite of historic and prehistoric properties reflecting a wide array of cultural contexts. They include everything from abandoned mills, farms, mining camps and stage stops in rural settings to foundations and refuse middens associated with domestic residences and industrial complexes in urban settings. The importance of cemeteries (marked and unmarked) is well recognized. Yet like other sites, even these commemorative places are often defaced or forgotten. The problem resonates in the text of a simple sign on the cemetery at the ghost town of Bodie, a California State Historic site, that reminds visitors that "this site is still in use."

The visibility of cemeteries, buildings, and standing ruins makes them relatively easy rallying points for preservation and ideal tools for public education. Prehistoric sites are more difficult to deal with because they are less visible, and with the exception of contact-period sites, they lack the associated documentation of historical sites. In may cases these "older" resources in our communities are reflections of past social and economic conditions and, in the case of prehistoric sites, the residue of cultures that are quite different from our own. The cultural separation between "past" and "present" often leads to the destruction of resources of local importance. The ability to protect local archaeological sites is linked to the realization that local sites are of significance and that there are many resources available to assist the process of site protection. The local historian can assist in the evaluation of local resources based on their knowledge of local history, their knowledge of where to find resources, and by their ability to educate the public.

The local historian can play an essential part in the illumination and dissemination of information on all types of archaeological sites. Their knowledge of local archives, researchers, and general history makes them key resource persons with respect to archaeological sites. Because early settlers' accounts often document the location of early historic sites and contact-period relations with Native Americans, the local historian often has information about archaeological sites that has not been reported to nor recorded by state and federal registers of prehistoric and historic properties. It is therefore important to integrate the local historian into the archaeological sites-management network of communication concerning the local, state, and national levels.

In recent years, archaeologists have begun to realize that their goals must include public involvement and education along with the traditional goals of archaeological site protection and scientific excavation. These goals mesh with the basic goals and responsibilities of local historians. Though the goals are shared, formal archaeological-site reg-

25

isters of each state are still not readily available at the local level; hence, information on archaeological sites has not been made available to the public. Below are guides to published materials, and World Wide Web resources on archaeological sites and the process of site protection (see bibliography and selected World Wide Web archaeological resource listings). It also encourages the local historian to integrate archaeology into their educational programs.

Every community in America has an archaeological heritage, which, if managed properly as a public resource, can help us recognize and celebrate the accomplishments of our predecessors. Archaeology brings the American legacy to life.
"Community Archaeology in
Alexandria, Virginia"

PAMELA J. CRESSEY

Archaeological resources within the community. The first step for the local historian is to link up with knowledgeable people to find out about archaeological resources. Make contacts with the faculty at your local college or university; in most cases they will be quite pleased to know of your interest. They often have students looking for projects and most have access to information that can help you get started. Ask them to put you in touch with the local SHPO (State Historic Preservation Officer) archaeologist or professional archaeological contract firms (lists of firms can be gained through your state SHPO or the Register of Professional Archaeology at <www. rpanet.org>).

A wonderful book aimed at protecting local resources is Susan Henry's *Protecting Archaeological Sites on Public Lands.* This volume, published by the National Park Service, is a practical guide that deals with archaeological resources that are not state or federally owned. It contains important bibliographic materials, a detailed summary of protection strategies, a very good guide to the process of archaeological resource assessment, and an important section called "Sources of Financial Assistance." This volume was written with local communities in mind and includes an address list for state historic-preservation offices around the country. Your state historic-preservation officer (SHPO) will be able to inform you about archaeological resources in your area.

Local historians have a solid working relationship with local historical societies and museums. To gain a better understanding of local archaeology they might also link up with local and regional archaeological societies. For example, groups like the New York State Archaeological Association, and similar groups in states such as Arkansas and Pennsylvania, have a strong avocational archaeology tradition. In many cases the local knowledge of archaeological sites far exceeds information that has been centralized at the state level. There is also a network of local not-for-profit historic site-preservation organizations, like the Preservation Association of Central New York, Inc. that have information on protecting historic properties including archaeological sites. The National Trust for Historic Preservation is a good source of information on local preservation groups (see list of website listings).

Federal law provides for the creation of Certified Local Governments, (CLGs), which allow the designation of "local" protected-sites status to archaeological sites and historic properties on a community level. Contact your State Historic Preservation Office for details concerning local CLGs in your area or to obtain information on the advantages of creating a process for local designation in your community. A few communities, such as Santa Fe, New Mexico, have well-conceived preservation plans that fully engage the potential of CLG designation to protect local sites (see Elliot, 1988).

Many communities, particularly in the western United States, are in close proximity to lands that are managed by state and federal agencies, including state parks, military bases, National Parks and National Forests, Bureau of Land Management lands, and properties managed by the Army Corp of Engineers. Most of these agencies have archaeologists assigned to the management of archaeological resources. These professional archaeologists can be of considerable assistance to the local historian in communicating knowledge of resources on public lands and in providing direction to assist the protection of archaeological resources on private property. For best results consult the local or regional office of the respective agency.

Archaeological resources within your state. The primary "formal" repositories of information on archaeological sites are at the state level. Under federal law each state is required to keep a register, or list, of archaeological sites and properties. In most cases, the list of archaeological sites is separate and independent from the National Register of Historic sites and includes all reported prehistoric and historic archaeological sites regardless of relative significance.

Many archaeological sites are located in rural, isolated, and unprotected areas, and because there is a history of looting and site destruction, information on sites, including their location, is restricted to professional archaeologists. In a few states, such as Florida and North Carolina, this information is available to the public. In almost every case an inquiry by a serious local historian will be viewed by the SHPO as a professional inquiry, and they will be forthcoming with information to assist that individual in order to enhance local knowledge of archaeological sites. Unfortunately, in many states the SHPO office is understaffed and may not be able to provide direct assistance (site visitation, evaluation of significance, filing for site protection); however, they will provide information to assist in documenting sites. They will also be able to put you in contact with academic and professional archaeologists who can make an evaluation of the site's significance. They can provide information on local community archaeological projects and events such as regional "Archaeology Weeks" and "Historic Preservation Weeks" that are organized in order to involve the public in archaeology and preservation.

National level resources. The National Park Service's Archaeology Division has primary responsibility for archaeological resources in the United States. They have published a long list of publications that explains federal laws governing archaeological resources. Two key lists of reference materials are the *Catalog of Historic Preservation Publi-*

cations and *Federal Historic Preservation Laws* (National Park Service 1990a and 1990b; some key federal publications, pamphlets, and bulletins are included in the bibliography under National Park Service).

The cornerstone of federal preservation law is the National Historic Preservation Act of 1966 and its several amendments. The publication *Held in Trust: Preserving America's Historic Places* (National Park Service, 1991) provides an overview of this Act. It is important to consider that this Act specifically includes archaeological sites among those historically significant to our nation's heritage. The Act establishes the mechanism for the establishment of the National Register of Historic Places. This register provides federal recognition to sites that are significant at the state and local level as well as those that are of national significance. It established an Advisory Council on Historic Preservation that advises the president and the Congress on historic-preservation matters, and it establishes a protocol for the Historic Preservation Fund. This fund provides matching grants to states, Certified Local Governments, Native American tribes, and the National Trust for Historic Preservation (see website listings for the National Park Service and the National Trust for Historic Preservation).

Archaeology and the local historian. The protection and preservation of prehistoric and historical resources is dependent upon the careful recording of information on sites and on systems of interpretation that make this information available and useable by schol-ars, planners, Native American groups, and the broader communities in which the resources are located. As caretakers of the past, local historians can assist planners and developers at the community level to gain a solid grasp of the resources located within the region for which they are responsible.

Local historians can also play a vital role in assisting the scholarly community and local planners in developing resource-management strategies that ensure that *all* significant resources are afforded protection from destruction. Archaeological resources are an important part of our "living" heritage. Local historians have the ability to link the local community with archival and resource information at the local, state, and national levels. It is hoped that local historians will be encouraged to get involved with archaeology and to utilize archaeological resources in interpreting local history.

See Christopher R. DeCorse, *The Record of the Past: An Introduction to Physical Anthropology and Archaeology* (Upper Saddle River, N.J., 2000); Elizabeth J. Kellar, "The Public Trust" (Unpublished Master's Paper, Anthropology Department, Syracuse University, 1996); George E. Stuart and Francis McManamon, *Archaeology and You* (1996). Also, Public Law 89-665: The National Historic Preservation Act of 1966; Daniel Haas, "Reaching the Public. Looking at the Past—Looking at the Future," in *Common Ground: Archaeology and Ethnography in the Public Interest*, 3/1 12–13 (Washington, D.C., 1998); Susan L. Henry, "Protecting Archeological Sites on Private Lands," National Park Service, Preservation Planning

Branch, Interagency Resources Division (Washington, D.C., 1993); William D. Lipe, Introduction to *Save the Past for the Future II: Report of the Working Conference* (Washington, D.C., 1995); *Catalog of Historic Preservation Publications*, Cultural Resource Program, National Park Service, Department of Interior (Washington, D.C., 1990); *Held in Trust: Preserving American's Historic Places— The National Historic Preservation Act of 1966, 25th Anniversary Report* (Washington, D.C., 1991); "Archaeology and the Federal Government," *Cultural Resources Management* 17(6) (Washington, D.C., 1994); The Native American Graves Protection and Repatriation Act, Special Report, *Federal Archaeology* 7/3 (fall/winter) (Washington, D.C., 1995); *Common Ground: Archaeology and Ethnography in the Public Interest*, 3(1) (Washington, D.C., 1998); Public Law 89-665 (16 USC 470) 1966. The National Historic Preservation Act; "Mapping Out a Career in Historical Archaeology," *Society for Historical Archaeology* (Tucson, Ariz., 1996); *With Heritage So Rich: A Report of a Special Committee on Historic Preservation*. United States Conference of Mayors (N.Y., 1966).

Selected world wide websites. Archaeological Web Pages <http://csbs.utsa.edu/car/archlink.html>: this site will link you to hundreds of archaeological websites both in the United States and around the world. It includes many of the sites listed below and will allow you to choose your path to a full range of archaeological resources.

National Park Service Archaeology Division <www.cr.nps.gov/nr/bulletins/archaeol>: general information on archaeology from the Department of the Interior and its archaeology divisions within the National Park Service. See also <www.cr.nps.gov/seac/seac>: an excellent public interest web site maintained by the National Park Service's Southeast Archaeological Center, this site focuses on public archaeology, research and education.

The National Trust for Historic Preservation <http://www.nationaltrust.org>: congressionally chartered, this organization publishes *Preservation* magazine and has personnel with knowledge of legal structures and resources. The National Trust has regional field officers who may be able to come to your community to provide assistance with your preservation projects and programs.

Register of Professional Archaeologists <http://www.rpanet.org>: this is a group of professional archaeologists who have demonstrated training and expertise and who declared their intention to work ethically within the field of archaeology.

Society for American Archaeology <www. saa.org>: general information presented by the largest professional and academic archaeology organization in the United States. See also <http://www.saa.org/AboutArch/participate.html> for public information and resources aimed at informing the public.

The Society for Historical Archaeology can be contacted at <www.azstarnet.com/~sha>.

DOUGLAS V. ARMSTRONG

See intellectual property rights; patrimony.

architectural pattern books. In the mid-nineteenth century, the American architectural landscape was increasingly shaped by the widespread circulation of pattern books. These were illustrated architectural manuals that defined taste by providing examples of appropriate, fashionable, and "modern" designs. Pattern books became popular during a period of great change in the building trades, and many builders relied on them to keep abreast of current fashions.

The earliest architectural publications in the United States were reprints of English books. Although Abraham Swan's *The British Architect* (1775) was the first architectural book published in America, it had appeared in London several decades earlier. Asher Benjamin's *Country Builder's Assistant* (1797), which was the first U. S. handbook that was not based on English or foreign sources, marked the beginning of a long line of increasingly influential architectural publications that continued through the nineteenth and twentieth centuries.

Pattern books evolved through several stages. The first of these were builders' handbooks, which typically included drawings of details or discussions of specific building problems, but offered few designs for complete buildings. These builders' guides, such as Owen Biddle's *Young Carpenter's Assistant* (1805) and John Haviland's *The Builder's Assistant* (1818), attempted to systematize building practice and to synthesize architectural knowledge into something of a science. In the 1830s, stylebooks began to appear. Unlike the builders' guides, stylebooks such as Alexander Jackson Davis's *Rural Residences* (1837) presented models for complete buildings within appropriately landscaped surroundings, and were aimed at a broader audience that included prospective clients as well as builders. Stylebooks typically included plans as well as perspective views of buildings in naturalistic settings; perhaps more importantly, they also stressed the tastefulness of their designs. Andrew Jackson Downing, author of *Cottage Residences* (1842), *Rural Architecture & Landscape Gardening* (1842), and *The Architecture of Country Houses* (1850), was one of the most famous proponents of a tasteful and appropriate domestic environment, arguing that thoughtfully planned dwellings played an important role in forming moral character. After the Civil War and through the later nineteenth and early twentieth centuries, books promoting mail-order house plans began to appear, followed eventually by catalogues marketing completely prefabricated houses. Mail-order plan books were simply catalogues of house plans that readers could purchase, and usually included multiple perspective renderings, floor plans, construction cost estimates, and price tables for working drawings. In time, building components and entire prefabricated houses could be selected from catalogues such as those issued by Sears Roebuck & Co. and Montgomery Ward and shipped by rail to waiting customers.

It is important to remember that, despite the popularity of pattern books in the antebellum period, literal copies of published designs were not particularly common. Most builders borrowed from these books selectively, working within a traditional architectural vocabulary and grafting stylish motifs onto more conservative forms. Exact copies of published examples became more widespread only later in the nineteenth century, when complete plans and pre-fabricated dwellings began to appear. Pattern books transformed American architecture not only by promoting change and novelty, but also by bringing fashionable designs within reach of an ever-widening audience.

See Linda Smeins, *Building an American Identity: Pattern Book Homes and Communities, 1870–1900* (Walnut Creek, Ca., 1999); Jan Jennings, "Cheap and Tasteful Dwellings in Popular Architecture," in *Gender, Class, and Shelter: Perspectives in Vernacular Architecture,* Elizabeth Collins Cromley and Carter L. Hudgins editors (Knoxville, 1995); Dell Upton, "Pattern Books and Professionalism. Aspects of the Transformation of Domestic Architecture in America, 1800–1860," *Winterthur Portfolio* 19 (summer/autumn 1984): 108–150; Gwendolyn Wright, *Building the Dream: A Social History of Housing in America* (Cambridge and London, 1983); Catherine W. Bishir, "Jacob W. Holt: An American Builder," *Winterthur Portfolio* 16, no. 1 (Spring 1981): 1–31; James L. Garvin, "Mail-Order House Plans and American Victorian Architecture," *Winterthur Portfolio* 16, no 4 (Winter 1981): 309–334; and Henry-Russell Hitchcock, *American Architectural Books, New Expanded Edition* (N.Y., 1976).

Note: The classic source for pre-1895 pattern books is Hitchcock's bibliography; probably the most useful secondary source for understanding the influence of pattern books is Upton's article.

Both are cited above. Following are some key builder's-guide and pattern-book authors to look for, although there are many others: Benjamin, Asher; Bicknell, Amos J.; Biddle, Owen; Davis, Alexander Jackson; Downing, Andrew Jackson; Fowler, Orson Squire; Haviland, John; Lafever, Minard; Palliser, Palliser & Co., Architects; Ranlett, William H.; Sloan, Samuel; Stickley, Gustav; Vaux, Calvert; Wheeler, Gervase; and Woodward, George E.

GABRIELLE M. LANIER

See architecture and the local historian.

architecture and the local historian. In countless venues where the concerns and imperatives of local history intersect with the subject of architecture, there is that inevitable question: "What style is it?" This is hardly surprising, for people who care about buildings want some sort of purchase on their meaning—their place in the scheme of things—and recognition of a building's "style" has become the most popular strategy for achieving this. The range of possible answers to the question "What style is it?" have a way of reassuring people that they understand what they are observing, yet hardly anyone stops to consider what the definitions of "style" may encompass and exclude. Equally obscure is any notion of what it means to identify a building as an example of some well-known stylistic designation such as "neoclassical" or "art deco." Local historians are wise to consider these matters, for they have a powerful impact on that most challenging task of discovering and elucidating the historical significance of a particular place.

Invocation of the term "style" as an explicit means of classifying art, sculpture, artifacts, and buildings originates in the eighteenth century, that great period of confidence in natural, rational, comprehensive systems of order. Definitions of "style" varied, but all included some notion that it referred to the manner in which an object was made beautiful or picturesque. This manner might include certain characteristics such as curving lines or elements such as classical columns. It also might involve intellectual or aesthetic underpinnings—often in the form of principles for discerning artistic integrity or beauty. In any case, considerations of "style" helped to identify significant affinities among some objects and distinctions between others. "Style" served many classificatory purposes, but not all. Its development as a useful concept paralleled yet another form of classification denoted by the word "type." For eighteenth-century writers, this term referred to the use of an artifact or building. "Type" has been replaced in modern parlance by the word "function." This point is worth making, for popular understandings of architectural "style" often presume that it accounts for every important aspect of a building, rather than just one.

During the nineteenth century, European analysts of art history and—later—of architectural history imparted to the term "style" the formidable teeth of differentiation, evaluation, and judgement as they attempted to sort out the history of artistic expression and to establish the origins and essence of aesthetic achievement. Now-familiar names for periods of art and architecture, including "Renaissance," "Bar-

oque," and "Romanesque" emerged from this endeavor. Scholars struggling to delimit and justify their discipline also developed systems—some of them aiming to achieve a "scientific" level of verity—for determining the quality of an individual building, object, or painting. This striving for scientific clarity also fostered the adaptation of Darwinian principles to art-historical purposes. So it was that the discipline became infused—although not everyone realized this—with the notion that historic styles of art and architecture exist to be discovered, naturally evolve over time, and serially replace one another.

The disciplines of art and architectural history arrived in North America near the turn of the twentieth century. Because these fields of inquiry were new here, practitioners found it necessary to legitimatize their particular brands of knowledge. One means of gaining a professional or scholarly credibility was to emphasize both the classificatory and the evaluative aspects of stylistic analysis. For many, authority accrued to the treatment of architectural styles as episodes in a march through time that was as distinct and progressive as stages in the evolution of living forms. For others, expertise devolved from the capacity to recognize the immutable qualities of individual architectural styles, to characterize them as essential and mutually exclusive—like elements in a periodic table. As a result of such strategies for explanation, buildings with blended, transitional, understated, or idiosyncratic manifestations of style often suffered from the perception that they were mutations or contaminations. A scholar need not strike an overtly censorious stance to invoke such thinking—though many did. "Retardataire," an inherently pejorative adjective for buildings that seem out of date or underdeveloped, made its appearance at the beginning of the twentieth century and has figured sporadically in conventional U.S. architectural histories ever since.

Other ambitious scholars found that the identification and analysis of new styles proved a likely path to recognition and influence. As a result, "Colonial Revival," "Arts and Crafts," and "Art Deco" became new links in the chain of acceptable names for styles of art and architecture. Soon these terms—long established as well as freshly minted—found themselves augmented, overlapped, or subdivided by categories with names like "Jeffersonian Neoclassicism," "Richardsonian Romanesque," "Wrightian," "Chicago School," "Prairie School," "Cottage Style," "Octagon Mode," and "Shingle Style." What these latecomers to the academic enterprise of classifying architectural styles have in common is that they are not attempts to characterize the unifying aspects of stylistic expression during a particular age. They refer instead to the work of an individual artist and his imitators, to a discrete school of design practice, to a region of origin and popularity, or to a predictable occurrence of particular materials, shapes, or surface motifs.

Academic architectural history hummed along well enough through the twentieth century with its inherent inconsistencies. On one hand, there was the notion that the "march of the styles" was a scientifically derived and rationally founded system of explanation subject primarily to repetition and oc-

casionally to refinement. On the other hand, there was an increasingly balkanized set of terms that were not mutually exclusive, not based on parallel criteria, and not drawn from a common definition for the term "style." Despite these intellectual incongruities, the most conservative sectors of the discipline somehow foundered on the notion that a building's style embodies its fundamental essence—and the irreducible core of its designer's intention. As late as the 1980s, courses in architectural history might with sincerity emphasize the "applicability of style recognition" as one of their chief goals. This reductive "style primacy" was certainly mitigated by the subsumption under "style" of a constellation of related matters that might be distinguished more precisely by words like "aesthetics," "fashion," "taste," "form," "monumentality," "patronage," and "authorship." The major contributions of this brand of architectural history include a reasonably clear sorting out of visible architectural attributes by period of origin, a literature that characterizes and differentiates the contributions of major designers, and the formation of an "honor roll" of buildings deemed indisputably important and influential. This is the "canon" of U.S. architecture that any informed person must be able to recognize.

Of course, this way of studying buildings ignores a host of issues pertaining to the practical, social, economic, political, and ideological processes of making, using, and altering buildings. Fortunately, at about the same time architectural history emerged as a discrete discipline in North America, a separate group of scholars working mostly outside the academy and often in isolation began attending to these many issues. Until recently, these investigators of architecture identified themselves as something other than "architectural historians." They were *antiquarians, preservationists, archaeologists, anthropologists, folklorists, cultural geographers, social historians, and—significantly—local historians. They have generated a rich and diverse, if scattered, legacy of description and analysis that has accorded serious attention— or acknowledged the necessity for serious attention—to almost every aspect of architecture and every facet of its context. Gradually these diverse practitioners have coalesced around this conviction and under the general though somewhat unwieldy terms "vernacular architectural history," "new architectural history," and most recently, "cultural architectural history."

Despite their ideals and practices of inclusiveness, most of these scholars chose to ignore architectural "style" as a meaningful basis for analysis. The more intellectual among them justified this strategy on the basis of the anthropological understanding of "style" as contingent or superficial—as the detritus that remains once an analyst has accounted for all of an artifact's substantial characteristics. "Style" is merely "cosmetic" in the estimation of one influential folklorist. Other scholars dismissed the matter of architectural "style" for a less rational reason: the term so thoroughly pervaded the language of academic architectural historians with their often limited concerns and discriminating ways.

During the past two decades, this unproductive scholarly polarization gradually has given way to a more thoughtful realization on both sides that architectural "style" is but one of many ways of investigating a building's history and establishing its significance. Thus focused attention on "style" reemerged, and concern for its differentiation from, as well as its connection to, a building's other characteristics attracted new attention. For the most part, those who invoke or address "style" in an intellectually defensible way either explicitly or implicitly draw on an influential definition posited in a 1953 essay by Meyer Schapiro, wherein he concluded that "style" is best understood as "a system of forms with a quality and a meaningful expression" through which the artistic intention of an originator or school of practitioners is discernible. He also identified style as "a vehicle of expression" by which a group of makers and users communicate "certain values of religious, social, and moral life through the emotional suggestiveness of forms." He concluded that "style" also could encompass the "qualities shared by all the arts of a culture during a significant span of time."

This broad but lucid definition accords with the work of those architectural historians who privilege "style." It also offers a basis from which scholars and practitioners of more varied stripe can invoke "style" in their work. Shapiro's formulation, as well as the numerous published elaborations and refinements of its principles, should prove serviceable to the enterprise of local historians. Ironically, it does not, and the reasons shed arresting light on the perplexities and opportunities that local historians confront.

The emergence of *historic preservation in the United States generated, among other important impulses, a popular concern for some way to understand, discuss, and respond to the variations among buildings that they found intriguing. Casting about for answers, people resorted, quite logically, to the authoritative literature on U.S. architectural history that had originated in the academy. From these texts they inferred the apparent primacy of "style." Once the question "What style is it?" gained currency with the general audience for and supporters of historic preservation, writers began publishing architectural manuals to meet a growing demand to identify and understand "style."

Guides-to-the-styles began to appear in the late 1960s, tumbling out of presses at the rate of one every two or three years. This cascade will undoubtedly outlast the twentieth century. That a fair proportion of these books focus on domestic architecture is one important indication of how anxious readers are to learn about the buildings most closely connected with their lives. It also suggests how important the enterprise of architectural identification and understanding is to the means and goals of local historians.

While the authors of these style guides enjoy varying levels of association with the academy, nearly all of them have absorbed one of two crucial lessons available to those who read conventional U.S. architectural history. This means that the style guides themselves fall into two general categories, both of which represent a challenge for local historians who wish to engage with architecture.

The first set of style manuals assumed an authoritative, discerning tone. It tended to confine itself to style categories of venerable pedigree, which leaves out a great deal and thus disappoints many readers.

Furthermore, once the question "What style is it?" has been satisfactorily answered with respect to a particular building, there remains the correlative task of assessing its fitness as a bearer of that style. Is it sophisticated or naive, elaborate or plain, elegant or clumsy? The answers to these questions are inevitably reductive; the instances of architecture for which the style guide has been consulted usually take on the quality of echoes—perhaps wan, sometimes exuberant—of stylistic essences that originated and reached full realization elsewhere. Thus the locality, however varied and complex its architectural heritage, seems derivative, cut-rate, perhaps even beggared.

Authors of the second sort of style manual have absorbed the notion that style designations, because they are paramount in architectural analysis, are capable of universal application and susceptible to free devising. More cognizant than their judgmental counterparts of the role they play in addressing a general and region-oriented audience, these guides have drawn on every imaginable basis for differentiating and designating architecture. Thus there is the "Quaker Style" and the "Shaker Style," the "Log Style" and the "Rammed-Earth Style," the "Prefabricated Style" and the "Mobile-Home Style," the "A-Frame Style" and the "Four-Square Style," the "Strip Style" and the "Commercial Style."

Discerning local historians and an increasingly thoughtful reading public have come to perceive these categories as indefensibly unparallel with bases in such disparate, ahistorical, and manifestly other-than-stylistic characteristics as ethnic or ideological origin, construction material, means of production, type, form, and function.

The pervasive and firmly rooted impulse to address architecture in terms of "style" and its constant refreshment through resort to guidebooks present local historians with a formidable dilemma. There is on one hand the subtle denigration of regionally distinct expressions and idiosyncrasies that the first, magisterially discerning, sort of guidebooks tends to foster. On the other, there is the classifactory muddle generated by the second, enthusiastically inclusive, type of guidebooks. In neither case is there any ground to be gained in overtly challenging the term "style." Where the popular understanding of architecture is concerned, "style" seems as fundamental and incontrovertible as gravity.

Surprisingly, shrewd local historians may find the effects of the magisterial guidebooks easier to manage. When locally numerous or individually prized buildings are left out or casually dismissed, these books unintentionally create opportunities for introducing other attitudes toward architectural value. Fresh attitudes, in turn, can generate architectural points of departure for more developed insights into the local past. Suppose there is no Italianate architecture in this town. Does economic stasis during the third quarter of the nineteenth century account for this local reality? How, indeed, were people making a living here right after the Civil War? Did the building trades stall altogether?

When did they recover and what were the results? Perhaps, in another community, the only building for which there is some guidebook counterpart is the house built by the manager of the local mill. What, then, does its clear affiliation with a recognizable architectural style have to say about its owner's values, resources, and frame of reference? Why are the factory buildings themselves, not to mention the housing of most mill employees, innocent of corresponding embellishment? What "style" are they?

In a different way, the inclusive guidebooks can also function as the texts for useful new lessons. The proliferation of designations that end in the word "style" may lack lexical integrity, yet they involve worthwhile attention to many different sorts of building that contribute in myriad ways to a distinctiveness of place. Furthermore, shrewd local historians can pick up where the badly discriminating style guides leave off, drawing interested readers toward the understanding that a two-room log dwelling constructed in 1820 and a forty-room log resort hotel built in 1920 figure in very different historical contexts and embody very different social meanings, despite their identical materials of fabrication.

Inclusive guidebooks can help demonstrate fundamental historical similarities as well as critical distinctions in chronology. In many rural areas, architectural styles such as Federal, Greek Revival, and Gothic Revival make their successive appearances on houses with the same plans and the same facade compositions. In these cases, the continuity of building form over time is the critical historical lesson; the sequential adoption and abandonment of stylistic motifs manifests a concern for fashion, but clearly there was no fundamental shift in the domestic order of the countryside.

In these and scores of other ways, local historians can persuade colleagues and constituents to abandon the censorious differentiation or conceptual sloppiness inherent in style guides by using them as the starting place for more historically accurate and compassionate ways of thinking. The trick is to keep a dialogue in play after the question "What style is it?" has been addressed. With ingenuity and enthusiasm, this dialogue can transform the confining process of style-designation into the expansive enterprise of discovering, through architecture, the faceted riches of each uniquely important place. For local historians, the frustrations of "style" and its petty uses are thus reconfigured into the rewards of "significance" and its worthy causes.

See John Milnes Baker, *American House Styles: A Concise Guide* (N.Y., 1993); Thomas Carter and Bernard L. Herman, "Toward a New Architectural History," in Carter and Herman, eds., *Perspectives in Vernacular Architecture IV* (Columbia, Mo., 1991), pp. 1–6; Dell Upton, "Form and User: Style, Mode, Fashion, and the Artifact," in Gerald L. Pocius, ed., *Living in a Material World: Canadian and American Approaches to Material Culture* (St. John's, Newfoundland, 1991), pp. 156–169; Dell Upton, "Outside the Academy: A Century of Vernacular Architecture Studies 1890–1990," in Elisabeth Blair MacDougall, ed., *The Architectural Historian in America* (Washington, D.C., 1990), pp. 199–213; Richard Longstreth, *The Buildings of Main Street: A Guide to American Commercial Architecture* (Washington, D.C., 1987); Dell Upton, ed., *America's Architectural Roots: Ethnic Groups That Built America* (Washington, D.C., 1986); Diane Maddex, ed., *Built in the U.S.A.: American Buildings from Airports to Zoos* (Washington, D.C., 1985); Richard Longstreth, "The Problem with 'Style,'" *Forum: Bulletin of the [Society of Architectural Historians] Committee on Preservation* 6 (1984), pp. 1–4; Virginia McAlester and Lee McAlester, *A Field Guide to American Houses* (N.Y., 1984); John C. Poppeliers, S. Allen Chambers, Jr., and Nancy B. Schwartz, *What Style Is It? A Guide to American Architecture* (Washington, D.C., 1983); Jules David Prown, "Style as Evidence," *Winterthur Portfolio* 15 (1980), pp. 197–210; Robert C. Dunnell, "Style and Function: A Fundamental Dichotomy," *American Antiquity* 43 (1978), pp. 192–202; Henry Glassie, *Folk Housing in Middle Virginia: A Structural Analysis of Historic Artifacts* (Knoxville, Tenn., 1975); Margaret Finch, *Style and Art History: An Introduction to the Theories of Style and Sequence* (Metuchen, N.J., 1974); Marcus Whiffen, *American Architecture since 1780: A Guide to the Styles* (Cambridge, Mass., 1969); Vincent J. Scully, Jr., *The Shingle Style and the Stick Style*

(New Haven, Conn., 1955); Meyer Schapiro, "Style," in A. L. Kroeber, ed., *Anthropology Today: An Encyclopedic Inventory* (Chicago, 1953), pp. 287–312; Vincent J. Scully, Jr., *The Cottage Style* (New Haven, Conn., 1949).

CAMILLE WELLS

archives and local history. Governments, organizations, and individuals create and assemble documents in the course of their daily activities. Most of these documents will eventually be discarded as no longer necessary for business, but a relatively small proportion of the records will be preserved because of its historical, legal or general cultural value. Those records having such long-term value are archival. In some usages, the term "archives" is reserved for institutional records. Archives can range in size and complexity from a thin manuscript volume of minutes kept by a local school district to the thousands of linear feet of military pension records preserved in the National Archives. The term "archives" can also refer to the location or agency responsible for the care of the permanent records of an institution. The archives of a local church might be contained in a file drawer under the care of the church officers or of a volunteer historian.

Records are often created and used with little or no thought of their long-term value. Federal and state *pension records for Civil War service were created to insure that those who were entitled to receive pensions were paid. A century later, those records are valuable to genealogists and historians who use them to recreate past lives. *Census and *tax records, originally compiled by local, state, and federal government for the purposes of collecting revenue and apportioning political representatives, are now used to trace migration patterns or examine the occupational structure of a community.

Records documenting a community may be divided among many types of archival repositories. Some will be in the immediate area, either in the local historical society or the offices of local governments. However, much significant documentation may also be available in state and federal archives, in regional and state historical societies, and specialized collections. Records of a defunct local church may have been transferred to a regional or national church archives. Records of a regional, but state-operated mental hospital may have been transferred to a state archives. Military service and pension records for Revolutionary or Civil War service can be found in both state and national archives. The papers of individuals and nongovernmental organizations may be scattered among different types of archives and manuscript collections. In addition to the collections documenting a locality or region, there are repositories specializing in particular subjects, ranging from the histories of special populations, including women, racial and ethnic minorities, religious communities, to topics from medicine or physics to the labor movement and reform. The papers of a nineteenth-century woman botanist who was also active in the women's suffrage movement could easily fall within the subject area of the local historical society where she lived and also within the collecting scope of a repository, perhaps far distant, interested in the history of science or in the experience of women.

There is no single source for locating information about archival collections. The National Union Catalog of Manuscript Collections from the Library of Congress, in both its older printed form and newer on-line version, provides national coverage. Many archives and historical societies, particularly in larger institutions, list some or all of their collections in the Online Computer Library Center (OCLC) or the Research Libraries Information Network (RLIN) on-line catalogs. In addition, there are guides to individual repositories and subjects.

Unfortunately, many repositories do not have either the time or the staff to contribute information about their holdings to the national guides and library catalogs. Researchers need to use multiple strategies to locate material. The published and on-line guides are useful but incomplete. Comprehensive research requires individual contacts with libraries, archives, and fellow researchers.

Researchers should expect to work with the reference staff of the archives or historical society. Letters of inquiry addressed to an archive should be as specific as possible. A brief explanation of your research topic may also be helpful. Often an archivist or librarian can suggest related material. Don't ask for "everything you have on the Civil War" if your subject is limited to life on the home front in a specific locality. Researchers should also be familiar with the secondary literature on their topic. Researchers often locate relevant mate-

rials by looking at footnotes and bibliographies in published histories. There is no need for a researcher to spend his or her time, or that of an archives staff, reading through boxes of records if the information required is readily accessible in a printed source. It is often a good idea to call in advance when first visiting an archives to verify their hours and the accessibility of materials. It is wasted expense to travel to a remote city only to find that the material you seek is in a remote storage area and cannot be retrieved for several days or has been loaned to another institution for an exhibit. Check also to see whether the material you need has been microfilmed or published. It may be possible to borrow or purchase microfilm rather than travel to a collection.

While archives and manuscript collections exist to support research, and most welcome any knowledgeable researcher, archives have a responsibility to ensure the preservation of unique and often fragile records. Archives have to protect the documents in their care from loss or damage. A diary kept by a schoolteacher in 1905 may have little monetary value, but if it is damaged by improper photocopying, or is stolen, it is still irreplaceable and its loss is a loss to history. Archives usually require that a researcher sign in to the reading room, provide identification and use materials under supervision.

Archives and researchers should be aware of potential *copyright issues involved in the reproduction and use of documents and images. Any plans for publication should be cleared with the archives. A local historical society may own a diary or a collection of photographs, but the copyright may remain with the original writer or photographer, or their descendants and heirs. It is the responsibility of the archives to inform persons wishing to publish direct copies or extensive quotations that the material may be covered by copyright, and it is the responsibility of the user to investigate the copyright status of any document or image he or she wishes to publish. In addition, archives will often charge a use fee for reproducing images from its collections.

CHRISTOPHER DENSMORE

Archives of American Art, The. The Archives of American Art was created in early 1954 out of the scholarly frustration of Lawrence A. Fleischman, who collected American art in Detroit, Michigan. The problem, as Fleischman saw it, was that the United States was large and the papers and memorabilia relating to those in the American art field were scattered geographically. Fleischman was also struck that in the aftermath of World War II there were only about nine books written about American art, yet there were over a hundred about Pablo Picasso alone. He felt that the field of American art deserved much more attention.

Fleischman created an organization to collect materials in one place for easier access for scholars. Dr. Edgar P. Richardson, then director of the Detroit Institute of Arts and a renowned scholar in his own right, seized upon the idea and added an important tool—microfilm. Thus, it would be simple to duplicate institutional records as well as materials that for various reasons could not be donated.

The Archives of American Art was chartered on November 11, 1955, and took up the challenge of gathering and microfilming material beginning with the holdings of the American Philosophical Society in Philadelphia. Foundations also provided substantial support to the Archives, and its collections began to grow.

Edgar P. Richardson, who had acted as director during the first organizing years, was replaced by William J. Woolfenden. In May 1970, the Archives of American Art joined the Smithsonian Institution in Washington, D.C.

The Archives now has over 13,000,000 items and has collecting, membership, and development initiatives reaching all over the country and abroad.

The holdings of the Archives of American Art cover the period from the founding of the United States to the present. It is the largest archive of primary source documentation on the visual arts in America. It includes over 5,000 collections of letters, diaries, sketches and sketchbooks, photographs, exhibition catalogs, scrapbooks, business records, and art periodicals totaling 13 million items. Also available are over 3,000 interviews, which are part of the Archive's oral history project, and 1,000 photographs related to artists' collections. There are invaluable records from galleries including sales books, price lists, publicity material and artists' files. The records associated with the seminal 1913 Armory Show are also available as are numerous art-school records. The collections are strongest in the period from the beginning of the twentieth century through the 1950s and include information on Latino artists, African American artists, and women artists. There is also strong documentation from the WPA of the New Deal era including oral histories and photographs.

The Archives' original material may be consulted, by appointment and without fee, at the National Museum of American Art/National Portrait Gallery in Washington, D.C. The most actively used holdings are available on microfilm through interlibrary loan or at Archives offices in Washington, New York, and San Marino, California, or at research centers in Boston and San Francisco. The Archives also has a website : <www.si.edu/artarchives>.

BARBARA FLEISCHMAN

Archives Week. Usually held in October, Archives Week is a program for raising public awareness about who archivists are and what they do. The idea, still in a fledgling stage of development, offers great potential for local historical groups with archival records and manuscripts collections as part of their operations.

The idea for an annual Archives Week program was first promoted in the late 1970s by the International Council on Archives (ICA). The North American impetus came from the New York State Archives and Records Administration, which began in the late 1980s. This program has expanded across a seven-state region, south through Virginia. Elsewhere, archival groups, particularly in Ohio, Kansas, and Arizona, have also developed annual programs, generally held during October.

Archives Week activities can include open houses, speakers, workshops, and exhibits that involve the public—from school-age youngsters to the elderly—and teach the value of historically important textual materials. Local historical societies, genealogical societies, and community history centers in public libraries frequently have materials, such as photographs, maps, and even newspaper clippings, that can be used in the annual observance. Most of the programs organized by professional archivists also have a poster for distribution focusing on the rich resources housed in archival repositories.

For the Archives Week idea to reach its full potential, more archivists and those with responsibility for manuscripts need to make a commitment to a program where it does not currently exist. Even so, the programs have grown, instilling confidence that the idea will continue to spread in the years ahead.

GEORGE W. BAIN

Armenians. See Appendix A.

Arminianism. The theological belief of James Arminius, a seventeenth-century Dutch Protestant theologian who rejected John Calvin's idea of predestination in favor of a belief in faith and good works. The Arminian belief is that all who believe in Christ can be saved and that atonement is universal.

armory. A place in which weapons and ammunition are stored and where meetings are often held.

ARNOVA. The Association for Research on Nonprofit Organizations and Voluntary Action is an international association promoting the study of non-governmental organizations and activities, including *philanthropy, voluntarism, and nonprofit entities.

Drawing its membership from all social disciplines, as well from the ranks of thoughtful practitioners, the Association supports a quarterly journal, *Nonprofit & Voluntary Sector Quarterly*; a newsletter; a website, <ARNOVAL@ wvnvm.wvnet.edu>; and an annual conference. Since its establishment in 1972 as the Association of Voluntary Action Scholars, the journal and annual meeting have been important venues for presenting and publishing sociological and historical studies of communities and community institutions.

Further information about ARNOVA and a complete index of articles published in *Nonprofit & Voluntary Sector Quarterly* can be obtained through its website <http.//www. arnova.org>.

PETER DOBKIN HALL

Ashkenazie Jews. See Appendix B.

Asian American history. American economic, political, and religious ambitions in Asia and Asian migration to America prompted some of the earliest works of Asian American history. Accordingly, trade, missionary labors, colonialism, the United States's Pacific destiny, and Asian exclusion and assimilation are dominant themes within that foundational literature, and Asian American history is commonly grouped under the rubrics of U.S. diplomatic history and the history of U.S. race relations. Prominent within Asian American historiography are three interpretive strands advanced by anti-Asianists

and cultural brokers; liberals; and Asian Americanists.

Central to the debate between anti-Asianists and cultural brokers are the questions over America's place within world history and the nature of U.S. history and society. William Speer, a Presbyterian missionary to China, published his *The Oldest and Newest Empire: China and the United States* (Cincinnati, Ohio, 1870). Contemporary concern over Chinese migration or "the Chinese question" motivated Speer to write a book that, he promised, would explain to Americans the true character and capacities of the Chinese by a cultural broker (someone who claims the ability to mediate between cultures). Speer's canvas is large and offers a history of Europe's fascination and encounters with Asia beginning with Marco Polo's late–thirteenth-century account of China. It provides an argument for American expansion because of the Republic's location, sitting at the confluence of Europe's civilization and Asia's wealth. The world's oldest empire—China—writes Speer, must give way to its newest empire—the United States—that was destined for "peculiar glory" in the meeting of East and West.

Those Pacific visions by cultural brokers like Speer arose in defense of America's westward expansions across the continent and the ocean that was the highway to Asia's raw materials and manufactures. These were the forerunners of the imperialists of the late nineteenth century who proclaimed America's manifest destiny in the Pacific and Asia. But they also sought to counter the anti-Asianists' claim that Asian migration to America threatened to tear the nation's economic, political, and moral fabric. Pierton W. Dooner's *Last Days of the Republic* (San Francisco, 1879), for instance, presented a case for the exclusion of Chinese workers in a genre called by Dooner "deductive history." The book is set in the future, but reads as an historical account of the United States's demise brought about by cheap Chinese labor that swamps first California and then the rest of the nation. In 1893, during the noonday of European imperialism, English historian Charles H. Pearson published his *National Life and Character: A Forecast* (London and N.Y., 1894), in which he predicted a final conflict for global supremacy between whites and nonwhites led by Asians. Nonwhite migration from the tropics to the temperate, white heartlands, warned Pearson, threatened to engulf white civilization and conjured up the specter of the "yellow peril," an idea then prevalent in Europe and America. For both the cultural brokers and anti-Asianists, especially after the advent of European and U.S. expansions to the tropics, what happened "out there" in the peripheries held growing significance for what happened "here" within the core.

Asians, like whites, offered to interpret Asian culture to whites and to contest the claims of the anti-Asianists. Indeed, to cultural brokers, the acculturation of Asians documented the falsity of the anti-Asianist contention that Asian cultures were at odds with European civilization and that they were unassimilable. Born near Macao in 1828, Yung Wing was schooled by missionaries before leaving for the United States in 1847 to further his education. After graduat-

ing from Yale in 1854, Yung returned to China, where he organized the government-sponsored Chinese Educational Mission that sent 120 Chinese youths for studies in the United States from 1872 to 1881. In his autobiography, *My Life in China and America*, published in 1909 (N.Y.), Yung endorsed the missionaries' claim that Christianity had the power to transform Chinese culture and that education could lead to the "reformation and regeneration" of China. Yung testified to "a metamorphosis in his inward nature," yet declared his "undying love for China."

In the early twentieth century, "liberals" joined the debate between cultural brokers and anti-Asianists. What distinguishes the liberal writers from their nineteenth-century predecessors is their belief in the progressive view of American history that conceives of the Republic as a nation of immigrants who were "pushed" by hard times and persecution and were "pulled" to these shores by the land's bounties and the society's freedoms and opportunities. The saga moves from despair to hope, from poverty to plenty, failure to success as immigrants struggle to make a home for themselves in the United States and achieve the "American dream." Liberals applied the historical template derived from the late-nineteenth-century European migrations to the simultaneous migrations from Asia.

Liberal writings might have marked a departure from previous Asian American histories, but they were also connected with the works of cultural brokers in that both sought to undermine the arguments posed by anti-Asianists and thereby defend not only Asian migrants but the ideals of American society and America's national interests as they saw them. Mary Roberts Coolidge's *Chinese Immigration* ([1909] Taipei, 1986) is clearly the most important liberal text, because it identified the historical problem as posed by the liberals and offered its explanation. Begun during the debate around the Geary Act of 1892 that extended the decade-long exclusion of Chinese workers, Coolidge's book delineated the processes whereby Asians became or were prevented from becoming Americans—that of inclusion or exclusion—along with their domestic and international ramifications. And despite subsequent compelling evidence that refutes and revises her version of Asian American history, Coolidge's statement of the problem and its explanation remain the standard treatment today.

Called the California thesis, Coolidge's account of the rise and nature of the anti-Chinese movement depends upon conditions peculiar to the time but also to the place. Pivotal was the gold rush that attracted to the state, according to Coolidge, Southerners who held racial prejudices against darker-skinned people, ignorant and greedy frontiersmen who viewed all nonwhites as inferiors, and recent immigrants such as the Irish who resented competition from the Chinese. East Coast Know-Nothing *nativism and xenophobia were additional ingredients exported to the California mix of hatred against the Chinese, who were vilified as scapegoats for the economic decline that followed the initial euphoria of instant wealth and the exhaustion of surface mining. In truth, maintained Coolidge, Chinese workers bolstered California's economy and the anti-Chinese movement tarnished the United States' reputation abroad and threatened its trade with China and Asia.

Although European immigration proved the rule for some liberals, the "Oriental question" seemed to pose an exception to the melting-pot notion to others. Robert Park, a sociologist like Mary Roberts Coolidge, and several of his colleagues and students at the University of Chicago during the 1920s and 1930s took a special interest in that "question." Park's race-relations cycle of migration, competition, accommodation, and assimilation described the European experience, but failed to account for the receptions of both Africans and Asians because of their "physical marks." Race constituted a barrier to their full participation in American life, Park concluded. Park's Survey of Race Relations that interviewed hundreds of Asians and non-Asians along the West Coast and publications that emanated from the "Chicago school" were enormously influential in reshaping and validating the liberal interpretation of the Asian-American experience. Still prevalent are the ideas drawn from the Chicago school such as Park's race-relations cycle, an approach to race relations that pivots on the white and nonwhite axis, the assumption of assimilation, European immigration's paradigmatic status, the focus upon urban communities, and the notion that minorities are "deviations" from the European "norm."

Asian Americanist writings depart from the liberal tradition in that they center upon the Asian American subject for and of itself. In their view, inaccurate are representations of Asian Americans drawn from European American models and by studies that conceive of Asian Americans as social problems and deviations or that ignore the aspirations and perspectives of the subjects themselves. During the 1920s and 1930s, with the coming of age of a second generation, Asian Americanists began documenting their lives and histories to record the realities of their past and present as they saw them, and to mobilize a sense of community and collective agency. Takashi Tsutsumi, secretary of the Federation of Japanese Labor, published in 1921 his *Hawaii Undo Shi* (History of Hawaii Laborers' Movement). He wrote to inform Japanese sugar-plantation workers about the injustices perpetrated by the sugar planters, and to present the union's version of the 1920 strike that involved 8,300 Filipino and Japanese laborers or about 77 percent of the total plantation workforce on the island of Oahu. Ernest K. Wakukawa's *A History of the Japanese People in Hawaii* (1938) was written in English and addressed the second generation, who, the author observed, often failed to appreciate "the achievements and accomplishments of the pioneers and their forebears." History, he hoped, would help them understand "their own status and problems."

Those Asian Americanist concerns and purposes are evident in contemporary texts such as Ronald Takaki's *Strangers from a Different Shore* (Boston, 1989) and Sucheng Chan's *Asian Americans: An Interpretive History* (Boston, 1991) that have become standard surveys of the Asian American experience. But the rise and now predominance of the Asian Americanist interpretation hasn't foreclosed its antecedents, and readers can still find remnants and variants of cultural brokers, anti-Asianists, and liberals in the comparative effusion of writings on Asian Americans today. In truth, although they might comprise distinctive strands, the three varieties of Asian American history overlap and form continuities as well as breaks. Cultural brokers held liberal ideals of America's identity and promise; Asian Americanists claimed the role of cultural brokers between wider society and "their" communities; and anti-Asianists and liberals contended their versions of the past and present were in the best traditions of the Republic's founders.

For local historians, the writings by liberals and Asian Americanists should hold the most interest. The sociological studies from the University of Chicago, for instance, offer exemplary accounts of Asian American communities in places like Seattle, Chicago, San Francisco, Los Angeles, Hawaii, and Butte, Montana. Key texts include S. Frank Miyamoto's *Social Solidarity among the Japanese of Seattle* (1939), and Paul C. P. Siu's *The Chinese Laundryman: A Study of Social Isolation* (N.Y., 1987). Asian Americanists, like the liberal sociologists, have stressed urban communities, mainly Chinatowns and Japantowns in California and New York. Exceptions include Illsoo Kim, *New Urban Immigrants: The Korean Community in New York* (Princeton, 1981); Robert N. Anderson et al., *Filipinos in Rural Hawaii* (Honolulu, 1984); and

Bruce La Brack, *The Sikhs of Northern California, 1904–1975* (N.Y., 1988). Asian Americanists have also studied rural communities primarily in Hawaii and on the West Coast, and local historians and history societies have published significant numbers of works designed principally to document the past and ensure a collective identity in the future. These include: Ethnic Studies Oral History Project, *Uchinanchu: A History of Okinawans in Hawaii* (Honolulu, 1981); Steven Misawa, ed., *Beginnings: Japanese Americans in San Jose* (1981); Chinese Historical Society of Southern California, *Linking Our Lives: Chinese American Women of Los Angeles* (1984); Ron Chew, ed., *Reflections of Seattle's Chinese Americans: The First 100 Years* (1994); Pepi Nieva, ed., *Filipina: Hawaii's Filipino Women* (1994); and Daisy Chun Rhodes, *Passages to Paradise: Early Korean Immigrant Narratives from Hawaii* (1998).

GARY Y. OKIHIRO

attainder, bill of. In English law, a bill passed by the legislature that decreed that certain crimes, especially treason, required the forfeiture of all property and civil rights. Such bills are expressly forbidden under the U.S. Constitution.

Australian local history. Interest in local history or community history (a recent term) in Australia has grown enormously in the latter half of this century. Since the nineteenth century, considerable historical collections have been amassed by the national and state libraries, the national archives, state historical societies, and over the past thirty years, by public libraries. While these collections have always been of interest to historians, it was not until the 1970s that attention was focused on local history. The federal Australian Heritage Commission Act of 1975, and subsequent state acts, which emphasized preservation and conservation of the built and natural environment, also created an upsurge of interest in local history generally. As a result of this legislation Heritage Councils and National Trust offices were formed in all states of Australia, and Australians were encouraged to actively participate in collecting, preserving, and managing their local historical resources. Museums, local historical societies, and local history collections in public libraries were established around the country, promoting the history of the local community, events, and people.

At the same time universities expanded their public and social history programs to include local history. As a result of these courses, professional and academic public historians have been responsible for the publication of many excellent local histories commissioned by local authorities. During the same period, amateur historians also produced an array of local and family histories. Most family histories have been written by enthusiastic amateurs. University programs, while supporting public and local history, have shown less interest in educating family historians so whilst there are some excellent family histories published, some publications have been limited.

Initially the emphasis of local history was on "settler/explorer history," the experiences of white settlers in Australia, but over the past twenty years this changed, and as a result local histories now are far more diverse, giving a voice to all Australians. Australia is now recognized as a multicultural society, and federal and state governments have legislated to protect Aboriginal heritage and culture, and Aboriginal people have introduced their stories in art, printed works, exhibitions, and multimedia. Ethnic communities have also claimed their place in local history, local museums and heritage organizations, and are actively engaged in presenting their stories to the community. Different perceptions on the development of Australia have not necessarily meant an easy path for local history. Local histories based on their cultural history and the personal experiences of different sectors of the population has meant that local history must be recognized as coming from a range of cultural perspectives. With authors coming from vastly different cultural backgrounds, some of these publications may well be contested histories that may cause upset in the local community, but they will ultimately bring a richness to the local community that would otherwise not be available.

What constitutes local history has now also been widened to encompass corporate and institutional history and histories of individuals, families, the natural and *built environment, houses, streetscapes, and different sectors of the community.

Local history in Australia today is in a curious situation. On the one hand, the community sense of local history is strong. Local authorities have been required, under legislation, to undertake inventories of *heritage places within

their boundaries. This has resulted in the collecting of documentary heritage about the locality, including family and corporate records, oral histories, and photographs. This in turn has resulted in a greater interest by local communities in their own heritage, which has resulted in people acquiring a sense of heritage, finding value in their own community and resulting in greater stress being placed on developing cultural *tourism.

To encourage visitors, councils are supporting a proliferation of pamphlets, booklets, and exhibitions promoting heritage walks, heritage places and local events and people. To support the interpretation and promotion of the heritage of the local community, collections of local historical materials are mushrooming in public libraries, but are still drastically underfunded. Heritage organizations, supported by the federal and state governments, are engaged in promoting strategies for the protection, conservation, and management of heritage places in local communities. Practitioners from a wide range of disciplines involved in the heritage industry—museums, historical research, conservation, archaeology, archives, and libraries—are being drawn together to support this, and the presentation and interpretation of local history to the community.

Local history has become cultural heritage with concerns at many levels: the natural and built environment, the collection of objects in local museums and local history collections, cultural tourism, and conservation. Conservation and presentation of the country's heritage as linked to the future of

Australia. The emphasis is on ensuring the cultural heritage as a mainstream activity supporting a national inventory of places, collections, and activities.

On the other hand, there are fewer professionally commissioned local histories being funded and published. Universities, in a period of stringent budget cuts, are concentrating on the broader public-history courses and reducing a particular emphasis on local history, although several are rethinking the needs of family and community historians who are not interested in undertaking the more traditional form of study, and devising special courses to suit them. Excellent academic local histories continue to be published but local government funds must now support all aspects of cultural heritage.

Conceptually there is confusion over the placement of local history in the broader cultural-heritage scene. The heritage industry is a powerful one, particularly cultural-heritage tourism, and the place of local history in tourism and the relationship between all the disciplines involved in presenting and preserving the history of the local community requires further exploration. While local communities are becoming enthusiastic about their heritage, often there is little understanding about where their community fits into the national cultural-heritage landscape. A gap remains between the enthusiastic local and the cultural-heritage professionals. With heritage becoming a viable industry, local communities see cultural tourism as an economic gain without necessarily understanding the need for advice and assistance from professional local historians.

Undoubtedly there is considerable interest in cultural heritage at a community level, but it appears the community wants its history presented in a palatable form: booklets, brochures, exhibitions, videos, websites, plaques, and events that emphasize cultural tourism. These formats provide an interesting but often superficial overview of the local community and its history, and there is a danger that larger well-researched publications may be overlooked. How to unite the scholarly and the popular remains an issue.

There is also a need to increase commitment to the development of local history collections in libraries and archives. As financial pressures occur at a national and state level, the major collecting institutions in Australia are no longer able to collect material relating to local communities. Unless local libraries develop collections, this material may well be lost. There is a need for public libraries to develop active collecting policies to ensure, as developments take place, that records of the peoples, events, places, and environments are acquired in all formats. As more and more government, commercial, and academic information becomes available only in electronic format, there is a real danger of this information not being retained. There is also a need for these collections to be made accessible electronically for researchers, historians, and the general public. Governments need to be convinced that local history is not only about the past but also about the present and the future, and histories of any type, including local histories, will not be written if the resources are not available.

Local history will continue to flourish, as a separate entity and within the broader cultural-heritage scene. Local history, through its depiction of the community and its peoples, is an important element in the creation of a sense of local identity. As Australia and the world changes, there appears to be a yearning for a tangible connection with the past.

Local history can be presented in many forms: as in-depth publications of local identities, places, events, and peoples; as more ephemeral publications, reenactments, events, and exhibitions; and as collections for students and researchers. All provide a rich tapestry supporting local communities. Local history in Australia is undergoing change but will be richer, more diverse, and in greater demand in the next century.

JAN PARTRIDGE

Austrians. See Appendix A.

automobile. The invention and evolution of the automobile, and their appearance in our communities, is an important local history topic because cars brought with them long-lasting changes that are interesting to research and important to our communities. There were, of course, personal attitudes about automobiles both positive and negative, but in addition, there was the competition between the automobile and the horse-drawn wagon, the need for more and better roads, the importance of laws, both state and local, to regulate ownership and use of automobiles, and there was the expansion of our communities and the homogenization of the population as the automobile allowed people to work and travel beyond a walk or tram-ride from home. In addition, there were many local carriage works that produced early cars; most of these did not last past the earliest days, but they are of local interest. The automobile caused the landscape of our communities to change, for they required roads, signs, parking places, and service stations. Automobiles stimulated *tourism, and this had an effect upon their destinations, while residents in those places responded in various ways. All of these things can be seen in photographs at the turn of the century, in newspaper articles, especially from 1900 through 1920, and in municipal records.

Later, some communities competed to be a destination for the new traveler, while others turned away from visitors who were thought not likely to spend enough money locally to make improvements for them worth undertaking. The automobile altered communities and attitudes about place. They demanded attention unknown earlier.

See Douglas A. Wick, *Automobile History: Day by Day* (Bismark, N.D., 1997); Clay McShane, *Down the Asphalt Path: The Automobile and the American City* (N.Y., 1994); John A. Jakle, *The Tourist: Travel in Twentieth-Century America* (Lincoln, Neb., 1985); and Warren James Belasco, *Americans on the Road: From Autocamp to Motel, 1910–1945* (Cambridge, Mass., 1979).

ℬ

Bahai. See Appendix B.

Balch Institute for Ethnic Studies.
Located in Philadelphia, this is one of the largest research centers for the study of America's immigrant, ethnic, and multicultural heritage in the United States. Founded in 1971 as an independent cultural institution, the Balch includes a museum, education center, and regular series of public programs as well as a major research library and archives. The Institute is named in honor of Emily Swift Balch (1835–1917) and her sons, Thomas W. Balch and Edwin S. Balch (both died 1927) who left instructions in their wills for establishment of a "library and auxiliary museum." The Balch Institute building, only a block and a half from the Liberty Bell and Independence Hall, opened in 1976.

Over the years, the Balch Institute's museum has sponsored multiethnic exhibits such as "Ethnic Images in Advertising," "Ethnic Images in Comics," and "Ethnic Weddings in America" as well as exhibits focusing on the experience of particular ethnic groups, including Poles, Italians, Jews, Chinese, and Japanese. Many of the catalogues of past exhibits, as well as interpretive essays, primary sources, and the card catalogue of the Balch Library are available on the website <www.balchinstitute.org>.

While continuing to gather resources about immigrants from many countries and periods, the Balch Institute currently has a particular research interest in newer immigrants to the United States, especially those who have come in larger numbers since World War II. In 1999, for example, the Balch opened a museum exhibit, "Live Like the Banyan Tree," on the experience of Indian immigrants, based on extensive ethnographic research in that community. Current research projects include Arab Americans and recent African immigrants. Many of these groups have seldom been studied in the American context, and have not had their communities shown to a wide audience.

Projects planned include research on recent immigrants from formerly Communist countries in Eastern Europe; Latino/Hispanic immigrants; Koreans; and Southeast Asian immigrants. These projects include oral histories, museum exhibitions, and published community profiles or guides. All these projects in the New Immigrants Initiative are based on extensive field research, and include advisory committees from the communities. The Balch Institute is committed to working with diverse communities and listening to their stories as part of the process of creating a public representation of immigrant and ethnic communities in America.

The Balch Institute serves as a center for education on American immigration, pluralism, and diversity. Over 25,000 school students a year participate in programs at the Balch and at schools in the community. In addition, Balch educators and staff serve as resources for numerous teacher-training workshops and for visiting university classes. The Balch Institute also sponsors programs on cultural diversity for corporate audiences and adult groups in the community.

The Balch Institute sponsors an extensive public programming series, including films, lectures, cultural demonstrations, and musical events. These are tied both to current exhibitions and to wider themes of pluralism and diversity reflecting issues in America's multiethnic society. An advisory group of leading academics assists in developing programs.

The Balch Library, which houses one of the largest multiethnic collections in the country, supports student study, advanced research, and genealogical investigation. Balch holdings contain material on more than eighty ethnic and racial groups, primary sources on more than thirty groups, and extensive research materials on multiculturalism, immigration, and diversity in the United States. The library contains approximately 60,000 volumes, 6,000 serial titles, 5,000 linear feet of manuscript collections, 6,000 reels of microfilm, 12,000 photographs, and other resources. Library books do not circulate, although books and microfilms are available through interlibrary loan. The Balch Institute serves as home to the Philadelphia Jewish Archives Center (a separate organization) and houses the library and archives of the Scotch-Irish Foundation. In addition, the Temple-Balch Center for Immigration Research is indexing eleven tons of ships' mani-

fests listing U.S. immigrants from 1850 through 1897. The manifests themselves are not available to the public, but many of the indexes have been published and are available in libraries including the Balch.

As noted, the archives include materials from dozens of ethnic groups, including many organizational and individual collections. The largest collections by ethnicity as of 1999, in order of size are: Slovaks, Multiethnic, Poles, Puerto Ricans, Germans, Italians, Greeks, Carpatho-Rusyns, Irish, Swiss, Latinos, Native Americans, Chinese, Jews, Swedes, African Americans, Scots, Japanese, and Lithuanians. These holdings are in English and in other languages.

The Balch Library and Archives have materials from national organizations and from many parts of the United States as well as some holdings from Canada. Collections are particularly strong in materials from the Greater Philadelphia and Eastern Pennsylvania areas. The library holds microfilms for hundreds of ethnic newspapers and magazines published in the nineteenth and twentieth centuries from many cities. Examples include Polish newspapers from Milwaukee, German newspapers from Chicago, Slovak newspapers from Pittsburgh, and Chinese newspapers from Vancouver. Local and national publications appealed to ethnic readers in English and other languages.

Balch holdings range from African American through Italian, Icelandic, and Irish, to Welsh publications. Newspaper files and editorial records include the Greek-language *Atlantis* (New York, 1894–1973) and the Philadelphia edition of the Yiddish *Forward* (1945–1960). The Balch has a significant collection of socialist, labor, and radical publications from this period.

Balch archival holdings for Asian American and Latino/Hispanic populations are growing. Multiethnic collections include papers of The Council of Spanish-Speaking Organizations (El Concilio) from Philadelphia and the Southeast Asian Resource Action Council (national, based in Washington, D.C.) The Balch archives include a significant collection related to the internment of Japanese Americans during World War II. The Institute holds records of many fraternal and mutual-support organizations. Cartoons, postcards, and articles illustrating ethnic prejudice and stereotyping are also well represented.

The museum collection of over 4,000 items is especially rich in objects brought, made, or used by immigrants and their children in the years from 1860 to the present. These include items and crafts associated with ethnic clothing and festivals, ethnic cuisine, work and business, and spiritual life. Games, posters, and commercial products showing ethnic images—whether of inclusion or of stereotypes—are a significant part of the collection.

Guides to the Balch archives and to the museum collections were published in 1992. At this writing, copies are still available, as are catalogues from many of the past exhibits.

The Balch Institute for Ethnic Studies is located at 18 South Seventh Street, Philadelphia PA 19106; (215) 925-8090; fax (215) 925-8195 <www.balch-institute.org> .

ROBERT TABAK

Balkan peoples. See Appendix A.

Baltic people. See Appendix A.

Bancroft, Hubert Howe (1832–1918). A turn-of-the-century historical entrepreneur, Bancroft laid the foundations for state and local history of California and the Pacific Slope. Born in Ohio, he came to San Francisco in 1852 where he began as a bookseller. He slowly added music, stationery, maps, printing and binding to his business. Around 1860, he began a project that would lead to the publication between 1874 and 1890 of a 39-volume history of the West, plus over twenty other books. His field was *Western History, from prehistoric times to the end of the nineteenth century; from the Rockies to the Pacific, and from Alaska to Central America.

Bancroft entitled his autobiography *Literary Industries* (San Francisco, 1890), and that pretty much describes how he produced his books. Recognizing that no single human being could research and write the books he envisioned, Bancroft set up a factory in which he hired assistants who collected books and manuscripts, interviewed, organized, indexed, and often even wrote first drafts of his material. Bancroft's firm printed, bound, advertised, and marketed (sometimes by pre-publication subscription) his books.

Both during his lifetime and since, critics have denigrated Bancroft's works, sometimes severely. He has been accused of sloppiness, inaccuracies, plagiarism, and prejudice (usually in favor of subscribers' points of view). Many academics simply cannot cope with the commercialism of the whole enterprise. Although there is merit in most of the criticisms, the fact remains that the Bancroft productions are still useful.

Bancroft's histories were lengthy, detailed descriptive and narrative works free of the philosophical frameworks that characterized so much nineteenth-century history writing in the United States. Thus, the local or state historian will find in Bancroft a mass of detailed information, often from sources no longer extant. The books were also heavily documented (on many pages, the footnotes were longer than the text!), providing present-day historians good leads to sources. A California or western local historian who ignores these volumes misses a valuable starting point.

RAYMOND STARR

Bancroft Library. The Bancroft Library began in 1905 when the University of California purchased the Hubert Howe Bancroft collection of research materials on the western United States and Latin America—a move that the university hoped would change its image from a minor teacher-training institution to a major research university. From that time forward, the Bancroft Library, which is housed on the University's Berkeley campus, has been one of the great research centers of the nation.

As noted, the library began with the Bancroft collection of over 16,000 volumes, which had been assembled since 1860 by Bancroft in order to produce and sell over sixty volumes of the history of the West. In time, the holdings ranged from pre-Columbian native cultures and the Spanish colonists, to 1905. The library included published items—books, diaries, travel accounts, memoirs, published documents, newspapers, maps, manuscripts public and private, and transcripts of oral interviews with many participants. In many cases, the Bancroft had the only copy extant of the item.

Since its inception, the Bancroft Library has continued to add material in support of its original collection until by 1998 it has over 400,000 volumes; 32,000 linear feet of manuscripts; 3,500,000 photographs and other visual images; 67,000 microforms, and 21,000 maps. That is supplemented by its Regional Oral History Office, which, since 1954, has been interviewing in order to fill in the gaps in the written record. Focusing on modern California, public affairs, government, and the arts, the office has over 1,250 oral-interview transcripts of their own, plus additional ones from other institutions that have been deposited there.

Anyone doing state or local history of the American West, especially California, should know of the Bancroft Library and its holdings. The Bancroft Library is located at the University of California at Berkeley, Berkeley, CA 94720-6000; (510) 642-6481; <www.lib.berkeley.edu/BANC>.

RAYMOND STARR

Baptists. See Appendix B.

Basques. See Appendix A.

Belgians. See Appendix A.

best-sellers. The earliest best-selling book was the *Bay Psalm Book* issued in

1640 and in 27 editions thereafter. During the eighteenth century, most readers in the United States sought out theology; among the Revolutionary generation, political philosophy was important, especially John Dickinson's *Letters from a Farmer in Pennsylvania* (issued in 1768) and Thomas Paine's *Common Sense* (1776). Susanna Rowson's *Charlotte Temple* (1791) was the first best-selling novel; James Fenimore Cooper and Washington Irving became the most prominent nineteenth-century authors. See Alice Payne Hackett and James Henry Burke, *Eighty Years of Best Sellers, 1895–1975* (N.Y., 1977). This book is usually found in the reference collection.

biographical dictionaries. There are a number of biographical dictionaries worth consulting:

Who's Who in America: A Biographical Dictionary of Notable Living Men and Women (Chicago, 1899–). This standard dictionary of contemporary biography is issued biennially and has constantly been expanded since 1899. Regional directories are designed to supplement this work (*Who's Who in the East*, etc.).

Who Was Who in America: Historical Volume 1607–1896 (Chicago, 1963; revised edition, 1967).

American Biographical Archive (London, N.Y., 1986–1991). This large microfiche set has entries from 368 of the most important English-language biographical reference works on the United States and Canada originally published between 1702 and 1956, reproduced in a single alphabetical sequence. An accompanying six-volume printed bibliography, *American Biographical Index* (London, N.Y., 1993), lists the collective biographies that are included on the microfiche, along with the names of the persons whose biographies are to be found there.

American National Biography, John A. Garraty and Mark C. Carnes, eds. (N.Y., 1999). Informed by recent historical scholarship and reflecting a high level of diversity, this set describes the lives of 17,000 people, both well known and obscure.

Dictionary of American Biography (N.Y., 1928–1937, vols. 1–20). Covering noteworthy persons of all periods, this work has signed articles with bibliographies. More than 13,600 biographies are in the basic volumes; periodic supplements bring the coverage forward in time.

The National Cyclopaedia of American Biography (N.Y., 1892–). Less selective than the *Dictionary of American Biography*, this voluminous set includes photographs.

Notable American Women: A Biographical Dictionary, Edward T. James, ed. (Cambridge, Mass., 1971–1980). Vols. 1–3: 1607–1950; Vol. 4: the modern period. This scholarly work includes biographies of more than 1,350 women.

Black Biographical Dictionaries 1790–1950 (Alexandria, Va., 1987). This microfiche set reproduces the contents of nearly 300 volumes containing biographies detailing the life and times of more than 30,000 nineteenth- and twentieth-century Afro-Americans.

Black Biography, 1790–1950: A Cumulative Index (Alexandria, Va., 1991), in three volumes, this is an alphabetical list by name, and provides some biographical information as well: birth and death dates, place of birth, occupation, and religious affiliation. Volume 3 has a separate index of women, and personal names listed by place of birth, occupation, and religion.

Encyclopedia of American Biography, John A. Garraty and Jerome L. Sternstein, eds. (N.Y., c.1996). This is a one-volume work with descriptions and evaluations of the lives of more than 1,000 persons, living and dead. Each entry has two distinct parts: factual and evaluative.

Biographical Dictionaries and Related Works: An International Bibliography of Approximately 16,000 Collective Biographies, Robert B. Slocum, ed. (Detroit, 1986). Collective biographies of persons of local interest can be found under the section entitled "United States: Local (States, Cities, and Regions)."

Dictionary of Canadian Biography (Toronto, 1966–1998), vols. 1–14. This distinguished work is organized by chronological periods, with the first volume covering 1000–1700. There is an index of names at the end.

MARTHA R. HSU

bird's eye view. The term refers to a landscape seen from above. In nineteenth-century America, prints with bird's eye views of towns and cities were immensely popular. Most of the prints are lithographs, a process that became commercial in America after 1820; lithography was much quicker and cheaper than etching or engraving. These prints, often in color, showed every building and landmark in the urban scene as well as some of the surrounding landscape. The idea of making such prints was not new, but what was distinctively American according to John Reps (*Bird's Eye Views: Historic Lithographs of North American Cities* [N.Y.: 1998]), was their sheer volume. By the time the fad died

Bird's eye view of Bismark, North Dakota

in the early twentieth century, there was one bird's-eye view lithograph of as many as 2,400 places, often in more than one version (Reps, p. 7).

Although prominent artists like Fitz Hugh Lane were known to produce these prints, most of the work was done by lesser-known artists who traveled from town to town soliciting enough orders to make a printing run profitable. These itinerant urban viewmakers were welcomed by town *boosters. In some cases, the "towns" depicted were in fact the fantasies of real estate promoters. However even the most accurate were highly selective. They tended to emphasize commerce and suggest an order and dynamism that did not exist at street level. Key parts of the city, such as scenes of squalor, vice, and congestion, were ignored. Nevertheless, local historians will find these wonderful views a treasure trove of information. Not only do they depict existing structures and their relationship to one another, they often included descriptive text and detailed vignettes of individual buildings.

NORMA PRENDERGAST

Blockson, Charles L., Afro-American Historical Collection. This archive, created by Charles L. Blockson, is devoted in particular to the history of African Americans and the Underground Railroad. It is located in Sullivan Hall, on the Main Campus, Temple University. The telephone number is (215) 204-6632; see <www.library.temple.edu/blockson>.

book dealer, notes from. Historical societies, and collectors of local history, will find that many dealers who handle

out-of-print and antiquarian books are a good source for acquiring material. Dealers who are local-history–oriented will try to stock whatever they can: books, pamphlets, maps, manuscripts, and other printed and written items. There are regional printed guides that list book dealers and their specialties and some public libraries also have publications listing dealers.

After locating several nearby dealers it would be profitable to visit them to see their mode of operation, and to inquire if they handle materials in your line of interest. Some work out of open shops, but many others work out of their homes, barns, garages, rental storage, or trailers, and an appointment is needed.

Once you have located one or more dealers who handle items in your field of interest, it would be good to visit them from time to time to see what new items have come into stock. If they issue catalogs, ask to be put on the mailing list. Choice items sell fast. The dealer should mail the parcel to you as soon as possible after receiving your check. Because of the volume of phone calls received on a catalog, a dealer who is working alone may take several days to process an order. After a catalog has been mailed out, he often has to spend the next two or three days answering the phone. To remain profitable, dealers must update their mailing lists, and drop those who have not placed an order after receiving several catalogs.

The relationship between the out-of-print and antiquarian book dealer, and collectors and historical societies is a two-way street. The dealer should provide accurate descriptions of the items he offers for sale, carefully pack ordered items for shipping, and be reasonably prompt in completing the transaction. He should notify his customers when items come into stock that he believes they may have an interest in. It is important to read the descriptions in catalogs very carefully and to know exactly what the item is before ordering it. If you phone in your order, most booksellers will be glad to give you further information about the material you are interested in. Follow the payment instructions given in the catalog. Most dealers are willing to make special arrangements to meet budget needs. People who are chronically late in paying are apt to receive no more catalogs.

There are a great many other items that should be collected to enhance the value of the library for researchers. *Identified photographs* are frequently one-of-a-kind photographs of local people and scenes. **Directories* mirror the importance of a town. If you study the directories of a now sleepy town you may find that it once was a hive of industry and commerce. *Newspapers* detail local events. *Church histories* and *biographies of ministers* contain facts and anecdotes not always found in standard town histories. *Business histories* not only provide local details, but often include the influence of the business on other areas of the country.

Catalogs issued by local factories illustrate the products made there, and no doubt some of those products are still being used. Local *celebration pamphlets*, common in the first half of the 20th century, often contain photographs taken expressly for the publication.

Broadsides (sheets printed on one side only) announced local events, of-fered rewards for lost cattle, solicited bids for work, and products for sale. *Folded view booklets*, mainly 1880–1910, offer town views of buildings and street scenes available nowhere else. *Maps*, both printed and manuscript, are essential to the study of local history. *Hotel registers*, signed by overnight guests, inform researchers of important personages who passed through the town, and when.

Manuscript letters and diaries containing accounts of local people and events offer a wealth of information to historians and genealogists. A single line in an otherwise mundane letter can be of value. For instance one sentence, "D.L. Moody the famous evangelist was in town last night and held a meeting at the Baptist Church," pinpoints where Moody was and what he was doing at a specific time. An ordinary looking *diary* from the 1860s with brief lines on weather and farm activity, became much more valuable when it was discovered it contained three pages describing the Confederate invasion of York, Pa. It must be remembered that handwritten and typed *manuscripts* are the basis of almost all written history.

From time to time *school district records* and *Justice of the Peace records* come on the market, and they provide the names of pupils and details of legal actions that occurred locally. Manuscript *business records*: ledgers, journals, invoices, and correspondence give information on the economic history of an area. General *store account books* are valuable for knowing what type of merchandise was used in a particular section, prices, and names of the residents within the trading district of the store.

Autobiographies, family genealogy, or *recollections, sketchbooks*, and other papers originally made only for the writer appear for sale from time to time. Other types of manuscripts include: wills, deeds, legal papers, personal account books, and account books of businesses.

Local pamphlets often cover a variety of topics. If the pamphlet was published locally it shows the workmanship of the resident printer.

What should be done with materials donated to an historical society? There are many horror stories of donated items being relegated to a dark corner, never used, and ending up being ruined by neglect. The society should tactfully refuse any item that does not fit in with their collections. Accepted material should be cataloged within a reasonable length of time and made available to researchers. On occasion the donor will put restrictions on the use of the papers, usually stipulating that they cannot be used for a certain number of years to prevent embarrassment for people still living. These restrictions must be honored. The papers should be processed, sealed, labeled, and put in a safe area.

HAROLD NESTLER

See copyright; intellectual property rights.

books of local history. See virtual shopping.

boosterism. A civic booster promoting his or her city is a familiar sight. Boosters put forward the virtues of their villages, small towns, and big cities to encourage progress, by which they mean economic development and growth. Boosters, in short, sell their lo-

cality. While leaders continue to hail the opportunities to be found in their city, the heyday of boosterism was in the nineteenth and early twentieth centuries, as community leaders competed with their rivals to attract business.

Who tended to be boosters? The most common image of the booster is Sinclair Lewis's character Babbit, a shallow, materialistic member of the middle class. His image is only partially correct. Historian Daniel Boorstin described the businessman as booster thus: "We might better characterize him as a peculiarly American type of community maker and community leader. His starting belief was in the interfusing of public and private prosperity" (Boorstin, pp. 115–16). Civic boosters were local elites—politicians, business leaders, lawyers and other people holding positions of prestige—who promoted their communities to the outside world. In the process, some scholars argue, they also created an identity for their community. Much of boosterism was about projecting a favorable image, an image that would attract new businesses and workers to an area. Boosters hailed progress through technological development and values that stressed the centrality of business in the community. Boosters placed great value on the latest in urban conveniences; at the turn of the century the streetcar and the railroad were the chief symbols of the age. The use of athletic teams as champions, and the related building of arenas and stadiums, has a long history. Boosters, whether bringing a new factory or a new stadium to town, often created controversy by using government funds to subsidize private ventures in the name of the common good.

Boosters represented a stable elite in a mobile population and a volatile economy. During the nineteenth century, boosters were concerned with building communities in a period of intense disruption. In the frontier town of Jacksonville, Illinois, according to an historian of the city, most of the "population at any given time were transient strangers" and only a small core of the residents had a long-term stake in the town's future (Doyle, p. 3). One outgrowth of booster's emphasis on progress was a call for tolerance in the name of stability and economic growth, sometimes leading boosters to overlook or ignore the grievances of workers. Boosters of *Middletown in the 1920s urged solidarity and quieted criticism for fear of discouraging new business, calling those who did not share in their civic vision "knockers" (Lynds, p. 222). Boosters also utilized a variety of methods for spreading their message. They joined middle-class associations, clubs, and lodges such as Rotary, Jaycees, and Lions. Business groups such as local trade associations and chambers of commerce played a large role. Boosters used their influence in the local governments to provide incentives for business growth, such as tax breaks and favorable zoning. They shaped local news coverage. Local newspapers could be as much about promotion as news. Boosters had deep roots and influence in the locality.

The message of the booster was intended to lure outsiders to the locality, but it was also supposed to change and control how residents viewed their community, especially in times of controversy or adversity. Occasionally their optimism could prove a hindrance to growth and change. Dalton, Georgia, boosters held economic interests in local mills because of their wealth and not necessarily because of their expertise in manufacturing textiles. The lack of technical skill meant that the mills began to fall behind. At the turn of the century, community leaders felt they had to celebrate economic trends, despite a slowing economy, lack of diversification, and the movement of young people to other areas in search of employment. To improve image and life, boosters promoted cultural events—both middle and high brow—as a method of economic development.

Boosters embraced a linear view of progress. A town's evolution, as they saw it, traced a course from industry and business in its rawest form to a role of leadership in culture and society. Examples of this can be seen throughout the nineteenth and twentieth centuries as towns and cities vied with each other for prominence. This was particularly true of the cities of the Midwest, especially Cincinnati and Chicago, where leaders often hoped to overtake New York City both economically and culturally. Museums, libraries, sports teams, and symphonies acted as proxy champions in the competition. For example, to overcome the city's reputation as the "hog butcher" of the world and to improve middle-class life, Chicago leaders brought highbrow culture to their city after the Civil War. Organizers intended the 1893 Colombian Exposition as more of an announcement that Chicago had arrived as a major city than as a celebration of Christopher Columbus's voyage. Cincinnati, also a center of butchering and industry, joined Chicago in this movement to improve the region's image. The first two decades following the Civil War saw Midwestern cities try to assume a leading place in cultural as well as industrial affairs.

Boosterism in the late twentieth century has taken a different turn. While growing cities, especially those of the Sun Belt, still exhibit boosterism in its purest form, many of the towns and cities that had been once so heavily touted have begun to decline. Small towns, in both image and reality, have declined since World War II. For boosters of such declining centers, the old linear evolutionary model of progress has become questionable. With decline the boosters sought to make use of history to provide examples of past glory and an exploitable past that could point to future growth. Leaders of such towns have embraced *historic preservation and *tourism as the answer to the community's problems.

Boosters interested in historic tourism often emphasis the "apex" of a community's history—the point at which the town was most successful or best dealt with a crisis. Thus, historic districts and local history museums generally emphasize a particular moment, presenting a clear, positive, lesson. Boosters and tourist officials often avoid the ambiguities of change. History as interpreted by local historians and preservation groups tends to be static, romantic, and one-dimensional, reflecting a neighborhood or theme at a certain time. Not surprisingly, past civic leaders, boosters in their own day, are featured. The historic districts and local history museums do preserve, in a limited way, material culture and history that otherwise would have been lost. Again, image and economic opportunity play a critical role. In 1978, the United States Department of Housing and Urban Development and the Massachusetts Department of Community Affairs argued for the economic use of history for community development: "Perhaps the single most important problem facing the New England mill towns is the problem of image. The overwhelming decline and collapse of the textile industry in the North has tarnished the image of these cities, not only in the eyes of the people from the outside but also in the eyes of the citizens themselves" (Hamer, pp. 118–19). Thus the modern *historic preservation movement relies on tourism and many of the same techniques that boosters have historically used to promote a better future.

See Richard O. Davies, *Main Street Blues: The Decline of Small-Town America* (Columbus, Ohio, 1998); David Hamer, *History in Urban Places: The Historic Districts of the United States* (Columbus, Ohio, 1998); Jon C. Teaford, *Cities of the Heartland: The Rise and Fall of the Industrial Midwest* (Bloomington, Ind., 1993); Douglas Flamming, *Creating the Modern South: Millhands & Managers in Dalton, Georgia, 1884–1984* (Chapel Hill, N.C, 1992); Andrew R. L. Cayton and Peter S. Onuf, *The Midwest and the Nation: Rethinking the History of an American Region* (Bloomington, 1990); Thomas, Bender, *Community and Social Change in America* ([1978] Baltimore, 1986); Don Harrison Doyle, *The Social Order of a Frontier Community: Jacksonville,*

Illinois, 1825–1870 (Urbana, 1978); Robert H. Wiebe, *The Search for Order, 1877–1920* (N.Y., 1967); Daniel J. Boorstin, *The Americans: The National Experience* (N.Y., 1965); and Robert S. Lynd and Helen Merrell Lynd, *Middletown: A Study in Modern American Culture* ([1929] N.Y., 1956).

PHILLIP PAYNE

See heritage.

borders and boundaries. Anyone who practices local history will quickly run up against borders and boundaries. Examining the history of a neighborhood, a community, a city, a township, a county, a river valley, or any other local area requires decisions about what to include and what to exclude. Borders and boundaries both separate and connect; they help to define what makes people unique as well as what they have in common. Borders and boundaries can be seen simply as survey lines on maps that delineate political subdivisions or mark the ownership of property. Borders and boundaries designate cities and towns; townships, counties, and parishes; states, provinces, and nations. In addition to circumscribing one place from another, political borders are contact points; they provide the framework that unites townships into counties, counties into states, and states and provinces into nations. Asking why a community or county is bounded in a particular manner can open up interesting and useful avenues of historical inquiry. In the United States, where private property has played a central historical role, we have systematically and elaborately divided the land into metes and bounds; sections, townships, and

ranges; lots and blocks, and so on. In addition to lines on maps, there are cultural boundaries that have influenced how people understand themselves and others. Although these differences are harder to define and delineate than political or property borders and boundaries, they have nonetheless played an important role in the unfolding story of local history.

While on the surface it may appear as though the surveyed lines that mark political subdivisions and property are quite distinct from cultural boundaries, closer examination reveals that they are often tightly intertwined. Cultural boundaries have established myriad overlapping and shifting fault lines that divide and distinguish groups of people one from another. Attitudes and values embedded within cultures have played a major role in the creation of historical memory and in the understanding of place—two variables that have powerfully influenced the construction of local identities. People are distinguished by virtue of living in a nation, state, province, county, township, city, or town. Because they reside in a particular place, they define themselves as different from those who do not; yet, what is outside of the boundary also helps to establish the context for what is within.

Benedict Anderson's *Imagined Communities: Reflections on the Origins and Spread of Nationalism* (London, 1983) and Seymour Martin Lipset's *Continental Divide: The Values and Institutions of the United States and Canada* (N.Y., 1990) both provide useful explanations of the cultural origins of modern national identities. *Continental Divide* does an especially good job of addressing significant, but sometimes subtle, differences that distinguish people. These observations on the cultural construction of national identity can shed light on the local history as well. Historically, Canada and the United States have been divided not only by political borders but also by different historical experiences and memories—experiences and memories that have influenced how they interpreted the past and how they understood themselves and each other. Former Canadian Prime Minister Pierre Trudeau neatly and dramatically encapsulated some of the key cultural differences between Canada and the United States when he described the relationship between the two nations as similar to "sleeping with an elephant." Residents of a rural town in New England, or a county in the upland South, or neighborhood in New York City, or a barrio in Los Angeles are as much members of imagined communities as they are of physical locations. Indeed, one of the challenges of local history is to untangle the overlapping and evolving imagined communities to which people belong based on factors such as race, class, gender, ethnicity, and occupation.

Bounding of land to validate ownership and facilitate sale offers another example of the historical blending of lines on maps with cultural distinctions. When European colonists surveyed their land and marked it with fences, their fences were cultural symbols of profoundly different attitudes towards land and the ownership of land between themselves and the Native Americans. William Cronon's *Changes in the Land* (N.Y., 1983) offers a good

introduction to those cultural attitudes. In 1785, the Confederation Congress passed an ordinance that established the rectangular survey system, which imposed a uniform grid comprised of sections, townships, and ranges on a diverse natural landscape. The rectangular survey reflected cultural attitudes towards the relationship between people and land, as well as deeply held beliefs on the nature of citizenship and the future of the new nation. Over time, the rectangular survey has had a major impact on the cultural geography of most of the United States. *Order upon the Land: The U.S. Rectangular Land Survey and the Upper Mississippi Country* (N.Y., 1976) by Hildegard Johnson would be a good place to begin an inquiry into the local significance of the rectangular survey system. Land in urban areas is also carefully subdivided into lots and blocks, the complexities of which are effectively and insightfully addressed by Kenneth T. Jackson in *Crabgrass Frontier: The Suburbanization of the United States* (N.Y., 1985).

Because borders and boundaries both separate and connect political subdivisions, parcels of land, and imagined communities, cross-border topics present a particularly rich and challenging opportunity for local historians. The range of potential cross-border topics might include the following: politics, commerce and industry, popular culture, crime, migration, tourism, sports, goods and services, financial activities, transportation, communication, and technical systems, rivers and streams, pollution, flora and fauna, energy, literature, ideas, heritage tourism, and so forth. In the end, the plethora of cross-border topics that present themselves for examination are circumscribed only by the range of human experiences and the curiosity and imagination of the local historian.

PHILIP SCARPINO

Bosnians. See Appendix A.

boundaries. See borders and boundaries.

broadsides. Broadsides are large sheets of paper printed on one side only, usually for purposes of advertising. Early broadsides were small and were sometimes referred to as handbills; today they are generally called posters.

breweries. Making beer has always been popular in the U.S. and Canada. See Frederick William Salem, *Beer: Its History and Its Economic Value as a National Beverage* ([1879] N.Y., 1972). Founded in 1970, the Brewers Association of Canada maintains a library at Heritage Place, Suite 1200, 155 Queen Street, Ottawa, Ontario, Canada K19 6LI. The phone is (613) 232-9601; the e-mail address <office@brewers.ca>; the Web address <http://www.brewers.ca>. The library consists of 500 books about the history of the brewing industry, taverns and inns, alcoholic beverages, beer and brewing, and houses statistical information about the brewing industry.

British Association for Local History. This organization, known as BALH, was created in 1982 from the Standing Conference for Local History. BALH publishes the *Local Historian. The address is P.O. Box 1576, Salisbury SP2 8SY, England.

See England, local history in.

brochures and pamphlets. These smaller-format publishing ventures are staples of the local historical society. They have been around for a long time and are less time consuming and less costly than books to produce. They are usually narrowly focused. Pamphlets and brochures can also be sold cheaply or given away, which allows historical material to get to a wide range of people.

buff. A buff, as in "history buff," is a devotee, a fan, or one whose hobby or passion is collecting specific items, attending specific events, or associating with a specific group. The term was first used in print in the 1930s, in a novel by Emmanuel H. Lavine, in a book entitled *The Third Degree: A Detailed . . . Exposé of Police Brutality* (N.Y., 1930 [reference from Harold Wentworth and Stuart Berg Flexner, *Dictionary of American Slang*, N.Y., 1960]). Lavine wrote, "there are several varieties of police buffs." The word has come to be used in a somewhat disparaging fashion, implying amateurism. A history buff is enthusiastic about some aspect of history without, the word implies, a serious, contextual knowledge. "Lol" is another such term. "Lol" refers to "little old ladies" and is usually followed by "in tennis shoes." Heard less frequently in recent years.

built environment. The term "built environment" refers to the shape, pattern, function, and appearance of our present surroundings that result from human intervention. The term is often used in opposition to the term "natural environment." However, the built environment includes designed landscapes and plantings. The term came into common usage in the 1950s among city and regional planners and was adopted by the historic-preservation community to indicate the broadest possible interpretation of the term "cultural resources."

W. BROWN MORTON III

Bulgarians. See Appendix A.

Bunyan, Paul. According to Richard M. Dorson, the "fame of Paul Bunyan rests not upon lumberjacks but on a profit-motivated advertising agent of a lumber company." Paul Bunyan was created in 1914 by William B. Laughead, who worked for the Red River Lumber Company. See Dorson's *America in Legend: Folklore from the Colonial Period to the Present* (N.Y., 1973) and *American Folklore and the Historian* (Chicago, 1971), especially chapter 8, "Local History and Folklore."

Bureau of Reclamation. Congress established the Bureau of Reclamation within the Department of the Interior in 1902 with the strong support of President Theodore Roosevelt. The Bureau of Reclamation's charge was development of water resources in the arid West. Reclamation developed over 180 water projects for irrigation, hydroelectric generation, and municipal and industrial uses. Other significant benefits of Reclamation projects include recreation and flood control.

Reclamation's records include correspondence, manuscript and printed reports, drawings and maps, films, videos, and photographs. Reclamation's original objective was to create new irrigated farms for families in the arid West. Because of that objective, Reclamation was especially interested in the communities and living conditions on and around its projects. Reclamation's early records, especially the photographs, document their efforts. In addition, there are early Reclamation photographs of Western *national parks and projects in the South where swamp and overflow lands were reclaimed.

Reclamation's records and photographs are found in several locations. Older, historic records of Reclamation have been transferred to the *National Archives and Records Administration. The older photographs are in the still-picture collection of the National Archives and Records Administration in College Park, Maryland. Many of those older images are duplicated in the National Archives holdings in Denver, which is the location of the vast majority of Reclamation's written, printed, and image collections that have been transferred permanently to the National Archives and Records Administration. More current records are retained in Reclamation's offices: Washington, D.C.; Denver; regional offices in Salt Lake City; Sacramento; Billings; Boise; and Boulder City, Nevada; and in over 20 area offices in the West.

BRIT STOREY

See water rights in the West.

Burned-Over District. The Burned-Over District is a portion of central New York that experienced repeated incursions of religious enthusiasms. The region was so identified and written about by Whitney Cross in his book *The Burned-Over District: The Social and Intellectual History of Enthusiastic Religion in Western New York, 1800–1880* ([1950] N.Y., 1965).

See religion.

business and industrial history as a local history subject. Business and industry offer great opportunities for historians of any locality. The history of any town or city, no matter how small, is intimately connected to the rise and fall of local businesses. "In American society," Mansel Blackford, Austin Kerr, and Amos Loveday have observed, "with the possible exception of a few utopian communities, towns and cities have been established, have existed and prospered, and have died for economic or business reasons." Blackford, Kerr, and Loveday, along with the American Association for State and Local History, have provided a valuable resource book for local historians seeking to develop business histories: *Local Businesses: Exploring Their History* (Nashville, Tenn., 1990).

Some businesses and industries of national (or international) significance are closely linked to a particular locality. The U.S. automobile industry is synonymous with Detroit, Michigan (the "Motor City"); and this industry has played a crucial role in shaping the history of Detroit. Pittsburgh, Pennsylvania, is likewise linked to the steel industry; and the rise and decline of steel manufacture in the United States is in many ways the story of Pittsburgh.

California's Silicon Valley and Massachusetts's Route 128 area have received much scholarly attention recently. These two distinctive localities have produced important innovations in computer technology since World War II in very different ways. Networks of small firms and producers in California created a flexible system for producing technological innovation, while a more rigidly structured system of large integrated firms in Massachusetts had greater difficulty in adapting to changing economic conditions. Textile manufacture in New England and the Philadelphia area also evolved in distinctive ways. While New England firms were large, integrated, and well-capitalized from the earliest days, Philadelphia's textile industry grew from a great variety of small, flexible firms (as chronicled by Philip Scranton). The details of each local story, therefore, were important factors in explaining the relative successes of each region. The stories of these industries are crucial to understanding much of the national history of the United States. Smaller, lesser-known industries are also often linked to particular localities. Dalton, Georgia, residents accurately refer to their town as "the carpet capital of the world." The area around High Point, North Carolina, has long been a major center of U.S. furniture production.

Economists and economic geographers call such clusters "regional agglomerations," and the study of these areas has become a major area of research within business history. A number of business historians have argued that many such industries are not simply located in a particular place, but grow out of a complex web of relationships that is closely connected to the rhythms of particular communities. Thus local history takes on added significance; the study of industrial agglomerations links local business history in important ways to broader fields of study. Former House Speaker Tip O'Neill famously remarked that "all politics is local." In the field of business and industrial history, it now seems that much, if not quite all, history is local. See Philip Scranton, *Proprietary Capitalism: The Textile Manufacture at Philadelphia 1808–1885* (Philadelphia, 1987) and *Endless Novelty: Specialty Productions and American Industrialization, 1865–1925* (Princeton, N.J., 1997).

RANDALL PATTON

C

Cambridge Group for the History of Population and Social Structure.

The Cambridge Group (CAMPOP) was founded in 1964 by a group of historical demographers based in the University of Cambridge, U.K. Led by Peter Laslett, and involving many nonacademic local historians, they have explored household and family composition and other familial issues. Drawing on English parish registers and other inhabitant lists of the sixteenth, seventeenth, eighteenth, and early nineteenth century, the group pioneered the English use of the family reconstitution techniques developed by the French demographer Louis Henry. Publications such as *The World We Have Lost* (N.Y., 1965) and *Household and Family In Past Time* (Cambridge, U.K., 1972), both edited by Peter Laslett, introduced family reconstitution as a research tool to many English-speaking historians. Other scholars in the group include E.A. Wrigley, who edited *Introduction to English Historical Demography* (London, 1966) and *Identifying People in the Past* (London, 1973). With R. S. Schofield, Wrigley wrote, *The Population History of England, 1541–1871: A Reconstruction* (Cambridge, Mass., 1981). Members of the Cambridge Group have contributed regularly to the journal *Local Population Studies* since it was first published in 1968.

Few local historians in North America are involved in local population studies. The work of the Cambridge Group can provide a wealth of ideas regarding the study of families and communities. Although the source documents may differ, the questions and issues addressed in the work of the Cambridge Group have the potential to open up many new aspects of local history in the North American context. Further, the example that the Cambridge Group provides in linking academic and independent scholars is one that could be employed elsewhere.

KENNETH G. AITKIN

Canada, local history in. Insofar as local history is the "historical study of how . . . people lived in relation to their local environments and to one another within identifiable communities," local history in Canada is the invisible history. It is done and often done well, and while embraced by an amateur tradition, is usually identified by professional historians as something other than local history, including regional or community studies, history of settlement, rural history, urban history, or even demography and family history. The recent two-volume *Readers' Guide to Canadian History*, for example, cites most of the best academic "local histories," but has no entry for "local history" in the subject index of either volume. With few exceptions, it does not cover the amateur contribution. There are complex reasons for this state of affairs, some found in the complex structures of Canadian national life; others in the logic of academic practice in Canada.

In respect to the former, Maurice Careless and others have argued that the Canadian identity is found, paradoxically, in the "limited identities" that make up the nation-state. This line of thinking has been supported by work of some social psychologists who have argued that Canadians tend to establish their local identities first, their national identity second: the reverse of the situation in the United States. Canada in the early twentieth century did not become a "melting pot," despite efforts to do so, and, making virtue out of necessity, opted in policy and practice for the "mosaic," or what in contemporary parlance is called "pluralism."

Canada is also a federation with powerful provinces, and the provinces have jurisdiction over local government and most of the "culture-forming" instruments, especially education, in the country. Even for research purposes, including the pursuit of municipal records, vital statistics, land records, and material on natural resources, the road runs through the provinces or their municipalities. Canada also covers an extensive land mass, of varying form and function. As noted by Margaret Ormsby, author of *British Columbia: A History* (Toronto, 1971), for any individual in such a huge landscape only a few places can evoke recognition.

All of this is to say that logic would argue for a very powerful local history tradition; the "limited identities" providing the very foundation for the nation itself. Instead, several things seem to have happened that militate against "local history," not the least of these being the possibility that "limited identities" or a "community of communities" is really not at the foundation of the Canadian national psyche.

Regardless, local identity is often conflated with national—or, especially, but not alone, in Quebec—with provincial history. Local history is not done for its own sake, but appropriated to demonstrate a larger political identity. In this respect, then, local history does *not* operate in the more neutral embrace of the "region," but the politicized one of the "Province" or the "Nation." Most recently, there has also emerged the recognition that individuals, especially in federations, can and perhaps must embrace many identities: local, provincial, and national identities can coexist (as well as many other "social constructions" of gender, class, faith, and so forth). Individuals often operate in terms of "unlimited identities." Finally, and in terms of current Canadian debates, privileging one identity (unless it is a national one) over all others is in some quarters anathema. Local history, in this regard, can be seen as impolitic.

As if this is not enough, the essence of local identity in Canada—what makes a place unique or special—is often rooted in powerful and extensive offshore influences. Settlement, wherever it occurred in Canada, was expensive, as H. A. Innis noted in *The Fur Trade in Canada* ([1927] Toronto, 1956), and therefore heavily supported either by metropolitan subsidy, often in the form of military expenditures, or by the production of "staples," which by definition depend on a metropolitan market. The local in Canada almost always grew out of the metropolitan, a defining theme, for example in Paul Voisey, *Vulcan: The Making of a Prairie Community* (Toronto, 1988), though it could be considered a matter of employing metropolitan concepts to underwrite local particularity. Similarly the influence of the United States on local identity—as well as national—has been pervasive, most typically, but not exclusively in communities founded by those first un-American Americans, the United Empire Loyalists. Finally, the complexity of the nation coupled with its 500-year process of European settlement and with a reemergence of native consciousness, has produced a mosaic of local history practice across the country. Natives, unintegrated in most local history to date, have struck out on their

own, heavily supported by academic professionals and national and provincial governments, and largely in terms of ethnohistory, rather than local history. Francophones, where in a minority—whether Acadians of the Atlantic Provinces, or other Francophones outside Quebec, such as Franco-Ontarians—have often developed their local history in terms of the Roman Catholic "parish," rather than the secular municipality. This is also partly true in Quebec, but there additional organizing principles prevail, including that of the seigneurial system, even though seigneuries were commuted in 1854, and, of course, in terms of the principle of the province itself and especially its "distinctiveness." On the positive side, such a search for identity has led not only to a high level of methodological sophistication, but also to a good deal of funding support for the study of the locality by academic historians; but like much local history in Canada, it is local history in aid of a larger project.

Academic practice has also underwritten the invisibility of local history in several respects. In the expansion of universities and their programs in the 1960s and 1970s, local history did not get on the agenda in Canada. The foundation of lively amateur endeavor was not built on, nor were there sufficient hirings of trained local historians in university departments to provide a focus of activity, or, perhaps more important, to establish the legitimacy of local history in the scholarly milieu.

The result was the writing of books and articles that had many of the characteristics of local history but were labeled as something else that had more academic respectability. Rather, the scholarly community tended to develop in two directions from the traditional emphasis on polity, economy, and external relations. One direction was toward "regional history," rooted in the "provincial" universities of a large, thinly populated nation. These changes are reflected in the professional renewal of existing regional journals such as *Acadiensis, Revue d'histoire l'Amerique français*, and *Ontario History*, and the development of new ones, such as *B.C. Studies*, replacing the old *British Columbia Historical Quarterly*.

A second direction was toward the studies of the social relations of gender, class, race, and ethnicity, exemplified in the journals *Histoire sociale/Social History, Labour/Le travail, Canadian Ethnic Studies* and *Atlantis*. Though this history is very often "micro-history," including in its locale, it is not usually focussed on "place" or the special identifying qualities of place. Rather, such history, insofar as it focuses on "place" does so to demonstrate the nature of structural changes in the economy or society due to "faceless forces" and thereby affirm some general process. Forms of "exceptionalism," and this would include "local exceptionalism," are greeted in some quarters with hostility. Volition is not usually an element of such history, either. Still there are some examples of such history that do remain sensitive to place, though they would not be considered local history as such, for example Voisey's *Vulcan* or Joy Parr, *The Gender of Breadwinners: Women, Men, and Change in Two Industrial Towns, 1880–1950* (Toronto, 1990).

As for other journals, *The Urban History Review/Revue d'histoire urbaine*, with its emphasis on place, tends to embrace both streams and neither, as does *Canadian Papers in Rural History*. Older journals, notably the *Canadian Historical Review, Queen's Quarterly*, and *U of T Quarterly*, as well as the *Journal of the Canadian Historical Association* (formerly labeled *Annual Report* and then *Historical Papers*), began by the 1970s to reflect the changed emphases toward regional and "social" history. Nominally "national" journals, the *Journal of Canadian Studies* and the *International Journal of Canadian Studies* have both been sensitive to the pluralist quality of Canada, but not particularly to its local history.

It is in these journals, and especially in their annual bibliographies—including that of the *Canadian Historical Review*, which has a section on "Regional and Local History"—that local history is generally found, if not always labeled as such. In sum, the job of the local historian in Canada is both huge and complex; and the academic resources to address local history are thin, whether in terms of person-power or willpower.

In terms of the history of local history, the earliest local histories in Canada—mostly county histories or the histories of towns—date from the colonial era, that is, prior to Confederation in 1867. The first county history in Upper Canada (now Ontario) was James Croil's *Dundas; or, A Sketch of Canadian History* (Montreal, 1861). Some of these early histories were frankly historical works; others, like Croil's, began as historical sketches that were intended as background to county "prize essays," solicited and published in the 1850s by provincial Boards of Agriculture. The essays were motivated in part by a Victorian sense of the progress achieved by the first generation of pioneers who had transformed the "howling wilderness," but they were also motivated by a dawning sense of colonial identity, and frequently by an attempt to assert a moral superiority for British Americans in an effort to distinguish their experience from that of their neighbors.

The late nineteenth century saw a redoubled interest in the history of the fast-disappearing pioneering generation, at least in English-speaking Canada. This interest was stimulated by celebrations in 1884 to mark the arrival of the loyalist refugees of the American Revolution into what is now the Maritimes, Quebec, and Ontario, and resulted in the founding of several local and county historical societies.

But there was also a realization that knowledge of the early days of local communities was vanishing, along with the pioneers' generation. Entrepreneurs in the United States were quick to capitalize on this new awareness of local history, moving into Canada and signing up subscribers for county land-ownership maps in the 1860s, and for a series of county-by-county "illustrated historical atlases" with extended historical and biographical sketches in the 1878–1880 years. These are catalogued in Heather Maddick, *County Maps: Land Ownership Maps of Canada in the 19th Century* (Ottawa, 1976), and in Betty May, *County Atlases of Canada: A Descriptive Catalogue* (Ottawa, 1970).

Some of these Americans extended their Canadian efforts to voluminous, stand-alone county history books with chapters on the various townships, and biographies or genealogies of subscribers and their families. A good example is Goodspeed's *History of Middlesex County*, Canada (Toronto and London, 1889). These efforts stimulated domestic historians and businessmen to follow suit, resulting in publications such as Thomas Miller's *Historical and Genealogical Record of the First Settlers of Colchester County* (Halifax, Nova Scotia, 1873) or C. Blackett Robinson's *History of Toronto and County of York, Ontario* (Toronto, 1885).

Where authors were local, they were frequently retired businessmen or wealthy farmers, or clergymen or newspaper editors, that is, men with education and leisure time to devote to research and writing. Women joined their ranks late in the century (Janet Carnochan in *Niagara* [Bellville, Ont., 1973] is especially well known), and even created institutional forms (such as the Women's Historical Society of Ottawa), but feminization of the genre seems not to have progressed as far as Kammen has observed in the United States.

As the capacity to draw upon oral recollections dimmed in the early twentieth century, the quality of eastern and central Canadian local histories deteriorated. Partly this was due to a democratization of authorship, and a tendency to rehash the contents of earlier works. The years after World War II, however, saw a proliferation of such amateur productions, receiving special impetus from federal encouragement and funding associated with the national centennial in 1867 and some subsequent provincial centennials, especially in Manitoba and British Columbia. The centennial promotions stimulated a copycat interest that has scarcely let up since, with the 100th or 200th anniversaries of many townships and municipalities providing the occasion for commissioned local histories, sometimes written by professional historians.

In the Prairie west, settled most intensively around the turn of the century, the centenaries of white settlement and the passing of the pioneer generation were again capitalized upon by commercial enterprises. Notable among these has been the Friesen company, a Winnipeg publisher of high-school yearbooks. The firm developed a template for local history books, canvassing rural communities for subscribers and sometimes supplying an author, as its predecessors had done a century earlier in Ontario and the Maritimes.

The historical chapters in these works tend to be thematic and to be overwhelmed by the genealogical sketches that follow. Friesen had determined early on that roughly five books would be sold for every early-settler genealogy included.

Many of the independent works produced throughout the country since World War II have continued to betray a democratization of authorship in a decline of original research and a tendency to rework and cannibalize earlier histories, notably the county atlases. Some of the best, however, break free from the thematic arrangement (churches, schools, social institutions) and draw upon local newspaper morgues to provide observant and often very useful chronological accounts. In doing so,

they sometimes break free as well from Whiggish progress as a central theme, or its common flip side, the nostalgia of an elderly author for the golden age of his or her youth.

Some of the best amateur studies were published by university presses, notably the University of Toronto Press, though since the 1950s nonacademic authors have been given short shrift. Amateur productions still continue to dominate the stream of county, township, and community histories flooding from the presses as Canadian academics have been slow to take the genre seriously.

An academic local history tradition did become established in the interwar years at the University of Western Ontario, in London, but it never achieved much importance outside the local area and has since foundered. Professor Fred Landon (1906–1969) received support from the university to establish a Regional Collection in the library in 1926–1927 because administrators conceived of Western as a regional school at a time when there were few universities in the province. In his *Western Ontario and the American Frontier* (Toronto, 1941), Landon expressed a sense of regional identity for southwestern Ontario in which he saw American influence as largely formative. In 1942, Landon established the mimeographed periodicals *Western Ontario Historical Notes* and *Western Ontario History Nuggets* to disseminate inexpensively the results of amateur and professional research. Landon was succeeded by his student J. J. Talman—like Landon, a librarian/historian.

Though other Western historians such as Fred Armstrong (also a historian of Toronto) and Roger Hall continued to write on southwestern Ontario subjects following Talman's retirement in 1970, and students continued to draw on the Regional Collection for resource material, the results are usually categorized as social or urban history. There never was a "Landon School," because neither Landon nor his successors developed a conception of local history, or a distinct methodology around which an academic program could evolve. In their own writings, neither Landon nor Talman made a firm break with antiquarianism.

It is perhaps symptomatic of the situation of local history in Canada that in the early 1970s historians and social scientists at the University of Western Ontario put forward an elaborate proposal for an interdisciplinary study of southwestern Ontario using the latest computer technology and the impressive array of material at the Regional Collection. But it was an indication of the academic's lack of commitment to place that no thought was given to producing a good history of the region other than as background to the more specialized topics, and that following refusal of Canada Council funding for the "Landon Project," little of the work was continued independently. Even the emphasis given the Regional Collection has been downgraded now that the university administration no longer views Western as a regional university with a special responsibility toward the residents of its hinterland.

As for resources, a beginning place for the study of local history in Canada is probably with the local history handbooks, most published following the centennial celebrations of 1967. The first was probably that complied by H. A. Stevenson and F. H. Armstrong, *Approaches to Teaching Local History* (Toronto, 1969). It was aimed at the classroom teacher, applied only to Ontario, and is now dated, standing in a sense between the old local history of the amateur and the unrequited local history of the professional. It also conveys the persistent and unfortunate sense that local history is mostly a matter for amateurs and school children. Still, it has a useful bibliography of some of the early local histories of Ontario. A second guide is the loose-leaf *Discovering Your Community*, published by the Young Ontario Committee of the Ontario Historical Society in 1984.

Others have been written for most of the provinces in Canada and these include: Gerald Friesen and Barry Potyondi, *A Guide to the Study of Manitoba Local History* (Winnipeg, 1981); and Saskatchewan Archives Board, *Exploring Local History in Saskatchewan* (Regina, 1980); Harry Baglole, ed., *Exploring Island History: A Guide to the Historical Resources of Prince Edward Island* (Belfast, PEI, 1977); Mary Frederickson, *Local Studies* (Halifax, 1977); E. J. Holmgren, *Writing Local History* (Edmonton, 1975); William B. Hamilton, *Local History in Atlantic Canada* (Toronto, 1974); Marie Nelson, *The History Handbook: Your Complete Guide to Writing and Publishing a Local History* (Calgary, 1973) and Hugh A. Dempsey, *How to Prepare a Local History* (Calgary, 1969). A bibliography for Ontario is Barabara B. Aitken, compiler, *Local Histories of Ontario Municipalities, 1951–1977: A Bibliography* (Toronto, 1978). Useful material can also be gleaned from Gerald Killan's study of the Ontario Historical Society, *Preserving Ontario's Heritage* (Ottawa, 1976). For material prior to 1950, consult the multivolume compilation by William F. E. Morley, *Canadian Local Histories to 1950: A Bibliography* (Toronto, 1967–1978).

As indicated above, the nature of academic practice in Canada and the structural imperatives of its history mean that local history, especially in current bibliographies, often masquerades as something else, even when the material is undeniably "local history." Often this material is slotted under "rural" history and counterpoised to "urban" history, for example Glenn Lockwood's fine township histories, notably *The Rear of Leeds and Lansdowne: The Making of Community on the Grananoque River Frontier, 1796–1996* (Lyndhurst, Ontario, 1996), *Smiths Falls: A Social History of the Men and Women in a Rideau Canal Community, 1794–1994* (Smiths Falls, Ontario, 1994), *Beckwith: Irish and Scottish Identities in a Canadian Community* (Carleton Place, Ontario, 1991), *Montague: A Social History of an Irish Ontario Township, 1783–1980* (Smiths Falls, Ontario, 1980). This practice has also embraced L. A. Johnson, *History of the County of Ontario* (Whitby, Ontario, 1973) W. H. Graham, *Country Matters in 19th-Century Ontario* (Peterborough, Ontario, 1988), F. C. Hamil, *The Valley of the Lower Thames, 1640–1850* ([1951] Toronto, 1973), and others that can be found in one of the few bibliographical essays to focus on a "Sense of Place," that of Bryan Palmer, in M. Brook Taylor, *Canadian History: A Readers' Guide*, Vol. 1, *Beginnings to Confederation* (Toronto, 1994). But Palmer places Donald Akenson, *The Irish in Ontario, A Study in Rural History* (Kingston and Montreal, 1984) as part of rural (as well as "settlement') history, though it is essentially a study of identity in two Ontario townships. Similarly Bruce Elliott's *The City Beyond: A History of Nepean, Birthplace of Canada's Capital, 1792–1990* (Nepean, 1991) is generally slotted under "urban" history, while his *Irish Migrants in the Canadas: A New Approach* (Kingston and Montreal, 1988) under "settlement," while both were influenced by his graduate studies in local history in England. Likewise, Voisey's *Vulcan* often appears as "urban" history or as the regional history of the Canadian prairies.

Ostensible "local history" can appear as "social history," as with Allan Greer's *Peasant, Lord and Merchant: Rural Society in Three Quebec Parishes, 1740–1840* (Toronto, 1985) or J. I. Little, *Nationalism, Capitalism, and Colonialism* (Kingston and Montreal, 1988), and *Crofters and Habitants: Settler Society, Economy and Culture in a Quebec Township, 1848–1881* (Kingston and Montreal, 1991) to cite some Quebec examples. Where French, local history in Quebec often operates from an *Annales tradition, which specializes in intensive and detailed regional economic and social studies. The influence of Fernand Braudel and his colleagues was imported by Quebeckers educated in France even before the seminal 1963 conference at the Université Laval that brought Quebec and French scholars together. The most notable study in the Annales tradition is probably Louise Dechene, *Habitants et*

Marchands de Montreal en 17e siecle (Paris, 1974). The Annales approach has also influenced work done at the provincial level, notably the economic and social history of Fernand Ouellet. But local and regional studies have also been fostered by the sense of Quebec "distinctiveness" that is implicated in tensions in federal–provincial relations. Separatist and federalist politicians alike continue to underwrite the study of Quebec society and culture where retrenchment is the order of the day in other sectors and other regions. The provincially funded Institut quebecois de recherche sur la culture (Iqrc) has produced a series of monumental historical volumes on Quebec's subregions, one of the most notable being that of Gerard Bouchard and his colleagues, at the Université du Quebec a Chicoutami, the so-called Saguenay Project, which has produced numerous papers and a number of outstanding books in French. Others include a regional study of the Outaouais, which has resulted in book of that name edited by Chad Gaffield, and another is currently underway on Quebec's main street, the Laurentian Project, led by Jean-Claude Robert, Norman Seguin, and Serge Courville. Courville, a geographer, is also responsible for a number of useful aids for local historians, including the bibliography in his *Entre ville et campagne: l'essor du village dans les seigneuries du Bas-Canada* (Quebec, 1991), itself valuable, and Courville et al, *Seigneuries et fiefs du Quebec: nomenclature et cartographie* (Quebec, 1988), and *Paroisses et municipalites de la region de Montreal au XIXe siecle (1825–1861): repertoire cartographique et documentaire.*

The production of local histories, both academic and popular, has also benefitted from cultural agreements signed periodically between municipalities and the Quebec Cultural Affairs Ministry. Both levels of government contribute to a fund for community- or government-initiated projects. The latest three-year agreement with Montreal totaled $42 million.

Despite their having no index citation to local history, the two-volume *Canadian History: A Readers' Guide* (Toronto), edited respectively by M. Brook Taylor for the pre-Confederation period and by Douglas Owram for the post are probably the best entry point in a search for local history in Canada, especially the chapters that reflect a regional or provincial organization. These will not only include relevant bibliographies, but also subject headings that will lead to material that can be construed as local history. For the Atlantic provinces, in particular, the indexes and notes to P. A. Buckner and John G. Reid, eds., *The Atlantic Region to Confederation: A History* (Toronto and Buffalo, 1994) and E. R. Forbes and D. A. Muise, eds., *The Atlantic Provinces in Confederation* (Toronto and Fredericton, 1993) should be consulted.

The growing importance of the Internet should not be neglected by anyone interested in local history in Canada. Of particular importance, the National Library of Canada has recently established the Canadian History and Society Research Service (CHSRS), which offers a range of services for "selected subject areas, themes, issues, historical events and types of documents." Contact Franceen Gaudet, of the Reference and Information Services Division, at <franceen.gaudet@nlc-bnc.ca>.

As the National Library of Canada is a library of deposit, a visit to its website, which provides access to its on-line catalogue, can be invaluable. A first stop to archival work should be the "Canadian Archival Resources on the Internet" site, maintained by the University of Saskatchewan Archives. It is found at <www.usask.ca/archives>.

As well, "Online Resources for Canadian Heritage" is maintained by the Canadian Museum of Civilization at its website: <www. civilization.ca>. For an urban history search—which also includes many references to local history, especially the Wellington County (Ontario) Project—an invaluable site has been put together by Gilbert Stelter for his Internet course "Reading a Community: Urban History at the Local Level." It can be found at <www.uo guelph.ca/history/urban>.

Finally, researchers should not neglect items in three national projects. First there is the *Dictionary of Canadian Biography*, which by death date has now moved into the twentieth century. Its indexes crosslist by place. The recent *Historical Atlas of Canada* (Toronto, Buffalo, 1987 and 1993) in three volumes is a synthetic and analytical atlas that has useful maps, though limited bibliographies. And the Canadian Institute for Historical Microreproductions (CIHM) has undertaken to copy on microfiche everything published about Canada or by Canadians. It is completed to the early twentieth century and is extensively indexed. It is available through most academic libraries, and is on the Web. Very useful material can

also be found in the multivolume "Champlain Series," which reproduces original documents and papers, carefully introduced and annotated in a scholarly fashion. Volumes include, of course, Samuel de Champlain's papers, and others ranging from the two volumes on the Town of York to Robert Reid's compendium on *The Ottawa Valley* to Jack Saywell's on *The Diary of Lady Aberdeen* (Toronto, 1960). Finally, in May 1999, the National Archives of Canada launched "ArchivariaNet" containing earlier compendiums of finding aids, manuscript and government record groups, but also such items as the 1871 manuscript census, enlistment records from World War I, and a selection from the Documentary Art and Photography collection. It can be found at <www.archives.ca>.

JOHN TAYLOR *and* BRUCE ELLIOTT

Canada, National Archives of. Called, until 1987, the Public Archives of Canada, the National Archives is one of oldest and most important cultural institutions in Canada. As national custodian of Canada's unpublished documentary heritage, the National Archives has records from many sources, relating to all aspects of Canadian life. It is a leading practitioner of the Canadian concept of "total archives," whereby archival institutions collect the records, in all media, of their sponsoring institution or level of government, and the records of private-sector individuals, groups, and organizations that complement or supplement the institutional holdings. Because of its national status, the National Archives collects the permanently valuable records of the Government of Canada and records of "national significance" from citizens and private associations.

Records of regional or local significance are generally acquired by provincial, municipal, university, church, or local museums and heritage centers throughout the country, not by the National Archives. Nevertheless, among many holdings of the National Archives will be found records of local interest.

Collections include extensive copies of early records from Great Britain and France relating to those countries' colonial administration of what is now Canada; files, reports, letterbooks, and studies from all federal government departments and agencies and from both the public and private sectors, maps and atlases, architectural plans and drawings, medals and photographs, documentary art (paintings, drawings, sketches, prints, and posters), motion-picture films, television and radio programs, sound recordings, and an increasing volume of computer-generated or electronic records. For the private sector alone, records include correspondence, diaries, journals, draft manuscripts, speeches, notes, and other papers of individuals and groups judged to have attained "national significance." The National Archives also has many records of pre-Confederation local government (i.e., before 1867) for what is now Ontario and Quebec: Upper and Lower Canada, and Canada East and Canada West. The records of the local administration of other colonies are located in the relevant provincial archives.

The National Archives was created in 1872 when an officer was appointed within the Department of Agriculture to care for historical documents in a nascent Archives Branch, then primarily focused on pre-Confederation records and copying programs overseas. In 1903, responsibility for preserving the records of the federal government was added. This expanded mandate was formalized by an act of Parliament in 1912 that granted separate departmental status to the renamed Public Archives of Canada. With the growth of the state in two world wars and the Depression, the government-records programs were much expanded after the 1950s, with a network of regional records centers being opened, and an increased focus to the present on records management and information policies. The 1960s and 1970s witnessed an explosion in numbers of staff, collections, media coverage, and buildings and facilities.

The National Archives now preserves its collections in vaults in the world-class Gatineau Preservation Centre (opened 1997). And it strives to make its collections available, subject to certain access to information, privacy, and copyright restrictions, to researchers from government, universities, the media, or citizens interested in history and genealogy. To reach the general public, in addition to extensive descriptions of its holdings, the archives produces brochures, slides, microfiche, and reference publications (including CD-ROMs); organizes exhibitions to highlight its diverse holdings and illustrate the country's history; maintains an Internet website (<www.archives.ca>) with information of how to contact the institution or consult these reference materials; and answers written and telephone inquiries about its holdings. Its microfilmed holdings are also available on interinstitutional loan.

The reference and consultation rooms are located in downtown Ottawa. The Archives may be reached by mail or in person at National Archives of Canada, 395 Wellington Street, Ottawa, ON K1A 0N3, Canada; by e-mail via the above-mentioned website; or by telephone: (613) 992-3884 for Reference Services generally; (613) 996-7458 for Genealogy Reference Services, or by fax: (613) 995-6274.

For other Canadian archival resources, readers could consult the Union List of Manuscripts in Canadian Repositories (2 vols., 1975, and supplements) and the Guide to Canadian Photographic Archives (1984). There are two very useful "clearinghouse" Internet websites with many links. "Canadian Archival Resources on the Internet" <www.usask.ca/archives/menu.html> allows searches alphabetically, or by type, region, or other headings (educational, associations, listservs), and has pilot information from the growing Canadian Archival Information Network (CAIN) that will eventually be an on-line index to the nation's archival collections. The "Canadian Council of Archives' Directory of Archival Repositories" at <www.cdncouncilarchives.ca/dir.html> lists the names, addresses, telephone and fax numbers, brief descriptions of holdings, hours of operation, etc., for hundreds of archives in the country.

TERRY COOK

Canadian military records. See military records, Canadian

Candlemas. The feast of the Purification of the Virgin Mary celebrated on February 2. Candlemas plays a role in folklore as it marked what would have been the end of winter in Great Britain; in the United States that day is usually about half-way through winter and is known as Groundhog Day.

Caribbeans. See Appendix A.

Carnegie Libraries. See library history.

celebrations. Over the past 50 years the nature of community celebrations has changed. At one time, we celebrated Independence Day or town founding day or some significant local holiday with sermons and orations, sometimes with community dinners for a town's elite, or picnics at the fairgrounds or church yard. Fireworks were primarily individually motivated and were often dangerous. It was a time of preachers, politicians, picnics, and parades.

In some places the parades became more elaborate, the marching punctuated with homemade floats, and around the turn of the twentieth century historical *pageants were introduced. David Glassberg has written of that era when the "Spirit of Pageantry" appeared in a gauzy dress to bless the festivities.

That changed. At midcentury, publicists and others became involved in *"boosting" communities and in attracting visitors to what were originally local events. Ron Powers, in his book *White Town Drowsing* (Boston, 1986), gives a vivid account of the Mark Twain Celebration planned and mounted in Hannibal, Missouri. Celebrations ceased to be homegrown affairs and became instead, slowly and inexorably, about a town's image, then about a place being able to attract others to it, to enjoy and appreciate but also to take away coffee mugs and T-shirts duly marked with place, date, and event.

States that once had modest offices to attract tourists now have development directors with several-million-dollar budgets to lure the visitor and book concessionaires. Local celebrations are now marketed with an eye to the tourist, to the "heads in the beds," "butts in the seats," and the bottom line; they are often organized not by local volunteers, but by paid events managers, and the measure of success is counted in the number of cars parked and hot dogs sold rather than by scouts marching not so neatly to the music of the local high-school band, the smell of hot dogs cooking in the park, and neighbors facing neighbors along Main Street each armed with a small paper flag.

See David Glassberg, *American Historical Pageantry: The Uses of Tradition in the Early 20th Century* (Chapel Hill, N.C., 1990); Michael Kammen, *Mystic Chords of Memory* (N.Y., 1991); Ron Powers, *White Town Drowsing* (Boston, 1986); W. Lloyd Warner, *The Living and the Dead: A Study of the Symbolic Life of Americans* (New Haven, Conn., 1959); and the movie, *Waiting for Guffman* (1997), available on video and brought to my attention by David Boutrous.

See also boosterism; emancipation celebrations; nostalgia; tourism; Yankee City Series.

cemeteries. See gravestones.

censorship. Local historians sometimes censor history. Consciously or without premeditated thought, this censorship is important to recognize because it limits the topics that we select; it colors our outlook about doing local history for the community in which we live; it sometimes skews the sort of history that the local public expects and gets from local historical societies and from local historians.

There is censorship that stems from the desire to portray our local past in the best possible light. In such cases, the historian restricts local history topics and bypasses important episodes because they might cause people to think ill of the community or of individuals—or of local history. These are inescapable motives for local historians who are dependent upon the community for additional information and new materials and whose audience is local townspeople. An "unreliable" local historian, that is, one who embarrasses area residents or who makes them uncomfortable, will soon find documents unavailable and people unwilling to cooperate.

Another form of local censorship involves what a historical society is willing to endorse as an exhibit, program, or research topic. Some historical societies, conscious of the need for local support and contributions, are loath to touch subjects that might become controversial; their motive is self-preservation and preserving good community relations. This is censorship that derives from the attitude that local history should be *boosterish of—or good for—the community. Our communities are avid consumers of local history because it provides tourist destinations and because local history provides good copy for publicity about place. It is also expected to make people knowledgeable about and feel good about the place where they live.

A third manifestation of local censorship comes in the form of disappearing documents; the motive is the same, but in this case it is the archivist that exercises a form of censorship. A friend, researching the lives of teenage girls in the nineteenth century, came across the record book of a home for unwed mothers. There was a good deal of information in the book about the girls, their ages, what happened to their babies, and where the mothers went from the home. On a second visit, my friend was told that the book had been lost. In that way, the keeper of the archive was able to censor what was studied and consequently, what was known about the local past.

In addition, some local historians censor the topics they research, concentrating on a few standard topics, neglecting study of local *crime, race relations and conflict, the actions of strikers and bosses, and *political topics of all sorts. These are legitimate subjects to pursue, but they are generally about divisive moments in our past; they do not promote a picture of a unified community or of a harmonious past. They do, however, reflect life, even as we know it today.

The final way in which local historians censor the past is by a preference for beginnings rather than an examination of the development of a community over time. There is a bias for the remote past, for those first to till the land, early institutions, and how the community grew from a rude place to one of enterprise, industry, and culture. A 106-page history of a city not far from my home devotes the first 80 pages to the period before the Civil War. This is surely a distortion: yet it is not an uncommon one, and it is often the way we perceive local history. Nevertheless, this bias for the earliest era to the exclusion of other, more recent topics, cheats us of fully understanding how the present came about and knowing that we, ourselves, are living in historical times.

Local historians do all of these things for the best of reasons, yet in doing so we short change ourselves and our communities. By presenting local history as always positive, we deny the fact that the past was as controversial as we know the present to be.

See boosterism; county histories; nostalgia; recent history.

Census, United States. The United States Census is the first wonder of the statistical world: a decennial census dating from 1790, and continually refined and expanded from that simple count of heads of households to the present multibillion-dollar effort. While the value of the census for understanding trends in the new country was recognized at the outset, realization of its value to historians came late. Joseph Hill, the head of the Census Bureau for the 11th Census told historians in 1909 that ". . . it would be very difficult to write history either social or economic or indeed political without statistics, and it would be a very defective economic or social history of the United States that ignored the statistics compiled by the United States census" (Joseph A. Hill, "The Historical Value of the Census Records," *Annual Report of the American Historical Association for the Year 1908* [Washington, D.C., 1909, vol. 1, p. 199]). He went on to extol the even greater utility of the census manuscripts. Although historians were slow to take up Hill's challenge—they were balked by the inaccessibility of much of the material—it is difficult today to imagine a local history that does not use census material. As more census content is digitized and made available for personal computers—much of it distributed on the Internet and the World Wide Web—it will become increasingly important for historians to understand and be able to evaluate and use census information.

Many cultures have employed some form of census for administrative purposes, usually for identifying taxable units, or men of fighting age. There are several censuses in the Bible: the misfortunes that befell the Israelites after David's attempted enumeration (2 Samuel 24 and 1 Chronicles 27) reportedly influenced many cases of noncompliance in the early American republic; and it was a version of the Roman census that brought Joseph and Mary to Bethlehem (Luke 2). Rome's periodic enumeration and classification of its citizenry provided the intellectual and historical precedent for all later European efforts, although no comprehensive nationwide census was attempted before the U.S. Census of 1790. At the instigation of the British Board of Trade, the American colonies were fre-

quently, if grudgingly, enumerated, but only as individual units. The accuracy of the results depended on the administrative ability of the governor and the political climate. Thirty-eight pre-Revolutionary censuses have been identified. These provided a tradition of census-taking and developed some expertise, particularly in the northern states. The 1774 census of Rhode Island, for example, may have been a model for the U.S. census of 1790. In *American Population before the Federal Census of 1790* (Gloucester, Mass., 1966), Evarts B. Greene and Virginia D. Harrington thoroughly review colonial census history and content. Only a scattering of these early censuses survive.

More directly, however, the origin of United States Census stemmed from the desire of the Continental Congress to apportion the debt incurred from the Revolution fairly among the colonies (Articles of Confederation, Article IX). Early in the Congress one important train of thought was that the basis for apportioning the debt should be the value of land and property in each colony. Methodological and logistic difficulties stymied efforts along these lines, and eventually it was decided to base apportionment on the number of households. Even this proposed "capitation" was never actually carried out, but the concept of proportional taxation based on a census carried over to the Constitutional Convention. There, it was ready at hand when the delegates sought a method of apportioning seats in the House of Representatives once the constitutional compromises were struck.

The Constitution calls for a complete enumeration of inhabitants every ten years for the purpose of apportioning the House (Article 1, sec. 2), and the first House of Representatives, consisting of 65 representatives apportioned by the Constitution itself, immediately authorized a census for that purpose, which was carried out in 1790. Federal district marshals, the only countrywide federal bureaucracy available, hired enumerators to count the heads of households in their judicial districts. There were no standardized forms or training. The postcensus check consisted of tacking the results up at two local gathering places in the district and inviting comments.

The manuscripts of the enumerators, the lists, or "schedules" of names, were collected by the marshals, who did the actual tallying for their districts. They then sent the tally sheets directly to the president. From these, clerks in the Secretary of State's office did the final tally and wrote up the report. The report was published and distributed to the states and to Congress. It was also made available to the public. The marshals placed the manuscript schedules in the district courts for safekeeping.

The population totals from the first census were disappointingly low—the first of many perceived undercounts. The Secretary of State, Thomas Jefferson, forwarded the report of the first census, a 56-page summary still missing the totals from South Carolina, to President Washington. After some disagreement about the apportionment formula, and the first presidential veto, 105 congressional seats were reapportioned for the election of the 3rd Congress according to the results.

There are several excellent histories of the United States Census: Carroll D. Wright, assisted by William C. Hunt, *The History and Growth of the United States Census* (Washington, D.C., 1900), remains indispensable. Wright provides the schedules for every census through 1890, along with instructions to enumerators, texts of the census laws, and extensive bibliographies. A briefer, but very useful overview of early census history is *Bureau of the Census, A Century of Population Growth: From the First Census of The United States to the Twelfth, 1790–1900* (Baltimore, 1967).

The first census established the procedural and publishing patterns for succeeding censuses. The public result was the summary report. The report of the first census was not ambitious, and only summarized data at the state level, but subsequent reports have grown in importance as more and more detailed information has been collected and summarized at local levels, such as county and town. The presentation of the data also became more sophisticated with more information extensively cross-tabulated. The census report is extremely useful to historians in itself. The report will tell the researcher, for example, how many white females there were in Tompkins County, New York, in 1850 and how many foreign citizens (but not yet how many naturalized females). It will report how many suspender-makers in New York State, but not how many in Tompkins County. The published summary reports are available at large libraries and the contents for all the population censuses from 1790 to 1940 have been indexed by Suzanne Schulze, *Population Information in Nineteenth Century Census*

Volumes (Phoenix, Ariz., 1983), and successive volumes.

A complete bibliography of all published census publications to 1945 is *Library of Congress, Census Library Project, Catalog of United States Census Publications, 1790–1945*, prepared by Henry J. Dubester, Chief (Washington, D.C., 1950); now reprinted and augmented with additional information as Kevin L. Cook, *Dubester's U.S. Census Bibliography with SuDocs Class Numbers and Indexes* (Englewood, Colo., 1996).

The materials behind the reports are just as valuable, and for local historians, perhaps more so. The unpublished, or manuscript, schedules contain the answers to the census questions collected for each household, or, after 1850, each individual person. The questions themselves varied from census to census, increasing in detail and scope each decade. In the first census, for example, there were only six questions: name of householder, race, free or slave, sex of free white householder and whether white males were above 16 years of age, or below. By 1880 there were thousands of questions (on many different schedules).

The manuscript schedules will tell the researcher, among other things, that a man named Horace Mack lived in Ithaca in 1850. He was twenty-five years old and had a wife and two daughters (known by inference). He was born in Connecticut, was a publisher by profession, and had real estate worth $750. This household- or individual-level information is available for most states and most censuses from 1790 to 1920. Personal information in later censuses

is protected by the "72-year directive," which requires a 72-year wait before the census schedules are made available to the public.

For a state-by-state listing of available census schedules, see *The 1790–1890 Federal Population Censuses: Catalog of National Archives Microfilm* (Washington, D.C., 1993).

The Census to 1850: The same basic pattern established in the first census was maintained for the next four censuses. The marshals remained the executors and their judicial districts were the basic census-collection units, although the reporting was by state and usually, but not necessarily, by county. Census logistics and reporting became the responsibility of the Secretary of State. The questions asked of each household were still few, and differed slightly from census to census, mostly in the way people in the household were grouped by age. The only name asked and recorded was still the head of the household. Questions about social characteristics, such as occupation and naturalization, began to be asked in 1820 and expanded each decade, so the 1840 census asked, in addition to the demographic information, about the number of people engaged in specific occupational categories, number in school, literacy of adults, and the number of insane.

The 1850 Census: The census of 1850 is often called the first modern census. Enumerators for this census were now hired on the basis of merit—trained, and, since 1830, provided with standard forms and printed instructions. Although the marshals were still in charge in the field, a temporary office, first established in 1840, coordinated the census effort centrally, now under the Secretary of the Interior. Census geography was regularized: the judicial districts were subdivided along the lines of known civil divisions, such as towns, villages, and wards, both for purposes of enumeration and summarizing data.

In terms of content there was a radical break from the old concept of the household as the basic census unit. From 1850 on, every free individual in the United States was enumerated by name, and his or her demographic and social characteristics were recorded. In addition to the standard questions of age, sex, free or slave (in slave states, separate slave schedules were used), occupational category was also recorded. Earlier censuses had experimented with questions on nativity and naturalization, but the 1850 census asked the state or country of birth. The head of the household provided information on the value of the family real estate. The individual's relationship to the head of the household was not asked but often indicated by the enumerator by indentation or some other means. In total, there were eleven questions.

1860–1920: The next six censuses grew in complexity, but the underlying pattern endured. An important development, after an explosion of questions in many different schedules, was to conduct special censuses, with specially trained enumerators, for many aspects of U.S. life such as manufactures and agriculture. In 1910, these were completely separate from the population censuses and formed the basis for what would become the Economic Census.

The first housing question occurs in 1890, and from that time the census content begins to evolve into the modern census triad of individuals, households, and housing. The Census Office became permanent in 1902, enhancing greatly the professionalism of the census enterprise. A particularly portentous event was the development of an automated counting machine using punch cards to tally the results of the 1890 census. Invented by Herman Hollerith, a Census Office clerk, this machine was a precursor of the modern computer. Hollerith left the Census Office to found what would become International Business Machines.

For a comprehensive guide to the questions asked in each census, along with the instructions to the enumerators, and illustration of the forms used see the Bureau of the Census's *200 Years of U.S. Census Taking: Population and Housing Questions, 1790–1990* (Washington, D.C., 1989). A more compact census-by-census review is "Research in Census Records," in *The Source: A Guidebook of American Genealogy*, edited by Loretto Dennis Szucs and Sandra Hargreaves Luebking (Salt Lake City, c. 1997).

Census Geography: One problem for historians has been the lack of consistent census-unit boundaries in small areas, so that valid comparisons can be made over time. Many states have changed boundaries or been carved out of earlier territories while counties have proved even more fluid, changing shapes and dividing as population shifted. Wards and then enumeration districts were used to divide cities into manageable units for enumeration, but the lack of a consistent submunicipal census unit before the tract was adopted in 1940, makes understanding neighborhood dynamics difficult.

Street addresses were not provided on the returns until 1880, so that enumerator routes must be reconstructed from directories. Despite the difficulties, interesting work in understanding local history has featured joining information from census schedules to reconstructed local maps or other geospatial data. See, for example, Michael P. Conzen, "Spatial Data from Nineteenth Century Manuscript Censuses: A Technique for Rural Settlement and Land Use Analysis," *The Professional Geographer*, 21 (September 1969): 337–42. The standard guide to census geography is William Thorndale and William Dollarhide, *Map Guide to the U.S. Federal Censuses,1790–1920* (Baltimore, 1987).

Historians and the Census—Accessibility: For many years the manuscript census schedules were scarcely used, at least by historians. Although mail requests for information from the schedules are recorded as early as 1850, extensive research was impossible without hands-on access. The establishment of a permanent Census Bureau in 1902 increased accessibility. The older schedules were inventoried and bound. The first census index, the 12-volume *Heads of Families at the First Census of the United States Taken in the Year 1790* was published in 1907–1908, but only the most intrepid genealogists made the trip to Washington to consult the fragile, otherwise unindexed schedules of later censuses.

Three important developments brought about a revolution in accessibility. The most important was the founding of the National Archives and the transfer of the extant schedules to them from the Census Bureau in 1942. The Archives applied the newly developed technologies of photostatic reproduction and microfilming to the schedules throughout the 1940s. This allowed for the distribution of the schedules, as well as guaranteeing their survival. Somewhat earlier, the Civil Works Administration had begun indexing schedules for the Census Bureau. Indexing began with the 1900 Census, and eventually resulted in the *Soundex indexes for the 1880, 1900, 1910, and 1920 censuses. These indexes, which are available on microfilm, are still not complete for all censuses. Accelerated Indexing Systems and other commercial genealogical indexing companies began indexing in the 1960s, and have produced printed indexes of the 1800–1860 censuses for most states.

Researchers hoping to consult the original paper schedules for 1900–1920 will discover that microfilming, for all its benefits, turned into a two-edged sword. Once the original census schedules had been microfilmed, they were destroyed by act of Congress with the acquiescence of the Archivist of the United States. And the move from the Census Bureau did not come in time to save the schedules of the 1890 census, which were partially burned in 1921, and then destroyed, possibly unnecessarily, in 1930, before they could be filmed or indexed.

The enumerations themselves are far from perfect. There are problems with compliance and accuracy. The indexes mirror their problems and add several of their own, but together they offer the local historian a magnificent resource for analyzing and understanding families, governments, and institutions, either captured in time or changing decade by decade.

For a state-by-state listing of census schedules, see *The 1790–1890 Federal Population Censuses: Catalog of National Archives Microfilm* (Washington, D.C., 1993). Szucs, op. cit., 104–8, has an excellent discussion of problems inherent in census data.

Nonpopulation Schedules and Censuses: Immediately after the first census, Thomas Jefferson and many others urged Congress to order census-takers to ask additional questions about social characteristics, agriculture, and the state of manufactures. The third census actually included a separate schedule of manufacturing questions, but this early experiment in economic census-taking was not successful. A sustained effort to gather agricultural information began in 1840 and continued until a separate Census of Agriculture was undertaken in 1925. Also in 1840, a special census of Revolutionary War veterans was made and separately published.

The 1850 census retained the agricultural schedules and added schedules for slaves, mortality, manufactures, and social statistics. The slave schedules were also used in 1860. Slave names were not recorded, but the schedules have been used successfully for historical research. The mortality schedules asked questions about anyone who died within the previous year and some other vital-statistics questions. The social statistics were an attempt to collect information about a wide range of social institutions within the enumerator's district: for example, how many libraries and schools, and taxes collected. These questions were not asked of individuals, but depended on the enumerators' research. Mortality and social-statistics schedules were part of the census through 1880.

In addition, there have been several population censuses that fall outside of the decennial period. In 1885, states were encouraged to take their own censuses, which would be partially paid for with federal money. Only a few states accepted the offer, but these schedules have survived and been microfilmed.

Finally, there was a special census of Union veterans of the Civil War in 1890. These are the only surviving schedules of the 1890 census, except for a scattering of counties.

In 1919, Congress authorized the disposal of the nonpopulation schedules from 1850 to 1880, but the objections of organizations such as the Daughters of the American Revolution forced the Census Bureau to offer the volumes to state libraries and historical societies. If they were refused, the DAR Library in Washington held them for safekeeping. The National Archives has since attempted to locate as many as possible for filming.

There is a complete discussion of availability and location of the nonpopulation census schedules through 1890 in Szucs, pp. 128–34. The fate of later schedules is reviewed by Louis Malcomb, "Non-Population Census Schedules: Description, Accessibility and Disposition," *Indiana Libraries*, 11/1&2 (1992): 23–34.

State and Local Censuses: Many states conducted their own censuses. Like the federal censuses, both the manuscript schedules and the summary reports are extremely useful. In addition to the states, some cities, such as Boston, conducted censuses. State and local manuscript schedules suffer from limited availability—most are not even microfilmed and many are not held in a central location. New York, for example, took regular censuses from 1825 to 1925. After tallying, the schedules were returned to the county clerks. Very few counties have preserved complete runs of the schedules entrusted to them, without missing years or damage. Indexes for state censuses are very rare, although the occasional county or town may have been indexed by a local group or individual. Library of Congress, *Census Library Project, State Censuses: An Annotated Bibliography of Censuses of Population Taken after the Year 1790 by States and Territories of the United States,* prepared by Henry J. Dubester (N.Y., 1948) is the standard bibliography of the published reports. All the censuses listed in this work have been microfilmed. For state censuses, see: *Microfiche Collection of Censuses of Population Taken after the Year 1790 by States and Territories of the United States* (Millwood, N.Y., 1970).

A very useful companion volume for the schedules has been prepared by Anne S. Lainart, *State Census Records* (Baltimore, 1992), who provides information on availability and additional bibliographies, along with extensive annotations. For a briefer overview, see Szucs, op. cit., pp. 134–36.

The Electronic Census: Microfilm technology and indexing of the federal censuses dramatically increased accessibility to census information. An even more dramatic rise in historians' ability to gather and analyze information from previous censuses is taking place now with the advent of the personal computer and high-speed networks. Many printed indexes are being entered into machine-readable databases or converted into database formats that are readable by personal computers. These are often distributed on CD-ROMs through commercial genealogical publishers. The disks have enough capacity to hold a complete index to the 1860 U.S. census, for example. Disks with even greater storage capacity (DVDs) are quickly becoming available and will undoubtedly be used to hold even larger and more complete indexes.

Since the indexes have been created mostly for genealogical purposes, they are limited to searches by name, frequently only the head of the household, and can't be searched by other attributes such as age, race, and occupation. Nevertheless, many academic researchers and historians have constructed elaborate databases for local geographic units by keying in all the information on the manuscript returns into modern survey or statistical software. As increasingly accurate scanning equipment and optical character-recognition programs are developed, it should become possible to develop statewide databases based on the historical schedules. These can then be enhanced with other sources of information, such as maps, nonpopulation schedules, voting records, tax lists, or any other individualized information.

CD-ROMs and related technologies

will undoubtedly remain important media for distribution and preservation of census indexes and data, but distribution is increasingly taking place over the Internet and in particular on the World Wide Web. Indexes residing on a central computer can now be searched from personal computers anywhere in the world. Page images of the census schedules can also be distributed in this manner. Many of the large genealogical sites on the World Wide Web already allow searching of their census CD-ROM collections online. Important genealogical sites with search engines are Ancestry: <http://www.ancestry.com>; and Family Tree Maker Online: <http://www.familytreemaker.com> and <www.familysearch.org>.

Ambitious projects are underway that will make vast amounts of census information available over the World Wide Web. One notable example is Edward L. Ayers, Anne S. Rubin, and William G. Thomas, *In the Valley of the Shadow* <http://jefferson.village.virginia.edu/vshadow2>. This project has cross-linked the indexes from 1840 and 1850 census for two counties, one in the Virginia's Shenandoah Valley and another in Pennsylvania, and added information from other manuscript sources such as church records. This is a test for a larger project cross-linking data from all the available census schedules for all Virginia counties.

There is also the Historical Census Project at the University of Illinois, which hopes to enter all the census data ever collected in a single massive database <http://www.library.uiuc.edu/aitg/maps/1870/htm/default.asp>. In the meantime, county-level data from summary reports from 1790 to 1960 are now available from Harvard's Historical Census Data Project: <http://fisher.lib.virginia.edu>.

The personal computer, high-density storage, and the Internet have combined to make more census data available more quickly and in more useful formats than ever before.

See also *The 1790–1890 Federal Population Censuses: Catalog of National Archives Microfilm* (Washington, D.C., 1993) and Robert P. Swierenga, "Historians and the Census: The Historiography of Census Research," *The Annals of Iowa* 50 (Fall 1990): 650–73.

ROBERT KIBBEE

See also demography.

Central and South Americans. See Appendix A.

charity. See philanthropy.

chattel. The word comes from the Latin for cattle and refers to articles of personal property both animate and inanimate.

Chicano history. Since the 1960s, a new generation of historians has been researching and writing about the history of the people of Mexican descent who live within the United States. This history has been called Chicano or Mexican American history, and it spans pre-Columbian times up to the present, with its focus of research being the greater Southwest, including Texas, New Mexico, Arizona, and California. Much of the published research in this field has concentrated on events and persons in the twentieth century, although there is a respectable body of work done on previous centuries.

It is difficult to generalize about Chicano history. There are many themes that have developed over the years. One strong theme has been the struggle of the Mexican American people to survive economically and culturally within the United States. This has meant studying the history of labor organizations, mutual-aid societies, political associations, and the like. Perhaps the best single text telling of this struggle remains the survey by Rudolfo Acuña, *Occupied America: A History of Chicanos*, 3rd ed. (N.Y., 1987). Other themes have involved the role of Mexican immigration in shaping the Chicano community: Richard Griswold del Castillo and Arnoldo De Léon, *North to Aztlan: A History of Mexican Americans in the United States* (N.Y., 1996) and David G. Gutierrez, *Walls and Mirrors: Mexican Americans, Mexican Immigrants, and the Politics of Ethnicity* (Berkeley, Calif., 1995). The theme of community building, both urban and rural, has been the subject of many monographs, too many to list. Perhaps the most outstanding are Arnoldo De Léon, *The Tejano Community, 1836–1900* (Albuquerque, 1982) and Gilbert González, *Labor and Community: Mexican Citrus Worker Villages in a Southern California County, 1900–1950* (Urbana, Ill., 1994).

Within the last thirty years, Chicano historians have created a new history, one that has never been told before, one that challenges the accepted approaches and themes in American historiography. Chicano history is still considered as marginal to the larger historical narrative. Being marginal, outside the mainstream, and relegated to the periphery, Chicano historians have been freer to experiment with methodology and approaches, with interpretations and categories. Since 1990, for example, more than forty monographs have appeared contributing to the development of Chicano history.

This is a part of Western history that has escaped the notice of most historians. Some of the titles of the more notable books published in the last four or five years: Rosaura Sánchez, *Telling Identities: The Californio Testimonios* (Minneapolis, 1995); James Sandos, *Rebellion in the Borderlands: Anarchism and the Plan of San Diego, 1904–1923* (Norman, Okla., 1992); Devra Weber, *Dark Sweat, White Gold: California Farm Workers, Cotton and the New Deal* (Berkeley and Los Angeles, 1994); Martha Menchaca, *The Mexican Outsiders: A Community History of Marginalization and Discrimination in California* (Austin, Texas, 1995).

This sample of the more than forty titles in Chicano history that have been published in the last decade indicates something of the diversity of interest and authorship. First of all, not all the authors are of Mexican descent: Sandos and Weber are only two non-Mexican Americans who have been interested in writing Chicano history; there are others. Secondly, there is a fair number of women authors and they are not all writing about women's history, but about a diversity of topics. Third, the topics being developed by Chicano historians are not necessarily "political"— in the pejorative way that some have characterized Chicano Studies. Sanchez's history is a sophisticated analysis of the unpublished narratives collected by *Hubert Howe Bancroft during the 1880s in California. Sandos' study is of the influence of the Mexican revolution on Mexican Americans in South Texas. Weber's is a history of the labor movement and governmental institutions during the 1930s among California farm workers, and Menchaca's is a historical study of a Mexican American barrio.

The point is that 150 years after the U.S.–Mexican War, a conflict that separated Mexican communities from each other, a new kind of historical legacy has emerged—one that now has a very respectable historiographical tradition. This kind of history is western history, and it has too often been marginalized or relegated to the "minority" categories of journals and conferences. It is time that it be considered as an integral part of the American Western experience.

For the readers who want a good introduction to this other kind of Western history, there are several classic surveys that have been republished in recent years. A readable and updated classic is Carey McWilliams's *North from Mexico* (Philadelphia, 1990); another well-written survey is Matt Meier and Feliciano Rivera, *The Chicanos: A History of Mexican Americans* (N.Y., 1990).

In many ways Chicano history is reviving and enlarging the field of Southwestern history, a field that has lost vitality within U.S. universities during the last several decades. Many local histories, especially of Texas and California towns and cities written by Chicano historians are especially valuable to local historians who want to see their region through different eyes. Much genealogical research has been done by New Mexican Hispanos and resulting publications sponsored by the Hispanic Genealogical Research Center have a wealth of local Chicano history. See <www.HGRC-NM-ORG>.

There are scores of works that could be discussed as examples of a developing modern Chicano history. Two categories of Chicano history that have been well developed in the past are "Political" and "Community" history. In the nineties there have been some fine works in these areas, such as Juan Gómez Quiñones's *The Roots of Chicano Politics, 1600–1940* (Albuquerque, 1994) or Martha Menchaca's *The Mexican Outsiders: A Community History of Marginalization and Discrimination in California*, but there have been many more works published in the categories of literary history and autobiography. It would seem that in the 1990s, Chicano historical scholarship has been more active in cultural and intellectual analysis than in researching community and political issues. There have been a number of excellent multidisciplinary anthologies published that include significant essays in Chicano political history and that interpret major issues in Chicano cultural and intellectual history. But their impact is diluted by the nature of anthologies. The major advance in Chicano historical scholarship has been in the careful elaboration of a view of the past that is sensitive to more than one perspective within a monograph book format. We have seen, for example, increased concern for the views of indigenous people and their interactions with Mexicanos, as in Douglas

Monroy's book, *Thrown among Strangers: The Making of Mexican Culture in Frontier California* (Berkeley, 1990) and Elizabeth Haas, *Conquests and Historical Identities in California, 1769–1936* (Berkeley, 1995). And there has been increased use of multidisciplinary approaches and diverse theoretical constructs as in books by Carlos G. Vélez-Ibáñez, George I. Sanchez, David Gutierrez, Zaragosa Vargas, and Steve Loza. There is no dominant paradigm or political approach that characterizes Chicano history in the nineties. The diversity of approaches in writing history has produced a growing body of literature that has gone far beyond the initial conceptualizations of the field.

RICHARD GRISWOLD DEL CASTILLO

children's history. Children's history is, like its namesake, a relatively young field. Until recently, adults captured almost all the historical attention. Beginning in the 1960s, as historians began to examine the lives of those ordinary Americans who had been at the margins of more traditional histories (such as people of color, workers, and women), children also began to come to the forefront. The field's relative "youth" grants opportunities to forge original and exciting paths of research. Local historians can explore, from local perspectives, a number of interrelated issues: the meaning of childhood as a concept, the history of how adults have treated children, and the history of how children themselves have experienced their youth.

All humans pass through childhood on the way to adulthood, but this period of life, while ubiquitous and universal, has acquired its meaning in the context of particular communities, circumstances, and generations. The experiences and expectations of Italian American immigrant children at the turn of the century, for example, were significantly different than those of white Colonial-era children, or young African American slaves. The histories of children living on farms have differed from those growing up in large cities. Girls and boys have often played different games, been assigned distinct chores, and been inculcated in gender-specific expectations for their future lives as adults. Over time, factors such as decreased infant mortality, fewer siblings, longer schooling, and increased rates of divorce, have all affected children's lives. The list goes on given that childhood is as much a product of cultural as of biological circumstances; local historians are likely to uncover a diverse set of adult expectations for children and childhood experiences, even within small communities.

Within a particular community, the intergenerational transmission of traditional cultural values, from adults to children, has much to tell us about what was deemed important within the group. Seemingly simple questions reveal much about the larger culture. When and where were children expected to be silent unless spoken to at the dinner table, to earn money for the family at a young age, or to achieve high levels of education? How, when, and why did such customs shift? And what does children's own transmission, among themselves, of games, songs, and codes of friendship, tell us about their particular historical moment and the future expectations that shaped their young lives? If the history of childhood offers a unique perspective upon local history, it also speaks to larger national concerns: family life, education, sexuality, leisure, and labor, among others.

Before undertaking a children's history project, a number of methodological issues are worthy of thought. First, what particular cohort of children will bound the study? One person might be interested in child care, another might look at Girl Scout troops, a third might explore high-school dances. Available source materials for each of these projects will likely differ. Children, especially young children, have left behind few of the documents that historians might normally use as evidence, such as laws or published speeches; in general, the younger the cohort of the children under consideration, the harder it is to uncover their own voices. A project about babies might uncover extensive evidence, including birth records, child-rearing manuals, and evidence of child-care arrangements, but would be unlikely to discover much about the feelings of babies themselves. Studies of older children, on the other hand, may provide better access (although hardly unmediated by adults) to evidence of youthful self-representation: school yearbooks; youthful fashions; and newspaper descriptions of dances, parties, or youth groups. Historians of twentieth-century childhood will usually find more material (including oral histories) than those working in earlier periods. Many historians of childhood have turned to institutional records, such as orphanages or juvenile detention centers, or prescriptive records,

such as child-care manuals and educational treatises. These kinds of documents are fairly accessible, but because they are usually written from the perspective of adults, they are often more useful for exploring adult expectations than for uncovering children's own experiences of youth.

The terminology of childhood is also worthy of consideration. From our contemporary vantage point, at the turn of the twenty-first century, 17-year-olds are considered "children," as well as "adolescents." These terms, however, are grounded in cultural rather than biological realities. Historically, particular eras have defined childhood and youth quite differently. Secondary reading (see sources suggested below) is invaluable in determining the relevance or irrelevance of our contemporary definitions. In addition, these readings allow local historians to put their evidence into the context of national trends. In some cases, the childhood practices of individual towns or regions may correspond to larger social norms, while in other cases they may reflect particular issues specific to that locality or community.

The following suggestions for research are not all-inclusive, but they are meant to underscore the variety of documents that local historians can use in writing children's history, whether it be a study of adult ideas about children, an excavation of children's experiences, or both.

Prescriptive literature illuminates adult ideas about how to raise children. What kinds of child-rearing manuals or precepts were considered valuable among the people of your study? What did these treatises suggest?

Newspapers and magazines may also have written about special events in the lives of children, such as the first day of school, summer recreation, sports events, and dances. How did the local paper describe appropriate parenting and childhood behavior, or admonish what it considered inappropriate? Was there a children's column or another venue for local children to participate in the print media?

Laws governing childhood have varied from locality to locality. In your region, what kind of child-labor legislation was proposed and enacted? What kind of resistance did it meet? At what age were girls and boys allowed to marry, leave school, drive a car, or consume alcoholic beverages? Under what conditions was corporal punishment allowed, or juvenile detention? When and why did these laws come into being? Why did they change, and how did such changes reflect larger community or national trends?

Schools reveal much about economic and educational expectations. When was the first school built? The first high school? What were the physical conditions of schooling? What kinds of books were used, and what pedagogical methods were stressed? Which children attended school, and for how long? What do we learn from this about socioeconomic expectations, gender, race, ethnicity? What changed over time, and what do such shifts suggest about the expectations of the larger society? Did the school maintain a newspaper, a yearbook, or prize-winning compositions, that might provide insight into student life?

Other institutions serving youth may have kept records: orphan asylums, churches or synagogues, local branches of the Boy Scouts, 4-H clubs, or Camp Fire Girls, and sports teams. What kinds of services and activities did they provide to children? When did these institutions begin, or cease to exist, and why? What did they mean for the children who participated in them?

Oral histories provide valuable first-hand information about childhood, by allowing access to the kinds of personal stories that are often absent from the public record. This information is often most useful where it can be cross-tabulated against other kinds of evidence. Some localities have repositories of already extant oral histories; in other cases, personal interviews are necessary.

Municipal records such as lists of births and deaths, or records of juvenile crime or delinquency, are also revealing. How many children were born to a family during a particular period, and what was the prevalence of infant mortality? Were grown children likely to stay or to leave the town in which they grew up? How do the answers to these questions differ by race, gender, ethnic group, economic class, and what do those differences tell us about the community as a whole?

The material culture and folklore of childhood illustrate how children were represented—for example, in photographs and paintings—while offering clues about children's experience. What were the material conditions of children's lives: did they share a bed, have their own room, have many toys and clothes or only a few? Where and when did they play? What were considered appropriate playthings for particular children, and why? In addition, the culture that children themselves propagated is a rich resource. What toys did they make for themselves, what songs did they sing, what clubs or sports did they initiate, and what do these artifacts tell us about how children understood their world?

See N. Ray Hiner and Joseph M. Hawes, eds., *Growing up in America: Children in Historical Perspective* (Urbana, 1985); Grace Palladino, *Teenagers: An American History* (N.Y., 1996); Elliott West and Paula Petrik, eds., *Small World: Children and Adolescents in America, 1850–1950* (Lawrence, Kan., 1992); Elliott West, *Growing Up in Twentieth-Century America: A History and Reference Guide* (Westport, Conn., 1996). Also see Philippe Aries, *Centuries of Childhood: A Social History of Family Life* (N.Y., 1962).

LESLIE PARRIS

See family history; toys.

China, local history in. Since the end of the Maoist era in 1976, interest in and production of local history has flourished in China. Among the wide range of such activities that have occurred during this period, three are particularly noteworthy: the public release of extensive materials on local revolutionary history, collection of written and oral historical reminiscences by ordinary people, and the compilation and publication of detailed county-level histories.

Since 1949, study of China's Communist-led revolution has occupied a place in the nation's overall historical consciousness similar in some respects to both that of the American Revolution and the U.S. Civil War. Like the American Revolution, the Chinese Revolution is closely associated with the symbols and founding myths of the country's political system; like the Civil War, China's revolution was a bloody fratricidal conflict whose emotional intensity and heroic sacrifices have made an enduring impression on the nation's collective memory. And like both of its U.S. analogues, the Chinese Revolution was as much a local as a national experience, and has become thoroughly woven into the fabric of the nation's local histories.

To a much greater extent than is true in the United States, however, the local diversity of China's revolutionary experience has until recently been largely overshadowed by a singular national narrative orthodoxy, one that focused on—and was in considerable measure constructed by—Mao Zedong (Mao Tse-tung) and a small circle of other party leaders. This orthodoxy stressed policies, events, and localities that were connected with Mao and his associates, and slighted those that were not.

Recent developments have reduced this Mao-centered emphasis and have expanded opportunities for the exploration of other aspects of the revolution. Among the most notable trends in this regard have been the publication of thousands of previously confidential pre-1949 party documents, and the concomitant appearance of new histories and biographical collections focusing on the revolutionary struggle in specific localities.

Many of the documentary collections are multivolume compilations of primary materials on the rural base areas that dotted the Chinese countryside during the 1930s and 1940s; while some of the secondary histories and biographical collections deal with areas as small as individual counties or cities. The amount of these materials is extremely large: published collections of primary documents concerning rural base areas centered in the single province of Jiangxi alone, for example, exceed 5,000 pages in length (albeit with some duplication), and the corresponding volume of reminiscences, biographies, and secondary histories is even greater. Although all of these materials focus mainly on the Communist Party's military activities and internal politics, they also frequently include information about regional social and economic conditions, and about the political dynamics involved in the emergence of local revolutionary movements. Both in their richness of detail and in the increasingly complex and multifaceted pictures they present of the interaction between party organizations and local societies, the new materials have enabled scholars to revise significantly their understandings of the history of the great revolutionary upheaval that brought the Communist Party to power.

A second trend in local history studies involves the collection of reminiscences of local life in the first half of the twentieth century. The most important institutional venues for the collection of these materials have been the various branches of a large organization known as the Chinese People's Political Consultative Conference (CPPCC), which in recent years has focused its energy on encouraging elderly Chinese from all walks of life to reminiscence on various aspects of pre-1949 life. The sheer volume of the reminiscences thus produced—referred to by the generic title "Materials on Culture and History" (wenshi ziliao)—is staggering. While only a percentage of them have yet been (or probably ever will be) published, the most comprehensive available index to those that have appeared in print lists about 300,000 articles; their combined bulk fills 10,000 or more volumes.

As impressive as the volume of reminiscences is their diversity of subject matter. The choice of topics is clearly somewhat influenced by government priorities, but even so the available memoirs cover a tremendous range of subjects. There are, for example, thousands of biographical sketches of local notables; hundreds of histories of individual local schools, commercial enterprises, and specialized handicraft industries; and many dozens of volume-length accounts of particular local events, personages, and activities, such as peasant uprisings, famous native sons, or the production and distribution of well-known local products. There are numerous articles on temple festivals, religious sects and unusual local customs; on bandit gangs, opium production and the depredations of "local tyrants"; on landlord militias, warlord armies, and the local impact of China's numerous twentieth-century wars; on landholding arrangements, marketing networks, and the intricacies of local taxation systems. There are, in short, articles on almost every imaginable aspect of life in the vast majority of China's several thousand rural counties and urban centers.

Despite some government oversight and influence over their publication, most bureaucrats and professional historians in China tend to disparage these reminiscences. They stress that the fallibility of memory, the low educational level of many memoirists, and the lack of rigorous prepublication fact-checking or scholarly peer review have led to many errors. By contrast, scholars outside of China have used the memoirs extensively. They argue that their Chinese counterparts are affected by elitist academic prejudices, and that whatever difficulties this literature pose are far outweighed by its wealth of information on aspects of local life that are otherwise little recorded.

A third trend in local historical studies has been the ongoing publication over the last fifteen years of an officially sponsored series of local *gazetteers (*fangzhi*) covering virtually every county- and city-level administrative unit in the country. Contemporary versions of a similar genre of historical works produced before 1949 through the cooperative efforts of local scholars and officials, the recent gazetteers attempt to provide a thorough, institutionally-oriented history of each unit from the early twentieth century down to the time of their publication in the 1980s or 1990s.

Thanks to detailed official prepublication guidelines, the gazetteers (each of which is 500–1,000 pages in length) are remarkably similar in layout and topical coverage, though they vary somewhat in overall quality. Variation is particularly notable in the quantity and quality of information they provide about pre-1949 history, in part depending on the survival of local archives and earlier gazetteers. For the post-1949 period, the gazetteers provide much more uniform coverage. All include a wide range of factual and statistical information—much of it chronologically arranged—on topics such as population size and distribution, customs and dialects, geography and land use, agricultural and commercial conditions, educational affairs, the size and functioning of local government and party organs, and biographies of local notables.

The material that these gazetteers contain is extremely valuable to historians. Besides providing an impressive amount of previously unknown or inaccessible information about individual areas, the uniform presentation of this information facilitates detailed comparison among localities, and also the construction of large-scale databases whose analysis can reveal broader trends and patterns concerning such topics as the evolution of the Chinese economy and political institutions, distribution of ethnic groups and dialects, and variation in local customs.

Each of the three types of materials on Chinese local history described above provides a different type of information and lends itself to a different use. Taken together, however, they offer scholars an unprecedentedly rich body of knowledge about how the most basic levels of Chinese society have coped with the tremendous upheavals that have wracked the country throughout the twentieth century.

STEVE AVERILL

Chinese. See Appendix A.

cholera. Cholera first appeared in the New World in the 1830s. Over the remainder of the nineteenth century, epidemics occurred with some frequency, especially in 1832, again in 1849 when Zachary Taylor declared a national day of fasting, in 1854 and 1866. It was especially deadly in the cities and on the trails west. See Charles Rosenberg, *The Cholera Years: The United States in 1832, 1849, and 1866* (Chicago, 1962).

Christian Science. See Appendix B.

Church of England. See Episcopal Church, Appendix B.

city. A large or important settlement. The word comes from "see" (from the Latin *sedes*, meaning "seat") or the seat of a bishop. The term is often used to distinguish an urban area from the surrounding countryside. Legally, a city is distinguished by its size, the fact that it has governmental power derived from the state, that it is incorporated, and that it has legally defined boundaries.

city directories. City directories are one of the local historian's most treasured sources. They can be a source of simple information regarding a specific person or site, or they can be used for sophisticated, usually statistical, studies that can explore a wide variety of topics. City directories appeared on the scene very early in the nation's history. It is likely the first one appeared in Baltimore in 1752; directories were published in Charleston, South Carolina, in 1782 and 1785. By the nineteenth century many communities had city directories, and they remained constant until replaced to a certain extent by the ubiquitous telephone directory. Even after the rise of the "phone book" they have continued in many cities in a variety of forms. The presence of a recent directory may be determined by consulting James A. Ethridge, ed., *Directories of Directories* (Detroit, 1980) but it will only list those in print at the time of its publication. The best places for local historians to find out if there are pertinent local directories would be the local library, historical society, or a local newspaper or printing company.

The information directories give the local historian varies. Some simply list name and street address. Most will list occupation—sometimes a simple designation such as "merchant," "chandler," "carpenter," and at other times a descriptive title and even where the subject is employed. Some will list a spouse's name, and, of course, later ones might list a telephone number. These directories were (and are) published primarily for business use, so they reflect that bias. They usually slight nonwhites, ethnic minorities, unskilled laborers, and often do not list women unless they are business owners. Obviously they list some information that might also be in a United States manuscript census, but city directories are likely to be published annually (unlike the decennial census), and may include additional information. Despite some shortcomings, directories can provide much information for historians.

The most obvious information would be about a person or a site. Did so-and-so live in this community at a given time? What was the person's occupation? When did that person change his or her occupation or residence? Who occupied a particular building at a particular time, and what might it have been used for? This information is especially helpful in seeking biographical information, data on a building (for an application for historical-site status, for example), or on a neighborhood.

City directories can also be used for more complicated and sophisticated research on localities or communities. For instance, Judith Liu used the city directories to find the location of Chinese laundries in San Diego, and to note the transitory nature of the Chinese population in that city (Judith Liu, "Celestials in the Golden Mountain: The Chinese in One California City, San Diego, 1870–1900," Master's thesis, San Diego State University, 1977). Don H. Doyle used the city directories to tabulate the social characteristics of Nashville's economic leaders in *Nashville in the New South* (Knoxville, Tenn., 1985). Stephen R. Thernstrom and Peter R. Knight's "Man in Motion: Some Data and Speculations about Urban Population Mobility in Nineteenth-Century America" in *Anonymous Americans: Explorations in Nineteenth-Century Social History*, Tamara K. Hareven, ed. (Englewood Cliffs, N.J., 1971, pp. 17–47) provides a succinct example of the use of directories, along with other sources, to measure in and out migration in a locality. Each of these historians also published more extensive studies using city directories and related sources (see Knight's *Plain People of Boston, 1830–1860* [New York: 1971]; and Thernstrom's *The Other Bostonians* [Cambridge, Mass., 1973], which are regarded as models of this kind of methodology).

If a local historian is going to use directories for something beyond very simple information, they should learn something about them and their characteristics. David Kyvig and Myron Marty give a good, brief introduction to city directories and a bibliography on them in *Nearby History: Exploring the Past around You* (Nashville, Tenn., 1982), pp. 72–73 and 85. More detail can be found in Gordon Lewis Remington, "City Directories and their Cousins," in Arlene Eakle and Johni [*sic*] Cerny, eds., *The Source: A Guidebook of American Genealogy* (Salt Lake City, 1984), pp. 387–404. The most extensive essays on problems of using city directories for social history are the essays in the back of the books by Knight and Thernstrom; they are especially helpful in indicating the limits of city directories as a source for local history. Those limits, however, should not obscure the fact that city directories are one of the most valuable tools available for the local historian. See also <http://www.city directories.psmedia.com>.

RAYMOND STARR

Civil War federal tax records. Historical data about the wealth of a community and of its individual property holders may be found in tax, land, probate, census, and credit records. However, those records provide only clues as to disposable income. Since 1913 the federal government has levied a tax on personal incomes, and the states began adopting income taxes around the same time. Both federal and state income-tax returns are confidential, and they are destroyed after audit and legal requirements have been satisfied. Fortunately the records of an earlier federal income tax, imposed during and immediately after the Civil War, are in the *National Archives and are available for research.

Before the Civil War, the U.S. government operated on revenue generated mostly by customs duties, land sales, and occasional excise taxes on liquor. During the Civil War years, the federal government had to find massive new revenues to help pay for the huge cost of the war and also to fund the growing national debt and stabilize the currency. In August 1861 Congress authorized a 3 percent tax on incomes over $800 per year. This tax was never implemented; it was supplanted by a revised income tax that was part of an omnibus "internal revenue" act passed in July 1862. This act imposed a plethora of new taxes, some of them still unmatched in their fiscal creativity. Businesses paid monthly duties on a wide range of products, "from ale to zinc." There were monthly taxes on the receipts of canal and ferry boats, and railroad and steamboat lines; on the surpluses of banking and insurance companies; and on auction sales. Proprietors of almost every kind of retail and financial business, as well as professionals like lawyers and physicians, had to pay a yearly license fee. Licenses were also required of hotels, taverns, restaurants, theaters, circuses, billiard halls, and bowling alleys. Every deed, mortgage, contract, stock, bond, pack of playing cards, and bottle of medicine or perfume had to bear an Internal Revenue adhesive stamp. Luxury possessions like carriages, yachts, gold and silver plate, gold watches, pianos, and par-

lor organs were taxed. Of course, alcoholic beverages and tobacco products were taxed. Even newspaper advertisements were taxed.

The income-tax rates were initially 3 percent on incomes over $600, and 5 percent on incomes over $10,000 per year. In 1864 the rates were increased to 5 percent on incomes over $600, and 10 percent, over $5,000. Collection of the income, excise, and direct taxes and duties was the responsibility of a Commissioner of Internal Revenue in the U.S. Treasury Department. Every state and territory under federal control was divided into one or more collection districts, each with an appointed collector and assessor. Taxpayers were required to submit lengthy, complicated forms listing their incomes and any items or transactions that were subject to tax or duty. Assistant assessors in each community compiled summary lists from the individual tax returns. Both the lists and the taxpayers' returns were forwarded to Washington. The internal revenue taxes remained in force for several years after the Civil War. Most of them, including the income tax but excepting excise taxes on liquor and tobacco, were repealed in 1872, effective July 1873. The individual tax returns were destroyed in 1895, but the summary assessment lists are today in the National Archives (Record Group 58).

The lists are organized by state, then by collection district, then by county, then by year. Annual and monthly lists for each county enumerate the taxes and duties paid in those periods. Like other records containing data on wealth, the Internal Revenue assessment lists from the 1860s must be used with caution. Most individuals paid no income tax, because of the $600 exemption and other deductions. However, the lists do identify the wealthier individuals in a community. The successive returns for 1863, 1864, and 1865 often indicate increasing incomes, the result of wartime prosperity and currency inflation. The listing of taxable items like gold watches and reed organs is an interesting indicator of middle-class aspirations. Assessment lists for a sample community in western New York often list such items for individual taxpayers for only one year; evidently the owners thought they should pay the tax on these prized possessions only once! The assessments on businesses likewise must be used with care, since few Internal Revenue employees were hired to enforce the laws. Another source of bias in the records is the fact that the district collectors, assessors, and assistant assessors were political appointees, not all of whom may have been completely honest.

The Internal Revenue assessment lists for the states and territories for the period 1862–1866 (excluding several Southern states) are available on microfilm. The subsequent assessment lists for income and direct taxes through 1872 (when they were discontinued), and for the remaining excise taxes through the end of the century are available only in their original format (paper) at the National Archives. There are some gaps in the lists, but overall the nineteenth-century Internal Revenue assessment lists are an abundant source of economic and social data for the community historian.

See Cynthia G. Fox, "Income Tax Records of the Civil War Years," *Prologue: Quarterly of the National Archives* 18:4 (winter 1986): 250–59, reprinted in *Our Family, Our Town: Essays on Family and Local History Sources in the National Archives*, ed. Timothy Walch (Washington, D.C., 1987), pp. 141–46; Kenneth W. Munden and Henry Putney Beers, *The Union: A Guide to Federal Archives Relating to the Civil War* ([1962] Washington, D.C., 1986), pp. 204–11; Robert B. Matchette and others, comps., *Guide to Federal Records in the National Archives of the United States*, 3 vols. (Washington, D.C., 1995) [Record Group 58 "Records of the Internal Revenue Service"]; *Guide to Genealogical Research in the National Archives* (Washington, D.C., 1983), pp. 246–50.

JAMES FOLTS

Civil War nurses. See nurses.

civilly dead. See Women's legal status.

clan. A clan is an aggregate of families who claim descent from a common eponymous ancestor from whom they draw their name. The ancestor may be a human being, a supernatural being or a totem (an entity in the natural world such as an animal, plant or heavenly body).

In *patriclans, descent is reckoned solely through the male sex. Female siblings are clan members, but their children are affiliated only with their father's clan. In *matriclans, the reverse is true: descent is reckoned solely through females, whose brothers are clan members, and usually take political leadership within the clan. Brothers' children, however, are affiliated with a separate clan: that of their mothers.

Marriage between members of the same clan is considered incestuous and sometimes punishable by death, thus clans are exogamous (out-marrying) groups. In patriclans and matriclans lineages form as sibling sets separate to form their own households and claim their own lands. Lineages become separate groups, although all members of a lineage can trace the links that connect them to the founding clan ancestor.

Hostile relations may develop between lineages, which nevertheless will reaggregate to confront a threat to their security posed by another invading group. If two clans reside in close proximity to one another, relationships between them may be structured according to specific rights and obligations (e.g., marital exchange, competitions, or the requirement that each clan conduct burial ceremonies for members of the other). This formal structure is termed a moiety organization—the division of a social unit into two groups based on both antagonism and mutual support.

LAURIS McKEE

class. See social class.

Cobblestone Publishing. Cobblestone Publishing's magazines let young people experience the pleasure of reading through an accurate, fascinating, and authoritative resource that is appropriate in the library, the classroom, and the home. The company's seven magazines—covering the areas of U.S. history, cultures and geography, world history, science and space, African American history, and general reading—educate and entertain through a creative mix of articles, primary-source documents, photographs, and illustrations as well as enjoyable activities, puzzles, and cartoons. Each theme-based magazine takes a "story behind the story" approach that provides readers with more than just facts and figures. Bringing a topic to life is the core of all you see and read in Cobblestone's publications.

Two teachers, looking for a way to promote reading and history to children, developed the idea for *Cobblestone* magazine in 1979. Their legacy is now a successful publication that makes discovering American history an adventure. The magazine explores all aspects of the American experience, but in much more detail than you'll ever find in any textbook. Through the years *Cobblestone* themes have ranged from the obvious—Lewis and Clark and Gettysburg—to less frequently told—Harlem Renaissance and Transcendentalism. All of *Cobblestone*'s 200-plus issues are still in print and available as back issues, which is also true for all other Cobblestone magazines.

These include *Calliope, Faces, Odyssey, Appleseeds,* and *Footsteps* launched to celebrate and explore the rich and courageous heritage of African Americans. Each theme-based issue reports on the many, and frequently overlooked, contributions that African Americans have made to our culture by looking beyond the ordinary and accepted. Recent issues investigate the many ways blacks participated in the Civil War and in the whaling industry as well as how blacks made up a large portion of the cowboy population.

The story of California provides the backdrop for *California Chronicles* magazine. This publication provides insight into the multifaceted events and developments that occurred in today's most populated state. Each issue brings young readers an understanding of the people, places, resources, and occurrences that helped make California the dream state for many.

What makes all of Cobblestone Publishing's magazines attractive to many people is their unbiased and accurate content. To develop this material, Cobblestone works with consulting editors, writers, historians, museum curators, and others who are experts in their respective fields. This quality-focused approach has earned Cobblestone praise and awards from the Parents' Choice Foundation, the Freedoms Foundation, and the Educational Press Association of America (EdPress). In 1998, EdPress named *Calliope* magazine as the outstanding young-adult publication of the year. In addition, Cobblestone's magazines are part of the recommended reading list for meeting the national Middle School Language Arts Performance Standards for English and Language Arts.

For libraries, the magazines of Cobblestone Publishing offer excellent resources for general reading, research or homework projects, or simply to enhance a young person's overall knowledge.

Cobblestone Publishing is located at 30 Grove Street, Peterborough, NH 03458; (603) 924-7209; <www.cobblestonepub.com>.

LOU WARYNCIA

co-ed. The term "co-ed," or "co-educational," first appeared in 1855 to indicate the education of both sexes in one institution. "Co-ed" was a term of derision, especially after 1870 with the debate about admitting women to men's colleges. Some feared that the education of boys and girls together would harm women; others worried about the effect upon the boys—especially if women students outscored them. Andrew Dickson White, Cornell University's first president, believed that the presence of women students would help "civilize" the men.

See education, history of.

commonwealth. A commonwealth is a body of people of an area organized as a community or a state; the archaic term was "commonweal," meaning of the general welfare. In the United States, Massachusetts, Pennsylvania, Virginia, and Kentucky are officially designated commonwealths.

community studies. Beginning in the 1960s, several trends in historiography combined to produce new community studies. Urban history flourished as historians tried to understand the profound changes taking place in the cities of the United States during the years of riots and urban renewal. The civil-rights movement and women's movement profoundly influenced historians who entered the profession during these same years, and they embarked on what came to be called the "new social history," emphasizing women, minorities, blacks, ethnic groups, workers—everyone except the traditional "great white men." Community studies soon reflected this same emphasis, as well as the impact of the *Annales school, which began in France in the 1930s and flourished in the 1950s, studying population groups by looking at demographic patterns. Historians learned about statistics and began to use computers to analyze vital statistics (birth, death, and marriage records) and wills to document communities through the lives of otherwise anonymous residents. Just as these trends began to gain a firm foothold in the academy, communities across the United States began to plan their own *celebrations of the nation's bicentennial in 1976 and produced a dizzying number of community histories of wide-ranging quality.

All of these studies focused on the community as a geographic place and on the events that happened within that place. They were, then, examples of local history, although they did not always have that label. As such, they provide local historians with innumerable examples of innovative uses of sources such as *census data, *city and business directories, newspapers, city council and county commission records, school board records, *vital statistics, plat maps of subdivisions, real and personal property tax records, utility-company records, insurance-company maps, and R.G. Dun & Co. credit records. They raised questions that can be asked about other communities such as patterns of suburbanization and the evolution of ethnic neighborhoods, and, most importantly, models of integrating events of local communities into broad national trends.

Some of the earliest comparative community histories set the standards for this integration of local events into national contexts. Carl Bridenbaugh's *Cities in the Wilderness: The First Century of Urban Life in America, 1625–1742* (N.Y., 1938) and *Cities in Revolt: Urban Life in America, 1743–1776* (N.Y., 1955) compared developments in five cities that were the bulwarks of European settlement on the Atlantic coast and, then, leading centers of the American Revolution. In the 1960s, Richard C. Wade analyzed westward expansion by comparing urban development in the Ohio River Valley in *The Urban Frontier: Pioneer Life in Early Pittsburgh, Cincinnati, Lexington, Louisville, and St. Louis* (Chicago, 1964) and then reinterpreted the history of slavery in *Slavery in the Cities: The South, 1820–1860* (London, 1964).

Some historians have continued to write comparative community histories and to provide broad national or regional contexts for local events. Examples of this genre include Richard R. Lingeman's *Small Town America: A Narrative History, 1620–the Present* (Boston, 1980), which includes everything from a detailed description of the early days of Virginia City, Nevada, to an example of small-town boosterism in the naming of Bucyrus, Ohio, for "the founder of the Persian Empire, with a prefixal 'bu' tacked on for euphony" (p. 111). Darrel E. Bigham's *Towns and Villages of the Lower Ohio* (Lexington, Ky., 1998) also fits this comparative model in its examination of towns from Evansville, Indiana, to Cairo, Illinois.

More frequently, though, historians have focused their work on one particular city or one specific aspect of the history of that community, using that emphasis as a way to deepen or expand our understanding of basic assumptions. Each monograph, therefore, reinforces the national story by adding rich and complex details or forces us to reexamine what we thought we knew. Examples of such urban histories, written in the 1960s, include Sam Bass Warner's *Streetcar Suburbs: The Process of Growth in Boston, 1870–1900* (Cambridge, Mass., 1962); Stanley Buder's *Pullman: An Experiment in Industrial Order and Community Planning, 1880–1930* (N.Y., 1967); and Zane L. Miller's *Boss Cox's Cincinnati: Urban Politics in the Progressive Era* (Chicago, 1968). All focus, in part, in how cities expanded and how neighborhood development was an integral part of a city's history.

The 1960s also saw a growing interest in *African American history and the beginnings of the "new *social history" that has come to dominate the historical profession. Gilbert Osofsky's *Harlem: The Making of a Ghetto: Negro New York, 1890–1930* (N.Y., 1963) is a classic in both urban and African American history. Suzanne Lebsock's *Free Women of Petersburg: Status and Culture in a Southern Town, 1784–1860* (N.Y., 1985); James Borchert's *Alley Life in Washington: Family, Community, Religion, and Folklife in the City, 1850–1970* (Urbana, 1980); and Jacquelyn Dowd Hall et al., *Like a Family: The Making of a Southern Cotton Mill World* (Chapel Hill, 1987) integrate the broad themes of *women's history, black history, and *labor history into the histories of specific communities. Urban historians have long been interested in immigration as an aspect of urban history, but works such as Ricardo Romo's *East Los Angeles: History of a Barrio* (Austin,

1983) shifted the emphasis from European immigrants to Hispanics.

Especially when based on dissertations, as was Lebsock's book, these studies are rich in detail for particular areas and meticulously documented. Therefore, they provide references for further research on that community. They also reflect the fact that universities located in major cities often emphasize urban issues and will encourage faculty and students to write about those cities.

By the early 1970s, historians were beginning to look at "cliometrics," the use of quantitative analysis, to examine community life. John Demos was one of the early pioneers in this approach with *A Little Commonwealth: Family Life in Plymouth Colony* (N.Y., 1971).

Since the 1960s, historians have been shifting their attention from Northeastern and Midwestern cities like Philadelphia, New York, Boston, Chicago, and Cincinnati to cities in the South and West. We still need far more studies of communities in the South, as well as in rural areas like *Appalachia and the Great Plains so that we can better understand the complexity of community history. David R. Goldfield has made important contributions to our understanding of Southern urbanization in *The City in Southern History: The Growth of Urban Civilization in the South* (Port Washington, N.Y., 1977); *Cotton Fields and Skyscrapers: Southern City and Region* (Baltimore, 1989); and *Region, Race and Cities: Interpreting the Urban South* (Baton Rouge, La., 1997).

Anniversaries are occasions to commemorate the past, often by publishing community histories. The nation's Bicentennial sparked the publication of such books for towns and counties large and small across the country. Similarly, centennials, bicentennials, and even tricentennials for some cities have led historical societies and commercial publishers to reprint long out-of-print local histories. Cincinnati's 1988 bicentennial celebration, for instance, included the reprinting of the Works Progress Administration guide, *Cincinnati: A Guide to the Queen City and Its Neighbors* ([1943] Cincinnati, 1987) and Henry Allen Ford's *History of Cincinnati, Ohio*, with illustrations and biographical sketches (Cleveland, 1881). Commercial publishers like Walsworth Publishing Company work with local historical societies to produce leatherette-bound, yearbook-type volumes that can contain a wealth of information on local schools, churches, businesses, and families. The quality depends on the research by local authors, and there are far too few sources cited to suit the needs of most professional historians. Too often, also, there is so much focus on the local events that it is hard to accurately analyze the community's place in its region or state. Nor do these works often include enough attention to women and minorities or institutions outside the mainstream of community life. Funding usually comes from individual subscriptions and advertisements from local businesses, so these are truly community histories.

One variant of these community histories is the ten-volume Foxfire series, which Eliot Wigginton edited between 1972 and 1993. The numerous volumes in the series document local folk traditions in *Appalachia, including information on music, folk remedies, and crafts. *Foxfire* had at least one local imitator, *Hickory and Ladyslippers: Life and Lore of the People of Clay County*, which students at West Virginia's Clay County High School published from 1977 to 1990.

In contrast to these local histories, we began to see a new genre of community histories develop during the 1980s—urban *encyclopedias for cities that are so complex that historians are daunted by the task of producing comprehensive monographs. These include *The Encyclopedia of New York City*, Kenneth T. Jackson, ed. (New Haven, Conn., 1995); the *Encyclopedia of Indianapolis*, David J. Bodenhamer et al., eds. (Bloomington, 1994); and *Cleveland: A Concise History, 1796–1990*, Carol Poh Miller, ed. (Bloomington, 1990). The editors of and contributors to these volumes are often professional historians who spend many years compiling scholarly articles on numerous aspects of city life, carefully placing the local story into a national context. The *National Endowment for the Humanities supported some of these projects.

Still, the bold synthetic approach to community history continues. The most dramatic version of this is *Gotham: A History of New York City to 1898* by Edwin G. Burrows and Mike Wallace (N.Y., 1998).

Interest in *historic preservation has generated interest in illustrated histories, architectural histories, and guides to local landmarks. Some are published by major presses and distributed nationally, some by local organizations and available only in local bookshops. One classic of this genre is John W.

Reps's *Town Planning in Frontier America* (Princeton, 1965). George McDaniel, *In Hearth & Home: Preserving a People's Culture* (Philadelphia, 1982) studied the housing and lives of rural African Americans in Maryland. *The Most Beautiful Villages of New England*, by Tom Schachtman with photographs by Len Rubenstein (London, 1997) profiles New England villages.

There are guides to the *architectural history of almost every major city and, often, publications documenting surveys of important landmarks through the *Historic American Buildings Survey and *Historic American Engineering Record, both programs of the U.S. Department of the Interior.

It is important not to overlook the numerous publications that local historical societies have produced to encourage children to be interested in community history. One model is *People, Space, and Time: The Chicago Neighborhood History Project, An Introduction to Community History for Schools*, by Gerald A. Danzer and Lawrence W. McBride (Lanham, Md., 1986). The Missouri Historical Society has also produced a series of *pamphlets on the history of St. Louis that are attractive, yet inexpensive and easy to distribute.

Community studies, therefore, are as varied as the communities they document and the authors who write them. Most importantly, since the 1960s, these histories have increasingly documented the rich diversity of local communities and the lives of all their residents.

BARBARA HOWE

Congregational Church. See dix B.

consultancy concerns and fees. fees.

controlling knowledge. See intellectual property.

copyright. Copyright governs the rights of authors, publishers, and consumers of artistic works, such as books, songs, plays, movies, choreography, photographs, paintings, sculpture, sound recordings, and works of architecture. A copyright is a legal right to control the reproduction and dissemination of an artistic work. In many countries, a copyright is considered to be a natural right of the author. In the United States, however, copyrights are granted to promote the public welfare by giving authors and publishers an economic incentive to create and publish new artistic works.

pyright Act of 1976, the
rtistic work is granted the
t to reproduce the copy-
, to distribute copies of the
work to the public, to per-
play the copyrighted work
and to prepare derivative
ch as translations or adapta-
ased upon the copyrighted
hese exclusive rights, however,
ject to a number of important
ions that are designed to balance
ghts of authors against the rights
nsumers, and to ensure that copy-
t does not unreasonably restrict the
ts of others to freely express them-
ves.

First, copyright protection extends
nly to those elements of a copyrighted
work that are original to the author. For
example, because facts are not originated by the author of a copyrighted work,
the copyright does not prevent a second
author from copying those facts, even if
the first author was the first person to
discover or report those facts. Instead,
copyright protects only the author's
original expression of those facts. Thus,
one author can prevent another author
from using the same sentences and
paragraphs used by the first author (or a
close paraphrase of them), but he or she
cannot prevent the second author from
expressing the same facts in his or her
own words.

Second, copyright protection does
not extend to any idea, procedure,
process, system, method of operation,
concept, principle, or discovery that is
contained in the copyrighted work, even
if those concepts or ideas are original to
the first author. Instead, copyright protects only the author's original expres-

sion of those ideas. According to the U.S.
Supreme Court, this limitation on copyright law (known as the idea/expression
dichotomy) is necessary to ensure that
the Copyright Act does not violate the
rights of free speech and press that are
guaranteed by the First Amendment.

Third, copyright protection is subject
to a number of express exceptions contained in the statute. For example, libraries and archives are permitted to
make single copies of copyrighted works
under certain circumstances. Schools
and churches are permitted to perform
or display certain works publicly in the
course of classroom teaching activities
and religious services, respectively. Certain nondramatic works may be performed publicly if no admission is
charged or if the proceeds are used exclusively for educational, religious, or
charitable purposes. The Act also contains comprehensive, highly detailed
and technical provisions governing the
retransmission of copyrighted works by
hotels and apartments, cable-television
systems, and satellite broadcasters.

One of the most important of these
limitations on the exclusive rights of
the author is the first sale doctrine. The
first sale doctrine permits the lawful
owner of an authorized copy of a copyrighted work (including the original) to
display that copy publicly, or to lend or
sell that copy to anyone else, without
the permission of the copyright owner.
An exception to the first sale doctrine,
however, prohibits the commercial
rental or lease of sound recordings and
computer programs, in order to prevent consumers from renting those
works for the sole purpose of making
unauthorized copies at home.

Finally, copyright protection is subject to the fair use doctrine, which permits a second author to borrow a small amount of original expression from a copyrighted work in creating a new work, where doing so would not unreasonably interfere with the copyright owner's ability to sell or license the copyrighted work. Examples include the use of quotations in a review of a book, and exaggerated imitation in a parody of the original work.

The fair use doctrine was originally developed in judicial opinions, and was later codified in Section 107 of the Copyright Act. Section 107 does not attempt to define fair use, but simply lists several potential examples and directs courts to consider four factors in determining whether a use is fair. The first factor is the purpose and character of the use: transformative uses, in which the borrowed material is used as a point of departure to fashion substantially original material, are more likely to be fair uses than reproductive uses, in which the borrowed material is copied without change or comment; and noncommercial or educational uses are more likely to be fair uses than commercial uses. The illustrative purposes listed in the statute include criticism, comment, news reporting, teaching (including multiple copies for classroom use), scholarship, and research. The second factor is the nature of the copyrighted work: borrowing material from factual works is more likely to be a fair use than borrowing material from works of fiction; and borrowing material from published works is more likely to be a fair use than borrowing material from unpublished works (especial-

ly where the unpublished works have the potential to be published by the copyright owner). The third factor is the amount and qualitative importance of the portion used, in relation to the copyrighted work as a whole. Borrowing a relatively small amount of the copyrighted work is more likely to be a fair use than reproduction of the entire work. The fourth factor is the effect of the use upon the potential market for or value of the copyrighted work. If the defendant's use would substantially diminish the revenue that a copyright holder would expect to receive by acting as a substitute for the original work, the use is less likely to be a fair use.

History. Copyright law evolved in England out of efforts by the Crown to control the use of the printing press by granting a monopoly on publishing to the Stationers' Company, a group of London printers and booksellers who were required to submit their publications for approval by official censors. Shortly after the official monopoly expired, Parliament passed the first copyright statute, the Statute of Anne, in 1710. It granted to authors the exclusive right to publish their works for an initial term of fourteen years, renewable for an additional fourteen years. After that, the work passed into the public domain, meaning that anyone was free to copy or publish it.

In 1789, the U.S. Constitution authorized Congress "[t]o Promote the Progress of Science and useful Arts, by securing for limited Times to Authors and Inventors the exclusive Right to their respective Writings and Discoveries." The first Copyright Act in the United States was enacted by Congress in 1790. Comprehensive revisions were made to the Copyright Act in 1831, 1870, 1909, and 1976. The 1976 Act has since been amended several times to accommodate new technologies and international trade considerations. Most importantly, in 1988 the U.S. enacted several amendments designed to allow the United States to join the Berne Convention, the most important international agreement concerning copyright protection. Additional amendments were made in 1994 to implement the Agreement on Trade-Related Aspects of Intellectual Property (TRIPs) adopted at the Uruguay Round of the General Agreement on Tariffs and Trade (GATT); and in 1998 to implement the World Intellectual Property Organization (WIPO) Copyright Treaty, and the WIPO Performances and Phonograms Treaty.

In general, works created before January 1, 1978, are governed by the 1909 Act (with some important modifications in the 1976 Act), while works created on or after January 1, 1978, are governed by the 1976 Act, as amended. The current provisions of the Copyright Act can be found in the first eight chapters of Title 17 of the United States Code.

Requirements for Protection. To receive copyright protection, a work must be "original." Courts have construed the word "original" to mean only that a work must have been independently created, and that it contain a minimal amount of creativity. Thus, a work that consists entirely of facts or data, or other public domain material, cannot be protected by copyright unless the preexisting material has been selected, coordinated or arranged in an original way. The author of such a work may receive a copyright in the original compilation, but the copyright protects only the original aspects of the work, and does not affect the copyright status of the preexisting material. Likewise, the author of a derivative work (a work based on one or more preexisting works) may receive a copyright if the preexisting material was used lawfully; but the copyright extends only to the original aspects added by the second author.

Under the 1909 Act, copyright protection was divided between federal and state law. State law, or common-law copyright, protected a work prior to publication. To receive a federal copyright, the work had to be published with a copyright notice, containing the word "Copyright" or the symbol ©, the date of first publication, and the name of the copyright owner. If a work was published without notice, the copyright was forfeited and the work fell into the public domain. To reduce the number of inadvertent forfeitures, courts distinguished between a general publication (the distribution of copies to any member of the general public), and a limited publication (the distribution of copies only to a select group of people for a limited purpose). Only a general publication without notice would place the work in the public domain. While the copyright owner was not strictly required to register the copyright with the Copyright Office, he or she could not renew the copyright or bring an action for infringement until the copyright had been registered and a copy or copies of the work had been deposited with the Copyright Office as required by the Act.

Publication ceased to be the dividing line between state and federal protection under the 1976 Act. For works created on or after January 1, 1978, federal copyright protection attaches as soon as the work is "fixed in a tangible medium of expression." A work is "fixed" when it is first placed into a tangible form. The Act allows copyright to protect works fixed in any medium, now known or later developed, regardless of whether technology is needed to perceive or reproduce it. Common-law copyright can still be used to protect works that have not yet been fixed; but for fixed works, the 1976 Act preempts all other state laws that provide rights equivalent to those provided by copyright.

The 1976 Act retained the requirement of notice when the work was published; however, it permitted the copyright owner to cure the omission of notice in some circumstances. Despite this provision, however, the notice and registration provisions continued to prevent U.S. membership in the Berne Convention, which prohibits conditioning the exercise of copyright on any such formalities. In order to join the Berne Convention, the United States eliminated the requirement of notice for all works published on or after March 1, 1989. It also eliminated registration as a prerequisite to filing suit for works created by authors from, or first published in, a foreign nation adhering to the Berne Convention. Registration is still a prerequisite to filing suit for all other works, however, including works by U.S. authors and works first published in the United States; and the Act retains certain procedural and remedial advantages for those who comply with the notice and registration provisions.

Ownership. A copyright is owned initially by the author or authors of the work. The authors in a work of joint authorship are co-owners of the copyright. The "author," however, is not always the person who created the work. Under U.S. law, a work created by an employee acting within the scope of his or her employment is a "work made for hire," and the copyright is owned initially by his or her employer. A specially commissioned work can also be a "work made for hire" if it falls within one of nine categories listed in the statute (such as a motion picture), and if the parties agree in a signed writing that the work shall be a work made for hire. If these requirements are met, the copyright is owned initially by the commissioning party.

A copyright owner may authorize another person to reproduce, adapt, sell, publicly perform, or publicly display the copyrighted work. Such an authorization is called a license. A license may be restricted in duration or geographically, and it may be either exclusive or nonexclusive. A signed writing is required to grant an exclusive license or to transfer a copyright.

Ownership of a copyright is distinct from ownership of the material object in which the work is fixed. Thus, the sale of an original work of art, such as a painting or sculpture, does not transfer the copyright to the buyer. The copyright is retained by the author, and the buyer (such as a museum or gallery) must obtain permission to reproduce the work. Likewise, the recipient of a letter does not have the right to reproduce the letter; the copyright is retained by the original author.

Duration. Like the Statute of Anne, the Copyright Act of 1790 provided for an initial duration of fourteen years from the date of first publication, and the copyright could be renewed for an additional fourteen years. The Copyright Act of 1831 increased the initial term to twenty-eight years; and the 1909 Act increased the renewal term to twenty-eight years, for a maximum duration of fifty-six years.

The 1976 Act changed the term of copyright for works of individual or joint authors to the life of the author (or longest surviving author) plus fifty years. For works made for hire, the term was the shorter of seventy-five years from the date of first publication, or one hundred years from the date of creation. Works first published before January 1, 1978 had their copyrights extended to seventy-five years from the date of first publication. Works that had been created prior to January 1, 1978 but that had not been published (and were therefore subject to common-law copyright) were given the same term of protection as new works; but in exchange for being forced to relinquish their common-law protection, which was in theory perpetual, the Act provided that such copyrights would not expire before December 31, 2002; and if the work was published before then, they would not expire before December 31, 2027.

In 1998, Congress passed the Sonny Bono Copyright Term Extension Act, which purports to extend the term of all existing and future copyrights by an additional twenty years. (The sole exception was for works created before January 1, 1978, that remain unpublished, which will still enter the public domain on January 1, 2003.) The application of the Term Extension Act to existing copyrights is being challenged in court on the ground that it violates the Copyright Clause of the Constitution, which provides that copyrights can only be granted "for limited times." Regardless of the outcome of this challenge, however, it will not affect the validity of term extension for works created on or after October 27, 1998.

The Term Extension Act did not attempt to revive copyrights that had already fallen into the public domain. As a result, the one statement that can be made with certainty is that works first published in 1922 or before have fallen into the public domain. If the Term Extension Act is upheld, works first published in 1923–1963 and properly renewed, and all works first published in 1964–1977 (for which renewal is automatic), will be protected for 95 years from the date of first publication. Works created before 1978, and first published in 1978–2002, will be protected for the term given to new works, or until December 31, 2047, whichever is greater. Works created before 1978, but not published in or before 2002, will be protected for the term given to new works, or until December 31, 2002, whichever is greater. Works created in 1978 or later will be protected for the life of the author plus 70 years; or for works made for hire, for the shorter of 95 years from first publication or 120 years from creation. As under the 1976 Act, all copyrights run to the end of the calendar year in which they would otherwise expire.

Infringement. When a copyright owner discovers that someone else is reproducing, adapting, selling, publicly performing, or publicly displaying a work without authorization, he or she has three years in which to commence an action for infringement. Such an action must be filed in a federal district court. To prevail, the copyright owner must demonstrate that he or she is the owner of a valid copyright; that the defendant has exercised one of the exclusive rights without authorization; and that the defendant's work is substantially similar to protected expression in the plaintiff's work. If the copyright owner does so, then the defendant bears the burden of proving that he or she falls within one of the statutory exceptions, including fair use.

If infringement is proved, the plaintiff will generally receive an injunction against any further infringing use of the copyrighted work. The court may also order that any infringing copies be impounded and sold or destroyed. The plaintiff is also entitled to recover any actual damages suffered as a result of the infringement, plus any profits earned by the infringer, to the extent they do not overlap. If the plaintiff cannot prove any damages or profits, it may elect to recover statutory damages in an amount fixed by the court within the range provided in the statute. The court also has discretion to award both costs and attorneys fees to the prevailing party. Criminal penalties of up to ten years in prison may also be imposed for intentional infringement, but as a practical matter criminal penalties are rarely enforced except against parties who commit large-scale infringement for commercial gain.

TYLER OCHOA

See intellectual property rights.

cornerstones. A cornerstone is a key building block inserted and usually dated while a building is under construction. It often holds a box, usually made of copper, in which contents are placed; that box is often called a "time capsule." The conflation of these two terms is common, although time capsule usually denotes a container in which items are put aside for a specific length of time at which point it is to be deliberately opened; whereas, the contents of a cornerstone usually remain in that stone until the building is demolished, or in a number of cases, until the building is renovated, which allows the cornerstone to be removed, and the contents, if any, seen.

In either case, a cornerstone provides an opportunity for materials from one era to be deliberately selected to be seen or recovered at another time. The question arises, what have people put in cornerstones and what might we consider putting in one to represent today to the future?

When the cornerstone placed in 1878 in St. Vincent's Orphanage in Columbus, Ohio, was reset, it was damaged, and the contents were revealed. In it, slightly damp and very fragile, were a crucifix, saints' relics, two postage stamps, five contemporary coins, four religious medals, five different German-language newspapers from Columbus in 1878, a postcard showing a picture of the orphanage, a picture of Pope Leo XIII, and a photograph of Sylvester Rosecrans, the first Roman Catholic bishop of Columbus. In 1998, when St. Matthew's Church in Detroit opened its cornerstone, sealed originally in 1926, observers found a typed history of the church with information about the "social climate of the day between blacks and whites," the trades in which many black residents were employed, and "verification of a long-rumored but never proven meeting between abolitionist John Brown and Frederick Douglass" (*The Detroit News*, September 21, 1998, p. B1).

Schools also have cornerstones. In Omaha in 1996, a 1922 cornerstone at the Papillion School was found. It contained the petition that had been issued regarding the expansion of the school and the information that the bond had been passed by a vote of 117 to 116. There was also a program from the dedication, the names of the Board of Education members and of all the students in the school that year. The time capsule at the Newton Memorial Hospital in Cassadaga, New York, revealed slides inserted in 1927 when the building was a tuberculoses hospital for children. Those slides showed that there had been 238 patients, and that their average weight gain over the eight weeks of treatment was $6^1/4$ pounds. "These items," reported the *Buffalo News* (May 4, 1996), "belong to the community."

Cornerstones and their contents have been unearthed in many public buildings, including city halls, and even police headquarters, such as the one in Tampa, Florida. When the old building was being turned into a police museum, included in the cornerstone was a 1961 letter written by John P. Griffin who hoped he would be there when the box

was opened. He wasn't notified in time to be present when that occurred in 1998, but Griffin, then age 73, did see his letter (*St. Petersburg Times*, July 31, 1998, "Police Crack Open Memories of '61").

Not only are time capsules and cornerstones opened, they are still being created. They are considered interesting school projects as well as community acts. In Washington in 1998, the headline read "Edmonds to Open, Bury Time Capsules." As an inducement to people to come to the cornerstone ceremony, they were promised that all attending would have their names preserved in the new box (*Seattle Times*, May 26, 1998).

Local historians, because we deal with the relics of the past, are often called upon to help decide what is appropriate to preserve for the future. From the past we learn that coins of the date, newspapers, lists of names, relics, trolley tokens, and other items are often considered best. Sometimes letters to the future are inserted. Often lists of important people are kept.

See salting the archive.

corporation. A corporation is a legal entity, usually made up of a group of people but sometimes of an individual. It differs from a company in that it is legally incorporated and, unlike a partnership, it remains as a corporation even if the participants change. A corporation may be public or private. Examples of public corporations are municipalities, water districts, and school districts. Private corporations, on the other hand, have no governmental duties. They may be formed as business organizations or for charitable purposes, such as assisting the poor or administering hospitals, asylums, or colleges. The United States, unlike England, does not have ecclesiastical corporations. Churches are incorporated like any private charitable organization.

costume history. Historical societies often harbor mountains of clothing that loom disconcertingly in back room, attic, or cellar. Unless a society has used the services of a specialist, the accumulation of ancestral apparel may exist in a state of neglect ranging from abuse to indifference. Everyone knows something needs to be done, but no one knows where to first grab that sleeping tiger, and the decisive moment is evaded. However, when the costume collection is brought into order, it becomes useful for study as well as for exhibits; the inclusion of clothing enhances other exhibits as well.

There are four basic concerns for a costume collection:

Physical well-being: It may be difficult to locate a specialist to help with identifying clothing, but it is not difficult to ensure its safety while awaiting identification. As with manuscripts, paintings, drawings, and furniture, clothing requires storage in reasonable climatic conditions to prevent or minimize damage from mold and fungus, vermin, dehydration, and acid formation. Temperature and humidity should be maintained at levels more or less comfortable for humans. Marking must be done in an archivally safe manner. Storage boxes and bags must be made from archivally safe materials, and the packing or hanging must be accomplished with the *support* (not compacting) of the garment uppermost in mind. Racks and shelves should be sturdy, clean, and resistant to corrosion and off-gassing of deleterious chemicals. There should be room enough for a work table, and aisles large enough to move about in without endangering the objects. The space needs to be accessible for regular cleaning to discourage infiltration by pests. Not the least of concerns is the need to handle clothing with gloved, or at least frequently washed, hands. Food is not to be allowed in the storage or work area.

Identification: Illustrated references are available to assist in the difficult task of identifying and dating clothing (see below). Nevertheless, it is easy to misunderstand the subtleties of style, so it is advisable to seek help from a specialist. Information entered into the collection catalog is worthless if the description is inaccurate or superficial; it must specifically identify details that clearly distinguish an item from others like it. In the case of a computerized catalog, it is important to settle upon consistent terminology that facilitates successful searches for particular items.

Accession and deaccession: Even the best-funded clothing collections occasionally experience the pinch of inadequate storage space. The fastest way to acquire a storage problem is to uncritically accept every offered donation. The best way to prevent such a problem is to establish a collection policy stipulating the time period, geographical area, quality level, and object type to be collected. A collection committee charged with the responsibility of evaluating potential donations is able to restrict acquisitions to those items that best enhance the collection. In addition, such an arrangement affords a mitigating, impersonal cloak of diplomacy when a donation must be declined. When the time comes to cull irrelevant, redundant, or shabby items that have been in the collection for decades, the job will be simplified if those sorts of things have not been indiscriminately acquired in the present.

Use: "Old clothes" have been closely associated in our lives with activities like children's play, Halloween parades, and theatrical productions; thus many persons find it difficult to adjust to regarding those familiar and fascinating objects as *museum artifacts.* Yet clothing is less able to withstand ordinary handling than most objects—respect for costume items is extremely important to their survival. Some items are retained for their value to the collection although they are too fragile to mount on mannequins, or even to exhibit flat. Discretion is required in selecting items to be made available for study or exhibit. There is no difficulty in deciding whether to allow clothing to be worn, because wearing clothing intended for preservation is inappropriate.

See Janet Arnold, *Patterns of Fashion 1: 1660–1860* (N.Y., 1964, 1972); James R. Blackaby, Patricia Greeno, and the Nomenclature Committee, *The Revised Nomenclature for Museum Cataloging* (Walnut Creek, Calif., 1988); Stella Blum, ed., *Harper's Bazaar 1867–1898* (N. Y., 1974); Nancy Bradfield, *Costume In Detail—Women's Dress 1730–1930* (Boston, 1968); Karen Finch and Greta Putnam, *The Care and Preservation of Textiles* (London, 1985); John Peacock,

20th Century Fashion (London, 1993); Lawrence R. Pizer, *A Primer for Local Historical Societies*, rev. ed. (Walnut Creek, Calif, 1991); and Naomi Tarrant, *Collecting Costume* (London, 1983).

SUSAN GREENE

Commerce, Department of. The Department of Commerce is a large, multifaceted federal agency that administers the diverse areas of International Trade, Technological Administration and Economic Statistics, and Oceanic and Atmosphere Administration. The Census Bureau, Patent and Trademark Office, and the National Weather Service are some of the better-known, if smaller, components of the department. The department does not maintain a central office outside of Washington. Most of the divisions and subdepartments are located in Washington, although some have regional offices. Phone numbers are listed in the United States Government Manual and the Federal Yellow Pages, which can be found in most libraries. The best way to contact the department is through the website: <www.doc.gov>.

The individual subdepartments are: Bureau of Export Administration <www.bxa.doc.gov>; International Trade Administration* <www.ita.doc.gov>; Bureau of Economic Analysis <www.bea.doc.gov>; Bureau of the Census* <www.census.gov>; Patent and Trademark Office <www.uspto.gov>; Economic Development Administration* <www.doc.gov/eda>; Minority Business Development Agency* <www.mda.gov>; National Telecommunications and Information Agency* <www.ntia.doc.gov>; National Institute of Standards and Technology <www.nist.gov>; National Technical Information Service <www.ntis.gov>; National Oceanic and Atmospheric Administration* <www.noaa.gov>. The starred agencies have regional or field offices.

JERRY BRISCO

controlling knowledge. See intellectual-property rights.

county historians. For decades, local historical societies and local historians have served their respective communities in recording and preserving the past for present audiences and future generations. Inspired in part by the nation's *centennial celebration in 1876, these organizations and individuals devoted to the preservation of grassroots history have shared, through written accounts, county atlases, museum exhibits, oral histories, tours, and special events, the rich stories and events that have affected their communities over the years. Through these means, they have proved themselves to be powerful and articulate advocates for the preservation of local community records and material culture as well as history educators committed to reaching a wider public.

While most local historians are connected with a particular community, village, town, or township, there are others whose responsibilities cover the entire county. These county historians may be affiliated with the county historical society; some, however, may claim the self-appointed or honorary title based upon their longevity in and extensive knowledge of their area. Their numerous and varied tasks include gathering stories and recollections of long-time residents, publishing newsletters and books, writing history columns for the local newspapers, assisting at the county historical society/museum, serving as a resource for schools, and assisting with family history and genealogical research. In most cases, there is no formal appointment to the post of county historian. There are, however, two examples of long-established county historian programs in the United States—one implemented by state legislation; the other, a partnership between a state agency and a private historical society.

In 1919, New York Governor Alfred E. Smith signed a bill, known as "The Historian's Law," which made his state the first to establish a formal network of appointed municipal historians. The bill's intent was to designate an individual in every community to serve as a resource for inquiries about local history and to assist the state historian in preserving historical records and memories. State historian Dr. James Sullivan believed that this network also would promote the preservation of primary sources at the local level and encourage the development of history programs statewide. The first official task of these municipal historians was to gather materials pertaining to New York's communities during World War I, a project that continued well over a decade. Since a few counties previously had appointed historians, those individuals assisted in the war research project, thereby laying the foundation for the next phase of history at the local level.

The New York State Legislature amended the civil code in 1933 to permit the appointment of a historian for every county. The legislation authorized these individuals, designated by the board of county supervisors, to oversee the activities of their respective county's municipal historians and to promote those goals established by the state historian. Under the direction of Dr. Albert Corey, state historian from 1944 to 1963, the county historian program expanded beyond the task of collecting war records and reminiscences. Rather, Corey redirected these historians' attention towards issues that affected their own work, namely, *historic preservation, public records, education, and advocacy. In so doing, he developed an active statewide network of local and county historians and strengthened their ties with the office of the *State Historian.

Recognizing the need to obtain a greater knowledge about their municipal responsibilities, local and county historians participated in workshops and seminars offered by state government agencies. Since these agencies did not specifically address matters pertaining to history nor provide a professional affiliation, the historians formed their own organizations—the County Historians Association (1967) and the Municipal Historians Association of New York (1971)—to provide more collegial support and in-depth training within the profession.

By the early 1980s, the Laws of the State of New York continued to include the position of "county historian" under the section "Divisions of History and Public Records." The law specified that each county board of supervisors had the authority to select the county historian, who would serve without compensation, unless the governing board decided otherwise. Once appointed, the historian was expected "to supervise the activities of the local historians in towns and villages within the county in performing the historical work recommended by the state historian, and . . . to prepare and to present to the board of supervisors a report of the important occurrences within the county for each calendar year." They were charged with tasks and responsibilities traditionally associated with being a historian: researching and writing on aspects of local history; interpreting the history of the community through public presentations; encouraging the preservation of historic manuscripts, records, artifacts, and buildings; and organizing local historical celebrations.

Although there were initially few requirements for holding the position of county historian, the state historian of New York has recommended certain professional standards for individuals occupying that office. Since the position requires greater administrative responsibilities than those at the municipal level, individuals who serve as county historians should possess at least a master's degree with a major concentration in American history or a related field. By law, county authorities are required to provide their historians with sufficient space in a fireproof structure to collect and maintain historical materials. The counties' boards of supervisors are also empowered to raise taxes and spend money for historical purposes, including historical buildings, erecting historical markers, collecting documents, preparing and printing historical materials.

The Local Government Records Law, effective August 1988, updated the 1933 Historian's Law, which had defined the initial tasks of local and county historians. With the increased awareness for preserving local government records, the 1988 law specifically addressed the new records-related activities for local and county historians:

Each local government historian shall promote the establishment and improvement of programs for the management and preservation of local government records with enduring value for historical or other research; encourage the coordinated collection and preservation of nongovernmental historical records by libraries, historical societies, and other repositories; and carry out and actively encourage research in such records in order to add to the knowledge, understanding, and appreciation of the community's history.

The state of Indiana launched a local-history–oriented program in the early twentieth century that served as a forerunner of a county historians' program organized decades later. The Indiana General Assembly, in 1915, authorized the creation of the Indiana Historical Commission to oversee the state's centennial celebration in 1916. In an effort to ensure statewide participation, the Commission planned commemorative programs in every county of the state and encouraged greater emphasis on local history through reinvigorated local and county historical societies. Following the state centennial and a two-year lull in activity brought on by World War I, Governor James P. Goodrich summoned the Commission members to organize a county-by-county history of Indiana during the Great War. Funding from the General Assembly provid-

ed support for this research and retrieval of historical materials, which often devolved to those individuals most familiar with the county's history.

In an effort to improve its communication with the local historical communities statewide, the Indiana Library and Historical Board, the governing agency for the Indiana State Library and the Indiana Historical Bureau, voted in January 1952 to approve the creation of the office of county historian. The Bureau, established in 1925 and renamed from the Indiana Historical Commission, would oversee the program. Based upon nominations from the historical community for each county, the Library and Historical Board appointed individuals to serve in these honorary, unsalaried positions. Duties specified for the new county historians included starting or nurturing county historical societies; stimulating attendance at the annual statewide history conference; notifying the State Library of available manuscript collections; keeping track of county records; gathering information for the Gold Star Honor Roll of World War II; and serving as local resource persons for schools and research inquiries. These individuals were deemed "a public-spirited group of men and women who cooperate . . . in preserving Indiana's historical heritage." For various reasons, this local history program gradually disappeared over the years.

The years surrounding the nation's bicentennial celebration brought renewed interest in and new commitments to strengthen local history programs in Indiana. During 1979, Pamela J. Bennett, director of the Indiana

Historical Bureau, and Thomas Krasean, then field representative for the Indiana Historical Society, joined their institutions to expand the state's local history program. Originating in a series of "Local History Today" workshops and lectures that reached out to and assisted local historical societies and local history practitioners, Bennett and Krasean reinstituted the county historian program in 1980–1981, a program defunct since the mid-1950s. By resuming this practice, the Bureau continued its emphasis on local history throughout the state, while the Society, in commemoration of its sesquicentennial in 1980, demonstrated a new commitment to providing history services at the local level. The Bureau and the Society, intending to improve historical communication and network statewide, produced a handbook for historians that described historical resources and services and offered regular training opportunities regarding working with local communities and their diverse constituents.

As in the original 1950s program, Indiana's county historians receive their two-year appointments jointly from the Bureau and the Society after being nominated by the local historical community. Each historian is expected to be "well acquainted with the county and its history," to be a clearinghouse for information on local history, and a resource for research inquiries. One important task of the county historian has been to "promote coordination and cooperation" among historical groups within a county in order to avoid duplication of efforts and to promote broader participation in doing history. The county historian also serves as the local representative of the Bureau and the Society, providing information about potential collections, assisting in identifying potential historical marker sites, encouraging the expansion of local history activities, and serving as an advocate for historic preservation and access to public records.

Other states have addressed the public's and local governments' interest in county history. The General Assembly of Tennessee, in 1965, passed legislation that created a county historian program with responsibilities similar to those of New York and Indiana. In the spring of 1999, representatives in the Pennsylvania legislature discussed the feasibility of authorizing county commissioners to appoint county historians. Critics expressed concern that the position could become a political appointment instead of one properly held by a trained professional historian or someone with extensive experience in local history.

Besides enumerating similar responsibilities for collecting and preserving, educating and serving as an information resource, county historian programs share a common (and somewhat disturbing) feature in that appointees serve without compensation. This clearly diminishes the importance of the unique skills possessed by historians, perpetuates the belief that anyone can do history, and ultimately implies that history, unlike other commodities, has no value in contemporary society.

County historians provide valuable services both to the community and the historical profession. As keepers of local memories and records, they help to preserve documents and artifacts that are useful in historical research, nurture an appreciation for history amongst a broader audience, assist in building collaborations among local historical organizations, and serve as advocates for history-related issues at the local level. With the arrival of a new century and a new millennium, states and counties, whether through governmental agencies and/or private historical institutions, should commit themselves to preserving the histories of their local communities. By supporting the initiatives of local and county historians today, the current generation will be able to leave a rich and detailed record for generations to come, thereby providing them with a greater appreciation of their origins and helping them to build towards the future.

See Robert W. Arnold III, *Documenting the Community: Suggested Records-Related Activities for Local Government Historians* (Albany, N.Y., 1994); McKinney's *Consolidated Laws of New York: Book 3B, Arts and Cultural Affairs Law* (St. Paul, Minn., 1984); State University of New York, *Historian's Guide: A Handbook for Local Historians* (Albany, N.Y., 1982); *Indiana History Bulletin*, vol. 57, no. 12, December 1980: 179–80; *Indiana History Bulletin*, vol. 29, no. 2, February 1952: 31–32.

DAVID G. VANDERSTEL

See community studies; county histories; local history in the U.S.; state historical societies.

county histories. Although some county histories appeared earlier, the peak decade for the publishing of county histories came between 1880 and 1890. Building on an interest in locality that emerged throughout the nation following the Centennial Celebration of the *American Revolution in 1876, publishers saw possibilities to make money by issuing county histories, *mug books, and compilations of biographies and the memoirs of prominent citizens. In some cases, the books were written locally, but in the main, compilers were sent out to solicit the aid of the public, to determine subjects and even write entries. These books were, for the most part, paid for by subscribers even before they were printed. Mug books were those books that contained pictures and biographies, inclusion depending upon one's willingness to pay.

P. William Filby in his *Bibliography of American County Histories* (Baltimore, 1985) improved upon and expanded Clarence S. Peterson's *Consolidated Bibliography of County Histories in Fifty States*, published in 1961. Marion J. Kaminkow included county histories in her five-volume work, *United States Local Histories in the Library of Congress: A Bibliography* (Baltimore, 1975). Filby states that some 5,000 county histories were published during the peak period. A number of them were reprinted in the 1970s and '80s, some with extensive name indexes. See, for example, *History of Randolph and Macon Counties, Missouri* ([1884], Marceline, 1983, with complete name index). Few county histories of the scope and size of the early books have been published since that time.

When county histories were written later than the nineteenth century, they were often limited in subject matter to the earliest times: see David D. Oliver

Centennial History of Alpena County, Michigan . . . 1837–1876 (Alpena, Michigan, 1903), or Rhoda C. Ellison, *Bibb County, Alabama: The First Hundred Years 1818–1918*, published in 1984. This interest in the settling generation has continued.

There are some consistent themes to be found in those nineteenth century books. Their authors complained in preface after preface that gathering the material and writing were hard work, but they recognized that the work had to be done and was pleasant despite the strain. They also feared their books would not come up to expectations, that some would think they had gone into "too much detail and that I have put in much that might have been left out" (A. S. Salley Jr., *History of Orangeburg County, South Carolina* [1898]). They also boasted, such as in the preface in *The History of Saline County* (Kansas, 1881) where the author notes that his book had been "carefully written and compiled." Meanwhile in the *History of Buchanan County and St. Joseph* (Missouri, 1899) the author insisted: "Accuracy our first aim."

Almost without exception, those nineteenth-century county histories were written because the old timers— the original settlers, or those with memory of the early days—were passing, and there was a need to get the story written down. But these books did more than preserve early history, for they selected which history it was that would be recorded, and they stated their intentions clearly. From *Holt and Atchison Counties* (Kansas, 1882), the preface notes that the book was written because "the energy and bravery of these hardy

pioneers and their descendants have made Holt and Atchison Counties what they are." The early settlers had made the wilderness "bud and blossom," something this author would like to encourage the younger generation stay around and replicate. The story of those two counties needed to be preserved in order to "hand it down to posterity."

In the *History of Jackson County Missouri* (1881), the author complains that "oral memory is sometimes at odds and gives conflicting versions of the same events" making it necessary for the historian to take "much care and delicacy to bring harmony to the story." While county histories most often record harmony, our local history was not always harmonious even though the discords are infrequently heard. Rather than a single note to represent the past, groups of chords are best, harmonious or disharmonious, a multitude of chords better represent the human condition.

See Richard Wohl and A. Theodore Brown, "The Usable Past: A Study of Historical Traditions in Kansas City," *The Huntington Library Quarterly* 23 (May 1960), pp. 237–59, reprinted in Carol Kammen, *The Pursuit of Local History: Readings on Theory and Practice* (Walnut Creek, Calif., 1996), pp. 145–63. See also John H. Long, ed., *Atlas of Historical County Boundaries* (N.Y., 1993); Joseph N. Kane, *The American Counties: Origins of County Names, Dates of Creation and Organization, Area, Population including 1980 Census Figures, Historical Data, and Published Sources* (Metuchen, N.J., 1983) and Bureau of the Census, *County Business Patterns, 1968–1977: 10-Year History: Employment and Payrolls,*

court records. Civil and criminal court records are a new and promising source of evidence for historians. The academic field of legal history has developed since the 1960s. Family and community historians have long used probate court records, because of their valuable information about family relations and material culture. However, records of other courts have generally lain untouched in courthouses across the land. The obstacles to use of court records for historical research are several: technical legal language; unfamiliar terms in Latin and French; incomplete indexes; poor storage conditions; loss of records; complex and confusing court organization and jurisdiction. Yet historians will find in court records ample evidence of the role that courts have played in maintaining community order, facilitating commerce, protecting the interests of the unfortunate, and, in many times and places, upholding the rights of the powerful. Records of a particular case—a lawsuit, a murder trial, a divorce or bankruptcy proceeding—may reveal striking details about the relationships and tensions in a family or community.

Each of the fifty states has its own judicial system, and superimposed on the state court systems are the federal courts (discussed below). Today every state has multiple levels of courts: a supreme court that hears final appeals (in Maryland and New York the court of last resort is called the "court of appeals"); a court that hears initial appeals (called the "court of appeals" in most states); a trial court of general jurisdiction (larger lawsuits, probate matters, other civil proceedings, and felonies); and municipal courts of limited jurisdiction (smaller lawsuits, misdemeanors). Some states have courts of specialized jurisdiction (for example, family courts that deal with juvenile violators). Court procedure and court organization have changed greatly over the past two centuries. During the nineteenth century, almost all the states simplified the complex system of writs and pleadings inherited from the common-law courts of England. (A modified form of common-law pleading persisted in Illinois until the 1950s.) During the twentieth century most states have simplified the structure of their court systems, reducing the number of courts and the overlapping jurisdiction among trial courts.

Despite the many changes in court organization and court procedure, the basic judicial remedies available in the Anglo-American legal system have endured for centuries. All the states in the United States except one trace their legal and judicial systems to England, usually via models established in the older states. (Louisiana's legal system is modeled on the continental civil law, as codified under Napoleon.) The once-separate courts of common law and equity, each with its own procedure and governing precedents (case law), have long since been merged into courts of general jurisdiction, both in England and the United States. (The first combination of common-law and equity jurisdiction in one court occurred in several of the American colonies. Today only Delaware has a separate equity court.) The remedies developed in the old English courts of common law and equity have been incorporated into the modern state and federal judicial systems.

The common-law courts of England and early America offered a limited number of remedies to a potential litigant: a plaintiff could seek to recover a money debt of one sort or another, or money damages for injury to a person or property, or possession of real or personal property or its monetary value. The usual mode of trial was by jury, and testimony was given orally. The documents produced in a typical debt case included: 1) a writ (sealed court order) summoning the defendant to appear; 2) the pleadings filed by the plaintiff and defendant; 3) a judgment roll summarizing the appearances, the pleadings, the result of the trial if one were held, and the court's determination; and 4) a writ ordering the sheriff to execute the judgment (collect the money, or sell property to pay the judgment creditor). (In many cases there never was a judgment, the parties having settled their dispute out of court.) All these documents were loaded with stilted legal formulas developed in the English common-law courts during the Middle Ages, and they usually reveal few details about the case.

The bulk of the business of the courts held by county judges and local justices of the peace was debt cases, which, though routine, can tell quite a lot about a family or community. A review of court docket books (case registers) or filed papers should reveal patterns of litigation—who were the creditors who brought lawsuits, who were the debtors who got into financial trouble? Civil court records can help explain changes in the fortunes of families and businesses, changes that are only alluded to in letters or newspapers. Some scholars have considered the civil courts to be debt-collection machines, favored by well-off merchants and lenders. However, this view is somewhat belied by the fact that many civil judgments, perhaps in most jurisdictions, were never satisfied. Many delinquent judgment debtors left town before the sheriff arrived to sell their personal or real property to satisfy the judgment. (Before the early nineteenth century, when imprisonment for debt was abolished, a judgment debtor could be jailed if he had no money or property with which to satisfy the judgment against him.)

Creditors certainly went to court to try to get their money, however slim their chances. But there could be other motives behind a lawsuit. A judgment placed a lien upon the debtor's real property, which advised the public of a bad credit risk. (Credit-reporting agencies did not appear until the mid-nineteenth century.) A lawsuit could be a means of harassing an enemy, though the plaintiff had to have grounds for the case. A civil complaint of "trespass" might really concern a criminal act; for example, an individual might sue for money damages after being beat up in a brawl. During the later nineteenth and early twentieth centuries the higher state courts were very busy with tort cases—particularly suits for personal injuries sustained in railroad, factory, or automobile accidents. Such cases can illustrate the impact of modern technology on a community or a family.

Equity jurisdiction originated in the office of the king's chancellor. In the later Middle Ages, the chancellor began to dispense discretionary "equitable" justice in the king's name, in what became known as "the court of chancery." That court offered important judicial tools and remedies not available in the common-law courts. Equity jurisdiction came to include supervision of trustees for the property of persons needing judicial protection (widows and orphans, lunatics and drunkards, insolvent corporations); foreclosure of mortgages; other disputes requiring an equitable remedy; and (in the United States) divorce and probate proceedings (in England those matters were traditionally handled by the church courts). The court of chancery could issue powerful writs (such as subpoena and injunction) to assist the other courts in doing justice. Courts of equity used no juries and often obtained evidence in the form of written depositions. Equity court records therefore contain much information about the facts of cases. And because of the nature and scope of equity jurisdiction, the records can be rich sources for social and economic history.

Until the twentieth century, criminal procedure was relatively simple, cases were swiftly resolved, and the resulting records were modest in volume. Judges of the civil courts (county or municipal) generally presided over the criminal courts as well (the largest cities had entirely separate criminal courts). The records of a felony case that went to trial typically consisted of the indictment or presentment, and the trial minutes naming the witnesses and jurors and stating the verdict and the sentence (if the defendant were found guilty). Until state and federal appellate court laws were somewhat liberalized around 1900, appeals by convicted criminal defendants were rare. The records of the minor criminal courts, which handled misdemeanors and violations, contain similar information. Despite their laconic nature, criminal court records can provide evidence of the types of crimes and punishments that prevailed in a particular community. The majority of criminal defendants have always been young males—evidence of a community's failure to socialize some of its youths.

The public's vision of the law and the courts is shaped by the sight of law libraries—seemingly endless shelves of reported state and federal cases, legal digests and encyclopedias, and treatises. This huge, elaborate apparatus of reported and analyzed case law is built on the relatively small number of court cases that raise unsettled points of law. Those questions are normally argued before and decided by appellate courts (though decisions of trial courts occasionally establish useful, though not definitive, legal precedents). The historian may want to learn how to use a law library (it is easier than it may seem), because those dull-looking case reports and the accompanying digests and indexes should lead to trial court documents and testimony that were transcribed for appellate court hearings. (Court stenographers make the transcripts only in event of an appeal.) The "record on appeal" and accompanying legal briefs from the appellant and respondent can be a wonderful source of information on the facts of the case, as well as on the legal arguments of the opposing sides. Records and briefs on appeal are typeset and bound like published books. However, they are prepared in very small numbers (usually just a few dozen copies) and are preserved as sets in only a few large law libraries in each state, or possibly in the state archives. (A copy of the record on appeal may be remitted, or sent back, to the trial court after the appeal is decided.) Printed records and briefs began to appear in federal and some state appellate courts in the early nineteenth century, and were in widespread use by mid-century. (The predecessor to the record on appeal was a manuscript transcription or summary of trial court proceedings attached to a writ of error or writ of certiorari, the common-law writs by which allegedly erroneous proceedings in a trial court were called up for review by an appellate court.)

Though the federal trial courts have always had a much smaller caseload than the state courts, federal court records can be useful sources for community history. The federal courts have operated since 1789 in both states and territories. Their jurisdiction embraces a wide variety of civil and criminal matters arising under the U.S. Constitution and federal statutes and treaties. Federal court records of particular interest for historical research include bankruptcy proceedings (the bankruptcy statute was in effect for several periods during the nineteenth century and continuously since 1898); prosecutions for violation of federal revenue acts (particularly excise taxes on liquor and customs duties); recovery of fugitive slaves (un-

der the acts of 1793 and 1850); admiralty proceedings involving ocean-going vessels, or their cargoes, owners, officers, or crew members (in 1845 admiralty jurisdiction was extended to inland navigable lakes and rivers); and strike- and union-breaking injunctions (particularly during the 1920s). Federal courts have been active in the fight against organized crime. In the nineteenth century, interstate counterfeiting rings were frequently prosecuted; in the twentieth century, illegal sale of liquor during Prohibition and racketeering activities more recently have kept federal courts busy. The jurisdiction of federal courts expanded significantly when they were authorized to hear appeals from determinations of regulatory agencies such as the Interstate Commerce Commission. The civil rights acts of 1964 and 1965 resulted in thousands of suits in federal courts in the southern states and elsewhere, challenging discriminatory practices.

Certain areas of federal court jurisdiction are shared with state courts. Under their constitutional "diversity" jurisdiction, federal courts may hear and decide a civil suit by a plaintiff residing in one state against a defendant in another state. (Businesses have often considered it easier to recover money from out-of-state debtors by suing in a federal court, rather than in a state court.) Naturalization of aliens is a federal function, today usually performed by the U.S. district courts. However, the higher state trial courts may handle naturalization proceedings, and they routinely did so for over a century. During much of the nineteenth century, violations of federal customs and excise laws could be prosecuted in either a state or federal court.

The federal court system is simpler in structure than most state court systems, but it has changed considerably over time. During the nineteenth century there were two federal trial courts, the district courts and the circuit courts. The jurisdiction of the two courts overlapped, with the U.S. district courts having the more limited jurisdiction. In practice, after the 1840s the district courts handled mainly criminal and admiralty cases, and the circuit courts, mostly civil cases. The circuit courts also heard some appeals from the district courts, but most appeals from those courts and all appeals from the circuit courts went directly to the U.S. Supreme Court for final review. In 1891 Congress established circuit courts of appeals as the main appellate courts in the federal court system (since 1948 those courts have been called "courts of appeals"). The district courts have continued as trial courts (the now-redundant circuit courts were abolished in 1911). Since 1891, appeals heard by the Supreme Court have been limited almost entirely to cases involving significant constitutional questions. Since 1789, every state has had at least one U.S. district court; today some states have as many as four districts. Originally the United States was divided into three circuits, each with a circuit court. More circuits were established as the nation expanded; since 1980 there have been twelve regional circuits of the U.S. Court of Appeals.

Special federal courts create some records relating to local communities and individuals. All claims against the United States for debts or damages were reviewed and decided by the Continental Congress or the U.S. Congress until 1855, when a court of claims was established. (Its present-day successor is the U.S. Claims Court.) During the later nineteenth century the Court of Claims determined many cases relating to damages inflicted by Confederate forces on Union loyalists in the Southern states during the Civil War, and by Indian raids on American settlers in the Western states. Federal military courts try officers and enlisted men for violations of military law. A Court of Private Land Claims, active between 1891 and 1904, determined numerous land titles deriving from the Mexican government in what became the Southwestern states.

Records of state and municipal courts are generally found nearby, in a county courthouse or a city hall; older court records may be in the state archives. Archival records of the federal courts for a particular state may be located much farther away, in one of eleven regional branches of the *National Archives. Except for naturalization records, relatively few older federal court records have been microfilmed, and they typically occupy over 60 per cent of the space in a National Archives regional branch.

On the history of Anglo-American law, see Charles Rembar, *The Law of the Land: The Evolution of Our Legal System* (N.Y., 1980) and John H. Baker, *An Introduction to English Legal History*, 2d ed. (London, 1979). Readable surveys of American legal history are: Peter Hoffer, *Law and People in Colonial America*, rev. ed. (Baltimore, 1998); Lawrence M. Friedman, *Crime and*

Punishment in American History (N.Y., 1993); Kermit L. Hall, *The Magic Mirror: Law in American History* (N.Y., 1989); and Lawrence M. Friedman, *A History of American Law*, 2d ed. (N.Y., 1985).

For help in understanding historical court procedure and court documents, see Arlene H. Eakle, "Research in Court Records," in *The Source: A Guidebook of American Genealogy*, edited by Loretto Dennis Szucs and Sandra Hargreaves Luebking (Salt Lake City, 1997), pp. 172–238; William E. Nelson, "Court Records as Sources for Historical Writing," *Law in Colonial Massachusetts 1630–1800* (Boston, 1984), pp. 499–518; Michael S. Hindus and Douglas L. Jones, "Quantitative Methods or Quantum Meruit?: Tactics for Early American Legal History," *Historical Methods Newsletter*, 13:1 (winter 1980): 63–74; Peter J. Coleman, *Debtors and Creditors in America: Insolvency, Imprisonment for Debt and Bankruptcy, 1607–1900* (Madison, Wisc., 1974); and Herbert A. Johnson, "Civil Procedure in John Jay's New York," *American Journal of Legal History*, 11 (1967): 69–80. Also useful for understanding old court procedure are contemporary manuals written for lawyers and justices of the peace; and the published legal papers of John Adams, Alexander Hamilton, Aaron Burr (microfilm), John Marshall, Daniel Webster, and (forthcoming) Abraham Lincoln.

On the federal courts and their records, see Robert A. Carp and Ronald Stidham's introductory text, *The Federal Courts*, 3d ed. (Washington, D.C., 1998); Erwin C. Surrency's detailed historical discussion of organization, jurisdiction, procedure, etc., *History of the Federal Courts* (N.Y., 1987); Robert B. Matchette and others, comps., *Guide to Federal Records in the National Archives*, 3 vols. (Washington, D.C., 1995); Loretto Dennis Szucs and Sandra Hargreaves Luebking, *The Archives: A Guide to the National Archives Field Branches* (Salt Lake City, 1988); *Guide to Genealogical Research in the National Archives* (Washington, D.C., 1983) (chapters on U.S. district court and naturalization records); *Prologue: Quarterly of the National Archives*, 21:3 (fall 1989) (special issue on research uses of federal court records); Peter A. Wonders, comp., *Directory of Manuscript Collections Related to Federal Judges, 1789–1997* (Washington. D.C., 1998).

General guides to published legal sources and legal history at both the federal and state levels include: Morris L. Cohen, *Bibliography of Early American Law*, 6 vols. (Buffalo, 1998) (pre-1861 materials only); J. Myron Jacobstein and others, *Fundamentals of Legal Research*, 7th ed. (N.Y., 1998); Stephen Elias and Susan Levinkind, *Legal Research: How to Find and Understand the Law*, 4th ed. (Berkeley, 1995) (intended for non-lawyers); Kermit L. Hall, *A Comprehensive Bibliography of American Constitutional and Legal History, 1896–1979*, 5 vols., and Supplement, 1980–1987, 2 vols. ([1984] Millwood, N.Y., 1991); Morris L. Cohen and others, *How to Find the Law*, 9th ed. (St. Paul, Minn., 1989); Erick B. Low, *A Bibliography on the History of the Organization and Jurisdiction of State Courts* (Williamsburg, Va., 1980); and "Guide to Legal History Resources on the Web," University of Texas at Austin, Tarlton Law Library:

<http://www.law.utexas.edu.rare/legal-his.html>. Reported (published) state and federal court decisions and opinions may be located through the multivolume *American Digest* or (more conveniently) through the *Federal Reporter* and the various regional and state reporters.

On legal terms and language, see *Black's Law Dictionary*, 6th ed. (St. Paul, Minn., 1990) and David Mellinkoff, *The Language of the Law* (Boston, 1963).

Some readable works that suggest approaches for using court records for community history are: David E. Narrett, *Inheritance and Family Life in Colonial New York City* (Ithaca, N.Y., 1992); Robert A. Silverman, *Law and Urban Growth: Civil Litigation in the Boston Trial Courts, 1880–1900* (Princeton, N.J., 1981); Lawrence M. Friedman and Robert V. Percival, *The Roots of Justice: Crime and Punishment in Alameda County, California, 1870–1910* (Chapel Hill, N.C., 1981); and Richard M. Brown, "The Archives of Violence," *American Archivist*, 41:4 (October 1978): 431–43 (strikes, vigilantes, outlaws, and the records that tell their stories); and Mary K. Bonsteel Tachau, *Federal Courts in the Early Republic: Kentucky 1789–1816* (Princeton, N.J., 1978).

JAMES FOLTS

crime, history of. Crime in the United States is a fluid rather than a static subject. Factors as diverse as religion, population density, technological advancements, social class, etc., have changed the notions of crime and the distinguishing characteristics of criminals since the country's founding.

Crime in the colonies was a product of numbers of people settling near each other. Clustered together, the colonists could defend themselves from environmental and native threats and help each other survive when weather and disease conspired to destroy a settlement. However, individuals in the nuclear settlement might reject the beliefs of the majority or endanger the welfare of the community. The three colonial geographical areas appear to have had distinctive ideas about crime. All of them held sacred the right of an individual to his person and his property, but variations in goals of a settlement led to regional variations in criminal statutes and in the application of justice. Several secondary sources offer helpful overviews of colonial philosophies regarding crime.

Settled by Puritans, colonial New England's ideas about crime centered early around religious beliefs and practices. Thus, the Bible, the Ten Commandments, and doctrinal writings and preaching dominated a community's judgment about criminal acts. Heretical views, violation of Sabbath restrictions, and even eccentric behavior were punishable by law. Conformity in thought and behavior, it was believed, led to the survival of the colony and the betterment of the individual; its opposite would lead to earthly chaos and eternal damnation. Accounts about nonconformists like Anne Hutchinson and the "witches" of Salem are easy to find, and state archives and other historical repositories preserve original documents from this period.

The Southern colonies with their plantation systems had concepts of crime that were more economically based. Colonists' motives for settling in these areas were to gain material rather than spiritual improvement. Since free labor contributed to the prosperity of isolated properties and the well-being of their inhabitants, laws governing behaviors were determined by individual plantation owners. Slaves, indentured servants, and apprentices owed total allegiance to their owners or sponsors. Punishments for infractions were meted out swiftly and often brutally, and masters did not need the authority of either court or community to discipline their own property. Slave narratives like *The Autobiography of Frederick Douglass* and *The Narrative of Sojourner Truth* give firsthand accounts of plantation justice.

The middle colonies, with demographically diverse populations, were somewhat more liberal in their views of crime, although slavery, indentured servitude, and apprenticeships were common in all areas well into the nineteenth century. *The Autobiography of Benjamin Franklin* offers a fascinating view of an apprentice's life in the middle colonies during the eighteenth century. The Protestant ethic and the Golden Rule seem to have dominated notions of proper and improper behavior in mercantile settlements. Thus in the 1750s, a notorious New York counterfeiter was hanged for his crimes. Densely populated communities meant a greater number of temptations, increasing possibilities for violating neighbors' rights, and rising ability to evade arrest and prosecution.

Crime in the last century might be seen as related to the "haves" and the "have nots." The first half of the nineteenth century was dominated by westward expansion and settlement and Irish and German immigration. Trailblazers and canal builders created pathways to the interior on which "boom towns" were soon strung. While new settlers attempted to recreate the orderly communities they had left, problems caused by transients and opportunists outpaced the citizenry's inclination to finance services and municipal improvements. Community ordinances burgeoned as tensions increased. Criminality was thought to be limited to the "have nots"; to be poor was to be a criminal in the early nineteenth century.

Canals brought not only new settlers, but also workers who were idle during months when the weather prevented construction and water travel. These workers, frequently Irish immigrants, loitered in frontier towns from late fall to early spring. Uneducated and unskilled, they could find few employments. Often, a community's first response to this situation was to create an alms house to which vagrants and drunks were sentenced because of their inability to pay for housing and sustenance. Alms houses might be thought of as benevolent institutions because they did provide shelter and structured work experiences for the inmates who might not survive on their own. On the other hand, alms houses can also be seen as institutions designed to rid a community of unpleasant, unsightly and unruly derelicts by restricting their freedom. Some communities, like Rochester, New York, have preserved alms-house registers that identify inmates by name, age, and nationality to the second generation. Nationality was very important to communities where births among immigrant populations outnumbered those among native citizens, threatening established political power.

Canals brought another problem. Canal boats were towed by mules or horses driven by young boys. The youngsters had little to do in off season and no means of support, and so many of them plagued canal-town businesses with pilfering and petty thievery. They spent their idle time with adult canallers, brawling, frequenting bars and brothels, and learning the colorful but lewd language of their elders. State houses of refuge were the earliest institutions established for juvenile delinquents, an attempt to separate young felons from an environment that might turn them into hardened criminals. Inmates farmed, attended an institutional school, and went to mandatory religious services. Those who were judged incorrigible could be sent to a seaport and sentenced to serve a term on an outgoing ocean vessel. State repositories, for example the New York State Archives, may hold registers of house-of-refuge inmates, if they exist. Names, ages, birthplaces, places of arraignment, criminal charges, and nationalities to the second generation may be found in the registers.

Newspapers illustrate the issue of crime during this period, quite often in a colorful way. Murders appear to have been infrequent, but assaults were plentiful. Drunk and disorderly was by far the most common crime, with vagrancy and wife beating coming in close behind. Criminals are listed by name, crime, and disposition of the case. In some cases, editors used stories of crimes as comic relief, particularly if the criminal was an intoxicated Irishman whose crime was against a fellow countryman. Names of established families rarely appear in crime reports, although there is an occasional mention of anonymous "rowdies" disturbing the peace on a weekend night. Newspapers are also a good source for reports of local government proceedings where new ordinances give clues about behaviors that offended mainstream citizens. Local ordinances regulating alcohol sales, Sabbath activities, and health practices, correspond to the increasing problems of rapidly growing communities and a moral-reform movement that paralleled westward settlement.

The social-reform movement shifted attention to crimes committed by the "haves" in the latter half of the nineteenth century. New waves of immigrants, handicapped by ignorance, by lack of skills, and usually by the inability to speak English, crowded into cheap housing in large cities. Slum landlords profited from them. Sweatshop operators exploited them. Politicians bought their votes. Social reformers such as Jane Addams sensitized Americans to abuses of economic power toward the end of the century. Again, newspapers have probably the best information on local developments of the period, particularly about local ethnic gangs engaged in illegal activities. Biographies of social reformers will detail the conditions in which victims lived.

Americans' notions of crime in the twentieth century have concentrated on acts of omission as well as acts of commission. Political dissension; abuse of economic, political, and military power; and misuse of technology have joined the list of misdeeds of the past.

The moral-reform movement peaked in 1919 when temperance advocates succeeded in outlawing the transportation and sale of alcoholic beverages. With Prohibition, crime became more sophisticated; organized criminal bodies set up networks for importing illegal substances and established "speakeasies." Indeed, many ordinary citizens themselves became accomplices in these activities. Beginning in the latter years of the nineteenth century, American criminals were increasingly romanticized in the press and in popular literature. Biographies of the notorious became as popular as stories of the merely noteworthy. Repeal of the Eighteenth Amendment in 1933 did not wipe out the mob, however, and it continued to profit from the sale of illegal—but for many—enticing, substances and the provision of illegal, but for many pleasurable, activities.

Political unorthodoxy became increasing criminalized, peaking with the notorious McCarthy hearings in the 1950s. Abuse of political power has continued to be a major concern throughout the latter half of this century, with Watergate and Whitewater scandals dominating headlines.

The best research sources for questions about local crime in the twentieth century will be local newspapers. In contrast to the last century and the early years of this century, today there is little suppression of scandal in the local press. Secondary sources abound and biographies are well detailed and documented. There are a number of books that outline early criminal activities, their detection, and judgments.

See Douglas Greenberg, *Crime and Law Enforcement in the Colony of New York, 1691–1776* (Ithaca, N.Y., 1976); Edwin Powers, *Crime and Punishment in Early Massachusetts, 1620–1692* (Boston, 1966); and Raphael Semmes, *Crime and Punishment in Early Maryland* (Baltimore, 1938). In addition, don't miss *Annals of Murder: A Bibliography of Books and Pamphlets on American Murders from Colonial Times to 1900*, Thomas M. McCade, comp. (Norman, Okla., 1961).

TERESA LEHR

Croatians. See Appendix A.

Cubans. See Appendix A.

culinary history. Food history is one of the last of the *social-history topics to get academic attention. It has proved to be an important means of investigating and understanding the past, for food history encompasses the history of technology, of the economics of place and of a household; it provides evidence of the use of local goods, and the availability of goods from afar. The history of food allows us to think about house planning, food storage, food preparation, and how that has been transformed over time; about food eaten at special meals, and daily fare; about food eaten in the home and out of doors, at sea, on picnics, on the trail, and in restaurants. In addition, the history of food requires that we look at gender roles in a household, at class, and at the role of the dinner table in family life. All of this lends itself to questions of change and continuity over time.

Scholarly work on the history of food is less than twenty-five years old, and historical societies are only now turning to food history as a subject for exhibit and display. Still, most historical societies have artifacts associated with food and food history in their collections; and for visitors, the history of food should be an accessible and interesting historical experience. An investigation of local food lends itself nicely to programs that involve the public. Ethnic foodways have long been a popular experience; brought into the historical society, culinary history provides an interesting way of expanding audiences.

See Donna Gabaccia, *We Are What We Eat: Ethnic Food and the Making of Americans* (Cambridge, Mass., 1998); Anne L. Bower, ed., *Recipes for Reading: Community Cookbooks, Stories, Histories* (Amherst, Mass., 1997); AASLH Technical Leaflet: *Interpreting Food History*, written by Sandra Oliver; *Food History News*, a quarterly newsletter also edited by Oliver (available at $15 a year at *FHN*, HCR 60, Box 354A, Iselboro, Maine, 04848); and *Food and Foodways* (published since 1985), which is international in focus. Also see Sandra L. Oliver, *Saltwater Foodways: New Englanders and Their Food, at Sea and Ashore, in the Nineteenth Century* (Mystic, Conn., 1995); and Jacqueline Williams, *Wagon Wheel Kitchens: Food on the Oregon Trail* (Lawrence, Kan., 1993).

cultural geography. See landscape.

cultural tourism. See tourism.

culture. See popular culture.

Curti, Merle. See: Trempealeau County.

Czechs and Slovaks. See Appendix A.

𝒟

Danes. See Appendix A.

databases for local history. Databases, collections of information stored electronically and retrieved automatically, can be found on the World Wide Web and in your local library. Some databases—those available on CD-ROM, for example—are produced by commercial firms and can be purchased for use on your own computer. Most of the information on the Internet is currently free to the user, although there are fees for certain databases and services.

There are many databases on the World Wide Web of interest to local historians, with more appearing every day. There are bibliographic databases, primary documents whose full text is readable on the Web, descriptions of libraries' archives, statistical materials, maps, and many other types of resources. Lists on the web of websites on particular subjects link you to more databases than you can easily examine, just as a library's catalog can lead you to more books than you can read.

In order not to become overwhelmed by the wealth of material available, one needs to know how to find useful websites, while skipping quickly over the irrelevant ones. There are several ways to do this. One way is via publications that evaluate and describe Web resources, such as The Scout Report <http://scout.cs.wisc.edu/scout/report/index. html>, where you will find recommended websites on many subjects. In addition, subject directories such as Yahoo! <http://www.yahoo.com> classify sites in a traditional, hierarchical structure of subjects, and are a good place to start your search.

Another way to find websites is by using search engines—programs written especially to facilitate finding information on the Web. There are many search engines, and their features vary. None of them can search every location on the Web; moreover, they will all produce slightly different results to your query. Some popular search engines are Alta Vista <http://www.altavista.com>; Excite <http://www.excite.com>; and HotBot at <http://www.hotbot.com>.

If you already know the uniform resource locator (URL)—the address—of a website, you can type the URL (http://etc.) directly in the box presented by your web browser when you click to open a location or page. Clicking on the links from that page can lead you to many other related sites in a continually expanding universe of information.

The Web is largely unregulated—anyone can create a webpage and put anything he or she wishes on it. When looking at material on the Web, you need to evaluate what you find. Some questions to ask: Who has made the information available? Is there an institutional or organizational affiliation? Is the information up-to-date? Databases and search engines are subject to change at any time. Keeping current with what is available and discovering additional resources is an ongoing process.

Below are listed some websites that may be useful to local historians. The first two contain census data; the third is a collection of nonphotographic representations of cities showing street patterns, individual buildings, and major landscape features. The rest are lists of Web databases of various types.

United States Historical Census Data Browser: <http://fisher.lib.virginia.edu/census>. This contains searchable files of detailed census data from each state and county from 1790 to 1970.

National Archives and Records Administration: <http://www.nara.gov>. This contains detailed descriptions of the collections and how to use them, as well as links to additional information.

Government Information Sharing Project: <http://govinfo.kerr.orst.edu>. This is a collection of searchable demographic and economic census databases, including the 1990 Census of Population and Housing; School District Data Book Profiles: 1969–1990; Regional Economic Information System: 1969–1996; Census of Agriculture: 1982, 1987, 1992; and U.S.A. Counties 1996.

Panoramic Maps 1847–1920: <http://lcweb2.loc.gov/ammem/pmhtml/panhome.html>. This site contains schematic views of towns and cities. This is one of the American Memory Historical Collections from the Library of Congress. To see the other collections, go to <http://rs6.loc.gov>.

Repositories of Primary Sources: <http://www.uidaho.edu/special-collections/Other.Repositories.html>. This is a listing of over 3,000 websites describing holdings of manuscripts, archives, rare books, historical photographs, and other primary sources.

Genealogy Resources on the Internet: <http://www-personal.umich.edu/~cgaunt/gen_web.html>. This contains an alphabetical index of websites useful for genealogical research. Click on a state to find information on the local level, if available.

State and Local Government on the Net: <http://www.piperinfo.com/state/states.html>. This is a list of pointers to state, county, and city government webpages.

American Women's History: A Research Guide: <http://www.mtsu.edu/~kmiddlet/history/women.html>. This is a guide to women's history resources, on and off the Internet. Click on "bookmarks" to find websites arranged by category.

Newsdirectory.Com: <http://www.ecola.com>. This provides links to almost 7,000 newspapers and magazines, some of whose back issues are searchable.

American and British History Resources on the Internet: <http://www.libraries.rutgers.edu/rulib/socsci/hist/amhist3.htm>.

This is a very long list of scholarly resources available on the Internet.

MARTHA R. HSU

Daughters of the American Revolution National Society Library. This library, founded in 1896, specializes in genealogy, U.S. local history, American Indian history, and American women's history. The archive contains genealogies compiled by DAR members and an extensive collection of U.S. *city directories.

The address of the Library is 1776 D St. NW, Washington, D.C. 20006-5392; (202) 879-3229; <www.dar.org>.

See *State and Local History Holdings in the DAR Library Catalogue*, vol. 2. (Washington, D.C., 1986).

day by day. There are a number of books that list the special events, anniversaries, and celebrations day by day.

See Leonard and Thelma Spinard, *On This Day in History* (revised by Anistatia R. Miller and Jared M. Brown; London, and Paramus, N.J., 1999); Paul Wasserman, ed., *Festivals Sourcebook: A Reference Guide to Fairs, Festivals, and Celebrations in Agriculture, Antiques, the Arts, Theater and Drama, Arts and Crafts, Community, Dance, Ethnic Events, Film, Folk, Food and Drink, History, Indians, Marine, Music, Seasons & Wildlife* (Detroit, 1984); and Chase's *Calendar of Events: The Day by Day Directory to Special Days, Weeks & Months* (Lincolnwood, Ill., 1937 and annually).

decorative arts. The term usually means all aesthetic objects that are not architecture or fine art, such as furniture, textiles, metalwork, and ceramics, but may extend to toys, jewelry, costumes, bookbinding and wallpaper. These objects can be studied in a number of ways: as articles to be collected by connoisseurs, as part of the history of art, the history of technology, or social history. In museums they may be grouped by period, style, region of origin, material, or function. For a good overview of scholarship trends see Kenneth L. Ames and Gerald W. R. Ward, eds., *Decorative Arts and Household Furnishings in America, 1650–1920: An Annotated Bibliography* (Winterthur, Del., 1989). While useful, this book includes no Native American references and few Canadian or Mexican American works. For Canadian works, see Donald B. Webster, ed., *The Book of Canadian Antiques* (N.Y. and Toronto, 1974).

The fact that relatively few survey texts of the decorative arts have been published in recent years reflects the great changes taking place in the field. The canon of important works and creators has broken down as has the emphasis on the material culture of the ruling class. Today, interest has shifted to what happened to an object after it left the shop rather than a close examination of the individual maker and his or her milieu. From early on, provenance has been significant because the mere fact that an object was owned by a prominent person conferred value on that object. However now the interest has shifted to the consumers themselves, no matter what their class or status in the community.

Typological histories that trace the evolution of particular forms have been important sources of information. The study of vernacular materials, regional variations, and patterns of change and diffusion has always been useful. Scholars are now moving beyond tracing the diffusion of certain forms, such as dining-room sideboards, to ask why there are shifts in taste and regional variations in forms. Increasingly they are studying the interaction of cultural and production centers with social and geographic margins.

The study of decorative arts is often multidisciplinary and increasingly difficult to distinguish from an interest in *material culture. Folklorists have offered new insights about visual thinking, and historians have learned the value of contextual studies from social scientists and anthropologists. Scholars have pointed out that objects have multiple contexts—social, cultural, political, ideological, and technological—all of which can shed light on a work's meaning and significance. The decorative arts are shaped not only by aesthetics, availability of materials, and craftsmanship, but also by trade disputes, price fixing, fuel supplies, or labor shortages.

Much work is being done on the ideology of material goods. Scholars have begun to examine why certain objects are sometimes desirable and sometimes out of fashion. Other researchers look for patterns of consumption and use that may have been too obvious to record at the time. As in other fields, scholars are currently paying more attention to ethnicity and class, often bringing a Marxist or feminist perspective to the task. For example, the interest in quilts that was stimulated by the Bicentennial has led to a broader discussion of women's issues.

This is an exciting time for those interested in the decorative arts, and local historians in particular can make substantial contributions to our understanding of the past. While eighteenth-century primary sources may be scarce, there is much material for nineteenth- and twentieth-century objects. *Photographs and trade catalogs are just two important sources. See E. Richard McKinstry, *Trade Catalogs at Winterthur: A Guide to the Literature of Merchandising, 1750–1980* (N.Y., 1984) and William Seale, *The Tasteful Interlude: American Interiors through the Camera's Eye, 1860–1917*, 2d ed. (Nashville, Tenn., 1981). For suggestions on research strategies, see Kenneth Ames et al., *Material Culture: A Research Guide* (Lawrence Kan., 1985). *The Index of American Design* (Teaneck, N.J., 1980) is a microfiche reproduction of over 15,000 renderings of all sorts of American applied and decorative arts. It was part of the Federal Art Project and Works Progress Administration in the 1930s. The originals are in the National Gallery of Art in Washington D.C.

NORMA PRENDERGAST

decree. A court judgment; judicial decision.

deed, title. Legal document that shows ownership, used to transfer property from one person to another.

demography. As the study of human populations, demography concerns itself with the collection of reliable data, the presentation of this data in useable formats, and the analysis of this data. Demographic investigation has become more important in local history since as early as the 1960s, when the focus of history in general changed from one centered almost entirely on the powerful and famous to a focus on the general populace and the lives they led. This new interest in *social history required the development of new tools for understanding the past, and one of these was demography, used hand-in-hand with statistical investigation.

The focus of demography is human populations, currently, in the past, and in the future. This interest can cover a broad range of human experience, including health issues such as epidemiology, migration patterns and population growth, birth rates, the effect of the environment on population, the ethnic or racial make-up of populations, economic issues, aging, family structure, and the role of women, men, and children in society. Broadly, demography focuses on any changes affecting populations in human societies, so its interest is always in assessing how these populations have changed or been changed over a period of time. Demography evaluates changes that have taken place in human populations and even projects what changes may occur in the future.

Since demography is grounded in statistics, anyone interested in using demography must understand how to make a careful empirical study. First, the historian must conceptualize the issue being studied. If interested in studying the growth of suburban populations after World War II, for instance, you must determine how to define the term "suburb" for the purposes of the study, narrow the geographical area being studied to a useable area, and determine exactly what "growth" to study. Second, the historian will have to determine where to find or how to collect data to illuminate this issue and will have to evaluate if this data is adequate for these purposes. For instance, the term "suburb" may not be a data element in any statistical sources, so you must determine if the data can be used adequately to identify suburbs in the process of development. Third, the his-

torian will have to determine how to measure this particular population issue. Will the historian merely measure gross population change or also evaluate the changing birthrates in this area? This empirical process then must be bolstered by analysis. Using techniques and standards of other disciplines, including economics, political science, sociology, and anthropology, historians need to evaluate this massaged data to draw reasonable conclusions.

There exist many sources of information for demographic data. The most common of these is federal census data, but many states and some localities (even churches) have at one time also enumerated their constituent populations. For instance, New York State for many years produced decennial censuses for years ending with the number five. With a little work, a historian could compare this data with that from the U.S. Census Bureau (whose years of enumeration end with a zero) to produce a more detailed evaluation of a population change. Much census data, including even data projections, is available online, and these computerized data servers can be a valuable source of information with a little effort. Rather than relying on the cumulated data, the historian can instead use the actual censuses. Using raw data, a historian can develop new ways of looking at or cumulating the data to carry out narrower studies of a particular region: for instance, ethnic patterns of settlement or family size in different parts of a county. The least likely, though still viable, source of information is to collect your own data. However, this is a difficult process, fraught with potential problems, including the problem of comparing data collected by different entities using different data standards.

One of the most common problems a local historian will find when dealing with demographic datasets is data resolution. What this means is that most data is more broadly defined than local historians would want. For instance, the U.S. Census Bureau's International Data Base (IDB) maintains various datasets on hundreds of countries and areas (usually territories of countries). This data server includes data and estimates covering the years from 1950 and projections out to 2050. But the data resolution is so broad (first by country, then subdivided by rural versus urban) that it provides little help for the local historian. Sometimes, data centers that focus on one state, such as the Pennsylvania State Data Center or the Louisiana Population Data Center, may have the information at a more valuable resolution, since these narrow down to at least the county. Many historians, however, will be interested in tracking by the township, village, city, or some geographic subdivision of a county that may not have been caught during any census or statistical collection.

The final step in demographic investigation is the evaluation of the data. First, you must ensure that you understand the metadata (or the definitions of the data). For instance, if a certain census collects information on who lived on farms, what was its working definition of a farm? Next, you must assess the chance for error (caused by misunderstanding, accidental mistranscription, etc.). Only since 1940, for instance, has the Census Bureau done random checks to determine the percentage of errors in federal enumerations, so be sure to understand the source of the data and how the collector evaluated or corrected for error. Often, you must determine how to use hard data to develop approximate data for the geographical district you are studying. After doing all this to arrive at reliable and reasonable numbers, you must carefully evaluate the data, noting changes over time, in terms of real numbers and percentages. Then you must combine this data with other sources of information (geographical conditions, maps, biographies of people, etc.) to conduct your analysis. Without the final step of analysis, demographers cannot make their final conclusions and the data remain only a collection of abstract numbers.

GEOFFREY A. HUTH

devise. Refers to a gift of land or buildings made through a last will and testament. Usually personal property that is not real estate is called a "bequest" or a "legacy."

diaries. Diaries have long been important to local historians and every local historical society has a cache of little black books in which people recorded their days. Sometimes writers did so in great detail, sometimes they worried about the state of their soul, sometimes the notations were simply farm activities such as shoveling manure or planting the back forty. There is a mystique about diaries: yet often they are cryptic and difficult to understand, or their enthusiasms are out of sync with historical interests. Yet, some are wonderful treasures that illuminate the events of the day or the personality of the writer.

The history of diary-keeping dates to the seventeenth century, when churchmen frequently kept accounts of their spiritual state. Over time, diary-keeping became more popular. In the United States, especially in the last third of the nineteenth century when small black diary books were available and inexpensive, many people kept diaries. In the mid-twentieth century, diary-keeping became a popular teen-age pursuit; diaries have been prescribed in some psychological treatments and used by feminist groups.

See Thomas Mallon, *A Book of One's Own: People and Their Diaries* (N.Y., 1984), in which he groups types of diary-keepers: "Chroniclers," "Travelers," "Confessors," "Prisoners." See also William Matthews, *American Diaries in Manuscript 1580–1954: A Descriptive Bibliography* (Athens, Ga., 1974), which lists brief descriptions of 4,889 unpublished diaries held in public archives. For example:

#2346 McCoy, Lt. Thomas Franklin. 1847. Mexican War journal, with 11th Pa. Inf.; camp life; guard duty; drilling; rumors; marching; skirmishes; many men dying from sickness; movement of troops; strategy; plans. Typescript of this diary is held at the Columbia University Library, N.Y.

See also Laura Arksey, Nancy Preis, and Marcia Reed, *American Diaries: An Annotated Bibliography of Published American Diaries and Journals* (Detroit, 1987) in two volumes, I: 1492–1844, II: 1845–1980. This book contains three full and helpful indexes, one to names, one to geographical places, and one for a variety of interesting and useful subjects.

Thomas Mallon notes that the words "diary" and "journal" are "hopelessly muddled. They're both rooted in the idea of dailiness." He quotes Dr. Johnson's *Dictionary*, which makes them more or less equivalent: Johnson defines a diary as "an account of the transactions, accidents and observations of every day; a journal."

dictionaries of biography. See biographical dictionaries.

Dictionary of Americanisms. Mitford Matthews was the lexicographer who compiled *A Dictionary of Americanisms on Historical Principles* (Chicago, 1951). This massive work documents American words and phrases, their meanings, and the first and some subsequent uses. For the phrase " all-American," for example, the entry, listing the first date of published use and the book or magazine where the usage appeared, reads:

1888 Outing Nov. 166/2 The All-American team . . . is composed of men picked from the ranks of the representative ball teams of America. 1920 Outing Nov.84/3 The little cripple, none other than Eddie Dillon, sometime All American, caught the ball and ran with it through the entire opposing eleven for another touchdown. 1949 Atlantic March 24/1 You can't be an All-American on a losing team.

See regionalisms; slang.

diocese. An ecclesiastical administrative unit under the jurisdiction of a bishop.

diphtheria. An infectious disease caused by a bacillus that is characterized by weakness, sore throat, and high fever. A membrane on the tonsils, which may interfere with breathing, is characteristic of this disease. This was a common children's disease in the nineteenth century; it was finally controlled by vaccination in the 1950s.

disease. See health.

documents on the Internet. See databases for local history; Internet, uses by historians.

domestic economy. The domestic economy consists of the total contributions made by all members of a household to the economic viability of the household. These contributions can be cash income from wage labor; home production of goods (e.g., food, clothing, candles) for use, sale or barter; or such vital work or services as child care, housework, or chores that have economic value that are performed by children. By taking into account the contributions of all members of households, historians now recognize the significant economic role that women and children have played in family life, at least in some time periods and locales. Some historians, influenced by Marxist historical emphasis on material conditions as the foundation of a society's values, have posited that women's critical economic contributions have made them more valuable in some societies, and therefore more valued and respected. Extended-family members (including the elderly), servants, boarders, apprentices, and others who live in the household also contribute to the domestic economy. The concept of domestic economy is frequently associated with an agrarian "subsistence economy" where every family member had to pull his or her weight for the family to survive. It is also often contrasted to the stereotype of the middle-class, wage-earning male head of household who single-handedly supports his, usually nuclear, family.

CHRISTINE KLEINNEGGER

domestic labor. Care of a home, cooking, and the laundry employed more women in the nineteenth century than any other occupation. Many of these workers were immigrant women, usually Irish or African American. In 1870 there was one domestic servant for every 8.4 families (Strasser, p. 163). Servants were prevalent in urban areas, in the South, and in places with large immigrant populations. For most of the nineteenth century, servants cost less than a technological solution such as indoor plumbing and electricity. Over time, and depending upon place, domestic servants were drawn from preferred groups and for some immigrant women, domestic service was seen as a good way to learn how to "become American."

See Faye E. Dudden, *Serving Women: Household Service in Nineteenth-Century America* (Middletown, Conn., 1983); Susan Strasser, *Never Done: A History of American Housework* (N.Y., 1982); Dolores Hayden, *The Grand Domestic Revolution: A History of Feminist Designs for American Homes, Neighborhoods, and Cities* (Cambridge, Mass., 1981); David Katzman, *Seven Days a Week: Women and Domestic Service in Industrializing America* (N.Y., 1978); and Eli Zaretsky, *Capitalism, the Family, and Personal Life* (N.Y., 1976).

domesticity, sphere of. See woman's sphere.

donation visits. In lieu of an adequate salary, or sometimes, of any salary, donation visits or donation parties were held to which parishioners brought gifts of food and sometimes money to a minister's family. These parties were frequently put on in the fall, after the crops were in, and before winter.

> *It's funny how our ancestors*
> *Would gather at the minister's*
> *And eat him out of house and home*
> *And call it 'A Donation.'*
>
> Daniel L. Cady,
> Rhymes of Vermont Rural Life
> (Rutland, Vt., 1919)

dowry. Property that a wife brought to a marriage; also called a marriage portion. A "dower Negro" was a slave brought by a wife to a marriage.

drama and local history. There are any number of reasons for historical societies and historians to consider the advantages of using drama. Dramatic presentations can increase the visibility of the local past. Taking history out of the museum and placing it on a local stage can increase and expand audiences beyond those who normally appear at society functions. In addition, as with *historical fiction, drama is often a way of exploring ideas about the past that the documents cannot fully support yet the historical event or situation suggests.

There is a long history of dramatic presentations of historical topics. Because of the format, however, and the need to attract and please audiences, the history presented is often skewed, and its characters stereotyped. Think of the portrayal of Native Americans on film, or of African Americans during the era of minstrel shows. Remember too, the controversy that some films generate when history is pushed to present one view or another in the name of artistic license.

The Great American History Theater, 30 East 10th St., St. Paul, MN; (651) 292-4323 is an Equity theater organization that commissions, produces, and tours plays that dramatize history, folklore, and social issues <www.bitstream.net/theater/hist.htm#perf>.

drama and local history, a case study. Our small-town historical society museum in Arizona wanted to reach an audience that does not normally frequent museums. Like all communities, we have stories to tell that are dramatic.

The idea was to produce a history *pageant. With grant money, a storyteller/playwright was hired to gather stories and transform them into *corridos*, poems and dramatic narratives. A script incorporated *music, storytelling, and dramatic vignettes featuring local historical events to show the development of the town. The writer acted as the director. The pageant walked a razor's edge at all times between straightforward history and creative storytelling.

Music typical of key periods covered in the script was included. Several professionals were hired to manage sound and video including professional actors who worked closely with volunteers. A professional actress/storyteller worked in the community as an artist-in-resi-

PHOTOGRAPH COURTESY OF *THE WICKENBURG SUN.*

Aaron Summers and Morris Baughman act a scene from "The Wickenburg Way."

dence for two weeks during the early stages of the production.

At the suggestion of the Arizona Humanities Council and the Arizona Commission on the Arts, the organizers consulted with a historian on script content and conducted an acting residency.

During a preview, evaluation sheets were made available to audience members. Most people stated that they had learned something about Wickenburg's history from the reading. Two-thirds stated that presenting history on stage is an effective way to teach history. Almost all appreciated the efforts and the participants appreciated being allowed "to work on such a rewarding project."

SHEILA KOLLASCH

due process. The right of due process is the right to legal protection through the courts. In other words, it prevents individuals or governments from depriving citizens of their legal rights without adjudication in the courts of the land.

Dun and Bradstreet. See financial and business records.

Dutch. See Appendix A.

dysentery. A disease, usually transmitted by impure drinking water, that inflames the mucous membrane and glands of the large intestine, causing pain and loss of blood. Outbreaks were common in the nineteenth century, especially among travelers to the West. See the discussion of dysentery in Lillian Schlissel, *Women's Diaries of the Westward Journey* (N.Y., 1982).

E

East Indians and Pakistanis. See Appendix A.

Eastern Orthodox. See Appendix B.

economic history. Only infrequently do local and regional historians look squarely at the issue of economics, yet so many of the topics that we tackle are, at heart, those that hinge on economic issues. In an important and interesting article, Paul Leuilliot declares what he calls his First Principle: "Local economic history of the 19th century leads into the present; it is related to our contemporary problems, our present-day preoccupations." Leuilliot argues that we must take into "account traditional aptitudes, available manpower, certain activities that often have long been carried on in a specific region, different types of regional growth, a locality's tendency to be thrifty and to store things up or to favor (or reject) a Malthusian spirit of enterprise."

Everyday life has an economic underpinning and tells us a great deal about a place. When new roads open, there is an economic impact; when a factory attracts workers from outside the area, that has a direct economic impact; when a college is founded, there is an economic impact upon producers of goods, availability of homes, modes of transportation, and the variety of commercial enterprises in a community. Advertisements promote new products and new desires, and these make a local economic impression. We need to expand our view of the past by looking at the ways in which the places we study reflect economic change and what that has meant to the people of that time and place.

The Economic History Association was founded in 1940. It is located at the Department of Economics, University of Kansas, Lawrence, KS 66045 and can be contacted by phone (785) 864-2847 or by fax (785) 864-5270. On the Internet, see <www.eh.net/EHA> or <eha@falcon.cc.ukans.edu>. The EHA publishes the quarterly *Journal of Economic History*.

For a commentary on the value of economic history, see Paul Leuilliot, "The Defense and Illustration of Local History," in Carol Kammen, *The Pursuit of Local History: Readings on Theory and Practice* (Walnut Creek, Calif., 1996), pp. 164–80.

See wages.

editing historical works. What does an editor look for in a good history manuscript? In the words of one historian, "Much depends on much." There are publishers and publishing venues for every conceivable work, and finding an appropriate press for work-in-progress, or for recently completed manuscripts, requires authors to be knowledgeable about the opportunities available to them. I have worked for a university press, and our editorial agenda looks very different from those of many of our fellow university presses, let alone commercial houses, regional trade presses, or textbook publishers. Nevertheless, I'm constantly struck by the proposals I'm sent that have surely gone to all manner of publishers in just the same form. Before I describe what I like to find in a publishing prospect, allow me to describe the part of the publishing universe I inhabit: the world of scholarly publishing. Seen through my eyes, that world may be a bit more comprehensible to an author—with some hints about other venues along the way.

As an acquiring editor responsible for my press's lists in American history, I go in search of approximately twenty new titles to sign and publish each year. To ensure that we get to publish the very best work available to us, I am proactive: I travel extensively each year, visiting campuses, and attending conventions; I read widely in American history; and I maintain lively correspondence with an extensive network of professional advisers and contacts. I must carefully formulate our agenda for the field, as it is necessary for scholarly publishers to focus our lists. By developing a distinctive profile to the work we publish in American history, I try to help our marketing effort by creating opportunities to offer prospective readers a group of books related by interest. I also look for books that will appeal to multiple readerships, and, of course, books that will appeal to the broadest imaginable collectivity, that elusive "general-interest" audience. Working for a university press, I seek projects that will uphold the standards of scholarship for which our parent institution is recognized; I look for books that are teachable; and I look for work that brings the very best scholarship to bear upon topics of interest in the wider world. I enjoy this perpetual quest, much as I expect a talent scout or a critic might in other contexts.

Like most editors, I am bombarded by unsolicited or "blind" submissions of projects each day. As one can find good manuscripts anywhere, from anyone, I look at each of these projects, in the hope of finding delight and profit in the unexpected. But because the principles of selection (like those embodied in any press's editorial agenda) are so well marked, our economic margins so tight, and our prior commitments so extensive, I can determine rapidly whether it makes sense to pursue projects or refuse them. As an editor, what do I look for?

First, I want to know: does the author have a good subject? As a history editor, I believe strongly in the importance of historical work: I believe that the preservation of the human record is critical to the endurance of a humane society, a virtue in and of itself. But there is a difference between a book and an archive, a chronicle and a narrative. In my search for books to publish I look for history that extends our common quest for the relationship between past and present. Only with assurances that an author has engaged a topic with this purpose in mind am I capable of determining the relevance and the appeal of a given project. I look for good stories, told with a purpose.

Second, I want to know whether an author writes well. If not, I must assume that efforts to read a book may likely be defeated, and its readership will therefore be drastically curtailed. The importance of the subject may still prevail over pedestrian writing for some of a book's core readers—but then, is it worth the chance? I need to judge.

Third, I try to gauge the likely audience for a book. How extensive will the market be? Is it a readership that our press is capable of reaching, given the preciousness of our marketing resources? Have we been successful in appealing to a particular audience with previous publications? How enduring will the market be—is a project time-sensitive?

Fourth, I need to attend to the economic considerations raised by the prospect of publishing any work. How long is the book that will emerge from a given project? How extensive an illustration program will the work require? How attractive will the finished product need to be in order for it to satisfy its likely purchasers? Will design and production be costly?

Finally, I want to determine how knowledgeable a prospective author is about the publishing process. Has the person been published before? Am I being approached by someone who knows what our press does best, and therefore has some understanding of what their own project is likely to contribute to our list? Can I have confidence that an individual will appreciate the intricacies of editorial collaboration, schedules and deadlines, the horizons of feasibility in marketing and promotion? In sum, will a prospective author be good to work with?

All of these considerations are related, even inextricably linked: an author who has published before may be more practiced in picking a topic; more experienced and adept in the writing and publication process; better known to an extended audience; and more attuned to the economic constraints presses must live with. But every author must write a first book, and the interplay of factors is often unique to each project, and yet so critical to anticipate, that a first-time author does well to try to address these concerns before approaching any publisher with their work.

Today, publishing good work in American history carries many of the dangers and difficulties that beset the publication of all scholarly books, even as the prospect remains exciting and even distinctive. All editors in scholarly publishing face the harsh realities of a sharply declining library market for our product; rising costs that force us to price our wares dangerously high; a growing disenchantment in the review media with first books (barely revised doctoral dissertations); and a declining readership for serious nonfiction. But American history remains one of the few academic specialties with a following among general readers, and the premium for finding and publishing good work that will appeal to them remains high. The competition between publishers for such projects is intense, and individuals—even first-time authors—can gain a hearing for their work among a number of presses.

An effective approach to a publisher by an author must cover many bases in the short time an editor is likely to spend in making a preliminary decision. I advise prospective authors to take some time studying the lists of the presses they may wish to approach. Do those houses actively publish in one's own subject area? Which publishers feature titles that would travel well with an author's own work? Are there intermediaries who might speak to editors on the author's behalf—or could be invoked in a cover letter? Often academic conventions furnish an occasion to speak directly with an editor; I suggest asking a question—say, "does your press's having published x mean that you're in search of similar works?" The same angle of approach may be taken in a cover letter that makes clear that an author has studied carefully the reasons for wanting to submit work to particular presses.

Like most editors, I look for an initial solicitation that consists of such a cover letter, the author's resume, a brief (3- to 5-page) prospectus that describes the project, a table of contents, and a sample chapter or two (the introduction, certainly, plus a fair sample of the work's substance). It is especially helpful to know how long the work is, and what illustrations it will require, if any. With such materials in hand, I can make a swift determination of a project's likely prospects at my press. Of course we're deluged daily with submissions of this kind—and it's always easiest to determine which projects we should decline immediately. Taking a closer look at projects with some prospect takes time. Still, it isn't too much to hope for an initial response from a publisher within a month.

When I receive a completed manuscript, I look carefully to see how well an author honors those conventions that good books require. I look for an introduction that invites readers to consider the book's subject. I want to see if an author is adept at avoiding the typical difficulties writers have in getting going: unnecessary signposting, throat-clearing, busy-ness, and other tics and quirks. Does the author provide readers with a compelling reason to read on? Can the subject matter be made to speak for itself through a telling example, say, one that quickly demonstrates the author's mastery of the subject, yes, but also the story in which the subject will unfold? I look closely at chapter titles: do they betoken the various aspects of the story, without succumbing to vagueness, or to unnecessary elaboration of particulars? (Currently I'm warring against academic pedantry in the form of two-part chapter titles, separated by colons!) I look with particular care at chapter openings and closings: are these sufficiently varied, or—a common malady—does each look just like the last? And do the transitions between chapters occur seamlessly? Here too, unnecessary "we just saw this, now we'll see that," or "first-I'll do this, then I'll do that" declarations often reveal a lack of confidence that is typical among first-time authors. (Intelligent authors will follow clear transitions without needing to be told they're being made.) In academic works, I'm immediately on the lookout for over-referencing, another common, costly malady; a confident author will provide a single citation where ten others may be found—without burdening the reader with all the rest. (Hint: these days, we look for a text-to-notes ratio of

4:1, no worse!) Finally and importantly, I want to be sure that a manuscript is no longer than it absolutely must be.

While it may have been necessary once (in writing a dissertation, say) to presume no prior knowledge in one's readers (typically, four members of a Ph.D. committee), that time has passed. In a "first look" at a manuscript, I'm anxious to determine the degree of mastery its author displays: over the subject, the story being told, and the conventions that make for a work of economy and grace.

As the electronic revolution relentlessly alters the publishing landscape, I remain optimistic about the future for books. For certain kinds of work, they remain the best way to convey knowledge in a lasting form. Writing a good book is hard, but it is always possible to improve one's work, and editors can help. When I look at a project for the first time, I want to find reasons to be confident an author has laid the necessary groundwork for a good collaboration to follow. While the dissemination of information is made easier all the time, authors and editors together must work harder to produce works of enduring value. That's what the best book publishing has always been about, and now only more so.

PETER AGREE

education, history of. The current scholarship on the history of education moves beyond the legislative story of how public elementary schools were formed. Today scholars are asking, who participated in the movements that ultimately instituted public schools?; why did supporters argue for schools to be managed at the state level?; and what purposes did advocates plan for public schools to serve?

In 1960, Bernard Bailyn, historian of New England and of immigration patterns to the United States, called for approaches to the history of public schools that would disclose the connections between education and national, state, and local histories. Questions like those above reestablish these historical links. Evidence gathered by historians Carl Kaestle (U.S.), Andrew Cayton (American Midwest), and R. D. Gidney and Bruce Curtis (Ontario) reveal that prior to 1850, the ranks of public school promoters were filled with society's leaders. Common among them were ministers, politicians, businessmen, educators, and journalists. Biographical records and manuscript collections exist for many; thus, local historians can readily analyze early public school supporters and how they fit into their state and provincial societies.

Local historians are also well placed to research why promoters fought to institute public schools. Historians such as Scott Walter and Susan Houston show that public school advocates in Indiana and Ontario, respectively, held deep concerns about the challenges their communities faced.

The period between the War of 1812 and the Civil War witnessed many changes. Immigration rates swelled in both the United States and Canada. Newcomers brought multiple languages, customs, religions, and ideas about democratic-based politics. In the midst of this influx, economic systems were changing from mercantilism to capitalism. Financial institutions such as banking and insurance were developing. Consequently, North Americans began moving from subsistence farming and cottage industries to commercial agriculture and manufacturing.

At mid-century, many North Americans detected growing idleness, drunkenness, and lawlessness in their burgeoning cities. In their search to form cohesive, prosperous, and peaceful communities, U.S. and Canadian leaders joined public-help organizations such as temperance societies and Masonic lodges, and they built churches. They also persuaded their legislators to create public schools. Local researchers can piece together the relationship between the fast pace of change and the growth of support for public education by tracing these factors in the lives of individuals and political, volunteer, and fraternal organizations during the antebellum period.

Proof that public school promoters sought to cure social ills and form coherent communities lies in their rhetoric. Their arguments permeate secondary literature about early American and Canadian public education history. Comparing sources from different periods across the North American national boundary highlights strong parallels in the reasons school advocates gave for creating public schools. First, school supporters wanted to create patriotic populations capable of intelligently fulfilling the roles of citizenship: owning property, voting, and perhaps even standing for public office. Thus, they contended that all children must be taught about their government and national history and that these subjects should be taught in a standard and ap-

proved fashion. Public schools could accomplish these goals, they reasoned, whereas traditional neighborhood, church, and subscription schools could teach these subjects only to varying degrees and from numerous perspectives.

School advocates asserted that public schools could instill morality in society by teaching all children common values. Christian ministers promoted this view, and even nonreligious figures such as Thomas Jefferson maintained that basic morals must be observed in order to sustain democratic nations. The values advanced by public school promoters synthesized ethical maxims from the Protestant churches and echoed dictums from the Jewish and Catholic faiths as well. Among them were industry, honesty, respect, and obedience; and restraint from stealing, adultery, and murder. Infusing these traits in the general population would curtail crime, laziness, and civil disorder while promoting harmony, cooperation, and prosperity, the school advocates argued. Conversely, they pointed out, the traditional network of schools could neither reach all youngsters, nor could it easily instill shared values.

Local scholars may gather primary documents such as speeches, editorials, and other rhetoric pertaining to public school creation in newspapers, journal articles, church sermons, correspondence, broadsides, or assembly-meeting minutes. By this effort, local historians will broaden our understanding of the purposes that public schools were meant to serve.

Furthermore, this research will uncover arguments of public school dissenters. Secondary sources state that opposition to public schools existed. For instance, historian Logan Esarey uses statistics from a referendum vote on education to show that one-third of Indiana voters did not want legislators to institute public schools in 1848. Other U.S. and Canadian historians, though less specific, indicate that many early residents resisted public schools. Scholarly opinions as to why some North Americans failed to support or else actively opposed public schools vary widely. Were detractors ignorant, or were they merely content with the customary network of schools? Did they oppose paying taxes for schools, or did they disapprove how the funds were to be distributed? Did they lack sufficient time and money to concern themselves with schools, or did they prefer local control over state or provincial control of schools? As yet, we have no clear conception of public school adversaries. Being close to the resources, local historians may lead this intriguing field of inquiry.

As the twentieth century ends, North Americans are again experiencing rapid changes. Many perceive a breakdown of basic values. Simultaneously, educators, politicians, and others debate the purposes of schools. Consequently, it is an opportune time to identify the original public school promoters and opponents and to outline their reasoning. Not only might the answers reconnect education with local and national histories, they might help create useful links between public schools and our societies today.

See M. Teresa Baer, "Education and the Perception of Equality: Defining Equality through the Establishment of Public School Systems in Indiana and Ontario, 1787–1852," M.A. thesis, Indiana University at Indianapolis, 1998; *Hoosier Schools Past and Present*, William J. Reese, ed. (Bloomington, Ind., 1998); Andrew R. L. Cayton and Peter S. Onuf, *The Midwest and the Nation: Rethinking the History of an American Region* (Bloomington, Ind., 1990); Bruce Curtis, *Building the Educational State: Canada West, 1836–1871* (London, Ontario, 1988); Susan E. Houston and Alison L. Prentice, *Schooling and Scholars in Nineteenth-Century Ontario* (Toronto, 1988); Carl E. Kaestle, *Pillars of the Republic: Common Schools and American Society, 1780–1860* (N. Y., 1983); *An Imperfect Past: Education and Society in Canadian History*, J. Donald Wilson, ed. (Vancouver, 1977); *Education and Social Change: Themes from Ontario's Past*, Michael B. Katz and Paul H. Mattingly, eds. (New York, 1975); *Essays on Education in the Early Republic*, Frederick Rudolph, ed. (Cambridge, Mass., 1965); Bernard Bailyn, *Education in the Forming of American Society* (N. Y., 1960); Paul Monroe, *Founding of the American Public School System: A History of Education in the United States, from the Early Settlements to the Close of the Civil War Period* (N. Y., 1940).

M. TERESA BAER

emancipation celebrations. African American emancipation celebrations commemorate events connected with blacks' struggle to end slavery in the United States. This commemorative tradition began in 1808, when Congress prohibited further importation of enslaved Africans into the United States. Enthusiasm for this particular commemoration died out, but the commemorative tradition revived when Great Britain abolished slavery in its West Indian colonies on August 1, 1834. Free black Americans saw this as a portent of American emancipation and held massive annual August 1 celebrations in dozens of northern communities that included parades, religious observances, speeches, music, feasting, and assorted amusements.

When U.S. slavery ended in the 1860s, Northern and Southern African Americans commemorated various dates associated with that event. Some continued to celebrate on August 1, while others, especially the freed persons in the South, commemorated Lincoln's Emancipation Proclamation, which went into effect on January 1, 1863. Still others celebrated various dates that had local or regional significance. During the nineteenth century, emancipation celebrations served many functions. They celebrated freedom, helped spread knowledge of African American history, facilitated political and social networking, and provided an annual gathering of blacks from small communities around a region who normally may not have had much opportunity to interact. Special excursion rates on trains made attendance more affordable, and black churches, veterans' groups, and fraternal lodges were often among the organizers.

Emancipation celebrations gradually lost their significance and were discontinued in many areas by the early twentieth century, continuing mainly in the South. As blacks migrated out of the South between the 1910s and 1960s, they carried their traditions with them.

The most resilient of African American commemorations of emancipation has been the once-marginal and regional "Juneteenth" tradition, which was initiated by Texas blacks in commemoration of the June 19, 1865 date when Union troops liberated slaves in that state. This tradition has been rediscovered and is now celebrated in many communities in all parts of the country.

In investigating the role these events played in local communities, local black or white newspapers, as well as prominent black papers from major cities, are an excellent source. Newspaper accounts provide a sense of who the local leaders were, and suggest the extent of interaction among African Americans from across a given region. Some key questions to consider when researching emancipation celebrations: What dates were commemorated by blacks in your community? When and why did these observances begin and how long did they continue? To what extent was there interaction with other black communities around the area? How were churches, fraternal organizations, literary societies, veterans' organizations, or other institutions involved? For scholarly discussion of emancipation celebrations, see Mitchell A. Kachun, "The Faith That the Dark Past Has Taught Us: African-American Commemorations in the North and West and the Construction of a Usable Past, 1808–1915" (unpublished doctoral dissertation, Cornell University, 1997); and William Wiggins, *O Freedom! Afro-American Emancipation Celebrations* (Knoxville, 1987).

MITCHELL A. KACHUN

emigrant. An emigrant is one who leaves another country to settle here. An immigrant is one who has come from a foreign country to settle here. The first word places the emphasis upon the country of origin from which a person is taking leave; the second focuses upon the act of arriving in a new country in which one wishes to settle. "Emigrant" is also used to describe those who left the eastern part of the United States to settle in the West. John Frémont noted in 1843 in his journal that he had come across a pack of cards that "marked an encampment of our Oregon emigrants" (*Exploring Expedition to the Rocky Mountains . . .* [New York, 1856], p. 14). "Emigrant" was also used in the 1840s for African Americans being sent by the Colonization Society to Africa.

eminent domain. The right of the government to seize property for the good of the majority of citizens.

encyclopedia making. Over the past two decades among the most interesting developments in local history is the proliferation of comprehensive regional encyclopedias. One of the first of the new breed of encyclopedias, in 1987, was *The Encyclopedia of Cleveland History*. This inspired *The Encyclopedia of New York City* and *The Encyclopedia of Indianapolis*. The success of the *Encyclopedia of Southern Culture* inspired a new generation of regional encyclopedias, including a revamped *Encyclopedia of the West*. A third genre of recent encyclopedias takes a statewide focus, including recent volumes on Kentucky and Utah. Many other encyclopedias are in process, including prospective treatments of Chicago, New England, the Middle West, Appalachia, New York State, and southern California.

The new breed of local and regional encyclopedias differs from their predecessors in a number of ways. At the turn of the twentieth century, a common form of regional encyclopedia was the illustrated prosopography of local worthies. While these encyclopedic works can offer much valuable historical information, on the whole their canons of inclusion and exclusion, even granting changes in historical taste, tend to be erratic. Many are flawed by cloying *boosterism. Another brand of local reference works was the glorified *gazetteer, utterly comprehensive in their scope, with an individual entry for almost every hamlet, hillock, and creek. An example is Walter Prescott Webb's mid-1950s *Handbook of Texas*, in four volumes, a model reference work, but nonetheless numbing in its thoroughness. Undoubtedly the best local reference works of an earlier generation are the still-invaluable Works Progress Administration (WPA) guides from the 1930s and 1940s. These guides dropped the encyclopedia format altogether, and were essentially sophisticated guidebooks, arranged topically and geographically, and having as one their purposes orienting the new visitor to the city or state. On the whole, the WPA guides are more useful for their accounts of the contemporary scene and the recent past rather than earlier history. Though often possessing high literary merit, the WPA guides were not rigorous in their scholarship, and for earlier history relied too heavily on questionable secondary sources.

The recent local history encyclopedias are scholarly, intended for readers interested in history rather than tourists. The encyclopedias are selective in their choice of entries and topics, and contain a mixture of longer thematic entries and briefer entries on significant individual persons, places, or things. This selectivity is both an intellectual and practical necessity, since almost all of the recent encyclopedias have been issued in one volume, thereby facilitating sales to the general public, rather than simply to libraries. The recent encyclopedias are collaborative, often relying on hundreds of authors, each writing in their area of expertise.

There has been much speculation on the reasons behind the increasing pace of production of encyclopedias of local and regional history. They are excellent vehicles for popularizing and disseminating current scholarship outside of the walls of the academy. Encyclopedias offer the chance for connecting to serious readers who do not frequent historical monographs; and a number of publishers and historians, for a range of financial and intellectual reasons, have leapt on the encyclopedia bandwagon.

Local encyclopedias also filled the need for substantial local histories. The "city biography," a comprehensive study of a particular locality from its founding to the present day, had its heyday from the 1930s through the 1950s. They were largely supplanted by smaller, discrete monographs of particular periods or topics, and few general local histories appeared. The interest in largescale histories were further undercut by the burgeoning interest in social history, which in the minds of its proponents undercut the need or relevance of traditional narrative histories. Though there is some heartening evidence of the return of the "grand narrative" to local history, local encyclopedias permit a coherent though decentralized approach to their topic. Encyclopedias certainly differ from traditional narrative histories. Experts view the locality from their own perspective, and there is no need to tie all the pieces together into one unified vision of the city or locality. Many topics that would either not appear at all or receive scant mention in a unified narrative can be treated at greater length in an encyclopedia; such as short entries on every important hospital or settlement house in an area, or entries on every significant sports team or military unit. Rather than the structure of a single narrative, the inherent serendipity and random juxtapositions of local and regional encyclopedias (especially those arranged alphabetically) make a very different, and much more interactive and personal way of learning and reading.

The future of the new breed of local history encyclopedias is rapidly changing. The emergence of new electronic information technology, which multiplies by many orders of magnitude of speed and access to information, is fomenting radical changes in reference publishing. No longer do the constraints and expenses of publishing large volumes limit the size of a reference work. Enhanced graphics and hyperlinks are transforming the rather drab, print-heavy look of the traditional encyclopedia. Some have questioned the need for encyclopedias in an era when a good search engine can find a website on almost any imaginable topic in a matter of minutes. The Internet is also a challenge to the economics of reference publishing; how can the labor-intensive process of producing quality reference works recoup development costs in a media where most information is available for free?

The new technology carries with it both great possibility and potential pitfalls. The freedom from space constraints can seem liberating to reference editors who have spent their professional lives fighting to keep encyclopedia entries to their assigned lengths, but this new freedom can breed laxness. One of the best features of recent local encyclopedias is that their selectivity inculcates editorial discipline, and the making of tough decisions about inclusion and exclusion. The freedom to post almost anything of any length on the Internet is to its advocates, a new form of democracy and, to skeptics, a form of electronic anarchy in which good, bad, and indifferent reference sources exist side by side, often requiring the scrutiny of experts to tell them apart. However, if the future of encyclopedias is on the Internet, like traditional publishing, electronic publishing will require authoritative reference works. The migration of local history encyclopedias to the Internet has already started. Fittingly, the pioneer of the new model of local history encyclopedias, *The Encyclopedia of Cleveland History*, was the first to appear on-line. Others will shortly follow. This is a challenging time for reference publishing; one hopes that amid much transformation, the basic criteria for excellent reference writing and publishing—accuracy, clarity, economy, and even-handedness—will remain unchanged.

See Howard Roberts, *The New Encyclopedia of the American West* (New Haven, Conn., 1998); David D. Van Tassel and John J. Grabowski, *The Encyclopedia of Cleveland History*, 2d ed. (Bloomington, Ind., 1996); Kenneth T. Jackson, *The Encyclopedia of New York City* (New Haven, Conn., 1995); John E. Kleber, *The Kentucky Encyclopedia* (Lexington, Ken., 1992); and Charles Reagan Wilson and William Ferris, *Encyclopedia of Southern Culture* (Chapel Hill, N.C., 1989).

PETER EISENSTADT

See mug books.

England, local history in. In 1979 a national working party chaired by Lord Blake proposed "a strong independent national organization for local history (in England and Wales)," together with a large number of other recommendations that, in essence, envisaged a national body organizing the provision of training, information, and advice, with the result that the *British Association for Local History (BALH) was established in 1982. Prior to this, in 1948, a national Standing Conference for Local History had been established under the auspices of the National Council for Social Service, and in 1952 the *Amateur Historian* was founded by the Conference. Later, its name was changed to the *Local Historian, and it continues to be published four times a year.

In England and Wales, the provision of libraries and largely county-based public record offices has been a statutory duty placed by central government upon county boroughs and county councils (and their successors), with the result that voluntary institutions acquiring and managing large collections of local historical records and books has never been the norm. Town and city museums have similarly been established and maintained by local councils, which is why local history societies in England have, almost exclusively, concentrated on organizing meetings, visits, and in some cases, publishing journals and occasional books.

1998 finds the organization of English local history weak at the center, nonexistent in the regions, extremely varied in the counties, and, for the most part, parochial at the local level. Local history "qualifications" continue to depend on the initiatives of individual colleges and universities, although in recent years some imaginative courses have been initiated by small groups, archives, and museums. A survey published in 1998 by England's archivists says that "the nation's archives are in urgent need of money to save them for future generations."

A recent directory of county-based local history associations and related umbrella groups published in *Local History Magazine* (March/April 1998) and on their website <www.local-history.co.uk> lists some 70 societies covering the 39 historical counties of England, 33 of which act as county committees concerned with the organization and promotion of local history within their counties. However, only 21 maintain lists of local history societies within their counties. We estimate that there are about 2,000 local history societies in England, many of which will have little or no contact with their county association, let alone any national organization. Ad hoc regional

structures have been created to organize local history fairs and other events, but when these have fallen by the wayside, so has the idea of regional cooperation, except in the case of the areas around Birmingham and Bristol, where strong umbrella groups crossing historic county boundaries have been established.

In addition, there are at least 13 county-based record societies in England that specialize in the transcription and publication of historical manuscripts and records in annual volumes for use by students and others. As well as county umbrella groups there are some 22 county-based archaeological and historical societies that, for the most part, have their roots in the days of antiquarianism and are regarded as more learned than the county associations, which are more popular in approach. Also, a number of county record offices and many local museums have their own voluntary organizations for users and friends.

Based on the known membership numbers for county associations and a few counties as a whole, about 100,000 people in England belong to a local history-related voluntary society of some kind. The numbers actively involved in some way, including adult students, probably does not exceed 5,000.

In sharp contrast to the plight of local history organization at a regional level, local history award courses, organized in regional centers by universities, are booming, with over 100 courses on offer in the autumn of 1998, with an estimated 2,000 students. In 1996 and 1997, *Local History Magazine* published local history student profiles based on replies to questionnaires distributed via course organizers. The findings show that: 70 percent of local history students are aged 50 and over; 50 percent travel more than 20 miles to attend their chosen course; 65 percent plan to sign up for another local history course upon completion of their current course; and that only 43 percent are members of a local history society.

In addition to the award courses, there are hundreds of local history evening classes across the country, together with other courses and day schools organized by archives, libraries, museums, and county associations. For many, this kind of activity has actually replaced the need to join a local history society. What these organized courses provide is access to resources, professional advice and support, together with the companionship of like-minded individuals.

Another measure of what is happening to English local history can be found in the area of local history publishing and periodicals. National and regional publishers provide the "consumer" with a never-ending stream of books based on old photographs, whilst restricting their publication of general local histories to counties and towns with sufficiently large populations to make such ventures viable. Books about sources and specific topics tend to be published by bodies such as BALH, the Historical Association, the Federation of Family History Societies (FFHS) and independent family-history publishers.

However, it is self-publishing by individuals and local history societies that accounts for the vast majority of local history titles published in England each

year. We think it fair to say the antiquarian tradition is alive and well, insomuch as many authors continue to present their readers with lots of "facts" and transcriptions, rather than interpret their evidence in relation to historical changes and developments in society, either locally and nationally. Visit any bookshop in England and you are likely to find a reasonably sized local history section.

Whilst most local history society journals in England are still exclusively for members, more and more societies are publishing popular journals for sale within their local communities. These magazine-type journals include articles about historic local events, celebrities and sport, whilst encouraging readers to share their reminiscences about the area. Alongside the entertainment are articles that offer historical perspectives in relation to nineteenth- and twentieth-century issues such as education, health, housing, employment, disability, race and, increasingly, the environment.

In all these areas, English local historians have had access to not only contemporary primary and secondary sources, but, in many cases, to the oral reminiscences of people with direct experience of the events or periods being researched. Local communities can now read articles and books about the history of their town or village in which they, or people they know, participate as witnesses. This is probably one of the reasons popular interest among enthusiasts in earlier periods of English local history has been considerably less than it might otherwise have been.

The past twenty years has also seen a rapid growth of *family history activity, and in many areas their members are far more active than local historians. Unfortunately there is little formal cooperation between family historians and local historians. In addition, the Historical Association continues to take an active interest in local history through its own national local history committee and publishing program, and in 1998 the Open University (OU) established the Family and Community Historical Research Society. Interestingly, the OU prefers the term "community history."

The rapid growth of information technology (IT) has also changed the world of English local history in so many ways that it would take a separate article to do justice to the subject. The late nineties saw the publication of several reports that relate to IT and its likely impact on the future course of local history in England, including *New Library: The Peoples* [*sic*] *Network* (Library & Information Commission, 1997), which says "community history and community identity" should be one of "the principal strands" of a £770 million vision to link all libraries in the United Kingdom via the Web. *Local History Magazine* regularly reports on IT issues and has published a number of articles in recent years covering such topics as the Internet, Optical Character Recognition (OCR), Geographical Information Systems (GIS), and digitization of records.

With so many voluntary groups and societies, as well as statutory bodies and educational establishments involved, it is clear that interest in English local history is alive and well, even if it lacks any real cohesion. After twenty years during which so much has changed, the time has probably come to look at the organization of local history in England again (Wales, like Scotland, should be in charge of its own destiny).

SUSAN GRIFFITHS *and* ROBERT HOWARD

England, local history themes. Local history has a long history in England. It started with antiquarians (mainly educated and leisured gentlemen) traveling through the country noting antiquities and searching for records relating to buildings and sites. They produced collections of information without any general themes emerging. During the nineteenth century, legal and administrative matters were added to this, and during the early part of the twentieth century, economic local history was also added. Increasingly, the work was done by academic historians (as well as leisured persons often working as volunteer archivists and archaeologists) who sought in the localities examples of national trends or the working out locally of national events such as the English Civil War or the Industrial Revolution. The *Victoria County History fossilized this form of local history with its emphasis on what may be called the "great people" (landlords and clergy) and great events approach to local history.

The real study of local history began in the 1950s. In part, this was inspirational, the work of a small group of great enthusiasts and their successors. In part, it was due to the adult education movement. In part, it was also due to increased access to records and other local history source material. But there may have been deeper reasons for this outburst—a local search for a sense of security in a rapidly changing society, faced particularly by increasing immigration and a threat to national identity.

Since then, English local history has gone through three clear stages. The first was a topographical and archaeological phase, in part associated with the work of the so-called Leicester School of Local History but more widely related to the contemporary environmental conservation movement. Medieval field systems; urban working-class housing; industrial archaeology; hedgerows; medieval churches and dissenting chapels; workhouses and almshouses; vernacular architecture—these formed some of the major themes of English local history during the sixties and early seventies. Exciting new revelations grew from looking carefully and discriminatingly at the manmade environment.

From the seventies, there came a sociological approach. Here the emphasis was on the word "community" (the term almost became a compulsory part of the title of every local history book that came out during this period). It was argued that history concerned people, not things. Local residence groups in villages, towns, and suburbs were studied intensively, and general conclusions were drawn about them. The search was on for the elements that local communities held in common. Here was laid the foundation of the study of "open" and "closed" communities, of occupational and ethnic groups, of women's local history (the current Open University initiative still contains much of this approach). The work was based on social science research, and the findings were almost always presented in the form of statistics. One key element in this sociological approach to local history was historical *demography, "population studies," which for a time became very popular throughout the country; people searching censuses, parish registers, and other records for common trends of population growth, decline, and crisis points. This approach related closely to contemporary concerns with largely urban social problems.

More recently, there is beginning to be an interest in anthropological approaches to local history. Here concern is more with "culture" (folklore and customs, local language, etc.), with people's perceptions, world pictures, and practices. Above all, the emphasis is on what is different in each locality or neighborhood group, rather than on what is common. Accounts are being related of what happened in this particular locality and why, not on whether such a story throws light on anything or anywhere else. This reflects contemporary concerns with a sense of cultural identity.

Major attacks have been launched from time to time by some academics on local history as being parochial and antiquarian. Much of this attack is, unfortunately, based on truth. But the answer they propose—regional studies—has its own problems. Regions cannot easily be recognized in the perceptions of people in the past; their sense of belonging was to village, county, and estate.

It is not clear where local history in its fullest form will go as information and communication technology (ICT) develops. But it will clearly keep pace with the development of newly emerging academic understandings and disciplines.

ALAN ROGERS

See Cambridge Group for the History of Population and Social Structure; Finberg, H. P. R.; Hoskins, W. G.; regionalisms.

English in North America. See Appendix A.

enfranchisement. To enfranchise is to set free or to liberate from slavery. African Americans were freed by the Emancipation Proclamation and other laws. African American males were enfranchised, that is, given the vote by the terms of the 13th Amendment to the U.S. Constitution, and by terms of the 19th Amendment, females—both black and white—were given the vote.

entail. An entail limits how and who may inherit land and houses, as opposed to land held by *fee simple.

environmental history. Two major literary works published right before and after World War II articulate themes that play a central role in understanding and interpreting the local environmental experience. *The Grapes of Wrath* (N.Y., 1939), John Steinbeck's Pulitzer Prize–winning novel, sympathetically chronicles the plight of tenant farmers like the Joads displaced from their homes in Oklahoma by drought and greedy absentee landlords who cared more for profit than people or the land. Shortly after the Joads abandon their farm and hit the road for California, Grandpa Joad dies. Seeking to understand the first of what would be many

tragic events, "Reverend" Casy explains "Grampa an' the old place, they was jus' the same thing. . . . He died the minute you took 'im off the place." With these words, and throughout the novel, Steinbeck addresses the connection between people and place, which is one of the key themes in understanding both the human experience and local environmental history. Steinbeck's characters also highlight the role of memory in assigning meaning and significance to place.

Ten years later, in 1949, Oxford University Press posthumously published *A Sand County Almanac and Sketches Here and There* (N.Y., 1949) by Aldo Leopold—forester, father of wildlife biology, pioneering ecologist, and one of the most important environmental philosophers of the twentieth century. Part I of *A Sand County Almanac* recounts the experiences of Leopold and his family on an abandoned farm that he bought in Wisconsin in the mid-1930s. Leopold's narrative combines a keen sense of the interdependent, reciprocal relationship between natural and human history with a subtle and effective treatment of evolution and ecology—two watershed concepts in modern environmental understanding. Anyone interested in local environmental history would do well to start with Part I of *A Sand County Almanac*, especially "Good Oak" and "Burr Oak."

Environmental history did not exist as a field until after the mid-1960s, and it emerged as a direct result of the post–WWII environmental movement. Americans had long been interested in nature, and there had been powerful and sustained conservation movements in this country in the early twentieth century and again in the 1930s. In the mid-1920s, the Izaak Walton League of America (IWLA) developed a strong following that included dozens of active chapters in the Midwest. Concerned about water pollution, drainage of wetlands, and other practices that threatened opportunities for fishing and hunting, the IWLA organized a successful nationwide campaign to establish the Upper Mississippi River Wildlife and Fish Refuge.

The post–WWII environmental movement was different from the earlier conservation movements; it drew its scientific and philosophical inspiration from the science of ecology, popularized by writers such as Aldo Leopold, Rachel Carson, and Barry Commoner. As was the case with evolution in the nineteenth century, ecology brought with it a seachange in the ways that people saw and understood the world around them. In the 1960s, the word "environment" first came into general use, often as a shorthand description of the natural world as a complex, interdependent life-support system of which people were a part. The passion and urgency and excitement of the environmental movement jump-started historians' interest in examining the interplay between people and the natural world. Scholars such as Thomas Dunlap, Samuel Hays, Susan Flader, Carolyn Merchant, Roderick Nash, and Donald Worster began to develop a body of literature that quickly took shape as a distinct field of study.

Within recent years a number of monographs have looked at local and regional environmental topics, but one of the most successful at developing a useful and understandable model for the interaction between people and nature is Richard White's *Organic Machine* (N.Y., 1995). Writing about the Columbia River, White describes the modern, reengineered river and its valley as an "organic machine" in which nature and technology, human and natural systems have been thoroughly intertwined and organized for the material benefit of people. The organic machine, which is a cyborg-like human creation composed of natural and artificial parts, is representative of the places that most of us inhabit in the late twentieth century.

In many ways, local environmental history is the story of the creation of place over time, as people acting on attitudes and values embedded in their cultures intentionally and unintentionally altered their surroundings. As scholars such as William Cronon have shown (in his *Changes in the Land* [N.Y., 1983]), Native Americans, largely through the use of fire, shaped the environment that Europeans found when they arrived in what they called the "New World." One of the great historical stories since European contact has been the dramatic making and remaking of the face of the land, a process that accelerated rapidly in the late nineteenth and twentieth centuries. Over the course of the twentieth century, fewer and fewer Americans have lived in environments that are "natural."

Cities, suburbs, small towns, farms, river valleys, lakeshores—all have environmental histories worth exploring. One way to begin thinking about local environmental history is to look at your local surroundings and ask: How did they get that way? This question directs attention to the evolving interplay between people and place and to the attitudes and values that underlay peoples' actions.

While there are plenty of things people did not create and cannot control, generally speaking the contemporary environment both locally and nationally is a human artifact; it is an example of human material culture. Archaeologist James Dietz has defined material culture as "that portion of man's physical environment purposely transformed by him according to culturally dictated plans." Local museums and historical societies routinely interpret the past using material culture.

Employing a definition of material culture that embraces the humanized environment allows these institutions to include the creation of place over time in the presentation of local history.

Environmental history offers exciting interpretive opportunities for local historians, but it presents challenges as well. All of us make sense of the past through the prism of our own culture. Topics such as the environment, on which there are likely to be strong and conflicting opinions, make it is disarmingly easy to slip into measuring people from the past against the knowledge and standards of the present. As is the case with other historical subjects, it is important to try to understand past interaction with the environment in the context of its own time. While there were people in the past who were stupid or greedy or deliberately destructive, most acted in ways that they believed would produce personal or social benefits. All too often, the expected benefits came packaged with significant unintended and unanticipated consequences. Indeed, in trying to understand cause and effect in the evolving relationship between people and the environment, unintended and unanticipated outcomes are at least as important as what they deliberately set out to accomplish. It is also worth remembering that not everyone has had the same environmental experience. Historically, people's relationships with the environment have been influenced by variables such as race, class, gender, and employment.

Examined imaginatively, almost any local topic can shed light on the creation of place over time and can contribute to an understanding of the intertwined accounts of human and natural history. Conner Prairie and Sturbridge Village, *living history museums in Indiana and Massachusetts, both feature country stores—their shelves stocked with products common to antebellum life. Each of those products could be the starting point for an environmental history. Together they can shed light on a developing economy, which linked those places to a worldwide trading network that converted the products of nature into products for people. Lyme disease, which is named for the Connecticut town where is was first isolated and discovered, is a relatively recently identified affliction spread by tiny ticks. Viewed through the lens of environmental history, lyme disease becomes a chapter in a saga involving the unintended and unanticipated consequences of changes in agricultural practices, reforestation, recovery of deer and other wildlife populations, suburban growth, and shifting attitudes towards animals and hunting.

Writing in *A Sand County Almanac*, Aldo Leopold said that "Many historical events, hitherto explained solely in terms of human enterprise, were actually biotic interactions between people and land." Leopold's words still suggest a model and a direction of travel for anyone interested in pursuing local environmental history.

PHILIP SCARPINO

ephemera. Handwritten or printed papers not meant for posterity, but that have survived and are now available for historical purposes.

episcopal. This word comes from the Latin *episcopus*, meaning of or pertaining to bishops. Its use denotes a church hierarchy in which a bishop is at the head, such as is found in the *Methodist Episcopal Church. For Episcopalian, see *Protestant Episcopal Church.

Episcopal Church. See Protestant Episcopal Church, Appendix B.

epitaphs. Inscriptions on gravestones or monuments commemorating the deceased.
See gravestones.

equity. In law it refers to so-called natural law or ethics. It has to do with moral principles rather than with the legal system. A second meaning is the amount that remains after all liens and mortgages are deducted from the value of a property.

escheat. A term that comes from feudal law and refers to those circumstances where there is no heir to a prop-

erty and so the estate reverts to the lord of the manor, or in the United States, to the state.

esquire. In England, esquire is a title that ranks above a gentleman and below a knight. It was commonly used for officers of the law such as justices of the peace and sheriffs. In the United States it commonly applies to justices of the peace and attorneys.

estate. This term refers to all property—either real or personal—and is not a legal definition. However, in the law there are a number of kinds of estates that are defined by the conditions under which the owner holds the property such as an estate in severalty (property held by one person) or estate in common (property held by two or more people).

Estonians. See Appendix A.

Ethical Culture. See Appendix B.

ethics and local history. Two types of ethics concern the conscientious local historian. There are the corporate ethics of the broader historical profession, the accepted norms of the majority of people who work in institutions dealing with the preservation or presentation of local history. The local historian also has recourse to another type of ethics, a tool kit that is part of her or his everyday community life: personal ethics.

The corporate ethics of the local history practitioner are formally set out in codes of ethics, such as the *American Association of Museums' very detailed 1978 text *Museum Ethics*, the National

Council on Public History's very general "Ethical Guidelines for the Historian," and the formal statements of principle and practice laid out by a wide variety of history-related professional organizations. Interested readers might see Theodore J. Karamanski, ed., *Ethics and Public History: An Anthology* (Malabar, Fla., 1990) and Gary Edson, *Museum Ethics* (London, 1997). The corporate ethics of the local historian are sometimes a reflection of professional training, perhaps in a public history graduate program. For those without the benefit of such training, professional development can provide exposure to the same norms of practice. Through reading publications like *History News*, participating in historical conferences, both regional and national, local historians learn the language, attitudes, and values of the larger historical profession. Codes of ethics and professional acculturation ensure that the hard-won experiences of senior practitioners are passed on to the rising generation of local historians. Unfortunately, after a flurry of activity in the late 1980s, the systematic discussion of historical ethics has waned, leaving practitioners with an attenuated set of professional ethics.

The strength and weakness of a corporate approach to ethics is that it reflects the experience of past professionals. Yet in the past generation, history as practiced on the local level in the United States and Canada has changed a great deal. The number and type of historical museums exploded in the 1970s and 1980s. Even with this expansion, the day is past when local historical museums or local history reading rooms in community libraries constitute the majority of institutions requiring the participation of the local historian. Today the story of our communities is also preserved and presented by local landmark commissions, Main Street organizations, *living history sites, consulting firms, genealogical societies, and reenactment groups. Each of these organizations brings its own approach to the past, be it buildings, families, neighborhoods, or battlefields. The means by which history can be presented by local groups has also changed the face of local history. Video and audio productions are no longer the province of a handful of expensive professionals. Desktop publishing has made local history dissemination easier, and websites bring local stories to an international audience. The exhibit in the historical society, once the principal mode of disseminating local history to the public, has been joined by tools unimagined in 1949 when the *American Association for State and Local History was created. When these new means of presenting our stories are added to the ever-widening range of stories historians are interested in exploring on a local level—from labor history to technology, from popular culture to gender and sexual orientation—the potential for venturing onto new ground is manifest. An ethical awareness based simply on an understanding of the norms of the profession is inadequate to the task of being an effective community history leader.

Unlike fellow historians working in the university or in state and federal agencies, local historians often work in an environment in which they are the only history professional, or in many cases the local historian is a volunteer without the benefit of graduate training. Also, the local historian is by definition rooted in a community. While an academician may pronounce with impunity on the foibles of people of the past, the local historian lives and works in a milieu where history's judgments have a more intimate and immediate impact. These and other distinctions between local history and the larger profession make it imperative that the local historian have an internalized, personal code of ethics that goes beyond the received wisdom of people who have operated museums or conducted oral histories in the past, but which instead grows out of reflection on the basic questions of the historical enterprise. Ethics for the local historian is not simply about following codes, but is the case-by-case making of moral choices.

Much of the background for making such choices is personal and reflects values deeply held and character formed through the years. Experience plays a role as well. There is no substitute for knowing the community in which you work, its personalities, and cultural fault lines. In dealing with controversial topics, for example, the lessons learned from past difficulties or the well-publicized debacle of the *Enola Gay* exhibit, can serve to reduce the possibility for conflict by bringing stakeholders in the community into the planning process. To be able to anticipate ethical challenges before they become dilemmas goes a long way toward defusing the potential for compromising deeply held values. Experience,

however, cannot always help us anticipate and defuse ethical challenges. The danger of asserting ethical principles that grow more out of our individual conceptions of history than any existing codes of ethics or canons of practice is that the local historian risks standing alone. This is sometimes inevitable, and the price of doing the "right thing" by your light can sometimes be a pink slip or the cold shoulder of your neighbors. For a particularly good case study concerning local historians and controversial topics, see Robert R. Weyeneth, "History, He Wrote: Murder, Politics, and the Challenges of Public History in a Community with a Secret," *The Public Historian* 16/2 (spring 1994): 51–74.

Particularly vexing are issues that pit personal values against clear professional responsibilities. There is little in the existing codes of ethics of public history that would guide the local historian in dealing with controversial topics. Admonishments from the *American Historical Association of the importance of "integrity" or from the *National Council on Public History to "represent the past in all of its complexity" are useful yardsticks, but they do not provide direct guidance to a historian working within a community where the past is intimate and immediate. In doing a history of a Midwestern community, I was once confronted with the challenge of narrating a petty political-corruption case, suppressed at the time, that led to the dismissal of an important local official. The incident was important in that it led to a change in leadership. The details of the case were not widely known at the time and therefore were not part of public discussion when it occurred.

The individual involved had cooperated with my research. I liked and respected him as a person. My decision was to reveal the incident but not to narrate it in great detail, and to try to place the end of the official's career in balance with his accomplishments. I felt very much caught between my responsibility to tell the whole truth, personal sympathies, and a recognition that my narrative was going to be the "official" record of a community and the evaluation of an individual's life. Certainly an investigative journalist would have afforded the incident much more print space, and another historian would have been perfectly within the ethical bounds of the profession to do so as well. My decision grew out of a web of personal considerations from religious values, long-shaped attitudes toward political institutions, frequent positive association with people in government service, and my relationship with the individual in question. Each of these were values that influenced the way I presented the past, although I sought to ensure that they did not override my overarching obligation to historical truth. While the assertion of personal ethics in local history is perhaps inevitable given the intimate nature of the work, it clearly puts the practitioner on a slippery slope. See the National Council on Public History, "Ethical Guidelines for the Historian," *Ethics and Public History* (pp. 76–77) and American Historical Association, "Statement on Standards of Professional Conduct," *Ethics and Public History* (pp. 97–103).

Historical ethics, like personal ethics, in the end reflect the type of human relations we seek to cultivate. Most existing codes offer guidance on our relationship with employers, colleagues, and the community. Strangely, professional historians have been much less explicit about the vital relationship between the historian and the people of the past. The local historian is especially engaged in the question of what does a museum or historical society owe to the past. The Oral History Association offers very thoughtful guidelines regarding the mutual rights of the historian and the living informant. The American Museum Association's *Museum Ethics* concerns the curator's responsibilities to the present, even the future. What of the dead? Do we have a responsibility to the people of the past? This is discussed in the Oral History Association, "Goals and Guidelines of the Oral History Association," *Ethics and Public History* (pp. 104–14) and by the American Museum Association's *Museum Ethics* (Washington, D.C., 1978).

More than in any other field of history the local practitioner has felt the tug of the past at their sleeve. In the nineteenth and early twentieth centuries local history was sometimes disparaged as, in Albert Bushnell Hart's words, the "worship of ancestors." Writing about deceased family members or others they knew, many early local historians were motivated by their bonds to the people of the past. During the last two generations local history has been consciously professionalized, with an increasing number of local historians having received at least some advanced training in the subject. As the philopietistic approach to the past has been gradually eroded, the local historian is left with the same ambiguous relationship with the dead as the academic historian. We read their mail. We save it for posterity. We use it to help our contemporaries better understand the communities in which they live and to appreciate our own humanity.

Their words and possessions are a treasured part of our "heritage." Local historians have a relationship based upon intimate association with those who left us historic houses we now operate as museums, dresses that we now exhibit as artifacts, and letters we now store as documents. But human relationships are based on reciprocity. What do we, as historians, owe to those who have given us so much? One might consult David J. Russo, *Families and Communities: A New View of American History* (Nashville, 1974).

Certainly we owe the people of the past our memory. The act of remembering is what local historians are doing when they arrange manuscripts, craft exhibits, and author histories. The corridors of memory are the space in which the dead are reanimated to suit the needs of the present. But utility alone cannot dictate how we use the memory of the past. Our debt to the people of the past includes the responsibility to remember them as part of a whole world that is past. The contextual integrity of the past balances the need to remember the past to suit present needs.

The dead are vulnerable to our probing. While laws govern the disposition of the physical body, the way a person is remembered is constantly being reevaluated. Are there questions we should not pose? Are there issues we should not explore? Should the veil of privacy be drawn over aspects of past lives? New scientific techniques expand the range of questions for which we can seek answers. Because we have the ability to find the answers, should we ask the questions? Thomas Jefferson has been subjected to a posthumous paternity test, Zachary Taylor to forensic examination almost 150 years after his death. Yet in these cases the new technologies were used to answer questions long raised in the past. More recently historical societies possessing materials related to Abraham Lincoln have been approached to allow genetic testing to determine if the martyred president had Marfan syndrome (a condition unknown in Lincoln's time) and unconnected to any aspect of his public career. Supporters of testing contend that knowledge that Lincoln had this disease would be heartening to people who currently suffer from Marfan syndrome (an inherited connective tissue disorder). In 1999, the Chicago Historical Society, which holds a large number of blood-stained items from the president's assasination, had to ask itself if Lincoln's DNA was as open to investigation as was his official correspondence. Such issues transcend the established bounds of historical ethics, and point to the need for further professional dialogue. This issue is discussed by Glen W. Davidson, "Abraham Lincoln and the DNA Controversy," *Journal of the Abraham Lincoln Association* 17/ 1 (1996): 2–26.

Historical museums have always been the physical embodiment of the bifurcated nature of history, embodying the things left by the past as well as the interpretation of those things into a narrative or exhibit. History was lived; history is remembered. Through preservation, curators of history perform their responsibility to the people of the past. Only through the unity and integrity of the historical record can the past live again as history. In interpretation the local historian can assume many roles, from prosecutor to defender of the dead. But whatever stance he or she may take, the subject is due full and unbiased interpretation of the historical record. Such a plane of objectivity is a noble fiction, but one toward which it is essential that all historians consciously strive. Local historians must fight against the trend, increasingly a problem in the academic sector, for authors to preface their interpretations with the qualification that they eschew traditional aspirations for objectivity in favor of an approach biased by gender, race, religion, or class theories.

The local historian who works with a society or museum takes on additional responsibilities. Open access to historical society collections (unless those collections have legal restrictions) is expected for all researchers. It is understandable that local historians will develop a strong, personal identification with their history, particularly if they are in the process of writing their own volume. Nonetheless, documents in a historical society collection should not be confused with personal property, nor should the history of a community be seen as a proprietary possession. Research results, of course, are private until published, but research materials should be made available to fellow historians.

The local historian works on the grass-roots level and has a responsibility to protect the full range of historical resources within their community, including documents, districts, buildings, and artifacts. The local historian's responsibilities include building historical consciousness in the schools, businesses, voluntary organizations, and government of their community. Most important of all, the local historian makes the results of historical research available to the community. While the act of writing local history can sometimes be a solitary pursuit, the mission of a conscientious local historian is to be an advocate for history within the community.

The good historian is the result of the fusion of personal ethics and professional ethics. Just as the local historian presents the story of a town in the context of its region and nation, historical ethics encourage us to build outward from the self. Our goal is a series of just relationships that unite the individual historian and the community, the living and the dead. The local historian is responsible to the people of the past, the community in which they work, and to the larger enterprise of history. It is a wonderful and exciting prospect to be in a place you know and mediate between the past and the present, but with it comes the challenge to represent history to your community.

THEODORE J. KARAMANSKI

See museums, and the matter of ethics.

Ethnic Heritage Act. Passed in 1972 by the U.S. Congress, it amends the Elementary and Secondary Education Act of 1965. The Ethnic Heritage Act recognized the multicultural nature of American society and promoted a greater understanding of the components of the population. Grants were made to plan, develop, establish, and operate ethnic heritage studies programs that were charged with creating curriculum materials, disseminating knowledge throughout the school system, training, and promoting research into the history, culture, or traditions of America's ethnic groups.

ethnic slurs. Many words commonly used in one era are considered unsuitable in another. Words used to identify people of a specific ethnic, racial, or religious group reflect upon the prejudices of people who uttered them. While local historians would not today use these terms themselves, these are words that often appear in the documents we use.

The question is how to deal with words we now consider offensive. If Walt Whitman, for example, talked about a "good nigger woman" who aided the soldiers wounded in the Civil War, it would be wrong to change his word within the confines of his quote to something acceptable today. Yet, except as a quotation, paraphrasing an objectionable term is one way of dealing with the problem. Change in the meaning and use of words is an important component of a local culture, and local historians might comment upon the fact that what at one time was commonly voiced, would not be considered appropriate at another.

See also ethics and local history; slang.

ethnicity. The very creation of communities in U.S. history often had an ethnic component. Clusters of immigrants moved together from homeland villages to places of residence in the United States that promised good land for farming or jobs needed for adjustment and survival. Thus, it was Silesian Poles who settled Panna Maria, Texas, in 1854. In a similar way, families of Dutch immigrants located in Carver County, Minnesota, in the 1870s. Historian Jon Gjerde, in his *The Minds of the West: Ethnocultural Evolution in the Rural Middle West, 1830–1917* (Chapel Hill, N.C., 1997), reveals that over 2,000 Norwegians moved from Fortun, a parish in western Norway, to Dane County, Wisconsin, around the same time. If the immigrant arrivals did not initiate a settlement, they often transformed it. Dubuque, Iowa, populated by English and Irish arrivals in the 1830s and 1840s, was heavily German by the middle of the nineteenth century. After 1880, Cambridge, Minnesota changed from a town of native-born Americans to one consisting mostly of Swedish newcomers.

Although cities invariably contained several ethnic and racial groups, specific urban neighborhoods could be ethnic settlements unto themselves. During the early twentieth century, Jews and Italians dominated life on the Lower East Side of Manhattan. Poles concentrated on the South Side of Pittsburgh. The Bohemian Flats neighborhood of Minneapolis, clutching a narrow strip of land alongside the Mississippi River, was essentially a village of Czechs, Slovaks, and Swedes. In the 1930s and 1940s, East Harlem was attracting newcomers from Puerto Rico. By the 1930s, as George Sanchez demonstrates in *Becoming Mexican American: Ethnicity, Culture, and Identity in Chicano Los Angeles* (N.Y., 1993), the Belvedere section of Los Angeles was home to over 30,000 Mexicans who were attracted by low rents and inexpensive housing. At the same time, the Boyle Heights area of the city was home to 10,000 Jews who found it a short commute to their jobs in the downtown area.

Newcomers inevitably relied on ethnic contacts to shape the economic life of their locale and of their group. Local economic conditions often attracted settlers in the first place. Thus, German Mennonites brought their skills in wheat farming to Kansas in the nineteenth century when land was available to them. In the same century, Chinese laborers were attracted to silver mines in California and coal mines in Utah. Early in this century the construction of interurban lines by the Pacific Electric Railway brought unskilled Mexicans to Los Angeles, many of whom settled in the Watts area. Sometimes the reverse was true: the existence of a large supply of immigrant workers attracted industry. Thus, cigar manufacturers located in Detroit in the 1920s due to the presence of thousands of Polish women who would work for relatively low wages.

Ethnic colonies not only seized portions of local labor markets, but also rapidly created countless numbers of neighborhood businesses. Small shops lived off ties forged by migration and ethnic settlement. German Catholics who opened a general store in Dyersville, Iowa, in 1858 became so successful that they expanded into the buying of grain and stocks. In 1915, the Chinese community of Locke, California, supported six restaurants and nine grocery stores. Jews on the Lower East Side around the same time patronized over 140 groceries and 130 kosher butchers. In San Antonio, Mexican vendors carried tamales and enchiladas in buckets and sold them in the streets. Donna Gabaccia, in her book *We Are What We Eat: Ethnic Food and the Making of Americans* (Cambridge, Mass., 1998), revealed that many ethnic enterprises eventually expanded to meet the demands of a mass market. An Italian-Swiss immigrant opened a cafe in 1828 that became Delmonicos, a famous New York restaurant. Domingo Ghiardelli began grinding imported chocolate in the nineteenth century and was soon selling goods throughout San Francisco. Germans mobilized to form the California Wine Association in 1894 to promote their product; the formation of the Italian Wine Makers Association soon followed. In recent years Koreans in the New York area have used ethnic ties to recruit workers from their homeland and open over 9,000 shops of all kinds.

Perhaps one of the most dramatic examples of ethnic enterprise influencing a local economy took place in the 1970s and 1980s in Miami. In the book *City on Edge: The Transformation of Miami* (Berkeley, Calif., 1993), Alejandro Portes and Alex Stepick explain how Cuban entrepreneurs reshaped the economy of South Florida. Building on ethnic connections between Cubans in Miami and Spanish-speaking companies in Latin America, these immigrants came to dominate local business. By 1979, over a half of all construction companies in Dade County were Cuban owned. When these entrepreneurs were no longer able to hire other Cubans because of the group's upward mobility, they turned to Nicaraguans, and, consequently, provided an economic base for another ethnic settlement.

The ethnic character of local America could lead to conflict as well as financial success. Tensions between Irish Catholics and native-born Protestants were strong in Philadelphia in the 1840s. Natives resented the fact that the Irish worked for low wages and competed for jobs. The Catholic newcomers were resentful of the practice of reading a Protestant version of the Bible in the public schools. The riots in the Kensington section of the city in 1844 resulted from this tension. In Grass Valley, California, in the 1850s, Cornish miners in search of gold competed with German and Irish men and fought with them in taverns on Saturday nights. During World War I, German Americans were often looked upon with suspicion, and the teaching of the German language was ended in many public schools. And in the 1940s, in Los Angeles servicemen attacked young Mexican males whom they held in contempt because of their ethnic background and the unusual "zoot suits" they wore.

Politics, however, offered an arena in which ethnic hostility could be resolved in less violent ways. Throughout much of American history, local politics was ethnic politics. In the nineteenth century there was a strong correlation between nationality and party. Irish Catholics tended to find a home in the Democratic Party apart from many Protestant groups like the Scandinavians who joined the Republicans. John Allswang, in his book *A House for All Peoples: Ethnic Politics in Chicago* (Lexington, Ky., 1971), explained how ethnic and religious differences made Prohibition a major issue in the city, one that often determined the results of mayoral elections. Anton Cermak, a Czech, actually mobilized Germans, Czechs, and Poles who opposed Prohibition and resented the anti-immigrant views of the Republican candidate to win the mayor's office in 1931. From 1930 to 1960, Italians living on "the Hill" in St. Louis could find jobs by contacting a local political boss like Lou Berra (Yogi's father). And in the 1980s Cubans not only came to play a major role in the economy of Miami, but transformed South Florida into a bastion of conservative, Republican power.

Additional information on the importance of ethnic identity in local history can be found in the many entries of the *Harvard Encyclopedia of American Ethnic Groups* (Cambridge, Mass., 1980). Valuable archival and newspaper collections regarding ethnic settlements can be found at the *Immigration History Research Center of the University of Minnesota, the *Balch Institute for Ethnic Studies in Philadelphia, the Asian-American Studies Center at the University of California in Los Angeles, and the YIVO Institute for Jewish Research in New York.

JOHN BODNAR

See ethnic groups by name or region in Appendix A.

ethnohistory and local history.
Ethnohistory is a subdiscipline of anthropology that seeks to reconstruct the cultures of historically recorded societies. Its aims and methodology are closer to those of local historians relative to other branches of cultural anthropology that in the past focused primarily on the study of living tribal societies. In contrast, ethnohistorians use historian's methods to recover and assemble data from the past in addition to using traditional anthropological methods.

Apart from creating a chronicle of events, the ultimate goal of the ethnohistorian is to reconstruct the cultural contexts and common understandings that shaped the actions of a particular historic group. Attention to language—expressed opinions and explicit or implicit premises, norms and principles justifying action—provides clues to widely held values. Thus, ethnohistorians use symbolic analyses and other anthropological theories and concepts to analyze and interpret their data.

For those local historians interested in pursuing cultural explanations of social phenomena, certain anthropological approaches can be useful and informative. Perusal of the journal *Ethnohistory* will demonstrate the range of research strategies and the breadth of inquiry that characterize this field. Below are a few examples of recent work by ethnohistorians and anthropologists whose research focuses on North American subcultures. These are selected to illustrate (minimally) the variety of subjects explored in cultural analyses of documentary data and/or oral histories.

The search for patterned behaviors and shared attitudes and opinions is a time-honored anthropological approach. The complexity encountered in multiethnic communities or in interethnic contacts, however, results in complicated, ambiguous, and often conflicting sentiments.

William H. Lyon, in his article "Navajos in the American Historical Imagination, 1868–1900" (in *Ethnohistory* [1988], 45:2, 237–76), studied documents and photographs of Indians from the late-nineteenth century, examined contrasting attitudes among Southwestern whites who lived in proximity to Navajo groups. Those who were assimilationists, evolutionists, and empiricists admired the Indians and their unique way of life. Other whites, whose attitudes were at best paternalistic, called for the demise of Navajo culture and demanded that Indians become "civilized." They deplored the cultural practices and the moral codes of Navajo culture, which differed from their own (the practice of polygyny was considered scandalous).

Russell K. Skowronek analyzed archival materials and archaeological data from early missions in northern California and found that after more than sixty years of intense Christian missionizing, the Ohlone Indians still conserved much of their original cosmology (see "Sifting the Evidence: Perceptions of Life at the Ohlone [Costanoan] Missions of Alta California," in *Ethnohistory* [1988], 45:4, 675–708). To the dismay of the Franciscan missionaries, they persisted in their traditions of dance, healing rituals. and mortuary practices (when individuals died, Indi-

169

an tradition required burning all their belongings, a practice missionaries deemed barbaric and wasteful). Ceremonies ritually reframe reality and emphasize certain shared ideals that give shape and direction to cultural lifeways. The conservation of Ohlone ceremonies was supported by archaeological finds in the missions' residential areas that included such artifacts as bone- and stone-sucking tools used by Ohone shamans.

Kinship analyses are central to many ethnographic studies, as the ideologies and structures that create and maintain families are embedded in their kinship systems. The rules and norms that govern kinship systems are cultural constructions and vary among societies. David Schneider found that the core symbol in the American kinship system is consanguinity. Although relationship is based on shared "flesh and blood," the biogenetic principle in reality is subordinated to cultural belief and practice. Schneider maintains that American notions of kin-relationship are not biologically derived, but are culturally constructed (see Schneider, *American Kinship: A Cultural Account* [Englewood Cliffs, N.J., 1968]).

In the bilateral system common in the United States, descent is reckoned through parents of both sexes. Conceptually, this system should generate an enormous kindred that would include as members *all* living descendants— siblings and offspring—of all of an individual's ascendants. Following the system's logic, all these persons are "blood kin."

Nevertheless, most American *kindreds remain relatively small. Individ-

ual selectivity is operative here, personal kindreds include only those kin perceived as "close," those to whom a particular person is willing to give his/her love and support. For example "blood kin" such as second cousins may fall completely outside an individual's family circle. The extension and shape of the kindred varies among subcultural groups. In multiethnic communities analyses of how families are defined and constituted can reveal patterns of alliance for mutual aid or for political action.

The kindred also can be fictively extended where there is mutual love and support. The use of kin-terms (aunt, uncle, sister, brother, etc.) between unrelated individuals refer to kin-like relationships. As culture is a system of symbols, the symbolic forms, "words, images institutions, behaviors—in terms of which people actually represented themselves to themselves and to one another" (Clifford Geertz, *Local Knowledge* [N.Y., 1983], p. 58) offer insights as to how a group constructs its social world.

Oral histories allow the ethnohistorian to reach back two or more generations in a family through the transmission of memories. A prime example of this method of reconstructing a lost way of life is found in Marriot's ethnographic novel of the Kiowa tribe. Marriott chronicles the first contact with white people and the subsequent changes in Kiowa culture over three generations (see Alice Marriott, *The Ten Grandmothers: Epic of the Kiowas* [Norman, Okla., 1945]).

There are, of course, problems to be dealt with in collecting oral histories, such as informants' selective recall (tendencies to remember happy events and forget sad ones), or reporting to conformity to cultural rules, rather than deviance or idiosyncracies in behavior. Such problems are discussed by Margaret Willson ("Oral History Interviews: Some History and Practical Suggestions," in Dennis Wiedman, ed., *Ethnohistory: A Researcher's Guide* [Williamsburg, Va., 1986], pp. 61–76).

The examples of ethnohistoric inquiry in American society given here are stringently limited. The point is that for those local historians interested in culture—in discovering the common understandings and shared meanings that motivate and color community actions—anthropological approaches have many rich strategies to offer.

LAURIS McKEE

See clan; family relationships.

ethnography. The term "ethnography" currently denotes a written description of life within a specific cultural group or a subgroup of a larger society. Ethnographic monographs may take an holistic approach, describing all aspects of a group's customary lifeway, or they may focus only on certain aspects of a culture such as family organization, economic practices, political structure, ritual and symbolic systems, or the effects of rapid cultural change on a local group. Ethnographies may be analytic or reflexive in orientation, but unlike ethnology (the comparative analysis of two or more contemporary or historical cultures), an ethnography is a description and analysis of a single group.

LAURIS McKEE

etiquette. Advice on etiquette often merges with works on housekeeping, medical care, letter writing, childrearing, business and legal forms, and lessons in elocution and public speaking. For etiquette book surveys see Sarah Newton, *Learning to Behave: A Guide to American Conduct Books before 1900* (Westport, Conn., 1994) and Deborah Robertson Hodges, *Etiquette: An Annotated Bibliography of Literature Published in English in the United States, 1900 through 1987* (Jefferson, N.C., 1989). There is also an excellent bibliograpny in John F. Kasson, *Rudeness and Civility: Manners in Nineteenth-Century Urban America* (N.Y., 1990). A brief examination of etiquette books will make clear that each generation is convinced that manners are declining. However the survey will also reveal that many standards of behavior thought to be age-old are in fact fairly recent innovations.

While seeming inconsequential, rules of etiquette in fact provide the structure of everyday life; they determine people's social identities and define their social relationships. The topic therefore provides the historian with an excellent means of examining social classifications: who is civil and refined, what is appropriate and inappropriate behavior. Manners define the relationship between the sexes, between adults and children, between employers and employees, and, especially, between rich and poor.

These issues are particularly important in the United States, where citizens pride themselves on being free of class distinctions. U.S. books on manners often repeat democratic pieties while at the same time preserving social distinctions and class privileges. In these works, class distinctions are turned into questions of "refinement" and matters of "taste." John Kasson argues that while the virtues of civility are necessary to a democratic society and to everyday social intercourse, "codes of behavior have often served in unacknowledged ways as checks against a fully democratic order and in support of special interests, institutions of privilege and structures of domination" (p. 3).

One can also see in these rules a response to the stresses caused by the rise of an urban capitalist society. Nineteenth-century rules of conduct were an effort to maintain bourgeois class and gender ideals at a time when the growth of large cities and their concomitant anonymity made it more difficult to sustain old social distinctions. Etiquette rules also attempted to balance the ideal of hard work and self-denial, so necessary to production, with the siren call of a consumer society offering instant gratification and self-indulgence.

By the early twentieth century, one could see in the rules of behavior a shift in emphasis from building "character" to polishing a "personality." See Warren I. Susmand, "'Personality' and the Making of Twentieth Century Culture," in John Higham and Paul K. Condin, eds., *New Directions in American Intellectual History* (Baltimore, 1979). Though the tradition of etiquette books

continues in the works of Leticia Baldrige and "Miss Manners" (Judith Martin), it can be argued that the true inheritors of this tradition are the vast array of psychological self-help books and that they have also been displaced by advertising and the attempt to shape an individual's "lifestyle."

See Gerald Carson, *The Polite Americans: A Wide-Angle View of our More or Less Good Manners over 300 Years* (N.Y., 1996); Sarah E. Newton, *Learning to Behave: A Guide to American Conduct Books before 1900* (Westport, Conn., 1994); Sarah Kortum, *The Hatless Man: An Anthology of Odd & Forgotten Manners* (N.Y., 1995); Deborah Robertson Hodges, *Etiquette: An Annotated Bibliography of Literature Published in English in the United States, 1900 through 1987* (Jefferson, N.C., 1989); and Arlie Russell Hochschild, *The Managed Heart: Commercialization of Human Feeling* (Berkeley, 1983).

NORMA PRENDERGAST

evangelical. An evangelical is a Protestant Christian who believes in man's sinful condition and the need for salvation, in the revelation of God's grace, and the necessity of spiritual renovation through the experience of faith. In the last two decades of the twentieth century, some Roman Catholics, seeking a more emotional experience of faith, have also been identified as evangelicals.

F

fact. See historical proof.

factor. An agent, dealer, or middleman.

failure and local history. Cycles of "boom and bust" are as characteristic of the American experience as the familiar "rags to riches" story. Although most people would rather perpetuate success stories and most local historical activities celebrate "the winners," personal, organizational, and regional failures should not be forgotten when recounting the history of a locality. By including the saga of the unsuccessful, the local historian provides a more complex and realistic perspective on the past.

In the nineteenth century, many communities that ultimately failed were founded on *utopian principles. The list is long and varied, including the Shakers, Fourierists, the New Harmony Community (in Pennsylvania and Indiana), the Oneida Community, and many others. While the social and economic programs of these particular groups did not stand the test of time, it is important that their stories be told so that the history of social reform and "alternative lifestyles" is fully recorded.

The failure of utopian social movements affected a relatively small number of communities, but economic downturns shaped the histories of many cities, towns, and villages. Most places have experienced agricultural and/or business growth and then decline. In some cases the economic downturns were overcome relatively quickly; in others, problems persisted for long periods. The "faded glory" of many upstate New York towns, as well as towns and cities in the Midwestern "Rust Belt," testifies to the tenacity of "hard times." Sometimes a community simply disappeared. The American West is not the only area where "*ghost towns" dot the countryside. U.S. history is replete with "panics" and "depressions," as well as lost opportunities and schemes that did not come to fruition. In some cases success for one area meant failure for another. The Erie Canal lead to the creation of great cities at Syracuse, Rochester, and Buffalo; it caused a loss of population and economic dominance for Geneva and Canandaigua, New York. By analyzing these larger movements and explaining their local impact, the local historian makes the history of the community understandable.

Large economic trends affect whole communities; personal failures are also reflected in history. The presence of poor houses, alms houses, and orphan asylums in most nineteenth-century towns and cities were symbolic of very personal tragedies. City and county jails, and state and federal penitentiaries are all indications of social ills that are still very much with us. For women, the existence of prostitution and welfare dependency represents personal difficulties that our communities have handled in different ways over time.

The sources for documenting personal and institutional failures may be difficult to find. One good source is old newspapers. Others include old bank records, labor-union records, bankruptcy records, and court records. This is an area where *oral history interviews can also be important.

As difficult as they may be, the stories of lost dreams and unfulfilled promises constitute a vital element in the histories of all communities. In retelling these stories, the local historian paints a fuller and more realistic portrait of the past while allowing for a better perspective on current problems faced by the locality. By dealing with failure as well as success, the local historian helps the community more fully appreciate their collective past, which should assist them in facing their collective future.

G. DAVID BRUMBERG

fairs. "World's fairs" have been important events—culturally as well as commercially—in modern industrial nations since the first one, held in Paris in 1798. Governments and businesses from many nations, but especially the host country, participate as exhibitors. The fairs are open to the public and generally last four to six months. The first in the United States was the Crystal Palace Exhibition in New York in 1853, an echo of the important Crystal Palace Exhibition in London in 1851. The great fairs since then are a record of many high moments in American life:

among them, the Centennial Exposition at Philadelphia, 1876; the World's Columbian Exposition at Chicago, 1893; the St. Louis World's Fair of 1904; and the Panama-Pacific International Exposition at San Francisco, 1915. A number of such special celebrations in the 1920s and 1930s gave further boosts to the love of history, historic buildings, and the concepts of historic preservation. Among these were the Sesquicentennial of Independence, 1926, and the Bicentennial of the Birth of George Washington, 1932, both of which focused attention on specific historic sites and on preservation concerns in general. Even future-oriented celebrations, such as Chicago's Century of Progress, 1933, and the New York World's Fair of 1939, focused attention on the past, if only as background to the wonders of the future.

See Leslie Prosterman, *Ordinary Life, Festival Days: Aesthetics in the Midwestern County Fair* (Washington, D.C., 1995); Robert W. Rydell, *All the World's a FAIR: Visions of Empire at American International Expositions, 1876–1916* (Chicago, 1984), and his *World of Fairs: The Century-of-Progress Expositions* (Chicago, 1993); Helen Augur, *The Book of Fairs* ([1939] Detroit, 1990); Frances Shemanski, *A Guide to Fairs and Festivals in the United States* (Westport, Conn., 1984); and U.S. Department of Housing and Urban Development, *The Urban Fair: How Cities Celebrate Themselves* (Washington, D.C., 1981).

JOHN PEARCE

fakelore. This term was devised by Richard Dorson (1916–1981), folklorist at Indiana University, to describe commercial, cleverly packaged, uncritical and random collections of stories presented as genuine folklore, such as those about Paul Bunyan, Joe Magarac, and Pecos Bill. He also railed against inauthentic presentations that simulated folk traditions, such as folk singers and folk festivals. Dorson's ire blazed during the 1940s when Disney and American propagandists created commercial versions of "national" folklore to unite the country. Dorson wrote, "fakelore is the presentation of spurious and synthetic writings under the claim that they are genuine folklore. These productions are not collected in the field but are rewritten from earlier literary and journalistic sources in an endless chain of regurgitation, or they may even be made out of whole cloth. . . ." See "Fakelore," in Richard M. Dorson, *American Folklore & the Historian* (Chicago, 1971).

Today, the idea of "invented tradition," the term used by Eric Hobsbawn and Terence Ranger, is being looked at more objectively as a part of the cultural process. In particular, scholars are now considering the image of the "folk" in popular culture that communities use for boosting their image, creating an identity, or carrying a sense of tradition. This process is also referred to in the scholarly literature, especially in Europe, as "folklorism" or "folklorisms."

See Regina Bendix, *In Search of Authenticity* (Madison, Wis., 1998); Venetia J. Newall, "The Adaptation of Folklore and Tradition (Folklorismus)," *Folklore*, 98 (1987), pp. 131–51; Hermann Bausinger, "Toward a Critique of Folklorism Criticism," in *German Volkskunde: A Decade of Theoretical Con-* *frontation, Debate, and Reorientation* (Bloomington, Ind., 1986), pp. 113–23; and Vilmos Voigt, "Folklore and 'Folklorism' Today," in *Folklore Studies in the Twentieth Century*, Venetia J. Newall, ed. (Suffolk, Eng., 1978), pp. 419–24.

SIMON BRONNER

See folklore and folklife.

family. There are many different types of families. Anthropologists have identified some helpful categories.

There are those with *unilineal descent*: *Clans are groups of people who claim descent from a common ancestor either through the male line (called patriclans) or a common ancestor through the female line (called matriclans). Phratries and moieties are generally loose associations of clans based upon historical or religious factors. Their functions vary. A moiety is a grouping of clans within a phratry often based upon myth and often defining eligible marriage partners.

Cognative descent defines individuals who can trace descent to a common ancestor or founder through either a mother or father's line.

There are families based upon *bilateral*, or two-sided kinship systems, that is, through both parents, which is how people in most Western counties trace kinship. These produce relationships that are known as kindred, which consist of all the people that a specific person recognizes as a relative. This kinship system does not usually hold large tracts of land in common nor is it as bound to traditional place and ideas. Thus kinship families are generally seen as more modern and as functioning well in a capitalistic society partially because of their flexibility and mobility.

For more detailed descriptions of family structure and function, see, for example, James Peoples and Garrick Bailey, *Humanity* (Minneapolis, 1994).

Our definition of family today includes, in addition to two parents and their children, single-parent families, blended families, and families where both parents are of the same gender.

LAURIS McKEE

See clan; family history; family relationships; household.

family history. Family history is a new field attracting scholars in the last three decades. Developing out of the "New *Social History" of the 1960s, social historians interested in family life formed part of a larger effort to reconstruct the private lives of everyday people. For them, "history from the bottom up" also meant probing the daily interactions of family members to understand the impact of family life on the individual as well as to understand the ways in which families resisted or supported the prescriptions of the larger society. Yet, the new family historians of the 1970s, 1980s, and 1990s did not break entirely fresh ground. Prior to their interest in family as a legitimate area of academic study, two other groups—antiquarians and behavioral scientists—pioneered both the historical materials as well as the theoretical context for the work.

Although the purpose of antiquarian and genealogical research differs in large part from that of family historians, it was the by-product of that diligent research that attracted historians. Indeed, the recovery work of antiquarians and genealogists developed and preserved vast collections of documentary materials—now available to family historians. Wills, deeds, town records, *census reports, *cemetery inscriptions, and a host of other *material culture artifacts as well as documents were the grist for their personal histories. Indeed many of the research methods such as collecting personal statistics from government documents like the federal census or town records or searching out material artifacts such as *photographs and personal documents were techniques developed by genealogists and antiquarians. While historians searched out the personal writings and published works of the highborn, political or military notables, antiquarians and genealogists mined more humble strata. The results of their painstaking explorations (and off-handed rummaging) often found their way into local archives and have become valuable collections today. In addition, many government documents such as the federal census manuscript schedules were microfilmed to meet the demand of their work. In the process of their work, these independent scholars created some truly remarkable repositories, such as the Salt Lake City library of the Church of Jesus Christ and Latter Day Saints.

While the genealogists and antiquarians scoured the countryside for documents and artifacts, the behavioral scientists—sociologists, psychologists and anthropologists—established theoretical models for understanding the structure and complexities of family relationships. To most of these researchers, the family provided a fundamental unit that seemed universal to most, if not all, human experience. To understand the construction of the individual, behavioral scientists examined the way in which that person's life came to be encapsulated, organized and shaped by the internal authority of the family. Moreover, social scientists theorized that the external forces working on the family could be resisted or reinforced depending on how the family unit responded to larger societal pressures. Initially, the theoretical work of social scientists became important to social historians when they began to focus on larger social groups delineated by religion, *ethnicity, economics, or skin color. Naturally, when interest in the family developed, this same theoretical base informed family historians.

The field of family history did not emerge with one seminal work or a particular school of historians, rather the earliest family historians simply chose families as the best subject group for their interests in other social forces. Bernard Bailyn's *Education in the Formation of American Society* (Chapel Hill, N.C., 1960) and Edmund Morgan's *The Puritan Family* (Boston, 1966) were not self-conscious attempts to create a new field. However, by 1970 John Demos recognized the emergence of family history as a new field in the foreword of his work, *A Little Commonwealth* (N.Y.). In his assessment, Demos noted that the appearance of works that could be categorized as "family history" proliferated, but, on the whole, the current body of scholarship lacked a solid set of "guiding themes and questions." All the same, Demos predicted that family history was an important new development in social history. He also observed that one of the most useful methods for exploring family life was through the study of local history. By confining his work to materials "indigenous" to Plymouth Colony, Demos hoped to construct as accurate a picture of family structure and relationships as possible.

By the early 1980s, more historians were actively working in the field, and, in the process, refining the direction that family history moved in the last decade of the twentieth century. More than just a method of recapturing the social experience of everyday people, the study of the family provides social historians an ideal "place" to explore the construction of race, class, and gender. A more inclusive approach for studying gender, relationships between generations and across ethnic lines, current methodology in family history attempts to weave the conventional "impressionistic" evidence with the quantitative evidence of social history. By Jacquelyn Dowd Hall and others, *Like a Family* (Chapel Hill, N.C., 1987) combined the interests of family, social, and economic historians to reconstruct the Southern cotton-mill communities. As *Like a Family* demonstrates, the family unit was the primary point of intersection between private and public life. Clearly, it is the place, metaphorically as well as physically, where human/social reproduction and production are linked. Since individual identity is generally formed in the context of family, the construction of race and class identity must also be part of that process. From this perspective, the evolution of American society is irrevocably linked to the influences both emanating from and acting upon the family units that make up the larger community.

Aside from the advantages, family historians have also recognized there are also inherent problems. How can those working in the field create a standardized definition beyond a single individual historian's work? Once scholars began to look at the family unit as a valuable category for analysis, they also began to understand the endless permutation of family models. Despite the fact that most cultures recognize some type of family arrangement, the forms and functions vary widely and are not always comparable. Even in the American context, the concept of family differed over time and across distinct cultural/sectional divides; this variation makes nonsense of descriptors like "traditional" or "modern."

In seventeenth-century New England, the social identity of family generally encompassed all who lived under one roof under the authority of the male head, but in practice many New England families were nuclear. In contrast, Native Americans' families typically included individuals beyond the "*household" members, and "households" were not necessarily defined by Anglo-patriarchal standards. Iroquois families, for instance, defined kin along *matrilineal lines and, though individual families may have shared distinct hearths within the family dwelling, Iroquois longhouses contained large extended-family units linked by a senior female relative. Should historians define a longhouse as a group of families or as one unit? In the slave quarters of southern plantations, African Americans attempted to maintain nuclear families around conjugal couples, but were often forced to rely on a broader definition of kinship due to the realities of slave life. Sale, work in the fields, and separation between neighboring plantations meant slave families functioned very differently from their white neighbors. How does a historian winnow out what a particular group desired as family patterns from what they were forced to accept?

In the nineteenth and into the twentieth centuries, as the market revolution helped to define a new U.S. middle-class, Americans more fully adopted a nuclear family model. The "cult of *domesticity" dictated that women remain in the home as caretakers, men become breadwinners, and conjugal couples with children form the appropriate family archetype. Again, there were obvious concessions to the exigencies of the industrial workplace. Despite the impact of hegemonic U.S. cultural ideals on immigrant families, alternative family structures persisted. Families who relied on factory labor for their subsistence often took in boarders and perhaps incorporated them into their family structures as more than just paying guests. Middle-class families often incorporated domestic staff into their lives as more than just household laborers.

In the West, the last half of the century was a time of enormous change for native people as assimilation became a national policy after 1880. The Dawes General Allotment Act encouraged native people to become individual landowners through the break up of reservations into family-run farms. Indian leaders argued loudly against the Dawes Act, pointing out that under their communal land-ownership system everyone was protected. As individuals, all Indian people would not have the benefit of access to land for cultivation or pasture. Despite great pressure, many tribal groups resisted and continued to operate in communal systems.

Other Americans developed new models of family and community life in clear protest to the prevailing industrial/nuclear trend. The Shakers rejected family altogether and opted for celibate separation of the sexes. Free love communities rejected "traditional" marriage and practiced plural or universal marriage. Some groups even abolished particular parent/child relationships and imagined a communal kind of parenting. The Mormons practiced their own version of plural marriage and also tinkered with mainstream American family structure.

Clearly, throughout the nineteenth century, American notions of what constituted "family"—or what it should be—remained unsettled. They seem to remain unsettled. The language of recent political debates over "family values" underscores that confusion. Certainly, the "ideal" family by mainstream American definition is the nuclear parent/children unit. Yet, the evidence points overwhelmingly to the fact that this is an ideal, and the reality is that many families in twentieth-century United States are not typically "ideal." Indeed, much of the interest in family history has been a direct result of the puzzling political rhetoric that invokes "traditional" family values with no clear indication of whose "tradition" and from what era these values emanate. Even if there were agreement as to what

"traditional" values are, there exists a great disparity between the "ideal" and the reality of family life.

As a result, family historians often find—willingly or not—a political dimension exists in their work. Often, political and social critics demand that historians provide definitive and concrete models that can inform their contemporary dialogue—with little understanding of the difficulty in developing broad generalizations. The shifting landscape of family patterns against the economic and social trends of any given period makes such particular observations extremely difficult. Instead, historians often find that there is great variation across time and space that militates against broad general models. As historian Stephanie Coontz noted, "What we [family historians] need to do is approach families as organic parts of a total yet ever-changing network of social interactions in which equilibrium is never achieved" (Stephanie Coontz, *The Social Origins of Private Life* [London, 1988], p. 16). Family should be understood in the historical context as a vehicle for governing and organizing individual behavior within the unit and as an interactive part of a much larger set of changing historical and cultural imperatives. This kind of cultural and historical relativity seems to lend itself well to another related field: local history. Coontz's own work demonstrates how fruitful such collaboration can be.

While Coontz produced a comprehensive study of the history of the American family, *The Social Origins of Private Life* and *The Way We Never Were* (N.Y., 1992), many of the works she drew upon for her study were local and community studies. Thus, for her larger synthesis, scholars of local or regional history provided the raw material in their particular histories of small places and minor groups. In short, both fields, local and family history, have much to offer each other.

Family history is now an important part of many college and university curriculums. A growing number of sessions at national conferences have been devoted to family history as well as several scholarly meetings held at Carleton University in Ottawa, Ontario, that focused entirely on the family. The National Council on Family Relations in Minneapolis, Minnesota, publishes a *Journal of Family History*. See Stephanie Coontz, *American Families: A Multicultural Reader* (N.Y., 1998).

SUSAN OUELLETTE

See antiquarian; Family History Library; genealogy, an archivist's view.

Family History Library of the Church of Jesus Christ of Latter Day Saints.

The largest genealogy library in the world is operated by the Church of Jesus Christ of Latter Days Saints in Salt Lake City, Utah. The five-floor library has 142,000 square feet of space and houses 278,000 books, 711,000 microfiche, and 2 million rolls of microfilm. Each year the church adds 1,000 books and 5,000 rolls of microfilm to the collection.

The library does not respond to telephone or written requests for research. However, many of the sources are on microforms in the 3,400 branch libraries located around the world. The library houses many local and community history books, family histories, maps, and all forms of records. Local branches have microform copies of many of these books and records; or they can be ordered from Salt Lake.

The library is located at 35 NW Temple Street, Salt Lake City, Utah, 84150; (801) 240-2331; <www.familysearch. org>. Admission is free. Four-hundred volunteers help an average of 2,400 daily visitors. The library is open Monday 7:30 A.M. to 5:00 P.M. and Tuesday–Saturday 7:30 A.M. to 10:00 P.M.

JERRY BRISCO

See International Genealogical Index.

family relationships. Families today come in many combinations and sorting out relationships can be difficult. Most confusion seems to center on cousins and cousins once removed. This might help: first cousins are the children of siblings. Second cousins are the children of first cousins. Use of the term removed—as in first cousin once removed—indicates a shift in the generations. Imagine an abbreviated family tree with a brother and a sister, their children (who are cousins), and their grandchildren (who are second cousins to each other). The relationship between one of the grandchildren descended from the sister, with one of the cousins descended from the brother— that is, with someone of the previous generation—gives you a first cousin once removed.

Step sisters and step brothers share one parent but not both. Blended families today include any number of new relationships, many not based upon blood ties.

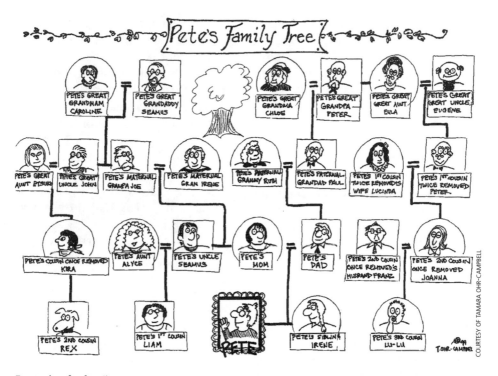

Example of a family tree.

Farm Security Administration photographs.

The Farm Security Administration (FSA) was created in the Department of Agriculture in 1937 to succeed the New Deal Resettlement Administration (RA). Its purpose was to assist farmers, but one of its most notable legacies is a series of photographs documenting American life. Under the direction of Roy Emerson Stryker, head of the special photo section of the RA and the FSA from 1935 to 1942, over 77,000 black-and-white photographs were produced by a number of outstanding photographers including Dorthea Lange and Walker Evans. Early on, these photographs documented rural life and the negative impact of the Great Depression, farm mechanization,

and the Dust Bowl. In 1942, the photography unit was moved to the Office of War Information and recorded the mobilization for World War II.

The collection is housed in the Prints and Photography Division of the Library of Congress. These world-famous photographs can be accessed through their website: <http//memory.loc.gov/ammem/fsowhome.html>. A number of them have been published in books on photography and in books of photographs from several states. The entire collection is available in microform with the photos cataloged by region and subject: America 1935–1946; Photographs of the U.S. Department of Agriculture Farm Security Administration; and United States Office of War.

See also Penelope Dixon, "Photographers of the Farm Security Administration: An Annotated Bibliography, 1930–1980," in *Garland Reference Library of the Humanities*, vol. 373.

NORMA PRENDERGAST

See Library of Congress; photography.

federal involvement with place names. Federal concern with geographic place names is associated with maintaining accurate published maps. For that reason the United States Board on Geographic Names is a function of the U.S. Geological Survey and has the responsibility of reviewing existing place names, proposals made to change existing place names, and proposals made to establish names for places where none had existed previously. To insure that local expertise is brought into this process, the U.S. Board normally works with a state-level names authority. This could be a committee of historians, geologists, archivists, and geographers who work together just for this purpose, or it could be an existing agency, such as a historical society, which serves as the names authority. It is this state authority that is primarily responsible for collecting the background information and documentation that the federal board needs to makes its decision, and for making recommendations regarding naming proposals. It is only the federal board, however, that approves or rejects the proposed name.

Historians often seek information on *place names and their derivation, and this research can sometimes be facilitated by consulting the federal database of geographic names, known as the GNIS, which is available on the Internet at the USGS website. Not all place names in local use can be found here, and for those established some time ago, records of their approval or derivation may not be available.

The mailing address for the United States Board on Geographic Names, is U.S. Geological Survey, 523 National Center, Reston, Virginia 20192-0523. The web address for this agency is <http://mapping.usgs.gov/www/gnis/bgn.html>.

PHILIP LORD, JR.

See place names.

fee simple. Property held in fee simple or fee absolute is owned unconditionally and will descend to the owner's heirs even if he or she dies intestate. It is distinguished from an entailed estate where there are limitations on who may inherit and under what circumstance.

fees, consulting. In the 1980s, there was an expectation that staff at our state-funded museum would be available to give advice without charge to volunteers responsible for the ever-increasing number of local history museums in New South Wales, Australia. Each year I would respond to about six requests in my field, some involving travel to a distant part of the state, with a requirement for overnight accommodation and meals. However, with the slavish adoption of the user-pay principle, the state museum where I worked now imposes a charge for consultancy services and travel expenses.

A number of retired and retrenched museum professionals are also now available to undertake consultancy work of various kinds. A wise director of a local history museum should find out what consultancy services are currently available from state museums as well as from private enterprise, and costs, before making any commitment.

As I now work as a museum/heritage consultant on a professional basis, I find it necessary to prepare a budget for each request, no matter how small. The first step is to obtain a brief. Usually this is prepared during a preliminary discussion about the project, as rarely does the client know exactly what is required and how long the task or project would take. (In some cases I might seek a fee to cover expenses, if the location of the meeting is remote.)

Once there is an agreed brief, the task of preparing a budget is simplified:

Consulting: Hourly rate with a minimum number of hours per session, usually three. The actual rate would depend on the nature of the work and the consultant's standing in the profession. If the client cannot describe the full scope of work or feels other tasks are likely to be added later, a specified number of hours is adopted with provision for a budget review at intervals.

Travel: If travel is by public transport (air or train) or I use my own vehicle (or a combination), I do make some allowance, depending on the location of the client and the nature of the tasks. In some cases, it is necessary to rent a car from a railway station or airport. If I am required to spend more than half a day in traveling, I usually request an allowance at half the consulting rates.

Accommodation and meals: I allow for three-star accommodation (average) if I expect to be away from my home/office for two or more days. While I operate on minimum costs, the amount would be substantially higher if the work is in a state capital.

Insurance: One of my regular clients requires: worker's compensation—even though I rarely employ anyone to assist me, although I do subcontract specialized support work; public liability—because my work may involve inspecting heritage structures that could be unsafe (so is crossing a busy road!); and professional indemnity—this is very expensive in Australia, but may be required by state government bodies and local government authorities. A separate insurance policy is required for each contract. The insurance broker recommends that the period of coverage should be extended for at least twelve months after completion of a contract. This adds considerably to the cost.

Telephone: I make provision for long-distance calls (details provided on Telecom statement), but I do not charge separately for local calls or e-mail.

Postage: Again some provision. Recently a client requested that I handle the distribution of copies of a draft report to a long list of people. From earlier experience, I found that the purchase of special envelopes, delivering envelopes to the post office, and actual mailing costs eats into a straight consulting fee.

Photocopying and binding: While I use my own photocopier for small tasks, production costs can be high. In addition, if there is a requirement that copies of reports be bound, it may be more efficient to use a service center for such a task. One client likes colored photographs in the final report, so this is included as a separate item in the budget.

Photography: Usually there is provision, but I charge at cost, since these services, including the supply of film, are on a mail-order basis, with digital photographs usually provided through e-mail and by mail on a CD-ROM. In general, I find that it is essential to maintain a photographic record of a project.

Subcontracts: A quotation from a subcontractor is attached to the main quotation. In some cases, an administrative fee of 10 percent is added to cover the paperwork and supervision in handling a subcontract.

Contingency: This is necessary so that any additional requests by the client can be met from the budget. I allow 10 percent of the total budget.

While some clients express initial concern at the size of the budget, I find my method much easier to explain because there is a sound basis and full details are provided. My main problem with the provision of quotations is the need to allow for the expanding nature of a project.

Beware of the client who says: "While you are looking at this heritage building, would you please take a look at two other buildings we want to do something with. While it is outside the contract, it won't take you long to let me have your opinion."

DESMOND KENNARD

fiction. See historical fiction.

filiopietism. A term for a child's debt to a parent, particularly to a father, and the child's proper regard for that parent. The word, when used to describe local history, refers to the way that nineteenth-century local historians honored and wrote about the founders of a community—in deferential, nonquestioning terms. While this might be an ideal way of parenting—and even that is suspect—it is not a good way of researching or writing history, for it cuts off questioning the past and seeking answers in favor of accepting the information given. Filiopietistic history is that which accepts an older idea that the only actors in history were the healthy, wealthy, and wise—unlike the trends of the past 25 years in which females, males who failed, those who left a place, and people of various ethnicities and races are also part of the local story. See local history themes.

financial and business records. These represent a valuable but underused resource for the local historian. Because they document the economic ups and downs of a locality, they provide a window into the dynamics of community relationships. Interactions between business elites, salaried employees, and laboring people can be made vivid using these records.

The R. G. Dun and Company Credit Ledgers constitute one of the most extensive and important aggregations of business records in the United States. Located at Harvard University's Baker Library, the collection contains about 2,580 volumes that encompass 249 linear feet of shelf space. Although the volumes span the period 1840 to 1895, the bulk of the material pertains to the 1850s, 1860s, and 1870s.

In 1841, Lewis Tappan established the Mercantile Agency in New York City to gather credit information on merchants in the United States and Canada doing business in the New York City area. By the late 1850s, the firm had been taken over by Robert Graham Dun and the business—by then the dominant player in the field—continued as R. G. Dun and Company until merging with the Bradstreet Company, forming Dun and Bradstreet, in 1933.

At one time during the nineteenth century, R. G. Dun and Company had as many as 2,000 local agents throughout the country who reported semiannually (more often if circumstances required) on businesses in their area. These reports were sent to the central office in New York City where they were recorded in ledgers arranged by state and then by county or city. This information was sold to individuals and business firms.

Although the main focus was financial, the reports often contain information of a personal nature regarding the owners and top officials in the concerns under scrutiny. The agents typically reported on the individual entrepreneur's background, marital status, church membership, involvement in civic affairs, reputation in the community, and previous business experience. It was not unusual for the agents to give their own subjective opinion of the business acumen and credit worthiness of the subject. In the case of this author, a report in the 1880s indicated that it was my grandmother, rather than my grandfather, who was the real "brains of the operation."

As these reports were relied upon by individuals and institutions contemplating the loan of money, they needed to have a high degree of accuracy. The R. G. Dun and Company Credit Ledgers present their subjects "warts and all" and therefore are a valuable source for anyone interested in getting the true history of a place. They are a good corrective to the optimistic *boosterism usually found in nineteenth-century newspapers and pronouncements of local governments and other public bodies.

The fact that the records are arranged by state and within each state by county or city makes them very useful for the local historian. This arrangement facilitates the examination of the major business entities within a locality. The presence of a name index in most volumes is another valuable feature.

There are some drawbacks to the Dun and Company records. The individuals and businesses reported upon tended to be the largest and most successful in an area, those making purchases outside the community and/or applying for credit. Thus, smaller enterprises do not always show up. The records are sometimes incomplete, and they can be difficult to read because of illegible handwriting and extensive abbreviation. Permission to publish any material from the records must be obtained from the Baker Library and Dun and Bradstreet. Perhaps the greatest difficulty for local historians is the fact that the Credit Ledgers are available only at the Baker Library at Harvard University.

If these impediments are too great, the local historian can explore the possibility of using financial records closer to home. Local banks, credit bureaus, chambers of commerce, better business bureaus, and other business-oriented concerns, including local businesses themselves, may be willing to allow the use of their historical records. Although such records are usually jealously guarded, the local historian may get access by assuring the firm that the records will be used in an evenhanded way for noncompetitive, noncommercial purposes. If the attempt is successful it will return dividends in a more well-rounded, informative historical analysis.

For more information, see James H. Madison, "The Credit Reports of R. G. Dun & Co. as Historical Sources," *Historical Methods Newsletter* (September 1975); and James H. Madison, "The Evolution of Commercial Credit Reporting Agencies in Nineteenth-Century America," *Business History Review*, 48, no. 2 (summer 1974). Baker Library at Harvard can be located at: <http://library.hbs.edu/>, which contains a list of the volumes available by date, and state and county.

G. DAVID BRUMBERG

Filipinos. See Appendix A.

Finberg, H. P. R. Finberg (1900–1974) started work as a typographer with a number of eminent publishers; he set up his own publishing concern and was responsible for the first edition of A. E. Housman's poems in 1929. He remained interested in printing and design all his life, remaining on the board of a major printing press and acting as advisor to H.M. Stationery Office in the U.K. He received international awards for his designs as late as 1965; involved in religious translation and publishing, he was acknowledged by the Catholic

Church with the award of the Knight of St. John. His local history interests commenced as an amateur. In 1949, he published *Tavistock Abbey: A Study in the Social and Economic History of Devon*, and with W. G. Hoskins a volume of *Devonshire Studies*. In 1952, when Hoskins left Leicester University, Finberg was appointed reader and head of the department of English Local History, a controversial appointment since this was his first academic post at the age of 52, but he was strongly supported by some of the major historians of the day. In 1963, he became the first professor of local history in any university in the U.K.; he retired in 1965 but carried on working until his death in 1974. He was a prolific author of local history, especially early medieval history, and of the West Country (e.g., collections of Anglo-Saxon Charters in Devon, Cornwall, the West Midlands, and Wessex, etc.). He, like Hoskins, with whom he collaborated on several ventures, was interested in *landscape history. He wrote about the study of local history (see *The Local Historian and His Theme* [1952]). He was editor of *Approaches to History: A Symposium* (Toronto, 1962); and with V. H. T. Skipp, *Local History: Objective and Pursuit* (Newton Abbot, England, 1967). He was one of the general editors of the mammoth *Agrarian History*, which continued after his death, and he served as President of the British Agrarian History Society 1966–1968. He was also interested in towns, producing, with Professor Maurice Beresford, one of the leading topographical historians, a handlist of *English Medieval Boroughs* (Newton Abbot, Eng., 1973). He was throughout his life a strong advocate of the link between academic and amateur local historians, promoting both national and local societies for the advancement of local history.

ALAN ROGERS

Finns. See Appendix A.

folklore and folklife. The materials of folklore and folklife are expressions of cultural tradition. Typically transmitted by word of mouth, custom, imitation, and demonstration, enactments of legends or games are socially shared and hence people can draw identities from them. Among the common social identities that folklore and folklife represent for people are family, ethnicity, religion, occupation, class, gender, region, age, and, significantly, community. The ties of folklore and folklife to community are apparent from the ways that tradition is used to signify, and adapt to, the place in which folklore is performed and persists through time. Insofar as such tradition is usually associated with cultural practices within communities, it reveals locality in the way it depicts the people who inherit and transmit their experiences, values, symbols, and concerns, and references the places that act as settings shaping identities. Its significance in local historical work is in its special evidence of local knowledge and cultural practice through time.

"Folklore" was a term coined by Englishman W. J. Thoms in 1846 to replace use of "popular antiquities" and "popular literature" for forms of cultural traditions. He had been inspired by the *Volkskunde* ("knowledge of the people") presented by Jacob and Wilhelm

Grimm in the early nineteenth century in what is now Germany. They collected ancient tales that shared similar plots from contemporary storytellers who included in their performances details of local sites and practices. The repetition and variation characteristic of oral tradition among ordinary people, they argued, formed valuable cultural evidence that could be used to trace international diffusion of ideas and at the same time the development of local and national traditions. Sir Walter Scott's collection of Scottish ballads and folk songs, also in the early nineteenth century, drew similar attention to an overlooked artistic tradition among ordinary people that recorded and significantly interpreted the meaning of historical events. The antiquarian and literary interests of many early "folklorists" in the British Isles identified folklore by its comparable, and relatively stable, textual forms—the lyrics of ballads, the plots of tales, the rules of games. Indicative of the local collecting enterprise was a massive "county folklore" series of books (published by "The Folklore Society," established in 1878) recording examples of oral traditions throughout England. In addition to showcasing artistry in oral performances, the collections also uncovered valuable references to groups and events that were regionally significant but not typically covered in documentary records. In these collections are found lasting themes connecting folklore and local history of finding traditions that illuminated the diverse, often unrecorded heritage of a nation at its roots, providing reminders of creativity in everyday life by ordinary people, and raising questions about the sources and spread of ideas in culture.

If the British folklorists tended to emphasize the "lore," others, particularly in Scandinavia and Germany, focused more on different communities of "folk," many of which had similarly been overlooked. The materials included social and material practices that bound a community, including crafts, housebuilding, and cooking. The significant context was social—the groups among whom the practices were functioning—and geographical—the landscapes and environments in which people were forced to adapt their traditions. For focus on everyday lives, the term "folklife" began circulating in the nineteenth century as a counterpart to folklore. Folklife scholars developed presentations of the social and physical contexts of ordinary groups in "folk" museums such as *Skansen* in Sweden. Organizers displayed traditional buildings, crafts, and landscapes representing deeply rooted, regional cultures of the nation. In showing the aesthetic patterns displayed and adaptations to the environment that such structures revealed, they hoped to discern the core and borders of cultures, the symbols by which social identities were communicated, and the relations of humans to their surroundings. They implied that such communities and their structures carried with them a pride in the ancient legacies, and often a shared racial stock, that aligned a nation-state with its culture.

To many Europeans, the United States appeared too new as a nation and too socially and physically diverse as a settlement to register significant findings for folklore and folklife research. As the United States underwent rapid social change in the nineteenth century, several writers took the lead in presenting literature and local historical chronicles that recorded and interpreted an emergent folklore in America. Notables such as Nathaniel Hawthorne, Washington Irving, and James Fenimore Cooper helped create an American literature based on their representation of local place legends, comic anecdotes of ethnic and rustic characters, folk-hero tales, and customs of "pioneer" practices. In cities such as Philadelphia and New York that were rapidly growing with newcomers, many immigrants, and industrializing, antiquarians took note of endangered traditions, even if they appeared to be of short duration compared with the "antiquities" of Europe and Asia. John Fanning Watson, for instance, published *Annals of Philadelphia and Pennsylvania in the Olden Time* (1830), he claimed, "to awaken the public to the utility of bringing out their traditions and ancient family records." He collected this material with questionnaires given to the elder residents who recalled the everyday practices of the past, and in the process, he recorded beliefs, crafts, foodways, and local legends. Before "folklore" was even coined, he called this material "traditionary lore," and went on to compile similar tomes for New York City, bringing out the cultural depth of American communities. He explained that the traditions taken from ordinary individuals' traditions gave insight into their perceptions (embedded in narratives) of what happened in the past—what they thought of as history—and he presaged a wider view of heritage, including everyday life and cultural expressions, extending the understanding of local historical legacies.

Although the United States was relatively new as a nation, many observers proclaimed that a rich and varied store of folklore indeed thrived there for abundant reasons: (1) the spread and extent of small settlements and ethnic-religious communities gave rise to a variety of local traditions and the transplantation of others; (2) the varied landscape, distinctive flora and fauna, and new encounters with the environment as settlers moved west inspired the narration of natural surroundings in the form of place names, beliefs, customs, and legends; (3) terrain and conditions unfamiliar to settlers forced adaptation of Old World material traditions in the form of foodways, architecture, clothing, and crafts; (4) isolation of some settlement pockets on mountains, in valleys, on islands, and along shores fostered the persistence of traditions; (5) encounters of settlers with American Indians and the mixing of races, classes, and ethnic groups encouraged cultural exchanges; (6) the creation and maintenance of a new republic with constituent regions and states resulted in national/state/regional rituals and performances, some of which became embedded into culture as they were accepted as traditions.

In 1888, an organization consisting mainly of writers, clergy, professors, museum professionals, and local historians formed the American Folklore Society "for the collection of the fast-vanishing remains of Folk-Lore in America." In the proclamation of the society's founder, William Wells Newell, is specific reference to local historical work when he called the "remains of a tradition which was once the inheritance of every speaker of the English tongue" as essential to the historian of American life as "the dust of letters and pamphlets" in local historical societies. He emphasized the direct experience of local traditions as they are spoken, sung, performed, and demonstrated, taken from people in their homes and communities as a necessary supplement to the analysis of human legacies. In its early years, the Society had an orbit of chapters devoted to local research in Philadelphia, Berkeley, Boston, and Hampton (an organization working particularly on African American lore), among others. In the twentieth century, regional and state societies formed and continued the spirit of local studies, including a few directly associated with historical societies such as the New York Folklore Society and Pennsylvania Folklore Society. This "fieldwork" orientation toward the interpretation of culture through the collection of living traditions, at the heart of the work of these organizations, is still part of the folkloristic enterprise. A revision of Newell's vision, however, for today's research is the embracing of folk as representing a communicative process used by people acting in groups. In this view, folk is not a level of society, but a type of learning and expression used by all people; it can be useful to reveal social needs and identities enacted in different settings. Further, the distinctions between the scope of folklore and folklife have arguably become less noticeable in the late twentieth century as cultural and historical investigators typically take into account material and social traditions.

Revisions of historical research to interpret the influence of everyday life, community events, and social movements on the American past have had the effect of engaging more historians in folkloristic methods of ethnographic fieldwork, comparative textual analysis, and cultural mapping. In the common discussion of history as "*heritage," and "legacy," for example, is a reference to the significance of traditions and the role of community in passing and adapting those traditions. Folklore, it is often stressed, is not false information or primitive practice; it is socially truthful because it reveals perceptions, ideas, beliefs, and biases—sometimes summarized as worldview—that helps answer questions about the meaning of local and national experiences. As historians have been engaged by folklore's revelation of community traditions, so folklorists have been attracted by the social orientations of local history that record families, neighborhoods, rituals, legends, and customs. Indeed, several classics of folklore collection come from rigorous research projects in local settings: Richard Dorson's *Land of the Millrats* (Cambridge, Mass., 1981); David Steven Cohen's *The Ramapo Mountain People* (New Brunswick, N.J., 1974); Lynwood Montell's *Saga of Coe Ridge* (Knoxville, Tenn., 1970); Richard Dorson, *Bloodstoppers and Bearwalkers: Folk Traditions of the Upper Peninsula* (Cambridge, Mass., 1952); and Harry M. Hyatt's *Folk-Lore from Adams County, Illinois* (n.p., 1935).

"A New Triangulation of Local Studies" of documents, oral traditions, and artifacts articulated in 1956 by New York State Historical Association director Louis C. Jones exemplified a growing vision of folklore studies in rewriting local histories: "What I want to see is a new kind of local history that considers not alone the political and institutional development of a community [but that] which really tells us how Everyman lived, the details of his work day, how he courted, loved, married, raised his family, accepted his responsibility in the social patterns of his time, and what he thought about these experiences." By the time of the Bicentennial of America's independence, a trend had been established in observances for local historical societies to highlight the everyday life, indeed folk arts, of their community's past. Folklore and folklife added to the historical record allowed for representation of plural groups, reflection on changing cultural experience in everyday life, and recognition of ordinary individuals in the story of the community.

Since the Bicentennial, many historical societies have taken up a call to folklore and folklife research to reveal cultural traditions of America's diverse communities. If there is not a national celebration to motivate the movement, there are often new considerations of conserving "cultural" resources that contribute to local pride and sometimes heritage *tourism. Economic development through festival promotion and folk-arts marketing, diversified audiences for community programming, and outreach to youth in schools with folklore and folklife relating to the local area are often the results. These considerations have been part of governmental involvement in cultural-resource management that has brought many folklorists into public programming, and many have had prominent roles in state historical and arts agencies. America's first official state folklorist, Henry Shoemaker, began work in 1948 for the Pennsylvania Historical and Museum Commission, and by 1990, over 40 states established such positions. In addition to academic institutions, regional and state societies, and research centers devoted to local and regional folklife studies, many agencies at the municipal and county level have also employed folklorists to guide local cultural research, organize archives, prepare publications, and mount exhibitions. The American Folklife Center in the Library of Congress, a national agency established by the Folklife Preservation Act of 1976, offers archives, publications, and technical assistance to encourage grassroots efforts. In 1998, the Center launched an ambitious "Local Legacies" project to gather examples of community traditions from every locality in America. The Smithsonian Institution, which has a Center for Folklife Programs and Cultural Studies, meanwhile has sponsored institutes for community investigators in folklore and folklife research. Universities regularly offer courses and workshops in folklore research (several, including Indiana University, University of Pennsylvania, and University of Texas offer a Ph.D. in it), and several have sponsored massive *encyclopedias of regional history and culture that have featured folklore and folklife sections (e.g., *Encyclopedia of Southern Culture*; *Encyclopedia of New England Culture*).

With the end of the twentieth century, challenges and opportunities continue for enhancing the role of folklore and folklife research within local history work. Among the challenges are taking into account newly formed communities with a variety of languages and traditions as part of local heritage. Folklorists have been instrumental in establishing exhibitions and documentary projects for local agencies on groups such as Vietnamese, Hmong, Ethiopian, Yemenite, Haitian, and Chicanos in the recent American experience. Other migrations of traditional groups such as the Amish and Hasidim to new localities require revisions of local history that should involve assessment of cultural traditions in the life of the community. The changing physical structure of communities invite questions that link folklorists in local historical settings to subjects such as patterns of suburbanization, retirement and recreational developments, and temporary settlements. More than recording the past, the ties of folklore and folklife to local history raise pressing issues of the changing, often endangered relationships of traditional communities to their natural as well as cultural environments. There is opportunity for local historical work that examines at the grassroots emergent social and environmental movements of great national impact. Indeed, the field experience of folklorists may inform local agencies that move outside their old headquarters to establish outposts within a variety of communities and offer cultural historical programming and services for cultural conservation. Archives and exhibitions are changing to accommodate new forms of information; technology, ranging from digital cameras to computers, allows for expansion and systematization of the material being recorded, enhancing access to records of what ordinary people said, sang, and made, as well as what they wrote.

See Simon J. Bronner, *Following Tradition: Folklore in the Discourse of American Culture* (Logan, Utah, 1998) and *American Folklore Studies: An Intellectual History* (Lawrence, Kan., 1986). Also, Jan Harold Brunvand, *The Study of American Folklore: An Introduction*, 4th ed. (N.Y., 1998) and *American Folklore: An Encyclopedia* (N.Y., 1996). The dean of American folklore is Richard M. Dorson; see his *Handbook of American Folklore* (Bloomington, 1983), *America in Legend: Folklore from the Colonial Period to the Present* (N.Y., 1973), *American Folklore and the Historian* (Chicago, 1971), *Buying the Wind: Regional Folklore in the United States* (Chicago, 1964), *American Folklore* (Chicago, 1959), *Bloodstoppers and Bearwalkers: Folk Traditions of the Upper Peninsula* (Cambridge, Mass., 1952). Also, Robert Georges and Michael Owen Jones, *Folkloristics: An Introduction* (Bloomington, Ind., 1995); Mary Hufford, ed., *Conserving Culture: A New Discourse on Heritage* (Urbana, Ill., 1994); Patricia A. Hall, "A Case for Folklife and the Local Historical Society," in *American Material Culture and Folklife*, ed. Simon J. Bronner, pp. 205–14 (Logan, Utah, 1992); Burt Feintuch, ed., *The Conservation of Culture: Folklorists and the Public Sector* (Lexington, Ken., 1988); Bruce Jackson, *Fieldwork* (Urbana, Ill., 1987); and Austin Fife, "Folklore and Local History,"

Utah Historical Quarterly 31 (1963): 315–23. Still useful is William Wells Newell, "On the Field and Work of a Journal of American Folk-Lore," *Journal of American Folklore* 1 (1888), pp. 3–7. Also, Barre Toelken, *The Dynamics of Folklore* (Logan, Utah, 1996); Don Yoder, *Discovering American Folklife: Studies in Ethnic, Religious, and Regional Culture* (Ann Arbor, Mich., 1990); and Elliott Oring, ed., *Folk Groups and Folklore Genres: An Introduction* (Logan, Utah, 1986).

SIMON J. BRONNER

food. See culinary history.

footnote. A footnote should be placed whenever an idea or a piece of information is not original to the writer or of common knowledge. The footnote, to the best of our ability, should tell the reader where to find the original. Thus, the book or other source of information should be listed, including author's name, the title, place and date of publication, and page:

Sandy Lydon, *Chinese Gold: The Chinese in the Monterey Bay Region* (Capitola, Calif., 1985) p. 237.

In this way another person can see what the original text looked like.

A magazine or periodical, called by librarians a "series" because these are issued in parts, would be footnoted by giving the author and title of the article, the name of the serial in which the article appeared, the number of the volume and the number of the issue:

Robert R. Archibald, "Time & Tempo, Stories & Survival," in *History News* 52:3 (Summer 1997) 14–18.

A newspaper follows the same form, although some pieces of information, such as the author and sometimes even the title of the article, might be missing:

The Cleveland Plain Dealer, 13, Sept. 1973, 4:1.

The last two numbers refer to the page on which the article is to be found, and the column on the page.

If information came from a record group, manuscript collection, oral interview, or church minutes in the green corner cupboard in the parsonage, the same rules obtain. Give the author, title, date, location of the source in which the item can be found; and if the container is one of many (a box of manuscripts in the attic, for example), list the identifying features so others can find it.

The general public does not like footnotes. Most readers, however, can comfortably skip the little superior numbers. The new footnote style of placing references at the back of the book listed according to the page number on which the reference appears, eliminates numbers and allows the reader to assume that for every quote there will be a reference.

There is also a device called a sneaky footnote in which as much of the identifying information as possible is written into the text. Thus, an author might state that "in the green file cabinets in the parish hall there are mottled old notebooks labeled 'Church Minutes' in which we read for September 16, 1896, that...." That information should get an interested reader close to the desired information.

The reason we use footnotes is another story altogether. We leave them behind like footsteps so that in the future other researchers seeking the same or different questions can understand and follow our pathways and expand upon them. While each historian creates a particular story or understanding of the past, footnotes link us into a generational chain of endeavor as we build upon and sometimes correct the work done by others.

A golden rule:
Leave footnotes unto others of the sort you wish others had left for you.

France, local history in. In France today, history, as an activity meeting certain social demands, can be divided into two worlds: The first world is that of professional scholars, usually university affiliated, who have mutually agreed upon the rules of their craft, and who make use of these procedures of scientific validation and data gathering. Then there is also the world encompassing the many forms of activity undertaken by individuals, members of various associations, and independent scholars, all of them "amateurs," who conduct historical research in the various archives for personal or family reasons, or for the benefit of some other collective body. It would take only a brief visit to the archival holdings in the regional departements to get an idea of the passion for *genealogy so evident in the reading rooms. This is where "local" history is done—"local" meaning that which is based in a village, town, commune, region, neighborhood, or individual estate, with practitioners often being particularly concerned with retracing a modest familial "saga." What distinguishes this type of historical research from scholarly history is not really the "geographical" dimension; that is, it is not the relative size of the research subject that distinguishes this research, since professional historians can also be interested in the history of a specific region. The distinctive elements are to be found instead in the nonprofessional status of local history writers, in the "do-it-yourself" aspect of their methods in contrast to the often quite elaborate formal methods of university researchers, and in their different motivations.

Nevertheless, there exists today a number of bridges between the two worlds, so deeply inscribed is the need for history in French society. Whether it is a matter of lectures organized by various associations or by "leisure-time universities"; journals aimed at popularizing scholarship; a flourishing marketplace for books of history; radio and television broadcasts; or, finally, certain initiatives undertaken within the archives or relating to exhibitions organized around their holdings, it is relatively easy for the two sides of "local" and "scholarly" history to find ways to come together in dialogue.

There is ample evidence of the French infatuation with history. History provides abundant references for speeches by politicians, and a grand "historical" spectacle such as that being devoted to General de Gaulle at the end of 1999, which can become a political event in Paris, complete with press commentary. The book market offers what is probably the best illustration of this "passion." Far from being cloistered away in publi-

cations by university presses and only providing the groundwork for a kind of secret commerce between specialized publishers, history reaches the larger public because all the great publishing houses (Hachette, Gallimard, Fayard, Le Seuil, Plon, and so on) have each developed respective series of titles in history. The extensive biographies published by Fayard, for example, have been so successful with the public that they have been imitated by rival houses. Professional and university historians have contributed to this public curiosity by offering works that popularize research intelligently: *Montaillou, village occitan* (1975) by the historian Emmanuel Leroy Ladurie was a veritable best-seller, having sold more than 200,000 copies, while the books of Georges Duby have made the French familiar with the Middle Ages. History is alive and well in multiple forms in the newspaper kiosks, starting with publications aimed at children (*Je lis des Histoires vraies* ["I read true Histories"], published by Bayard, and *Arche~o Junior*, to name only two) continuing on to periodical journals aimed at the "grand public," such as *Historia*, or *Historama*, older and more traditional publications. Printings that run into several hundred thousands and the regular evolution of new periodical titles underscore the dynamism of this market. History has been a presence in both radio and television since the 1960s; the diversification of broadcast channels has opened up new venues for history that feed the curiosity of its various public audiences, familiarizing them with new documentary "sources," such as the cinema. Finally, the newest media efforts have also made a place for history: in the domain of recreational/ educational CD-ROMs, the game "Versailles, Intrigue in the Court of the Sun-King," designed with the support of the national museums, has created something of a stir, giving rise to similar productions.

This success and the multiple possibilities of satisfying both the most demanding expectations and the simple desire for "chronological exoticism" find their origin partly in the importance accorded in France to the teaching of history as part of the education of children and adolescents. Modifications to scholastic programs in history and changes made with respect to sequence or schedule in the history curriculum can be the object of vast debates and consultations among scholars and other parties with an interest in the educational system (the Ministry of Education, teachers, national education supervisors, parents' associations). If history plays such an important role, it is because it is felt to be a discipline that contributes to the formation of a "civic conscience"; it constitutes, in the final analysis, one of the pathways toward the formation of a "national identity." It is through the intermediary of history and a certain number of momentous "founding" historical events such as the 1789 Revolution or Liberation in 1944 that French society represents itself to itself, setting forth its contradictions and its conflicts, seeking out its elements of consensus.

The "Sunday historian" and the *amateur can exercise their activity in the most prosaic of ways; it is nevertheless a fact that the dynamism of local history is only one facet of a social need that has profound cultural and ideological roots.

Local history has had a noble pedigree. In the sixteenth century, the tendency toward the reinforcement of nation-states in Europe was accompanied by the birth of "national histories." But from the sixteenth century into the beginning of the seventeenth, the jurists, clergy, and magistrates of various localities also took it upon themselves to write local "monographs" devoted to a town, a village, or a province. These works in most cases function emblematically: they affirm the prestige of the newly elite classes; they define the identity of a local collective body; they try to reinsert a locality in the context of a broader history, with more or less mythological colorations. Certain attributes of "traditional" local history are already there: the attention paid to multiple anecdotes, the identification of grand personages as significant actors, the preference for a recitation of events rather than an analysis of ruptures and evolutions. But local history more particularly saw its heyday beginning in the 1830s, when history was viewed with romantic sentiment, and again in the last quarter of the nineteenth century. There, a rise of interest in folkloristic curiosities and a broadening in the discipline of history came together to stimulate activity in local history by the development of scholarly societies. This infatuation then translated its energy into the publication of numerous articles and books, which are now often methodologically out of date and superceded by the availability of the archives, but which in a number of cases still offer useful services.

Local history, which had apparently been marginalized by the increasing professionalization of the discipline from the beginning of the twentiethth century, was resurrected in the late 1960s. The atmosphere following the protests of May 1968 and the difficulties of finding university jobs led some young historians to promote a movement toward doing history in a non-academic environment, employing the framework of associations formed around shared themes or research interests, and proposing to construct a "history as seen from below." The first consequence, felt by the entire field, was to draw attention to "excluded" and "silent" groups in history. The second was the development of new research practices, notably *oral history, which attempted to give back to these excluded groups the power of testimony, that written sources had denied them. This history broached themes pitched by the contestatory movements of the 1970s: the theme of "identities," then a cause taken up in demonstrations by militant regionalists, such as the Basques, Bretons, or Occitans; the theme of *"roots," useful at the time to the various movements to save from oblivion not just rural traditions but also those of an industrial society in full mutation; the theme of "memory," of interest in the effort to understand the permanence of certain engagements or of certain social or regional "temperaments" (for example, the "Camisards" of Cevennes, or the Vendee of 1793). This renewed attention to local history sparked interesting initiatives: oral history, from that point on, had full privileges in the national archives, and the methods for conducting interviews that would constitute the oral archives had been refined. If the first enthusiasm for this "history as seen from below" suffered because of the disappointment the militants felt at the beginning of the 1980s, it nonetheless remains true that what was left over from those associations then active in local history has remained rich: at the beginning of the 1990s, a survey of groups interested in local history tallied their numbers in the several hundred (between 800 and 1,000). These associations range from venerable scholarly societies that bring together local historians from across the entire country, to associations of women publishers of newsletters with a more or less private circulation; there are also recently created associations that have been formed around the organization of an exhibition, or in response to some operation of urban action, for example, an association seeking to re-establish the spaces of an old neighborhood, or again, a group mobilized by the elimination of a factory.

One of the essential contributions of this kind of history has been to incite historians to confront the work of memory. Shorn of its most militant aspects, the theme of collective memory has become an instrument for political consensus, recognized by the highest authorities of the State when the president of the republic named 1980 the year of *heritage, but also a horizon of cultural expectation, "cultural horizon d'attente." This recognition has by now evolved into a kind of commemorative and patrimonial syndrome.

The growing success of the French public's reception every autumn to the "days of heritage" and the impact of the 1789 bicentennial celebrations, which from the outset grew out of a veritable explosion of local initiatives, testify to this phenomenon. This proliferation turns out, however, to be problematic; first, because of its tendency to religiously safeguard all the traces of a past that one is in fear of losing. The number of protected monuments multiplies; these traces are inventoried encyclopedically, but without, however, any attempt to place them in the context of some constructed ensemble that makes sense.

Another problem arises because this devotion to memory clearly does not forge any common identity, but may lead to a plurality of local identities, compartmentalized entities each concerned with its own defense, each recognized independently from the others. This "mosaic of individual of memory" (*mosaiques de memoires particulieres*), to use Pierre Nora's phrase, may satisfy the appetite for history in French society, but the ever-present accompanying risk is that of turning history into a mere instrument in the service of memory, which is by principle selective, emotionally subjective, and, indeed, tends toward over-simplification. Whatever the injunctions may be that weigh down on historians as a whole, history is, first of all, the putting into order of materials that have come from the past, a reconstruction of meaningful chains of events, and an effort of analysis and impartial understanding.

In the two articles he published on the relationship between local history and general history, which appeared in 1967 and 1974 in *Annales: Economies,* *Societes, Civilisations*, a journal edited by Lucien Febvre and Fernand Braudel, the historian Paul Leuillot sketched out problems in the conversation between these two sides in the field of history and said he feared that the scholarly side could become closed off and unresponsive to the needs expressed by society. Subsequent publications taking a serious approach to popularization may have been a response to this worry, as has been the participation of career historians in journals respected by the profession yet turned toward a larger public. But the part accorded to the "local" as such can be quite minor or very perfunctory in these "national" publications. When one looks at the specialized literature that has in these last few years been devoted to the "history of history," one is obliged to note the absence, or the marginal, "unscientific" character of local history, even while it forms a part of the general state of history as practiced in contemporary French society (Antoine Prost, Gerard Noiriel). There is no entry for local history in the *Dictionnaire des sciences historiques* [*Dictionary of Historical Sciences*], published by the Presses universitaires de France (PUF) in 1986 under the direction of Andre Burguiere, though there are articles on "oral history" and "collective memory," topics that, in this context, connect to a method or to a type of epistemological reflection given validation by professional historians. There is no mention at all of local history in the work *Passes recomposes: Champs et chantiers de l'Histoire* [*Pasts Recomposed: the fields and pathways of History*], directed by Jean Boutier and Dominique Julia, published in 1995 in the series *Autrement*. An initiative such as the publication by Seuil of a *Guide de l'Histoire locale* [*Guide to Local History*], 1990, with the eloquent subtitle "Let's Do Our History," is the exception that proves the rule. Directed by university academicians (Alain Croix and Didier Guyvarc'h), bringing together the contributions of teachers and university professors often engaged in the life of professional associations or scholarly societies, this work aims at democratizing the practice of history by putting the rules and methods of scientific historical research in the hands of amateurs. As such, it goes back to an "engaged" approach to the practice of history, one that is not necessarily endorsed by all.

In certain quarters, one might see the relations between "*amateur" historians and professional historians evolving toward increasingly greater separation. In the course of the twentieth century, the world of historians and the practice of history have been marked by an ever-reinforced professionalization. Between the early 1960s and the early 1990s, the number of tenured historians in French universities almost quadrupled, growing from around three hundred to nearly twelve hundred. The "monopoly" of these professionals is exercised for the most part in the fabrication of a kind of history recognized for its scientific and editorial values. In addition, research has become internationalized, and the circulation of scientific information has accelerated and broadened. These conditions, while encouraging growth in comparatist approaches and contributing to the explosion of interest in history and the proliferation of its objects, have led to a decline in status for the genre of the regional monograph, now seen as a piece of "total history," of which local history could appear as an embodiment. Exchanges with other disciplines in the human sciences, such as geography or sociology, have placed at the fore studies of networks, for example, in *urban history, to the detriment of studies grounded simply in one, unique space.

But one may want to acknowledge, on the other hand, that certain developments in professional scholarly research offer new resources for local history. Studies inspired by the "microhistory" coming from Italy (Carlo Ginzburg, Giovanni Levi) can be fertile ground for an approach to "local" history that would agree to adopt the methods and scientific criteria of professional historians. Indeed, the professionalization of the "craft" or "trade" of the historian has led to the definition of a set of rules imposed as constitutive on the practice of history. The historian must know how to exploit his sources, written or not, by respecting a method of critical reading; he must constitute the corpus of his primary material, the archives, with the aim of addressing a problem that has been defined beforehand. Such an approach to local history, adopting these principles, would still lack the academic validation that would grant him scientific recognition. At this important stage—"every history being easy to swallow if it is well done"—we need to imagine the possible complementary forms between "local" history and professional scholarly history.

There are institutional "spaces" or settings that allow "amateur" and professional historians, or "specialists" such as archivists, to meet in contexts that organize opportunities for dialogue between "local" history and "scholarly" history. It is necessary to underscore the formidable amount of field work accomplished in France by professional archivists in assembling and preserving the collections of the regional departments. Today their traditional mission of document conservation is matched by new ones: introducing and maintaining up-to-date technological supports of communication (microfilm, CD-ROM); finding ways to keep the old sources in view (regular exhibitions organized around the "memory of a department"); and, finally, taking on a pedagogical role toward their readers (offering courses on how to read and make use of old documents). Maintained by local groups, some departmental archives regularly publish rather sumptuous brochures, which are intended to accompany a temporary exhibition, but which also allow on each occasion for a collection or a series of documents to be introduced, for new acquisitions or publications relating to the department to be mentioned, and for the use of the archives and their services to be explained.

Some of these "spaces" for dialogue refer back to an older "heritage": such is the case for the Annual Congress of Scholarly Societies, the meetings of which are most often organized around topics defined by university-affiliated scholars, with papers coming from authors with diverse backgrounds but who are principally teachers in upper and secondary education. But any comparison to academic forms of scientific exchange, such as the colloquium, is fairly primitive, and the temper of these meetings is a long way from expressing the dynamic liveliness of the exchanges between professional and amateur historians in the course of the last few decades. The *Rencontres d'histoire locale* [*Meetings on Local History*], set up at Nantes at the end of the 1980s, are probably closer to the "realities of the field." Since 1998, the annual festival *Rendez-vous de l'Histoire* [*Meetings on History*], founded in Blois by the former French Minister of Culture Jack Lang, bring together the elements that make for success in the exchanges between amateurs and specialists. *L'Association des professeurs d'histoire-geographie* [*The Association of Teachers of History and Geography*] in secondary education plays an essential role in the *Rendez-vous de l'Histoire* meetings, serving as a relay among research professionals, teachers, and various publics (elementary and high-school students, and families). This festival proposes debates that make use of university faculty, films, exhibition halls, and may be organized around a topic highlighted by current events or by a revival of historiographic interest: for 1998, the theme was political crime in history; in 1999, the fruits of the earth; for the year 2000, the theme is utopia. Anything or anyone that touches on the practice, consumption, indeed, the "staging" of history, can find a place here: publishers, journals both scholarly and popularizing, the large "cultural" media (which can serve as sponsors), but also universities, student associations, as well as societies of local history and archival collections. Such diversity does not come without ambiguity: the professional historian will find here both a public audience and a court of judgment, as will the amateur, even as the hierarchy between these two is still far from being abolished. As a consumer of cultural commodities, the "honnête homme" of the disappearing century may stand informed, his appetites satisfied.

However, the purist scholar may find that one has to sacrifice too much in this genre geared toward "media effects" and toward celebratory commemorations that are eagerly anticipated by a larger public but play loose with scientifically established "truth." In fact, it remains a simplification to pose the debate in these terms. The success of the *Rendez-vous de l'Histoire* can be attributed to the fact that its sessions synthesize several aspects of the social demand placed on the discipline. As a veritable showcase, it superimposes different forms of knowledge and different forms of the circulation of historical information.

And in order to remove "false problems," it is appropriate when one is beginning to develop some kind of "historian's project" to know what the social needs are that one is contributing to satisfying. Is it a question of constructing a rigorous research method? Is it a question of teaching or popularizing in the best sense of the term? Is it a matter of answering to an individual approach, for example, of discovering a family memoir? Each of these levels in the practice of history does not come without some responsibility. Can the amateur historian stay totally ignorant of the conventions for utilizing archival documents and manuscripts or those employed in historical papers, if he aspires to being read, and not simply remain working in an isolated and "egocentric" activity with no real collective usefulness? At its best, local history, in the secrets that it unravels, in the information it succeeds in establishing, and in the archives that it brings to light, participates in the general progress of historical knowledge and of an understanding of the world.

As for the teacher who has to spark his pupils' interest by what touches them closest to home and who has to stay locked into "modern" methods for teaching civic conscience and critical thinking, can he seriously remain oblivious to the thematic, indeed methodological, evolutions in the discipline he teaches?

Is he not in a primary position to take the achievements of the discipline and articulate them for the benefit of local resources in a manner both popularly accessible and scientifically rigorous? Finally, what would be the point of a university-based history, disillusioned and closed in on itself, whose only calling lay in the corporate world and with no regard—except perhaps critical—toward the expectations of the public and society? Without its being so much a question of setting aside the required criteria for scientific history, the demand in local history puts professional historians in the position of having to confront pressure towards democratization in the practice of history and in the diffusion of information. Assuredly, the ways of responding to this social need already constitute a sort of engagement and an attitude with respect to history.

See Gérard Noiriel, *Qu'est-ce-que l'histoire contemporaine?* (Paris, 1998); Antoine Prost, *Douze leçons sur l'Histoire* (Paris, 1996); Jean Boutier and Dominique Julia, eds., *Passés recomposés. Champs et chantiers de l'Histoire* (Paris, 1995); Alain Croix, Didier Guyvarc'h, eds., *Guide de l'Historie locale. Faisons notre histoire!* (Paris, 1990); André Burguiere, ed., *Dictionnaire des sciences historiques* (Paris, 1986). And see also Françoise Zonabend, *The Enduring Memory: Time and History in a French Village*, trans. Anthony Forster (Manchester, Eng., 1984); and Philippe Joutard, *La legends des Camisards. Une sensibilité au passé* (Paris, 1977).

VINCENT MILLIOT
translated by Emoretta Yang

See Annales School; social history.

free boarders. In many communities, laws were passed to give hogs and other domestic animals free rein to forage for food, in which case they were declared to be free boarders. Other communities restricted animals to a common land or to an owner's care and thus denied them the right to be free boarders.

Freedom of Information Act. James Madison once observed that "a popular government, without popular information, or the means of acquiring it, is but a Prologue to a Farce or a Tragedy—or perhaps both." For most of our history, however, Americans had no way of obtaining essential information about the workings of government agencies or the kinds of information those agencies had in their files. All of that finally changed—for the better, Madison would surely have said—with congressional adoption of the Freedom of Information Act (FOIA) in 1966 and the Privacy Act in 1974. Those measures would subsequently be revised, most recently in 1996, but the principles they embody—openness and accountability—remain firmly in place.

The FOIA provides that "any person"—not only citizens but also permanent resident aliens and foreign nationals—may obtain the records of federal agencies regarding policies, actions, and expenditures except where there is a compelling need to maintain confidentiality. The Act covers cabinet-level departments (such as the Defense Department), executive branch agencies (such as the Federal Bureau of Investigation), the independent regulatory commissions (such as the Environmental Protection Agency), and federally controlled corporations (such as the Tennessee Valley Authority). The FOIA does not apply to Congress, the federal judiciary, or the president and his advisory staff. Although the act is applicable only to federal agencies, all the states and some localities have passed similar measures granting citizens access to their records. In 1978 the Supreme Court declared: "The basic purpose of FOIA is to ensure an informed citizenry, vital to the functioning of a democratic society, needed to check against corruption and to hold the governors accountable to the governed" (*NLRB v. Robbins Tire & Rubber Co.*, 437 U.S. 214, 242 [1978]).

Under the terms of the FOIA, most federal records must be made available to the public, but certain crucial material may remain under lock and key.

The most frequently invoked exemption includes classified documents, such as those relating to military plans and weapons, which, if released, "reasonably could be expected to cause damage to the national security." Other exemptions are provided for internal government memoranda that are part of an ongoing process of decision-making; information contained in personnel files or medical records the disclosure of which would jeopardize individuals' privacy rights; and documents whose release would interfere with law enforcement investigations.

In 1974 abuses of power unearthed during the Watergate investigations led Congress, first, to amend the FOIA to make it more difficult for agencies to withhold information under the existing exemptions, and, second, to pass a far-reaching companion measure, the Privacy Act. This enables individuals to obtain copies of records the government has about them, to request that inaccurate records be corrected or deleted, and even to sue an agency if it refuses either to provide or correct the records. Unlike the FOIA, the Privacy Act may only be used by United States citizens and permanent resident aliens, not by foreign nationals, and only to obtain access to records retrievable under an individual's name or some identifying number. The agency may also charge individuals for the costs incurred in searching, reviewing, and duplicating records requested under the Privacy Act (although educational and noncommercial institutions, and the news media, need only pay the costs of duplication).

In 1986 the Reagan administration succeeded in toughening the standards for the release of government records, particularly those having to do with criminal investigations. In the 1990s, however, President Bill Clinton moved to minimize the restrictions on public access to government information. In October 1993 President Clinton urged all federal agencies to observe the "spirit" as well as the "letter" of the FOIA. Attorney General Janet Reno, noting that the measure sought to achieve "maximum responsible disclosure of government information," established a new "foreseeable harm" standard for responding to FOIA requests that tipped the scales further in the direction of making information available.

On October 2, 1996, President Clinton signed the Electronic Freedom of Information Act Amendments of 1996 (E-FOIA), which make it possible for individuals to have electronic access to government records. The amendments require agencies to make previously requested records available for copying without a request if the agency has determined that the records "have become or are likely to become the subject of subsequent requests for substantially the same records." Agencies had to make such records, and an index of them, available in their reading rooms by March 31, 1997. The indexes were also be made available over the Internet by December 31, 1999. Further, the E-FOIA require agencies to provide guides to assist individuals in requesting records. These guides must include indexes of the agency's information systems, and these indexes, too, will eventually be available on-line.

The information individuals need to use the FOIA, the Privacy Act, and the E-

FOIA is, in fact, already available on the Internet. Among the many sites devoted to the topic, perhaps the most useful is the First Report by the House Committee on Government Operations (103rd Congress, 1st Session, Report 103–104, 1993), *A Citizen's Guide on Using the Freedom of Information Act and the Privacy Act of 1974 to Request Government Records* <http://www.cpsr. org/cpsr/foia /citizens_guide_to_foia_93.txt>. This report not only contains a wealth of information, but also provides examples of sample letters that might be used to file requests.

The FOIA, the Privacy Act, and the E-FOIA establish the presumption that records in the possession of government agencies and departments are accessible to the people. Before 1966 the burden was on the individual to establish a right to examine such records (a right, incidentally, having no statutory basis and no remedy at law if denied). As the House Committee on Government Operations notes: "With the passage of the FOIA, the burden of proof shifted from the individual to the government. Those seeking information are no longer required to show a need for information. Instead, the 'need to know' standard has been replaced by a 'right to know' doctrine. The government now has to justify the need for secrecy." As a result of the 1996 amendments, those seeking information will find their task to be an infinitely easier one.

In signing those amendments, President Clinton asserted: "The Freedom of Information Act has played a unique role in strengthening our democratic form of government. The statute was enacted based upon the fundamental principle that an informed citizenry is essential to the democratic process and that the more the American people know about their government the better they will be governed." James Madison would have agreed, for as the "Father of the Constitution" once said: "Knowledge will forever govern ignorance, and a people who mean to be their own Governors must arm themselves with the power which knowledge gives."

RICHARD POLENBERG

freehold. A freehold refers to land, buildings, or other immovable property that are held in *fee simple. The property may be held through a lease rather than owned outright, but the lease must be for 99 years and be renewable in perpetuity. The term also refers to oil and gas leases.

French. See Appendix A and Canada, local history.

Friends, Society of. See Quakers, Appendix B.

frontier thesis. Frederick Jackson Turner's frontier thesis was the dominant explanatory model of American Western history during the first half of the twentieth century. Presented at the World's Columbian Exposition in Chicago in 1893, Turner asserted that the key to understanding the history of the United States was the frontier experience. The frontier thesis offered a scenario where successive waves of American settlement advanced "civilization" at the expense of native and natural "savagery." Trappers and traders represented the first wave of infiltration, followed shortly by permanent settlers and the establishment of advanced agriculture. The arrival of cities and manufacturing marked the end of the United States' frontier era. According to Turner, this process of settlement marked more than a period of national expansion, for the distance of the wilderness from Old World influences and institutions created a uniquely American culture that valued individualism and democracy.

Lauded when it first appeared and displaying remarkable resilience for much of the century, the frontier thesis has fallen into disfavor among many contemporary historians. For the text of the frontier thesis, see Frederick Jackson Turner, "The Significance of the Frontier in American History," reprinted in *History, Frontier, and Section: Three Essays by Frederick Jackson Turner*, with an introduction by Martin Ridge (Albu-querque, 1993). On Turner's life and influence, see Allan G. Bogue, *Frederick Jackson Turner: Strange Roads Going Down* (Norman, Okla., 1998).

ROBERT PHELPS

See Western history and local historians.

fundamentalism. This is the name given early in the twentieth century to the conservative movement within Protestantism characterized by intense affirmation of biblical authority. The origins of the modern fundamentalist movement began in the 1820s with the ideas of the Englishman John Nelson Darby. Any member of a religious group who remains attached to the earliest phase of that religion may be called a fundamentalist. See David O. Beale, *In Pursuit of Purity: American Fundamentalism since 1820* (Greenville, S.C., 1986).

G

gardens. Even grand gardens seldom outlive their makers. Nevertheless, gardens are profitable starting points for examining local history. The very meaning of a garden is an interesting topic. Since the first American gardens were carved out of the wilderness, they came to represent order and security. America, as the new Eden, was often thought of as a garden, and gardens were a metaphor for God's providence. Their abundance was represented by cornucopias and flower baskets that ap-peared in a number of contexts, from quilts to paintings to furniture.

As Patricia M. Tice points out in *Gardening in America, 1830–1910* (Rochester, N.Y., 1984), a well-worked garden was a sign of the agrarian ideal that underlay Americans' sense of themselves from Thomas Jefferson until the rise of industrialism. Gardens assured economic and social stability as well as independence from Europe. Productive gardens were a reward for industry, and gardening was seen as a morally uplifting activity. In the nineteenth century, worried about what they saw as the degrading effects of cities, Americans founded school gardens to teach moral virtue to new immigrants and the poor.

Individuals and groups interested in public health were also drawn to gardens. Besides the healthful effects of fresh air and exercise that gardening provided, it was thought that frequent turning of the soil filtered away the city's unhealthy germs and miasmas. However, the produce of these gardens was sometimes regarded as the source of cholera outbreaks caused by watering with polluted water.

Exploring the crops grown in kitchen gardens gives us insights into the American diet. Fresh vegetables and fruit originally played a minor role. The earliest gardeners grew vegetables that would store well over the long winter: potatoes, cabbage, carrots, parsnips, beans. By looking at seed lists and nursery catalogs we can see changing eating patterns and the influence of various immigrant groups who brought with them new fruits and vegetables.

One can also study class distinctions. As cities expanded and processed food became more available, the poor came to depend on suburban truck gardens for fresh vegetables because the cost of land and the expense of maintaining a kitchen garden were quite high. Thus kitchen gardens came to be status symbols and were used to grow exotic and expensive items. Over the years they became ever more elaborate and labor intensive.

Ornamental gardens were also expensive and uncommon in the first quarter of the nineteenth century.

Though flowers were grown in the earliest gardens, they were grown for their medicinal qualities not their aesthetic value. These gardens were often laid out as if they were agricultural fields: in rectangular blocks with the plants in rows. This style of gardening can still be seen in rural America where dahlias and gladioli often stand in rows beside beans and chard.

The design of American ornamental gardens has been largely based on European and English models. In the nineteenth century, there were two main types of gardens—informal and formal. The formal styles more or less derived from French and Dutch models, while the informal style was a miniaturized version of eighteenth-century English landscape design. The idea that streets of houses should be fronted by uninterrupted lawns derives from this tradition and has become a characteristic that visitors from abroad cite as peculiarly American. The European cottage garden where vegetables, fruit, and flowers grow in a random pattern is unusual in America and its presence often suggests a garden designed by an immigrant.

In the late nineteenth century, a third approach to gardening developed based on the work of the English gardeners Gertrude Jekyll and William Robinson. These gardens were often associated with Arts and Crafts–style houses. They consisted of herbaceous borders organized by color and were popularized by magazines like *Country Life in America* and *House and Garden*.

Books of advice are another excellent source for studying history. America's foremost nineteenth-century landscape designer, Andrew Jackson Downing, wrote extensively on the design of both houses and gardens. One can find many examples of houses derived from his designs, and a close reading of his books can reveal much about American attitudes. For example, in his edition of the popular English book, *Mrs. Loudon's Gardening for Ladies and Companion to the Flower Garden*, Downing commented that the portion related to the kitchen garden had been omitted in the American edition "as not likely to be of much value here." Flower gardening was a suitable occupation for American ladies, vegetable gardening was not.

One can also study the effects of various inventions on the craft of gardening. Urbanization allowed the formation of nurseries and seedhouses to serve the increasing number of gardeners. These enterprises often adopted industrial techniques such as standardized packaging and division of labor to cut costs. They also developed new varieties of flowers and vegetables. While the earliest varieties were often named after the place where they originated, later nurserymen resorted to promotional names such as the "Mortgage Lifter" tomato.

Some inventions had a dramatic effect on the design of gardens. The mass production of the lawnmower in the 1870s meant that lawns became affordable. Previously they had had to be scythed, an expensive proposition. With lawns came all sorts of lawn games like badminton, croquet, and lawn tennis. Outdoor furniture became popular along with a wild array of garden ornaments whose iconography would reward the enterprising historian.

The organization of horticultural societies and garden clubs is another excellent way to study local history. These were organized for a number of purposes: the dissemination of scientific knowledge, the holding of fairs and competitions, and the distribution of free seeds. Some had libraries and a few prominent ones developed cemeteries that were amongst the first public parks. For example, the Massachusetts Horticultural Society sponsored Mt. Auburn Cemetery in Boston, and there are numerous similar examples. The minutes and records of garden clubs offer fertile ground for studying local communities.

Finally, gardens themselves can be studied using old records, diaries, books, and archealogical techniques. Their restoration is itself an instructive process.

See Rudy J. Favretti, *Landscapes and Gardens for Historic Buildings* (Walnut Creek, Calif., 1997); Ann Leighton, *American Gardens of the 19th Century* (Amherst, 1987); and A. J. Downing, ed., *Ladies Companion to the Flower Garden* (N.Y., 1860).

NORMA PRENDERGAST

See culinary history.

gay history. To the extent that people have thought about the role lesbians and gay men have played in the development, enrichment, and preservation of American communities, they have associated the sexual minority with the history of the nation's larger cities. New York, Boston, San Francisco, Los Angeles, and Chicago, among other cities, have been seen as destinations for gays. When considered at all, the story is singular: homosexuals leave their home-towns all over America and move to Greenwich Village or West Hollywood to find self-realization, acceptance, and to found communities of their own. The gay experience has been character-istically viewed as an escape from the towns and villages of the country. This "escape" has remained one defining pattern of the lesbian and gay experi-ence, but not the only one.

In fact, most American localities had lesbian and gay citizens who stayed home, where many of them played cru-cial roles in civil life, education, church, and social life, and in the preservation of local history and traditions that are so important to American culture. And they spent their time as most people do, in the daily rounds of family life and in making a living.

The invisibility of the gay experience in local history has two principal causes. There has been an abiding prejudice against same-sex love since before the nineteenth-century invention of the categories of hetero- and homosexual. In addition, most gays made a secret of their inclinations and lived a life re-ferred to as being "in the closet." That closet was the silence imposed by cul-ture on the gay person and it was also the private world gays created for them-selves. To find lesbians and gay men in home places requires that one be willing to see the people and lives behind the euphemisms, such as the term "Boston marriage."

Local theater and music, choirs, and other cultural activities were places where gay men and women participat-ed, but they did so as individuals. The same is true of those gays who became teachers and librarians, and those in-volved in the preservation of a commu-nity's traditions. Think of the most per-formed and admired play about Amer-ican small-town life, *Our Town*. Thorn-ton Wilder was a closeted gay man and in the play the Stage Manager suggests the existence of social misfits who "read" as gay and reflect what Wilder knew from experience. William Alex-ander Percy, the Mississippi writer, kept his gay life confined to his poems and his sojourns away from Greenville, all the time writing movingly about a number of other subjects. He was an important local as well as national cul-tural figure.

The host of gay women and men who formed so vital a part of the culture of American places needs to be acknowl-edged when they are encountered. They deserve respect for the significant roles they played in the elaboration of the American town as a fact and an ideal of American life. The significant partici-pation of lesbians and gay men in cur-rent local history, preservation, and cultural activity in America's smaller places—within and without the urban sprawls—is easier to recognize and ac-knowledge now, since so many gays have "come out" of the closet whereas in earlier times they would have been unidentified. We need also to remem-ber that the sexual minority was and is in every class, in most families, and among the ordinary people who built and lived in all our towns. Local histori-ans have access to these truths about the commonality of people, whose differ-ences in sexual orientation may have had to be secret in earlier time but no longer need be. The result will be a more democratic, accurate, and nuanced understanding of America's local histories, and also the revelation of how little sexual orientation has or need divide people when their common interests and feelings, homes, and towns are concerned.

See John Howard, ed., *Carryin' On in the Lesbian and Gay South* (N.Y., 1997); D. Michael Quinn, *Same-Sex Dynamics Among Nineteenth-Century Americans: A Mormon Example* (Urbana, Ill., 1996); and Neil Miller, *In Search of Gay America* (N.Y., 1989).

ROBERT DAWIDOFF

gazetteer. According to the *Oxford English Dictionary*, the word "gazetteer" originally meant journalist, one who worked for a gazette. In time, it came to refer to a geographical index or dictionary. The earliest published in England was L. Echard, ed., *The Gazetteer or Newsman's Interpreter: Being a Geographical Index* (London 1704). Although the word sounds old-fashioned or quaint, gazetteers are still being published today.

genealogy, an archivist's view. They come in little packs, or in busloads. They're there in the mornings waiting semipatiently for the doors to open. They're there to be gently shooed out when you close up at night. They make more visits, ask more questions, write more letters, they visit your website more often than any other part of your constituency. They are genealogists.

The major difference between genealogists and local historians is that local historians are primarily concerned with groups—organizations,

schools, churches, societies; while genealogists are concerned with individuals and families. And, while a historian can turn to another subject if the records are too scant to support a research project, the genealogist works with whatever resources are available.

Any organization connected with local history will be a magnet to people whose ancestors once lived in the area, however briefly. They can be important supporters of your organization and its work.

Genealogy is a research-intensive interest/pastime/obsession. Gathering any substantial amount of genealogical and biographical information about one's ancestors often involves a significant investment in time, money, and effort. Because of the time and expense involved, genealogists tend to be (but are not always) at the older end of the population spectrum. Many are now computer literate.

Genealogy, when done well, is a research discipline. Any serious genealogical inquiry involves considerable research into the traces of our ancestors to be found in the records that have survived to the present day. This research can, and often does, extend over many years. For that research to be useful, the results must be carefully documented, and citations to sources used need to be included in any finished product.

The first step in genealogical investigation should be to put down, in some organized fashion, what is known about one's ancestors and their families. The second step is to gather whatever information can be obtained from relatives. There is a good chance someone in the family has already done some of this work and this research should be appreciated.

At some point, though, the actual research begins. Exactly what records may be of help will vary according to what particular information is missing, what time period and exactly where one's ancestors lived. There are numerous genealogical guides (see the suggestions at the end of this essay) that give detailed descriptions of what records and other resources are available and where they can be consulted. Some key genealogical records may be held by the federal government, such as records of the U.S. censuses, passenger lists, military and pension records for service in the country's various wars. The originals of these are generally found in research libraries, although many may also be available on microfilm. Some resources will be found in county repositories, such as courthouse records: vital records (civil records of birth, marriage, divorce, and death), probate records (i.e., records concerned with the settling of an estate), land records, tax rolls, and court records (including naturalization or citizenship records). Others are more likely to be housed at the local level, such as newspapers, church and cemetery records, manuscript records of all types (letters, journals, organizational records, etc., including materials gathered by previous historians and genealogists). It is with these resources that a local historical organization can be most useful.

The best response of a historical agency is to have its records well cataloged, organized, and available. It is often helpful to work with other record-holding agencies, such as the local courthouse, library, and archival agencies. The more a historical society knows about area records, the more helpful it can be to genealogical researchers, for being able to refer researchers to other resources is a valuable service.

The *Family History Library of the Church of Jesus Christ of Latter-Day Saints (Mormons) in Salt Lake City is a special resource. Because of the importance in Mormon theology of gathering family history, the Family History Library has acquired, primarily by microfilming, genealogical source records from around the world. A network of local libraries, called Family History Library Centers, allows researchers who cannot get to Salt Lake City an opportunity to borrow records and use them locally. In addition, the Family History Library has compiled two major databases of genealogical information under the name Family-Search.

The Ancestral File is an index of genealogical material submitted by many people; the *International Genealogical Index (IGI) is a massive index to a wide range of "vital records," information from around the world. Family-Search is available at all Family History Library Centers and at many other genealogical libraries and repositories.

The Family History Library is but one of many important archives. Many public libraries have genealogy/local history collections and in some cities there are large and useful collections. Every state has at least one major resource institution, such as a state historical society, state archives, or state library with important materials.

There are, in addition, resources available on the Internet. Many organizations serving genealogists have a website and many more soon will. Some of these sites are little more than advertising, but more and more are making resources available in this novel way. See in particular <www.family-search.org>, the site created by the Church of the Latter Day Saints. A great deal can be accomplished on the Internet, but certainly not everything.

In addition to the many researchers primarily interested in their own ancestors, there are a few who go beyond that to research entire communities or particular groups. Some gather and publish genealogical resource materials, others teach people how to "do" genealogy. Still others provide support to genealogical societies, local libraries, and even local historical societies. They help process material, and they respond to inquiries. Genealogists can be an important source of support to any local historical society. And, because of their numbers, they can be a political force as well, providing backing in the never-ending battles for funding and support.

The literature on genealogy is vast, but a first-rate introductory book is (despite its unfortunate title) *The Complete Idiot's Guide to Genealogy*, by Kay Ingalls and Christine Rose (Indianapolis, 1997). An excellent guide to state and county records is *Ancestry's Red Book: American State, County & Town Sources*, edited by Alice Eichholz (rev. ed., Salt Lake City, 1992). For more in-depth discussion of a wide range of genealogical resources, see *The Source: A Guidebook of American Genealogy*, edited by Loretto Dennis Szucs and Sandra Hargreaves Luebking (rev. ed., Salt Lake City, 1997); and Kory L. Meyerink, ed., *A Guide to*

Published Genealogical Records (Salt Lake City, 1998). In addition to these, many societies offer classes in genealogical research, and some have regular programs about various aspects of the field. Some large societies hold substantial seminars or multiday conferences, where genealogists meet and learn. The largest gatherings are annual conferences sponsored by the National Genealogical Society (located at 4527 17th St, North, Arlington, Va., 22207-2399; [800] 473-0060; <www. NGSGENEALOGY.ORG>) and the Federation of Genealogical Societies (at P.O. Box 200940, Austin, Texas 78720-0940; [512] 336-2731, fax: [512] 336-2732; <www.fgs.org>).

Institutes, such as those held annually at the National Archives and Samford University (800 Lakeshore Dr., Birmingham, Alabama, 35229; [205] 726-2011) offer concentrated education in specific aspects of genealogical research.

While beginners will always outnumber experienced researchers, genealogical research can be challenging and rewarding. You will never run out of ancestors to learn more about.

JAMES L. HANSEN

genealogy, African American. Traditionally, elder Africans provided oral history that linked generations, placing their families within a definable period in U.S. history. This allowed a descendant to connect a loved one with local events, which helped explain the emergence and perpetuation of particular values and habits within a family from one generation to the next. Such oral history found its way into written texts as early as 1880, when profiles were presented about formerly enslaved Africans or descendants who became members of the Jubilee Singers of Fisk University. Two years later, George Washington Williams, a former Civil War soldier of the United States Colored Troops, authored *A History of the Negro Race in America* ([1883] N.Y., 1968) and in 1883, he proposed that the Negro Historical Society be established.

Eight years later, the Reverend Edward A. Johnson wrote *School History of the Negro Race in America*. This 1891 text, like those before it, reflected positively on the African's presence in America. Before the nineteenth century came to an end, the voice of Paul Laurence Dunbar found its place in print through the poetic work, *Lyrics of the Lowly Life*—a tribute to the many Freedmen who survived enslavement, including his mother and the more than 180,000 black men who had fought for their freedom. The stage had been set, and numerous other writers responded to the charge, including John Wesley Cromwell with his text, *Negro in American History* (Washington, D.C., 1914), which was published by the American Negro Academy. In all these books, the role of the black soldiers of the Civil War was highlighted.

During 1925, Dr. Carter G. Woodson, heralded as the father of Negro History Week, published an important work through his Association for the Study of Negro Life and History, Inc. The text, *Free Negro Heads of Families in the United States in 1830* ([1924] N.Y., 1968) enhanced the process of reclaiming black ancestry. It provided a vehicle for identifying many of the 319,000 free persons

of African descent. Benjamin Quarles devoted an entire book, *The Negro in the Civil War* (Boston, 1953), to placing the soldiers within local historical context. The process of reclamation was once again magnified by the publication of Alex Haley's *Roots (N.Y., 1976), which was made into a television miniseries in 1977. The television drama greatly influenced a new generation at a time when the study of black history was being urged throughout the country.

One of the first indications of the impact of this emerging search for ancestral lineages was the founding in 1977 of the Afro-American Historical and Genealogical Society (AAHGS) in Washington, D.C., by James Dent Walker. That same year Charles L. *Blockson and Ron Fry authored *Black Genealogy* (Englewood Cliffs, N.J., 1977), a most resourceful tool for the aspiring family historian. See also Debra L. Newman Ham's *Black History: A Guide to Civilian Records in the National Archives* (Washington, D.C., 1984); and Sandra M. Lawson, *Generations Past: A Selected List of Sources for Afro-American Genealogical Research* (Washington, D.C., 1988). The stage had been set for millions of African Americans to enter research libraries, local, regional, and national, with the confidence and resolve necessary to search for their roots.

Today, researchers are aided by <Afri geneas@Ms.State.edu>, an Internet listserve moderated by Valenda Nelson at Mississippi State that serves as a forum for family research. In addition, in 1998, the American Society of Freedmen's Descendants (ASFD) was established by charter members from twelve states and Canada. This organization, with Sylvia Cooke Martin as president, serves as an educational lineage society devoted to the scholarly pursuit of ancestry of the formerly enslaved Africans in America. Hartwick College, located in Oneonta, New York, serves as the host site for ASFD, as well as its sister organization, United States Colored Troops Institute for Local History and Family Research. All of these efforts, in addition to new case studies in historiographic genealogy, reveal a rather remarkable journey made by African Americans in reclaiming their ancestral roots.

HARRY BRADSHAW MATTHEWS

genealogy, Jewish. There has been growing interest in Jewish genealogy over the past two decades, but that interest has exponentially accelerated with the availability of computers and the Internet. This genealogical interest has three principal goals: tracing the individual's forebears; locating the individual's living relatives; and understanding the lives and development of the family.

There was little interest in genealogy among the early Jewish immigrants to the United States. The American ethos of a democratic country where a person succeeded on the basis of ability reduced the importance of family connections. Like other U.S. immigrants, most Jews came to the United States because of the promise of better economic conditions. Unlike their fellow immigrants, most Jews were not well-integrated into the societies of the countries they left, so no outpouring of nostalgia drove an interest in genealogy. If there was nostalgia, it was for a commu-

nity that no longer existed because war, oppression, or mass migration had devastated it.

The return to genealogy is really a return to roots in more than one sense. Jewish genealogy reaches back to the Bible. Genesis carefully traces the family relationships between its characters. This tradition has been carried on in rabbinic circles as some families have produced large numbers of rabbis over the century. Any rabbi who writes a book will normally include as a preface his genealogy, which may be complete, or males-only, or rabbis-only, and often attempts to connect the author to one of the great leaders of the past, such as Rashi or the Baal Shem Tov.

Most American and Canadian Jews are descended from the great wave of immigrants from the Russian Empire and Galicia (from 1880 to 1920, a part of the Austro-Hungarian Empire). A smaller, but significant, number came from Germany and neighboring lands after the failed revolutions of 1848. A much smaller group are Sephardic Jews, descended from those Jews expelled from Spain and Portugal at the end of the fifteenth century who settled first in London, Amsterdam, and Rouen, then came to the New World. Some are refugees from the devastated Europe of World War II. In the 1990s, Jews began arriving from the former Soviet Union, often seeking the descendants of relatives who left the Russian Empire a century ago.

The first task of the person seeking his genealogy is to gather an *oral history of his family. Just as "one peek is worth a thousand finesses" in bridge, genealogy is much simplified by being told what to look for and where to look. Most helpful is knowing the town of origin in Europe, which is sometimes more easily discovered in conversation than by examining the records.

Family oral history should be done first because it is a transitory asset. Barring fire or other disaster, the records will be equally available in the future. But the persons who carry the oral history age every day. Death will silence them completely; mental deterioration may scramble their memories irretrievably; and macular degeneration or glaucoma may render them unable to identify the persons in their family photo albums.

Oral history also puts flesh on the skeletal records. Genealogy is more than who begat whom. It is the way families lived and interacted. Stories about holiday celebrations, business partnerships, shared vacations, cousins' clubs and the like are unlikely to appear in official records or in yellowed newspaper columns, but they are available from older relatives. Though oral history seems a slender reed upon which to build anything, as memories play tricks after only a few years, the experience of most genealogists is that family stories are remarkably accurate and, even when they are deficient in some details, useful if carefully investigated.

Simultaneously with collecting oral history, one needs to collect records. Oral history needs to be documented, and one often discovers whole branches of a family by an informed look at vital records.

The common conception of the stable Jewish family could not be further from the truth. As early as the 1850s, Russian Jewish communities had a high rate of divorce unequaled anywhere in Europe, ranging from 15 percent in some towns to 45 percent in others. These figures do not include de facto divorces where the husband emigrated and simply remarried in the new country without having divorced his wife left behind in the old country. Also, mortality was high among young men, and even higher among young women. This left many young widows and widowers shopping for new mates and finding them; so the concept of "my children, your children, and our children" was more prevalent in 1895 than in 1995. Records can make sense of these shifting family affiliations.

Most records are local. They are kept by the city or county and only occasionally gathered into statewide or province-wide archives. They are seldom kept nationally. Sometimes older records are kept by religious group, and most Jewish genealogists find significant numbers of intermarriages and conversions, both into and out of Judaism. There is little uniformity in the records or the methods of search or the local rules of access. Hours are long, and it is easy to become discouraged.

Into this breach has come the computer. An informal Jewish genealogy chat group called JewishGen has appeared at <www.jewishgen.org> providing Frequently Asked Questions (FAQs) and Infofiles that take the novice through approaches to particular genealogical problems, and providing a daily forum for asking people around the world for their expertise, their help, or if they are related. JewishGen also maintains online the Family

Tree of the Jewish People (FTJP), to which any person can submit his family tree for publication and correlation with others. In 1999, FTJP contained more than 300,000 names. Perhaps the most significant aspect of JewishGen is the help participants offer each other. I can easily look up a California obituary for a person in Florida while someone in Philadelphia takes photos of my ancestors' *gravestones there. JewishGen also provides an on-line *gazetteer for locating places with historical Jewish populations, many of which no longer exist.

A second major contribution of the computer for persons with U.S. families is the Social Security Death Index. This database lists dates of birth and death for individuals for whom a death benefit was paid from the mid-1960s to the present. It also provides the key to getting further information about individuals by obtaining copies of their social security applications, which have extensive personal information, from the federal government.

Third, some states and provinces are beginning to put their indices to some vital records on the Internet as searchable databases. Thus, the amount of actual research one can do without leaving home has greatly expanded.

Genealogy is important in Mormon Church doctrine. Because of this, the Church tries to accumulate microfilms of every vital record it can find, as well as any index available, and maintains *Family History Centers in most major U.S. cities. For the cost of mailing, any of the Church's microfilms can be sent to your local FHC within a couple of weeks. So it is not necessary to travel to major records centers because the Mormon Church is willing to bring the records to you. See <www.familysearch.org>.

With the disintegration of the former Soviet Union, the Mormon Church is becoming even more helpful to Jewish genealogists. Teams of Mormon microfilmers criss-cross Poland, Ukraine, and Belarus filming vital records. While these records are difficult to use because there are no indices, teams of volunteers have created indices for Poland and Lithuania so that entire communities can be reconstructed.

Jewish Genealogy has also benefited from increased publications and support groups. *Avotaynu*, an excellent quarterly journal, has expanded to publish monographs, both practical and scholarly. There are Jewish genealogical societies that meet regularly in about 70 different cities, and an international association of Jewish genealogical societies that ties them together. There are special-interest groups that concentrate on particular areas (Galicia, Kielce-Radom, Belarus), and groups that band together to raise money and share knowledge about particular towns.

A generation's work in social history has also helped the Jewish genealogist flesh out a family. We now have studies of birth-control methods used by immigrant women at the turn of the century; patterns of work among men, women and children; and recreational habits. While we cannot be sure that our ancestors fit the common mold, we can relate the results of those studies and speculate about whether our ancestors were more likely to have conformed.

Most of the genealogist's work concerns records. With practice, one learns what data is likely to be present in what records, and how available the records might be. As a general rule, federal government records are housed at the *National Archives, regional archives, or the originating agency; state records, at a state library or archives, department of health, department of vital records, department of motor vehicles. Found closer to home are local records, such as those at a marriage license bureau, department of health, department of vital records, register of wills, register of deeds, register of voters, orphan's court, probate court, city or county archives, business license bureau, or school board. There are also newspapers that can be located at the *Library of Congress, local university or public libraries, genealogical or historical societies; and maps, at the Library of Congress, U.S. Geological Survey, or local tax assessor.

Below is a list of the sorts of facts a genealogist might like to know and the sorts of records that might contain valuable information. Bear in mind that the United States is decentralized, so the agency that designs the forms decides what questions to ask and may change the questions over time. For example, in less than two years of existence, there were three different forms for World War I draft registration, each asking somewhat different questions. Also, jurisdictions differ in the privacy they accord records and the degree of indexing provided. In Massachusetts, all vital records (with a few exceptions, such as adopted persons' original birth certificates) are open to the public and are indexed alphabetically in five-year indices. In Maryland, there are annual indices that are arranged chronologically but separated by first letter and first vowel of surname, but death records are not open to the public for 20 years, while the wait for marriage and birth records is 100 years. For this reason, it is useful to consult a variety of sources for each item of data sought. For example:

Date of birth: census, birth certificate, marriage certificate, death certificate, immigration manifest, naturalization petition, social-security death index, social-security application, voter registration, driver's license, draft registration, alien registration, passport application, business license application, obituary, gravestone.

City of birth: census, marriage certificate, death certificate, immigration manifest, naturalization petition, social-security application, draft registration, alien registration, passport application, obituary.

Date of marriage: marriage certificate, naturalization petition, alien registration, obituary.

City of marriage: alien registration.

Date of death: death certificate, social-security death index, gravestone, obituary, probate records.

City of death: social-security death index, obituary, probate records.

Place of burial: death certificate, funeral-home records, obituary, probate records.

Family relationships: census, birth certificate, marriage certificate, death certificate, immigration manifest, naturalization petition, social-security application, draft registration, alien registration, passport application, obituary, gravestone, probate records.

Physical description: naturalization declaration of intent, driver's license, draft registration, alien registration, passport application.

See Alexander Beider, *A Dictionary of Jewish Surnames from the Kingdom of Poland* (Bergenfield, N.J., 1997), and his *Dictionary of Jewish Surnames from the Russian Empire* (Bergenfield, N.J., 1994); *Avotaynu: The International Review of Jewish Genealogy* (Bergenfield, N.J.); Arthur Kurzweil, *From Generation to Generation: How to Trace Your Jewish Genealogy and Family History* (N.Y., 1994); Beider, *Ancient Ashkenazic Surnames: Jewish Surnames from Prague (15th–18th Centuries)* (Bergenfield, N.J., c.1994); Gary Mokotoff and Sallyann Sack, *Where Once We Walked: A Guide to the Jewish Communities Destroyed in the Holocaust* (Bergenfield, N.J., 1991); Shmuel Gorr, *Jewish Personal Names, Their Origin, Derivation and Diminutive Forms* (Bergenfield, N.J., 1991); and Alfred Kolatch, *Complete Dictionary of English and Hebrew First Names* (Middle Village, N.Y., 1984).

Guides to Records include: Aleksander Kronik and Sallyann Sack, *Some Archival Sources for Ukrainian-Jewish Genealogy* (Bergenfield, N.J., 1998); Susan Wynne, *Finding Your Jewish Roots in Galicia* (Bergenfield, N.J., 1998) and Miriam Weiner, *Jewish Roots in Poland: Pages from the Past and Archival Inventories* (N.Y., 1997); Harold Rhode and Sallyann Sack, *Jewish Vital Records, Revision Lists and Other Jewish Holdings in the Lithuanian Archives* (Bergenfield, N.J., 1996); Dorit Sallis and Marek Webb, *Jewish Documentary Sources in Russia, Ukraine and Belarus: A Prelimi-*

nary List (N.Y., 1996); Sallyann Sack, *A Guide to Jewish Genealogical Resources in Israel* (Bergenfield, N.J., rev. ed., 1995); Dmitri Elyashevich, *Documentlnye Materialy po Istorii Evreev v Arkhivakh SNG i Stran Baltii* (in Russian) (St. Petersburg, Russia, 1994); Arthur Kurzweil and Miriam Weiner, *The Encyclopedia of Jewish Genealogy*, vol. 1: *Sources in the U.S. and Canada* (Northvale, N.J., 1991); and Estelle Guzik, *Genealogical Resources in the New York Metropolitan Area* (N.Y., 1989).

Useful for social history: Raphael Patai, *The Jews of Hungary: History, Culture, Psychology* (Detroit, Mich., 1996); Masha Greenbaum, *The Jews of Lithuania: A History of a Remarkable Community 1316–1945* (Hewlett, N.Y., 1995); and Irving Howe, *World of Our Fathers* (N.Y., 1976).

There are a number of genealogies: Chaim Freedman, *Eliyahu's Branches: The Descendants of the Vilna Gaon and his Family* (Bergenfield, N.J., 1997); David Zubatsky and Irwin Berent, *Sourcebook for Jewish Genealogies and Family Histories* (Bergenfield, N.J., 1996); and Neil Rosenstein, *The Unbroken Chain* (2 vols.) (N.Y., 1990).

For children, see Ira Wolfman, *Do People Grow on Family Trees? Genealogy for Kids and Other Beginners* (N.Y., 1991).

HERBERT LAZEROW

generation. In general, a generation is reckoned to be thirty-three years.

Gentile. Gentiles are those, to Jews, who are not Jewish. The term usually refers to Christians; for Mormons, a Gentile is a non-Mormon.

geological surface maps. See maps.

German, local history today. The tradition of village history in Germany goes back to the antimodern movements of agrarian fundamentalism ("Agrarromantik" and "Heimatschutz") in the last decades of the nineteenth century. Since then, many village-centered articles and monographs have been written by local teachers, pastors, and other village officials, sometimes even by archivists. From a professional point of view, their value may vary. In the Nazi period the interest turned to genealogy, which was often connected with sharp racist purposes. For instance, village genealogical lists ("Ortssippenbücher") were broadly backed by the political authorities.

Some other books and articles are often connected with anniversaries. For these purposes during the last years, young historians without academic positions have been engaged by some communities to prepare village or small-town histories. Although the conditions are not always favorable—they are mostly hired for one or two years—this was one of the ways by which an influx of academic ideas flowed into localities. Another way has been the influence of workshops, which are sometimes connected with the local branches of the "new social movements" such as environmentalism.

In the 1950s and 1960s, village history was not of academic interest, partly because of its earlier ideological abuse. At the end of the 1960s, however, new attempts were beginning, based on contemporary changes in the German countryside—on the one hand—and new insight, gained by agrarian sociology, on the other.

Although the villages were rapidly losing their importance as economic units, a kind of village consciousness still survived. This contradiction—*"Ungleichzeitigkeit"* in the terms of the Tübingen philosopher Ernst Bloch—was a challenge to new approaches in historiography. A Tübingen group of historians and ethnologists concentrated on the Swabian village of Kiebingen to trace the roots of this sense of village "communalism." It split into various conflicting factions and alliances, the reasons for which could be found in cooperation and competition processes of the past, especially during the nineteenth century.

From the methodological point of view, local history became one of the major modernizing forces in German historiography as a whole. New topics appeared, like demography, family and gender history, which had been neglected for a long time. Local historians became familiar with *"histoire serielle"* and oral history. An outstanding monograph by Kurt Wagner on Körle in Nothern Hesse centered on the nineteenth century and on the impact of agricultural and industrial change on village relationships. Andreas Gestrich saw the sharpest break in village history in the experience of World War I, especially among men.

Wagner's study does not omit the political background. He provides new insight into the dissociation of traditional political forces at the end of the Weimar Republic and the formation of Nazi Rule within the village. Friedeburg's monograph on "traditional community protest" in Hesse, though it is not strictly a community study, shows the growing importance of village factions and especially of anti-semitism in nineteenth-century Hessian village politics.

Swabian villages, however, continued to be the heart of German community studies because of the abundance and variety of village-centered sources. David Sabean and Hans Medick were the first to trace these systematically back to the seventeenth century. Methodologically, both their books reflect "the anthropological turn" that was characteristic of an influential wing of German historiography in the early 1980s. (See Hans Medick, *Weben und Überleben in Laichigen 1650–1900 Lokalgeschichte als Allgemeine Geschichte* [Gottinger, 1996]; and David Warren Sabean, *Property, Production and Family in Neckarhausen, 1700–1870* [Cambridge, Eng., and N.Y., 1990].)

Sabean's book might be regarded as "traditional" insofar as he underlines the importance of nineteenth-century changes. He concentrates, however, on the question of how a system of kinship lines, family, household and inheritance conflicts, individual strategies and ideological attitudes, which had been established in the eighteenth century, had to be adapted to those processes of fundamental change. He gained some unexpected results, finding industrialization and commercialization strengthened the kinship networks instead of weakening them and led to a system of strict endogamy, hitherto unknown in a village of partible inheritance.

Medick in "his" Swabian community evaluates the benefits and costs of pro-to-industrial production for a local population. As to the methodological principles, Medick, in accordance with Italian "micro-storia," stresses the linkage of different types of sources concerning the same person. So, he can show that in the eighteenth century while material welfare was on the increase among the Laichingen weavers, the mortality rates of children and adults were becoming higher. This contradiction was balanced among the inhabitants by intensive religious feelings, organized in local *pietist circles. Paradoxically, this mixture of Swabian business, productivity, and piety succeeded in surviving up to the twentieth century and found its niche in capitalist society.

In both books local history addresses more general purposes. David Sabean for instance, considers "the varieties of human society" as "a sequence of specialized adaptations to different economic circumstances," which could be studied best on a local scale (Sabean, p. 9). In spite of the subtlety of these outstanding contributions, the question remains, how will local history, especially in its grass-root forms, follow this very professional way, or even whether it should do so.

WERNER TROßBACH

Germans. see Appendix A.

ghost towns, an American view. Ghost towns often bring to mind tumbleweeds skimming along a dusty street lined with the faded facades of abandoned buildings of the Old West era. The well-preserved, former mining camp of Bodie, California, comes to mind. Most ghost towns, however, are sites—illusive, difficult to locate, with standing structures such as houses, saloons, churches, stores, and perhaps a jail the exception. Though concentrated in the western half of the United States, ghost towns can be found in almost every state. Many were short-lived, such as the boom-and-bust towns of the California Gold Rush. Others were long lived like Calabazas, Arizona, inhabited since the 1600s, which became overshadowed as a port of entry by Nogales, Arizona, and died by 1883.

Towns become ghosts for many reasons. When natural resources dry up, towns fade away. Exhausted mines— coal in Iowa, gold in California and Alaska, silver in Nevada, lead in Colorado, iron in New Jersey—cause people to seek their livings elsewhere. As prices for copper fell, mines in Arizona closed. Timber runs out; people move on.

Changes in the way goods and people are transported can cause a town to die. The now-familiar demise of a town by-passed by a new freeway has it roots in the old town bypassed by the railroad. Even when the railroad gave rise to new towns such as Skiddy, Kansas, the town can die because the tracks are moved elsewhere or as in the case of Fairbanks, Arizona, the train no longer stopped there.

Other reasons for towns to die include school consolidation, financial panic/depressions, and politics (the town that became county seat usually survived).

Today, ghost towns are a source of pleasure for backcountry exploring and are a good way to introduce one to studying local history. Sources include oral histories from people who have lived in the towns or who are descendants of residents. Local archives, libraries, and historical societies house family histories, newspaper accounts, letters, diaries, memoirs, maps, state and county records, and photographs. The remains of the towns themselves, especially the cemeteries, also speak about their residents.

See Larry Wakefield, *Ghost Towns of Michigan*, vol. II (Holt, Mich., 1995); Daniel C. Fitzgerald, *Faded Dreams: More Ghost Towns of Kansas* (Lawrence, Kan., 1994); Remi Nadeau, *Ghost Towns and Mining Camps of California: A History and a Guide* (Santa Barbara, 1992); Arthur D. Pierce, *Iron in the Pines: The Story of New Jersey's Ghost Towns and Bog Iron* ([1957] New Brunswick, N.J., 1990); Eric N. Moody, *Flanigan: Anatomy of a Railroad Ghost Town* (Susanville, Calif., 1985); David M. Gradwohl and Nancy M. Osborn, *Exploring Buried Buxton: Archaeology of an Abandoned Iowa Coal Mining Town with a Large Black Population* (Ames, Ia., 1984); and Thelma Heatwole, *Ghost Towns and Historical Haunts in Arizona* (Phoenix, 1981).

Many websites can be found by plugging "ghost towns" into a search engine. A most useful website can be found at <http://www. ghosttowns.com>.

KATHLEEN PAPARCHONTIS

ghost towns, an English view. Towns and villages become totally uninhabited, or have the number of inhabitants greatly reduced for a number of reasons. As one writer (M. W. Beresford, *The Lost Villages of England* [London, 1954]) put it, "a village was as mortal as a man."

Perhaps the most obvious reason for a change in size was economic: for example, the township put up during a gold rush then abandoned when the claims became uneconomic to mine. Or the agricultural settlement abandoned when unsustainable farming practices have been followed. Or the civic or ecclesiastic government moves its administration or courthouse, and as a result, the settlement grows poorer and shrinks.

Sometimes settlements are abandoned in the face of natural disaster: cliff erosion or volcanic threat, for example. In other cases, settlements are moved to make way for reservoirs, military areas, and other activities not compatible with human habitation.

Where the settlement is owned by a single landowner, personal decisions to change the land use (moving from mixed farming to sheep, or to landscaping for a great house) can result in the settlement being moved.

Settlements can move for other reasons: attraction to a new religious center or transport node such as a railway station or canal wharf—this has the effect of creating a "ghost town" at the old location.

While the people are gone, or reduced in number, the settlement can live on in many ways: in the political/ecclesiastical landscape, in buildings, in archaeological remains, in placenames, and in local tradition.

PAT REYNOLDS

godparent. A godparent is one asked by parents to sponsor a child at the time of baptism. Customs vary as to the godparent's responsibilities thereafter.

government. See local government records and local government research topics.

grassroots history. An early use of the term "grassroots" dates to 1876 when the Black Hills were described as having gold everywhere, "even in the 'grass roots'" (see Richard I. Dodge, *The Black Hills* [N.Y., 1876]). Later uses of the term imply getting down to basics.

In 1940, Constance McLaughlin Green wrote an essay entitled "The Value of Local History" (in Caroline F. Ware, *The Cultural Approach to History* [N.Y.; reprinted in Carol Kammen, *Pursuit of Local History* (Walnut Creek, Calif., 1996, pp. 90–99)]) wherein she wrote that to understand the importance of American history one had to look locally. "There lie the grass roots of American civilization," she noted. The term, thereafter, has meant the history closest to the people.

Theodore Blegan begins his book *Grassroots History* (Minneapolis, 1947) with the comment that "the pivot of history is not the uncommon, but the usual, and the true makers of history are 'the people, yes.'" He insists that the essence of history should be to grapple with the "need to understand the small, everyday elements, the basic elements, in the large movements." That grassroots history recognizes the importance of the simple, Blegan wrote, "however complex and subtle the problem of understanding the simple may be."

gravestone inscriptions. There are many compilations of gravestone inscriptions. This is from *Permanent New*

Yorkers, by Judi Culbertson (Chelsea, Vt., 1987):

> *Here I lie by the chancel door;*
> *They put me here because I was poor.*
> *The further in, the more you pay,*
> *But here I lie as snug as they.*
> (Anonymous)

gravestones. Becoming nearly as fragile as paper documents, gravestones offer insights into many kinds of topics—such as biographical, artistic, cultural, and social to name a few—besides a community's history.

Genealogists use gravestones to trace individuals. Dates inscribed on stones verify other documentary evidence and clusters of stones in family plots sometimes lead to previously unidentified relatives. Epitaphs, like one composed in 1771: "Here lies as silent clay/Miss Arabella Young/Who on the 21st of May/ Began to hold her tongue," sometimes reveal amusing personality traits.

Symbols on the stones denote military service, occupations, fraternal and religious affiliations, and professions. Researchers can reconstruct the lives of early stonecarvers by identifying stylistic trademarks in images, plotting sites where stones appear, and occasionally discovering carvers' initials inscribed at the base of stones, sometimes even, below ground.

From colonial times to the present, tombstones have reflected changing styles of ornament. The death's head, common before the American Revolution, reflects the austerity of Puritanism. The winged-soul image that followed demonstrates a more liberal artistic taste, paralleling the optimism of the new country. Greek and Egypt-

ian motifs duplicate the early-nineteenth-century interest in classical designs. Voluptuous statuary and funereal symbols like the tree stump, the severed flower bud, and the lamb characterize the Victorian period. Modern stones, some with amusing decoration, such as a set of golf clubs, a sailboat, or a gun, reflect the individualism of the person they memorialize.

During the late nineteenth and early twentieth centuries it was common for distinctive cultural groups to reserve cemetery sections for their own people. Stones in these areas often use language and symbols that distinguished the culture; for example, the Star of David, portrait medallions, Eastern and other variations of the cross. And the rising popularity of buying monuments for pets and incorporating images of celebrities on tombstones reflects changes in American culture.

Burial plots have always been separated according to social classes. In larger cemeteries, barren paupers' grounds are distant from landscaped plots reserved for the affluent. Even in small-town and country settings, plain stones memorializing African Americans sit on the fringes of old burying grounds. Hedgerows and iron railings separate prominent families from each other and from other social classes. And, of course, impressive mausoleums and fine sculpture define the resting places of more prosperous residents.

One problem with using very early gravestones as historical documents concerns the accuracy of dates and spelling. At the end of the eighteenth and early nineteenth centuries, carvers were often illiterate itinerants who arrived at a household long after the loved one(s) had departed. Spellings may also vary; inscribers of early stones commonly misspelled words or ran out of space, necessitating the insertion of missing letters above the omissions. Verifying data with other documents can assure accuracy.

Finding particular tombstones can present problems as well. While large cemeteries have full-time staffs and carefully kept records, it may be difficult to find the person(s) responsible for graveyards in smaller communities. Fortunately, a Works Progress Administration project during the Depression encouraged some municipalities to inventory the cemeteries in their jurisdictions; some of these include inscriptions on the stones. Inventories, if they exist, may be found in local libraries and/or historical societies. However, monuments mentioned in them may no longer exist. Hidden family plots must be searched for in fields and woods near farms.

Due to natural and human factors, gravestones are disappearing as historical documents. Alternating freezing and thawing weather splits slate and sandstone, which maintain the clearest carvings for the longest time, shearing off sections of a gravestone's face. Acid rain erodes the carvings on more porous stones, obliterating imagery and messages. Careless mowing of burial plots chips away at the bases of tombstones. Researchers, anxious to record a significant find or an attractive motif, thoughtlessly apply damaging substances to capture a rubbing or a photograph. Graveyards have been perennial haunts of pranksters who think that tipping over a monument is a daring deed. And the late-twentieth-century development of the memorial park, with its unadorned markers imbedded in the ground and its characterless mausoleums and urn cubicles, has little research appeal.

Fortunately, groups of citizens who recognize the values of gravestones have banded together in "Friends" organizations. These volunteers raise consciousness by leading tours, sponsoring photographic publications, and giving illustrated lectures. Money raised through their efforts is used to repair damaged monuments and to help with maintenance. School curricula often incorporate research in local cemeteries, thereby instilling in youngsters the value of these stones. In several large cities, cemeteries have become stops on tour-guide itineraries.

The Association for Gravestone Studies (AGS), begun in 1977, is an organization devoted to "furthering the study and preservation of gravestones." Broadening its focus from New England graveyards to a national and finally an international scope, the AGS holds annual conferences, publishes a quarterly newsletter and an annual journal, *Markers*. It also advises interested groups and individuals about gravestone preservation, research, and education. Information may be obtained from the Association of Gravestone Studies, 278 Main Street, Suite 207, Greenfield, Massachusetts 01301; (413) 772-0836; <ags@javanet.com> and <http://gemini.berkshire.net/ags>.

One place to discover where "noteworthy" (and a few notorious) people are interred is <www.findagrave.com>.

The researcher can search by names of persons, by burial sites, and by "claims to fame." Many of the entries also have accompanying photographs of the monuments, and some even have street maps attached. The website also has a valuable bibliography of publications about regional gravesites and can lead a researcher to other resting places of local celebrities.

See M. Ruth Little, *Sticks & Stones: Three Centuries of North Carolina Gravemarkers* (Chapel Hill, N.C., 1998); Theodore Chase and Laurel K. Gabel. *Gravestone Chronicles* I (Boston, 1997); David C. Sloane, *The Last Great Necessity: Cemeteries in American History* (Baltimore, 1991); Francis Y. Duval and Ivan B. Rigby, *Early American Gravestone Art in Photographs* (N.Y.,

1978); and Harriett Merrifield Forbes, *Gravestones of Early New England and the Men Who Made Them 1653–1800* (Boston, 1927).

TERESA K. LEHR

Great Awakening. Between 1726 and 1756, the Great Awakening consisted of a series of religious revivals, spurred by the preaching of George Whitefield, Theodorus Frelinghuysen, Jonathan Edwards, Samuel Davies, and others, that swept from Maine to Georgia.

Greek Orthodox Church. See Appendix B.

Greeks. See Appendix A.

Gypsies. See Appendix A.

---

habeas corpus. The term is Latin for "you have the body." It refers to a legal writ used to free an individual from illegal confinement, a guarantee that a prisoner is given due process of law. In the United States, it is the constitutional guarantee against false imprisonment.

Haitians. See Appendix A.

hamlet. The word "hām" comes from Old English, meaning homestead; a hamlet is a cluster of residential, incidental, and possibly agricultural build-

ings without a municipal designation. Sometimes a hamlet is called an unincorporated *village.

Harvard Encyclopedia of American Ethnic Groups. See Appendix A and ethnicity.

health care, as local history topic. The subject of health care has become increasingly complicated in the past two centuries. Early Americans believed in simple theories of diseases and their treatments, casual methods of educating physicians, and basic solutions to the problems of health-care financing and delivery. However, the end of the nineteenth century experienced an explosion of knowledge about diseases and how they affect the human body. This brought about a multifaceted revolution in medical science and has mushroomed into the complex systems that exist today. In the early years, physicians attributed disease to one of two causes. The first, an imbalance of fluids in the body, led to the heroic remedies of bleeding and purging. This simple theory required a rudimentary curriculum. A man could assume the title of "doctor" by merely attending a two-year series of lectures at one of the medical colleges associated with Eastern universities. Or he could call himself "Doctor" by taking a few courses at a local school of medicine and apprenticing to a local physician for a few years. Many of the schools of medicine were located in small but growing communities; their durations were short, and they often relocated to more promising locales. Records of these establishments are rare, but the schools' existence can be established by searching announcements in local newspapers or listings in city directories.

In the late 1800s, as germ theory of disease gained adherence, surgical methods improved, other theories proliferated, and medical training expanded. Publication of the highly critical Flexner Report in 1910 led to a standardization of medical education. Originally, medical training distinguished between two specialties: medicine and surgery, the former being the most prestigious because of its greater rate of success. As knowledge about the human body expanded and as technology became more sophisticated, however, curricula in colleges of medicine became more involved and lengthy. Medical libraries at universities with schools of medicine often have excellent collections that trace the progress of medical education.

The miasmic theory held that contagion originated in the noxious odors arising from stagnant pools and untreated sewage, and that inadequate drainage spread disease in crowded communities. This belief led to local ordinances requiring individuals and businesses to clean up their properties, particularly during epidemics. Minutes of local government bodies show increasing attempts to control the spread of disease by regulating the environment. These concerns evolved into additional public health measures in the early twentieth century. Municipalities appointed city physicians, monitored drinking water sources, and established milk stations that distributed certified milk for infants. Later, visiting and district nurses educated citizens; free clinics examined school children; immunization clinics became routine. Newspaper articles document these public health movements.

Because health was predominantly a family issue, few early physicians could make a living by practicing medicine alone. The public's growing interest in good health during the last quarter of the nineteenth century, however, gave increased prestige to medical practitioners. Medical societies, formed to influence health-care legislation both at the state and community levels, gained prominence and power at the turn of the century. Academies of medicine, designed to isolate the profession from pretenders—quacks and patent medicine purveyors—established libraries and scheduled lecture series to keep local physicians abreast of new discoveries and to share observations with one another.

Toward the end of the Depression, medical associations identified increasing government intervention as a new threat to their autonomy and position. Malpractice insurance, hospital and medical school policies, and an educated public further eroded their position during the latter half of the twentieth century. Medical societies and academies of medicine in midsized to large cities have preserved many of the documents that help tell this story.

In rural America, too, during the early nineteenth century, health care was primarily a family affair. As settlements turned into villages and towns and the number of physicians increased, the rich and the middle class—who could afford the services of medical practitioners—were treated in their own homes.

The impoverished sick, on the other hand, were a serious problem in the close environments of growing cities. Benevolent societies, overseers of the poor, officially appointed city physicians, pest houses, and almshouse infirmaries were early attempts to help the poor and to isolate them. The third quarter of the nineteenth century saw a shift in attitudes toward hospitals, originally established for the poor. Physicians recognized that their wealthy, private patients would also benefit from a

hospital stay. Accordingly, hospitals added luxurious, private rooms to accommodate more affluent clientele. Gradually, clinics and dispensaries helped the middle class who could, for small fees, receive treatment that allowed them to continue working. The establishment of hospital insurance during the Depression finally made hospital stays affordable for every economic level in a community.

In older cities where there were medical colleges, early hospitals were established to treat the sick poor. These institutions, established by physicians and local business and political leaders, became demonstration sites giving students clinical experience, and removing patients from disease-ridden environments. Immigration and westward expansion prompted religious groups and charitable organizations to create hospitals in new communities. Toward the end of the nineteenth century, competing medical theories spurred the establishment of additional hospitals promoting homeopathic and other therapies. Local contributions, donated medical services, and volunteerism were the life blood of these institutions. Church collections, subscriptions, public appeals, and community contributions supported hospitals, activities that were well documented in local newspapers. Records, photographs, and relics, collected and preserved for institutional anniversaries, are frequently available to researchers. In addition, centennial and sesquicentennial celebrations have produced some histories and exhibits, and more recently, this information has been chronicled electronically.

As the twentieth century progressed

and communities became more dependent on hospitals for health care, individual physicians established small private hospitals in outlying towns. From the mid-twentieth century on, federal aid for local health care, particularly from the Commonwealth Fund and the Hill-Burton Act, encouraged small communities to build, equip, and staff their own hospitals. Newspaper accounts document these movements. Records for private hospitals are rare. Community hospitals have been required to keep good records, but they are often stored in out-of-the-way places. Public-relations personnel may have a sense of where to find information, but lack of time and human resources makes historical research in such institutions difficult.

Training for nurses was formalized after the Civil War when a few hospitals established schools. As an understanding of the causes of disease grew, training for nurses became more complex, and hospitals relied on student nurses' services. Two-year programs expanded into three-year programs as the twentieth century opened. During the first quarter of the twentieth century, the movement to require the registration of nurses was successful. This fact, combined with an increasingly complex curriculum, reassigned nursing chores to graduate nurses. Nursing shortages, notably during the world wars, contributed to the training of adjunct nursing personnel: practical nurses, nurses aides, and others. During the second half of the twentieth century, increased specialization and technological advances have led to the establishment of four-year, degree-granting nursing programs at local colleges and universities. Unable to compete with these new programs, hospital-based schools of nursing gradually closed. Nurses' alumni associations and military organizations have proudly preserved their documents and material culture, sometimes within the hospitals that ran the schools.

See Paul Starr, *The Social Transformation of American Medicine* (N.Y., 1982).

TERESA LEHR

herbal. A book with descriptions of plants giving their medicinal uses. The first herbals were written in ancient Greece around the fourth century B.C. Because the reader needed to correctly identify the plants in order to use them medicinally, most herbals were illustrated. The credit for the first herbal of indigenous drugs designed for the former British North American colonies goes to Samuel Stearns, a colonial physician. His landmark work entitled, simply, *The American Herbal* was published in Walpole, New Hampshire, in 1801 and focused on the organic and inorganic materia medica indigenous to both North and South America.

heritage. Heritage is an elusive and frequently misunderstood word-concept that has meant diverse things to different people in varied times and places. Although it came into very common usage during the last quarter of the twentieth century (excessively invoked at times, often to the point of cliché), it had assorted predecessors, such as the word "patrimony," which has cognates in all cultures where romance languages are used, such as *pat-*

rimoine in French and *patrimonio* in Portuguese.

At the end of the nineteenth century and early in the twentieth, when colonialism reached its peak, many observers in Europe and the United States assumed that some of the world's people (such as themselves) had a history, whereas others in less "developed" societies had seemingly timeless cultures that existed beyond the boundaries of history. Nevertheless, both types of societies had "heritages" even though that particular word was not yet widely used. The concept itself, however, certainly was. But heritage is not a broader or a more inclusive notion than history or culture. Rather, it is a different kind of concept, more value-laden, that can selectively draw upon or cut across the other two.

In recent decades, as heritage has been increasingly invoked for purposes of commercial promotion and cultural *tourism, many professional scholars have felt that the word-concept has been degraded, particularly when used casually, confusingly, or interchangeably with history. Hence, David Lowenthal (a historical geographer) wrote the following in 1996: "Heritage is not a testable or even a reasonably plausible account of some past, but a *declaration of faith* in that past. Critics castigate heritage as a travesty of history. But heritage is not history, even when it mimics history. It uses historical traces and tells historical tales, but these tales and traces are stitched into fables that are open neither to critical analysis nor to comparative scrutiny." That is a harsh judgment, yet understandable given the many abuses during immediately preceding decades.

Heritage may be appropriately perceived and understood in many contexts: national, regional (e.g., Southern or Yankee heritage), ethnic, racial, and religious (denominational, sectarian, or even a particular parish with a strong sense of tradition and identity). It is also suitably used in connection with ceremonies and rituals, cuisine, folklore, festivals, and distinctive styles of dress. There are, of course, numerous combinations of these categories and subcategories that are described and understood as heritage, such as the blues and jazz being vital in the African American heritage.

It should be acknowledged, however, that heritage is invoked intensively in a positive, even celebratory manner. It is applied to those aspects of life that people affirm and wish to remember—quite often uncritically. Groups are entitled to take pride in their heritage, but not in the ersatz versions that have been invented for commercial purposes or to validate a sense of superior identity. Above all, people should not blithely assume that pride in heritage is the same thing as historical information and understanding. Ideally, an enthusiastic interest in the former may stimulate an increased desire and appetite for the latter.

It also needs to be recognized that important institutions and organizations exist whose legitimate purpose is to preserve historical knowledge *and* to promote a sense of heritage. Examples include state and local historical societies, the *National Park Service, the *National Trust for Historic Preservation, the *Society for the Preservation of New England Antiquities, and the

Association for the Preservation of *Virginia Antiquities.

History and heritage are less like fraternal twins and more like second cousins: related but not intimately so. Ideally, they ought to be collaborative friends rather than conflicted foes, as Lowenthal discerned to be the case so often in the later twentieth century.

See David Lowenthal, *Possessed by the Past: The Heritage Crusade and the Spoils of History* (N.Y., 1996); and Michael Kammen, "History is Our Heritage: The Past in Contemporary American Culture," in Kammen, *In the Past Lane: Historical Perspectives on American Culture* (N.Y., 1997), pp. 213–25.

MICHAEL KAMMEN

heritage tourism. See tourism.

Hispanic Americans. See Appendix A.

historian, a or an. There are two schools of thought concerning the use of "a" or "an" preceding historical, historian, history, and other words that are derived from Greek, which had no letter "h." According to a learned and charming article by Wendell Tripp, entitled "How to Disenvowel a Charging Historian" (*Wisconsin Magazine of History* [Spring 1970]), the *h* sound that we hear today was represented by a symbol called a *spiritus asper* (s.a.). Thus, the Greek word would have been preceded by "a." The s.a., however, gave way to our modern *h*, consequently many people use "an" believing it the correct article.

This is something about which people will probably always disagree. For the sake of sanity and unity in this volume, we have elected to follow the Greeks and use "a." So: a historian might wrestle with a historical problem when writing a history of her hometown.

Those wishing to avoid the problem altogether might consider Wendell Tripp's solution, which is to insert an adjective. Thus, he suggests we praise a good history written by a careful historian who considers a thorny historical problem part of a day's work.

Historic American Buildings Survey. The Historic American Buildings Survey (HABS) is the oldest of the federal historic preservation programs, founded in 1933 as relief employment during the Great Depression. It is the last remaining WPA-era cultural program. HABS's mission is to document historic American buildings through the production of architectural measured drawings, large-format photographs, and written histories.

HABS was the brainchild of Charles E. Peterson. In a 1933 memorandum to his superiors in the National Park Service, he wrote:

The plan I propose is to enlist a qualified group of architects and draftsmen to study, measure and draw up the plans, elevations and details of the important antique buildings of the United States. Our architectural heritage of buildings from the last four centuries diminishes daily at an alarming rate. The ravages of fire and the natural elements together with the demolition and alterations caused by real estate "improvements" form an inexorable tide of destruction destined to wipe out the great majority of the buildings which knew the beginning and first flourish of the nation. . . . It is the responsibility of the American people that if the great number of our antique buildings must disappear

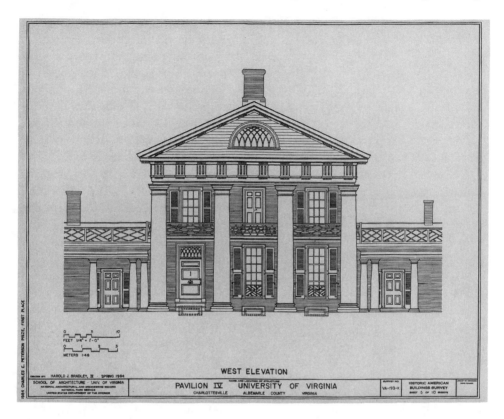

WEST ELEVATION

PAVILION IV   UNIVERSITY OF VIRGINIA
CHARLOTTESVILLE   ALBEMARLE COUNTY   VIRGINIA

through economic causes, they should not pass into unrecorded oblivion.

The list of building types . . . should include public buildings, churches, residences, bridges, forts, barns, mills, shops, rural outbuildings, and any other kind of structure of which there are good specimens extant. . . . Other structures which would not engage the especial interest of an architectural connoisseur are the great number of plain structures which by fate or accident are identified with historic events.

Peterson's proposal quickly received the support of the *National Park Service, the *Library of Congress, and the American Institute of Architects, the three organizations that continue to operate HABS cooperatively over six decades later. The National Park Service

produces the documentation, the Library of Congress cares for the collection and makes it available to the public, and the American Institute of Architects provides technical support through its Historic Resources Committee.

The primary use of HABS documentation is for the stewardship of historic buildings by providing baseline records of existing conditions to help with planning maintenance or restoration work. It also preserves in graphic and written records buildings that have been lost to demolition, natural disasters, or accidents. The HABS collection contains documentation on over 35,200 historic buildings, including 53,300 measured drawings, 193,000

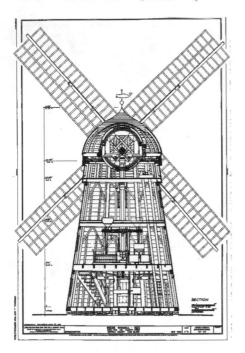

and ships—through the production of measured and interpretive drawings, large-format photographs, and written histories. Prior to 1969, documentation of engineering and industrial sites had been produced by HABS. All of the documentation is in the public domain and is accessible to the public through the Prints and Photographs Division of the Library of Congress in Washington, D.C. HAER documentation may be researched and viewed online at the Library of Congress' "Built in America" website at: <http://memory.loc.gov/am mem/hhhtml/hhhome.html>.

The HAER program was begun in response to a growing concern that early-American achievements in engineering and industry were being lost, through abandonment or replacement prompted by technological improvements, at a pace that did not allow historical perspective to evaluate their significance. It is operated under a 1969 Tripartite Agreement among the National Park Service, the Library of Congress, and the American Society of Civil Engineers. The National Park Service produces the documentation, the Library of Congress cares for the collection and makes it available to the public, and the American Society of Civil Engineers provides technical support through its History and Heritage Committee. In 1987, support of the HAER program was expanded through a protocol that included the other founding engineering societies: the American Society of Mechanical Engineers, the Institute of Electrical and Electronics Engineers, the American Institute of Chemical Engineers, and the American Institute of Mining, Metallurgical and Petroleum Engineers.

photographs, and 123,700 data pages. Approximately one-third of the buildings documented have been subsequently lost, a figure that reflects the program's emphasis on documenting endangered buildings.

Information about the program may be found at its website <http://www. cr.nps.gov/habshaer/habs> and in the book, *Recording Historic Structures* (Washington, D.C., 1989).

JOHN A. BURNS

Historic American Engineering Record.
The Historic American Engineering Record (HAER) of the *National Park Service is a companion program to the *Historic American Buildings Survey (HABS). Founded in 1969, HAER documents historic American engineering, industrial and maritime achievements—such as bridges, dams, canals, railroads, highways, factories,

The primary use of HAER documentation is for the stewardship of historic engineering and industrial structures by providing baseline records of existing conditions to help with planning maintenance or restoration work. The interpretive drawings explain archaic industrial processes and engineering designs. It also preserves in graphic and written records structures that have been lost to technological or economic obsolescence, demolition, natural disasters, or accidents. The HAER collection contains documentation on over 7,000 historic engineering and industrial structures, including 3,000 measured and interpretive drawings, 60,000 photographs, and 49,000 data pages.

Information about the program may be found at its website, <http://www.cr.nps.gov/habshaer/haer>, and in the book, *Recording Historic Structures* (Washington, D.C., 1989).

JOHN A. BURNS

historic monuments. See monuments.

historic preservation. Although the first major sites to be preserved in the United States were those seen as significant in national history—Washington's Hasbrouck House headquarters at Newburgh, New York, and his home at Mount Vernon, Virginia, both saved in the 1850s—their expression of history was in their immediate, tangible presence in a very specific locale. Thus their national history was also local history. Throughout the nineteenth and twentieth centuries, developments in local history were reflected in the growth of types of historic preservation activities, and developments in historic-preservation often influenced perceptions of local history. One of the best ways to study the development of local history in the United States is to examine historic preservation in the last two centuries. Since the sites, objects, folkways, and other subjects of historic preservation are "real," they also provide wonderful places from which to examine changes in historiography, and in myth-making, and in the very uses of history by professionals, amateurs, and casual observers. Because historic preservation has such deep local roots, local history museums and historic sites have become central to understanding "a sense of place" in the context of our lives. Both historic preservation and local history have played major roles in the continued maturing of our abilities to tell the stories of the nation.

Broadly viewed, historic preservation is a process for incorporating elements of the past into the present and future. It includes the identification, recording, study and, where appropriate, preservation and continued use of selected tangible structures, landscapes and objects, and selected intangible cultural expressions such as folkways. Historic preservation also includes methods of education and presentation of what has been identified, recorded, and interpreted. It includes the tools for identification and recording (such as *archaeology and *oral history), the tools for planned preservation and continued use (such as conservation, preservation planning, and preservation law), and the tools for presentation to a great variety of people, such as heritage education, heritage *tourism, museum programs and the techniques of media presentations.

Though the term "historic preservation" did not become current until the twentieth century, a growing number of sites, structures, and objects were saved for preservation and interpretation in the sixty years after the Civil War. This work included the acquisition of the first state and national parks. A number of the parks—and of the other sites saved—focused on memorializing one of four particularly prominent historical themes: pioneers and the pioneering spirit, George Washington and the American Revolution, the Civil War, and Native Americans. In the same period, the first local, regional, and national preservation organizations were formed.

Worship of Washington extended to almost any place he had been, as suggested by the proverbial, "Washington slept here." Before the end of the century, a site had been preserved simply because Washington had rested there on his way to battle. In the old Maryland Senate chamber where Washington had stood before the Continental Congress in 1783 to resign his commission, a historical-minded supervisor of the 1859 renovations made measured drawings of the woodwork that had seen that remarkable day; those drawings became the basis for the 1904 restoration of the room. Even Washington's mother was memorialized, with the Mary Washington Monument at Fredericksburg, Virginia, completed in 1889, by the Ladies Monument Association. In 1890 Mary Washington's house in Fredericksburg became one of the first projects of the new Association for the Preservation of

*Virginia Antiquities, which acquired the house to prevent its being bought and disassembled for re-erection as an exhibit at the Columbian Exposition in Chicago.

Following the Civil War, Americans needed to mark and preserve places important to both sides. They placed markers on graves, monuments on battlefields, and monuments to the women of the homefront. They saved trench lines, and shell holes and cannon balls in the walls into which they had been shot.

Throughout the intervening years, in every part of the country, civilian sites have been piously preserved for their association with the leaders of each side. In 1889, the state of New York established the Grant Cottage State Historic Site, at Mt. McGregor, New York, and, in 1895, the John Brown Farm State Historic Site at Lake Placid, New York. Several sites associated with the life of Jefferson Davis were preserved. In 1900, in Montgomery, Alabama, The First White House of the Confederacy became the first Confederate domestic site saved—although, it would have to be saved again, later.

Meanwhile, pioneer struggles were represented in historical monuments and sites preserved in the later nineteenth century, some representing settlers and pioneers of the earliest days, others representing pioneer struggles of the recent past. The Hannah Dustin Monument, a state monument erected in 1874 at Penacook, New Hampshire, commemorated the 1697 kidnapping of Hannah by Indians, and her subsequent escape. Mission churches and other Spanish colonial sites were saved in California and New Mexico, as was the Adobe Palace in Santa Fe. In 1890 the state of Idaho set aside places on two trails to the west. One was the City of Rocks, near Almo, Idaho, a natural landmark on the California Trail where pioneers had carved their names on the rocks; the other was Register Rock, near American Falls, Idaho, a place on the Oregon Trail where pioneers had also inscribed their names.

Even as the remaining struggles were carried on to force the Indians onto reservations, historic sites important to *Indian history began to be saved. In 1891 Minnesota acquired Itasca State Park in Clearwater County. Itasca contained a number of important Indian archaeological sites. In the same year Fort Ancient Earthworks, near Lebanon, Ohio, was saved for its two important Indian archaeological sites, a prehistoric Hopewell-culture hilltop enclosure and the Fort Ancient Village site, circa 1600.

In 1873 a committee was created for the restoration of Independence Hall. In 1876 An Old-Time New England Farm House was shown at the Centennial Exposition itself. Other preservation activities of 1876 illustrate the breadth of interest in preservation, for properties as distant and disparate as the Old South Meeting House in Boston and the old mission church of San Luis Obispo, California, were saved from demolition and ruin.

An important turning point in attitudes about preservation came at the third annual convention of the American Institute of Architects, held in 1869, where AIA president Richard Upjohn gave a paper on the colonial architec-

ture of New York and New England, recommending collection of data. By the 1870s and 1880s, measured drawings and other recordings began on a relatively large and systematic scale, and by the 1890s the first typological architectural histories were published.

In the same era came the impetus for the 1872 saving of Yosemite as the first national park, this forty years before the *National Park Service existed. The growth of ideas about the conservation of natural places, an important part of the changing preservation scene of the late nineteenth century, is seen everywhere in the nation today. In Massachusetts in 1891, a group of leaders formed the Trustees of Reservations to save important examples of Massachusetts landscapes, and in Philadelphia in 1893, Bartram's Garden was acquired as a historic site.

In the 1880s, 1890s, and early 1900s, some very ordinary sites and structures were studied and saved by a variety of local, regional, and national organizations, agencies, and actions. But by the 1880s and 1890s the states began acquiring historic properties at a rate of about one a year, and the acceleration continued into a major movement of state governments into historic preservation by the early 1900s.

In 1889, the first statewide preservation organization was created, the Association for the Preservation of *Virginia Antiquities, and their first three projects indicated the range of their interests: the old church ruins at Jamestown, the Powder Horn at Williamsburg, and Mary Washington's house at Fredericksburg.

In 1889–1903, a range of governmental and private actions pointed toward some of the future patterns for preservation. In 1889 Congress authorized the establishment of Casa Grande reservation in Arizona to save the ruins of a prehistoric Native American structure. In 1895, Allison Owens suggested a landmarks preservation society for New Orleans. Also in 1895, Andrew H. Green outlined the idea of a nationwide preservation organization, subsequently developed as the American Scenic and Historic Preservation Society. In the 1890s the Daughters of the American Revolution and the National Society of Colonial Dames of America were founded, eventually taking on hundreds of preservation projects over the next century.

Professionalization in the planning of preservation began to be developed. In 1890 the American Institute of Architects created its Committee on Historic Sites. Beginning in 1902, Professor A. D. F. Hamlin of Columbia University systematically examined European approaches to the scientific conservation of structures. In 1903, at Bruton Parish Church in Williamsburg, Reverend W.A.R. Goodwin began to dream of restoring not only the church but the major part of the town. Efforts were being made to broaden our whole vision of our cultural roots, and to begin to create a museum profession. The *American Association of Museums was founded in 1906, one of many steps toward professionalism in the fields related to historic preservation.

Private preservation became a major activity in this same period. For example, in 1904 the Hubbard family of Chestertown, Maryland, restored Widehall, their old house on the waterfront.

"What do you suppose is wrong with Mrs. Hubbard," friends are said to have asked, "she's gone out buying used furniture for her house." The image of finding an old house to restore and refurnish would soon be understood by a growing segment of Americans. A number of museums encouraged the use of buildings and objects to teach history, often through period-room exhibits. In 1913–1914 officials of the Metropolitan Museum of Art began searching for actual period paneling to install in a whole new "American Wing," and in 1914 the Public Museum in Milwaukee began plans for a "colonial village."

The rate of acquisition of historic sites by the states, which had begun to accelerate in the 1890s, doubled in each of the first four decades of the twentieth century, often linked to natural conservation through state park services, such as the very first one, Indiana's, in 1918. The themes represented by state historic sites continued to be those of the grandeur and the hardship of settlement and pioneering westward, the memorialization of Native Americans, of George Washington and the Revolution, of the Civil War, and of battles won and lost, including those of the local and regional governments.

The increasing range of historical sites that Americans thought worthy of preserving are suggested by several new types of sites of the 1910s: an elm tree marking the site of a famous Indian speech, a former portage point for the canoes of fur traders and explorers, three early U.S. military posts, an Ohio Company Land Office, an early settler's house that had been immortalized in a poem, the Bunker Hill Monument, the buildings of Old Economy, and the site of the 1874 Black Hills gold rush.

The federal government had been involved in historic preservation since the days of the early republic, particularly through the continued ownership by the War Department of hundreds of forts, arsenals, and armories, and by the Navy Department of dozens of navy yards and similar complexes. Yosemite and the other national parks were other precursors of Park Service work. But major, direct federal involvement in historic preservation was one of the great achievements by preservationists in the twentieth century. The Antiquities Act of 1906 authorized the president to protect archaeological and historical sites on federally owned or federally controlled land—the first time a preservation principle was made national law. This was followed by the creation of the National Park Service in 1916, the Historic Sites Act of 1935, the chartering of the *National Trust for Historic Preservation in 1947, the National Historic Preservation Act of 1966, and a host of other actions.

In the 1920s, preservation projects included the recreation of settlement groupings. At a homely level, groups of historic structures suggesting earlier land-use patterns were represented in such state projects as Pike's Stockade, in Conejos County, Colorado, a 1925 replica of a log stockade built by Zebulon Pike in 1807; or Fort Shantok, in Montville, Connecticut, the site of a Mohegan Indian village, established as a state historic park in 1925, the first attempt on the East Coast to understand life patterns of the Native Americans there.

The concept of recreating the entire town of Williamsburg, Virginia moved such village projects to the forefront of preservation. In 1926, Reverend W. A. R. Goodwin interested John D. Rockefeller, Jr. in buying various major structures and sites in Williamsburg, in order to recreate the setting of the eighteenth-century capital of Virginia. In the decades after 1926, the Williamsburg project grew to include restoration of more than 80 original structures and the recreation of some 300 others, with the development of a corps of architects, landscape architects, contractors, archaeologists, and interpreters. The recreated Williamsburg became one of the most popular projects ever conceived, one of the first great successes of the age of automobile *tourism, and a powerful force in the general culture. The Colonial Revival style of the 1930s is very largely in imitation of the Williamsburg style, and Williamsburg buildings were models for official buildings in many other states.

The Williamsburg idea was related, at first distantly, and later, more closely, to Scandinavian museum villages, that were assembled from buildings typical of a given rural region, in which "folk-life" was exhibited. Scandinavian scholars of folk cultures had begun creating these as early as the 1880s, the most famous being Skansen. The "collected village" became a prominent part of American historical activism after World War II. A striking early example is Old Sturbridge Village, near Sturbridge, Massachusetts, which opened in 1946. The concept was exported to Canada in the 1950s, when Upper Canada Village was created from buildings that would otherwise have been drowned or destroyed in the building of the St. Lawrence Seaway. Individual projects of the midcentury and later combined the general "saving" thrust of the old model, Mount Vernon, with the new "accuracy of interpretation" associated with Williamsburg.

Articles about the collections at Williamsburg, in such publications as *The Magazine Antiques*, produced a greater enthusiasm for collecting and for the Williamsburg method of exhibition, in ostensibly "real" room settings. After World War II this was further reinforced by articles about the Winterthur Museum near Wilmington, Delaware, which opened in 1952; by those about the new National Trust and its properties and restorations; and by publicity surrounding the multimillion dollar recreation and refurnishing of Tryon's Palace at New Bern, North Carolina. In the 1960s, further impetus came from the tremendous publicity about the Kennedy administration project to refurnish the White House "authentically."

In the 1920s and 1930s the development of automobile tourism contributed to the interest in the establishment of state historic sites. Automobile tourism is the force behind state highway-marker programs, which in turn became the framework of a limited kind of historic sites survey program. The creation of state and national highways—U.S. Routes 1, 17, 40, 66—lead to the study of old roads themselves, and the identification of historic transportation structures, beginning with West Virginia's 1924 establishment as a historic site of the Wheeling Suspension Bridge.

The *Historic American Buildings Survey (HABS), begun in 1933, was another step toward a national program. One of the less-known, but very important, actions of the Franklin Roosevelt administration was the Historic Sites Act of 1935, which strengthened HABS, created the National Historic Sites Survey to identify *National Historic Landmarks, and enlarged the National Park Service involvement in historic parks. The National Historic Sites Survey was probably most important for the concept of thematic or contextual study of historic sites, and for developing ways to integrate standard historical documentary research and the new kind of research: minute examination and interpretation of sites and structures themselves.

One notable theme was the attempt to collect evidence about "high-style" American architecture and furniture, and codify the styles of American architecture and *decorative arts. Henry Francis du Pont's Winterthur collection of American decorative arts led to the creation of the Winterthur Program in Early American Culture in 1952, and to a number of related programs in the study, conservation, and interpretation of objects. A similar study program for industrial history was connected with the Hagley Museum in Delaware.

Another notable theme was the collection of evidence about more "ordinary" lives. Pennsylvania established a program to study and interpret the life of an eighteenth-century religious sect when it acquired the Ephrata Cloister in 1930–1945. In 1931 the state of Kentucky established the Mountain Life Museum, at London, with log buildings and objects depicting pioneer life. Other similar sites followed.

In 1938 Stephen Clark created the Cooperstown Museum, at Cooperstown, New York, and started planning a training program. Henry Ford, beginning in 1936, created the Henry Ford Museum and Greenfield Village at Dearborn, Michigan. The museum housed a splendid collection of the objects illustrating mechanical history. To this, Ford added a large collection of American decorative arts and material culture items in a series of room settings housed in a building whose design was based on Independence Hall. To Greenfield Village, Ford moved a hundred historic buildings, including his own birthplace, Thomas Edison's Menlo Park laboratory, the Wright brothers' bicycle shop, and other exhibits related to the great inventive and industrial history of the United States. He also moved structures from other parts of the country and other parts of the world, creating an early version of what the late twentieth century would call a "theme park."

From the 1950s through the 1990s, both academic studies and specialized organizations helped preservationists focus on ever-wider aspects of the historical record. Although in 1964 a National Trust property committee member could still say, "After all, there is nothing after 1780 worth looking at," that position was radically altered in that very year, by the Trust's acceptance of the Gothic Revival Lyndhurst at Tarrytown, New York (1837 and later), and of Frank Lloyd Wright's Pope-Leighey House of 1940. The broadening of the definition of preservation was further strengthened a few years later by the listing of Wright's masterpiece, Fallingwater, near Ohiopyle, Pennsylvania, as a National Historic Landmark and the acceptance by the National Trust of Philip Johnson's 1949 Glass House at New Canaan, Connecticut, as a historic house museum.

Accompanying these efforts to enlarge the scope of concern for "high architecture" was the growing interest in collecting data about more ordinary sites and structures, as well. Preservation groups with an antiquarian bent had begun recording "ordinary" data early in the century, an outstanding effort being that of the *Society for the Preservation of New England Antiquities, which, in addition to preserving and exhibiting dozens of individual structures throughout New England, had created the New England Museum, with exhibits of many building techniques, and the important journal, *Old-Time New England*, probably the first to print the minutiae of early building contracts and details of building techniques. In 1980, architectural historians and cultural geographers created the Vernacular Architecture Forum, paralleling the British Vernacular Architecture Group.

These efforts were enhanced by the development of historic-sites survey techniques, begun by some of the state landmarks organizations in the 1950s, and then enlarged in the State Historic Preservation Offices, following the passage of the National Historic Preservation Act of 1966. As State Historic Preservation Offices began to carry out the survey mandated by the 1966 act, they developed a cadre of young surveyors.

Historic-sites *archaeology began to be used, on a regular basis, as an important tool. The National Historic Preservation Act of 1966 made archaeology a cornerstone of preservation by requiring that an archaeologist be on the staff of every state historic preservation officer, and that the survey work to be carried out included identifying archaeological sites. Archaeological identification was required as a percentage of the cost of federal building projects. Hundreds of thousands of archaeological sites were recorded in the 1960s–1990s, the number of professional archaeologists employed in preservation work grew dramatically, and archaeologists made a major contribution to all preservationists in teaching methods of "thinking anthropologically" about historic sites and patterns of use, methods that fit well with "the new *social history."

"Thinking scientifically" was also present in the development of such techniques as dendrochronology ("tree-ring dating"), first developed for prehistoric structures in the Southwest, but later used with great success in the East as well. "Thinking curatorially" was yet another path of development in the 1960s–1990s, especially in the transfer of principles and techniques of scientific conservation of materials from fine-art works to distressed houses and archaeological fragments.

By the 1980s, *material-culture studies were the most important academic approaches to preservation. In 1964 Columbia University's Graduate School of Architecture and Planning became the first institution of higher education in the United States to offer courses in historic preservation; in 1967 it became the first to offer a degree program (Master of Science in Historic Preservation). In 1983 Mary Washington College in Fredericksburg, Virginia, created the first academic department of historic preservation, offering a B.A. in Historic Preservation. By the year 2000 there were dozens of undergraduate and graduate programs and courses in historic preservation, public history, and related aspects of "applied history" continuing the links between historic preservation and local history.

In the late twentieth century, preservationists came to accept the inclusion of historic engineering and transportation sites and structures, as well as commercial and industrial ones, as deserving historic-preservation study. But even though aspects of those subjects were present in the early projects, attention to commercial, industrial, and engineering sites per se was slow to develop. The first great wave of nostalgia focused on the covered wooden bridges as they began to be destroyed at a high rate.

Full attention to commercial, industrial, and engineering sites only appeared amid the rising tide of preservation activities of the 1960s and after, with the focus of such specialized groups as the Society for Industrial Archaeology and the Society for Commercial Archaeology, and the efforts of national engineering societies to develop their own programs to identify and mark structures important in their history. The establishment of the *Historic American Engineering Record gave full legitimacy to these fields, which were also enormously enriched by the attention caused by beneficial changes in tax programs of the 1970s and 1980s.

In the two decades after World War II, there was a marked acceleration in the creation of local historic-district programs throughout the United States. One of the most important processes in establishing a historic-district was that of drawing the boundary around an area, defining what was inside the boundary as "historic" and what was outside it as "not historic." It had been necessary to draw such boundaries in the historic district designations of the 1930s—for instance, boundaries for the Vieux Carre, the old French quarter in New Orleans—defining the area where the special controls and special tax benefits applied. But the large number of historic districts that were being identified on a regular basis during the 1950s and early 1960s required a more regularized approach. By the mid-1960s there were dozens of historic districts, located in many regions of the country, with strong local review powers. They were the harbingers of the many hundreds of such districts that were developed later.

Efforts to found a national preservation program had been made as early as 1895. But only in 1947 was the first national preservation body formed, which would continue as an important actor in preservation: the National Council for Historic Sites and Buildings, transformed in 1949 into the congressionally chartered National Trust for Historic Preservation in the United States of America. The National Trust was intended to be a private, nonprofit, membership organization, providing national leadership and preservation education, as well as preservation assistance to its individual and organizational members, and owning historic properties operated both for the public benefit and as models for other owners of historic properties.

The use of the term "National Trust" was an echo of that name as used in England. However, the two organizations developed on very different tracks, especially with regard to property ownership. In England, the National Trust acquired numerous large houses with large acreages, in part because such gifts could pay part of heavy estate taxes ("death duties") imposed after World War II. The farms, forest lands, and towns acquired with the English properties often provided incomes sufficient to maintain and improve them. Gradually the English National Trust became one of the largest landowners in England, second only to the Crown. Another major difference was the involvement of the English National Trust in the conservation of natural areas, as suggested by the full title of the organization, "The National Trust for the Conservation of Places of Historic Interest or Scenic Beauty." Of great importance was the English National Trust summer school program, "The Great Houses of England," familiarly known as "the Attingham course" from the name of the house where students were first housed. This was followed by similar courses sponsored by the National Trust of Scotland, the Irish Georgian Society, and preservation groups on the Continent.

In the United States, however, the National Trust for Historic Preservation, without any official involvement in the conservation of natural areas, slowly acquired a small number of properties, usually with only relatively small amounts of land, virtually all of them inadequately endowed. Although many educational programs were developed, none of the efforts to create "an American Attingham" quite succeeded. A recurring problem has been the struggle for funds sufficient to operate the Trust properties. Although the Trust staff has developed a number of valuable programs at its properties, the greater contributions of the Trust were those connected with various locally focused technical programs, for instance, the National Main Street Center, the National Center for Preservation Law, and important projects for rural preservation and maritime preservation. Perhaps the Trust's most outstanding contribution was the leadership that resulted in the passage of the National Historic Preservation Act of 1966.

In 1964 the National Trust began a major effort for an enlarged overall national preservation program. The need for such a program was perceived by cities (through the U.S. Conference of Mayors) as well as preservationists. Massive highway building projects, begun as a Defense Highway System in 1954, grew into the Interstate Highway System. It had drastic effects on cities. Well-intentioned urban renewal projects were also damaging to the fabric of cities. Large sections of cities were acquired and demolished to create building plots for low-income housing and for major new buildings intended as part of the economic restructuring of the cities. In all too many cases, the new housing worked less well than the old, and the many new projects never materialized at all.

The passage of the National Historic Preservation Act of 1966 radically changed the role of historic preservation in American culture. The Act instructed the secretary of the interior to enlarge the National Register of Historic Places to include properties of state and local significance, through programs to be developed with the states and territories; to provide for protection of the listed properties against threats resulting from federal programs; and to provide financial assistance for both "survey and planning" and "acquisition and development" of such properties. To carry out these programs, the secretary of the interior asked each governor to appoint a state liaison officer (later, state historic preservation officer) assisted by professional staff.

The National Historic Preservation Act of 1966 was one of several dramatically important congressional acts of the period 1966–1975, of which the other most important were perhaps the 1966 Department of Transportation (DOT) Act, which included an absolute prohibition ("section 4f") of any DOT funding of a transportation project that required the taking of historic sites or structures; and the National Environmental Policy Act (NEPA) of 1969, which established a series of levels of review of federal projects for their potential effects on the environment. The highest level of review was that requiring an Environmental Impact Statement (EIS), and the best of these documents are tributes to the holistic approach toward the care of the natural and human world that was envisioned and carried out in the decades following 1969. Specific actions inspired by these acts and the climate of the 1960s and 1970s included the 1969 release by the U.S. Department of Housing and Urban Development of the first national preservation film, "How Will We Know It's Us?" In 1973 the president proclaimed the first observance of National Historic Preservation Week, an observance celebrated every year since then.

Other actors in the cities, both before and after the passage of the National Historic Preservation Act of 1966, were the city preservation organizations, the growing number of city (and county) historic-preservation commissions, and the various official and unofficial "Main Street" organizations of the 1970s and 1980s. In 1974, Seattle, Washington, became the first city to appoint a person to a job that resembled "preservation officer"; the position was called "city conservator." In 1975 the first national conference on the economic benefits of historic preservation was held in Seattle, under the aegis of that office. In 1975 Frederick County, Maryland, became the first county to appoint a county historic-preservation officer. In 1978, the U.S. Supreme Court, in the case of *Penn Central Transportation Co. v. City of New York*, ruled that New York City's preservation law was constitutional, thus giving strong legal backing to historic-district laws in general.

The tax-benefit programs of the period after 1976 were especially important in greatly increasing private investment in the rehabilitation of old office buildings, factories, and other commercial properties. The programs began to give such buildings a special depreciation benefit similar to that given to new commercial buildings as an economic stimulus after World War II. Other developments of the 1980s and 1990s included understanding the "cultural landscape," and including folklife elements in the sites and structures around which they occurred, something called "cultural conservation."

Simply put, in the 1990s the most important characteristic in historic preservation—as in local history—was its continued growth in intellectual vitality.

See Carter L. Hudgins, W. Brown Morton III, and John N. Pearce, "Preserving America" (unpublished manuscript); William Murtagh, *Keeping Time: The History and Theory of Preservation in America* (Pittstown, N.J., 1988); *The National Parks and Cultural Conservation* (Washington, D.C., 1987); John N. Pearce, "Dates Every Preservation Student Should Know" (offset; Fredericksburg, Va., 1986); Charles B. Hosmer, Jr., *Preservation Comes of Age: From Williamsburg to the National Trust, 1926–1949* (Charlottesville, Va., 1981); Philip D. Spiess, II, "A Chronology of Significant Preservation Events in the United States, 1966–1978" (offset; Washington, D.C., 1979); Charles B. Hosmer, Jr., "Introduction," *Material Culture and the Study of American Life*, Ian M. G. Quimby, ed. (N.Y., 1978); *A Guide to State Historic Preservation Programs* (Washington, D.C., 1976); Charles E. Peterson, "Historic Preservation U.S.A.: Some Significant Dates," *The Magazine Antiques*, February 1966; and Charles B. Hosmer, Jr., *Presence of the*

Past: A History of the Preservation Movement in the United States Before Williamsburg (N.Y., 1965).

JOHN N. PEARCE, W. BROWN MORTON III, *and* CARTER L. HUDGINS

historical fiction. On the subject of historical fiction, historians have two responses. One group absolutely disdains it. The other group embraces it as interesting, as an alternative way of expanding the audience for local history, as a means of telling historical truths that cannot necessarily be documented in the sources, and as being entertaining.

There have been times when historical fiction was our most popular literary form. George Dekker notes that, over time, "nothing has sold as well as historical fiction." Dekker points to Sir Walter Scott and his Waverley books (ca. 1814) as the origin of the historical romance in which the novel develops a historical consciousness by "multiplying the variety of natural and social forces that impinged on its characters' behavior." Dekker claims too, that the development of the historical novel forced professional historians to rethink their research methods and extend the "range of interests and motives surveyed in their accounts of historical causation." Historians, who have expanded their ways of researching and writing history, might claim that this enrichment has actually come for other reasons, though it would be hard to ignore the popularity some historical fiction has with the public.

Ernest E. Leisy, who studied and categorized historical fiction, claims there have been three periods when Americans have turned to this genre. The first

was the era following 1813 when the nation was creating its own identity. In *The Spy* (1821) James F. Cooper followed the pattern established by Scott in his portrayal of a family divided by partisan interests during the American Revolutionary War.

> An historical novel is one which grafts upon a story actual incidents or persons well enough known to be recognized as historical elements.
> —Paul Leicester Ford

The second period, according to Leisy, was at the end of the nineteenth and the beginning of the twentieth century. This era coincides with the appearance of the *local color and regional novels that depended upon the development of place and character as well as events. Leisy's third phase includes the decades between the 1930s and 1950s. The star attraction during that era might well be *Gone with the Wind*, which Dekker cites as the most famous and best-selling twentieth-century American historical romance; Edith Wharton's *The Age of Innocence* and William Faulkner's *Absalom, Absalom!* he calls "the greatest."

Leisy defends historical fiction as being more than escapist literature, for "it satisfied many tastes," and it "satisfied the need of the human mind for a story." He saw it full of suspense and drama, broadening the reader by allowing us to see people more fully than was the case in books of history. Leisy wrote that historical fiction "attracts us to the past" as it satisfies the reader with "color, pageantry, and the love of excitement"; it is, he claims "concerned with historical truth." More importantly, Leisy believed that historical fiction led to a belief in "national homogenity" and that it was satisfactory reading because it is concerned with truth—a statement that many people might dispute today.

What is true is that historical fiction has attracted writers of all sorts of abilities and that the stories it tells are usually vivid and full of authentic detail. That detail, of course, is what tends to make historical fiction seem so truthful to its readers. Consider the enthusiastic reaction to Charles Frasier's *Cold Mountain* (N.Y., 1997), which was full of the author's precise knowledge and often arcane and interesting vocabulary.

> *. . . any narrative which presents a day and a generation is of necessity historical.*
> —Owen Wister

Historical fiction has also taken a prominent place in our schools. In preference to using books of history, there has been reliance among some elementary school teachers on historical fiction as the basis of their lessons. This could be seen as a good thing since these books are interesting and generally well written; they are full of small and telling details; the attractive illustrations add to children's understanding of a different era or time. This could also be seen as a failure on the part of historians to produce books and pamphlets that are useful to classroom teachers.

In 1991, recognizing that many novelists have profoundly deepened our understanding of the past, the Society of American Historians created a biennual prize for historical fiction, called the James Fenimore Cooper Prize for Historical Fiction. The first four winners are: 1991–1992—Noah Gordon, *Shaman*; 1993–1994—Tim O'Brien, *In the Lake of the Woods*; 1995–1996—John Edgar Wideman, *The Cattle Killing*; and 1997–1998—Richard Powers, *Gain*.

In addition to those books that are written intentionally as pieces of historical fiction, the novelist John Hersey observed that "the superior novel of contemporary events will in time come to be regarded as a historical novel." See George Dekker, *The American Historical Romance* (Cambridge, Eng., and N.Y., 1987); A. T. Dickinson, Jr., *American Historical Fiction*, 2d ed. (N.Y., 1963), which contains an annotated bibliography of books from colonial to contemporary times; Robert A. Lively, *Fiction Fights the Civil War* (Chapel Hill, N.C., 1957); and Ernest E. Leisy, *The American Historical Novel* (Norman, Okla., 1950).

historical markers. In nearly every state there exists some form of official "state historic-marker" program, with signs erected along the roadside to identify places of local or regional significance. Few programs remain as active today as when they were first created, and for many, these cast metal plaques are from another age, when the pace of travel, and the speed of our vehicles, was far more leisurely than it is today.

But the intent in all these programs is the same: to identify for the traveler some place of interest that they other-

For instance, if using a *photograph, get rid of that old cliché "photographs don't lie," and recognize that a photograph is a mediated source just like a written one. Has the photographer altered the picture? Has the photographer altered lightness/darkness to affect the image projected? Has the picture maker selected or posed subjects in a way that makes a point, but perhaps distorts "reality"? Christopher M. Lyman's fascinating book *The Vanishing Race and Other Illusions: Photographs of Indians by Edward S. Curtis* (Washington, D.C., 1982) gives some good insights into how photographers shape their pictures.

If looking at a material object, how do we know it reflects a time, a period, or a value system; or how it relates to a specific incident? You probably would have to use studies of comparable material objects to find out how yours fits into the scheme of things. Thus Ivor Noel Hume in *Martin's Hundred* (N.Y., 1982) drew heavily upon research on pipe stems to place into context those his researchers found at the Virginia site, and to determine much information about life in that seventeenth-century Virginia establishment.

The use of oral sources, either interviews by the historian or previously recorded interviews found in research collections, can be especially tricky. The historian has the dual problem of the reliability of the oral source's memory—and also the problem of how the sources' responses may have been affected by the interaction with the interviewer. In general, historians need to ask the same questions they would of any source (as described above), but also to recognize the unique opportunities and limits of oral sources. A good guide and example of some of the treacheries of oral sources is Barbara Allen and Lynwood Montell, *From Memory to History: Using Oral Sources in Local Historical Research* (Nashville, 1981).

If you are pretty sure of the validity of your sources, the next question might be: How many sources do you need to "prove" something? Some people suggest three (responsible journalists often use that guideline). But what if there is only one or two? After all, we are dealing with the past, and the record is usually pretty spotty. You do not reject an historical argument just because you do not have three sources; you next look to see how that evidence is used. You use the whole context of the historical presentation, the evidence, the patterns the pieces of evidence create, the reasonableness of the judgment of the historian, to see a pattern. History seldom produces "hard facts"; it usually produces the most probable interpretation based on the evidence and logic available.

The terms used to refer to the processes described above are "inferential" and "demonstrable" proof. If you have several pieces of evidence that prove something to a reasonable person's satisfaction, that kind of proof is called "demonstrable." Clearly, that is what historians would like for everything. But historians seldom get such secure evidence; they have to rely upon circumstances, context, conjecture—in other words they often have to "infer" from spotty evidence. This is called "inferential" proof; it is something like a prosecuting attorney's case based on circumstantial evidence.

Another problem the historian has to deal with is the historian per se. If historians are asking the questions, examining the evidence, and synthesizing and interpreting it, then we have to know about the frame of reference and biases and prejudices of that historian. If you are reading history, you have to ask about the author in order to know how to evaluate the piece. If you are the author, then you need to consider your own frame of reference. Are you allowing basic beliefs and assumptions about gender, race, ethnic or national groups, or institutions, or even individual people to affect your evaluation and interpretation of your evidence? Only when you know the frame or reference of the historian has not been allowed to intrude, can you seriously consider whether something is "proved."

History will have the most credibility if it follows the rules of evidence and interpretation and only presents what the evidence provides. There are other ways, however, in which historians might present their work.

One is through dramatic or literary presentations. Obviously, to do this the historian/ dramatist is going to have to create conversation, attribute thoughts, compress characters, and exaggerate conflicts and resolutions. Thus their history will not meet the rigorous rules of the academic historian. But, the dramatic production or a novel may be able to capture the "spirit" of a person, a time, and a place more effectively than a heavily documented scholarly piece. An engaging drama or novel could have even more impact on an audience than a scholarly piece. For example, Michael Sharra's novel about the battle at Get-tysburg, *Killer Angels: A Novel* (N.Y., 1974) includes characters created to represent certain points of view regarding the Civil War; it provides sound insights into the nature of the entire conflict in a manner much more accessible to a public audience than a scholarly monograph.

Such works will not have the credibility, especially among academics, of more narrowly focused historical creations, since they have to be judged on the rather intangible standard of whether the author has accurately and effectively presented the spirit, mood, character of a person, people, or a time. Nonetheless these kinds of works do serve a useful function in making history more accessible to a wide audience.

Regarding historical proof, the "truth" of the matter is that since historians are human beings dealing with human subjects, there can never be perfection. The best the historian can do is to learn a few basic tests of the validity of evidence and interpretation, and then rely upon reasonableness and responsibility as they assemble their historical stories.

RAYMOND STARR

See drama and local history; historical fiction; historicism.

historical societies. We often hear complaints from local history societies—complaints about lack of members, lack of interest among the existing members, lack of active support, of membership getting older and there not being enough younger persons in the society.

Not all local history societies are like this, of course; but most societies have gone through phases like this. The solution to these problems is thought to be the search for new members, especially activists. All we need to do, it is sometimes argued, is to find someone who has recently retired or who in some other way has the time, energy and resources to do the work; get a new press and publicity officer or membership secretary, bring some younger persons onto the committee, get someone to take over the editing work or the promotion work for the journal or newsletter, etc. Such changes sometimes bring happy results. But often local history societies find it hard—amidst all the competing claims on volunteers—to get the attention for their work they feel they deserve.

And if we look at the way in which voluntary organizations work, it is possible to argue that this may not be the best way to promote a healthier local history society, that there are other strategies that can be followed. It may be useful to look at modern understandings of how voluntary organizations grow and remain healthy if we are to plan for our own local history society.

How do societies grow?

A model has been developed of voluntary bodies that sees them like a set of Russian dolls (or perhaps, easier to envisage, of concentric circles). At the center are the initiators, those persons who have the time, energy, and keenness to develop new ideas, to be creative, to begin new activities. There will always be very few of these. Behind them, and closely associated with them, are the activists: those who work hard to promote the society; who serve on the committee or on working groups; who do the work, often behind the scenes, of putting the journal or newsletter together. They will promote the society to the outside world. They will be rather more numerous. Then there are the people I call the "responders": those who are less creative than are initiators and activists. These are the reliable helpers, those who set up exhibitions, help with transport, plan and organize the outings, get the list of lectures put together and sent to the printers, put up posters, etc.

Beyond these, there is the still larger number of persons who may be called the "attenders." They come to events more or less regularly, they turn up at outings, they visit the exhibition. They do not wish to do more than this, but they do their bit.

And beyond these there are the rest of the (inactive) members who do not come to many events, but receive the newsletter and pay their subscription because they wish to belong. This in many cases is a still larger number than the attenders. Some local history committees feel unhappy that there are so many "inactive members," and therefore they seek to chivvy them up all the time. This only makes the inactive members feel uncomfortable, which is the way to make them leave! This would be a pity.

So much for the membership. But beyond this, to every voluntary body there is a most important group, what has been called "the interested constituency": those people who are interested in the history of their locality, who will buy the magazine (if there is one) or other publication, who will turn up at exhibitions, who will read the comments in the local newspaper and talk about it at home or in the pub. Without a strong "interested constituency," no local history society will last for long.

Before we discuss this picture with a view to seeing what it tells us about how to develop a healthy or unhealthy local history society, some general comments are necessary. First, this model was developed in connection with religious bodies, and I have adapted it to local history societies. It will be important for you to test this against your own local history society and to make your own analysis of your society in similar terms. The titles I have given to each sector are of course my own; you could come up with your own titles. Secondly, it is important to realize that the different sectors are not hard and fast; in many cases they will shade imperceptibly from one to another, and some of them may have subdivisions. Again, you will need to define your own society membership in your own terms.

There are, of course, healthy and unhealthy voluntary bodies. It can now be argued that a healthy voluntary body is a balanced organization—that is, each sector gets bigger and bigger until the interested constituency exceeds the whole of the society's membership. And it is not one where people are jumping straight from the "interested constituency" to become "activists"; this is relatively rare. It does of course happen some times, but it is not the normal way. Rather, it is one where there is a small but steady current or flow of persons from one level to the one immediately above it. The healthy society is one where one or two persons from the interested constituency will wish to become inactive members; where one or two inactive members will become at-

tenders, where one or two attenders will respond to requests for help, etc.

An unhealthy society, on the other hand, is one where there is a small but steady downward drift—where some of the initiators become less creative, where some of the activists need to be invited to do something before they do the work (i.e., have become responders), where some of the responders no longer respond, etc. The "dropdowns" (or dropouts) are the key feature of these societies.

The trick is knowing how to build a healthy society. The policy of a healthy local history society is not to seek new committee members, but it is to encourage gently one or two persons operating at one level to begin operating at a slightly higher level.

I believe that the key concern of every local history society is simply to build up the general interested constituency. It is not to try to get new members— they will come. It is to promote a general appreciation and understanding of local history among the people of the local community in every which way you can. This in turn will gradually increase membership in a small way, and the upward cycle will be strengthened.

But this can only happen if the active members of the local history society are outwardlooking; if they make it quite clear that new members are welcome, that the society is open. I know many people who say, when it is suggested that they join such and such a society, that they cannot join because it is a "closed" society. The members are seen to know each other well and to relate closely and exclusively, and this puts off other people. People operating at one level do not feel they can join the circle immediately above them because it seems to be a closed circle.

A healthy local history society seems to me to be one that is concerned first and foremost with the general interest in local history in the community—not with itself as a society. If its active members really want more people to appreciate and become active in local history, then they do not need to spend lots of time in committee meetings bemoaning the lack of support for the society—support will come of its own accord. If societies spend their time doing things for the outside world, the rest will follow.

A famous archbishop (I can't remember who it was!) once said that the Church was one body that existed solely for the sake of those who were not its members. Much the same is true of a local history society. If we work to build up and strengthen the interested constituency, I feel certain that we will find our own society growing. If, on the other hand, we work to strengthen our society in a cliquish way, I feel certain that we will soon notice signs of decline.

ALAN ROGERS

historicism. The term refers to particular beliefs about the nature of history and historiography. It implies that history should be conceived as a professional discipline and conducted as a rigorous science that requires objective research based on primary sources. Historicism rejects value judgments and metaphysical speculations. Instead, it insists that the historian should use rational methods and rigorously examine and evaluate his or her sources. Historicism is primarily identified with a worldview dominant in the nineteenth-century German academic world. For example, while historicism theoretically opens up all spheres of human activity to historical study, in fact, it has tended to focus on Europeans and the political life of nations.

Historicism has come under attack in recent years from a number of sides. Because historians are products of their culture, critics have pointed out that absolute objectivity is impossible. Others have suggested that since history is usually written as a narrative, the historian perforce fills in gaps, guesses at intention, surmises about cause and effect, and generally engages in what scientists call "smoothing the data" in order to form a comprehensible narrative. These critics suggest history is thus more akin to literature than to science. Still others have argued that language itself is a cultural construct and in fact bears little or no relation to "reality." The New Historicists, including Stephen Greenblatt, while sharing these ideas about language, rejected the notion that the texts forming the basis of history were unconnected to reality. Instead, they argued that these texts were shaped by the same forces that shaped society at large, but cautioned that they therefore had, like works of literature, multiple meanings.

Such attacks question the very notion that history can be written at all. Therefore, contemporary historians have taken account of these criticisms by varying their approaches and using more sophisticated methods. A benefit of this criticism has been to greatly diversify the scope of historical studies—a situation that has favored those engaged in small-scale histories, such as local historians. For a clear overview of the problem, see Georg G. Iggers, *Historiography in the Twentieth Century: From Scientific Objectivity to the Postmodern Challenge* (Hanover, N.H., 1997).

NORMA PRENDERGAST

See historical proof.

historiography. The accumulation of historical writing and knowledge from previous generations about a subject. A review of that which has been previously written about a subject.

History Day. See National History Day.

***History News* and *Dispatch*.** In December 1940 the former Conference of State and Local Historical Societies was dissolved and reformed as the *American Association for State and Local History. The new association published its first bimonthly newsletter, *State and Local History News*, six months later. The eight-page newsletter shared with its membership news from the field of state and local history along with association business. Interesting to note from those early newsletters is the association's support of and partnerships with the WPA *Historical Records Survey and the *National Park Service. Since that first issue the newsletter has changed its title, its print style and length, its frequency, and its city of publication several times. Now published from the AASLH permanent headquarters in Nashville, Tennessee, the newsletter known at one time as *History News*, then *History News Dispatch*, is called *Dispatch*. *History News* is the title of the association's mag-

azine. Currently *Dispatch* is published monthly and *History News* is published quarterly. The address is *History News*, AASLH, 1717 Church Street, Nashville, Tennessee 37203-2991; (605) 320-3203; fax (615) 327-9013; <history@aaslh.org>.

LAUREN BATTE

History Workshop. The History Workshop is a group of historians based at Ruskin College, Oxford University in England, who are concerned with the history of working-class men and women from the eighteenth century to the recent past. *History Workshop Journal* (formerly *History Workshop*), the semiannual journal of the group, began in 1976 as a journal of socialist and feminist historians. The journal continues its commitment to discover new sources of historical knowledge, and an enthusiasm for enlarging the boundaries of historical inquiry in the exploration of everyday life of working-class people. Among the many important monographs written by members of the History Workshop are two edited by Raphael Samuel and published in England: *Village Life and Labour* (1975) and *Miners, Quarrymen and Saltworkers* (1977).

Local historians will find *History Workshop Journal* and monographs from group members useful sources for information on research methods and findings. Many of these studies report research on the fundamental aspects of social culture past and present, including, labor, poverty, crime, education, family, and gender issues, often based on studies of rural communities and urban neighborhoods. *History Work-*

shop Journal is indexed or abstracted by the following on-line services: America History and Life and Social Science Citation Index. Tables of contents of recent issues, as well as subscription information can be found on the World Wide Web at <www3.oup.co.uk/hiwork>.

KENNETH G. AITKEN

holidays. The word "holiday" comes from the Old English word "haligdaeg," meaning "holy day," and the earliest days of celebration were those associated with the church calendar. Holidays in the United States are both religious and civic, and a few are even commercial.

See Hennig Cohen and Tristram Potter, *The Folklore of American Holidays* (Detroit, 1999); Jack Santino, *All Around the Year: Holidays and Celebrations in American Life* (Urbana, Ill., 1994); Timothy Gangwer, *American Holidaze* (Houston, Tex., 1991); Hennig Cohen, *America Celebrates! A Patchwork of Weird & Wonderful Holiday Lore* (Detroit, Mich., 1991); and Wicke Chambers, *The Celebration Book of Great American Traditions* (N.Y., 1983). An older but standard work is Jane M. Hatch, *The American Book of Days* (N.Y., 1978).

For African American holidays, see Barbara Eklof, *For Every Season: The Complete Guide to African American Celebrations* (N.Y., 1997); and James C. Anyike, *African American Holidays: A Historical Research and Resource Guide to Cultural Celebrations* (Chicago, 1991).

Arbor Day. Celebrated the last Friday in April, which is a good planting date in most of North America, Arbor Day, or the day set aside to plant trees, has been observed by presidential proclamation in 1970, 1972, 1988, 1990, 1991, and 1993. There is a committee for National Arbor Day that has proposed a set date and annual celebration. The headquarters are at 63 Fitzrandolph Road, West Orange, N.J., 07052; (201) 731-0840. See N. H. Egleston, *Arbor Day: Its History and Observance* (Washington, D.C., 1896).

Armed Forces Day. Celebrated on the third Saturday in May, this holiday was first celebrated in 1947 and pays tribute to Americans who served in the military.

Bill of Rights Day. This holiday, held on December 15, marks the adoption of the Bill of Rights following its Ratification by Virginia in 1791. The holiday was proclaimed by President Franklin D. Roosevelt eight days after the attack on Pearl Harbor in order to dramatize the contrast between the U.S. and the Axis governments. This day is not widely celebrated.

Christmas. See Stephen Nissenbaum, *Battle for Christmas* (N.Y., 1996); Penne L. Restad, *Christmas in America: A History* (N.Y., 1995); and William Burnell Waits, *The Modern Christmas in America: A Cultural History of Gift Giving* (N.Y., 1993).

Columbus Day. The second Monday in October marks Columbus's landing in the Americas, which actually happened on October 12, 1492. The first Columbus Day was observed in New York on the tercentenary and it was proclaimed a holiday by President Benjamin Harrison in 1892. Celebration of Columbus Day in 1992 became problematic. Native Americans observed that North America was already their home when Columbus arrived.

Election Day. See Kate Kelly, *Election Day: An American Holiday, An American History* (N.Y., 1991).

Flag Day. July 14th is set aside as Flag Day, observing the day in 1777 that the Continental Congress requested a national flag.

Halloween. Alvin Boyd Kuhn, *Hallowe'en: A Festival of Lost Meanings* (Chesapeake, Va., 1992); and Jack Santino, *Halloween and Other Festivals of Death and Life* (Knoxville, Tenn., 1994).

Independence Day. July 4th celebrates the adoption of the Declaration of Independence. It was first observed with elaborate community celebrations and recognized as a holiday by Massachusetts in 1781. It quickly became the nation's birthday. See Len Travers, *Celebrating the Fourth: Independence Day and the Rites of Nationalism in the Early Republic* (Amherst, Mass., 1997); Michael G. Kammen, *Mystic Chords of Memory: The Transformation of Tradition in American Culture* (N.Y., 1991); and Fred Somkin, *Unquiet Eagle: Memory and Desire in the Idea of American Freedom 1815–1860* (Ithaca, N.Y., 1967).

Labor Day. Labor Day, the first Monday in September, celebrates America's working men and women. The Knights of Labor proposed the holiday and sponsored the first Labor Day parade in New York, which drew 10,000 workers. The parade was followed by picnics, dancing, and fireworks. The holiday now marks, for students, the end of summer.

May Day. See Philip S. Foner, *May Day: A Short History of the International Workers' Holiday, 1886–1986* (N.Y., 1986).

Memorial Day. Celebrated the last Monday in May, Memorial Day began in tribute to soldiers killed in the Civil War. Patriotic societies in the United States promoted Memorial Day, which began in Waterloo, New York, and it has been officially recognized by law since 1949. After World War II it was expanded to commemorate casualties of all U.S. wars.

Thanksgiving. Feasts of thanksgiving have long been part of Native American celebrations. The Pilgrims held a feast of thanksgiving after landing in Massachusetts in 1620. Until the Civil War, thanksgiving observances were religious and patriotic. President Abraham Lincoln called for a Day of Thanksgiving in 1863 to be observed the fourth Thursday of November. President Franklin D. Roosevelt moved the holiday to the third Thursday of November to allow merchants a longer Christmas shopping season. It was returned to the fourth Thursday of November in 1941. See Lou Rogers, *The First Thanksgiving* (Chicago, 1962).

Patriots' Day. Celebrated the third Monday in April, Patriots' Day commemorates the battles of Lexington and Concord, April 19, 1775. The Sons of the American Revolution promoted the celebration of this day, which is a legal holiday in Massachusetts and is observed in other New England states. It is the date of the Boston Marathon.

Presidents' Day. This holiday, celebrated on the third Monday in February to combine Lincoln's birthday, February 12, and Washington's birthday, February 22. Lincoln's birthday was celebrated, beginning in Illinois in 1892, by all states but those in the former

Confederacy, excepting Tennessee. Washington's birthday was officially observed first on February 22, 1800, the year after George Washington's death. Observance was occasional until the centennial of his birth in 1832.

Veterans' Day. November 11th marks the signing of the Armistice ending World War I, in 1918. The day was first observed in 1919, but was expanded in 1953 to commemorate veterans of all wars. The day was legally recognized by Congress in 1954.

See celebrations; day by day.

Hoskins, W. G. Hoskins was born in 1908 in Exeter, which became the center for much of his local history work. He went to Exeter College of the South West (later Exeter University) and afterwards taught in Bradford. In 1931, he was appointed lecturer in economics in University College, Leicester, and in 1938 completed his Ph.D. degree with a thesis on the history of Exeter in the seventeenth and eighteenth centuries (a book on this theme was published in 1935, *Industry, Trade and People in Exeter 1688–1800*). During the Second World War Hoskins worked for the Board of Trade, and on his return to Leicester in 1945, he became a lecturer in economic history and later reader in a new Department of English Local History. A prolific writer, his key works came in the late 1950s, with *Midland Peasant: An Economic and Social History of a Leicestershire Village* (Wigston Magna, Eng., 1957) and *Local History in England* ([1959] London; and N.Y., 1984), the seminal work revised and updated regularly, to which all general studies of local history look back. Although like *Fin-

berg he believed that local history was an advanced study, not a subject for undergraduates, he nevertheless encouraged many amateurs to study the history of their own area. He wrote on the West Country, especially Devon, and on landscapes in *Making of the English Landscape* ([1955] London, 1970), which broke new ground and became a standard and authoritative work, going through several editions.

Hoskins advocated getting out into the countryside, looking at the topography (*Fieldwork in Local History*, 1967), but his interest in urban communities was confined to early market towns, not to industrial centers (these were taken up by other local historians such as Maurice Beresford at Leeds). Hoskins had strong views about modern developments like the car and even the railway: he believed that the industrial revolution had destroyed all that was beautiful and valuable in English life, and modern cities and highways were anathema to him. Many of the ideas he pioneered, especially those relating to vernacular buildings such as the Great Rebuilding of England in the sixteenth century, opened whole fields for further research and elaboration. He built up a strong Department of English Local History with money from several trusts, concentrating on agrarian history and topography; but it was his successor, Finberg, who developed the ideas relating to local communities that Hoskins first suggested.

Hoskins was a popularist for local history, not only through his writings, but also through radio and later through television. He was, however, not an easy person to get on with, frequently being very critical of other people's work; from 1951 to 1965, when he left Leicester for Oxford (as a reader in economic history), he found himself out of sympathy with that academic scene. During these years, he served on a national commission on common lands, which resulted in legislation for the preservation of commons. In 1965, he returned to Leicester as professor of English Local History on the retirement of H. P. R. Finberg; his inaugural lecture was on *English Local History: The Past and the Future*; but he retired after only three years in Leicester in 1968 at the age of 60. He returned to Exeter and continued writing and lecturing; his campaigning style on occasion resulted in litigation, until his death in January 1992 at the age of 83.

ALAN ROGERS

See landscape.

house museums. Historic house museums range from humble to grand, from those of one specific period to others with the accumulated layers of continued occupancy. They are connected to a single individual or representative of a group of people or significant architecture. They may be furnished or unfurnished. Guided by docents, volunteers or professionals, or by self-activated electronic devices or passive text panels, visitors to historic house museums achieve a unique connection to the past.

House museums are the most common type of history museum and are often underfunded and dependent on volunteer staff. Nevertheless, historic house museums can provide spaces for

discussing *social history, *economic history, *political history, and *material culture.

From the beginning of the historic house museum as an entity, a pattern emerged. A group of like-minded citizens organized to purchase and preserve a building of particular architectural interest or one associated with an historic event or personality. The first historic house museums were established in the 1850s. These structures were chosen for their association with American heroes and usually dated from the American Revolution and the early national period. The state of New York purchased and preserved the Hasbrouck House in Newburgh, New York, as the site of George Washington's headquarters from April 1782 to August 1783. In 1856, the Mount Vernon Ladies' Association formed to preserve Washington's home on the banks of the Potomac River. Mount Vernon underwent its first restoration beginning in 1859. Also in 1856, the state of Tennessee purchased the Hermitage, home of President Andrew Jackson, hero of the Battle of New Orleans in 1815 and seventh president of the United States. In 1888 the Association for the Preservation of *Virginia Antiquities became the first state organization formed to preserve historic structures. The APVA has expanded its holdings from Jamestown Island, site of the first permanent English settlement in North America, to more than 34 properties reflecting the history of the commonwealth. The *Society for the Preservation of New England Antiquities was founded in 1910 and today manages 35 properties in New England that document the architectural and social history of that region. The decade of the 1920s witnessed the formation of the Thomas Jefferson Memorial Foundation, which operates Monticello, and the beginning of John D. Rockefeller's partnership with the Reverend W. A. R. Goodwin that resulted in the creation of Colonial Williamsburg.

Historic house museums offer three-dimensional educational spaces where, through multiple layers of interpretation, visitors learn about the occupants, their tastes, and their times. The most successful historic house museums incorporate contemporary scholarship and primary source materials to achieve authenticity of furnishings and accuracy of interpretation. Whereas earlier furnishings more often reflected modern tastes in decoration and focused on the owners, today's historic house museums reflect research using probate inventories, looking at contemporary paintings and prints, and conducting microscopic paint analyses. For house museums that have been open for several generations, changes can be dramatic and unexpected. When paint analysis at Mount Vernon and Gunston Hall resulted in certain rooms being painted bright green or blue, the colors forced a reevaluation of ideas about taste. Research into contemporary paintings and prints suggested that oriental carpets, which so often graced the floors of historic houses, were, in fact, more indicative of twentieth-century interior design than eighteenth-century taste.

Interpretation in historic house museums generally celebrated individuals, almost always white men, who achieved wealth and status of who made significant contributions to the establishment of the United States. Women, immigrants, Indians, and enslaved Africans rarely appeared in the interpretation. In the last quarter of the twentieth century, however, curators and historians have developed more inclusive interpretations of their historic houses both to present a more representative history and to attract a more diverse audience. The bicentennial in 1976 combined with patriotic interest in American history and a growing awareness of the loss of the historical *built environment to urban renewal. As Americans' greater mobility and discretionary income resulted in increased *tourism and generated revenue for locality, historic house museums have begun to advertise their unique attraction more aggressively to visitors through signage on nearby highways, colorful brochures, and informative websites. To attract local audiences on a continuing basis to basically static furnished rooms, staff of historic house museums have developed programs, such as dressing the rooms for summer or decorating the house for Christmas.

The Wickham House, an 1812 National Historic Landmark now part of the Valentine Museum, Richmond, Virginia, in many ways reflects the changing attitudes toward historic house museums throughout the twentieth century. Founded as the Valentine Museum in 1892, by 1928 the museum had purchased three rowhouses adjoining the Wickham House and renovated the interiors of those houses for gallery and storage space. The Wickham House then underwent a two-year restoration that resulted in a series of rooms that reflected periods of the decorative arts available to Richmonders from the late 1700s through the 1870s. Although known as the Wickham-Valentine House, for the first and last owners, the history of the house as a residence to four owners was ignored in favor of an interpretation that treated the furnishings as curios. In 1985 the museum staff refocused the interpretation of the house as a neoclassical structure and home to John Wickham, a prominent Richmond attorney, his family and his slaves. Architectural research resulted in an extensive historic structures report and paint research revealed the extent and complexity of the original wall paintings. The house remained open throughout the restoration and the interpreters were given daily updates on research into the Wickham family and their slaves who inhabited the house. In 1993 scripted conversations recorded on compact discs and operated by remote control by the interpreter added a new dimension to the guided tour of the house. In all the restored rooms, visitors eavesdropped on conversations between the Wickhams as well as conversations among the slaves. The new interpretation emphasized that the Wickham House was home to thirty-one people by 1820, the Wickhams as well as the domestic workers. Interpretation of the spaces within the house also emphasized the use of the spaces to reflect the division between public and private spaces, work and leisure spaces.

Historic house museums may represent significant architectural features that can produce unique interpretive challenges. A rare survival of Jacobean architecture is located in Isle of Wight County, Virginia. Although built and owned by several generations of Allens, the house is known as Bacon's Castle for its brief association with Nathaniel Bacon, who in 1676 led a rebellion against Governor Sir William Berkeley. Bacon forced Arthur Allen, son of the house's builder, to flee the house for supporting Berkeley. Interested in the unique architectural elements, the Association for the Preservation of Virginia Antiquities opened Bacon's Castle as an historic house in 1983 and began a research and restoration project that has refurnished the house according to Allen family inventories dating between 1711 and 1755. The docent must tread carefully to make clear to the visitor: (1) the history of the Allen family, (2) the architectural significance of the house, (3) why the house is named for Bacon, and (4) why the furnishings reflect the material culture of wealthy Virginians in the early eighteenth century.

Local history and popular culture combine for a particular interpretive challenge in the Molly Brown House, owned by Historic Denver, Inc. Maggie Brown, popularized on stage and in film as the "Unsinkable Molly Brown," purchased the three-story structure in 1894 with her husband J. J. Brown. Although the docents clearly explain that the Browns spent little time in the house, and, in fact, rented it as a single-family dwelling and then as a boarding house, they acknowledge the association of the house with Maggie Brown's successful escape from the sinking White Star liner *Titanic*. By the end of the tour, visitors are aware that Maggie was never known as Molly and that the house reflects the lifestyle of Denver's upper middle-class at the turn of the century.

Some historic house museums exist as architectural remnants of the built environment. Both Hampton, owned by the South Carolina Department of Parks, and Drayton Hall, owned by the *National Trust for Historic Preservation, are examples of preserved historic houses. Built between 1738 and 1742 by John Drayton and occupied continuously by the family until 1974, Drayton Hall had neither electricity nor plumbing. Changes to the house over time were minimal and the Trust consciously chose to present the house as a unique architectural survival. Hampton, home to the Rutledge family of South Carolina, was restored by its last owner, the writer Archibald Rutledge, who, at his death, left the house to the state. Rather than attempt to furnish the house, the state of South Carolina determined to open the house as an architectural restoration in progress.

Preservation, restoration, and interpretation of historic houses today draws from a large body of resources and experiences gathered by curators and interpreters. The most successful historic house museums blend contemporary scholarship and primary research disseminated by interpreters trained and encouraged not only in historical research methodologies, but also in public presentation to diverse audiences. The variety of historic house museums offers visitors connections to lifestyles of the wealthy and the not-so-wealthy in America. Whereas earlier houses stressed grandeur and conspicuous consumption, visitors today may see restored homes of the working class, immigrants, slaves, and Indians. Historic house museums document the literary heritage of America, as well as its political and economic history.

See Patricia West, *Domesticating History: The Political Origins of America's House Museums* (Washington, D.C., 1999); William J. Murtagh, *Keeping Time. The History and Theory of Preservation in America* (N.Y., 1997); Sherry Butcher-Younghans, *Historic House Museums. A Practical Handbook for Their Care, Preservation, and Management* (N.Y., 1993); Thomas J. Schlereth, *Cultural History & Material Culture. Everyday Life, Landscapes, Museums* (Charlottesville, 1992); Peggy Coats, "Survey of Historic House Museums," *History News* 45, no. 1 (1990): 26–28; and Laurence Vail Coleman, *Historic House Museums* (Washington, D.C., 1933).

BARBARA C. BATSON

See libraries in house museums.

household. The simplest definition is that a household consists of those who dwell as a family under one roof and who have emotional and economic ties or responsibilities to one another. Thus, a household might be a traditional or nontraditional family.

Boarders are people in a household who pay rent for room, or board, or for both. They are listed in the census as residents, but they have no emotional tie and their presence is in exchange for payment. Boarders are viewed by Virginia Yans McLaughlin in her study *Family and Community: Italian Immigrants in Buffalo, 1880–1930* (Ithaca,

N.Y., 1977) as a way for women to earn money for the family without leaving their homes and still stay within the confines of *women's sphere.

housing, public. In the United States the term refers to housing built and owned by a public agency. The first public housing was federally funded during the New Deal through the Emergency Relief and Construction Act. Around 1937, the program was decentralized through the U.S. Housing Act, which authorized the payment of federal funds to local housing authorities. There are currently a wide number of housing programs, some of which involve private as well as public money.

Humanities Council. See state humanities councils.

Hungarians. See Appendix A.

Huntington Library. Founded in 1919, the Henry E. Huntington Library specializes in English and American printed books, literature, English history to 1837, and U.S. history, with special emphasis on California and the American West. It has a splendid collection of rare books, prints, photographs, and a gallery and gardens. The staff is exceptionally knowledgeable and helpful. The address is 1151 Oxford Road, San Marino, Ca. 91108; (818) 405-2101, (622) 449-5720; <www.huntington.org>.

Hutterites. See Appendix B.

hydrotherapy. A medical treatment of internal or external use of water. It was a popular cure in the later nineteenth century and led to the development of a number of spas. Hydrotherapy is still used today in the form of hot or cold packs on injuries, cool baths to lower fever, and physical therapy in swimming pools to treat various injuries and weaknesses. See Roy Porter, ed., *The Medical History of Waters and Spas* (London, 1990); Susan Cayleff, *Wash and Be Healed: The Water-cure Movement and Women's Health* (Philadelphia, 1987); and Jane B. Donegar *"Hydropathic Highway to Health": Women and Water-cure in Antebellum America* (N.Y., 1986).

I

Immigration History Research Center. The Immigration History Research Center (IHRC), established in 1965, is a unit of the University of Minnesota's College of Liberal Arts. Its mission includes the development and administration of a research collection, widely regarded as one of the nation's richest resources for the study of American immigration. These materials concentrate most heavily on the epic migration to America of the nineteenth to early twentieth centuries, and document the subsequent transformation of immigrant populations to ethnic communities up to the present. Over 5,000 linear feet of manuscript materials (approximately 1,000 individual collections) are joined by approximately 48,000 books, pamphlets, and bound serials; and 4,000 newspaper and serial titles. A 446-page guide to the Center's collections was published in 1991; in addition, its manuscript collections have been catalogued via the Research Libraries Information Network for national as well as local on-line access.

The significance of these materials is attested to by the fact that each year the IHRC attracts an eclectic research constituency, including local, national, and international scholars and students, media professionals, writers and artists, genealogists, amateur historians, and secondary-school students and teachers. Products emanating from this research include scholarly monographs and articles, television and radio programs, novels, student dissertations and research papers, family histories, public presentations, and exhibitions.

In conjunction with the building of its collections, the IHRC has promoted research in and teaching of the history of migration and ethnicity through a variety of programs and activities: conferences, publications, research grants, exhibits, public outreach programs, and contributions to the instructional life of the university. Among the conferences and symposia have been those devoted to the Finnish, Italian, Greek, Slovenian, and Arabic-speaking immigrants, as well as to Minnesota's ethnic language schools and East European communities. In addition to the proceedings of several conferences, the Center has published a number of bibliographies, research tools, and an occasional journal, *Spectrum*.

Given the transnational character of migration, the Center has over the years worked in developing collegial relations with research institutions and scholars in other countries. With its counterparts in Canada, Europe, South America, Asia, and Australia, the IHRC has arranged or facilitated exchanges of scholars and students, as well as research materials, collaborated on conference programming, and participated in cooperative microfilming efforts. These connections have increased in recent years and will become a growing part of the IHRC's mission as rapid enhancements in international communication expand opportunities for productive and imaginative collaboration.

The IHRC's "Documenting the Immigrant Experience" has been identified as one of "101 Official Projects of Save America's Treasures," a public–private partnership between the White House Millennium Council and the *National Trust for Historic Preservation. The IHRC is located at the University of Minnesota, 826 Berry St., St. Paul, MN 55114; (612) 627-4208; fax (612) 627-4190; <wurlx001@maroon.tc.umn.edu>.

JOEL WURL

indenture. The term refers to a contract or deed between two individuals. The word comes from the ancient practice of tearing or cutting a contract in two using a jagged (indented) line. Fitting the two pieces back together was proof that it was a true contract. Most often, indenture refers to a contract between a master and an apprentice in which both parties have obligations and responsibilities to one another. The contract usually is in force for a set period of time.

independent historians. An independent historian is defined principally by self-employment. She earns income in two ways, as a contract historian or as a freelance writer. The contract historian works pursuant to an agreement with an individual, company, or governmental institution. The most likely private firm is the archeological company producing cultural resource studies for the United States Government.

The freelance writer chooses his subject based on personal interest, the availability of material, and the likelihood of sales.

The independent historian and the academic historian normally share the same academic qualifications and methods. In most cases, they also share an interest in teaching. A more recent type, the *public historian, shares with the independent historian an interest in the affairs of a particular community, though his salaried employment puts him into the academic camp.

Both academic historians and independent historians face similar constraints on their intellectual freedom. The independent historian is subject to the pressures of the marketplace. The academic historian is subject to the pressures of the employing institution. However, both have compensating advantages.

The primary professional concern of the independent historian is to maintain access to the rich research materials available at the principal research libraries in America. As private universities face economic challenges, they tend to limit access to their costly sites to registered academics. Privately generated databases and indexes, such as the H. W. Wilson Company abstracts and indexes, are paid for through universities, leaving independent historians at the mercy of policies set by the library and the data group. Independent historians, therefore, stress the value of public access in order to insure that the full range of knowledge is available for dissemination.

Independent historians may be found in the established national historical organizations as well as the occasional regional organization such as the Institute for Historical Study in Berkeley, California, and the Association of Independent Historians of Art. A number of them belong to the National Coalition of Independent Scholars. Many are found on the listserv called H-Scholar, edited by officers of the National Coalition.

Since independent historians are not constrained by a particular workplace, they are free to live wherever they choose. Their choice frequently leads them into the local history of their community. Interesting places seem to draw resident independent historians.

The independent historian is defined above all by her self-employment, not by the topics she works on. Karen Reeds, for example, works in New Jersey, where her biggest project is an exhibit on the history of medicine in that state, paid for by New Jersey–based pharmaceutical corporations. But she also lectures at the National Library of Medicine on the history of St. Johnswort and writes for *The Cambridge History of Science* on medieval medicine.

Among the better-known, now-deceased independent historians have been Bruce Catton, Bernard deVoto, Barbara Tuchman, Cicely Veronica Wedgwood, Catherine Drinker Bowen, Constance McLaughlin Green, and, of course, Henry Adams.

WILLIAM D. REEVES

Independent Sector (IS). A national umbrella organization representing nonprofit organizations. Its membership includes the major grant-making foundations.

Through aggressive lobbying, public-relations initiatives, and sponsorship of research, Independent Sector has been the single most important force in promoting public understanding of nonprofit organizations and in encouraging the development of technical assistance to help local nonprofits. It has built university-based programs in nonprofit management and public policy. The IS has also produced important studies and reference works, most notably the *Nonprofit Sector Almanac* (San Francisco, 1993, 1996).

The IS address is 1200 18th St., NW, Suite 200, Washington, D.C. 20036; (202) 467-6100; fax (202) 467-6101; <www.indepsec.org> and <info@indepsec.org>.

PETER DOBKIN HALL

Indians. See American Indian history.

Indochinese. See Appendix A.

inflation. See wages.

influenza. A disease characterized by acute inflamation of the throat and bronchi, accompanied by neuralgic pains and prostration. See Alfred W. Crosby, *Epidemic and Peace, 1918* (Westport, Conn., 1976); and Richard Collier, *The Plague of the Spanish Lady: The Influenza Pandemic of 1918–1919* (N.Y., 1974).

insurance maps. See maps; Sanborn fire insurance maps.

intellectual property rights. Generally speaking, property is anything that can be possessed and disposed of in a legal manner, and we usually think of property as either "real" property (or realty, such as buildings or land) or tangible personal property, all that we personally own of value that is not realty. Intellectual property is another kind of property, an *intangible* personal property represented by knowledge, lore, and various forms of personal expression. The best known legal right of intellectual property is *copyright, legal protections for individually created works of literature, drama, architecture, choreography, art, music, motion pictures, and sound recordings. These rights of original authorship apply to any thoughts or concepts that can be expressed in tangible form—that is, in writing, film, recording, or art. Such works are protected from unapproved use, modification, reproduction, distribution, performance, or display. These legal rights are outlined in the Copyright Act of 1976 (as currently revised) and last from the creation of the work to the author's death plus 70 years. While patent and trademark rights are similar, less commonly known intellectual property rights are identified in the Visual Artists Rights Act of 1990, which protects an artist's right of attribution to a work of art and the integrity of the art from unauthorized change.

It is important that museums, historical societies, and researchers be aware of laws protecting intellectual property, since the transfer of ownership of an object does not, unless otherwise specified, also transfer copyright or artist's rights. In other words, a museum can own an object, but not the right to modify, copy, or distribute it, and perhaps even to display it. Nor could a museum repair a work of art if that resulted in significant changes to the artistic integrity of the work. There are "fair use" provisions that can allow limited legal use of copyrighted materials for educational and other purposes without the author's approval, but this must be carefully determined on a case-by-case basis. These and other issues, such as the duration of copyright, depend in part on when a work was first created, as copyright protection has changed over the years and thus varies for materials created at different times.

Less well-known intellectual property is the traditional knowledge of native peoples. Much of this traditional knowledge is acquired by special training, is owned as property by an individual or a group, and may even be sacred or patrimonial in character. Contemporary legal battles over patents for traditional knowledge of medicinal plants, and recent requests that the U.S. Patent and Trademark Office protect tribal symbols all illustrate this issue. Native American tribal governments are also restricting research access to and use of traditional knowledge, including oral histories, songs, and representations of traditional designs. The right to use such information, especially if it was acquired before human-subjects-rights policies, may be disputed. Accordingly, institutions should discuss the status of information they have from tribal sources. For many native peoples this is, like repatriation, another important human rights and legal issue, and thus should be handled openly, sensitively, and expeditiously.

JAMES D. NASON

See American Indian history; copyright; heritage; museums, and the matter of ethics.

Internal Revenue Records. See Civil War Federal Tax Records.

International Genealogical Index. Genealogical resources of the Church of Jesus Christ of Latter Day Saints maintains two large databases that can be utilized to research family names. The Ancestral File catalogs 35 million names that are organized into families and pedigree charts. The International Genealogical Index (IGI) is a listing of all individuals who have had ordinances performed for them in the church temples since 1843. Both files give dates for births, deaths, marriages, baptisms, and christenings (in all denominations).

The Church maintains 3,400 *Family History Centers or libraries, in 64 countries. These centers have computers linked to the church database. The largest library is in Salt Lake City, Utah, and the second largest is in Mesa, Arizona. The main libraries are usually open Monday through Saturday. The smaller centers, located in local church buildings, are open one to four times a week, or by appointment. Locations and hours can be obtained from the church family history website <www. familysearch.org> or by calling (800) 346-6044. Direct-line ancestry for both files may be accessed on the family search website. Viewing entire family groups' listings and pedigree charts, however, must be done at the centers, where volunteers are always on hand to aid the researcher.

The Family History Library Catalog consists of two million rolls of microfilms that have census data, biographies, family histories, databases, community histories, passenger lists, and other information. The individual centers carry some of the microfilms and others can be ordered from the central Salt Lake Library.

JERRY BRISCO

See genealogy, and archivist's view.

Internet, uses of by local historians. Writing a summary of local history on the Internet seems a daunting task. A broad-based search using any of the popular search engines yields some 20,000 "hits" or sites for the terms "local history." In efforts to attract residents and tourists, many localities include sections on their local history in their informational websites, which can be accessed through city.net (<http://www. city.net>), the Virtual Tourist (<http:// www.vtourist.com>), or a number of other meta lists. These brief capsule histories contain some information of interest to the general audience, but they are not useful to the professional or amateur historian interested in serious local history research.

In addition, there's something almost paradoxical about "virtual" local history. In visiting local history sites on the Internet, one perhaps loses the sense of place so important in local historical studies. But because it facilitates communication and exchange of information over wide geographic distances and allies historians and practitioners doing local history, the Internet possesses vast potential for sharing information, not only regarding content, but perhaps most importantly information about methods and techniques in local history.

On examination, therefore, one can discover a number of valuable Internet sites that contain much more than advertisements or enticements to visit. The Internet contains a wealth of information on history of interest to scholars and the general public, and there is a good portion of local history material included.

Electronic discussion groups, or e-mail lists, are a growing and accessible part of the Internet. H-Local, the H-Net list for state and local history, began in 1994 and at present (1999) numbers 670 participants. Topics discussed range from broad discussions of academic versus "amateur" local historians, to practical matters such as how to preserve documents. Subscribers also share helpful information about their specific local history projects, which, given the range of localities made possible by electronic discussion, are interesting primarily for methodological issues, that is, questions related to teaching and practicing local history rather than the content of specific projects.

There are also a number of electronic mailing lists for state history, including discussion groups for California, Georgia, Indiana, New York, New Jersey, Ohio, and Virginia. The Publhist list for Public History, housed at Indiana University, includes local history topics in its discussions of Cultural Resource Management (CRM), and offers information about graduate-school programs in public history. Genealogy lists abound for discussions of local and family history, with the Roots-L list and the associated <rootsweb.com> domain offering a good starting point for viewing what lists are available (<http://www.rootsweb.com>).

For content-based Internet websites, of special note as a model for local histo-ry on the Internet is the award-winning Valley of the Shadow Project by Professor Ed Ayers of the University of Virginia (<http://jefferson.village.virginia.edu/vshadow2>). Ayers has compiled a huge amount of material on two communities during the Civil War: Franklin County, Pennsylvania, and Albemarle County, Virginia. His site boasts an exhaustive run of contemporary newspapers, census material, and letters and diaries detailing life in the two communities during that critical time in American history. The site is fully searchable, and it enables visitors to "be their own historian" in the best sense of the phrase, by offering access to a virtual treasure trove of primary resources.

Websites of several state historical societies also contain valuable local history resources. The most extensive include the Arizona Historical Society (<http://www.azstarnet.com/~azhist/index.html>), the California Historical Society (<http://www.calhist.org>), the Indiana Historical Society (<http://www2.indianahistory.org/ihs1830>), the Kansas State Historical Society and related collections at the University of Kansas (<http://history.cc.ukans.edu/heritage/kshs/kshs1.htm>), the Minnesota Historical Society (<http://www.mnhs.org>), the Virginia Historical Society (<http://www.vahistorical.org>) and Library of Virginia (<http://leo.vsla.edu/lva>). These and a number of other state historical organizations feature online exhibits and holdings catalogs. For non–state-specific sites, the *American Association for State and Local History maintains a Web presence (<http://www.aaslh.org>) where virtual visitors can find links to a range of resources, including, of course, information about the AASLH's own projects and grant opportunities.

A number of local historical societies maintain high-quality Internet sites. The most interesting and extensive is probably the Chicago Historical Society (<http://www.chicagohs.org>), which features changing online exhibits on the history of Chicago, and "On the Paper Trail," a special section on how researchers use the Society's collections in their studies. The San Diego Historical Society (<http://edweb.sdsu.edu/sdhs>) is also very well done. There are literally tens of thousands of other private local historical societies with websites. Some of these local organizations are accessible through state pages, such as the Vermont Historical Society's special list of local societies (<http://www.state.vt.us/vhs>).

As local history organizations get more sophisticated in their Web usage, and more money becomes available for local history Internet projects, there will probably be much useful material made available on the Internet. At this point, however, most of the local sites contain the most rudimentary information about hours of operation and how to visit the area.

Colleges and universities also maintain sites of interest to local historians. These can contain information about courses and programs in local and public history, such as the Web presence of Arizona State University (<http://www.asu.edu/clas/history/grad/pubhist.html>), Indiana University and its associated National Council on Public History (<http://www.iupui.edu/it/ncph/ncph.html>), and the public his-

tory page of North Carolina State University (<http://social.chass.ncsu.edu/~slatta/ph.html>).

Because of the global nature of informational exchange on the Internet, it is difficult to summarize or predict its impact on local history. The spread of the Internet may result in the breakdown of the parochial nature of some local histories as sharing information across local, state, and national boundaries can aid in placing local history in context of national and world history. The development of additional projects such as the Valley of the Shadow, which allows researchers to formulate their own questions, can only increase the interest in local history and historical research.

TOM COSTA

interpretation and local history. Our written history is the product of the information that has come to us from the past, as it is organized and filtered through the mind of the historian, and as it reflects the time in which it is being written. All history writing involves interpretation and reinterpretation.

Most of what we consider to be historical sources were not created as such; they began as private letters, diaries, reports, etc. They are incomplete, in that they do not necessarily explain all that an historian might want to know. In addition, not all the necessary documents about a person, event, or trend survive, so knowledge of the past is incomplete, and what has come down from the past to us sometimes does so by serendipity.

The historian searches in the archives and elsewhere for information. If that search is thorough, the historian might find as much as there is to be found; the historian, however, might fail to look for everything that still exists. So the amount of information on a given topic is sure to be incomplete because of a historian's shortsightedness, or lack of time, or because the material necessary for an explanation has not survived or wasn't created in the first place. In addition, the historian organizes the material unearthed and then attempts to make it tell its story. In doing so, the historian brings to the undertaking all that he/she has read, learned, and his or her prejudices and inclinations, historical likes and dislikes. The historian therefore creates of the source material a narrative that is embellished in the context of what he or she knows. And thus, the source material has been interpreted by the particular historian.

In addition, the historian exists in a particular time and place, and that time informs many of the questions that the historian asks. In this way, new questions are posed of the past. While the material to answer those questions always existed, it took a particular point in time to have the question become of importance to the historian who then expands our knowledge of the past by the act of asking. And this too creates an interpretation of the past.

Thus, the materials from the past create a picture that might or might not be complete, but certainly skews the subject in some way; the historian by the type of search that is undertaken, by the organization made of the material and by the knowledge brought to the subject skews the subject anew; and the times in which the historian works bring yet another point of view into play giving the subject a particular interpretation.

This is one of the reasons that history will never be a science where the result is replicable, but is an art, for each person who makes a search will bring to the subject a subjective view.

In *Everyman His Own Historian* (N.Y., 1935), Carl Becker wrote: "In every age history is taken to be a story of actual events from which a significant meaning may be derived; and in every age the illusion is that the present version is valid because the related facts are true, whereas former versions are invalid because they were based upon inaccurate or inadequate facts" (p. 248).

Interpretations and reinterpretations are the natural result of the historical process. Interpretation can, however, disconcert the public who seek the surety of knowing. History, as taught, has often been presented by teachers as if it were a subject of right or wrong answers; it is that, of course, but it is so much more.

intestate. The legal condition of dying without making a will and thus allowing the laws of a particular state to dispose of one's assets. Dying intestate also means that the next of kin will have to apply to probate court to settle the estate. In legal documents, the term can also refer to the person who has died.

inventories. "The archaeological historian," noted Ivor Noel Hume in his essay "Material Culture with the Dirt on It," "sees a side of life that rarely finds its way onto paper and is rarely manifested in objects of museum quality. He becomes the custodian of the commonplace, the treasurer of trivia, but from it can emerge the features of hitherto faceless masses, without whom there could be no social history, nor any *material culture."

Inventories provide ways of peering into the personal environment of an individual or household. Even the daily life of a community can be illumined by a series of related inventories. Some wills contain detailed information. Fortunately, counties and other local governments usually have archives of records that include inventories, usually probate or intestacy inventories.

For examples of research making good use of this kind of resource, see Jayne Nylander's *Our Own Snug Fireside* (N.Y., 1993) and *SPNEA's *Bed Hangings* (Boston, 1961). In 1987, the annual proceedings of the Dublin Seminar for New England Folklife focused on the topic, "Early American Probate Inventories," which resulted in *Early American Probate Inventories*, Peter Benes, ed. (Boston, 1961), a publication rich in advice for the novice inventory-researcher. If there is any question about the relevance of material culture to the study of history, refer to *Material Culture and the Study of American Life* (N.Y., 1978), Ian M. G. Quimby, ed.

Conclusions based on inventory findings must be made with appropriate caution. Inventories that look "complete" or "incomplete" may not be so; it is advisable to take the opportunity to review as many examples as possible to develop a sense for that which is ordinary or extraordinary. There are four ways in which inventories might confuse or mislead the unwary.

Unintentional Errors. Even today, it is unreasonable to expect everyone to have a high level of organizational skill.

It might be assumed that the ablest or most responsible person available for the job was asked to perform the task of taking and recording an inventory, but in more sparsely populated communities, the "ablest" might have left something to be desired. In the nineteenth century or earlier, literacy and numeracy were far from universal. Occasionally inventories exhibit conceptual and graphic chaos. Often the handwriting is, in itself, a major obstacle to communication. In such cases, there is no assurance of accuracy. However, the lack of expected items does not necessarily indicate a job done poorly.

Appropriately excluded information. Some inventories are remarkably brief, or at least seem to lack the sort of contents the researcher expected to find. The obvious explanation would be that the possessions were, indeed, few. If the owner was sharing a household as a grandparent, newcomer, or partner, the list might be short. A wife's belongings were sometimes excluded. Perhaps an important heirloom, like a rifle, was passed on to the next generation in advance of the occasion for the inventory. In some cases, belongings may have been given over to settle debts.

Inappropriately excluded information. There is no way of knowing what was left off a list surreptitiously. The only assurance of accuracy is that these lists typically were made by two men who were well known in the community, and the community was probably intimate enough to have a fairly good idea of how well they did the job. Except in the rare case of blatant collusion or fraud, it seems likely that most inventories were honestly prepared.

Different standard of reporting. Cultural practices influenced what was selected to be listed, for which the researcher must be on guard. The religious traditions of the owner or the inventory-taker—even his or her degree of conservatism—should be kept in mind as the list is evaluated. A man's estate once included all his wife's possessions, except perhaps, for trivia like her needles. Women's rights to ownership began a slow process of upgrading, especially in the nineteenth century. Widows came to be acknowledged as beings in need of sustenance apart from the public dole and were finally guaranteed a portion of the husband's estate. Eventually, a wife's belongings ceased to be listed as a matter of course on her husband's inventories. With the grand changes brought about by improved transportation and the Industrial Revolution, came an increase in ownership of small things like chairs, teacups, dresses, and books. Reflecting this, inventories tended to be both more complex and more detailed.

SUSAN GREENE

Irish.　See Appendix A.

Italians.　See Appendix A.

J

Japanese.　See Appendix A.

Jehovah Witness.　See Appendix B.

Jews.　See Appendix B.

journals.　See state historical journals.

journeyman.　As distinguished from an apprentice, foreman, or master, a journeyman is a worker who has learned a handicraft or a trade. An apprentice is one who is still learning; a foreman is one who directs others in work; a master is one who has learned a trade, become a journeyman, and teaches others.

judicial records.　See court records.

$\mathcal{K}$

kindred. The nuclear family traces its descent from both parents, and this is called a kindred system. How a family defines itself determines from whom it can expect aid and favors and to whom it has responsibilities. There are a number of ways of defining who is one's kindred.

See clan; family relationships; household.

knitting. As a craft or art, knitting in England dates to the Elizabethan period although it is far older than that.

Knitting in the United States dates from at least the Massachusetts Bay Colony. While the original knitting guilds in Europe were male, by the end of the Industrial Revolution it had become a predominately female occupation. See Anne L. Macdonald, *No Idle Hands: A Social History of American Knitting* (N.Y., 1988); and Shirley A. Scott, *Canada Knits: Craft and Comfort in a Northern Land* (Toronto, 1990).

Koreans. See Appendix A.

L

labor history and the history of communities. Throughout history, earning one's daily bread has been a defining characteristic of human existence. Today, Americans spend one-third of their productive adult lives working. In the nineteenth and eighteenth centuries, it was half or more. How its inhabitants have traditionally earned their livelihoods determines not only the relative wealth of a community, but its institutions, social structure, and even the physical conditions of its environment. The availability of work is an important factor in the birth and growth of communities; its absence explains their decline and demise.

These insights are, of course, commonplace to most students of history. Nevertheless, it has only been in recent decades that professional labor historians have turned from the study of institutional and political labor history to the roots of worker history in community sources. In this new approach, workers are studied as complex human beings whose behavior in the workplace can be explained by examining their roles as members of communities, voters, racial minorities, women, and immigrants, not just as union members. In general, this new historical perspective is the result of the view that ordinary people's lives are just as important in history as those of famous leaders, powerful politicians, or wealthy businessmen. Several articles summarize this new historigraphical trend in labor history. Among the many are David Brody, "The Old Labor History and the New: In Search of an American Working Class" in *Labor History* 20 (1979), pp. 111–26; David Montgomery, "To Study the People: The American Working Class," *Labor History* 21 (1980), pp. 485–512; and Robert Ozanne, "Trends in American Labor History," *Labor History* 21 (1980), pp. 513–21.

The innovative way that historians presently view the history of *work has profound implications for the study of local communities. Just as union members and workers should also be seen in their dimension as members of local communities—voters, churchgoers, members of fraternal organizations, or newcomers from abroad—the study of the inhabitants of a local community should also include their roles as workers, whose lives are greatly influenced by what happens on the job. Work is such an important part of people's lives, that more often than not people rely on it to derive a sense of self-worth and identity. That is why labor unions have often provided a way for activists to maintain a sense of dignity and self-respect, just as they were relied on to guarantee decent working and living conditions. And that is why unions have been a constant presence in workplaces and communities since the beginnings

of the Industrial Revolution, almost two hundred years ago.

See James B. Gardner and George Rollie Adams, eds., *Ordinary People and Everyday Life: Perspectives on the New Social History* (Nashville, 1983); and Kenneth Kusmer, "The Concept of Community in American History," *Reviews in American History* 7, no. 3 (1979), pp. 380–87. Excellent methodological suggestions can be found in Jeremy Brecher, *History from Below: How to Uncover and Tell the Story of Your Community, Association, or Union* (New Haven, Conn., 1986); and Dennis Harison, *Working History: A Manual for Researching and Writing Labor History in Cleveland, Ohio* (Cleveland, 1984).

In other words, the history of a community is the history of its people, including all aspects of their lives. Often a community is defined by the degree of involvement of its population in local politics, by the voluntary work in charitable institutions, by membership in fraternal organizations, or by the rallying in support of victims of a natural disaster. The historical record shows that workers and union members were often at the center of these activities, providing the impetus and the solidarity that cemented community ties. While often portrayed as a sequence of violence and conflict, the history of labor is more often a tale of solidarity and support. The cigar makers, the carpenters, or the toolmakers who belonged to local Central Labor Unions in the nineteenth century were craftsmen who took pride in their work. They felt they had a stake in their jobs and in their communities. In her 1983 study, Helena Flam showed that at the turn of the twentieth century, highly skilled and home-owning workers in Paterson, New Jersey, participated freely and effectively in the city's politics. They contributed to what Flam called a "laborite democracy." See her "Beyond Democracy: Work, Credit, and Politics in Paterson, New Jersey, 1890–1930," Columbia University Ph.D. thesis, 1983.

Examples of community studies that include working people and labor in their accounts are numerous. See in particular the works of Anthony F. C. Wallace, *Rockdale: The Growth of an American Village in the Early Industrial Revolution* (N.Y., 1978), and *St. Clair: A Nineteenth-Century Coal Town's Experience with a Disaster-Prone Industry* (N.Y., 1987); and Gregg Andrews, *City of Dust: A Cement Company Town in the Land of Tom Sawyer* (Columbia, Mo., and London, 1996).

There are many other cases in which the investigation of local sources showed that people's experience in the workplace affected the character of the communities in previously unheard of or forgotten ways. Binghamton, in upstate New York, is a case in point. The recent historical study by Gerald Zahavi, based on oral histories and on company records, biographies, and labor magazines revealed that nearby Endicott was a veritable "industrial village," where Endicott Johnson, a local shoe manufacturer, provided housing, medical care, pensions, and recreational facilities for its workers. The benefits were given and received in the entire community, rather than in the workplace, thus tying all the aspects of people's lives to their jobs. The manufacturer coined the phrase "square deal" to convey his special relationship with the community. Although not prone to unionizing, his workers were able to negotiate better working conditions and wages as part of their bargain. See Gerald Zahavi, *Workers, Managers, and Welfare Capitalism: The Shoeworkers and Tanners of Endicott Johnson, 1890–1950* (Urbana, Ill., 1988).

Binghamton is also a good example of how abundant local sources can be. *Working Lives*, a study of the local history of work initiated by the local Roberson Center and partly funded by the county and the historical society, stressed that local repositories had a wealth of information pertaining to Binghamton workers that had been untapped for years. See Ross Mcguire and Nancy Grey Osterud, *Working Lives: Broome County, New York, 1800–1930* (Binghamton, N.Y., 1980).

Account books of mills and craftsmen, payroll records, labor contracts, city and county histories, business correspondence, local newspapers, and city directories are some of the sources contained in the public library and in the historical society. They detail the development and growth of the cigar industry, of glassmaking, tanning, and furniture making, and show that, contrary to common opinion, local unions had a varied and interesting history. The Knights of Labor, the Central Labor Union, and a variety of skilled-trades' organizations were a constant presence in the community.

Preserving labor history. If individual workers seldom had the time to personally document their lives, the institutions that they founded in their communities for collective action offer rich insights into aspects of this subject. The bulk of the nation's most important international labor unions have found homes for their archives. A large percentage of the records of 700 AFL-CIO city or regional central bodies, however, still require placement. More significantly, most of the records of over 60,000 local affiliates of American unions—many of which prove rich resources for the social and political history of the communities of which they are a part—have not yet been placed in a historical repository. The trend toward merger among American labor unions in the last decade, moreover, has resulted in the elimination of many long-lived locals and, sadly, the resulting loss of their records. See Daniel J. Leab and Philip P. Mason, eds., *Labor History Archives in the United States: A Guide for Researching and Teaching* (Detroit, 1992).

The State Historical Society of Wisconsin at Madison housed the first major labor history collection in the United States. Built by Professor John R. Commons and his colleagues at the University of Wisconsin and in the Society, this premier collection served as the basis for Commons's monumental *Documentary History of American Industrial Society*. The Society has continued its collecting in this area to the present time. Other state historical societies such as those of Illinois and Ohio and the Western Reserve Historical Society have joined in preserving labor history. Historical societies in major industrial cities frequently acquire major labor collections. Most prominent in this regard is the Chicago Historical Society, but there are also significant labor collections in the Buffalo and Erie

County Historical Society, in the Rochester Historical Society in New York, and in many others around the nation.

Beyond these repositories, the bulk of major international labor union records are either housed in specialized repositories such as the George Meany Labor Archives in Silver Springs, Maryland, or as part of the archival programs of colleges and universities. There are major labor manuscript collections in institutions of higher education in California, Georgia, Illinois, Maryland, Ohio, Michigan, New Jersey, New York, Pennsylvania, Texas, and Washington.

Statewide surveys of local labor union records have been conducted in Wisconsin, Illinois, and New York, and efforts to preserve important local records have been made in these states. Much more still needs to be done if important local history is not to be lost.

Local union records typically consist of union-meeting minutes, officers' correspondence, grievance records, local publications, photographs, and memorabilia. They can provide valuable documentation regarding local working conditions and, frequently, on local politics. Community historical repositories must begin to view the preservation of such documentation as the necessary complement to the preservation of other forms of community economic and business records.

Membership minute books form the core of most local union records. They are treasured by succeeding generations of union officers and may extend from the founding of the local through the present. It is not uncommon to find local minutes dating from the late nineteenth century. Such records are, of course, particularly fertile resources for local historians and genealogists. Other forms of membership records may also be particularly valuable for genealogical research.

When preserved, the correspondence of local union officials offer useful insight on the relations of these organizations with their national bodies, their lobbying activities, organizing activities, and support for community social agencies. Local unions also frequently maintain documentation relating to the local impact of work stoppages.

Newsletters offer personal details about the lives of the local members, insights into accidents, and work stoppages, or other incidents of importance that are frequently published by locals. They proudly chronicle the activities of local members serving their nation in time of war and the participation of the membership in local charitable activities.

Formal printed histories were often commissioned for important local union anniversaries. These are typically well illustrated, detailing the history of the locals and the biographies of its officers. They also frequently contain shop-floor pictures of union members at work and detailed descriptions of community businesses that employ union labor.

Local unions frequently keep collective-bargaining agreements with local employers long after the plant or company has ceased to be a factor in the local community. They offer important insights into the hours, wages, and working condition of the unionized worker in the community.

Photographs of local events such as Labor Day marches and picnics are almost always preserved by local officers, as are photographs of members engaged in a wide variety of activities from picketing to team sports.

The fraternal roots of craft unions are evident in the wide variety of ritual memorabilia they used in connection with union activities. Common were elaborate officer insignias, ritual handbooks, and artifacts such as Labor Day sashes, and a wide variety of membership pins and badges. Most locals had a banner emblazoned with the seal of the national union, the name and number of the local union, and an official local seal. Such items add substantial graphic interest to community history displays.

Beyond the important documentation and artifacts that can be obtained through local labor unions, records that were never before thought of as specifically pertaining to "labor" turn out to be very rich sources on the lives of working people. These include *diaries, letters, local newspapers, *city directories, parish registers, old county histories, *census records, fire insurance maps, and minutes of various organizations' meetings, just to mention a few of the available sources in local historical societies, public libraries, and museums.

Diaries and letters may tell us of the hard work and low wages of women in early textile mills, of their aspirations and often difficult choices, and how a farm girl could find the strength and motivation to join a strike. Census records may reveal the age at which children started working, what foreign country the immigrants in the community came from, in what neighborhoods people with given occupations lived, or whether married women worked outside the home. In addition, some local and state historical societies have sponsored oral-history projects that contain a wealth of insights into people's perceptions of their working lives. Finally, old *photographs sometimes have great documentary value. They might reveal that blacks and whites worked side by side in a particular shop where racial segregation had been assumed. Or photographs of the annual Labor Day parade may depict all sorts of groups marching behind their banners, not just labor activists, thus showing community-wide support for the meaning of the celebration. The exploration of local sources has delivered many such "surprises" to the local historian, and may reveal many more. Such discovery is a gratifying and fulfilling process, that not only gives due attention to all the members of a community, but may reveal its true character.

PATRIZIA SIONE *and* RICHARD STRASSBERG

landscape. Landscapes are products of the mind's eye, scenes composed through the act of framing disparate elements of the environment together into a coherent whole. In documenting and interpreting landscapes, local historians often examine three things: the interaction of nature and culture in a particular site, the relationship of the site to the larger world, and the diverse ways that local residents and outsiders have thought about the site as a place.

Landscapes reflect how successive generations of local residents adapted to their natural surroundings and, more often than not, remade those surroundings in accordance with their economic goals and cultural ideals. The interaction of nature and culture in American history is perhaps most evident in agricultural landscapes, where native plants were replaced with regular rows of whatever commodities farmers deemed most valuable. The reshaping of nature extended to water as well as to land, as evident in the canals dug for transportation and power, the rivers dammed for electricity and irrigation, the swamps drained for new housing developments. Even wilderness landscapes bear evidence of the human hand, whether the carefully constructed "wild" look of New York's Central Park, a reflection of the mid-nineteenth-century romantic ideals of its designers, Frederick Law Olmsted and Calvert Vaux, or the uninhabited wilderness landscapes created in the West by the removal of Indians to reservations.

Cultural landscapes include buildings as well, such as meetinghouses and churches, storefronts and factories, apartments and private homes. Their construction reflects the influence not only of economics and the environment, but also of prevailing social relations and ideologies. The impressive Greek Revival facade of the big house on a Southern plantation contributes to a landscape of power and domination, just as the vine-covered suburban cottage based on a design from an Andrew Jackson Downing *patternbook contributes to one of middle-class Christian nurturance. Over the past 100 years, many designed landscapes have been explicitly historical, such as the town commons developed by village improvement societies in New England at the turn of the century to emphasize the colonial character of where they lived. The interpretation of landscapes is not limited to physical descriptions of the land and buildings; indeed, social characteristics not always evident to the eye, such as inhabitants' ethnicity and race, often contribute the most to the distinctive character of a landscape. Whether urban neighborhood or rural village, landscapes have been characterized less by the architecture of the buildings than by the habits of the people who live in them.

Local historians also investigate how particular landscapes relate to one another within regions and across the larger society. The mansions of Pittsburgh cannot be understood apart from the coal fields of southwestern Pennsylvania or the iron-ore mines of Michigan's Upper Peninsula. Many towns owe their look and feel less to local conditions than to national forces, such as the grid Congress imposed over much of the nation with the Northwest Ordinance of 1787 to facilitate the sale of western lands, a regular pattern still visible from the air. Across America, landscapes have been shaped indelibly by the railroad, and after World War II by the *automobile, the development of a national interstate highway system, and the growth of national retail chains using a standardized architecture easily recognizable from the roadside. More subtly, they have been shaped by Federal Housing Administration mortgage policies that favored the construction of new single-family suburban homes over the renovation of older, more densely settled urban neighborhoods. Analysis of the relationship of landscapes to one another, and to national land-use policies and trends, helps the local historian understand the position of the local landscape in the larger world.

Finally, local historians investigate how local residents and outsiders, past and present, have themselves interpreted the land. Views of the land exist in *maps, paintings, and *photographs; in promotional literature aimed at tourists, and travelers' accounts written by them; in memoirs, newspaper articles, and stories about places handed down in the community. If landscapes exist in the eye of the beholder, and different observers have different perceptions of the environment, then local historians of landscape need to explore how particular views of the land become the prevailing ones in a particular time, and gained physical expression through land-use legislation. When some residents see a field as vacant awaiting development while others see it as already full of life requiring protection, which side wins out and why? Local historians can also explore, through public programs, the diverse environmental perceptions of contemporary local residents, the special places in the community and the memories and environmental values residents attach to them.

Understanding landscapes is essential to the task of local history. It is literally what makes local history local— about a place. Beyond researching the history of past landscapes, local historians often seek to document and preserve landscapes deemed significant by contemporary communities. They also organize public programs that represent local residents' experience of place, collecting memories and photographs.

While such programs may be of interest to outsiders, they are of far more importance to local residents. Such programs create environmental value by helping local residents to see the specialness of otherwise ordinary places in their community and to make informed decisions about the future of their environment.

The best introduction to the study of cultural landscapes, with examples of landscape analysis from different regions of the United States, are anthologies by Donald Meinig, ed., *Interpretation of Ordinary Landscapes* (N.Y., 1979); Michael Conzen, ed., *The Making of the American Landscape* (Boston, 1990); and Paul Groth and Todd Bressi, eds., *Understanding Ordinary Landscapes* (New Haven, Conn., 1997). The latter includes a superb bibliography of basic works in landscape studies.

Also near the top of any list of exemplary landscape studies are the essays of John Brinckerhoff Jackson and his former student John R. Stilgoe. Jackson's essays range from New England to the Southwest, and have been collected in a number of volumes, including *Landscape in Sight: Looking at America*, Helen L. Horowitz, ed. (New Haven, Conn., 1997). Jackson's *American Space: The Centennial Years* (N.Y., 1972) offers a fascinating portrait of American landscapes in the decade after the Civil War. Among Stilgoe's works are *Common Landscape of America, 1580–1845* (New Haven, Conn., 1982); *Metropolitan Corridor: Railroads and the American Scene* (New Haven, Conn., 1983); *Borderland: Origins of the American Suburb, 1820–1939* (New Haven, Conn., 1988); and *Outside Lies Magic: Regaining History*

and Awareness in Everyday Places (N.Y., 1998).

Local historians seeking to incorporate landscape history in public programming will be inspired by Dolores Hayden, *The Power of Place: Urban Landscapes as Public History* (Cambridge, Mass., 1995).

Finally, the *National Trust for Historic Preservation and the *National Park Service have published several guidelines for local communities seeking to document and preserve historically significant cultural landscapes. Among many useful publications are National Register Bulletin no. 18, *How to Identify and Evaluate Designed Historical Landscapes* (1987), and National Register Bulletin no. 30, *How to Identify, Evaluate, and Register Rural Historical Landscapes* (1988). An up-to-date list of federal preservation resources is available at <www.cr.nps.gov/nr>.

DAVID GLASSBERG

See parks.

land warrant. A document issued by a local U.S.-government land office to the purchaser of public land. It usually states the amount of land and describes the land and its boundaries.

Latter-Day Saints. See Appendix B.

Latvians. See Appendix A.

lease/leasehold. A document spelling out an agreement between a landlord and a tenant. The agreement usually specifies a set period of time. Leasehold refers to a property held under a lease agreement.

Leicester School of Local History.

The so-called Leicester School of Local History in the United Kingdom was until recently the main academic powerhouse for local history in England.

It began in the 1950s when Dr. W. G. *Hoskins (at that time a lecturer in economic history at the university) began to produce studies in local history. His first works had general titles (for example, *The Midland Peasant: A Study of Wigston Magna*, written in the 1940s but only published belatedly in 1957) such as would be appropriate to general economic and social history; but in 1959 his seminal work, *Local History in England*, was published. After absence from the university because of the war, on his return he was appointed head of a separate department of English local history with the title of "reader in local history." Hoskins left Leicester in 1951 to go to Oxford. Funding for the new department and its extensive library was obtained from a private foundation (the Marc Fitch Fund), and the first professorship (chair) of local history at Leicester was held by H. P. R. *Finberg, who came to the university not from an academic background, but from publishing. When Finberg retired in 1965, Dr. Hoskins returned to Leicester as professor of English Local History, retiring in 1968 to his home in Exeter. The Department of English local history continued under various successive heads, although it offers only postgraduate courses, not undergraduate courses. It remains today the only university department of English local history, although an increasing number of other universities in the United Kingdom have appointed individual professors of local (and regional and family) history, but without a department. Centers of local history and/or regional history exist in several universities such as East Anglia, Exeter, Lancaster, Leeds, Nottingham, and Sussex, mainly concentrating on research with some teaching of undergraduates and postgraduate students; and some specialist centers such as the Cambridge Centre for the History of Population and Social Structure have also been developed.

Leicester remains unique with its emphasis on English local history in the round. From the start, it took two distinctive approaches to local history. It started out by defining local history as topographical history, including rural settlements, peasant housing, landscapes, and the manmade environment. A second theme soon emerged from this primary interest, the history of the development of "local communities" from their origin to their decline. Both Finberg and Hoskins took a nostalgic view of local history as being essentially concerned with villages and small towns, thus tending to see the industrial nineteenth century as a period of "decline" of local communities, and the technological twentieth century as the age of the death of local communities, views not shared by all their successors at Leicester. Leicester pioneered many studies of historical landscapes and communities. Attention has been confined to England; the early members of staff argued that Wales, Scotland, and Ireland had distinctive local histories. The members of staff and the students of this "school" of local history have been prolific in the works they have produced. Many of these studies have been published by Leicester University Press. The publishing of academic local history has been a feature of the university for many years.

The topographical and "community" approaches to local history were the main focus for many years. But some members of the department widened this approach to economic history (Dr. Joan Thirsk's studies of agriculture and rural industries), historical sociology (Dr. Alan Everett's studies of nonconformity), and anthropology (Dr. Phythian-Adams' studies of folklore, etc.). And recently the community focus has been widened to include wider groupings (*pays*, provinces and regions). However, local neighborhood and residential groups remain a key element for the department; although in other universities, as local studies in academic institutions have grown in strength, the emphasis has moved more to regional studies and away from village and parish and estate.

It is important to note that, although the Department of English Local History has remained until today somewhat marginal to the main history departments at the University of Leicester, local history studies have been a feature of other parts of that university. This is particularly true of urban history. Building on the work of another economic historian at Leicester, Dr. J. Dyos, the Center for Urban History was created there. Publications (including an urban history yearbook) have also appeared in this area of study, especially through the work of Dr. Peter Clark. In the light of this widespread interest in historical locality studies, it is not clear at the time of writing if the De-partment of English Local History will remain a separate feature of the university or be assimilated into a wider school of historical studies.

ALAN ROGERS

libraries. There are an estimated 120,000 libraries in the United States, with the following breakdown: 4,000 college and university libraries; 93,000 library/media centers in schools serving grades K–12; 9,000 public libraries (with an additional 6,400 branch libraries); and some 12,000 special libraries serving corporations, museums, law firms, newspapers, hospitals, etc. This last category would include libraries in local historical societies and museums. Canada has almost 3,000 academic, public and special libraries.

The origin of libraries can be traced to about 3000 B.C. in what was then called Mesopotamia (now Iraq) from the time when our ancestors began to keep records. They first had to learn to write—to put down in graphic form some evidence of their experience, observation, and thought. When they began to save these records for religious, legal, economic, or sentimental reasons—from that point we had libraries and librarians.

There is a rich published literature tracing the history of libraries with two major themes—constant change, and survival and growth. There has been constant change in the contents of libraries from clay tablets (in Mesopotamia) to papyrus scrolls, to the book, to microforms, to computer databases, and to the World Wide Web. Constant change has also occurred in the locations of library collections from temples, churches, and monasteries, to the massive buildings of the British Museum Library and the *Library of Congress, to futuristic digital and virtual libraries. There has been constant change in the role of the librarians from high priest and civic official to slave librarians (in the time of Rome), to the scholar librarian, and to the modern librarian with the standard MLS degree. But there are also new variations such as knowledge worker, information manager, and cybrarian.

For over five thousand years, libraries have not only survived, but overcome many obstacles such as floods, fires, tyrants, vandals, inquisitions, wars, book burnings, budget crises, and predictions of their demise. During the past century each great information technology development—film, radio, mass-produced paperbacks, television, and computer—has brought with it predictions of the end of libraries. But libraries have continued to grow, adapt, change and become even more important in the new information age.

In the United States and Canada the first libraries were established through private collections brought by the early settlers and through the establishment of colleges such as Harvard (1636), which began with a collection of books. Social libraries during the eighteenth and nineteenth centuries developed, established by voluntary associations of people of similar income, educational and social level, but open to all who could pay the required fee. These social libraries began to convert to tax-supported, free public libraries during the latter half of the nineteenth century, particularly with the advent of Carnegie library philanthropy.

During 1886–1917 Andrew Carnegie gave money for the erection of 1,679 public-library buildings in 1,412 U.S. communities, and for public-library buildings in 116 communities in Canada. Carnegie had two requirements: each community was to provide a site and agree to support the Carnegie library through local taxation. The latter requirement solidified and expanded the development of public libraries in the United States and Canada.

Libraries are currently going through many revolutionary changes—perhaps the greatest in their 5,000 year history. We are living in the midst of an information revolution comparable to the impact of the invention of printing during the fifteenth century. Information formats are constantly changing. There is a shift from paper to digital form. There is also a shift from building library collections to providing access through networking. And yet books are not disappearing. Indeed book production continues to increase worldwide. Libraries continue to face the challenge of change and the need to respond to the information needs of society.

Public libraries continue to play a special role, since their goal is to provide free access to unrestricted information for all segments of society from preschool child to senior citizen and to all educational, income, and occupational levels. Local public libraries are natural allies of those interested in state and local history. They often are repositories of local history collections and are usually willing to cooperate on joint activities and programs with historical agencies.

It is ironic that libraries, whose major role is the preservation of the graphic record of civilization, have not done well in the preservation of their own historical record. There is an opportunity here for assistance and encouragement from local historians and local historical agencies.

See George S. Bobinski, *Carnegie Libraries* (Chicago, 1969); Wayne W. Wiegand and Donald Davis, Jr., eds., *Encyclopedia of Library History* (N.Y., 1994); Michael Harris, *History of Libraries in the Western World* (Metuchen, N.J., 1995); and Robert Wedgeworth, ed., *World Encyclopedia of Library and Information Services* (Chicago, 1993).

GEORGE S. BOBINSKI

libraries in house museums. Time after time while visiting *historic homes the guide shows you the library. I usually crane my neck and nearly fall over the guard rail, trying to see what titles the previous occupants owned. It so happens that there are a great many valuable books, and no doubt manuscripts, in these libraries that are not doing anyone any earthly good. Frequently they are dusty and drying out. Bindings are fragile. Of course, these books should never be sold, but they should be better cared for. I often say to myself: what a waste! It would take a bit of organization, but I think a plan should be formed to make use of these books. This is what I suggest:

Each historic home open to the public, and with a library, should make a brief inventory of all the books, pamphlets, and manuscripts; the inventory should list: author, title, date, and subject. This data should be sent to a central headquarters, where knowledgeable historians would make a Union

Catalog of the important titles. This Union Catalog could be printed and made available to serious historical researchers. The books should remain in their respective libraries, but be made available to qualified researchers, who would have to go the particular library to see the book, or books, or manuscripts. In that way the books would remain where they belong and would not get lost or mishandled by curious but not serious persons.

Such a Union Catalog would take a considerable amount of planning, but in the long run it certainly would be well worth the effort. A great many of these historic homes were, of course, owned by people of great importance, and their libraries certainly must contain valuable material not available anywhere else.

HAROLD NESTLER

Library of Congress. The Library of Congress has one of the world's premier collections of U.S. and foreign genealogical and local history publications. The Library's collection began as early as 1815 when Thomas Jefferson's library was purchased. In August 1935, a "Reading Room for American Local History and Genealogy" was opened. Over the years the collection has greatly expanded. The Library currently has more than 40,000 genealogies and more than 100,000 local histories.

In addition, the Library of Congress possesses related material of great significance such as archival resources, biographies, church histories, *city directories, *folklore collections, as well as geographical and historical works. Important resources can be found in the special collections of manuscripts, *maps and atlases, microforms, newspapers, *photographs, rare books, CD-ROMs and other electronic forms, housed in various divisions of the Library.

Fortunately, the Library has a number of outstanding tools to help the researcher access these collections. *The Library of Congress: A Guide to Genealogical and Historical Research*, by James Neagles (Salt Lake City, Utah, 1990), is a comprehensive handbook for the Library's genealogical collections and an inventory of the Library's vast city directories collection. It also gives an in-depth description of material in the Geography and Map, Newspapers and Current Periodicals, and Microform collections.

The Library of Congress provides many resources and services via the Internet, all of which are described or available from the Library's home page at <http://lcweb.loc.gov>. The Local History and Genealogy Reading Room's home page (<http://lcweb.loc.gov/rr/genealogy>) provides general information about the reading room, including the full text of the reading room's bibliographies and guides as well as links to other Internet sources on local history and genealogy. Most importantly, both these home pages provide access to the Library's online catalog. The Library is also beginning to offer some digital versions of books in the collection.

Aside from the digital versions of a few local histories, only material in microform is available for interlibrary loan; however, these microforms include a significant part of the genealogical collection. To identify titles on microfilm, consult *Genealogies Cata-*

loged by the Library of Congress since 1986: With a List of Established Forms of Family Names and a List of Genealogies Converted to Microfilm since 1983 (Washington, D.C., 1991). The Library's photoduplication service can supply photocopies of items if there are no copyright restrictions.

Many of the Library's 21 reading rooms offer essential sources for the local historian. The Local History and Genealogy Reading Room offers specialized card catalogs that index *genealogy, heraldry, and local history in the collections. The Reading Room also offers public Internet terminals, two of which permit searching on Ancestry's Library, an Internet site with access to more than 400 searchable genealogical databases. Two workstations contain the CD-ROM created by the *Family History Library in Salt Lake City, Utah, and provide access to the Ancestral File, the Family History Library Catalog, the *International Genealogical Index, the Social Security Death Index, and the Military Index. This high-tech tool is an important complement to the Library's resources; the Family History Library Catalog also serves as an in-depth index to many books in the Library of Congress collection.

The Library's historic Main Reading Room, through its catalogs, 70,000 volumes of print reference works, and a wide variety of CD-ROM and online databases, is the primary entrance to the Library's general collections. It is the principal reading room for work in the social sciences and humanities. Here one may research the history of medicine, or look up biographical details about pioneer doctors or even the history of a particular hospital. Similar research material is available about other professions and religion.

The Microform Reading Room has a collection of directories from selected cities and towns, dating from the colonial period to as recently as 1960. This microform collection is complemented by the New York City telephone directories from 1878 to 1959, plus those of selected towns in surrounding areas of New York and New Jersey. Other important microform collections include:

- Slave narratives, which are interviews with former slaves recorded between 1936 and 1938 by the Federal Writers Project. (Copies of the original transcripts are in the Manuscript Division.)
- The Barbour Collection, which indexes vital records transcribed from pre-1850 records for most Connecticut towns.
- Massachusetts Vital Records to 1850, and for some towns until around the beginning of the twentieth century.

These microforms are supplemented by the Library's extensive collection of unclassified city directories in paper. All book material cataloged by the Library is searchable on the online public catalog of the Library of Congress.

In the Manuscript Reading Room the researcher will find a wealth of material, including the Draper Manuscripts, the American loyalists collection, and, for German Americans, microfilm of the Hamburg ship-passenger lists from 1850 to 1873. The Alaskan Russian Church Records, 1772 to 1936, may also be helpful to researchers.

The Geography and Map Reading Room has material that can help researchers identify geographic locations. County atlases from 1825 onward show land ownership; some 1,500 county land-ownership maps date from the early nineteenth century; and ward maps are essential for obtaining ward numbers needed to undertake census research in major cities. *U.S. Geological Survey Topographical Quadrangles from the 1880s are helpful in locating cemeteries as well as boundary lines described on plats and deeds. Fire insurance maps from 1867 to the present in the *Sanborn collection indicate the size, shape and construction of dwellings in 12,000 cities and towns.

The Newspaper and Current Periodical Reading Room houses a large collection of U.S. and foreign newspapers on microfilm and in hard copy. The Reading Room's reference collection has a number of helpful indexes to newspapers, and abstracts of marriage records, death notices, *obituaries, and other data from a wide variety of local newspapers.

The Rare Book and Special Collections Reading Room includes material such as the Confederate States Imprints, *almanacs, printed documents of the Colonial Congress and the colonial governments of New England, and the Charles H. Banks material on early Pilgrim families in Massachusetts. Also available are a large number of local histories, published and unpublished genealogies, pre-1861 city directories, and the Library's collection of works published prior to 1801.

Other reading rooms of particular help in genealogical research are the European, Hispanic, Asian, and the African and Middle Eastern reading rooms.

While the Library is rich in collections of manuscripts, microfilms, newspapers, photographs, maps, and published material, it is not an archive or repository for unpublished or primary-source county, state, or church records. Researchers seeking county records will need to visit the courthouse or a library in the county of interest, the state archives, the Family History Library in Salt Lake City or one of its Family History Centers, all of which might have either the original county records or microform copies.

JUDITH P. REID

Lithuanians. See Appendix A.

living history museums. Living history is a technique of museum presentation and interpretation that attempts to create and animate a historical context or environment. Living history exhibits engage museum visitors through live interpretation and demonstrations as well as by providing sensory experiences that represent, evoke, and even try to recreate past life. Living history techniques have been embraced by many museums, particularly outdoor museums and historic sites. The majority of living history sites and museums focus on pre-industrial rural life on farms and in small villages or on military history in restored and recreated forts. With its high entertainment value, living history has been adopted by many historic sites and outdoor museums, which often are more closely tied to tourist visitation and admission revenues than are traditional museums.

The Association for Living History, Farm, and Agricultural Museums (ALHFAM) brings together over a 1,000 museum institutions, professionals, and practitioners who are engaged in living history. Embracing a range of definitions of living history practice, ALHFAM calls itself "an organization of people who bring history to life." Such efforts most often include interpreters performing historical work and trades, domestic activities including historic foodways, as well as *gardens, crops, and livestock. Living history sites most often depict pre-industrial periods and settings.

Sites and museums that fully embrace living history strive to create a total historical context and environment. They select a date or period of presentation and attempt an authentic restoration of buildings, landscapes, furnishings, and costumes, eliminating or minimizing intrusions that "are not period." In living history farm museums, these restorations sometimes include back-bred livestock and crop varieties that reflect and even preserve the genetic characteristics of the past. At the same time, certain amounts of modern intrusion and anachronism remain inevitable.

Most living historical programs are presented by interpreters dressed in period costume, who speak to visitors in one of two styles or voices, known as "first" and "third person." Using techniques of improvisational theater based on research, first-person interpreters speak as individuals of the past, conversing as if visitors were time travelers to the interpreter's place in history. In first-person interpretation, the time is the "period" of the presentation; visitors are enticed into the historical time frame, and questions are limited accordingly. Third-person interpreters describe the past from the time frame of the visitor, normally not attempting to impersonate a historical character. This offers third-person interpreters greater freedom to respond to visitors and explain the past in the context of the present. Many living history museums and sites selectively employ both techniques, providing general third-person interpretation with first-person "impressions" offered as historical vignettes. Some use third-person guides to introduce visitors to first-person interpreters, assisting visitors in making the transition between present time and "period." Others employ a "modified third-person" technique that allows interpreters who are based in present time to embrace the historical period, describing "things we do" in the historical context.

The achievement of high-quality living history presentations is challenging and expensive, requiring significant commitments to staffing, ongoing training, and supporting research. The popularity of the living-history farms movement and of military reenactments has led to a proliferation of pre-industrial farms, villages, and forts that sometimes seem to mimic each other while they ignore other periods and themes of history, such as the urban and industrial past and the histories of immigrants and ethnic minorities. A nostalgically attractive living history site, perhaps enhanced to appeal to a tourist audience, may idealize the realities of past life and work, while the enthusiasm for the past of some living history interpreters may inadvertently compromise the educational value of their sites.

Despite these pitfalls, living history can offer exciting, multisensory museum experiences that can captivate the interest of visitors and staff alike. The power of living history lies in its merging of educational interpretation and entertainment value and in the immediacy of its ability to engage museum visitors and stimulate their interest in ways that static exhibits cannot.

A partial list of museums that conduct significant living history programs includes the following: Fort Ross (California); Bent's Old Fort and the White House Ranch (Colorado); Mystic Seaport (Connecticut); Conner Prairie and Historic Fort Wayne (Indiana); Living History Farms (Iowa); Homeplace 1850 (Kentucky); Washburn-Norlands Living History Center (Maine); Old Sturbridge Village and Plimoth Plantation (Massachusetts); Fort Michilimackinac and the Henry Ford Museum & Greenfield Village (Michigan); Fort Snelling and the Oliver Kelley Farm (Minnesota); the Farmers' Museum, the Genesee Country Museum, and Philipsburg Manor (New York); Old Salem (North Carolina); Pennsbury Manor (Pennsylvania); Colonial Williamsburg, Jamestown Settlement, the Museum of Frontier American Culture, and the Yorktown Victory Center (Virginia); Old World Wisconsin; the Ronald V. Jensen Living Historical Farm (Utah); the Ukrainian Heritage Village (Alberta); the Fortress of Louisbourg (Nova Scotia); Black Creek Pioneer Village, Old Fort William, and Ontario's Sainte-

Marie Among the Hurons and Upper Canada Village. This list is not exhaustive. A growing number of museums and historic sites conduct successful living history programs.

See Association for Living Historical Farms and Agricultural Museums <http://www.alhfam.org>; Jay Anderson, *A Living History Reader. Volume I: Museums* (Nashville, Tenn., 1990), and Jay Anderson, ed., *Time Machines: The World of Living History* (Nashville, Tenn., 1984); and Warren Leon and Margaret Piatt, "Living History Museums" in Warren Leon and Roy Rosenzweig, eds., *History Museums in the United States: A Critical Assessment* (Urbana, Ill., 1989), pp. 64–97.

DAVID A. DONATH

See culinary history.

local and regional history in the U.S. See local history in the U.S.

local government records. County and municipal records document business processes and decisions, define prerogatives, track expenditures, defend the actions of local governments and record the routine of government. "Record" means any book, paper, map, photograph, or other information-recording device, regardless of physical form or characteristic, that is made, produced, executed, or received by any local government or local government officer pursuant to law or in the transaction of public business. Records may occur in any format or in many formats. Counties, boroughs, parishes in Louisiana, towns, townships, cities and villages— also known as general purpose local governments—create records on a daily basis. Approximately 5 percent of those records will be archival, with permanent research value for legal, historical, or other purposes, and on rare occasions, because of some identification with a famous person or event, some intrinsic value as well. Information contained in local records sometimes may be highly detailed and include important historical or genealogical information incidental to their original purposes.

While counties are generically similar to one another, they are particular and unique in their histories and structures. No two of them conduct their public business identically. Counties are often surrogates for federal or state programs, with funds passing to and through them to carry out a federal or state agenda. There are many more municipalities in the United States than there are counties, and while they also are structured in similar fashions, they too are unique in the way they apply themselves to the public business, a condition that may vary even more from state to state. Functions of local government that are the responsibility of municipalities in one state may not be so in another. In some states, for example, public education may be a function of county or city governments, while in others school districts may be independent or quasi-independent special-purpose local governments.

Records provide an evolutionary trail through the growth and development of local governments, illustrating the development and history of governments as they became broader purveyors of public services, taking on roles—especially since the Great Depression of the 1930s and since World War II—unforeseen when they were established originally. Records are generated following such functions of local government as public health, public safety, public education, ownership or use of real property, social services, collection and expenditure of revenues, or public works. Because of the particular characteristics of county or municipal government, records for similar functions can vary widely in their creation, scope, content, organization, accessibility, and physical form, as well as the range of dates that such records may cover. Records from the early years of very old communities are different in almost every respect from contemporary records.

Not all public records may be available for public use. Some records are confidential and cannot be made available to the public, as may be the case with adoption or divorce records. Other records may be excluded from public use even under the various "sunshine laws" regarding *freedom of information, because they regard ongoing contract negotiations or confidential personnel matters. The uneven and frequently unsystematic acquisition and deployment of computer and other information technologies may also make access to records difficult, particularly when legacy software and obsolete hardware have not been replaced or information systematically converted to the next generation of technology. Finally, by no means do all local governments possess articulated programs of records and information management and archival administration, so that, while current records may be well maintained and accessible, older records or archival records may be lost,

badly damaged, or stored haphazardly and without controls in scattered sites.

Many important records are the responsibility of municipal or county clerks or registers. The best-known responsibility of the county clerk is as register of land documents, the recording and indexing of deeds, mortgages, mortgage satisfactions, and similar records. Municipal clerks are often the clerks of their legislative bodies and may also serve as registers of deeds and of vital statistics, keepers of minutes and as the administrative interface with the general public. All clerks may serve as agents for various state functions or as official receivers of documents for recording or filing.

Land-use records. Found in county and municipal governments, they may include the usual deeds and mortgages, but also records relating to environmental management, toxic spills or waste dumps, landfill openings and closures, site-plan and zoning reviews and decisions, environmental quality-review records, official maps, subdivision documentation, and tax records. Building safety records can include building permits, code enforcement and inspection reports, and building condemnation and demolition records. The materials found in these records may include surveys, maps, blueprints, photographs, specifications, and detailed plans. Although often voluminous, such records contain valuable information on siting, design, construction, occupancy, use and alterations to the *built environment. Tax records such as assessment rolls contain information on the owner, occupant or user of property; assessed value; dates when constructed or modified; changes in property ownership; neighboring properties; and lot or building dimensions. Early tax records may also reflect local responsibilities regarding militia service by adult male citizens and indicate special assessments and include lists of those eligible for duty or already serving. Environmental health records most often relate to community sanitation, sewage disposal systems, water supply, lead paint, and asbestos abatement. Many land-use–related records are created and maintained in electronic formats such as Geographic Information Systems, systems of computer software with the capability to manage, analyze, and display geographic data in a highly sophisticated manner.

Administrative records. Administrative records contain a wealth of material on the origins and operations of local government. Both general- and special-purpose local governments keep minutes of their governing bodies, boards, commissions and panels. Minutes document hiring and firings, actions of the board—including, where applicable, passage of local laws, resolutions, and ordinances; accounts of hearings, discussion and approval of contracts and expenditures; and all the business of governing bodies and their subsidiary and specialized lesser boards. Minutes from smaller local government entities may be quite detailed and personalized or simply a general account of the proceedings of meetings. Minutes may be subjective in content and can reveal, sometimes unintentionally, a portrait of a given board, time, or community. Minutes can be an important source of community history and contain biog-

raphical or other genealogical information. Administrative records also include the documentation of expenditures and revenues, payrolls, oaths of office, personnel files, correspondence, plans, reports, and a wealth of other information about the daily operation of local government.

Vital records. Important information may also be found where municipal or county clerks are registrars of births, deaths, or marriages. In some states, vital records of this sort are considered state records, and local officials who keep them act as agents of state government. In states where public education was or is a function of general-purpose local governments, school attendance registers, annual reports, and similar materials may be filed with a county or municipal clerk. These are important records for legal, historical, or genealogical purposes: a researcher, for example, of the post–World War I Spanish influenza epidemic may find significant raw data in death certificates. In some states, access to these records is broader and more open than in others. In many states, access to these records is restricted to some degree. Access to some school records may be restricted under the Federal Education Rights and Privacy Act (FERPA).

Public-safety records. The activities and functions of sheriff's departments, police and fire departments, building-code inspectors and similar agencies are documented by public records, some of which may be unavailable to researchers for legal reasons. Records in this category can document trends in crime, public protection, fire prevention and arson investigation, ambulance and paramedic activity, and the deployment of related resources. These records contain demographic information and a range of historical data. Early records of a city or county jail may include admission registers of prisoners detailing even the contents of their pockets, while police blotters contain descriptions of arrests and related information on a very local level.

Social-program records. Such records are often seen as "welfare records." They provide a long-term portrait of a given community and its care for its poor or disabled citizens. Early records may include Poor Rolls listing indigent citizens and the records of local almshouses supported by local government. Rolls often note reasons for indigence such as "lunatic," "widow," or "crippled," and reflect both the state of the community and the values it associated with poverty, mental illness, and the use of public resources to support individuals unable to support themselves. Modern records comprise the full panoply of social service programs, may not be fully available to the public, and are often enormously voluminous.

Public-works records. Public-works records document the construction and maintenance of the public infrastructure: buildings, roads, bridges, and the like. Records may contain legal research on rights of way and eminent domain, surveys, maps, drawings, elevations, plans, contracts, specifications, agreements, environmental impact statements and reviews and a range of related materials. Documents regarding locally or nationally famous architects, engineers, or planners who were contracted for specific projects may be found as

well as significant information of purely local importance regarding the layout of communities, parks, streets, and highways, and the construction of firehouses, court buildings, monuments, city halls, and other structures.

Court records. The structure of court systems varies greatly from state to state and has evolved and changed from the very beginning of the nation. Court records reflect the entire range of judicial jurisdiction and function, with case files that deal with petty and capital criminal cases and civil litigation from the most minor of contested issues to cases of national significance. Probate or surrogate courts settle wills and safeguard the estates of minors or the incapacitated. A huge amount of social, legal, and other information can be found in court records, although statutes or judges may seal certain cases, by type or specifically. Court records are voluminous, and the records of modern courts increasingly so, reflecting the litigious nature of society and other trends.

Public health records. Many county and municipal governments have in the past operated or are now operating hospitals, clinics, treatment programs of various sorts, laboratories, medical examiner's and coroner's offices, boards of health and health departments, departments of mental hygiene, and other health-related facilities and programs. Records from municipal or county facilities can include registers of patients or inmates, provide environmental or epidemiological data and illustrate the history and development of local health care and the factors that drove the creation of corresponding treatment efforts. Such records may be

The Amateur Historian until 1968. The journal, published quarterly, contains editorials, several well-researched documents, reader queries, illustrations, and a review of recent publications, including both books and periodicals. Address: 21 Lower Street Hanrham, Salisbury, Wiltshire SP2 8EX UK. Cost of an overseas subscription is £22.

Local History. This English local history magazine is published by The Local History Press and edited by Robert Howard and Susan Griffiths. It appears six times a year and contains articles about local history, book reviews, and a popular "Noticeboard" that accepts short inquiries, notices of events, and job postings. The address is 3 Devonshire Promenade, Lenton, Nottingham, NG7 2DS England; <editors@localhistory.co.uk>. Cost of a subscription is £20, or £25 airmail.

local history in the U.S. Local history can be considered in a number of ways, for people have come to their interest in local history—in the history of the place where they live—by various approaches. The compass of local history has many directions, each a "true north" to those who embark upon a particular path. There are people who organized state and local historical societies with the intention of preserving and exhibiting the documents and artifacts of the past. There are individuals who have published documents of local history or written books about particular places. But local history is also approached by those who become interested in a particular aspect of material culture such as "train buffs" or individuals who preserve and record the information in cemeteries. There have always been collectors of local items, from quilts or local imprints, to the products of a particular industry such as stoneware jugs or buttons. There are people who trace local genealogical records, and there are the preservationists. They, too, are all local historians.

Local history also refers to the past of a place itself: to what happened, what was recorded, what was preserved, what has been written and said about a place. Local history, which seems to be the simplest, the most straightforward of disciplines, is actually a most complicated arena of activity. To draw all these strands together is not easy—or tidy—and here it can only be done with broad strokes, to give a general sense of all this activity. It is my hope that this overview leads readers to other essays in this book that tell particular stories in greater detail. See, for example, community history, state historical organizations, gazetteers, mug books, publishing local history, heritage, popular culture, and the new social history. Also see the readings listed at the bottom of this entry.

The United States emerged from the eighteenth century more a promise than reality. It was a nation in the process of creating itself, defining what it would become. Focus was upon its future; an individual's loyalty, then, and even for a time thereafter, was more to locality or state than to the idea of the nation.

At the very same time that this national experiment was getting underway, there emerged the first of the state historical societies with a somewhat contrary purpose than that of the new nation. The Massachusetts Historical Society (MHS), created by Jeremy Belknap and friends in 1791, proposed to collect and preserve and discuss the past of that one state so that its contribution to the previous war and the exploits of its sons would not be lost in the rhetoric of nation building. In 1804, with a focus upon its own past, the New-York Historical Society came into being. In each case, these organizations were elitist and intent upon preserving the historical materials that documented their own past—and present. The MHS encouraged ministers around the state to write histories of their towns—a call that a number of clergy heeded. In New York, the Historical Society gathered contemporary materials along with the documents and books of the past. In addition, it circulated a questionnaire asking about the current condition of the population. They did not wait, as Belknap wrote, "like oysters" for a sea of papers and books to wash over them, but set out on a quest for what each could find and collect. These organizations set as goals the preservation of the past so that their people and exploits would not be swept unheralded into the big picture, their colorful and particular beginnings and achievements lost to memory.

During the decade that followed, other states created historical societies. Maine instituted its in 1822, as did Rhode Island. New Hampshire created one in 1823, Pennsylvania in 1824, Connecticut the following year. In 1831 Virginia followed suit, Vermont in 1838. Then in Kentucky a group of men organized the Filson Club in 1838. These were all private organizations, meeting places for men of leisure and with the ability to pay fees, and with interest in listening to learned papers. The role of these organizations as repository and library was foremost, their field of concentration was the state. In the face of nationalism, these organizations looked inward and promoted the history of residents of the state.

That decade also saw the creation of the Historical Society of Ohio. The Western Reserve had been opened for settlement following the Revolutionary War, peopled in great part by settlers from New England. In 1790, Ohio was uncharted land; by 1800, it had been admitted as a state. In 1822 the state legislature approved a bill to create a historical society. Nothing happened at that time, but nine years later the legislature approved a charter for the Historical and Philosophical Society of Ohio that met in Columbus. The importance of this organization is that Ohio did not have two centuries of prior settlement and identity to preserve, nor ancient documents that needed care, because in 1831 it had only been a state for 22 years—not even a generation old. Still, its residents had a historical society to chart their arrival and the growth of their communities, indicating the importance these people placed upon what they had done in settling the frontier and also on their subsequent deeds. If older state organizations sought to preserve their identities in the midst of union and to preserve their rightful place in the creation of the nation, Ohio's motives were different. In Ohio, the historical association was intended to record recent history.

During the next 15 years, other state historical organizations appeared with the same purpose. Even without a long-recorded past, newer states created historical societies to enhance their own identity. To them history, even if it was of the recent past, was something that mattered.

It should be noted that at the same time, there was one attempt to create a national historical society. In Washington, D.C., Peter Force organized the American Historical Society in 1835 with the idea that it become the nation's organization of remembrance. John Quincy Adams was its president. The AHS held two meetings, issued one volume of *Transactions* in 1839, and collapsed.

Local history, of course, is not just the story of historical societies. It is also the accumulation of books and articles written to chronicle state or region, city or town. Though these organizational and scholarly activities at times intersect—such as in the documentary publishing ventures of some of the older historical societies—at other times they can be thought of as dependent but distinct, for many of those who have written about local history have initiated the projects themselves and have worked alone.

The earliest local histories have been declared by almost everyone to have been an *antiquarian enterprise. This was history written by people who were often writing about their own families while recording the history of place, much the same way that the New England pastors had written about church and town as one. David Russo calls these early histories "subliterary," and he points out that in the early phase, 1800 to 1860, most of them were the only books their authors wrote. These histo-

ries were of deep personal concern; the audience was local, and the authors worked in isolation from others concerned with the writing of local history. Many of the earliest writers were quite adept, and their books are replete with classical allusions, although none but a few of those early authors were primarily writers. The most notable exception to this generalization would be Ralph Waldo Emerson, who wrote his history of Concord in 1832.

What can be said of these books is that they were promotional of place, sometimes written in competition with histories and promotions of other, nearby places. This is true of the 1842 *History of Binghamton* (New York), created to rival the *History of Cooperstown*, a town not far away. These early books strove to show the refinement brought to once-frontier sites, the local enterprise, the duty to ancestors owed by the young who were increasingly looking westward, and the ties that one should have to place.

While local histories appeared in this first period in the East and even well into the Midwest, there were relatively few local historical societies in municipal units smaller than the state. According to Walter Whitehill, in his *Independent Historical Societies* (Boston, 1962), there were but 65 local historical societies in the entire country by 1865. He lists nine in the state of Ohio; seven each in Massachusetts and New York; three each in Illinois, Indiana, Pennsylvania and Vermont; two each in Connecticut and Iowa, Rhode Island, and Virginia (p. 350). He doesn't account for the others. By contrast, there were 2,000 societies listed by 1900.

There were other directions people took as they engaged in local history in the years before the Civil War. *Genealogy was one of those. The New England Historic Genealogical Society was begun in 1845 and others followed.

The real flowering of local history, both municipal and county, occurred after the *Centennial Celebration in 1876. Those who could, made their way to Philadelphia; others followed the suggestion made by President Grant that they endeavor to write the histories of their communities. Not only did individuals take up the challenge, so did publishing companies such as D. Mason Company, in Syracuse, New York, Everts and Green in Philadelphia, and a host of others all across the country. Canny editors sent compilers into America's counties to gather material for the massive county histories that adorn all our shelves. These often-maligned books remain invaluable, despite their lack of references and their disjointed narratives. They do contain gold, as we who pan through them know.

If we look at bibliographies of the local histories listed in the collection of the Library of Congress, under Alabama or Maine or Michigan, we can see the effect of this post–Centennial surge of interest in local history. In Michigan, for example, county histories appeared in the 1870s and 1880s for 41 of the state's 55 counties. Only two counties had histories written earlier, the remainder had histories published in the 1890s. This was a common pattern in many states.

There were a variety of types of books created during this era. Some were centennial booklets, others local directo-
ries or books of historical records, and of course, there were biographical and portrait books, known as "mug books," in which one paid to be included. For the most part, the county histories that appeared were long, as was the one for Kent County (Michigan), which was over 1,400 pages: it was meant to be encyclopedic and authoritative, but not a book anyone was expected to sit down and read. This sort of book set an odd precedent that has hung on throughout the twentieth century: local history was expected to answer questions but not necessarily to be a literary work, nor one in which a theme or argument was developed.

As David Van Tassel reports, with the creation of the *American Historical Association in 1884, the era of the local historian was expected to come to an end. Van Tassel implies that with the advent of "scientific" or "scholarly" history, local historians were no longer needed, nor could history, national or otherwise, be trusted any longer to the hands of the *amateur. The local historical society was to continue collecting documents, caring for them, and it would, one supposes, continue to sponsor lectures and occasional exhibits, but the writing of local history could now be passed along to those trained to do it properly. Things did not work out exactly as Van Tassel suggests, however, for academic historians concentrated on national issues, for the most part, writing for a broad audience, while the amateurs continued their works aimed at people at home. They wrote local and county histories; many contributed history articles to newspapers. But in truth, interest in local history did not prosper after the turn of the century as the audience for local history began to fade.

What did appear in the years leading to the twentieth century were numerous county historical societies. Many were organized during the post–Centennial era, some to continue, a number to falter, disappear, and then later to burst suddenly to life again. In addition, most of those states without historical societies created them: California, Alabama, and Colorado in the 1880s; in the 1890s, Washington and South Carolina chartered historical societies; West Virginia created its society in 1905. In all, eleven state organizations appeared at this time.

After the advent of the twentieth century, some forms of printed historical materials changed. Technology made picture books popular and a more popular format for local history. There were past-and-present books, numerous souvenir booklets, and volumes of memoirs.

The thrust of all this publishing—and there was a great deal of it—was to record everything possible so that nothing would be lost. The pioneer generations were gone, and the children of the pioneers were aging. Memory was not to be depended upon, and multiple versions of the past flourished. "Harmonizing" is a word often used in the prefaces of books in this period. The history offered was harmonized, or the author hoped it would harmonize the varying accounts then in circulation. These books were meant to have the last word. And in some ways they did.

By century's end, mug books declined in popularity, probably victims of their original appeal: if anyone with enough money could appear in one, the idea of exclusivity was surely degraded. And to how many such books would any one man subscribe? Gazetteers and directories of community information were popular for a brief time, books that were little more than glorified business directories. And there were illustrated histories. In Oregon, for example, between 1901 and 1909, most of that state's counties had illustrated histories to boast of. In the state of Washington, 21 counties had an illustrated history published between 1901 and 1909.

Most local history to this point had been written by men. Usually they were from the leisured class, writing about their own family and their associates. There were, of course, some exceptions. In Iowa, in the 1850s, a county history was written by a woman. In Maine, a number of women were involved in writing local history, beginning with Mrs. Clara Baines Martins's account of Mt. Desert Island, published in 1867. In Alaska, where local history writing began in 1901, Dazie M. (Stormstadt) Brown wrote *Sitka, the Beautiful* in 1909.

Women's involvement with the writing of nineteenth-century local history, however, is infrequent. Yet, during the 1930s and 1940s, more and more women's names appear, a number of them drawn from the ranks of newspaper writers. The other trend that brought women into the ranks of local history writers can be found in the 1940s when local history began to be considered a proper subject for schoolchildren, and books aimed at this audience appeared. Ethel Schuyler's 1941

History of Menominee County, written for the schoolchildren of that Michigan county, is one of the earliest of this trend, which continues to this day. For better or worse, local history seems, when present in the curriculum, to be located in the primary grades, to be taught by teachers who are untrained, for the most part, in historical methods.

Publishing local history and interest in local history subsided considerably between 1930 and 1970. Historical societies faded, considered by many to have little appeal. During the 1930s it was difficult to celebrate a community's progress in the face of the Depression, though some places managed a celebration such as the one in Newburyport, Massachusetts. In the 1940s there was war, and in the 1950s local history was not much on people's minds. In 1952 Wyoming became the last of the states to create a state historical society. In the 1960s the country focused upon its own anguish of war and on civil protest.

Local history was not, however, down and out in these years. Despite the general lack of interest in the subject, new ideas about history were being developed. Urban history, begun in the 1930s by academic historians and others, picked up again after the war. In addition, civil rights protest throughout the nation in the late 1950s and 1960s brought about the need to understand the origin of the country's treatment of blacks and women, of Native Americans, and of America's ethnic diversity. Activists translated these interests into political action, followed by historical research and eventually by academic programs. Students in the 1970s and onward attended classes in women's studies, Indian history, and African American history looking for answers to the questions of the day. Race, class, and gender became standard ways of discussing the present and thinking about the past.

State and county historical societies reflected these new interests and introduced topics previously unconsidered. This did not happen everywhere, of course, nor was it always greeted enthusiastically by trustees or the community. In addition to new topics of interest, the 1970s and 1980s saw an increase of students in college and new academic programs, especially the introduction of museum studies programs. Still, academic jobs were few and many educated young people sought and found jobs in historical societies, often in states and counties to which they had no previous ties. They began the process of professionalization of these organizations, bringing to them training, new academic interests, and fresh insights.

It was the celebration of the Bicentennial of the American Revolution and the presentation on television of Alex Haley's *Roots that energized current interest in the locality, just as the *Centennial had done a century earlier. The Ethnic Studies Act was also important, as was historical-preservation legislation that passed both nationally and in the states. Americans, shaken by national current events, looked homeward to local history to explain who they were. While many people remained in or near their hometowns, at least a quarter of all Americans lived in a state in which they had not been born: mobility had shaken up the population and redistributed people across the land.

It was often the newcomers who asked questions requiring research in state and local historical societies, and it was often the newcomers who wondered aloud about their new localities. In response, local historians faced new questions, and—prodded by professional organizations such as AASLH—expanded the topics they researched. In addition, too much can not be said about the importance of the preservation movement that encouraged activism on behalf of local domestic architecture and those public buildings that give character to towns and villages. This translated into an activism our communities had not previously seen. Sometimes jarring or challenging to local historical societies, it brought with it new energy and renewed focus upon place.

Not only did the exhibition of local history begin to change in this post–Bicentennial era, so did the writing and publishing of local history. At first, publishers reprinted the older nineteenth-century histories, often with an updated index of names or a new preface. Some new histories focused upon earlier times. In Colorado, for example, in 1980 one local history looked only at the first 100 years of Garfield County; in Alabama, a book entitled *Autauga County: The First 100 Years* appeared in 1972; in 1984 there was a book about Bibb County, Alabama, that covered only the years 1818 to 1918. But there were more contemporary books, as well. Some were well-written accounts, many were thematic in approach; some asked questions about place, a number of them attempted to look at twentieth-century social or cultural topics. At this time, too, there were influences on local

history stemming from academic writers who identified themselves as urban, cultural, ethnic, or as "new-social historians." They, in turn, sent a host of graduate students to investigate local archives creating what Raymond Starr has called "accidental local history," that is, local history written not to understand a locality, but to explore a major theme that just happened to be played out there. Kathleen Neils Conzen has noted that 7 percent of dissertations written in 1969 had a local focus, while the number was 20 percent by 1976.

Starting in the 1970s, but gaining strength in the 1980s, there was everywhere a revival of historical societies. State organizations hauled out musty exhibits and sought to portray diversity. Some of this interest was generated internally, some came about because of the availability of grants for new initiatives, some stemmed from the public, reflecting a concern for the history of places closer to home. Programming reflected new academic interests and the concerns of trained personnel.

At the local level, not only were county museums re-energized, but new town and specialized organizations tied closely to place were also born. In my county, for example, there had been two historical organizations in 1976—today there are seven. Nationally, there were over 13,000 organizations listed in the AASLH *Directory of Historical Organizations* in 1960; over 15,000 societies, associations, museums, and other history organizations are expected to fill the 2000 edition of that book. This has been a mixed blessing. While local history is attended to and nurtured, these groups are initiated and run by volunteers whose emphasis is on the smallest geographic unit—often to the exclusion of the context and comparisons that one might wish for. This local emphasis has energized people to take an interest in the past immediately about them and has, in many cases, aided in the collection of documents and the preservation of some worthy architectural structures such as old schoolhouses, churches, and former industrial buildings into which many of them have moved.

On the other hand, this localizing trend has also denied that same energy and monetary support to county organizations that have suffered from lack of funding for needed modernization of storage, archival retrieval, presentation, and programming. *State humanities council funding is available to these organizations, but most often grant money requires new programming initiatives rather than support for operational funds or more adequately paid personnel.

Despite problems, the 1980s and 1990s emerged as a time of surprise and delight for those of us involved with local history. Small publishers, along with commercial book packagers, brought out new books. State and regional historical agencies provided speakers for expanded programming, and there was grant money from a number of sources, private, state, and federal.

There was genuine public interest in place. This can be seen in the growing numbers of people ranging across the population spectrum who have joined local historical societies. Membership everywhere is rising and coming from a variety of people in a community who attend lectures and classes, who view exhibits, and fill the ranks of volunteers. Not only are these new people members of historical societies, they expect to be represented in its programming and archives.

There are some interesting questions to ask about local history. There have been many changes over time, while some things have remained constant. What has stayed the same? For the most, part the focus upon a geographical unit defined local history in the past and continues to define it today. This has fostered loyalty, but it is also a form of local shortsightedness. Our towns and villages do not exist in isolation, and our histories should not be explored as if each local historian were a miner in his or her own shaft. Instead of digging a vertical line to the past, we should think in terms of a honeycomb of lines, each intersecting other historical efforts at various points where comparisons can be made, insights gained. Regional emphasis will provide needed context.

While the field of local history has changed, many of the types of books written by amateurs have remained constant. Illustrated histories continue to be popular, often in the form of "now-and-then" books comparing the present configuration of a community to that of the past. These books often serve as a warning to a community concerning changes made, of the structures that have been lost in the course of change and development.

Local history is still boosterish, even if the form that it takes today is not the same as that of the 1850s, or 1880s. Today *boosterism in communities can be seen in tourist literature, as towns are touted for their interesting and curious historical associations with the past. The hope is that visitors, new residents, and industry will be attracted.

The topics of local history are still focused upon the origins of a community and on land. But this is changing. There is, perhaps, a less reverential eye cast on local history today than in the past, and that is a good thing. Still, we need to consider the topics we undertake and to broaden them.

There have been significant changes in local history, as well, in the ways we think about, research, and present it. The audience for local history has expanded. Historical societies' collections and exhibits reflect a broader interest in all aspects of the past and in many of the different types of people who have lived or passed through a place. Local programming continues to feature the railroads that served a place, but to this traditional interest there have been added other topics that explore the varieties of experiences that have been local. Women's history, that of African Americans and ethnicity, have promoted an interest in all classes, and in the diversity of the past. This has expanded and enlivened the study of the past.

Another change is the fact that local history is now often spoken of as useful. Where once the research and writing of local history was antiquarian, today, it is to local history that preservationists, environmentalists, lawmakers, and community development officers turn.

The pathways to local history will always be various. Individuals with an old house will become curious about its origins and find themselves engaged in local history research; others will hear a lecture and become involved; still others will arrive in a community and seek to understand its past and its folkways. Some will come from academe, others will arrive in a town with a degree in museum studies or preservation or a commitment to public history. There will be environmentalists hoping to understand contours on the land or railroad buffs looking for the places Car #67 traveled. Some will see local history as *genealogy, while others will regard it as the place to study costume, or *culinary history, or the rise of citizenship participation in volunteer activities. Each will bring strengths; each will contribute to our local knowledge of place.

See Carol Kammen, *On Doing Local History: Reflections on What Local Historians Do, Why, and What It Means* ([1986] Walnut Creek, Calif., 1997); David J. Russo, *Keepers of Our Past: Local Historical Writing in the United States, 1820s–1930s* (Westport, Conn., 1988); William P. Filby, *A Bibliography of American County Histories* (Baltimore, 1985); Kathleen Neils Conzen, "Community Studies, Urban History, and American Local History," in Michael Kammen ed., *The Past Before Us: Contemporary Historical Writing in the United States* (Ithaca, N.Y., 1980); Marion J. Kaminkow, *United States Local Histories in the Library of Congress: A Bibliography* (Baltimore, 1975–76); Walter Muir Whitehill, *Independent Historical Societies* (Boston, 1962); and David D. Van Tassel, *Recording America's Past* (Chicago and London, 1960).

CAROL KAMMEN

See county historians; filiopietism; local opinion/national opinion; mug books; state historical organizations.

local history journals. See state historical journals.

local history museums. See museums.

local opinion/national opinion. The idea of public opinion in the United States is typically treated as a simple matter, though it is widely regarded as an important component of a democratic political culture. In the 1990s, our national politicians employ "pollsters" or public-opinion analysts as a matter of course and use their findings not just to gauge the public mood but to help determine their own positions on vital issues. In this age of poll-driven politics, genuine political leadership seems destined to become purely a thing of the past. But what is public opinion? And how is opinion at the local level (where polling is less prevalent) related to opinion at the national level?

Public opinion refers broadly to the views held by citizens about public issues, particularly as measured through opinion polling but also as displayed in public debate. While public-opinion experts do analyze the views held by particular sociological segments of American society (i.e., women, African Americans, college graduates), the media and other commonplace discussion generally treat "public opinion" as a national aggregate, with little or no attention to local or regional variations. This notion of an aggregate, national public opinion is clearly a reification of a more complex, multifaceted phenomenon. On at least one level, "national opinion" in the United States is comprised of many "local opinions," just as the United States as an "imagined" national community is comprised of countless local communities, communities that vary more widely than the national poll numbers suggest. Over the course of U.S. history, however, local communities have increasingly conformed to national norms on matters of public opinion, as on other matters.

In the nineteenth century, the United States expanded into a continental power linked by rail and telegraph. Yet it remained a loosely linked chain of what the historian Robert Wiebe has aptly called "island communities." In this period before "public opinion" became readily quantified, national opinion consisted essentially of opinions on national matters expressed by newspapers and magazines with national reach and by prominent political figures, particularly office holders and party leaders. But in an era of high voter turnout and strong party loyalty, local discussion was generally vigorous, and local leaders played a significant role in shaping local opinion. By the late nineteenth century, what Wiebe has elsewhere called "the national class" was markedly ascendant in terms of shaping public debate as well as political economy. Still, local opinion often varied more widely than national opinion, and there were distinct local and regional variations in the views expressed and the patterns of debate. In the late nineteenth century, for example, Socialist views attained a certain prominence and respectability in parts of the Midwest, while white supremacist views ultimately gained (or regained) a dominant position in the South.

Over the course of the twentieth century, the relationship between local opinion and national opinion has changed dramatically. At the century's end, local and regional variations continue to exist in certain regards, but they have clearly declined. The growth of national institutions—including the federal government, nationwide communications and transportation systems, national print and broadcast media, and national membership organizations—has tied the former "island communities" together in a seamless web that is now becoming wired to the world. Throughout much of the twentieth century, though, local opinion has probably displayed greater variation, richness, and texture than the focus on nationally constructed public opinion has suggested.

At the national level, public opinion, even as quantified by the polls, is framed by public debate. Public debate, in turn, is framed by the national media, political parties, and national membership associations ranging from civil rights groups and organized labor to trade associations and lobbying groups. Membership organizations like civil rights groups and labor unions provide a useful window onto the relationship between local and national opinion. They are comprised of local chapters, yet they aspire to speak with a unified voice in the national debate of issues affecting their memberships. From the 1950s to the 1970s, for example, George Meany and other leaders of the AFL-CIO spoke to the nation on behalf of organized labor, but not all union members agreed with Meany's views, and these disagreements were more commonly expressed within union locals than in national conventions.

Such national organizations operate somewhat like funnels, or perhaps more like locks in a canal. Since at least the middle of the twentieth century, the national leadership of, say, the NAACP or the UAW, have attempted to sway public opinion as well as public policy. The national leadership must contend with or respond to a range of opinion among its branches or locals, but it attempts to regulate the views that get into the national conversation. In the early Cold War years, for example, some NAACP chapters expressed leftist views at odds with the national leadership's on both domestic racial issues and foreign-policy matters. It was imperative to the Association's national leaders to contain these views within its own ranks and to project a more moderate, reformist voice into national debates, and they were reasonably successful in doing so. In this case and in general, the national debate is the key sphere where public opinion is shaped, though local variation adds shading to the picture.

JOHN FOUSEK

See economic history; labor history and the history of communities; technology.

local history societies. Over the past 25 years there has been a proliferation of local historical societies, evidence of an interest in local history and in place. Their presence is also a comment about older historical agencies, such as county and state historical agencies, whose programs and interests tend to focus upon the larger unit leaving those from smaller geographic areas or with particular interests dissatisfied. These new, small organizations are, for the most part, run by volunteers, often focused around a building, and are financially insecure.

See local history in the U.S.; state historical societies.

local history workshops. Local history workshops (sometimes called research groups) grew up in the United Kingdom in the 1960s. They took two main forms. One was a movement that emerged from the post–WWII adult education program. This consisted of local study groups, provided with professional tutorial assistance by adult education agencies such as the Workers' Educational Association (WEA), various university departments of extramural studies (or adult education), and other bodies. Such groups undertook a joint study of an aspect of the history of their own locality, and wrote up and published their findings in some form or other (sometimes in book or booklet format, sometimes in other forms such as an exhibition or radio program, etc.). Many useful studies were produced: for example, Bernard Jennings' *History of Nidderdale* (Yorkshire) in 1967. Training and other forms of support were provided, and adult education agencies often helped with the costs involved in such group work. A training manual for such group work was published, *Group Projects in Local History* (Alan Rogers, ed., 1977); this included general chapters on "working with groups" and "group writing" as well as more detailed examples of local history projects. This movement was particularly strong in local population studies, and a regular journal for such groups was published.

It is important to distinguish these groups from the other local history, and especially family history, groups that formed at this time, in which all the members were pursuing their own studies and meeting to share experiences. Local history workshops' members combined together to share their work. The value of this approach was not only that the groups could cover more ground and more sources than could be handled by a single local historian in the same time, but also that they encouraged creative work from a number of persons who may not have done such work alone. They showed that different group members had complementary knowledge, experience, and talents. And in them, knowledge was shared among the group and throughout the community rather than belonging to an individual expert. But much depended on the leadership and, in the case of publication, the editorial skills available to the group. Several of these groups did not produce published work, but their educational value was still very high. And other such research groups resulted in longer-lasting local history societies.

This movement spread into United States in the early 1980s, most notably in the East Tennessee "Hard Times Remembered" project. But it died out in the United Kingdom as funding for adult education changed and local history courses in adult education became certificated. The emphasis is now once again on the education of individuals who are expert on the history of their region or on some local history theme. Even population history groups are now rarer. A research report in 1993 by Joan Unwin of Sheffield University attempted to provide evidence of the social and educational value of study groups such as these—not just in local history but also creative-writing groups and natural history groups—but the workshop approach has hardly survived current trends in adult education.

The second form of workshops was the History Workshop movement. This started at Ruskin College, Oxford, again in the 1960s. Students at the college engaged in research into topics that drew on their own working-class experiences and expertise in regular seminars, and several publications resulted from their work. Once a year, a large and very informal two- or three-day meeting of social (mostly socialist and later feminist) historians gathered to discuss a large number of pioneering studies, not all but several of them on themes of local history. These workshops widened interest among historians more generally in areas of radical social history, focusing on gender, ethnicity, the very poor, disadvantaged groups, marginal and often overlooked groups of workers such as quarry workers, children, etc. There was often a political agenda in these debates. Reports of these meetings were produced, and from 1976, an annual journal entitled *History Workshop* was published. From 1980, the annual History Workshop more often than not moved out of Oxford to other parts of the country; it became more closely tied to the formal education system, especially in the polytechnics, and more professional in its membership. These workshops tended to have more local history papers in them than the Oxford History Workshops. In addition, "Local History Workshops" were held briefly, from time to time, in various other venues. The movement has declined, largely because of the death of its primary inspiration, Dr. Raphael Samuel.

ALAN ROGERS

See Cambridge Group for the History of Population and Social Structure; England, local history in.

ℳ

Lutherans. See Appendix B.

Macedonians. See Appendix A.

manifest destiny. This term has been used by those who believed that it was the destiny—or the right—of the United States to govern the entire Western Hemisphere, as in "our manifest destiny to overspread the continent." Julius W. Pratt, in an article in the *American Historical Review* (XXXII [1927], p. 798) entitled "The Origin of 'Manifest Destiny,'" traced its first use in the House of Representatives to Robert C. Winthrop of Massachusetts on January 3, 1846, when Winthrop stated "the right of our manifest destiny to spread over this whole continent." But the term was not original to Winthrop. Pratt found it used in the New York *Morning News* on December 27, 1845, in an editorial entitled "The True Title" in which editor John L. O'Sullivan stated that it was the "right of our manifest destiny to overspread and possess the whole of the continent." O'Sullivan was editor of both the *Morning News* and the *Democratic Review*. He had written in a *Democratic Review* editorial, on July 9, 1845, that it was the "fulfillment of our destiny to overspread this entire North America." While the December use of the term was in association with the debate over Oregon, O'Sullivan first used the concept of "manifest destiny" in a discussion of the annexation of Texas.

manuscript. Any document written by hand such as a letter, diary, report. Manuscript also refers to the unpublished text of a book prior to publication; its abbreviation is "ms." or "mss.," in the plural.

maps. The written history of a local community, whether state, city, village, or county, tries to answer questions about what happened, when, why, who was involved, how events occurred, and where they happened. Maps provide significant, although partial answers to the where and when questions of local history. They give history a place and show how that place looked at a particular time. The natural landscape of a place and its transformation by human presence and use is an integral part of community history. Maps are a key resource for telling this story. Maps supply information about large issues, such as where a community was first settled, the direction and size of the community's growth, where its roads were, when they were built, and perhaps most importantly how those roads changed the community. They also answer very specific questions about specific *place names, individual family landholdings, and even about the construction of individual buildings in a city or village.

Maps are an important resource for local historians, but they also must be used carefully and balanced with the evidence found in other primary documentation. Local maps use elements such as scale, and symbols that, while they may attempt to provide an accurate depiction of a village or city, are not a perfect description of the real world of that community. Cartographers may include a wide range of skills and knowledge. For instance, a fur trader in the Rocky Mountains in 1840 drawing a sketch showing various Native American tribes, a partly trained surveyor mapping a route through the Shenandoah Valley for a Civil War general, or a highly trained mapmaker creating a detailed topographic map using satellite imagery are all depicting a part of the earth, but the maps are all to some extent distortions of the real world. Maps are made by people living within a particular political, social, and cultural context, and they may have motivations other than a wish to create an accurate map of a place. Perhaps a map was made by a residential land developer who wants to show only the good features of a place and neglects to show an existing industrial development. Or a military leader may defend his actions at a particular battlefield and might not depict the positions of troops completely. Misinformation— whether purposely shown, or due to the lack of cartographic skill, or because of the necessary distortion inherent in the use of tools such as scale, projection, and symbols—makes it incumbent on local historians to use maps with care. Local historians using maps may find it necessary to evaluate and substantiate the information found on particular maps with other documentation, including that found in *gazetteers and local *city directories, land-

survey records found in government archives, and other maps.

Cartographic depictions of the natural and human landscape of America have been made since the colonial era. Although surveyed and drawn in colonial America, these early maps were usually engraved and printed in Holland, England, France, and elsewhere until the late eighteenth century. The westward movement after the American Revolution provided an additional impetus to produce more and increasingly accurate maps. Large numbers of individual farms and other landholdings, the growth of towns, villages, and cities and the expansion of the transportation network of canals, roads, and railroads led to a rapid increase in the number of maps of counties and other local communities. State maps and atlases were produced in the early nineteenth century and cities were repeatedly mapped. By midcentury, county wall maps issued by commercial map publishers were regularly produced and beginning immediately after the Civil War, county atlases were published including detailed maps of all the towns and villages in the county. Later in the century and continuing into the early twentieth century, many counties had updated atlases produced of their communities. Urban centers, both large and small, benefited from the publication of insurance maps, beginning after the Civil War and continuing to the present day. These maps were the most detailed and accurate maps of urban neighborhoods ever produced and are a significant resource for local historians. In addition, panoramic maps, also known as *bird's-eye views, of many urban communities were lithographed in the late nineteenth century. The establishment of the United States Geological Survey and the creation of many state geological surveys also occurred in the late nineteenth century. These federal and state agencies over the past century have produced thousands of geological, hydrological, soil survey, transportation, and many other maps that may be useful resources for local historians.

Maps, both government and commercially published, may be found in a variety of institutions, including libraries, archival repositories, government records offices, historical societies, and private collections, especially in the offices of surveyors and attorneys specializing in the practice of real estate law. Many important map series have been microfilmed, including thousands of insurance maps of cities and villages in the United States, the U.S. Geological Survey's geological maps, and many county atlases. Increasingly, users will find many historical maps of states and local communities, including a range of maps from colonial depictions to insurance maps, digitized and available for viewing on the Internet. These scanned images of maps along with the vast numbers of maps available through the use of geographic information systems dramatically increase the cartographic resources available for local historians. Many libraries and archival repositories have cataloged their maps online into national bibliographic databases such as OCLC and RLIN (Research Libraries Information Network), as well as their own local online catalogs. These databases for maps of local communities are a useful tool for local historians in search of significant historical information about their community.

JAMES CORSARO

See Sanborn maps.

marriage. The study of courtship and marriage, as a historical topic, is relatively recent. Historians have documented interesting shifts concerning the idea of love, courtship, and marriage. This is a topic that can be researched in local letters, diaries, and church records; it can also be approached as an oral history project as local historians look for changes over time concerning these topics and related subjects such as engagements and wedding customs. See Karen Lystra, *Searching the Heart: Women, Men, and Romantic Love in Nineteenth-Century America* (N.Y., 1989); Ellen K. Rothman, *Hearts and Hands: A History of Courtship in America* (Cambridge, Mass., 1987); and Carl Degler, *At Odds: Women and Family in America from the Revolution to the Present* (N.Y., 1980).

Masons. The archive for this secret organization is located at the Scottish Rite Supreme Council Library, founded in 1888. The address is 1733 16th Street, NW, Washington, D.C. 20009; (202) 232-3579; fax (202) 387-1843; <http://www.srmason-sj.org>.

material culture. Material culture is the physical evidence or remains of the human past, including objects (also called artifacts), the *built environment, and the land. In addition to the physical evidence itself, material culture entails the interpretation or historical meaning of such physical evidence. Historians can extract meaning from a seemingly mute object by studying it in the context of its historical time and place—the economy, social institutions, demographic patterns, and cultural mores. Material culture is as important a source of local history as the more familiar documentary evidence found in *city directories, newspapers, *tax rolls, and *census records.

An object may be utilitarian, decorative, or symbolic of a society's values and beliefs—and often all three. Identifying an object usually includes determining when and where an object was made, by whom, of what material and method of manufacture, and its aesthetic style (e.g., Colonial Revival, Art Deco, vernacular). At one time the emphasis of artifact study was connoisseurship—an appreciation of fine and rare (and often expensive) objects, and their makers. In recent decades, interest in the history of common people has broadened material-culture investigations to include everyday objects (representative instead of rare), regardless of "aesthetic" significance or value. Studying how an object was used and by whom, instead of focusing merely on the maker, has more fully fleshed out the social history of material evidence.

Like the maxim "all politics is local," so, too, is all material culture local—for the obvious reason that all *things* come from *somewhere*. In the case of the built environment and the land, they are virtually synonymous with locale. An object was made somewhere and was used in one or often more locales. The origin of an object (where it was made) and its provenance (origin plus the history of what has happened to that object since

its origin) are about *place* as well as makers and owners/users. A locale is situated in a region, a nation, and ultimately it holds its place in the larger world. Thus, an object might have multiple and far-reaching meanings—it might be a product of one community in the style of a region, represent a national trend, and be exported and used around the world.

See, for example, J. Ritchie Garrison, *Landscape & Material Life in Franklin County, Massachusetts, 1770–1860* (Knoxville, Tenn., 1991); Henry Glassie, *Pattern in the Material Folk Culture of the United States* (Philadelphia, 1968); and Glassie, "Meaningful Things & Appropriate Myths: The Artifact's Place in American Studies," in *Material Life in America, 1600–1860*, Robert St. George, ed. (Boston, 1988), pp. 63–92.

CHRISTINE KLEINNEGGER

matrilineal. A society where descent is traced through the female line and membership defines an individual's primary social relationships and responsibilities within the natural and supernatural world. Matrilineal is not the same as matriarchy, which is where women rule. The Hopi of northeastern Arizona live in a matrilineal society.

See clan; patrilineal.

medicine, history of. See health care, as local history topic.

memoirs. Every historian wants to get as close to his or her subject as possible—close in time and close in proximity to the topic. Eyewitness accounts are thus highly valued by the historian. There are many types of these, such as a diary or journal entry (preferably made as soon after the incident as possible), perhaps a newspaper quotation of an eyewitness taken on the spot, maybe an oral interview (although that will usually be conducted at a much later date), and a memoir.

Memoirs are accounts of a subject's life or experiences, supposedly by the subject. On the surface they would appear to be excellent first-hand accounts of past events; in fact they may not be. Some are ghostwritten, although that is not too likely for local ones. Memoirs are usually prepared years after the events recorded, and thus the subject's memory has filtered the past through layers of life experiences or involvement with issues. Even if that is not the case, the account will be shaped by the author's desire to recount the story of his or her life as they want it remembered, rather than as it was. Think of the word "memoir" as meaning the subject's desire to shape the world's "memory" of that person. Yet another problem may be the actual knowledge of an event possessed by the memoirist. The author may accurately remember the event; *may* be consulting diaries and journals and letters from the time of the event; but the author *may* also be unconsciously remembering the past as it was described over the years.

If used with care, memoirs can be useful to the local historian: they certainly provide evidence of the memoirists' values and point of view and they may provide factual information regarding the events of the past. Wherever possible, however, the historian should try to find collaborating evidence in order to guard against the pitfalls of memoirs as histor-ical sources. The best guide to dealing with this troublesome source is Carol Kammen, *On Doing Local History: Reflections of What Local Historians Do, Why, and What it Means* ([1986] Walnut Creek, Calif., 1995), pp. 58–61.

RAYMOND STARR

Mennonites. See Appendix B.

Methodists. See Appendix B.

Mexicans. See Appendix A; also see Chicano history.

***Middletown* study.** During the mid-1920s, sociologists Robert S. Lynd and his wife, Helen Merrell Lynd, selected Muncie, Indiana, as the locale for their study of social change in American society. Their work resulted in the landmark study *Middletown: A Study in American Culture* (N.Y.), first published in 1929. In 1935, Robert Lynd returned to Muncie to investigate the impact of the Great Depression on the city; *Middletown in Transition: A Study in Cultural Conflicts* (N.Y., 1937) was the result. The strengths of the Lynds's works are many, but of particular value to sociologists, historians, and anyone interested in the study of the United States at the local level is the breadth of their investigations. Both works about Muncie are classics not only because they are lively and intensive, but particularly because the Lynds avoid the myopia to which authors of local investigations often succumb.

Robert and Helen Lynd selected Muncie (population 38,000) not because it was a particularly outstanding city, but rather because its unremarkability made it a fine specimen of American life and culture. In many respects "Middletown," as the Lynds dubbed it in an effort to conceal Muncie's identity, was a microcosm of national society. Between January 1924 and June 1925, the Lynds and their research associates lived in Muncie and insinuated themselves into the small city's life. They went to community meetings and attended church services; researched documentary material and compiled statistics; conducted interviews and distributed questionnaires. The Lynds did not embark upon the project to prove a thesis about life in the nation, but rather they armed themselves with the belief that, no matter the locale, there are a limited number of fundamental things in which humans are engaged. They reduced these to six areas: work, home life, education, leisure, religion, and community life. Rather than arriving at broad conclusions, the Lynds sought to suggest "possible fresh points of departure in the study of group behavior." Technological change, and especially its positive and negative aspects, is a central theme in the initial Middletown study. And although they shied away from conclusions, the Lynds' study emphasizes an ambivalence about progress. They paint a portrait of a city looking toward the future while trying to hang on to tradition. Upon returning to Muncie in the midst of the Depression, Robert Lynd discovered what investigators of localities found throughout the nation: that the federal government had become an imposing presence at the local level and that cities increasingly surrendered their autonomy to Washington.

The *Middletown* studies are valuable to social scientists investigating other localities because the Lynds effectively demonstrated that Muncie was, indeed, a typical American city. The extensive quantitative and qualitative data provide useful reference points for comparison and furnish interesting reading for anyone wishing to catch a glimpse of American life during the 1920s and 1930s. Today, the Center for Middletown Studies, located at Ball State University in Muncie, collects materials and supports further research on the city.

See Dan Rottenberg, ed., *Middletown Jews: The Tenuous Survival of an American Jewish Community* (Bloomington, Ind., 1997); Dwight W. Hoover, *Middletown: The Making of a Documentary Film Series* (Chur, Switzerland, and Philadelphia, 1992), and *Middletown Revisited* (Muncie, Ind., 1990); Theodore Caplow, *All Faithful People: Change and Continuity in Middletown's Religion* (Minneapolis, 1983), and Caplow et al., *Middletown Families: Fifty Years of Change and Continuity* (Minneapolis, 1982).

JEFFREY S. COLE

Midwest. West and north of the Ohio River, and extending to the Dakotas, Nebraska, and Kansas is a geographic region known as the Midwest or Middle West. This area includes the states of Ohio, Indiana, Illinois, Michigan, Wisconsin, Iowa, Minnesota, Missouri, Kansas, Nebraska, South Dakota, and North Dakota. Geographically, economically, politically, and culturally these states maintain aspects unique to themselves, but reflect unifying features. Almost all of this land came from either the Old Northwest or the Louisiana Purchase and entered the Union through the Ordinance of 1787.

The origins of the term the "Midwest" date to the early nineteenth century. Geographer James Shortridge traced the concept of the "Middle West" to 1827 in an account by a Cincinnati editor named Timothy Flint. Flint had been describing the Second Great Awakening, and referred to the prevalence of religious activity in "the middle western states; chiefly Tennessee." This description framed the Middle West in reference to the north and south, rather than east and west. By the late 1890s, the term had come into common usage and often referred to Kansas and the Dakotas. Geographers reached the current twelve-state understanding of the Midwest by 1920.

The Midwest is well-defined by geographic features. It is cradled by two great rivers and divided by one of the largest in North America. The land forms of the region progress from woodlands in the east, to prairie in the center, plains in the west, and forest in the north. Conrad Richter described the woodlands as a "sea of solid treetops broken only by some gash where deep beneath the foliage an unknown stream made its way" (*The Trees* [N.Y., 1940], p. 4). The prairie regions of Indiana, Illinois, and Iowa represent the stereotypical Midwest and the prairie plains of the Dakotas, Kansas, and Nebraska are an extension of this geographic region. The tall grass of the Grand Prairie of Illinois, or rolling land of Iowa offered fertile soil, as did the short-grass prairie plains of the Dakotas, Nebraska, and Kansas.

These prairie regions unify the central and western sections of the Midwest. The northern forests of Michigan, Wisconsin, and Minnesota yielded acres of trees for national consumption.

Agricultural production also defines the Midwest. The Midwestern states contain the most fertile soil in the nation, and agriculture attracted most of the earliest settlers. In the second half of the nineteenth century, the Midwest served as the nation's breadbasket. Corn, soybeans, and wheat are primary crops, as are hogs and cattle. The Midwest also has a strong industrial base, especially with regard to automobile production. Michigan is famous for its automobile industry, but Ohio, Indiana, and Illinois also contribute to national automobile production. Wisconsin is the location of numerous papermills, and Minnesota is home to companies such as 3M and General Mills.

Lewis Atherton described the culture of the Midwest in his groundbreaking 1954 work, *Main Street on the Middle Border*. Atherton considers the factors of church, school, and home as the educators in Midwestern life. He acknowledges that it is impossible to enforce cultural uniformity, but middle-class values helped shape the region. Shaped by the Second Great Awakening and Protestantism, these principles include trust in Divine Providence, honesty, and the Protestant work ethic. Today urban sections of the Midwest continue to diversify, and smaller towns with light manufacturing attract numerous immigrants, particularly from Central and South America.

The Midwest is politically divergent. The region has been marked by conservatism, but radicalism in many forms can be found in each state. North Dakota gave rise to the Non-Partisan League, Iowa the Farm Holiday Association, and Indiana proved to be a stronghold for the Ku Klux Klan. The boot heel of Missouri was a tempest in the 1930s when the National Southern Tenant Farmers' Union rebelled against the system of sharecropping. Robert M. LaFollete of Wisconsin, William Jennings Bryan of Nebraska, and Father Charles Coughlin of Michigan present additional examples of Midwestern radicalism. This spirited tradition is as much about being American as it is Midwestern.

Because the Midwest is in the center of the nation, it has borders that reflect other regions. Residents of southern Ohio, Indiana, Illinois and Missouri are as much Southern as they are Midwestern. The Upper Peninsula of Michigan and northern Wisconsin and Minnesota hold their own distinctive customs and dialect. The Dakotas, Nebraska, and Kansas reflect the geography and culture of the Great Plains. The mix of urban and rural in the Midwest helps it remain a distinct and diverse region. Because of its isolation from the coasts, Midwesterners are often depicted as rubes and yokels. Though not without its prejudices, the Midwest is home to the most literate and some of America's best-educated populations. The Midwest is the heartland of the United States and a representation of the nation.

See Lewis C. Atherton, *Main Street on the Middle Border* (Bloomington, 1954); Alan Bogue, *From Prairie to Corn Belt: Farming on the Illinois And Iowa Prairies in the Nineteenth Century* (Chi-

cago,1963); James A. Madison, ed., *Heartland: Comparative Histories of the Midwestern States* (Bloomington, Ind., 1988); James R. Shortridge, *The Middle West: Its Meaning in American Culture* (Lawrence, 1989); and "The Emergence of the 'Middle West' as an American Regional Label," *Annals of the Association of American Geographers* 74(2): 1984, pp. 200–20.

LEO LANDIS

military service records, Canadian. The first Canadian military records date from the early 1600s. There is a native experience that predates this, but it was not documented until Europeans arrived. From this time until Confederation and nationhood in 1867, Canadian record-keeping reflected the priorities and concerns of, first French (until 1763), and thereafter British soldiers, sailors, and administrators. After Confederation, the federal government increasingly came to see the Canadian military experience as an essential component of national sovereignty and of the national memory. Since that time it has collected records ranging from the tactical level up to civil–military and command relationships, from limited conflicts like the Fenian Raids (1866, 1870), the North-West Rebellion (1885), and the South African War (1899–1902), to the First (1914–1918) and Second (1939–1945) World Wars, the Korean Conflict (1950–1954), and peace-keeping operations (1948 to present).

Researchers will find these records fairly easy to use. While some are held at regular and reserve units in bases, armories, and museums throughout Canada, the vast majority of Canadian military records are deposited in two locations in Ottawa, Ontario: the *National Archives of Canada (NAC), and the Directorate of History and Heritage (DHH) in National Defence Headquarters (NDHQ). The Canadian War Museum (CWM) in Ottawa also has a large collection of military artifacts and vehicles, several important memoirs, and a photographic collection.

The NAC has organized its military documents into two categories. Government records are divided into Record Groups (RGs) for government departments, several of which include military documents. For example RG 9 includes nineteenth- and early-twentieth-century Militia and Defence records; RG 150 contains the records of the Overseas Headquarters in World War I; and RG 24, by far the largest, holds twentieth-century material including documents from World War II. The second category of NAC documents is Manuscript Group records (MGs). These consist of personal papers, memoirs, private correspondence, and diaries. Each RG and MG has computerized and printed Finding Aids, and the NAC has a website that lists RG holdings. Personnel records are also available and some of those from WWI are on the website. The Archives also has research assistants on call to help historians find what they are looking for. Because there is a wait of about a day for document delivery, researchers should contact the NAC in advance, in order to have some materials ready upon their arrival.

The DHH holdings are more specialized, because they consist of documents originally held by the historical sections of the three armed services, and, after 1968, the Canadian Armed Forces. Although about half of this collection has been transferred to the NAC, DHH holds the original references, along with conversion lists that cross reference to the NAC records. DHH Reading Room hours are restricted but the documents are held onsite.

National Archives of Canada (NAC) is located at 395 Wellington St., Ottawa, Ontario K1A ON3; (613) 995-5138 for general information; (613) 992-3884 for reference services; fax (613) 995-6274; <www.archives.ca>. The Directorate of History and Heritage (DHH) can be contacted through National Defence Headquarters, Major-General George R. Pearkes Building, 101 Colonel By Drive, Ottawa, Ontario, K1A OK2. The research facilities are located at the Charles P. Stacey Building, 2429 Holly Lane, Ottawa, Ontario. fax (613) 990-8579; <www.dnd.ca/hr/dhh>. The Canadian War Museum (CWM) is located at General Motors Court, 330 Sussex Drive, Ottawa, Ontario K1A 0M8; (819) 776-8600 or toll free (800) 555-5621; fax (819) 776-8623. The research facilities are located at Vimy House, 221 Champagne Avenue N., Ottawa, Ontario; (819) 776-8652; <www.civilization.ca/cwm/cwmeng/cwmeng.html> or <jean-francois.bussieres@civilization.ca>. See also Owen A. Cooke, *The Canadian Military Experience, 1867–1995: A Bibliography*, 3d ed. (Ottawa, 1997).

ROBERT CALDWELL

military service records, U.S. The National Archives Building in Washington, D.C., contains military service and pension records for veterans from the Revolutionary War through the early twentieth century.

Regular Army: Enlisted personnel: 1789–October 31, 1912; officers: 1789–June 30, 1917

Navy: Enlisted personnel: 1798–1885; officers: 1798–1902

Marine Corps: Enlisted personnel: 1789–1904; some officers: 1789–1895

Coast Guard: 1791–1919

Confederate States: 1861–1865

Veterans Records: Claims files for pensions based on federal military service, 1775–1916 or bounty land warrant application files relating to claims based on wartime service, 1775–1855.

To request copies of any of these records, submit NATF Form 80. To obtain forms, write to the National Archives and Records Administration, Attn: NWCTB, 700 Pennsylvania Avenue, NW, Washington, D.C. 20408-0001, or send an email to <inquire@nara.gov>. Provide your name and postal mailing address, specify the form number, and state the number of forms you need (limit six per order).

The National Personnel Records Center (NPRC) in St. Louis, Missouri, has records of the following personnel (earliest Official Military Personnel Folders at NPRC):

Air Force: Officers and enlisted September 25, 1947

Army: Officers separated July 1, 1917; enlisted separated November 1, 1912

Navy: Officers separated January 1, 1903; enlisted separated January 1, 1886

Marine Corps: Officers and enlisted separated January 1, 1905

Coast Guard: Officers and enlisted separated January 1, 1898

To request a search of personnel records held at the NPRC, submit a Standard Form 180, Request Pertaining to Military Records, to the address indicated on the form. To request a file, the researcher needs to have the soldier's name and unit. For enlisted personnel, the service number is required. Copies of the form are available from the NPRC at 8600 Page Boulevard, St. Louis, Mo. 63132, or from the NARA website at <http://www.nara.gov/regional/mprsf180.html>.

The July 12, 1973, fire at the National Personnel Records Center destroyed about 80 percent of the records for Army personnel discharged between November 1, 1912, and January 1, 1960; and 75 percent of the records for Air Force personnel discharged between September 25, 1947, and January 1, 1964 (with names alphabetically after Hubbard, James E.). There is no index of the records that were destroyed; researchers need to submit an SF 180 to find out if a record survived.

MARY RYAN

mining, hard rock. Let's begin with a few simple distinctions: hard-rock mining involves the extraction of ores containing precious or semiprecious metals. The methods of extraction range from the primitive—pans and sluice boxes—to the most sophisticated—vertical shafts and diagonal or horizontal drifts cut with expensive and labor-intensive industrial equipment. The ores sought—the rocks in which the metals are embedded—are quite literally hard. They contain gold, silver, copper, zinc, manganese, and assorted other and less valuable resources. Coal, both bituminous and anthracite, is "soft" rock mining and hence distinct; lead, tin, and iron ores are hard enough to qualify, but the methods of extraction are not the same as those used for hard rock.

That said, let it also be noted that there are some obvious similarities among all three types of mining: whether for copper, coal, or iron, the taking of ores from the ground was hard and dangerous work. It was work shunned by all who could find something else and better to do, meaning most of the native born; mining of whatever sort was disproportionately immigrant in its workforce. Similarly, it was often outside corporate control and there was a measure—often a very large measure—of labor violence. Particularly in their early years, mining regions tended to be demographically, and as a consequence, socially out of balance. They were overwhelmingly male, and the female component included few wives and homemakers. Historians would be advised to look elsewhere for evidence of the cult of domesticity, except as men performed "domestic" chores. Add to this list of similarities the inherently evanescent nature of mining as a form of enterprise. Mining towns literally consumed themselves; miners, by definition, worked with exhaustible resources. Once exhausted, the towns had no immediate reason for being; ghosts were all that remained. And finally, mining regions offer some of the most striking and strikingly ugly man-made environments on the face of the planet. They are historically and culturally fascinating places, but they have been roughly handled.

There are some other and historically determinative distinctions between hard-rock and other mining operations. First, with the exception of some tentative gold mining in colonial Georgia and North Carolina, hard-rock mining was a Western and hence "colonial" enterprise. Second, and with no exceptions, hard-rock mining towns were sited entirely on the basis of the resource that sustained them. No attention was paid to weather, water resources, food supplies, transportation facilities—either in place or projected—grand vistas, or any of the other criteria of town site selection. Little wonder that they were known as "camps." People live in towns; they pitch and break camps. Those camps were located where the ore was, and the ore would one day run out. More often than not, the ore was high in the Rocky Mountains in hard-to-reach places of no particular appeal when reached. There were camps that became towns, but no one of sound mind would have located a town in the places occupied by Butte, Montana (with a population approaching 100,000 by 1915); Goldfield, Nevada; Leadville, Colorado; Kennecott, Alaska; or even Nevada City, California. It is one of the nicer ironies of Western history that many of these camp towns—Aspen and Telluride, Colorado; Park City, Utah; and Ketchum, Idaho, among others—have gone from *ghost or near-ghost towns to opulent and pretentious resorts. But wherever found and whatever their longevity, hard-rock mining towns provide revealing points of entry into some important and fascinating history.

DAVID M. EMMONS

monuments. The artifacts of the past sometimes have a way of making us uncomfortable. In the climate of the 1990s, with our concern for fairness and inclusion, we often encounter in the commemorated local historical past evidences of other ways of thinking that are out of step with our own. We discover when we stop to read *historical markers and civic statues, that some are wrong, others skewed; that some place names reflect the past as it used to be discussed, not as we today would prefer to discuss or think about it; and that public monuments sometimes reflect particular, exclusive past events without consideration to how others might view them.

Sanford Levinson's book, *Written in Stone: Public Monuments in Changing Societies* (Durham and London, 1998) discusses a number of interesting topics, such as the statues of Confederate generals striding on horseback down Monument Avenue in Richmond, Virginia, a city with a large African American population; or the Memorial to the Confederate Dead located on the State House grounds in Austin, Texas; or the Liberty Monument in New Orleans that recalls the 1874 takeover of the Louisiana government by members of the White League. These are but a few of the pieces of public statuary that we may today find inappropriate. Levinson quotes Kirk Savage: "A public monument represents a kind of collective recognition—in short, legitimacy—for the memory deposited there." Statues do not, he insists, "arise as if by natural law." Levinson also discusses the current display of the Confederate flag over three state houses.

Newer highway markers reflect the historical interests of our own time, so that, all over the country, we encounter monuments that reflect history's latest concerns, such as African American or women's history. This righting of the record reflects our need to be inclusive of aspects once ignored.

*Place names, especially those of geographic features, can also bring us up short. This is true of Massacre Lake in Nevada or Massacre Rock in Idaho. Located along Route I-15 the Idaho name commemorates an Indian raid made on passing emigrants in 1862. We know now from the work of a number of historians, but especially that of Jesse Unruh (*The Plains Across: The Overland Emigrants and the Trans-Mississippi West, 1840–60* [Urbana, Ill., 1979]), that this might or might not have been the case and that most "massacres" were hardly that. "Massacre," of course, worries us because of how the word has been used to place blame on Native Americans for events that were more complicated than conventional European-style pitched battles between adversaries. We recognize today that there is more than one way to look at historical events.

What do we do about the monuments of our past that make us uncomfortable? We cannot always remove an offending historic marker from along a roadside—nor should we, necessarily—but we can erect others to tell more of the story than the original offers. And we can make sure to explain to the public about the changing nature of historical interpretation, about the ideas that inform the history we present. We can stress, as Carl Becker did, that history is both the past and what happens in the mind of the historian, who brings to the documents his or her own questions and historical understanding, as well as the interests, concerns, and historical understandings of the era in which he or she lives.

These debates about the changing past are one way of teaching a public used to thinking of history as static—having learned in school that history consists of right and wrong answers. Instead, what we know and how we understand depends very much upon who we are and the times in which we live. As ideas change, so do historical fashions—not to dress up the truth—but to better understand it.

Moorland-Spingarn Research Center. This archive is a repository of information about all aspects of the history and culture of people of African descent. It is located at Howard University, in Washington, D.C. 20059; (202) 806-7240; fax (202) 806-6405; <http://www.founders-howard.edu./moorland-spingarn>.

Moravians. See Appendix B.

Mormons. See Appendix B; Family History Library; International Genealogical Index.

mug books. Mug books are nineteenth-century compilations of photographs and biographies of prominent men. Most often, inclusion was determined by one's willingness to pay a fee to be included. The word "mug" came to refer to the face, probably from eighteenth-century drinking mugs that

were made to represent a human face, such as Toby mugs. In time, "mug" meant an ugly or a criminal face. Photographs taken after an arrest are called *mug shots.* See Oscar Lewis, "Mug Books," *The Colophon* 17 (1934).

mulatto. An offspring of white and black parents, defined variously by states' laws. Mitford Mathews, in *Dictionary of Americanisms upon Historical Principles,* traces the word "mulatto" to a designation of land or soil "of a brownish color." He lists the 1805 use of the word "mulattress" to identify women of mixed race. "Biracial" or "even mixed" would be the terms preferred today.

municipal corporation. This term refers to a political body authorized under state law and created by local residents. It is also called a municipality. The municipal corporation has the power to tax, spend, borrow, regulate, and exercise the right of eminent domain.

municipal records. See local government records

museums, and the matter of ethics. Ethics, or moral philosophy, deals with what is right or wrong, proper or improper, in human behavior and decision-making. Although the formal study of ethics in Western society began with such ancient Greek philosophers as Aristotle, every society has developed its own standards of ethics. In our society, concepts of ethics are understood to apply only to those actions that persons or groups can voluntarily make—that is, where a choice is possible, and where the choice is based on knowledge. In other words, being forced to do something, or to act with inadequate information about the choices, is not an ethical situation. Ethics, then, refers to the classification of voluntary and informed actions or decisions as being either right or wrong in relation to some standard accepted by a society.

There are several different approaches to the study of ethics. "Normative ethics" refers to any ethical system that is based on fixed rules or principles that apply to all actions and decisions. For example, the museum ethical view in conservation that all object treatments should be reversible is a fixed, or normative, principle. It is not subject to change, or even to special conditions—as we've seen in the debates over the treatment of the Parthenon's stones.

There are two types of normative ethical systems—teleological (or consequentialist) and deontological (or nonconsequentialist). Nonconsequentialist (deontological) ethics are based upon an intrinsic rule or principle that universally applies in all cases regardless of what consequences might result from a given action or decision. An example is the ethical principle that one should not kill. But consequentialist (teleological) ethics are not based on absolute principles per se, but also look at the consequences of an action. Thus, it may be wrong to kill, unless killing will save others. Most, if not all, museum ethics are consequentialist in nature. In the example given above, for instance, the ethical principle about reversibility of treatments is based on the idea that an irreversible treatment might ultimately cause harm to an object, an undesirable consequence.

Another approach is called "ethical relativism," which is based on the idea that there is no one set of ethical principles that apply in all societies at all times. In other words, ethics are particular to one society in one period, and may change. Ideas about what kinds of actions are ethically proper for curators in personal collecting, for example, have changed within our society through time. We can also see that new ethical approaches in conservation that recognize Native American standards and treatments for sacred objects (a different approach to the idea of object integrity) are ethically relative.

Finally, there is also "situational ethics," which holds that ethical decisions may vary depending on the particular context, or situation, in which the decision must be made. Many classic, museum ethical debates over, for example, the use of funds from the sale of deaccessioned objects to repair a building, are based on this conceptual approach. Today, many elements of professional museum codes of ethics are situational in nature.

It is clear that the significant increase in professional museum concerns over ethics in this century is related to changing standards, changing working conditions, changing notions of professionalism, and even changes in laws. This continuing dynamic will undoubtedly lead to further issue-based ethical discussions. These are important for the profession, as is our understanding about the distinctions in the kinds of ethics, or ethical systems, that form the foundation of such discussions.

JAMES NASON

See ethics and local history.

museums, several views.

From Michigan: The number of local history museums in the Great Lakes region is growing. Rooted in community pride, many spring into being because of threats to a community's historic cultural resources. Most run on the vision and energy of volunteer leaders and are operated by volunteers, or a volunteer staff under the direction of minimally paid staff. They are very much a part of the communities they serve. Grass-roots museums provide meaningful services to their neighbors and offer unique learning experiences to visitors of all ages.

A good portion of the nation's cultural artifacts are found in local history museums. Yet, most do not have the means to preserve delicate artifacts and documents to the same degree possible in a large museum or archive. In addition, the treasures of small museums are often unknown to researchers and scholars. However, in the local history museum, the diary or the finely pieced quilt help tell the local story. This accessibility and familiarity is very important to a community's identity. State and regional training programs offer advice to small museums, promoting the care and use of their cultural assets.

Many rural communities in the Great Lakes region recognize that elements of their cultural and natural landscapes are in jeopardy. It has been proved that a strong "sense of place" is key to stewardship of these resources. By knowing about a locality, its past and present, residents can begin to see their own place in time.

Local history museums are by their nature community based. The scope of their history-keeping activities is limited to a specific geographic and cultural area and they draw a significant number of community members into their activities. Community members provide knowledge, talent and the artifacts, and they pay the bills—they are involved in all aspects of a local history museum for it tells their stories; it is their museum.

LAURA J. QUACKENBUSH

From Virginia: At the James Monroe Museum and Memorial Library, in Fredericksburg, Virginia, founded in 1927, we have one "old" goal and three "new" ones.

The old goal is, of course, to continue to care for, add to, and interpret our collection of objects, books, and manuscripts related to the life, times, and influence of James Monroe (1758–1831), fifth president of the United States (1817–1825). This includes using the full panoply of interpretive programs, at our site and others, including videos and all other available media, to reach audiences ranging from local to international.

The three "new" (or at least, "newer") goals are: (1) deepened support of scholarly research; (2) continued experiments and developments in "telling stories"; and (3) continued development of the museum as a player in the whole life of the community.

The deeper support of scholarly research will take the form of cooperation with our sister institution, the James Monroe Presidential Center, created by the Board of Visitors of Mary Washington College in 1998 (both the Center and the Museum are owned and operated by Mary Washington College, a Commonwealth of Virginia institution). In 1999 the college created "The Papers of James Monroe" (within the James Monroe Presidential Center) with a long-range publishing program that we expect will lead to increased scholarly writing and increased popular presentations related to Monroe. It will also add to the story of the creation of the continental republic, and the story of the establishment of the position of the United States among the nations of the world.

The continued experiments and developments in "telling stories," including interactivity where appropriate and potentially successful, will allow us to pursue the important goal of true discourses with our many audiences. Visitor-studies information and our own surveys will be used to test our success.

JOHN N. PEARCE

From Australia: Local history museums are alive and well in Australia. Since the 1980s, a system of chapters was created in New South Wales, the oldest Australian state. A chapter comprises museums and art galleries within a zone or a number of local government areas, operating under the aegis of Museums Australia NSW Branch, but having a measure of independence. While there is a formal organizational structure, its strength is usually dependent upon the energy of the local chapter coordinator to organize regular meetings, usually at a different local history museum each time. Chapters have been encouraged as a means of overcoming what is regarded as the tyranny of distance, isolation, and cost of travel.

In the case of the Southern Highlands and Illawarra Regional Museums Chapter, there is a broad aim to improve the quality of displays, enter into partnerships with the state museums for training and access to conservation facilities, acquire specialized knowledge from museum professionals, engage in group marketing and to operate as a network of experienced volunteers.

This chapter is now in the process of preparing a five-year plan to ensure that there is a strategy in place to cope with anticipated future issues:

- Aging of volunteers.
- Easier access to training programs, particularly at the university level. (This includes the high costs of fees, travel, and accommodation.)
- Entering into partnerships with primary and secondary schools now that the curriculum has a substantial heritage content.
- Attracting youth into museums and art galleries as workers.
- Improved marketing to ensure a better flow of visitors.
- Discourage overlap between museums in adjacent areas.

Since World War II, there has been an explosion in the numbers of local history museums, normally associated with local government. For a while there was a tendency to regard any old council or shire building as being suitable for operation as a museum or art gallery, even if it was in poor condition, leaked in wet weather, and had inadequate interior spaces. While many of these buildings are still being used, local government in general is becoming more appreciative of the specialized needs of museums and art galleries, as well as the services they offer, often complementing the role of local libraries. In several cases, there is a willingness to fund extensions and to provide assistance in kind.

Local history museums in New South Wales also receive assistance from the Ministry of the Arts and through a newly developed foundation. The Ministry provides grants for a wide range of museum activities, including conservation projects, exhibitions, training, and the acquisition of new computers.

DESMOND KENNARD

music. Music and musicians can be a valuable tool for local historians. Music often recounts events of local significance, it helps fashion local identity, and its style can yield important insights into local values. In addition, because musicians are often at the center of a community's social life they can be valuable repositories of its history.

For centuries, musicians have set local incidents to music. The music—ranging from the tale of murder in the North Carolina mountains like "Omie Wise," to a *corrido* ballad of Mexican heroes on the Texas–Mexico border in "Gregorio Cortez," to a song of catastrophy in the Pennsylvania mines in "The Avondale Disaster"—helped spread the word about local happenings in communities plagued by illiteracy or a lack of newspapers. Current events were as often sung about as read.

Moreover, because these songs were frequently passed down, they became an essential part of the community's collective memory.

Music also helps mold a sense of local identity. Fabled musicians and the tunes they created are proudly claimed by the communities in which they grew up or lived. Even whole genres can become an important part of local identity, such as the blues in the Mississippi Delta, or polkas in the upper Midwest.

Historians should not overlook what values lie hidden in the music's style and performance. (See Alan Lomax, *Folk Song Style and Culture* [Washington, D.C., 1968].) The transformation from congregational singing to church choirs, for example, is as important a shift in values as it is in musical practice. The historian, then, should ask a series of questions of the music: Who participates? When? How is it passed on? What skills are considered necessary to participate? What function does the music play in the community? These questions will uncover a host of closely held though often unarticulated beliefs and assumptions.

Finally, musicians can be important informants because their craft has traditionally played a vital role in community life. Musicians often travel extensively and meet many people. As a result, many come to know a great deal about a community's landmarks, history, and its people.

In short, music should not be viewed as simply entertainment. Instead, it can provide local historians with valuable insights into the community's history, sense of identity, and values.

325

The Society for American Music's webpage address is: <www.American-Music.org>.

GAVIN JAMES CAMPBELL

muster roll. A list of those who have enlisted in a military effort. These are sometimes found in county courthouses, state archives, or in local historical societies.

myth. See folklore.

National Archives and Records Administration, The. NARA is our national record-keeper. By law, NARA is charged to safeguard records of all three branches of the federal government. Its mission is to assure federal agencies and the American public of ready access to essential evidence documenting the rights of citizens, the actions of government officials, and the national experience. NARA preserves and provides access to such records through a national network of records services facilities from Washington, D.C., to Washington State, from Atlanta to Anchorage, including ten Presidential libraries. NARA currently holds approximately 5.5 billion pages of textual records; 5 million maps, charts, and architectural and engineering drawings; 16 million still photographs and graphics; 16 million aerial photographs; 300,000 reels of motion-picture film, 200,000 video and sound recordings, and 12,000 machine-readable data sets. Much of the archival material, including special media such as still and motion pictures, sound recordings, maps, and electronic records, is housed in the National Archives at College Park, commonly called "Archives II" and in the original National Archives building in Washington, D.C. Eighteen regional records services facilities from Atlanta to Alaska house records from the federal courts and the regional offices of federal agencies in the geographic areas they serve. Thirteen of these regional facilities include regional National Archives holdings of major primary-source interest to historians. More material resides in NARA's records centers, where agency-owned records are held as long as needed before destruction or transfer to the National Archives.

In addition, the NARA contains a unique resource in its ten *Presidential libraries, one for each president from Herbert Hoover to George Bush, except for Richard Nixon, whose records are in NARA's Nixon Presidential Materials Project. Presidential libraries may not be obvious sources of local history material, but researchers may find useful material among the records and papers from the Office of the President, presidential commissions, the president, his family, associates, and members of his administration.

Another part of NARA, the Office of the Federal Register, publishes the daily Federal Register, a record of government proclamations, orders, and regulations; the weekly Compilation of Presidential Documents; and the annual Code of Federal Regulations, along with the U.S. Government Manual and Public Papers of the Presidents. It is also responsible for receiving and documenting electoral-college certificates for presidential elections and state ratifications of proposed constitutional amendments.

Anyone may use the National Archives. You do not need to be an U.S. citizen or to present academic credentials or a letter of recommendation. To use original records, you must have a researcher card. Also, you must be at least 14 years old, and you must show valid identification that includes a photograph to receive a card.

A great number of records have been recorded on microfilm both to preserve the records and make them more available to researchers. There are now more than 3,000 microfilm publications. You do not need a researcher card to examine microfilmed records. NARA's online microfilm database (<http://www.nara.gov/nara/searchmicro.html>) allows you to search for descriptions of microfilm publications by keyword, microfilm identification number, Record Group number, and NARA location.

Types of Records held by NARA are arranged by numbered "record groups." A record group comprises the records of a major government entity, such as a cabinet department, a bureau, or an independent agency. For example, Record Group 59 contains "General Records of the Department of State," and Record Group 29 holds "Records of the Bureau of the Census." Most record groups also contain records of predecessors of the organization named in the title. Records in all NARA locations across the country provide information on actions that affected everything from the entire nation to the individual home. While records in the Washington, D.C.–area document actions at the national level, the holdings of NARA's regional records services facilities document federal policies and programs at the local and regional level. The federal government documents people's lives in many ways, such as in census records and records of immigration, military service, and employment, to name but a few of the most obvious. Some examples of record groups useful for local history research are surveyed in the following paragraphs.

Records created by the Department of Agriculture and its agencies and the Bureau of the Census are rich resources for studies of rural America, documenting changes in farming practices, home life, and socioeconomic conditions. Through census enumeration district maps, one can trace urban growth. Important sources for the study of business history are censuses of manufactures and industry, patent records, court cases, and Civil War–era tax records. See articles on *census records and *military service and pension records.

Descriptions of the effects of and recovery from natural disasters may be found in several record groups, including records of the Weather Bureau, the Red Cross, the Office of the Chief of Engineers, District Courts, Naval Districts and Shore Establishments, and the U.S. Senate and House of Representatives.

The exploration and settlement of the West is documented in expedition records of the Geological Survey. Towns often sprang up around military installations; post returns and quartermaster records are valuable resources for tracing the interaction between civilian and military communities. Records relating to land claims may be found in records of the Bureau of Land Management, the Veterans Administration, and the U.S. Court of Claims.

The history of industrialization and urban living are well documented in U.S. District Court records. For example, a researcher studying auto manufacturing in Detroit will find a wealth of information in early bankruptcy and antitrust cases. Prohibition and gangsters are also well documented in Chicago, New York, and Philadelphia court records.

A local history study concentrating on the Civil War era will find valuable information in these records: census (population and nonpopulation schedules); Internal Revenue Service (assessment lists); Provost Marshal General's Bureau (draft records); Office of the Quartermaster General; Adjutant General's Office; Bureau of Refugees, Freedmen, and Abandoned Lands; District Courts of the United States; U.S. Army Continental Commands; Commissary General of Prisoners; War Department Collection of Confederate Records; Southern Claims Commission, Accounting Officers of the Department of the Treasury; barred and disallowed Southern Claims, U.S. House of Representatives; U.S. Court of Claims; Civil War prize cases, U.S. District Courts; Civil War Special Agencies of the Treasury Department; and the Treasury Department Collection of Confederate Records.

Resources for studies of *Indian communities include record of the Bureau of Indian Affairs, the Indian Health Service, various army records, and records of the U.S. Congress. NARA facilities in the western states are exceptionally rich in records relating to Native Americans. Applications for enrollment and final rolls of the Five Civilized Tribes list thousands of citizens and freedmen in Indian Territory at the turn of the last century, and records of field offices allow the researcher to form a vivid picture of the daily interaction between federal agents and the native population.

Records relating to areas that were directly under federal jurisdiction are often found in their own record groups: Records of the Government of the District of Columbia, the Government of Virgin Islands, the Government of American Samoa, the Panama Canal, the Puerto Rico Reconstruction Administration, and the Bureau of Insular Affairs (the Philippines, Cuba, and Puerto Rico). The New Deal and the two world wars saw the creation of a great many new government agencies. The Works Progress Administration, Civilian Conservation Corps, Federal Theatre and Writers Projects, and Tennessee Valley Authority, among others, put people to work and changed the communities they lived in. During World Wars I and II, the government imposed controls on food, housing, and other resources to ensure ample supplies for soldiers at the battle front. These emergency measures are documented on the national and local levels in the records of the U.S. Food Administration, U.S. Housing Corporation, Office of the Housing Expediter, the War Industries Board, and Office of Price Administration, among others.

Although paper records make up the vast majority of NARA holdings, *photographs, motion pictures, sound recordings, *maps, architectural and engineering drawings, and computer datasets provide a wealth of opportunities for the researcher. Most records on these media will be found in the National Archives at College Park, but NARA facilities nationwide contain significant nontextual holdings. For example, in the regions you can find aerial photographs from the Soil and Conservation Service and the Bureau of Mines, maps and charts from the Bureau of Land Management and the Federal Highway Administration, architectural and engineering drawings from the General Services Administration and the War Assets Administration, motion pictures from the Office of Scientific Research and Development, and photographs from the U.S. District Courts Bureau and the *National Park Service.

Photographs from the Environmental Protection Agency's DOCUMERICA project of the 1970s record community life across America. Famous photographers such as Russell Lee and Dorothea Lange and anonymous photographers in the local government bu-

reaus documented the effects of the Great Depression and the New Deal. Maps and photographs from the Western surveys trace national growth to the Pacific Coast. Aerial photographs give an exacting view of those same areas in the modern era. Census and economic statistics stored in electronic format reveal details about communities and industries. Architectural plans of public buildings are an invaluable source for *historic preservation projects. Films created by federal agencies, such as the Community Services Administration or the Extension Service, and donated collections, such as the Ford Film Collection, enable the viewer to see aspects of twentieth-century American life firsthand. No matter how large a list such as this grows, the diligent researcher is sure to uncover more resources and more ways to use them.

While the records described above may be found in NARA's facilities in the Washington, D.C., area and its regions, some bodies of records are concentrated in or are unique to the regional records services facilities. Original records of U.S. district courts constitute the largest record group in all the regions and offer countless research opportunities. Commonly used *court records include naturalization papers (declarations of intention and petitions for citizenship), bankruptcy case files, *copyright and patent files, and claims of various sorts. Nine locations (Anchorage, Atlanta, Chicago, Denver, Fort Worth, Kansas City, Laguna Niguel, San Francisco, and Seattle) hold records of the Bureau of Indian Affairs and the Bureau of Land Management. Records relating to Chinese immigration and the impact of the Chinese Exclusion Acts may be found in nearly every location. Records unique to a single NARA facility include enrollment cards for the Five Civilized Tribes, in Fort Worth; World War I draft-registration cards and Tennessee Valley Authority records, in Atlanta; records relating to the sinking of the *Titanic* and *Lusitania*, in New York; records of the Government of American Samoa, 1900–1906, in San Francisco; and records of the Pribilof Islands Program, 1870–1985, in Anchorage. Thirteen facilities have extensive holdings of National Archives microfilm publications that reproduce, with introductions and annotations, some of the most frequently requested records in NARA custody. Every location that has microfilm has federal population censuses for all states, 1790–1920; Revolutionary War military-service records; and passenger arrival and naturalization records. Additional microfilm publications usually reflect the special interest of the area served by the regional facility.

NARA is continually expanding the availability of its resources through the Internet. The NARA homepage (<http://www.nara.gov>) guides visitors to such resources as our "Research Room," "Online Exhibit Hall," "Digital Classroom," "Archives and Preservation Resources," and *Prologue*, NARA's periodical magazine, as well as several other locations. Each regional records services facility has its own home page, accessible from <www.nara.gov/regional/nrmenu.html>. The Federal Register page (<http://www.nara.gov/fedreg>) gives access to its publications, which include the daily *Federal Register*, the Code of Federal Regulations, the United States Government Manual, Weekly Compilation of Presidential Documents, and the Public Papers of the Presidents. The NARA Archival Information Locator (NAIL) (<http://www.nara.gov/nara/nail.html>) is an online catalog of NARA holdings nationwide (including those in presidential libraries and regional records services facilities). NAIL already contains more than 3,000 microfilm publications descriptions; 400,446 archival holdings descriptions; and 124,000 digital copies of NARA's most popular and significant manuscripts, photographs, drawings, sound recordings, and other documents. The database is searchable by title, subject, or other keyword. NAIL is the prototype for the online Archival Research Catalog in which all of NARA's holdings eventually will be described. But already, via the Internet, you can begin research in NARA's resources from your home, office, or library computer.

NARA Publications and Online Resources:
• NARA's homepage: <www.nara.gov>.
• NAIL (NARA's prototype searchable database): <www.nara.gov/nara/nail.html>.
• Information about NARA's regional records services facilities: <www.nara.gov/regional>.
• Information about the Presidential libraries: <www.nara.gov/nara/president/address.html>.
• Information about NARA publications (both free and for sale): <www.nara.gov/publications/pubindex.html>.

- *Guide to Federal Records in the National Archives of the United States* (1996): <www. nara.gov/guide>.

  Guides to Records in the Regional Records Services Facilities:
- *Chinese Immigration and Chinese in the United States: Records in the Regional Archives of the National Archives and Records Administration, RIP 99*: <www.nara.gov/revions/findaids/chirip.htm>.
- Anchorage: *Protecting Alaska's Native Population With Federal Records*: <www.nara.gov/regional/findaids/ancprote.html>.
- Atlanta: *Guide to Records in the National Archives—Southeast Region, Atlanta, Georgia*: <www.nara.gov/regional/findaids/atlgdtoc.html>.
- Archival Holdings Related to Family History at NARA's Southeast Region: <www.nara.gov/regional/findaids/atlgenea.html>.
- Archival Holdings Related to African American History at NARA's Southeast Region: <www.nara.gov/regional/findaids/atlblkhs.html>.
- Archival Holdings Related to the Far East at NARA's Southeast Region: <www.nara.gov/regional/findaids/atleast.html>.
- Boston: *Guide to Records in the National Archives—New England Region, Boston, Mass., RIP 89*: <www.nara.gov/regional/findaids/bosgdtoc.html>.
- Chicago: *Guide to Records in the National Archives—Great Lakes Region, Chicago, Ill., RIP 96*: <www.nara.gov/regional/findaids/chigdtoc.html>.
- *U.S. District Court Naturalization Records at NARA's Great Lakes Region, Chicago:* <www.nara.gov/regional/findaids/chinatur.html>.
- Denver: *Guide to Records in the National Archives—Rocky Mountain Region, Denver, Col., RIP 97* (1996): <www.nara.gov/regional/findaids/dengdtoc.html>.
- Fort Worth: *Guide to Records in the National Archives—Southwest Region, Fort Worth, Tex., RIP 84* (1994): <www.nara.gov/regional/findaids/ftwgdtoc.html>.
- Kansas City: *Guide to Records in the National Archives—Central Plains Region, Kansas City, Missouri, RIP 87* (1994): <www.nara.gov/regional/findaids/kangdtoc.html>.
- Laguna Niguel: *Guide to Records in the National Archives—Pacific Southwest Region, Laguna Niguel, Calif., RIP 86* (1995): <www.nara.gov/regional/findaids/laggdtoc.html>.
- *List of Naturalization Records at NARA's Pacific Region, Laguna Niguel:* <www.nara.gov/regional/findaids/lagnatur.html>.
- *Checklist of Archival Holdings Related to World War II at NARA's Pacific Region, Laguna Niguel:* <www.nara.gov/regional/findaids/lagww2.html>.
- *List of Case Files (1888–1933) from the Sawtelle Disabled Veterans Home, Los Angeles:* <www.nara.gov/regional/findaids/lagdav.html>.
- New York: *Guide to Records in the National Archives—Northeast Region, New York, New York, RIP 94* (1996): <www.nara.gov/regional/findaids/nycgdtoc.html>.
- *New York Chinese Exclusion Index*: <www.ancestry.com/ancestry/search/3307.html>.

- Philadelphia: *Guide to Records in the National Archives—Mid-Atlantic Region, Philadelphia, Penna., RIP 93* (1995): <www.nara.gov/regional/find aids/phigdtoc.html>.
- San Francisco: *Guide to Records in the National Archives—Pacific Sierra Region, San Francisco, Calif., RIP 88* (1995): <www.nara.gov/regional/find aids/sangdtoc.html>.
- *Records in the National Archives: Pacific Sierra Region for the Study of Ethnic History*: <www.nara.gov/regional/findaids/sanethnc.html>.
- *Records in the National Archives: Pacific Sierra Region for the Study of Labor and Business History:* <www.nara.gov/regional/findaids/sanlabor.html>.
- *Records in the National Archives: Pacific Sierra Region for the Study of Science, Technology, Natural Resources, and the Environment:* <www.nara.gov/regional/findaids/sanscite.html>.
- Seattle: *Guide to Records in the National Archives—Pacific Northwest Region, Seattle, Wash., RIP 85* (1994): <www.nara.gov/regional/findaids/seagdtoc.html>.
- *Box Contents List: Bureau of Prohibition Records (RG 56) at NARA's Pacific Alaska Region, Seattle:* <www.nara.gov/regional/findaids/searg56.html>.

Print-only publications:
- *Guide to Genealogical Research in the National Archives* (1985).
- *Our Family, Our Town* (1987).
- *The Trans-Mississippi West, 1804–1912: A Guide to Federal Records for the Territorial Period* (5 volumes).
- *Department of State* (1993).
- *Department of Justice* (1994).

- *Department of Agriculture* (1996).
- *Department of the Interior (Secretary of the Interior and Commissioner of Railroads)* (1996).
- *Department of the Interior (Geological Survey, National Park Service, Fish and Wildlife Service, Offices of Education and Territories, and Bureaus of Reclamation and Mines)* (1997).
- *Prologue: Quarterly of the National Archives and Records Administration*: contains articles based on research in NARA records <www.nara.gov/publications/prologue/prologue.html>.

Microfilm catalogs:
- *National Archives Microfilm Resources for Research: A Comprehensive Catalog Review* (1996): <www.nara.gov/publications/microfilm/comprehensive/compcat.html>.
- Census records: *The 1790–1890 Federal Population Censuses* (1997): <www.nara.gov/publications/microfilm/census/17901890/17901890.html>.
- *1900 Federal Population Census* (1996): <www.nara.gov/publications/microfilm/census/1900/1900.html>.
- *The 1910 Federal Population Census* (1982): <www.nara.gov/publications/microfilm/census/1910/1910.html>.
- *1920 Federal Population Census* (1992): <www.nara.gov/publications/microfilm/census/1920/1920.htm>.

Subject catalogs:
- *American Indians* (1995): <www.nara.gov/publications/microfilm/amerindians/indians.html>.
- *Black Studies* (1984): <www.nara.gov/publications/microfilm/blackstudies/blackstd.html>.
- *Diplomatic Records* (1986): <www.

nara.gov/publications/microfilm/diplomatic>.

- *Federal Court Records* (1987): <www.nara.gov/publications/microfilm/courts/fedcourt.html>.
- *Genealogical & Biographical Research* (1983): <www.nara.gov/publications/microfilm/biographical/genbio.html>.
- *Immigrant & Passenger Arrivals* (1991): <www.nara.gov/publications/microfilm/immigrant/immpass.html>.
- *Military Service Records* (1985): <www.nara.gov/publications/microfilm/military/service.html>.

Federal Register Online Publications: Federal Register publications, including the daily *Federal Register*, the *Code of Federal Regulations*, the *United States Government Manual*, and *Weekly Compilation of Presidential Documents*, are available through GPO Access: <www.access.gpo.gov/nara>.

To inquire about prices and order copies of publications other than Federal Register products, please contact: NARA Customer Service Center (NWCC2), 8601 Adelphi Road, College Park, Md. 20740-6001; (800) 234-8861; fax: (301) 713-6169.

Guides to records in the regional records services facilities may be obtained directly from the regions. See the list of addresses of NARA facilities in Appendix D.

MARY RYAN

See military service records, U.S.; Soundex.

National Coordinating Committee for the Promotion of History. Since 1982, the NCC has served as a national advocacy office for the historical and archival professions. A consortium of 53 organizations, the NCC focuses on federal funding and policy issues that have an impact on historical research and teaching, access to government information, the employment of historians, public policy relating to history, historic preservation, and the dissemination of historical information. The NCC operates from an office in the American Historical Association headquarters building on Capitol Hill in Washington, providing testimony at congressional hearings, presenting briefings to NCC member organizations, participating in advocacy strategy sessions, and writing legislative updates. In January 1995, the NCC began publishing regular "NCC Washington Updates" on the Internet through the H-Net. These reports provide current information on developments at federal agencies, court cases, federal regulations, and legislation. An archive of over 200 past updates can be seen at <h-net.msu.edu/~ncc>.

In the 1980s, the NCC played a key role in the passage of legislation to separate the National Archives from the General Services Administration. In the early 1990s, the NCC assisted in the development and passage of legislation that established procedures to assure a reliable documentary report of major U.S. foreign-policy activities through the State Department's Foreign Relations of the United States series. The NCC has supported federal funding for the National Endowment for the Humanities, the National Archives, and the grants program of the National Historical Publications and Records Commission. Additionally, the NCC has kept the scholarly community informed about proposed changes to the *copyright law and the dismantling of the House Historian's Office. At the NCC, there is never a dull moment.

The address of the National Coordinating Committee for the Promotion of History is 400 A Street SW, Washington, D.C. 20003; (202) 544-2422.

PAGE PUTNAM MILLER

National Council on Public History.
See public history.

National Endowment for the Arts.
Founded in 1971, the NEA supports folk arts, dance, design, arts in education programs, literature, museums, music, and theater. It is concerned with public policy concerning the arts, arts management, law and art, and the history of government involvement with the arts. The address is 1100 Pennsylvania Ave. NW, Washington, D.C. 20506; (202) 682-5400; <http://arts.endow.gov>.

National Endowment for the Humanities.
This agency was founded in 1971 to support a wide variety of humanities programs. The address is 1100 Pennsylvania Ave. NW, Washington D.C. 20506; <www.neh.fed.us> or e-mail <dmyrick@neh.fed.us>.

National Historical Public Records Commission (NHPRC).
Congress established the NHPRC originally in 1934 as the National Historical Publications Commission, an independent agency within the National Archives responsible for encouraging the publication of historical documents of national significance. In 1964 it was given funding to help carry out this mission. More than 800 volumes, and over 6,000 microfiche and microfilm reels, in approximately 300 historical-documentary–edition projects have been published under the NHPRC's auspices. In 1974 its mandate was increased to include efforts to preserve nonfederal records and manuscripts of national significance. Today the NHPRC is a 15-member body, chaired by the Archivist of the United States, and composed of representatives of the three branches of the federal government and of professional associations of archivists, historians, documentary editors, and records administrators. As a statutory body affiliated with the National Archives and Records Administration, the NHPRC supports a wide range of activities to preserve, publish, and encourage the use of documentary sources, created in every medium ranging from quill pen to computer, relating to the history of the United States. Its grants (approximately $6 million in 1999) go to state and local archives, colleges and universities, libraries, historical societies, and other nonprofit organizations. Through its support of State Historical Records Advisory Boards (SHRABs) it encourages state funding for preservation of locally significant documents and records. The National Archives and Records Administration is located at 700 Pennsylvania Avenue, NW, Room 111, Washington, D.C. 20408-0001; (202) 501-5610; <www.nara.gov/nara/nhprc> and <webmaster@nara.gov>.

CONSTANCE SCHULTZ

National History Day. This is a year-round program that uses history to challenge elementary and secondary-school students to improve their research, analytical, and communication skills. Its origins date to 1974, when faculty at Case Western Reserve University sponsored a history fair for Cleveland schools. The program spread quickly: at the first national contest in 1980, nineteen states participated. Funding from the *National Endowment for the Humanities stimulated further expansion over the next decade. Now funded by a variety of means, including contributions from corporate and individual donors, National History Day has become truly national: in 1998, 600,000 students from forty-eight states and the District of Columbia participated. At the local and state levels, History Day sponsors include museums, historical societies, archives, universities, and state humanities councils.

Each year, participants research topics related to a broad annual theme, such as "The Individual in History" or "Triumph and Tragedy in History." While students may choose national or world history topics, many choose to study local people and events. In seeking sources, some students visit historic sites, museums, or archives, while others conduct oral history interviews or correspond with experts. They present their findings in research papers, museum-style exhibits, original dramatic performances, or multimedia documentaries. History educators, public historians, and others volunteer as judges at district and state contests, held in the spring. The year culminates with the national finals each June at the University of Maryland in College Park.

Annually, more than 40,000 teachers participate in National History Day. To support their efforts, the program in recent years has developed pedagogical materials, including lesson plans, research guides, and tools to foster active learning and the use of primary sources. The national and state programs sponsor summer institutes and workshops, allowing teachers opportunities for continuing professional development.

As a result of the national competition and its growing role in teacher education, National History Day has become one of the nation's leading educational programs. As one teacher observed, "History Day is the only program where students use a great deal of research to synthesize information and produce a product. It is the only program where students have to truly know their subject, write well, be interviewed and know about research."

The address for National History Day is O119 Cecil Hall, University of Maryland, College Park, Md. 20742; (301) 314-9739; <www.thehistorynet.com//NationalHistoryday>.

BEATRIZ B. HARDY

National Park Service. Concerned about America's receding Western wilderness on a trip to the Dakotas in 1832, the artist George Catlin suggested that the government preserve some part of it in a "nation's park." Catlin's vision was partly realized when Congress granted Yosemite Valley to California for a state park in 1864. Eight years later, Congress reserved the spectacular Yellowstone country in the Wyoming and Montana territories "as a public park or pleasuring-ground for the benefit and enjoyment of the People." There being no state there yet to manage it, Yellowstone remained under the U.S. Department of the Interior as a national park—the world's first place so designated.

Other national parks followed in the 1890s and early 1900s, including Sequoia, Yosemite (to which California returned Yosemite Valley), Mount Rainier, Crater Lake, and Glacier. A parallel interest in protecting prehistoric Indian remains on federal lands led Congress in 1906 to pass the Antiquities Act, authorizing presidents to reserve significant cultural as well as natural features as national monuments. Theodore Roosevelt proclaimed the first 18 national monuments, including El Morro, New Mexico, containing ancient inscriptions, and Arizona's Petrified Forest and Grand Canyon. Congress later converted many national monuments to national parks.

The need to better manage these areas led Congress in 1916 to create a new Interior Department bureau, the National Park Service. The law made the NPS responsible for Interior's parks and monuments and directed it "to conserve the scenery and the natural and historic objects and the wild life therein and to provide for the enjoyment of the same in such manner and by such means as will leave them unimpaired for the enjoyment of future Generations."

The first NPS director, Stephen T. Mather, vigorously promoted park tourism and expansion of the park system through such eastern additions as Shenandoah and Great Smoky Mountains national parks in the Appalachians. Under Horace M. Albright, his successor from 1929 to 1933, the system expanded topically as well as geographically with the acquisition of Civil War battlefields, presidential sites, memorials, and other historic properties, many transferred from other federal agencies. The park service was now truly national and deeply involved with historic as well as natural preservation.

Beginning in the 1930s, the NPS also became involved with areas selected primarily for their recreational value. The scenic Blue Ridge and Natchez Trace parkways were launched as Depression relief projects. In 1936, the NPS assumed responsibility for Lake Mead National Recreation Area at the reservoir created by Hoover Dam, the first of a dozen reservoir-based additions. A year later Congress authorized Cape Hatteras National Seashore, the first of 14 national seashores and lakeshores. In 1972, Gateway and Golden Gate national recreation areas in New York City and San Francisco became the precedents for other urban recreation areas serving Cleveland, Atlanta, and Los Angeles.

By the end of the century the national park system comprised more than 275 areas from Maine to American Samoa. The NPS also administered a range of programs supporting natural and historic preservation and recreation outside the parks. Among them was the *National Register of Historic Places, which identified historic properties in both public and private ownership, made them eligible for preservation assistance, and gave them a measure of protection against impairment by federal projects. Through its management of the parks and such additional programs, the NPS had become the focal point of federal concern for natural and historic preservation and outdoor recreation in America.

BARRY MACKINTOSH

National Portrait Gallery. The National Portrait Gallery maintains the Catalog of American Portraits, a collection of images and data for more than one million portraits in public and private collections. These include one-of-a-kind images—paintings, sculpture, drawings, miniatures and silhouettes—plus a few rare daguerreotypes. In the manual file, one can find a photograph of the portrait, and standard cataloging information such as dimensions, condition, description, provenance, biographical sketches of the artist and sitter, bibliographic references and any archival correspondence and primary research material. There is also a searchable database of 65,000 records that allows one to search by a number of criteria such as subject, medium, setting, objects depicted, provenance, time or style period, and region. The latter database covers prints and photographs as well as paintings. The website is <www.npg.si.edu>.

In addition, the National Portrait Gallery shares a library with the National Museum of American Art containing 100,000 volumes and over 1,000 serials. The library also has an extensive collection of clippings and pamphlets on American art. Contact the library by telephone at: (202) 357-1886.

The National Portrait Gallery's research facilities are open to the public, preferably by appointment, weekdays 10–5. One can also write, phone, fax, or e-mail questions to the research staff. There is a nominal fee for copies of archival material. Write: Catalog of American Portraits, National Portrait Gallery, Smithsonian Institution, Washington, D.C. 20560-0213; telephone (202) 357-2578; fax (202) 786-2565; e-mail: <npgweb@npg.si.edu>.

National Register of Historic Places. Every state and community has places important to its past. In recognition of this, the *National Park Service, within the United States Department of the Interior, expands and maintains the National Register of Historic Places. This is the nation's official list of districts, sites, buildings, structures, and objects significant in national, state, and local history, architecture, archeology, engineering, and culture. The Register recognizes the value of places as diverse as a dugout shelter of an Oklahoma pioneer settler, the Breakers Mansion in Newport, and a 12,000-year-old prehistoric site. In addition to providing recognition of a property's historic significance, listing on the National Register brings consideration in planning federal or federally assisted projects, eligibility for federal tax benefits, consideration in decisions about coal-mining permits, and eligibility for federal preservation grants.

Places selected by Congress to be historical units of the National Park System and National Historic Landmarks, designated by the Secretary of the Interior for their significance to all Americans, are listed automatically in the National Register. Under the National Historic Preservation Act of 1966, as amended, other places may be nominated by states, federal agencies, and American Indian tribes. State, federal, and tribal preservation offices run programs to look for and evaluate buildings, sites, and other physical remnants from the past. Then they nominate to the National Register of Historic Places those they decide are historically or culturally important. Most nominations come through state historic-preservation officers. The professionals in state historic preservation offices work closely with local governments, historical organizations, and the public in locating and researching places that might qualify for recognition in the National Register.

National Register criteria for evaluation are written broadly to accommodate the country's rich history. To qualify, places may: (a) be associated with events that have made a significant contribution to the patterns of our history; (b) be associated with the lives of persons significant in our past; (c) embody the distinctive characteristics of a type, period, or method of construction; represent the work of a master; possess high artistic values; or represent a significant and distinguishable entity whose components may lack individual distinction; or (d) have yielded or be likely to yield information important in prehistory or history. Places may meet one or more of the criteria; must possess integrity of historic location, design, workmanship, feeling, and association; and generally, though not always, be at least fifty years old.

By 1999, the National Register listed more than 70,000 historic properties.

Because historic districts often include hundreds of significant buildings and other features, these listings represented about one million resources, approximately 90 percent of which are important at the state and local level. The National Register maintains a file on each listed property, with a physical description, geographical information, one or more maps, an explanation of historical significance, a bibliography, and at least one black and white photograph. Frequently, files contain additional information.

A computerized database called the National Register Information System (NRIS) makes it possible to find places linked geographically or according to historic themes, dates of significance, past or present uses, or associations with important individuals. Anyone can search the database by state or county by calling up the NRIS, found on the National Register's home page on the World Wide Web (<www.cr.nps. gov/nr>). With appropriate software, it is possible to search by other characteristics as well. More complex, customized searches require the assistance of National Register staff. The most recently published cumulative list of registered places is the *National Register of Historic Places, 1966 to 1994* (Washington, D.C., 1994).

Published guidance in National Register bulletins assists those evaluating properties for possible nomination to the National Register. In addition to bulletins explaining how to apply and how to fill out registration forms, there is guidance on identifying, evaluating and documenting cemeteries, battlefields, mining resources, archeological sites, landscapes, lighthouses, and other types of cultural resources found in many communities. Bulletins are free upon request, and many are available on the Internet.

The National Register promotes awareness and use of historic places in various ways. Through its "Teaching with Historic Places" program, it offers curriculum materials, workshops, and written guidance on using historic places effectively in the classroom and on forging productive partnerships between educators, historians, preservationists, and others. The program has created almost 100 lesson plans based on places listed in the National Register. A series of travel itineraries entitled "Discover Our Shared Heritage" provides self-guided tours linking places listed in the National Register. Topics and destinations represented in these travel itineraries include areas rich in Hispanic heritage; cities, such as Chicago, Baltimore, Seattle, Detroit, Washington, D.C.; communities across the country; and routes determined by themes, such as the Underground Railroad, Civil Rights, and women's history. Both lesson plans and travel itineraries exist in published form and on the World Wide Web, which provides one-stop shopping for information about many National Register programs and activities at <www.cr.nps.gov/nr>.

The address and telephone number of the National Register of Historic Places are: National Park Service, 1849 C Street, NW, Room NC400, Washington, D.C. 20240; (202) 343-9536.

CAROL D. SHULL *and* BETH M. BOLAND

National Trust for Historic Preservation. This private, membership organization was founded in 1949 to bring attention and provide education about the nation's architectural treasures and curiosities. The organization publishes *Preservation News*. The headquarters is at 1785 Massachusetts Ave., NW, Washington, D.C. 20036; (800) 944-6847 and (202) 588-6000; <http://www.nthp.org>.

See historic preservation.

National Women's History Project. The National Women's History Project (NWHP) was established in 1980 to promote the recognition of multicultural women's history in schools and communities nationwide. It originated and continues to lead the annual promotion each March of National Women's History Month and August 26 as Women's Equality Day.

The office is the national clearinghouse for women's-history programming, projects, and resources. Its staff provides information, referrals, and technical assistance free of charge on a year-round basis. Their website (<www.NWHP.org>) extends this service worldwide.

By issuing a Women's History Catalog, the NWHP brings women's-history information to people wherever they live or work. In addition to books from small and large presses, the NWHP itself has developed and published many curriculum units, program planning guides, video programs, posters, and display sets.

The NWHP provides staff support to a nationwide participant organization, the Women's History Network, pub-

zational activities, and perhaps their most prized feature to the historian are the *obituaries. Many newspapers have included local history, either in the form of frequent feature stories, or as regular columns. The advertising in newspapers may be one of their most important offerings; they can be used to study economic issues, taste, values and attitudes, as well as to identify and explain local businesses. Thus newspapers can be the source for information on almost every aspect of local life.

So what is the problem? The problem is that newspapers are not always reliable. Especially in the first century of their existence, newspapers usually represented a political party, and thus everything printed in them represented the party's particular bias. Others showed the economic interests of their owner or publisher or of the dominant interest of an area; thus a newspaper in a Texas oil town would not be too likely to report on the pollution of the air and water caused by that industry. Certainly a newspaper published by a church or the labor movement would be more interested in representing its point of view rather than "just the facts." Until very recent times, newspapers most likely reflected their white ownership and reported little of the life of nonwhites or many ethnic minorities in the community. The historian would have to know a great deal about the paper, in order to be able to evaluate its information.

Beyond the problems of point of view, there is the simple matter of accuracy. Almost anyone who has been interviewed by a newspaper or had an experience reported in the newspaper has been horrified by the distortions in the printed material. Newspaper reporters have never been experts in all topics (indeed in most small-town newspapers one person was often the reporter, writer, editor, publisher and printer!) and their reporting suffered from lack of full understanding of the information. Or perhaps the paper has relied on second- or third-hand accounts, or accounts submitted by interested parties. In every case, the newspaper is limited by time available and thus often lacks the opportunity to research fully—or even verify—their findings. Thus, even if bias is not a problem, accuracy is.

Does all of this mean local historians should not use newspapers? Absolutely not. In the first place, there is much factual information that is essential and that may not be available anywhere else. One should just be careful not to assume that the newspaper contains *all* the pertinent information on a topic. Newspapers are also valuable sources for values and points of view within a community; as advocates, they may also be a factor affecting the evolution of a town. And, at the very least, they may provide the researcher a good starting point on the road to more and better information.

If newspapers are tricky to use, they are even more tricky to find. There have been so many published, and often for such short periods of time, that they are very hard to locate. There are directories of currently published papers, and there have been many efforts at union catalogs of newspaper holdings, including a number of state and local ones; a good starting bibliography can be found in Lorreto Dennis Szucs, "Newspapers," in Arlene Eakle and Johni Cerny, *The*

Source: A Guidebook of American Genealogy (Salt Lake City, 1984), pp. 407–26, although a number of projects have been undertaken since 1984. An example would be the California State Library Foundation's *Newspapers in California* (Sacramento, 1985), which includes a bibliography of newspaper history in California, surveys of collections of newspapers within the state, lists of newspaper morgues (the newspaper's own archives of clippings and files), location of newspaper holdings by county and city published, and by title, and by depositories. It also mentions indexing where available (see below), and newspaper-clippings collections. Another publication by the same organization, *Newspaper Holdings of the California State Library* (Sacramento, 1986), provides an exhaustive list (by newspaper title) of all holdings in the state's major library. Although hardly complete, these kinds of collection guides are excellent "starting-point finding aids." Although the local historian should seek published finding aids, most will have to locate local newspapers by scouring the holdings of state and local libraries, archives, museums, historical societies, and the archives of local newspapers.

Once the historian locates newspapers, how can items be found within them? That can be a problem, since the historian may be dealing with long runs of many-paged daily newspapers. One way is to simply go through a paper, page by page. For some kinds of information, one may use sample pages by working through every tenth issue, for instance. Every historian's dream is that there might be an index. There are indexes to many major national newspapers and a number of local newspapers or libraries have indexed local newspapers; these are seldom mentioned in published finding aids, so the historian should ask at local depositories. If using an index, the historian must be aware of its limitations. What are the subjects being indexed? Remember that the determination of those subjects will reflect the values and biases of the times and the person doing the index. For example, in pre-1960s New York, when most people assumed racism was a problem only in the South, local newspapers were not likely to include racism in their indexes. How thorough is the index? Does it include topics only? Proper nouns? Just names? Places? Does the index cover the entirety of the newspaper? How thorough is it? There is a way of testing an index. Pick a page and identify several items that you think should be in the index; then check the index to see if they are there. That should give the historian a general idea of the appropriateness and thoroughness of the index.

A new finding aid is coming into existence. Beginning in the 1990s, some newspapers began going online, and some have even begun to go back and place their earlier issues on computer. In those cases, the user will then have available the word and subject indexing on the computer system.

Considering the problems in finding, evaluating, and using newspapers, some might think they are more trouble than they are worth. That would be a mistake; despite the problems they present, newspapers are probably the most widely used single type of source in local history writing.

RAYMOND STARR

Nigerian local historiography. As with most of Africa, the interest in the past and the consciousness of history is deep and enduring among all Nigerian groups. The development of local historiography can be discussed under three broad categories: oral traditions, Islamic historiography, and modern writing in English and indigenous languages.

First, history was traditionally recorded through a variety of oral methods—as myths, songs, poems, ceremonies, genealogies, praise poems, rituals, place names, commentaries, stories, parables, proverbs, etc. In areas with kingdoms, there were court historians devoted to the memorization and recitation of traditions. Oral histories have provided valuable data for contemporary authors in reconstructing the past. Initially distrusted in the Western academy, the use of oral histories is one of the major revolutions in history after World War II. Oral histories show a developed sense of historical consciousness, the deliberate attempt to use history for identity construction, power legitimization, and social control. Whether in the past or present, oral histories are a core component of local histories, as they privilege the knowledge of elders and the need to respect tradition even while accepting change. Current efforts to document traditions reveal their importance, as well as the need to preserve data before much of it disappears. With the rise of modern technologies, current events are being captured in print, audio, and video. The unresolved question remains how to collect and preserve many dimensions of the past, even for such a recent era as the first half of the twentieth century.

With the spread of Islam after the eleventh century A.D., the second historical tradition emerged, especially among the groups in the north where Islam slowly took root. Islam brought the language of Arabic, both in its spoken and written form, in addition to religious and social transformations. Nigerian Muslims, notably preachers and scholars, developed the skills to write and to record events. As early as the sixteenth century, a distinguished writer had emerged in Borno, a huge empire in the northeast: Imam Ahmad ibn Fartuwa, author of two books on Mai (King) Idris Alooma's reign and wars of expansion (1569–1619). In 1658, another Imam, Muhammad Salih ibn Isharku, wrote an account on the Borno's capital city of Ngazargamo. Of all the accounts of cities, the best known is the *Kano Chronicle*. The most prestigious body of Arabic writings is associated with the leaders of the nineteenth-century Islamic revolution, Shehu Uthman dan Fodio; his brother, Abdullahi dan Fodio; and his son, Muhammad Bello. They all justified the need for an Islamic *jihad*, and provided guidelines for attaining a good government and corruption-free society.

. Islamic local histories are very important. As written histories, they have enhanced our capability for understanding the history of Nigeria since the eleventh century, especially in the Sudan. As Islamic scholarship tends to be all-encompassing, the writings yield substantial information on religion, politics, diplomacy, warfare, trade, and power rivalry. They do have their bias toward Islam, thus explaining why they condemn "paganism," Christianity, and practices not sanctioned by Islam. Today, this tradition continues to flourish, in various Quranic schools where Imams continue to preach, teach, and write. Many of these Imams continue to express their ideas in pamphlets and radio broadcasts that circulate all over the country. As in the past, the aim is to use writing to change society, promote morality, and ensure conversion to Islam.

A third category is associated with Western contact that began in the fifteenth century, leading to the imposition of colonial rule from ca. 1900 to October 1, 1960. As Christianity and Western education spread, a new elite emerged. Eventually, an academic culture also took hold, with the establishment of the University of Ibadan in 1948. As the role of western education expanded and became influential, so too did the historiography associated with writing in English and indigenous languages. The earliest recovered work is the diary of a trader in the Niger Delta, dated 1787. The most cited is the 1789 autobiography of the former slave, Olaudah Equiano. Other liberated slaves also wrote, and the most famous was Ajayi Crowther—a Yoruba, the first African bishop, a pioneer in the efforts to make Yoruba a written language, and an author.

The successful works by Crowther and the increase in the number of educated Nigerians led to the greater production of local histories in the nineteenth and twentieth centuries. Usually chroniclers, the authors used their skills and education to turn oral histories into written form. Among the most famous authors are Samuel Johnson, historian of the Yoruba; Jacob Egharevba, who wrote on the Bini; William Moore, on the Itsekiri; and Akiga Sai, on the Tiv.

The majority of the chroniclers sought to preserve local traditions and knowledge. As witnesses to the rapid changes wrought by Christianity, Islam, and colonialism, they were alarmed by the erosion of indigenous values and ideas, and saw history writing as a way of restoring what was lost. The chroniclers were equally motivated by patriotism. To them the history of their places and cities were great and enduring; their people had great heroes and leaders, and they were all part of the march of civilization. It is clear that most authors show bias for the history of their people, sometimes exaggerating achievements and under-reporting failures. It is also true that they often use traditions indiscriminately, since they tend to regard myths and folktales as "histories." However, chronicles represent the most flourishing aspect of local history, without which many communities would never even be represented in historical accounts or libraries. Local patriotism remains the primary instigator for many authors who dedicate their spare time to writing.

As Nigerians struggled to obtain independence, nationalists broadened the terrain of writing by adding the genre of polemics, manifestos, and *memoirs. On the one hand were cultural nationalists who simply wanted to use history and writing to reclaim glory for Africans. Writing to them was an expression of nationalism. On the other hand were those who regarded writing as an anti-colonial weapon, by resorting to great rhetoric, polemic, and propaganda. Such famous politicians as Nnamdi

Azikiwe, Saheed Zungur, and Obafemi Awolowo were also great writers whose works provided a strong foundation for the emergence of academic history from 1948 onwards.

Academic history has actually strengthened the development of local histories, while of course promoting national and continental histories. Many M.A. and Ph.D. theses have examined the histories of local communities, intergroup relations, the impact of Christianity and Islam on many ethnic groups and societies, and the long-term impact of globalization and the incorporation of Africa into the western capitalist system. These works are generally detailed narratives, and the authors tend to disregard theoretical concerns in the disciplines or any pressure even to connect their works to so-called universalist literature. In other words, the context remains essentially local, as the authors dwell more on what is important to their people than what their colleagues in the Western academy find innovative. However, although local, these works are relevant to the disciplines. On the one hand, they continue to show how societies are vibrant and actively engage in finding solutions to their problems. On the other hand, they present Nigeria to Nigerians in such a way that the latter can be proud. This is an attack on the Western discourse of knowledge, which has presented Africa with non-Africans as the audience. Thus, local history can be an effective counter-discourse that aggressively corrects the still-pervasive negative external image of Africa. It is also "relevant history," in the sense that communities see themselves in historical accounts and, although they may not agree with everything that scholars say, they nevertheless are proud to be part of history: not relegated to footnotes but brilliantly explored in the main bodies of texts.

See Toyin Falola, *Yoruba Gurus: Indigenous Production of Knowledge in Africa* (Trenton, N.J., 1999), and "Trends in Nigerian Historiography," *Trans-African Journal of History* 1, 2, (1981), pp. 97–112. The following works were edited by Toyin Falola: *Yoruba Historiography* (Madison, Wisc., 1991), *African Historiography: Essays in Honour of J. F. Ade Ajayi* (London, 1993), and *Pioneer, Patriot and Patriarch: Samuel Johnson and the Yoruba People* (Madison, Wisc., 1993).

TOYIN FALOLA

See oral history.

Norwegians. See Appendix A.

nostalgia. Initially the term "nostalgia" was the province of medical doctors. In the nineteenth century, nostalgia had a pathological meaning: it was a form of melancholia brought on by acute homesickness. Used to describe the homesickness felt by sailors and soldiers, the term lingered in usage until World War II. The origins of the word are Greek, denoting home and pain. Only in the twentieth century did nostalgia take on its more modern meaning: wistful memories of an earlier time, a longing for the simplicity of some golden age. F. Scott Fitzgerald's *The Great Gatsby* (N Y., 1925) represented how American literature had assimilated the theme.

Not surprisingly, historians have often viewed nostalgia as antithetical to historical thinking and used the term as a pejorative. Christopher Lasch devoted an entire chapter to the topic in his book, *The True and Only Heaven* (N.Y., 1991). The larger point of his book, was a critique of the idea of progress. To Lasch, nostalgia was the mirror image of progress. Speaking of progress, he wrote: "The assumption that our standard of living (in the broadest meaning of the that term) will undergo a steady improvement colors our view of the past as well as the future." "It gives rise," he continued, "to nostalgic yearning for bygone simplicity—the other side of the ideology of progress." In short, Lasch saw nostalgia as the abdication of memory and the enemy of historical analysis.

Nostalgia gained wide currency in historical writings in the 1990s as the field of (public) history and memory coalesced. A seminal contribution to the field was Michael Kammen's *Mystic Chords of Memory* (N.Y., 1991). Published in the same year as Lasch's book, Kammen's was a sweeping treatment of the construction of national myths and commemorative activities. Speaking of Americans during a period of rapid change and adjustment, Kammen noted: "Nostalgia meant more to them than consolation. It provided identity, integrity, and perhaps even a sense of security—however false."

Kammen was one of the first commentators on the *heritage boom taking place in the years following World War II. In the writings of Kammen—and David Lowenthal, another critic of heritage—the terms "nostalgia" and "heritage" were related if not necessarily synonymous. In an essay included in *In the Past Lane* (N.Y., 1997), Kammen explained the difference: "Nostalgia tends to be history without guilt while this elusive thing called 'heritage' is the past with two scoops of pride and no bitter aftertaste." Whereas Lasch was deeply critical of nostalgia, Kammen saw the phenomenon as sometimes benign but often illusory, or self-deceiving. Later in that same volume, he wrote: "There is nothing necessarily wrong with nostalgia per se, but more often the phenomenon does mean a pattern of selective memory. Recall the good, forget the unpleasant."

Kammen harbored deep concerns about public conceptions of the past and how nostalgia and heritage informed the popular imagination. But he saw opportunity as well as danger. "One of the most welcome features of the heritage surge," Kammen wrote, "involves the development of contacts, even enduring relationships, between popular and academic history." While Kammen pointed out the ups and downs of heritage, it remained for others to articulate a more positive idea of nostalgia.

Historian John Lukacs wrote about the public's near mania for history in *Historical Consciousness* (New Brunswick, N.J., 1994). He argued that our evolving historical consciousness in the last three or four centuries was an underappreciated fact of Western civilization. While Lukacs criticized what he called the bureaucratization of history, he took seriously popular interest in the past. Lukacs noted how the term "old-fashioned" had lost its pejorative meaning, while "modernism" had lost its charm. Who would prefer "modern cooking" to "old-fashioned cooking," he asked? He also disagreed with intellectuals (even Dante) who associated nostalgia with pain. He recalled how his memories of better times during and after hardship experienced during World War II had given him pleasure. For Lukacs, nostalgia was good, and evidence of our historically conscious age.

In 1998, Jackson Lears wrote the most ardent defense of nostalgia to date. Lears wondered whether nostalgia might be taken seriously and used to inform a critical approach to the past. Unlike Lasch, Lears believed nostalgia was our best defense against a simple-minded notion of progress: "Renewed respect for nostalgia could provide a powerful antidote to linear notions of progress—by underwriting the conviction that once, at least, in some ways, life was more humane and satisfying than it is today." Nostalgia might also help to eliminate the jargon of inevitability from our political discourse.

Nostalgia's problem, Lears reasoned, was that it never gained intellectual authority. Medical elites had used nostalgia to label how poorly provincials had responded to the need for mobility in modern society. He singled out liberal intellectuals such as Richard Hofstadter and Arthur Schlesinger Jr. as exemplars of a cosmopolitan view that "cut off rich veins of historical thought—including, significantly, books on American regions and rivers, efforts to construct the past of a particular place." He was quick to emphasize, however, that both the right and the left had used nostalgia to "discredit their opponents without engaging their substance."

The meaning of nostalgia has been contested over time and put to diverse uses.

See Jackson Lears, "Looking Backward in Defense of Nostalgia," *Lingua Franca* 7 (Dec./Jan. 1998): 59–66; Michael Kammen, *Mystic Chords of Memory: The Transformation of Tradition in American Culture* (Ithaca, N.Y., 1991), and *In the Past Lane: Historical Perspectives on American Culture* (N.Y., 1997); David Lowenthal, *Possessed by the Past: The Heritage Crusade and the Spoils of History* (N.Y., 1996); John Lukacs, *Historical Consciousness: The Remembered Past* ([1968] New Brunswick, N.J., 1994); and Christopher Lasch, *The True and Only Heaven: Progress and Its Critics* (N.Y., 1991).

DAVID McMAHON

nurses, Civil War. Nursing was just beginning as a profession for women at the start of the Civil War. Middle- and upper-class women braved losing their social status as much as they risked their lives among the hardships of the army hospitals.

It was an era when bacteria were but an unproved medical theory and any body of water was believed to be suitable for drinking; when nurses stooped over or lifted patients bedded on the ground or on low cots; the threat to the nurses' health and hardihood was acute. Many nurses became ill and some died in the service.

Civil War nurses were a varied lot, from all classes, religions, and ethnicities. Most of what we know of them is from the journals, memoirs, diaries, and letters of middle- and upper-class white women and from those of white male doctors who observed their work. Suzy King Taylor, educated in a clandestine school in Charleston, left us a journal from the viewpoint of an African American woman who worked in the Union hospitals on the South Carolina coast. The best information about Civil War nurses comes from their own writings. Many nurses published book-length versions of their stories in the years after the war; others were published later by families or interested scholars. Other stories by nurses appeared in periodicals.

Two books about doctors contain useful bibliographies including primary material by nurses. See *Doctors in Blue: The Medical History of the Union Army in the Civil War* (N.Y., 1952) by George W. Adams; and *Doctors in Gray: The Confederate Medical Service* (Baton Rouge, La., 1958) by H. H. Cunningham.

See also Steven Louis Roca, "Presence and Precedents: The USS *Red Rover* during the American Civil War, 1861–1865," *Civil War History*, 44:2 (June 1998): 91–110; Jane A. Schulz, "The Inhospitable Hospital: Gender and Professionalism in Civil War Medicine," *Signs* (winter 1992): 363–92; Suzie King Taylor, *Reminiscences of My Life: A Black Woman's Civil War Memoirs*, Patricia W. Romero, ed. (N.Y., 1988); Ann Douglas Wood, "The War within a War: Women Nurses in the Union Army," *Civil War History* 18:3 (September 1972); Emily V. Mason, "Memories of a Hospital Matron," *Atlantic Monthly* 90 (1902): 305–18, 475–85; Mary A. Gardiner Holland, *Our Army Nurses* (Boston, 1897); Emily Elizabeth Parsons, *Civil War Nursing: Memoir of Emily Elizabeth Parsons* (1880); and Louisa M. Alcott, *Hospital Sketches* (Boston, 1863).

MARY WHITE

nursing home records. "Nursing home" is a term often used to cover a wide variety of nonhospital institutions. These include rest home, retirement home, old-peoples' home, home for the friendless, assisted-living center, rehabilitation center, long-term-care facility, skilled-nursing facility, poor house, work house, almshouse, poor farm, home for the aged, and "asylums" of all sorts. Since a nursing home is a business, although generally a not-for-profit one, it produces documents similar to those found in any corporate archive, including annual reports. The internal publications along with marketing and public-relations materials such as press releases, brochures, and newsletters can help the researcher tell the story of a home's operation, architecture, and human experiences.

Traditionally, homes were founded by religious groups, benevolent societies, fraternal organizations, groups of medical personnel, and concerned citizens. Fundraising records and minutes of trustee meetings may provide information about the history of such philanthropy in the community. Once the home was operational, how was it financed? Budgets, annual reports, and other finance records can describe endowments, donations of cash and materials, as well as the fees charged for services, entrance fees, insurance coverage, government subsidies, and whether residents were ever required to sign over assets in order to be admitted.

On a broader level, the historian might consider the home's place in the context of national movements in health or old-age care. Was the founding of the home a result of reform movements of the Progressive Era or of the benevolence movements of the nineteenth century? Was it always a nursing home? How have services changed? How is the home's philosophy changing now? Information for these topics may be found in board minutes, medical committee reports, reports made by the home's director to the board, and interviews with the present director.

In discussing the home as an employer, its role in the community is examined. In terms of work, how have employee titles and duties changed over the years? Have they followed national trends? Similar questions can be asked in tracing the development of departments such as admissions, food service, and activities. For all of these areas, records from the home's archive may be supplemented with newspaper stories. Diaries and oral histories from residents and former employees can also support this data.

Another facet of an institution's history is its resident population. Resident rosters as well as residents' possessions, papers, and photographs lend humanity to the operational story. In the case of retirement homes, residents often leave behind material culture including clothing, grooming aids, decorative objects and artwork. A study of these objects can color and clarify everyday life within the sheltered community.

Also of interest is the building itself. Deeds, plans, and construction work orders as well as reports from the board's grounds and building committees can fill in the reasons for the building's present configuration and appearance. Furniture, equipment, and interior and exterior finishes are other things to consider.

Finally, interviews with the home's neighbors can yield oral histories and photographs from people who have lived alongside the institution for many years. These can be an invaluable source of objectivity and fresh perspective for the historian.

The history of a nursing home may be written on commission from the institution or an independent scholar may see the importance of the home as part of the community's history. In any event, the writer must be sensitive to the feelings of the staff, residents, and possibly their relatives, especially if there has been a scandal or controversy. The writer must also be aware of *copyright laws pertaining to private, unpublished papers, and be familiar with local privacy laws that may impinge on the use of medical or other institutional records for publication.

CYNTHIA OGOREK

O

obituaries. An obituary is a published report of an individual's death. It generally supplies information about the death itself (the time, place, and cause), the funeral, and the interment. An obituary, however, also includes details about the life of the deceased. This can include alternate names (such as a married woman's maiden name), a birthplace, parents' names, places of residence, schools attended, places of employment, military history, names of spouses, names of children, names of siblings, religious affiliation, and membership in fraternal organizations, clubs, or other groups. An obituary is a miniature biography, and for many it is the only time that their life stories are presented in a public forum. Much of this information may not be easily attainable elsewhere, making obituaries invaluable to researchers. Also, the details presented in an obituary can supply the researcher with ideas for other avenues of investigation.

It should be remembered that the information in an obituary can go through a variety of filters. The person writing the obituary may not have known the subject personally. It is only notables who have their obituary data confirmed prior to their death and the writing of one's own obituary is generally a late-twentieth-century phenomenon. The writer may not even have dealt directly with the informant reporting on the deceased. The informant, usually the bereaved, may not have been thinking clearly at the time of the interview and may not have had firsthand knowledge of many details being reported.

Over time, different individuals have been responsible for the composition of obituaries. Obituaries, to be distinguished from death notices, have usually been written by journalists and are considered news items. They have become such a specialized form of *newspaper writing that today some papers supply the writers' bylines. In the late nineteenth century there were even freelance writers commissioned by the deceased's loved ones to author the obituary. It is also not uncommon for obituaries to be submitted by family members and friends. Who is writing the obituary is influenced by the period, the newspaper, the locale, and the deceased's place in the community.

Death notices differ from obituaries in that a fee is charged for their printing. They are often administered by the advertising department. Thus, the author of a death notice is more likely to be the funeral director or someone who knew the departed. The length may not then reflect the individual's standing in the community, but the estate's solvency. In actuality it is often very difficult for a researcher to distinguish obituaries from death notices and there is a trend, in some parts of the country, to charge a fee for obituaries, which is blurring the lines even further.

When searching for obituaries, all newspapers published in the area at the time of death should be consulted. Neighboring newspapers may supply differing amounts of information, as well as differing information. Discrepancies may be found among the various obituaries, making the search for all published reports important. While the community newspaper is usually the most frequent source for the local historian to investigate, obituaries also appear in other types of serial publications, at the local, state, and national levels. For example, the newspapers of religious denominations can be very useful, even for nonclergy subjects. Newsletters and magazines published by schools, professional organizations, clubs, and fraternal organizations can also be sources for obituaries. They can supply insight into different aspects of a person's life. *The Confederate Veteran* is a historic national publication known for the usefulness of its obituaries. Newspapers published by minorities and foreign language papers can report on members of their communities who may have been ignored in the mainstream publications.

Comprehensive indexing is rare for local newspapers; however, the rise of genealogical publishing in the last 30 years, has seen an increase in the production of books of abstracts and specialized indexes to such papers. Some of these publications focus exclusively on obituaries and death notices. Such tools can assist the local history scholar in locating obituaries when the date of death is unknown. It is, of course, a stroke of luck if the newspaper one is investigating has such a publication, and it covers the period needed.

Clipped obituaries can often be found in vertical, surname, family, *genealogy, or obituary files compiled by, and/or held by, libraries and archival institutions. These files are usually arranged by the individual's last name. Unfortunately, it is common that the items in such files do not include complete citations, which can hinder some research. Obituaries can also be found in family Bibles and in scrapbooks, held in both institutions and in private hands. Such scrapbooks can be the products of family members or of community chroniclers. Scrapbooks can be useful, for they bring together a large number of obituaries, usually tied together by some theme, such as family name or time period, and often include clippings from a variety of sources. Other institution types that should be consulted for obituary files are funeral homes, churches, cemeteries, and newspapers.

While obituary publications with a national focus are not usually useful to the local-history scholar, there are some that can assist with community research. For example, both the *Avery Obituary Index to Architects* and the *Biographical Dictionary of American Architects (Deceased)* can lead to information on architects who may have worked in the community. Such sources could assist in confirming a commission, or aid in the evaluation of an architect's professional development and style.

There is also a number of sources that document the deaths of U.S. doctors. Such national sources, however, tend to be expensive and are often only held by larger public or academic libraries.

The rise of the Internet has greatly facilitated the dissemination of obituary information worldwide. There are numerous sites where obituaries are posted, abstracted, indexed, and discussed. Modern newspapers allow for access, from a distance, to contemporary obituaries through their webpages and online archives. Some of these are fee driven, some not. Some provide full-text obituaries, and some simply provide the citation. There are newspaper databases that allow searching not only by name but also by such factors as town, occupation, or reported cause of death, thus easing the use of the obituary as a tool to evaluate social trends. Websites focusing on older obituaries are generally the product of genealogists and genealogical groups, as well as research institutions. Genealogy listservs often include in their discussions the posting of obituaries discovered by the list's members.

Commercial databases that index a number of newspapers (generally larger papers), such as LEXIS-NEXIS, can also provide access to contemporary obituaries. UMI Obituaries is one such database that focuses exclusively on obituaries. A very useful database is PERSI (PERiodical Source Index), which includes in its indexing references to obituaries that appear in a wide variety of genealogical and local history periodicals.

Obituaries are more than informational sources; they are also cultural documents reflecting the times in which they were written. While the number of people whose deaths are reported in the news has increased greatly since the eighteenth century, even in small local papers social factors influence what death is reported and at what length. Over time gender, race, and ethnicity have determined who warranted an obituary, at what length, and at what level of detail. Obituaries are a reflection of their community. They also can tell us a great deal about our changing attitudes towards death, how we report on this great eventuality, and how we mourn the passing of the various members of our community.

An excellent starting point for locating obituary sites on the web is the metasite Cyndi's List of Genealogy Sites on the Internet. As of July 23, 1999, her obituary page (www.cyndislist.com/obits.html>) contained links to over 80 sites. The links are arranged alphabetically by title and include sites for both contemporary and historic obituaries. While the vast majority of sites listed relate to the United States, there are some international links. The GEN-OBIT listserv is also included.

Cyndi's List is updated regularly, and inactive links are removed in a timely manner. Another metasite of interest is The Obituary Links Page (<www.geocities.com/Heartland/Bluffs/7748/obit/obituary.htm>). It can also be reached via Cyndi's List. The Obituary Links Page eases browsing by arranging its links both by location (state) and by surname. It also includes links to other similar sites.

Both PERSI and UMI Obituaries are easily available to the general public through subscription to Ancestry.com, the Web presence of Ancestry Publishing, a leading genealogy publisher (<www.ancestry.com>). Ancestry members also have access to an assortment of other obituary databases (<www.ancestry.com/ancestry/DB-List.asp?GroupID=26>). The descriptions of these databases are excellent and can be very useful in and of themselves. They include such information as the number of obituaries in the database, the date range, and, in some cases, a brief publishing history of the newspaper in question, along with contact information, if appropriate. Ancestry offers free access to new databases for ten days. Interested parties can obtain Ancestry's free e-mail newsletter to keep abreast of what databases are being added to the selection.

The Newspaper Association of America maintains a very useful site that allows quick access to contemporary newspapers. Try <NAA@Hot links> to access newspapers online. The major focus of this site is papers of the United States, arranged predominantly by state, but links have also been compiled for Canadian and international papers. Also, there is a page that includes weekly and alternative papers.

MARY MANNIX

Old Home Days. These community celebrations historically have lasted as long as a week or as little as a single day. The movement began in 1899 when New Hampshire sponsored the first Old Home Week. The idea spread quickly to neighboring states and Canada, then faded in importance after World War I. These celebrations are ex-periencing a modest revival in the shortened form of Old Home Day or Days. No state currently coordinates a general Old Home celebration as several states did early in the century, but individual towns and villages have their own Days. They usually occur in late summer and still are concentrated in New England.

The idea originated with Frank Rollins, a successful Boston entrepreneur who returned to his native New Hampshire and ran successfully for governor. Rollins thought that *nostalgia for place of birth and upbringing was a widespread phenomena that could be harnessed to help revitalize the state's rural economy. The plan was to invite those who had left their hometown back for a sustained communal celebration. Local folks would have to clean things up, returnees (like Rollins himself) who had been successful elsewhere would be encouraged to contribute to some local cause, and everyone would have a fine time visiting, reminiscing, and participating in the weeklong series of events. New Hampshire state legislators provided funding for promotion and Old Home Week became a reality. Over 50 New Hampshire towns participated that first time. Maine joined its neighbor the following year, Vermont the year after, Massachusetts in 1903. At its peak, the Old Home Week movement probably involved the participation of between two and three hundred individual towns.

Local history always played a prominent role in Old Home celebrations. Many communities staged elaborate *pageants in which residents reenacted what they considered the most important events in town history; prominent citizens—frequently men who had written or were in the process of writing the town history—delivered lengthy orations on the past; returnees were taken on "excursions" to local historical sites; collectors displayed old relics; conversations during the free time included lots of reminiscing about life "back then." Occasionally the script of a pageant was published and sent to everyone who had returned. Some group almost always assumed responsibility for publishing the historical addresses. To be sure, Old Home Days involved lots of nonhistorical activities such as bonfires and picnics, but without celebration of the past the movement would have attracted few followers. Even in today's modest revival of the institution, the emphasis remains historical.

Literature on Old Home Days is sparse. Two older essays are Thomas Anderson, "Old Home Week in New England," *The New England Magazine* 24 (August 1906): 673–85; and an anonymous article entitled "New Hampshire's Great Midsummer Festival" in *The Granite State Monthly* 61 (June 1929): 219–29. Recent literature includes Terence Hines, "The Seals of Old Home Week," *The American Philatelist* (November 1997): 1022–27; and chapter five of Dona Brown, *Inventing New England* (1995). Many histories of specific New England towns contain material on Old Home celebrations. For two good examples, see the committee-written *Sandwich, New Hampshire 1763–1990* (1995) and Ronald and Grace Jager, *Portrait of a Hill Town: A History of Washington, New Hampshire 1876–1976* (1977).

JERE DANIELL

oral history. There are two distinct sources for the widespread and growing interest in oral history in recent decades, and each has relevance for the practice of local history.

The first source flows from the recognition that reliance on traditional written documentation is insufficient for more recent history because so much of significance in modern life is simply not captured by such documents. With telephones replacing letter writing, with few crucial meetings or events recorded or noted in detail, with the accelerating onslaught of paper matched by the shrinking number of truly substantive and meaningful documents, those interested in the history of any community, business organization, government agency, or family, have needed to go beyond the conventional record simply to find out what happened—much less to place it in any framework of understanding. Oral history—the generation, collection, and consequent study of historic documents generated through systematic, recorded interviews—has been one attractive response to this documentary challenge.

A second source of interest flows from the recognition that the traditional documentary record is, in the nature of things, biased towards those with the power, privilege, and the institutional or social standing that generates records in the first place. It is necessarily history from the top down, seen through the eyes of powerful institutions, the press, and those people whose memoirs and letters are more likely to be written, collected, preserved, and published. In this light, oral history has been attractive as a way to alter the historical record fundamentally, not just to supplement it. Oral history has thus appealed to many as a route to a more democratic history, often written "from the bottom up," by bringing into view those whose experiences, memories, perspectives, and understandings have rarely been included at all as part of history.

Each of these perspectives inevitably comes into play in documenting a community, region, or local institution. But it is important to realize that these are not identical impulses, nor are they even necessarily harmonious. In many projects, significant choices and trade-offs may have to be made between the goals of deepening the historical record and of altering the angle of vision and inclusion more profoundly—that is, whether to use oral history to find better answers to older questions, or to use it to ask and answer very different questions altogether.

As this suggests, turning to oral history is no magic answer to the complex challenges facing local historians, no instant connection to "the voice of the people" or "the way it really was." It is, rather, a complex and powerful historical tool to be used with care and sensitivity.

But in this light, even the inherent limitations and disadvantages of oral history offer corresponding opportunities of particular use in the local history setting. For instance, many see oral history as problematic because it necessarily relies on individual memory so centrally; because it involves, by definition, looking back at history and experience from a later vantage; and because oral history is shaped by the questions,

comments, and responses of the interviewer. The resulting document is not simply a record of what the interviewee had to say, since questions produce answers, and those questions make the interviewer an integral part of the resulting document.

Oral historians respond that every type of historical document has its own peculiarities, problems, and capacities; one needs to be just as careful in assessing the historical meaning and reliability of a newspaper editorial, a government report, or a diary entry. Just as these documents can be extremely valuable once their particular qualities are taken into consideration, so too oral history interviews become more historically meaningful, rather than less so, when seen as documents providing a unique window onto memory, individual and collective, or as a dialog about historical experience that shows its changing meaning over time and that joins a participant's experience and the perspective of the inquiring expert. Such insights help us see how people understand, represent, and make use of their own history. In this way, oral histories become revealing documents about culture, values, family, and community rather than simply records of facts and events.

In all these ways, oral history enriches the record for local history, and also the process by which this history is preserved, communicated across time and generations, and made a resource for community dialog in the present. But these very qualities suggest one important caveat: for the real value of oral history to flower, it is important see it as an on-going process. Interview projects have to be carefully planned, and the resulting documents have to be organized, listened to, studied, used, discussed, and brought into the broader process of historical interpretation. Far too many communities have embarked on oral-history projects with great enthusiasm, but deflected or avoided decisions about the more complicated next steps—whether practical ones of organizing, indexing, and transcribing the tape collection so that it is usable, or more demanding ones of editing, selecting, and incorporating oral history documents in actual documentary products or community processes. The result, much too often, is shoe boxes of unorganized, unindexed cassettes and the rapid evaporation of a group's interest and enthusiasm, since deciding what to do with an oral history collection, and doing it, are so much more daunting, frustrating, and costly than the fun of plunging ahead with interviewing.

The best advice for novice oral historians, then, is to become more familiar with oral history as a tool and as a surprisingly rich ground for new insights and understandings, and to think carefully, from the start, about what to do with the oral history and how—to see oral history as a broader process of local history-making rather than only as narrow document collecting.

There are many, many resources available to assist the new oral historian in the local history setting, and to help more experienced ones see their work in a new and more powerful light. The Oral History Association, now headquartered at Dickinson College in Carlisle, Pennsylvania, is one important source of information. The Association publishes the *Oral History Review* and a useful pamphlet series, and holds an annual convention that routinely brings together academic, media, educational, and community practitioners in a refreshing and stimulating meeting. For further information, see the OHA home page at <omega.dickinson.edu/organizations/oha>, which also posts the very helpful OHA Evaluation Guidelines, a checklist for the design and assessment of any oral-history project.

Two extremely useful anthologies of articles and essays on oral history are Willa Baum and David Dunaway, *Oral History: An Interdisciplinary Anthology*, 2d ed. (Walnut Creek, Calif., 1996); and Robert Perks and Alistair Thomson, *The Oral History Reader* (London, 1998). Baum has also written the still-useful *Oral History for the Local Historical Society*, 2d ed. (Nashville, Tenn., 1977). Among the best of the "manuals" on oral history are Donald Ritchie, *Doing Oral History* (London, 1995); and Edward Ives, *The Tape-Recorded Interview: A Manual for Fieldworkers in Folklore and Oral History* (Austin, Tex., 1995). Ives's book has also been rendered in a half-hour video, *An Oral Historian's Work*, which is particularly useful for introducing and training community oral historians (Northeast Historic Film, Blue Hills, Me. 04615; [207] 374-2736).

For useful broader reflections growing out of concrete oral-history projects, see Paul Thomson and Hugo Slim, *Listening for a Change: Oral Testimony and Community Development* (London, 1995); Paul Thomson, *The Voice of the Past* (N.Y., 1994); Alessandro Portelli, *The Death of Luigi Trastulli and Other Stories: Form and Meaning in Oral History* (Albany, N.Y., 1993); and Michael Frisch, *A Shared Authority: Essays on the Craft and Meaning of Oral and Public History* (Albany, N.Y., 1990).

MICHAEL FRISCH

Organization of American Historians. Founded in 1907, the Organization of American Historians is the largest professional society created and sustained for the investigation, study, and teaching of American history, from the local to the national level. Its 12,000 members include a wide range of independent historians; college and university professors; archivists, curators, interpreters, and other public historians; teachers and students; and institutional subscribers. OAH publishes the *Journal of American History* (a quarterly) containing scholarly articles, roundtables, exhibit and film reviews, and approximately 150 book reviews per issue. Their *OAH Newsletter* (a quarterly) provides news for professional historians, news of the organization, and conference, grant/award, and job opportunities. *The Annual Meeting Program* describes sessions, meetings, book exhibits, and local off-site sessions/tours at the four-day conference held each spring. The OAH *Magazine of History* is a quarterly publication for teachers of history that includes teaching lessons that often draw on state and local resources. To assist with public advocacy initiatives important to all historians, OAH participates in the *National Coordinating Committee for the Promotion of History and the National Humanities Alliance, as well as other out-

reach and advocacy efforts. Every year OAH keeps its members informed about trends affecting professional historians. These include changes in funding for research, new teaching standards, government initiatives at the national, state, and local levels for preservation of historical resources, the evolution of heritage *tourism, and the public's connection to history. In addition, OAH maintains a direct link to public and local historians through its Public History Committee and, since 1994, its National Park Service (NPS) Committee. OAH and *National Park Service have cosponsored four site-specific conferences and sent teams of historians to review historical interpretation at five park sites. Beginning in August 2000, the organization will cosponsor an annual regional meeting at a different university each year designed to reach nearby academic, public, and independent historians.

The OAH is located at 112 N. Bryan St., Bloomington, Ind. 47408; (812) 855-7311; <www.indiana.edu/~oah>.

JOHN R. DICHTL

organizations, men's civic. During the 1990s, "manhood" and "masculinity" emerged as an exciting new field of historical inquiry. Much of this scholarship work focused on men as members of fraternal organizations, fire companies, political parties, professional societies, and similar voluntary associations, most of which were rooted in the life of the emerging towns and cities of the nineteenth century.

Books and articles on the subject proliferated, as did sessions at the conventions of the *Organization of American

Historians and the *American Historical Association, among other groups.
What puzzled many observers was the
fact that this subject could in any way be
perceived as new. Until recent decades,
wasn't nearly all history the story of
men? And if any particular men warranted special scrutiny, wouldn't it be
those factory hands, farmers, slaves, migrant laborers and so on whose stories
tended to be missing from the historical
record rather than the middle-class men
who frequented clubs, lodges, and business and professional associations?

Several factors converged to stimulate interest in the history of men in
such organizations. The most important was the rise of *women's history in
the 1970s and 1980s. Women's historians documented how women forged
close ties by joining missionary and
Bible-study groups, reform and temperance societies, and similar organizations: whatever their ostensible purpose, such societies nurtured a common consciousness among women and
helped confer gendered meaning upon
their lives. It required no remarkable
leap of intuition to realize that the organizations men created and joined, often to the exclusion of women, performed some analogous role in defining the attitudes and norms of middle-
class men and masculinity.

A second reason for the heightened
visibility of men's organizations was
their remarkable penchant for generating and preserving historical records.
Social historians, desperately intent on
discovering the voice of real people in
actual communities, found that the local archives often consisted almost entirely of such documents. In wood-pan-
eled lounges of the fraternal lodge, lined
with photographs of leonine figures in
bizarre uniforms, researchers spotted
bookcases and cabinets containing
leather-bound membership rolls, annual booklets, and dusty volumes celebrating annual dinners and special events,
and all manner of intriguing ritualistic
artifacts. In the basement of the public
library, researchers discovered molder-
ing bound volumes (or brittle microfilm) of newspapers, most of whose
pages were devoted to the seemingly
ubiquitous activities of the men's political parties, lodges, professional associations, and sports clubs. In some musty
neglected attic of the town hall, researchers located the resolutions, budgets, and political squabbles pertaining to
the growth (and, often, the eventual
abandonment) of the men's voluntary
fire companies, military organizations,
and the like.

Such sources were irresistible to social historians not merely because the
sources were so abundant, but also because they offered detailed and often
exhaustive information about particular persons. Men's organizations, then,
provided a means of redressing a frequent complaint about the new *social
history: that it too often seemed devoid
of real people.

Yet there is a tension between the appeal of the particular and the need to
transcend it. Often the writer-re-
searcher becomes so immersed in the
details of a lodge or baseball club or
political party that their work is of
solely *antiquarian interest. The larger
need is to cultivate these rich sources
so as to generate hypotheses about why
men founded such organizations and

so often chose to exclude women from them. *Tocqueville had perceived the ubiquity of voluntary associations as a peculiar trait of American life; he failed to remark upon the extent to which such organizations were segregated by gender and why.

Local men's clubs and societies were often components of regional or national organizations. Local variations among the various organizations were to some extent mediated by the homogenizing influence of the national bodies. The local militia unit was subject to organizational and cultural constraints imposed by state and national bodies; but the national bodies were themselves influenced by the particular concerns and demands of various local organizations. In this subject as in so many others, an understanding of the local community helps illuminate larger historical processes, and vice versa.

See Mark C. Carnes, *Secret Ritual and Manhood in Victorian America* (New Haven, Conn., 1989); and Mark C. Carnes and Clyde Griffin, eds., *Meanings for Manhood: Constructions of Masculinity in Victorian America* (Chicago, 1990).

MARK C. CARNES

organizations, religious. Most religious bodies support and sponsor church-related organizations, such as Mite Societies, the Dorcus Society, the Solidarities in the Roman Catholic Church, or Hadassah for Jewish women. To be looked for are those times when the groups agree to come together across denominational lines, possibly to sponsor something like a temperance crusade or a missionary to the poor. At oth-

er times, they work alone or only for a particular congregation.

Roman Catholic orders, from the earliest appearance of the Jesuits in the seventeenth century and the Ursuline nuns in the early eighteenth century, are discussed by Lawrence J. McCrank, "Religious Orders and Monastic Communalism in America," in *America's Communal Utopias*, Donald E. Pitzer, ed. (Chapel Hill, N.C., 1997). This includes a useful bibliography and chronology.

See organizations, men's civic; organizations, women's; women's history.

organizations, women's. Women's organizations flourished after the Civil War, though denominational societies were older. Many women's groups were founded in the last quarter of the nineteenth century with philanthropic or literary and self-improvement objectives. Among the earliest of these was Sorosis, founded in 1868 in New York City by Mrs. Jennie C. Croly when women correspondents were prevented from attending a dinner given by the New York Press Club in honor of the visit to the city by Charles Dickens. That same year the New England Women's Club was founded in Boston.

See works by Karen Blair, *The Torchbearers: Women and Their Amateur Arts Associations in America, 1890–1930* (Bloomington, Ind., 1994), *The History of American Women's Voluntary Organizations, 1810–1960: A Guide to Sources* (Boston, 1989), and *The Clubwoman as Feminist: True Womanhood Redefined, 1868–1914* (N.Y., 1980).

See organizations, men's civic; women's history.

$\mathcal{P}$

pageants. For the first 30 years of the twentieth century, American communities large and small staged pageants, usually featuring large casts of townspeople. The themes of these extraordinary affairs were community development and progress, in which change was seen as a graceful transition that incorporated the values of the past. These pageants contained contradictory themes while stressing the unique identity of each place. David Glassberg has noted that these pageants were a blend of "progressivism and antimodernism." Advocates of pageants viewed them as instruments of "communal transformation, able to forge a renewed sense of citizenship out of the emotional ties generated" (Glassberg, p. 284). By the late 1920s, however, community pageantry dwindled to be supplanted by large-scale, more "professional" productions.

See David Glassberg, *American Historical Pageantry: The Uses of Tradition in the Early Twentieth Century* (Chapel Hill, N.C., 1990); and W. Lloyd Warner, *The Living and the Dead* (New Haven, Conn., 1959).

See drama and local history.

Pakistanis. See East Indians, Appendix A.

palimpsest. Palimpsest originates from the Latin; it means "scraped again." Thus a parchment or a tablet may be used once, imperfectly rubbed clean,

and used again. If it is used a third time, that would be a double palimpsest.

So too, our communities can be considered as a palimpsest, on which generations write the evidence of their stay over the remains of those who were there earlier. The word is also a reminder that things remain from the past, sometimes faintly, sometimes much in evidence, and as time progresses new evidence of occupation can be seen along with the old. In thinking about old houses, we might remember that the furnishings were updated over time and therefore an eclectic collection might be in evidence rather than expecting every house to consistently represent a particular period. Think of our own homes: in them there are early pieces of furniture as well as those acquired later. The accumulation speaks of changing fashions, of new economic circumstances, and of an ongoing collection rather than one that is static.

pamphlets. See brochures and pamphlets.

parish histories. See Roman Catholicism, Appendix B.

parks. Municipal, regional, and state parks, including greenways, preserves, waysides, and recreation areas, can be windows to a rich past. Many parks contain one or more historic places that preserve or commemorate important aspects of local history or prehistory; sometimes, the history of the land before it became a park reveals much about local social or environmental concerns at a particular period of time; and oftentimes pre-park history can tell us something about individuals or groups beyond the founding families or the local gentry. Parks are especially associated with past activities of local women's clubs and garden clubs, local chapters of conservation organizations such as the Izaak Walton League, and patriotic societies such as the Daughters of the American Republic. In addition, many parks contain outstanding examples of rustic architecture that link them, historically, to a nationwide movement in the 1920s and 1930s when landscape architects across the country collectively created a distinctive naturalistic architectural style for parks. Others may be good examples of designed *landscapes associated with individual landscape architects or civic planners. Moreover, because parks are public spaces, they offer abundant opportunities for interpreting local history as well as natural history. For this reason, parks are ideal components of heritage areas.

In addition to local libraries, historical society collections, regional repositories, and the recollections of longtime residents, researchers may find useful information in the respective state historic-preservation offices: reports and surveys of historic buildings, structures, and objects (such as outdoor sculpture), and prehistoric sites. Websites may contain facsimiles of documents and historical images that pertain to even the smallest communities; see, for instance, the "American Memory—*Library of Congress" website: <http://memory.loc.gov>. Linda Flint McClelland, *Building the National Parks: Historic Landscape Design and Construction* (Baltimore, 1998) contains a thorough history of the evolution of park rustic architecture. Good contextual background on the American park movement and the influence of federal spending on parks in the 1930s may be found in Peter J. Schmitt, *Back to Nature: The Acadian Myth in Urban America* (Baltimore, 1990); and Phoebe Cutler, *Public Landscape of the New Deal* (New Haven, Conn., 1985). On the history of city planning and urban parks, see William H. Wilson, *The City Beautiful Movement* (Baltimore, 1989). Essays contained in *A Breath of Fresh Air: Chicago's Neighborhood Parks of the Progressive Reform Era, 1900–1925* (Chicago, 1989) explore the history of urban parks and social-welfare campaigns. Robert E. Grese, *Jens Jensen: Maker of Natural Parks and Gardens* (Baltimore, 1992) and Lee Hall, *Olmsted's America* (Boston, 1995) explore the design ideals of two of America's most influential landscape architects. Examples of local history associated with state parks and the roles that local citizens play in establishing and protecting parks may be found in Thomas R. Cox, *The Park Builders: A History of State Parks in the Pacific Northwest* (Seattle, 1988); Roy W. Meyer, *Everyone's Country Estate: A History of Minnesota's State Parks* (St. Paul, 1991); and my own *Places of Quiet Beauty: Parks, Preserves, and Environmentalism* (Iowa City, 1997).

REBECCA CONRAD

See landscape.

passenger lists. Passenger lists contain information about the millions of immigrants who arrived in the United States between 1820 and 1945. A vast majority of the available passenger lists are housed at the *National Archives in Record Group 36. These lists were compiled in compliance with an 1819 Act of Congress that required ships entering U.S. ports from foreign countries to file a list of passengers with the collector of customs. The lists contain name of ship, the master, the port of embarkation, date of arrival and port of arrival. Included are names of each passenger, age, sex, occupation, name of country of origin, country of intended settlement, and information concerning the cause of death if it occurred en route. Where the original list has not survived, there is often a copy or an abstract. These can also be found in Record Group 36.

In 1893, the information collected was standardized so that the reports from all ports were the same after that date. There was also increased information about immigrants, including their ability to read and write, marital status, nationality, last legal residence, destination beyond the port of entry, town, city or country of birth, and previous U.S. residence for those returning to this country. Passenger lists also contain information regarding a passenger's self-reliance and moral character; if the passenger had bought his own ticket or if a contractor had paid for the passage; the amount of money under 30 dollars held by the passenger, what sort of luggage the passenger arrived with, name of relatives or friends that the immigrant hoped to join, if the passenger had been a public ward or had been in prison, and if the passenger was a polygamist. There is also information about the health of the immigrant.

The National Archives has published a *Guide to Genealogical Research in the National Archives* (Washington, D.C., 1982) that includes an introduction to the use of ship passenger lists and a table of information about the availability of information. In addition, *Immigrant and Passenger Arrivals: A Select Catalogue of National Archives Microfilm Publications* (Washington, D.C., 1983) provides more details about which lists are available. *Soundex is used to search the large name indexes.

While the name indexes contain important information, it is important to remember that the book indexes are even more complete and should not be passed by. They are arranged chronologically by date of arrival.

See Frank H. Serene, "American Immigrant Families: Ship Passenger Lists," in Timothy Walch, ed., *Our Family, Our Town: Essays on Family and Local History Sources in the National Archives* (Washington, D.C., 1987). See also the National Archives Microfilm Publication M1066, *The Registers of Vessels Arriving at the Port of New York from Foreign Ports, 1789–1919*, and the *Mortan-Allan Directory of Ship Arrivals*.

See also <www.balchinstitute.org>. Under the link for Ship Manifests there is a great deal of information about passenger lists. See also <http://rstg.roots web.com> for passenger lists that volunteers are posting on this site.

patrilineal. A society where descent is traced through the male line, claiming that descent from a common, often distant, ancestor. Patrilineal is not the same as patriarchies, where rule is centered in men, such as in families that followed biblical injunctions and where the patriarch's word was law, where religious, social, and political functions were often linked to land and possessions.

See clan; matrilineal.

patrimony. Patrimony is property that is inalienable and essential to the cultural and historical identity of a group, community, or nation. Patrimony, viewed globally, is perceived as the collective heritage of humankind. When inalienable property—be it an object, idea or real property—becomes alienated, it may still remain in the inventory of a universal collective heritage. However, it most certainly falls outside the control, access, and use of the community for whom it holds the most meaning. When alienated property is returned to the people and place of origin, it has been repatriated.

In contemporary times, patrimony, cultural property, repatriation, and reparation have become leading topics in national dialogues and international conventions. 1n 1970 the Convention on the Means of Prohibiting and Preventing the Illicit Import, Export, and Transfer of Ownership of Cultural Property was adopted by the United Nations Educational, Scientific and Cultural Organization (UNESCO). Sixty-four countries, including the United States, are parties to the Convention. The 1970 Convention extended the definition of patrimony to include objects of importance for *archaeology, anthropology, history, literature, art, science, antiquities, furniture, musical instruments, and archival materials. The Convention established international guidelines for the protection of patrimony of all kinds by all nations. The Convention encouraged an international effort to curb illicit trade in objects of cultural patrimony and recommended repatriation of materials that were illicitly removed from their place of origin.

While the United States did not adopt the basic tenets of the 1970 Convention until 1983, it did enter into a treaty of cooperation in 1971 with the government of Mexico providing for the recovery and return of stolen archaeological, historical, and cultural properties. In ensuing years the United States entered into executive agreements with the governments of Peru, Guatemala, and Ecuador. In 1983 the Convention on Cultural Property Implementation Act authorized the president of the United States to impose import restrictions on designated types of archaeological and ethnological materials on a nation-by-nation basis. Specifically, archaeological material must be of cultural significance, at least 250 years old, normally discovered as a result of scientific excavation, clandestine or accidental digging, or explorations on land or under water. Ethnological materials were defined as the product of a tribal or nonindustrial society and important to the cultural heritage of a people because of their distinctive characteristics, comparative rarity, or contribution to the knowledge of the origins, or development of history of that people.

The focus of executive and international agreements was on Third World nations, tribal, or nonindustrial societies. At the same time, Third World nations and indigenous peoples were also creating their own laws and local ordinances to protect their patrimony and cultural properties. In the United States, most states have never written or revised statutes that would protect Native American and Hawaiian burial sites. In some states, statutes require private landowners to report the presence of burials on their land to a state agency and participate in repatriation of remains to the appropriate Indian community or tribal government authority. The Native American Graves Protection and Repatriation Act (NAGPRA), enacted in 1990, is to date the most comprehensive law concerning the disposition of cultural properties and patrimony of Native Hawaiians and Native Americans. NAGPRA and its provisions have been heralded as the single-most important piece of national cultural property legislation ever adopted by the United States. Among its provisions are four specific categories of cultural property that are subject to repatriations: (1) sacred objects, (2) objects of cultural patrimony, (3) human remains, and (4) funerary objects. Sacred objects include specific ceremonial materials needed by Native American religious leaders for the practice of traditional Native American religions by their present-day adherents. Cultural patrimony includes materials that have ongoing historical or cultural importance central to an Indian tribe or Native Hawaiian organization. The Native American group must have considered objects of cultural patrimony inalienable at the time the object

was separated from such group. Human remains includes the physical remains of a human body of a person of Native American ancestry. Funerary objects are items that were placed with or near individual human remains at the time of internment or at a later time as part of a death rite or ceremony of a culture. As national cultural-property legislation, each of NAGPRA's provisions has a corollary in traditional U.S. property law. NAGPRA does ensure that Native American property rights are acknowledged and respected along with those of all Americans. The implementation of NAGPRA rests with the collaboration and cooperation of all parties directly involved with the use, care, and protection of tangible and intangible cultural properties.

In the international arena, efforts continue toward resolving the ongoing theft of cultural properties, unlawful excavations, and illegal export of national and community-specific properties. In 1993, the Institute for the Unification of Private Law drafted the *International Return of Stolen or Illegally Exported Cultural Objects*. This document, which has taken the form of a treaty agreement, is under consideration by member states.

In addition to the legal and political issues associated with the protection of patrimony, there are also the humanistic considerations of mutual understanding and mutual respect. Many of the discussions to date have been about finding acceptable language for writing policy or developing an agreeable set of guidelines that meet the intent of laws or acts. Nation-to-nation, government-to-government, and person-to-person interactions and consultations over disposition of cultural patrimony have required increasing levels of mutual understanding and mutual respect between and among parties who are working diligently toward finding a common ground. This process and the growing awareness of the historical experiences and the perspectives of others is long overdue and may serve to inform humankind on how best to preserve an essential element of its identity and heritage: its patrimony.

HARTMAN LOMAWAIMA

See heritage; intellectual property rights; repatriation.

pattern books. See architectural pattern books.

peculiar institution. According to *A Dictionary on Americanisms*, the first usage of this term in print occurred in 1842, in James S. Buckingham's book *The Slave States of America*, published in London. Buckingham wrote: "Slavery is usually called here 'our peculiar institution.'" The term appeared again in 1856 in *The Literary Messenger* (XXII, 243/1): "There is a certain class of minds who see in every effort of the kind, some imaginary thrust at the 'peculiar institution.'" The phrase was also a code for slaves themselves. In 1860, the *Charleston* (S.C.) *Mercury*, on 11 December announced: "I met . . . the 'peculiar institutions' carrying lightwood up the back steps. . . ."

University of California historian Kenneth Stampp wrote his book about American slavery, *The Peculiar Institution*, in 1956 (N.Y.). The term has been in common use since then.

pension records. See military service records, Canada; military service records, U.S.

Pentecost. Pentecost is celebrated by Jews seven weeks after the second day of Passover; it is called Shavuous. Christians celebrate Pentecost on the seventh Sunday after Easter. It commemorates the descent of the Holy Spirit on the Apostles and is also called Whitsunday.

Pentecostal. Named at the beginning of the twentieth century, Pentecostal Christians have few doctrinal differences with the tenets of their original denominations. They participate in exuberant worship services in which they experience God's immediate presence by speaking in tongues, called *glossolalia*, a phenomenon that occurred among Jesus' disciples at Pentecost. Pentecostals also believe in divine healing and a small group, starting in 1909 in Cleveland, Tennessee, practiced snake handling. See George W. Dollar, *The New Testament and New Pentecostalism* (Minneapolis, 1978).

perambulation. We associate the word "perambulation" with William Lambarde (1536–1601), author of *The Perambulation of Kent*, published in 1576 and regarded as the first work of local history. This term came into common use in England, before the publication of Ordnance Survey maps in the later eighteenth century, to designate an annual walk around the boundaries of a parish with the rector who would recite prayers at various points. Used today, the word means leisurely walking, during which one can gain a close knowledge of a geographic region, its botany, topography, and recorded history.

See editorial, *History News* (summer 1997).

philanthropy. A natural topic for local and community historians, for, as Robert H. Bremner shows in his book *American Philanthropy* (2d ed., Chicago, 1988), philanthropy is an essential and defining aspect of American culture, and thus it looms large in the history of a locality. The investigation of philanthropic activities also provides insights into the values and attitudes of the locality involved, including ways in which the philanthropic values and the volunteer associations they generated served as a cement to bind the community together, a process Don Harrison Doyle illuminated in *The Social Order of a Frontier Community: Jacksonville, Illinois, 1825–70* (Urbana, 1983). In addition, there is likely to be a wide variety of pertinent sources available.

What is meant by philanthropy? It is volunteer activity in the fields of charity, relief, and social, educational, and humanitarian reform. (Since religion and education are topics unto themselves, they are excluded from this article.) Thus, through philanthropy we can look at the work of individuals and of organizations that have tried to make their community, or the world, a better place. That can mean taking care of the destitute and needy (food, shelter, medical care, child care, health care), providing tools to help people help themselves (as in a settlement house or educational programs), and the development of parks and recreational features,

libraries, and other cultural institutions. Another significant aspect of the subject would be relief activities, such as relief for victims of natural disasters, war, or economic catastrophes.

What kind of sources are likely to be available? Much philanthropy is generated by organizations, and they leave records—minutes, correspondence, newsletters, etc. Philanthropy is often driven by one or a group of individuals, so one could look for their papers and recorded comments. Since many philanthropic activities are at least semipublic, there might be material in local governmental units, such as county, city, school district, or special district archives. National and state governments often collected and published statistics and other material on particular philanthropic topics. Since much of the activity of charitable organizations is relatively public, newspapers and, where they exist, local magazines, can be very fruitful sources for information.

How might a local historian approach some of these topics? One way is to develop the history of a charitable organization in the community, as Thelma Lee Hubbell and Gloria R. Lothrop did in "The Friday Morning Club: A Los Angeles Legacy," *Southern California Quarterly* 50 (March 1968): 59–90, which exemplifies a study based primarily on an organization's archives. Another approach is to look at philanthropy in general. In "The Beginnings of Philanthropy in San Diego, 1900–1929," *Southern California Quarterly* 71 (summer/fall 1989): 227–73, Raymond Starr drew mostly on secondary sources to summarize the large extent of philanthropy in San Diego. He pursued the thesis that to a great extent philanthropy shaped the nature and identity of that locality, and also used the topic as a mechanism to explore the cultural roots and nature of the community as well. The article illustrates many of the kinds of topics included in the subject, and suggests many kinds of pertinent sources. For an example of how the study of an individual philanthropist can illuminate both local and national history, see Gregg Hennessey, "George White Marston and Conservative Reform in San Diego," *Journal of San Diego History* 32 (fall 1986): 230–53, in which the author makes good use of an individual's written records to tell his story.

RAYMOND STARR

photography. Most local history institutions, regardless of size, level of professionalization, and degree of funding, maintain photograph collections. Museums, historical societies, archives, and libraries (academic, public, and special) all collect photographs. It is not uncommon for folklorists, oral historians, and historic preservationists (surveyors, commissions, and lobbyists) to own photograph collections. Also, many offices, both in the government and the private sector, create photographs in the performance of their daily duties. Real estate developers, railroads, and utility companies are just three examples. Photographs are everywhere and can be produced by almost anyone. Due to this abundance, photographs are documents even the smallest, most poorly funded, local history institution can easily acquire.

These collections include many types of photographs as well as examples of many different photographic processes and formats. Common examples include: cased photographs, cartes-devisite, cabinet cards, stereographs, and postcards. They may represent a number of processes: daguerreotypes, ambrotypes, slides, negatives, and polaroids. They can all be useful. At times even a very "bad" photograph, with little to no aesthetic appeal, can serve a useful purpose. The only image left of a house long gone may have a thumb covering the top gable yet still be treasured.

The type of phototgraph and the photographic process used can often help date these images. If the photographer is known, dates relating to a photographer's career, such as when a studio was located at a certain address, can often be used to tentatively date an image. It may also be possible to track the history of the studio, using directories, the census, and advertisements. Images can also be dated by a careful examination of the subjects' *costumes or by other such clues in the photograph. Conventions that apply to painted *portraits also apply to photographs and can be useful in interpreting the image.

Photographs can be exceptional documentary devices. They supply a record of events, places, peoples, and things that may not be documented in any written record. Photographs can, however, lie. A photographer can control what they want the viewer to see and may be shooting with a bias or certain intent. As with any type of document, the truth they are presenting should be confirmed with other source types, if possible.

While photographs may be easy to obtain, they are not so easy to care for. They should be stored in a climate-controlled environment, in archival containers (boxes, folders), protected from light, dust, humidity, and severe temperature changes. Photographs are a very impermanent medium. Differing photograph types also have different storage and processing needs. This should be kept in mind when they are acquired. Photographs can be found in scrapbooks of mixed media and, of course, a wide variety of photo albums. Some of these albums can be inherently destructive to the photos. Beautiful, unique historic images may have been placed in magnetic photo albums, permanently damaging the image and requiring a conservator, and a substantial fee, if it is ever to be removed, and it may never be removed. Yet, this image can still be tremendously valuable to the right researcher.

How a researcher gains access to the images in a photograph collection differs with each facility. Photographs have often not received the intensive cataloging necessary to make them easily available, because cataloging images can be very time consuming. Photographs are almost always unique; they therefore require original cataloging. Many photographs held in archival collections will be arranged by provenance, which emphasizes the office of origin and not the subject matter, making them difficult to access.

Cataloging can be seen as a preservation measure. The more thoroughly an image is cataloged, the less likely it will be handled for inappropriate reasons. If there is no detailed finding aid, a re-searcher would then, in some cases, need to actually look at a large number of photographs to find what they need, thus increasing the potential for damage to the image. Some institutions create surrogate images, either photocopies or copy photos, for researchers to consult in just such situations, keeping the pulling of the originals down to a negligible number.

Photography was invented in 1839; therefore, it is impossible to locate photographs of anything that occurred prior to that time. While this may seem obvious, it is not uncommon to encounter a patron who "must" have a photograph of a person who lived in an earlier period. Color photography did not reach true commercial success until after 1935. Nineteenth-century "color" photographs were hand tinted.

A strong photograph collection can be a wonderful public-relations tool. Probably a more varied group of patrons are interested in pictures than in other types of primary sources. When an image is reproduced for publication, particularly when it is used in a magazine or newspaper, the name of the institution is brought before a new and larger audience. It is very important when allowing the distribution of images, especially for commercial purposes, to always make the patron aware of any *copyright concerns. In an ideal situation, where the donor held the copyright, the rights were signed over to the institution in the deed of gift. But this does not always happen, and it is not unusual for a local history institution to have no idea who holds the copyright for a sizeable portion of their photograph collection. The institution also needs to be aware of any changes, such as cropping, that will be done to the image and will need to decide whether such alterations will be allowed. If an image is to be used in a publication, a credit line should be required. This should be specified in a written policy; it is also wise to request a copy of the final product. The sale of images for reproduction will bring the name of the institution into the public eye, but it can also serve as a money-making venture. Reproduction fees will probably not make an institution rich beyond all dreams, but it might finance a few archival boxes.

The World Wide Web has allowed an increasing number of people to access photographic collections. The best-known example is "American Memory," a product of the National Digital Library Project of The *Library of Congress (<http://memory.loc.gov/ammem/amtitle.html>); however, it is possible for many very small, poorly funded institutions to put a sampling of their collection on the Web, increasing the visibility of their institutions and their holdings. Digitizing a photo collection, or a portion of a collection, is a useful access tool, but it is not a permanent preservation measure, though it does potentially limit the need for access to the original photographs. When an institution places images on the Web, they need to carefully consider whether they want to control who uses their images and in what ways that can be controlled.

Photography is also a way to promote contemporary documentation. It can be especially useful when working with children, but the idea of using adults, perhaps even amateur photographers, should not be overlooked. Sending these interested parties out to photograph vanishing houses, *cemeteries, their own neighborhoods, and local events is a way to promote interest in your institution. It also gives the participants a sense of what history is and may get them to look at their own world in a new way. Further, it may add many useful images to the collection. It is hard to get people to write insightful diaries and letters of value to future historians, but it is not hard to get them to take photographs.

A local history collection's finest photographs not only supply evidence and help to document another time or place, but they also make the viewer think. Thus, they not only assist with research, they also stimulate research. At times images can raise more questions than they answer. Photographs can be very powerful documents; they can move us in a way that most textual documents do not. This is why photographs are worth the time, effort, and expense needed to maintain them.

See Susan Sontag, *On Photography* ([1977] N.Y., 1990); and Michael Lesy's books, *Dreamland: America at the Dawn of the Twentieth Century* (N.Y., 1997), *Time Frames: The Meaning of Family Pictures* (N.Y., 1980), and *Wisconsin Deathtrip* (N.Y., 1973).

The George Eastman House library contains a comprehensive collection of nineteenth- and twentieth-century literature on photography and motion pictures, including important works on the history of photography. There are also more than 400,000 photographs and negatives, dating from the invention of photography to the present, as well as an outstanding collection of early photographic equipment. The George Eastman House International Museum of Photography and the Film is located at 900 East Ave., Rochester, NY 14607; (716) 271-3361, fax (716) 271-3970; <www.eastman. org>.

MARY MANNIX

COURTESY OF THE HOWARD COUNTY HISTORICAL SOCIETY

This photograph is from the collection of the Howard County Historical Society in central Maryland. Until the historical society's acquisition, the photograph was in private hands. It is a gelatin silver print, in a postcard format. The names of the photographers, Holmes & Bishop, are clearly visible in the lower left hand corner. Nothing is known about these photographers.

On the back of this postcard is written in pencil, "Suzanne Bancroft Carroll and CCC at Doughoregan Manor—25th Anniversary." Suzanne is the white woman, CCC is her husband, Charles Carroll of Carrollton. The Carroll family was the most prominent family of this county in the eighteenth and nineteenth centuries. The family's founder was one of Maryland's signers of the Declaration of Independence. The Carrolls are not only a very well-known family at the local level, but also at the national level. Thus, the Carrolls are a well-documented family, and it would probably be very easy to date this photograph if one believes the information written on the verso. Since this photo was in the hands of a branch of the family prior to its donation, the notation was most likely written by a member of the family and may well be accurate. Suzanne and Charles's 25th wedding anniversary was in 1914.

It is very easy to confirm who the white man and woman are, and it would be very easy to obtain basic information about their lives. It would also be easy to confirm the photograph's location, even with the small portion of the structure visible. Doughoregan Manor is an important eighteenth century house, still owned by the Carroll family. One might also find a newspaper account of the anniversary day. However, sadly, nothing is known about the two black women in the photograph. This is all the more ironic and frustrating for, while it is useful to the institution to have such a fine photograph of two members of the Carroll family, the image is most valuable to the institution for its portrayal of the two black women. Not surprisingly, due to this history of the county and the institution, this historical society holds very little primary source material documenting the history of the county's African Americans. This photograph is, therefore, an incredible find, even though these women are unnamed.

It is assumed that the two women were servants at the Manor. Census records should be searched for potential names. Any management records of the Manor, if they still exist and are accessible, may help identify these women. Any diaries, journals, or calendars kept by either Suzanne Bancroft and/or Charles Carroll may offer some insight. Interviewing members of the area's black community, whose families worked at the Manor either as slaves or freedman, could also be useful. On the other hand, these women might have come to the Manor with Suzanne Bancroft when she arrived as a young bride. Research into her family, her family home, and the individuals who worked there may also be called for. There are twentieth-century materials relating to a black family who was affiliated with a branch of the Carrolls; perhaps there is some connection with that family and these women.

This photograph showing two wealthy white aristocrats and two black women dressed in their finest attire, is a striking image. One cannot look at it without wondering what was the nature of their relationships and other intriguing questions. If we could somehow step into the image, into 1914, what sights, sounds, and smells would we encounter? What sort of celebration took place on that day? What was life like on the Manor for its owners and its many servants? The image, like most photographs, is thus a glimpse into the past and a powerful spur to further research.

pietist. Originally this term referred to seventeenth-century German religious persons who emphasized repentance, faith, regeneration, and sanctification. In general, pietists are those who stress the devotional over the intellectual aspects of the Christian religious experience.

place names. American place names provide a deep repository of information about a place and those who named it. The majority of place naming in the United States happened in the last 300 years. These names are newer than their counterparts in the Old World, and so, many of their reasons for use are still accessible.

Place names come in several types. George R. Stewart in his 1970 *American Place-Names* provides a classification scheme by "mechanism of origin" rather than motivation of the namer. There are ten classes in this system, ranging from simple descriptive names (such as Black Rock) to commemorative names (Lincoln City), from manufactured names (Texarkana) to transfer names (Cambridge, Mass.). This system helps in organizing large groups of names and in understanding why places may be named what they are when no other information is available.

The study of place names—toponymy, a subdiscipline of onomastics—is embedded in such fields as geography, anthropology, history, and linguistics, among others. For the local historian, understanding the reason local places were named what they were can help in

PHOTO COURTESY OF JON CRISPIN

understanding what the place was like when first settled, what events occurred there, the attitudes of the folks living there to outside events, or what the place meant to the world outside of it. For example, there are several Moscows in the United States that were named because Napoleon was defeated by the residents of Moscow, Russia, in 1812. This event provided an example of courage and standing up for oneself that folks in their little towns thousands of miles away wanted to be a part of (an example of a commemorative name). Other Moscows were named because folks there had come from places that were already named Moscow (a transfer name). And then there was the Moscow that no longer wanted to be associated with the original one when the 1917 Revolution tainted the name, and so the village in New York became Leicester instead. Why Leicester? To conform with the post office and township already named for Leicester Phelps, the son of a prominent judge.

Much of the study of the origins of names has been done by a variety of researchers, some as graduate theses, others as independent scholars curious to know why places were named what they were. An early compilation is that put out by the United States Geological Survey of the Department of the Interior in 1902, *The Origin of Certain Place Names in the United States* by Henry Gannett (Williamstown, Mass., 1978). Gannett used as his sources a variety of *gazetteers and histories to then put in dictionary form this collection of place-name origins. The New Deal agency, the Works Progress Administration, which published the wonderful *American Guidebook* series for each state in the 1930s and 1940s, had its researchers find the origins of many place names. Much of this work has not been published, but that which has is very useful and comprehensive. See, for example, *Palmetto Place Names* (WPA of South Carolina, 1941). Since these works appeared, there have been many placename books published for most of the country. When using these, it is best to avoid the ones that restrict themselves to "The 1001 Names of..." These cannot tell the whole story. Compilations like Helen Carlson's *Nevada Place Names: A Geographical Dictionary* (1974) are much more useful because in-depth research has gone into the study of every name in the state. The USGS today provides the scholar of place names with the Geographic Names Information System, a searchable database of all the names in the country, some with their name origins. GNIS can be accessed on the Web by going to <www.mapping.usgs.gov>.

People name where they live, first, simply as a matter of identification, but

375

the name they give their place then usually means something more than the words themselves. And place naming continues. Today we see naming going on in suburban subdivisions, in street names, in naming or renaming of hills and mountains and streams. Each version of a place name holds a story that provides an insight into us as we are when we participate in naming the land.

REN VASILIEV

See maps.

Poles. See Appendix A.

political history. "All politics is local," wrote former Speaker of the U.S. House of Representatives, Tip O'Neill. By that he meant that most of the time Americans are firmly rooted in their local traditions and concerns when they participate in the political arena. In his own political life, and in his suggestions to others, as he recounts in his autobiography, *Man of the House: The Life and Political Memoirs of Speaker Tip O'Neill* (1987), O'Neill never forgot to keep in close and constant contact with the local community from which he had come, the Irish neighborhoods of Boston and Cambridge, Massachusetts, never to lose touch with the friends and neighbors with whom he had grown up, and never to forget their concerns. The reward for him and others like him was electoral victory, and the reputation that they took to their graves: that they never forgot where they came from even as they rose to the highest positions within the American political nation.

The notion that all politics is local has more than a public-relations element to

it, or the demonstration of psychological bonding between leaders and those they lead. In O'Neill's statement lies a number of critical components of U.S. politics through the years. First, there are always local matters that take on political weight, for example, local planning decisions, taxation and development issues, as well as matters related to social concerns: schools, local behavioral ordinances and the like. The U.S. governmental process has always vested much power in local governments about these matters, and local power struggles result in sharp disagreements when one person's or group's idea or requested action is unwelcome, useless, or devastating to another individual or group. Roads may connect people to markets, schools, and churches, but they also cut through someone's property or change the quality of life in another corner of a town. Where does one put necessary but intrusive community services? "Not in my backyard" is the familiar refrain of many, despite the general benefits gained by all. Such difficulties lead to extensive debate and battles at the electoral and administrative levels to resolve issues that affect people differently. Robin Einhorn's study of the battles over taxation policy in nineteenth-century Chicago, *Property Rules: Political Economy in Chicago, 1833–1872* (Chicago, 1991), suggests the continuing relevance and power of such local concerns.

O'Neill's claim that all politics is local has another dimension as well. More often than not, political perspectives and electoral choices at the state and national level have traditionally been set by the experiences of individuals in their original social nexus. A number of community studies—for example, Don Doyle's study of Jacksonville, Illinois, in the mid-nineteenth century, *The Social Order of a Frontier Community: Jacksonville, Illinois, 1825–1870* (Urbana, Ill., 1978)—examines how these small-scale socioeconomic dynamics led to political commitments and activity. It is in their formative experiences in home, neighborhoods, and school, that most Americans develop outlooks, commitments, and prejudices, which they then take into larger arenas. The nation's uneasy cultural diversity, often first encountered at home and among neighbors, promoted intense political conflict. Another very useful study by Jonathan Rieder, *Canarsie: The Jews and Italians of Brooklyn against Liberalism* (Cambridge, Mass., 1985), demonstrates how much this remains true in the twentieth century when local battles over housing and schools continue to create searing political confrontations.

In particular, such local divisions led to one's choice of political party. Scholars of voting behavior, such as Paul Bourke and Donald DeBats in *Washington County: Politics and Community in Antebellum America* (Baltimore, 1995), have discovered that amid the closeness of statewide and national elections, at the local level—in townships, wards, and precincts—electoral choice is not all that divided, but highly committed to one party or the other from unit to unit, depending on the ethnic, religious, and economic nature of the people who cluster together in such small-scale places. Different townships, often next to one another, populated by different ethnic and religious

groups, have voted differently from one another and have persisted in such differential behavior over long periods of time.

In short, as Samuel P. Hays has effectively argued in his study of the late nineteenth and early twentieth centuries, *American Political History as Social Analysis* (Knoxville, Tenn., 1980), when people voted Democratic or Republican, for Abraham Lincoln, Grover Cleveland, Woodrow Wilson, Theodore or Franklin Roosevelt, their choice was set less by the quality and nature of the arguments offered by the parties in their national campaigns than by how such arguments were refracted through prisms established in the local neighborhoods where voters had originally ingested their political understanding. It is also of some note how much such refraction was rooted in memories stretching far back in the history of different groups, in the persistent hatred between Irish and British, or Protestants and Catholics, of acts of oppression from long ago, still remembered and passed on from generation to generation. Similarly, Lee Benson's study of New York State in the 1830s and 1840s, *The Concept of Jacksonian Democracy: New York as a Test Case* (Princeton, N.J., 1961), underscores how the tensions that developed between different groups in the New World—between New England "Yankees" and Dutch "Yorkers," for example, as they came in often unfriendly contact in colonial and early national New York over issues never subsequently forgotten—had enormous staying power on the political scene.

U.S. politics always has had a strong

organizational component to it, particularly in the structures and actions of the political parties. Political life in the United States originated in local meetings of the party faithful in town, district, and county conventions, where issues were framed and articulated, resolutions passed, and delegates selected to take each locality's message to the next level of political organization such as state conventions. Local newspaper editors trumpeted their party's cause in a persistent drumbeat of demands, reminders and exhortations addressed to the farmers, workers, and merchants of their neighborhood. Campaign rallies were held in local towns and county seats, addressed by local candidates and reminding everyone of their faith and commitment. Finally, on election day, local party organizers mobilized their followers to get them to the polls, watched over the count at the end of the day, and led celebrations of victory or lamentations about their defeat through the streets and pathways of thousands of local venues. Before the days of radio, movies, and television, such local focus was the heart of the political process and even in a more complicated and far-reaching communications age, many of these activities still occur, echoing moments when much political activity had strong local flavor to it.

That partisan commitment also worked upward to shape the stance of the national parties. Where should power lie in the American situation: primarily at the level of the national government? Or should power be left to state and local governments who are allegedly more attuned to local needs and wishes? Such arguments over the locus of power have remained a constant of U.S. political confrontation over two centuries as the champions of local control of one's destiny have never lost their force even as the power of the national government has grown beyond measure. In the early years of the republic, Jeffersonians championed state and local power against the national commitments of the Hamiltonian Federalists. As many scholars have demonstrated, throughout the nineteenth century Democrats persisted in that commitment to local control against Whig and then Republican efforts to expand the power of the national state. See, for example, my *The American Party Battle, 1828–1876* (Cambridge, Mass., 1999).

Interestingly enough, these arguments between the national parties were always shaped by localist perspectives. Democrats firmly argued that the American nation was a wonderful coming together of distinct localities each of whose individual freedom and security within the nation could only be guaranteed by weak governmental power at the center. In contrast, their opponents argued that only the power of a strong national government could guarantee and advance the economic viability and social security of different communities. In the twentieth century, the positions of the two national parties shifted significantly, the Democrats becoming the party of national power, the Republicans that of state and local predominance, but the nature of the general arguments recognizing the vitality of localist commitments and outlooks remained potent even as the nation dramatically changed.

This persistent localist dimension to political choice, activity, and confrontation, underscores the need for historians to work extensively in local research resources, in small-town newspapers and village courthouse records that help us recapture the issues and events of interest in different places, while providing insight into the perspectives of the people living there. Political historians have learned that they have to reach beyond the large cosmopolitan newspapers, the *New York Times* and the *Washington Post*, to recapture the pith and flavor of what lies behind national outcomes and perspectives. In a research project concerning New York state politics before the Civil War, for example, the scholars involved made sure that they pored over local newspapers, at least one from each party, in every county of the state. These were filled with news of local meetings, of sharp confrontations over one matter or another, with letters and editorials of a highly focused nature, all of which captured, as expected, the localist dimension present, and its interaction with the larger perspectives and issues being argued far away that were shaped and enriched by their origins in the local venues of the state. Research in local historical societies also produced a great deal of biographical and other material, about those politically involved, and the issues and actions that rarely made the larger newspapers or the manuscript collections of national figures. In local libraries, historical societies, and county courthouses, lies much gold for students of U.S. political history.

JOEL H. SILBEY

poll tax. The term comes from *poll*, meaning "head," and is thus a head tax that is levied upon certain classes of citizens—such as adult males or voters. In this it is distinguished from an income tax, property tax, or sales tax, which are based on a person's income, property, or on a financial transaction. Such taxes were common throughout the United States before the Civil War, especially in the colonial period, but even as late as 1923, thirty-eight states still collected a poll tax. Beginning in 1877 the poll tax gained notoriety as the primary means by which Southern states in the aftermath of Reconstruction restricted access to the ballot. Though aimed primarily at ending African American political participation, the poll tax along with a number of other voter qualifications helped disfranchise many poor whites as well. The tax was usually fairly minimal—$1 was common—and was not collected unless the individual intended to vote. Nevertheless, the tax often involved inconveniences designed to limit the number of people who paid. In some states, for instance, voters had to pay the tax up to eighteen months ahead of time. When they went to cast their ballot, they then had to produce proof that they had paid the tax. Moreover, some states required those who paid to also pay for of all the previous years when they were eligible to vote, whether they had voted or not. Because most poor whites and blacks were deeply in debt, such sums proved impossible to pay. State officials did not prosecute those who never paid the tax if they did not attempt to vote, since the penalty for not paying the tax was loss of suffrage. Although upheld by the

Supreme Court for over fifty years, poll taxes for federal elections were abolished after passage of the Twenty-fourth Amendment in 1964. Two years later, the Supreme Court struck down all poll taxes for state and local elections as well.

poormaster. This municipal official, usually elected and funded with tax monies, was in charge of dispensing the dole to those in need.

popular culture. Popular culture is a word-concept often used rather casually and in various ways. It can best be understood in relation to what it is not: high or elite culture, folk or vernacular culture, or mass culture. The first, high culture, has existed for centuries, but received its clearest definition in the nineteenth century as the best that has been thought and said in the world. The second, folk culture, is as old as humankind and refers to a wide range of ordinary and local activities and products, from domestic architecture to the songs distinctive to a particular subculture. The third, mass culture, is a twentieth-century phenomenon made possible by mass communication, mass production, and new technologies of efficient distribution.

Popular culture is usually understood as reaching a much wider audience than folk culture but a smaller one than mass culture. It is associated with commercialized modes of creating and distributing products designed for edification or leisure, such as religious tracts written to disseminate the Protestant Reformation or household objects meant to appeal to the expanding middle class of the eighteenth and nineteenth centuries.

In the United States, popular culture is most closely associated with the entrepreneurial desire to make a profit by filling the leisure needs of people in all social classes. Prime examples would be the minstrel show, the songs of Stephen Foster (and, subsequently, the sale of sheet music), dime novels, wild-west shows (associated with Buffalo Bill, especially), the circus (associated with P. T. Barnum, particularly), burlesque and vaudeville, and participatory sports.

Popular culture has been regarded as more interactive and participatory than mass culture. But there are phenomena that illustrate an era of overlap between the well-established existence of popular culture and the advent of mass culture. Silent film, comic strips, and comic books became mass culture when they become syndicated nationally. Radio became part of mass culture when local stations joined national networks during the 1930s. Baseball played in small communities for the pleasure of the community is popular culture, whereas baseball broadcast on national television exemplifies mass culture. Mass culture is more likely to be spectatorial and often passive by comparison to the participatory aspect of popular culture.

MICHAEL KAMMEN

population statistics. See vital statistics.

portraiture. What distinguishes a portrait from other works of art is the artist's attempt to convey individual character, not just outward appearance.

In looking at portraits today, we may miss that sense of individual character and put it down to the artist's incompetence. Paintings of different individuals done by the same artist often show a familial resemblance because each artist had conventions for painting features that were repeated throughout their careers. However, literary sources suggest that contemporaries saw real likeness in the portraits. In fact, the problem of likeness is a knotty one. The pendulum has swung back and forth between mimesis (imitation of reality) and idealization. Idealized portraits were often tied to a belief that images of heroes should inspire and teach us lessons of civic and moral duty.

If identifying the sitter is a problem, the painting itself may provide clues. The names of the sitters were sometimes included on the frame or written on a plinth or on some other object within the painting. In America, it was common for objects associated with the sitter's trade or profession to be a prominent and identifying part of the composition. Guides to symbols, such as James Hall, *Dictionary of Subjects and Symbols in Art* (N.Y., 1974), may be helpful.

There are many conventions associated with portraiture. Artists often repeated poses, and sitters were sometimes charged extra if they wanted a new pose. Since everything in a painting serves a purpose, a close examination of the entire work is invaluable to an understanding of what the sitter and the painter wished to convey. Wayne Craven, in his article "Colonial American Portraiture: Iconography and Methodology" in *The Portrait in 18th-Century America*, Ellen G. Miles, ed. (Newark, N.J., 1993), suggests studying *etiquette books and dancing manuals contemporary with the portrait. These manuals advised people on how to stand or walk and would have influenced a sitter's pose. The tradition of classical rhetorical gestures was another important influence on both painters and sitters.

Portraits were one of the most common types of American painting in the eighteenth and nineteenth century. While American portraits of the Federalist period and first decades of the nineteenth century were heavily influenced by English models, by the 1830s that influence waned, and sitters preferred a more romantic and intimate image. The 1839 invention of the daguerreotype forever changed the market, allowing many more people the opportunity to commission or own a portrait. However, photographers continued to maintain the conventions of painted portraits.

For small photographs of 4,045 portraits of prominent Americans from the colonial period to the twentieth century, see Hayward and Blanche Cirker, eds., *Dictionary of American Portraits* (N.Y., 1967). If you are trying to locate a particular portrait, see Cuthbert Lee, *Portrait Register* (Biltmore, N.C., 1968).

NORMA PRENDERGAST

See photography; technology.

Portuguese. See Appendix A.

postcards. Government-issued postcards began in Austria in 1869 with the *Korrespondenz Karte*. Some years earlier in the United States, John P. Charlton of Phliladelphia obtained a copyright for a privately printed card decorated with a small pattern. In 1873, the U.S. government issued postal cards of its own, costing one penny each. These were stamped on one side where the address would be added, and plain on the reverse side. Picture postcards in the United States date from 1893. At first these cards carried a picture on one side, the stamp and address on the reverse, and the only space on which to write was around the border. These cards cost two cents to send until 1898, when all postcards could be mailed for one penny. In 1907, the U.S. Postal Service allowed writing on the card next to the address.

The subjects of these first postcards were either sentimental or of particular scenes or buildings, so early postcards are often useful for the local historian in seeing how buildings or streets once appeared. They are often used in "then-and-now books" that document the changes in a community from one time to another. There are a number of books devoted to the cards of a particular locality, and early postcards are sought by collectors.

An annual directory of postcard collections, from those in the Asbury Park Public Library to those in the Wake Forest College Archives, is published by Postcard Collection Directory, Lake County Museum, 27277 Forest Preseve Drive, Wauconda, IL 60084.

Presbyterian Church. See Appendix B.

presidential libraries. Presidential libraries are maintained by the National Archives. Hours of operation vary at each Presidential library and museum. Visitors are encouraged to contact the sites directly for more information. The holdings of each library vary.

Office of Presidential Libraries
National Archives at College Park
8601 Adelphi Road
College Park, MD 20740-6001
(301) 713-6050; fax (301) 713-6045

Herbert Hoover Library
210 Parkside Drive
P.O. Box 488
West Branch, IA 52358-0488
(319) 643-5301; fax (319) 643-5825
e-mail <library@hoover.nara.gov>

Franklin D. Roosevelt Library
511 Albany Post Road
Hyde Park, NY 12538-1999
(914) 229-8114; fax (914) 229-0872
e-mail <library@roosevelt.nara.gov>

Harry S. Truman Library
500 West U.S. Highway 24
Independence, MO 64050-1798
(816) 833-1400; fax (816) 833-4368
e-mail <library@truman.nara.gov>

Dwight D. Eisenhower Library
200 Southeast Fourth Street
Abilene, KS 67410-2900
(785) 263-475; fax (785) 263-4218
e-mail <library@eisenhower.nara.gov>

John Fitzgerald Kennedy Library
Columbia Point
Boston, MA 02125-3398
(617) 929-4500; fax (617) 929-4538
e-mail <library@kennedy.nara.gov>

Lyndon Baines Johnson Library
2313 Red River Street
Austin, TX 78705-5702

(512) 916-5137; fax (512) 478-9104
e-mail <library@johnson.nara.gov>

Nixon Presidential Materials Staff
National Archives at College Park
8601 Adelphi Road
College Park, MD 20740-6001
(301) 713-6950; fax (301) 713-6916
e-mail <nixon@arch2.nara.gov>

Gerald R. Ford Library and Museum
Gerald R. Ford Library
1000 Beal Avenue
Ann Arbor, MI 48109-2114
(734) 741-2218; fax (734) 741-2341
e-mail <library@fordlib.nara.gov>

Jimmy Carter Library
441 Freedom Parkway
Atlanta, GA 30307-1498
(404) 331-3942; fax (404) 730-2215
e-mail <library@carter.nara.gov>

Ronald Reagan Library
40 Presidential Drive
Simi Valley, CA 93065-0600
(805) 522-8444; fax (805) 522-9621
e-mail <library@reagan.nara.gov>

George Bush Library
1000 George Bush Drive West
College Station, TX 77845
(409) 260-9554; fax (409) 260-9557
e-mail <library@bush.nara.gov>

primary and secondary sources. A primary source, in handwriting, voice, or print, is one created contemporaneously with an event or later by witnesses to an event or an era. This is the material by which history is known.

A secondary source is one that is conscientiously created to record or explain an event, person, trend, or place using all available material, including primary sources. A diary is a primary source; a book about diaries or one relying upon the information in a diary is a secondary source.

In examining the materials with which local historians work, J. D. Marshall has developed an interesting argument that local historians are prone to believe that "facts": that is, information from primary sources are more important than arguments or ideas about the facts. He calls this a form of "primitive antiquarianism," as opposed to scholarship. Marshall deals with this in chapter 3, "The Problem of Antiquarianism," in his book, *The Tyranny of the Discrete: A Discussion of the Problems of Local History in England* (Louth, Lincolnshire, Eng., 1997). This is an interesting and valuable book with which many historians will heartily disagree. That is, of course, no reason not to seek it out.

Protestant Episcopal Church. See Appendix B.

public history. Public history is a relatively recently defined field of history. Most public historians credit the late Robert Kelley of the University of California at Santa Barbara with coining the phrase "public history" in 1976, and with creating the first graduate program to train historians in this new area. Kelley was a traditionally trained and academically employed historian who discovered that his particular knowledge of *water policy in California interested attorneys and policymakers who wrestled with contemporary problems and disputes over that limited commodity in the West. Kelley's experience working in the legal arena combined with the shrinking academic market for historians in the 1970s convinced him that historians were ignoring an opportunity to revitalize their profession.

Professor Kelley and his colleague, G. Wesley Johnson, pioneered the practice of public history by producing the first academically trained public historians. Johnson and Arnita Jones, executive director of the National Coordinating Committee for the Promotion of History, furthered the public history movement in the late 1970s by helping to found a professional organization, the National Council on Public History (NCPH). The NCPH organized in 1979 and incorporated in Washington, D.C., the following year. At its second annual conference in 1980, the NCPH voted to make the newly minted professional journal, *The Public Historian*, the organization's official publication.

Robert Kelley defined public history in the first issue of *The Public Historian* as "the employment of historians and the historical method outside of academia" (Robert Kelley, "Public History: Its Origins, Nature, and Prospects," *The Public Historian*, vol. 1 [1978], p. 16). Kelley and other early public historians recognized that historians have worked professionally outside of the academy at least since the 1930s, principally at publicly funded historic sites. But, in the academic job crisis of the 1970s and early 1980s, many established historians saw the emergence of public history as a vehicle for the employment of graduate students in new venues. One of the best-known anthologies on public history, *Public History: An Introduc-*

tion, published in 1986, acknowledges the vocational aspect of the field by illustrating the wide variety of jobs held by historians outside the university. The authors of *Public History* reflect the diversity of public historians, many of whom work for corporations, public and private museums and historical sites, as well as for federal, state and local agencies.

Many introductory syllabi for public-history courses still define the field as a function of employment. However, this definition is far too narrow for most practicing public historians. When not employed as academic historians, public historians gain very little commonality of purpose or perspective by using a definition of what they are not. It is also inaccurate in that many public historians hold at least adjunct status at universities. The presence of a substantial number of directors of public history graduate programs in the National Council on Public History also suggests that public historians cannot and should not dissociate themselves from their academic brethren. As public historians have engaged with their "publics" during the last quarter of the twentieth century and have honed their skills, they have increasingly recognized the importance of broadening the field's definition.

Methodological emphasis is one way to further define the nature of public history. Public historians are quick to note that they are professional historians first and public historians second. They are trained to employ the same methods and analytical approaches that all historians utilize. A reliance on primary-source material, the critical comparison of documentary evidence, and a healthy dose of skepticism characterizes the work of the public historian. But a willingness to operate outside the sometimes-narrow focus of academic history has allowed public historians to experiment with sources and approaches not usually found in a traditional graduate program. Public historians have been quick to embrace the analytical techniques of other disciplines, such as archaeology, anthropology, geography, as well as numerous natural sciences. You are as likely to find a public historian working in the field with a hard hat or a compass and alidade as you would sitting in a library perusing a manuscript collection.

Although interest in these allied disciplines is not unique to public historians, they have often been more willing than their academic brethren to recognize the value of an interdisciplinary approach to historical inquiry. This methodological openness translates into an acceptance by public historians of the "team approach" to research. The use of historical or interdisciplinary research teams is one of the principal features that distinguish public history graduate programs from graduate training in other fields of history.

The method of public history also includes the way in which historical thought is communicated to various "publics." Public historians are sensitive to their audience and many would suggest that the way in which we define our audience differentiates public history from other fields of history. While many historians have been criticized for a tendency to write only for their colleagues, public historians recognize the impor-

tance of demonstrating the value of historical thinking to larger groups and interests. This point is ably demonstrated in another classic anthology of public history, *Presenting the Past: Essays on History and the Public* (1986), which continues to be used in many introductory public history courses.

All historians employ similar means to communicate their findings through reports, books, lectures, and displays in multimedia format. But the published monograph remains the principal means of disseminating historical knowledge in an academic setting. Public historians, of necessity, have been forced to abandon the traditional written monograph for more accessible modes of communication. Public historians look first to their nonhistorian audience when devising a scheme for what Leslie Fishel has called the "delivery" of history ("Public History and the Academy," in Barbara J. Howe and Emory L. Kemp, eds., *Public History: An Introduction* [1986], p. 11). They incorporate the oral record, the visual arts, and an interpretation of physical remains as often as they reduce their findings to a written report or a book. The emphasis is on ensuring that history reaches as wide a community as possible and public historians are not bound to a particular format to accomplish this goal.

Public history has distinguishable features that set it apart from other areas of history. However, as the field matures, fewer practitioners look to those aspects of their work that separate them from other historians. Rather, they focus on the skills and insights into the past that draw all historians together. Public historians are not confined to any particular topical or geographical area of history. Although it is true that many public historians have long-standing connections to local history—given the interest in employing public historians shown by local historical groups, museums, and interpretive sites—the field also has a growing international perspective. Public historians in the United States have forged strong links to their counterparts in Canada, Australia, and New Zealand, as well as to colleagues in Europe, where they are often known as "applied historians." In many respects, public historians now see themselves not as defined by where or how they work, but by their interest in making professional history more visible and accessible to larger numbers of people. In this sense, public history may be characterized more as an attitude or perception about the use and value of history, than as a distinct field of history.

The National Council on Public History, as the premier organization for public historians, reflects this conceptualization of public history. The NCPH is not the first or the only organization that represents public historians. National groups, such as the Society for History in the Federal Government, and local organizations, such as the California Council for the Promotion of History, attract public historians. There also are working committees on public history in the two major historical organizations, the *American Historical Association and the *Organization of American Historians. But the NCPH is an organization that views itself as an "umbrella" group, capable of representing the broad interests of all

practitioners of public history. Through annual meetings, publications such as *The Craft of Public History: An Annotated Select Bibliography* (1983) and *Careers in Public History* (1989), and through advocacy, the NCPH seeks to provide what one past NCPH president has called "common ground" for the gathering of all historians who recognize "that history matters" (Philip Scarpino, "Common Ground: Reflections on the Past, Present, and Future of Public History and the NCPH," *The Public Historian*, vol. 16 [1994], p. 21).

See James B. Gardner and Peter S. LaPaglia, *Public History: Essays from the Field* (Malabar, Fla., 1999); Susan Porter Benson, Stephen Brier, and Roy Rosenweig, eds., *Presenting the Past: Essays on History and the Public* (Philadelphia, 1986); Barbara J. Howe and Emory L. Kemp, eds., *Public History: An Introduction* (Malabar, Fla., 1986); David F. Trask and Robert W. Pomeroy III, eds., *The Craft of Public History: An Annotated Select Bibliography* (Westport, Conn., 1983).

ALAN S. NEWELL

publishing local history with a specialty publisher. Local history publications have a limited audience and market. This is a major factor in choosing a publisher for a local history. Specialty publishers are small companies that devote most of their resources to one subject area. Some publishers are retail oriented, others sell to private markets as opposed to the large publishing houses who direct their energies towards a broad, mass market. This type of publisher may be looked upon as a consultant or facilitator. Their responsibility is to make the book ready for production, control costs, and oversee the printer's work.

Most specialty publishers are involved in the creative processes of manuscript development, editing, design, and production. Specialty publishers are smaller companies and devote most of their resources in one subject area of book production. Book packagers differ only slightly from a specialty publisher in that they will take the entire process from the research phase, through manuscript preparation, to the completed book. In preparation for a publisher, several questions must be answered. First, who is the audience? Will this be a pictorial "coffee-table" book or a text with few illustrations? How many words and photos will be included? Will this be an in-house publication or shopped out to a freelance designer? How will it be funded and distributed?

A preliminary draft or detailed outline should be prepared before locating a publisher. This early work will answer most questions and ensure that all the salient details are covered. It will be easier to edit the manuscript at this point than after the contracts have been signed and a word and photo limit imposed. A 30,000-word manuscript means every word, text, captions, appendices, indices, title and dedication pages, footnotes, advertisements, donor/subscriber lists is counted. Every photo is counted as so many words, generally about 250, which represents the space the average photo will occupy in the publication. That means that if additional photos are added, then 250 words will have to be edited out of the

text, or alternatively, additional text can be added by removing photos.

Selecting the mode of production is next. Since the advent of desktop publishing, just about anyone can make a manuscript "camera-ready" for the printer. However, there is more to bringing a book from an idea to a finished product. Publishing in-house is time consuming. This means that the historical society will take the publication from research to writing, copyediting, scanning photographs for insertion into text, proofing, oversight of the printer and bindery and marketing—a long job that will tire even the most dedicated volunteer. Many desktop books have come off the press with muddy illustrations, blurry or too-small type on cheap paper and with a cover that will not grab the purchaser's attention and make the sale. Cost overruns for last-minute changes, corrections, or alterations can make a $20 book double in price. The unforeseen also contributes to the cost.

It is the publisher who provides the expertise to help a client avoid the pitfalls involved in the production of a book. Publishers can handle the design, making the publication pleasing to look at—a major point for sales—and help avoid costly mistakes that escalate the cost of the publication.

In choosing a publisher, several factors should be taken into account: for instance, the track record and timeliness in finishing the project; the quality of the product and materials used, as well as flexibility in printing. How does the color duplication look? Do they electronically "clean up" old photos? Is there quality control from design to the end product? How do they work with the client? How are they on cost containment? Do they deliver on time?

In working with a publisher, the society is responsible for authenticating the historical accuracy of the manuscript. If editorial control is needed along with design control of the project, that should be stated in the contract. It is also the society's responsibility to obtain permission to reprint photos and text that are not their property. It is also a good idea to have an agreement with the author about copyright and reproduction rights.

The publisher will require 25 to 50 percent of the publication's cost at the time of signing the contract. In addition to the basic publishing costs there are author fees, reproduction costs, photo fees, research fees, mailing fees, shipping costs, advertising, and marketing costs.

A marketing plan should be developed from the start. Things to be considered: an institutional sponsor who could receive a prominent place in the book; advertisements could be solicited for inclusion in the book; loans or grants could be sought to help defray costs or underwrite a specific phase of publication; donors could be solicited and receive recognition.

Prepublication sales should begin as soon as a delivery date is set, with a special reduced price to society members. Local booksellers could be contacted to act as outlets. However, in planning the price of the book, it should be taken into consideration that booksellers, especially the larger ones, will want a 55 to 60 percent reduced price, with mailing costs the responsibility of the historical society. Therefore a $39.95 list price would mean that the outlet would want $22 off the top.

PHIL MAPLES

See editing.

Puerto Ricans. See Appendix A.

Q

Quakers. See Appendix B.

R

Rappites. See Appendix B.

recent history. For a long time, many local historians favored research on the origins of a community, especially the settling generation, and initial patterns of development. These are surely important topics, but the later history of a town or village is equally important and recent history cannot be ignored. Relatively few local historical societies or historians deal with the recent past. In some cases this is because of personal preference or because the archives do not support more recent research. These issues need to be addressed. The millennium has spurred a good deal of interest in looking back at the twentieth century, which is certainly a good thing, although research materials will need to be collected.

Some important topics reflect our national history. These concern the effects of Prohibition on a locality; suffrage; war; economic depression and times of economic growth; the turmoil of civil rights; and the abortion issue.

These topics, and many others, allow us to look at the way a local community reacts to change. The sources are in the local newspaper, in local memory, and in documents that are just now appearing, some of them, in local repositories.

Other topics are those that emerge from the locality: a local flood or fire, urban renewal, the consequences of an interstate road or airport, the decline of a neighborhood, or the rise of new housing that creates new patterns, landmarks, and needs. The decline of agriculture in some places, or the loss of a business, are good ways of investigating how a community responds to stress or change. The introduction of new people into a place is another way of looking at community institutions. *Philanthropy has changed over time and is important to understand.

Some topics reveal change over time: how Main Street has adapted and possibly declined, going from being the hub of a town's commercial life to being perceived as a problem to be solved or coped with as the mall draws people away; how the population has dipped and risen over the century and who comprises the mass called the "townspeople." How occupations have changed, from those prevalent in the early census to video and computer stores that dot the commercial landscape today; how culinary habits changed over time, and how the way we have shopped is different now than it was a century ago. Women's and children's lives have also moved in interesting ways; these can and should be documented using printed evidence and also the memories of those people who have lived through shifting ideas about the lifecycle.

The history of the twentieth century is vast and mostly unexplored by the local historian. One of my favorite topics is the point at which the automobile was introduced and the changes it brought about—from the need for street signs and laws, to the shift away from local general stores to shops and services in a larger nearby community; from the ways in which an automobile allowed the family mobility for vacation and sightseeing travel, to the ways in which the family car was used, and who drove it. How the car displaced public transportation in a community is an important story as is how *nostalgia for the trolley, for example, has grown as we tire of cities clogged with cars that we are often unable to park. While scholars look at the *automobile in terms of change and mobility in a larger picture, the local community response to the car has yet to be fully probed.

The twentieth century is very much a blank canvas in terms of our local history. The sources are there for an interesting exploration of this recent time, but sometimes the documents are different from those we have used from earlier eras. One of the advantages of engaging in more current topics is the opportunity to use *oral history to plumb local memories. Another is that local reaction to current topics is often enthusiastic, for suddenly the historical society is touching upon and commenting on the times of their lives.

See sixties (the 1960s and local historians).

regional identity. See regionalisms; virtual shopping.

regionalism. Regionalism and the meaning of "place" have been persistent themes in American history, linking specific geographic locales with the people who have inhabited those spaces. "Place absorbs our earliest notice and attention," wrote Eudora Welty, "it bestows upon us our original awareness. . . . Sense of place gives us equilibrium; extended, it is sense of direction too." A nation always on the move, Americans crave roots; a nation shunning permanence, we dream of a "homeplace."

Lewis Mumford, one of America's most creative thinkers about cities, planning, technology, and the human condition, identified the "region" as one of the cures for the myriad problems of modern twentieth-century America. The region, he argued, with its small-scale patterns of life, ecological and human balance, and traditions of indigenous people, would counteract the ills associated with a stultifying national consolidation, rampant consumerism, economic centralization, and urban decadence. Central to this bulwark was Mumford's conception of the regional museum, which he described in *The Culture of Cities* (N.Y., 1938) as portraying "in compact and coherent form the actual environment . . . the place: the work: the people in all their ecological relations." The mission of such a museum was to give people a way of "coping with the past, of having significant intercourse with other periods and other modes of life, without confining [their] own activities to the molds created by the past."

Mumford's work on regionalism was written in the context of intense public, academic, and governmental interest in regions from the 1920s through the 1940s. There had always been nostalgic reexaminations of particular localities throughout American history, especially in areas undergoing economic modernization and dislocation. The historian Frederick Jackson Turner (see *frontier thesis) and others in the 1890s produced serious studies of the role of regions in American history and life. But the increasing bureaucratization of U.S. society after World War I, and the alarming deficiencies of the national economic system revealed by the Great Depression spurred renewed and widespread interest in the cultural roots of America, in the various regions that collectively defined the nation. Sociologists at the University of North Carolina, Southern Agrarians at Vanderbilt University, New Deal bureaucrats, artists such as Grant Wood and Ben Shahn, writers from William Faulkner to Sinclair Lewis, musicians and composers such as Woody Guthrie and Aaron

Copeland, and many others all looked to the regions to find the meaning of America, according to the historian Richard Maxwell Brown. The objective of much of this examination was reform and renewal, with the implicit (and often explicit) assumption, similar to Mumford's analysis, that what was most vital and real about the United States could be located in the regions.

As relative prosperity returned to America in the 1950s and 1960s, as the Cold War encouraged a consensus interpretation of U.S. history, and as homogenizing influences such as the interstate highway system, television, and the jet airliner seemed to reduce the significance of regional identities, there was a quiescence in the study of regionalism. Since the 1970s, however, regionalism has again received considerable attention. The persistence of distinct regional traits, the increasing interest in local and family history, the revitalization of the historic preservation movement, the academic interest in history "from the bottom up," efforts at decentralization, and ironically, a backlash from the pervasive homogenizing forces of modern society have all contributed to this "new" regional revival.

In addition to a plethora of academic studies of U.S. regions since the 1970s, and new governmental programs aimed at regional collaboration, many universities have established regional study centers such as the Center for Great Plains Studies at the University of Nebraska, the Center for the Study of Southern Culture at the University of Mississippi, and Appalachian State University's Center for Appalachian Studies. Museums and other cultural agencies have also focused on regions and many museums throughout American history have collected regionally. As early as 1820, Cincinnati's Western Museum consciously sought to collect regional artifacts that would instill in the city's inhabitants a regional identity and an unparalleled knowledge of the "region in which our destinies are fixed," according to one of the museum's founders. But the Western Museum quickly failed in its mission, partly due to the lack of financial resources. Under the rubric of "heritage *tourism," more museums are turning to collaborations and partnerships to both fund their missions and to help instill in their patrons a more nuanced interpretation of regional identity. Continuing in the tradition of John Cotton Dana and his innovative Newark Museum, and in ways reminiscent of Mumford's concepts, many museums and historical societies have restyled themselves as "history centers," becoming virtual community centers for a wide and diverse range of regional educational programs.

Broader regional coalitions have been encouraged at the state and federal government level. National heritage areas and corridors, under the sponsorship of the *National Park Service, have sprouted since the 1980s, and represent regional collaborative efforts between historical and cultural organizations to define and interpret the distinctive traits of specific regions. America's Heritage River Program is a similar attempt to encourage a regional identity around the nation's great rivers. Individual states have also started their own *heritage area programs. All of these initiatives are focused on specific historical legacies of

individual regions. But similar to the efforts of the New Deal period, they also include economic and social renewal as principal goals, and closely link *historic preservation, economic (re)development, and tourism. The *National Endowment for the Humanities, in addition, plans in the first decade of the twenty-first century to create ten regional humanities centers across the United States, each to focus on the study of a region's history, people, and culture.

There is a certain contradiction, of course, in this interest in regionalism. At the same time that we Americans demand unfettered mobility, fast-food restaurants, and discount superstores, we also crave rootedness, a "sense of place," authenticity, and distinctiveness. We want Lake Wobegon, but we just hope there's a Wal-Mart somewhere nearby. Michael Steiner and Clarence Mondale, in *Region and Regionalism in the United States*, suggest additionally that the very vastness of the United States creates a paradox, "that the larger and more expansive a nation, the more urgent is the need of its citizens for distinctive regional identities." As Nathaniel Hawthorne once confided to a friend, "New England is quite as large a lump of this earth as my heart can really take in."

This complexity and even ambivalence about regionalism and the "real" America, however, is the type of issue of immense interest to a new breed of regional scholar. Steeped in such fields as American studies, postmodernism, and cultural studies, these researchers study not only the "reality" of a region's past, but also more amorphous topics such as how regional identity and consciousness are formed, the "invention" of region, regional relationships of power, and the shifting and overlapping definitions of regions. Edward Ayers and Peter Onuf, in *All Over the Map: Rethinking American Regions*, remind us, for example, that U.S. regions "were never bounded and complete entities."

Instead, regions "have always been complex and unstable constructions, generated by constantly evolving systems of government, economy, migration, event, and culture." Regions are not, and never were, static entities, and a certain measure of flexibility is thus required in their study.

Most of all, however, regional study requires an intimate knowledge of place. In *A Continuous Harmony*, Wendell Berry wrote of his understanding of regionalism:

The regionalism that I adhere to could be defined simply as local life aware of itself. It would tend to substitute for the myths and stereotypes of a region a particular knowledge of the life of the place one lives in and intends to continue to live in. It pertains to living as much as to writing, and it pertains to living before it pertains to writing. The motive of such regionalism is the awareness that local life is intricately dependent, for its quality but also for its continuance, upon local knowledge.

The search for local knowledge, for regional renewal, for answers to complex questions about region, for the identification and preservation of distinct regions, is "every American's search," according to the geographer Pierce Lewis, "for reassurance that there are places, however remote, that will survive our frenetic passion for mobility, places where we can go and find the genius loci, alive, healthy, and benevolent."

See Charles Reagan Wilson, ed., *T. New Regionalism* (Jackson, Miss., 1998) John L. Thomas, "Coping with the Past: Patrick Geddes, Lewis Mumford and the Regional Museum," *Environment and History* 3 (1997): 97–116; Edward Ayers, Patricia Nelson Limerick, Stephen Nissenbaum, and Peter S. Onuf, *All Over the Map: Rethinking American Regions* (Baltimore, 1996); Alvin Rosenbaum and Marcy Mermel, "Why Now is the Time to Rethink Regionalism," *Colloqui: Cornell Journal of Planning and Urban Issues* 10 (spring 1995): 31–37; Barbara Allen and Thomas J. Schlereth, eds., *Sense of Place: American Regional Cultures* (Lexington, Ken., 1990); Michael Steiner and Clarence Mondale, *Region and Regionalism in the United States* (N.Y., 1988); M. H. Dunlop, "Curiosities Too Numerous to Mention: Early Regionalism and Cincinnati's Western Museum," *American Quarterly* 36 (1984): 524–48; Richard Maxwell Brown, "The New Regionalism in America, 1970–1981," in William G. Robbins, Robert J. Frank, and Richard E. Ross, eds., *Regionalism and the Pacific Northwest* (Corvallis, Ore., 1983), pp. 37–96; Pierce Lewis, "Defining a Sense of Place," *Southern Quarterly* 17 (spring/summer 1979): 24–46; Jay Mechling, "If They Can Build a Square Tomato: Notes Toward a Holistic Approach to Regional Studies," *Prospects* 4 (1979): 59–77; Wendell Berry, *A Continuous Harmony* (San Diego, 1970); Merrill Jensen, *Regionalism in America* (Madison, Wis., 1951); and Lewis Mumford, *The Culture of Cities* (N.Y., 1938).

DEAN HERRIN

See Appalachia; Midwest; regionalism, approaches to; regionalisms.

gionalism, approaches to. Regionalism is the concept that cohesive geographical areas that do not correspond to established state or national boundaries provide useful categories for either economic planning or academic study. Regionalism as an economic-development tool thrived during the New Deal in the 1930s and produced the internationally famous Tennessee Valley Authority. The Delaware River Basin Commission, Appalachian Regional Commission, and over a dozen other federally sponsored regional planning groups were created in the 1960s and early 1970s. Several regional entities have been organized by state governments without federal sponsorship.

Academic study of regions takes several forms. Every well-established discipline in the humanities and social sciences has produced its own library of regional monographs. In three disciplines, writing on regional subjects is especially rich. Students of language and literature have analyzed regional dialects, have created a subfield of English that concentrates on *"local color" writers such as Mary Murfree, Sara Orne Jewett, and Bret Harte, and in general have accepted regionalism as a helpful intellectual instrument in making sense of the spoken and written word. Geographers are even more dependent on regionalism. By definition concerned with differences defined by space, they have a long tradition of emphasizing the limited usefulness of looking at the world, continents, or individual nations primarily in terms of governmental boundaries.

The third discipline is history. Time serves historians just as space serves geographers. Regions have always had a high profile in writings about American history. The concept of *New England dates from the seventeenth century. The idea that the United States can be divided into culturally distinct Northern, Southern, and Western regions originated in the early national period. As settlement spread across the Great Plains and the Rocky Mountains, the original West became the *Midwest, and historians began writing about regions they labeled the "Far-west" or "Pacific Northwest." The world of professional historians accepted both the "history of the South" and the "history of the West" as areas of specialization in which one could get a Ph.D., expect to find jobs advertised, and write for journals devoted to scholarship on their regional field. Regionalism, in short, plays an important basic role in the world of historical writing and teaching.

Local historians can benefit from consulting the literature of regionalism. One challenge facing anyone trying to write family, neighborhood, town, or county history is to explain how events and broad patterns of change outside their specific geographical subject helped shape what took place locally. For example, someone writing about a family living seven generations in a Georgia county should not only know a reasonable amount about state and national history, but should also consult relevant entries in the *Encyclopedia of Southern Culture* (Chapel Hill, N.C., 1989), Charles Wilson and William Ferris, eds., and in the *Encyclopedia of Southern History* (Baton Rouge, La., 1979), David Roller and

Robert Twyman, eds. Allan Carpenter has produced encyclopedias on the Mid-, Central-, and Far-west. A four-volume *Encyclopedia of the American West* by Charles Phillips and Alan Axelrod came out in 1996; an updated version of Howard Lamar's encyclopedia on the same region was issued in 1998. Local historians may also find useful sections from the dozens of both popular and academic history books about specific regions in print at any one time.

Many books about regions in general and regionalism itself have also been published. They include Richard Broadhead, *Cultures of Letters* (Chicago, 1993); Robert Dorman, *Revolt of the Provinces: The Regionalist Movement in America, 1920–1945* (Chapel Hill, N.C., 1993); Michael Bradshaw, *Regions and Regionalism in the United States* (Jackson, Miss., 1988); Michael Steiner and Charles Mondale, *Region and Regionalism in the United States: A Sourcebook for the Humanities and Social Sciences* (N.Y., 1988); and Martha Derthick, *Between State and Nation: Regional Organizations in the United States* (Washington, D.C., 1974).

JERE DANIELL

regionalisms. Regionalisms are those words in a language whose use is restricted regionally. A regionalism may be restricted to a multistate region of the country, a single state, part of a state, or even to an individual city. Even a word common to many parts of the country may be a regionalism as long as it is not common in the country as a whole. For instance, although the word "icing" is used across the country, it is a regionalism since it is used less frequently in the northern and Pacific regions of the country. The word's synonym, "frosting," also ranges across the country, but its use is infrequent in the southern half of the country and heavy in the northern and western regions. This example shows that a person from New England or California is much more likely to use the term "frosting" in cases where a person from the South would probably use "icing." Interestingly, the synonymous term "filling" is found scattered across the Southern states. We can establish these facts because of the intensive work in linguistic geography that has taken place over the last several decades. Linguistic geography carefully plots the regional distribution of words, so that we can confidently state that someone using the term "Kaiser blade" (a swingblade) in casual conversation probably lived in the lower Mississippi Valley, and most likely in Mississippi itself.

People often portray regionalisms as quaint dialect terms, interesting only for their divergence from the standard dialect of a language. But such words do the important business of communicating and have most of their value as an object of study because of the light they shed on the people using the words. Such words can show us interesting distributions of words, a region's solution to lacunae in vocabulary, and a region's interest in maintaining a separate identity. Regionalisms can serve as a way for a group to form a separate geographic identity, and as such they are common in both the rural and urban sections of the country.

As with any words, regionalisms do not maintain an immutable status within any speech community. Some escape the province of one region and become standard terms. For instance, "enchilada" was once considered a regionalism confined to California and the Southwest, but now it is a standard food term in American English. Also, these regional words do not remain in use indefinitely. With the change of generations, we add new words to our vocabularies as others slip away. The Rhode Island term, "eaceworm," meaning "earthworm," is now obsolete, though it was once considered that state's most common term to describe that animal. "Elbedritsch," a Pennsylvanian term for the quarry of a snipe hunt, is beginning to drop out of currency.

Increased mobility and the rise of the mass media over the course of the twentieth century have led to the diminution of regional differences in speech in the United States, but linguistic shibboleths remain. During President Clinton's first term in office, he used the term "Adam's off-ox" to the consternation and bemusement of much of the national media. Used chiefly west of the Appalachians and common in Arkansas, this term is usually used in phrases like "I don't know him from Adam's off-ox." Although everyone understood what Clinton meant by this term, few people in the media were familiar with it or even understood that an "off-ox" is the ox on the righthand side (the far side from the point of view of the driver) of a yoke of oxen.

The range of some regional terms is determined by natural geography itself. For instance, the term "muscadine," a type of American grape, is confined primarily to the range of the fruit itself. A "blue northern" is a cold northern wind that signals a rapid decrease in temperatures and is restricted to Texas, which is where that wind occurs. Similarly, "chinook" is used in the Northwest to describe a wind in that part of the country. The range for the term "fox and geese" (a game designed to be played in the snow) is isolated to the northern, snowy states. The range of "Jersey mosquito" (any large mosquito) is limited almost entirely to New York, New Jersey, eastern Pennsylvania, as well as to the southern New England states, where the word in fact appears to be common.

Some regionalisms arise because they describe an activity limited to or more common in one part of the country. For instance, the verb "fire-hunt" (to hunt animals by shining lights in their eyes at night) is found chiefly in the southern and midland parts of the country, indicating possibly that the activity is more common there than elsewhere. In North Carolina the synonymous term "fire-lighting" is the common term. The near-synonymous "headlighting" is used chiefly in Texas and northern Michigan. "Forty-two" is the name of a card game apparently invented and played almost exclusively in Texas. Although known in other parts of the country, the true range of "lutefisk" centers on Minnesota and its surrounding states and almost nowhere else, since this delicacy is common where Scandinavian immigration was common. The word "baga," a foreshortening of "rutabaga," is common in Michigan, Wisconsin, and Minnesota, probably in part because that is a region of the country where the vegetable is more commonly consumed.

Foreign languages are often the source of regionalisms, since different regions have had contact with different languages. "Motte," restricted almost entirely to Texas, means "a grove of trees, especially if in an open prairie." The source of this word is believed to be the Norman English word "motte," which Irish immigrants brought to Texas in the nineteenth century. "Haole" is a common Hawaiian-language word used in English to describe non-Polynesians, especially whites. The term "killifish" describing a small minnowlike fish, appears isolated to extreme southeastern New York state, especially Long Island. The first element of this term is the Dutch "kill," meaning stream, and this term remains a current regionalism and is common in geographic names throughout the Hudson Valley and other areas of Dutch settlement. "Lagniappe," with its myriad pronunciations, is found chiefly in the Gulf states and especially in Louisiana, since that is where the French language had the greatest effect on the language. The term "gumband" (derived from the German *Gummiband*, meaning a rubberband) is now rare but was used chiefly in Pennsylvania, where the German language continues as a presence.

Many regionalisms serve as examples of a region's inventiveness in naming parts of their world. "Hallway" is used most frequently in Tennessee to mean the aisleway or open space in the middle of a barn or, by extension, the space between two buildings. "Darning needle" is a term for dragonfly that is especially common in New York and New Jersey. The similar term, "devil's darning needle," has a similar regional distribution but is much rarer. The use of the term "mall" meaning a highway median strip was almost entirely restricted to upstate New York, just as "maniportia" (*delirium tremens*) is restricted to Maryland. Similarly, the term "dropped egg," meaning "poached egg," is virtually restricted to New England. The word "duck," used to mean "cigarette butt," is confined to the southeastern United States. The onomatopoetic "jugarum" is used almost exclusively in the Northeast to mean "bullfrog."

With these examples in mind, it is important to remember that errors in identifying regionalisms are rife, even when carried out by professional language watchers making comparisons of national varieties of English, such as British and American English. Also, all speakers of a region will not necessarily use a particular regionalism even if it is common to that region. Absolutes are lacking. For these reasons, any decisions made about regional linguistic variation should be made only with adequate documentary proof and should probably still contain caveats ("used chiefly in Delmarva," "more common in western New York and the upper Midwest," "apparently restricted to the Ozarks," etc.). One of the best sources of information on regional American English is *The Dictionary of American Regional English*, three of whose planned five volumes have been published so far. Although a well-respected and dependable dictionary, some of its conclusions are based primarily on data now decades old, so caution should be used even when using this resource.

GEOFFREY A. HUTH

See slang.

relics. See patrimony.

religion, history of. J. Gordon Melton's *Encyclopedia of American Religion* (Detroit, 1993) contains 1,730 entries. Many of the listed organizations are tiny, scarcely more than moveable office addresses that will disappear before the next religious census. However, the vast array and diversity of institutions that remain suggest a reason why local historians are often the best recorders of what is most interesting about American religious life. Even American churches with large national followings look very different from place to place. American Baptists, with their various conventions and multitude of independent churches, are a classic case in point.

In studying American religion, local historians have sometimes focused on regions. Whitney Cross's *The Burned Over District* (Ithaca, N.Y., 1950) became a model, prompting studies of religion in the Hudson Valley, in southern California, and in *Appalachia. The geographical concentration of some important American religious groups—the Mormons, the Seventh-Day Adventists, the Amish—make them important subjects of local study. For the same reason, Native American religions lend themselves to the talents of the local historian.

From the *region, local historians move down to towns—the communitarians of Amana, Iowa; the Hasidic Jews of Sharon Springs, New York; the Swedenborgians of Bryn Athyn, Pennslyvania; the New Age groups of Sedona, Arizona. Some religious movements erupt for accidental reasons in a particular area and produce sensational headlines—as, for example, the Branch Davidians in Waco. Local historians more properly concentrate on connections between religion and place that develop over a long period of time.

Place can also be part of a large urban landscape. The various ethnic neighborhoods in New York, Boston, Baltimore, Chicago, New Orleans, Santa Fe, and Los Angeles have been sites where immigrants have reinvented the religious traditions of Europe, Asia, Africa, and Latin America. Studies of American Catholicism have long emphasized the local differences that separate ethnic parishes. Robert Orsi, with his studies of the Madonna shrine at Mount Carmel Church in New York City and the St. Jude statue at Our Lady of Guadalupe Church in Chicago, has demonstrated the important cultural issues that can be read from the ritual practices of a single church.

Local historians interested in American religions can make excellent use of interviews. A major challenge is to record oral testimony about the traditions of groups whose written documents are thin. The small African American churches of the South are an example. So are the many scattered Pentecostal churches whose local practices vary enormously. Local historians especially need to collect the written and oral records of recent immigrants to the United States—from Latin America and the Caribbean, from Asia, and from the Near East. These will be enormously important later in understanding Islam in the United States, Catholic vernacular religions of refugees from Central America, and the practices of Asian churches that dot the neighborhoods of all major cities.

In their various endeavors, local historians must not neglect the help they can get from sociologists and anthropologists who are often explicitly trained to focus on the local and particular. Their studies reveal how local history is not parochial history but a chance to interpret religious practice in concrete situations that reveal the connections between the lived experience of religion and large questions about public and private life. Local history has tied religion to family practices, to gender construction, to the creation of class, to nationalism, and to an immense range of other social and cultural issues.

See Margaret Washington, *"A Peculiar People": Slave Religion and Community-Culture Among the Gullahs* (N.Y., 1988); Robert Orsi, *The Madonna of 115th Street: Faith and Community in Italian Harlem* (New Haven, Conn., 1985); Mary Ryan, *Cradle of the Middle Class: The Family in Oneida County, New York. 1790–1865* (Cambridge, Eng., and N.Y., 1981); and Paul Johnson, *A Shopkeeper's Millennium: Society and Revivals in Rochester, New York. 1815– 1837* (N.Y., 1978).

R. LAURENCE MOORE

repatriation. Repatriation refers to the return of culturally significant objects to their country or culture of origin. The future of repatriation as an ethical concept and operational process is clearly embedded in its past. The massive international collecting of objects for personal and museum collections in the post–World War II period led to not only extensive looting of archaeological sites, but also to increases in object smuggling, collection thefts, and the loss of many traditional cultures' material heritage. By the 1960s, these conditions caused serious professional as well as political and social concerns, with both nations and native communities alarmed and outraged by the loss of national treasures, including sacred objects and objects of *patrimony. The resulting 1970 UNESCO Convention urged that nations find better ways to protect their *heritage and to ensure the return of stolen cultural objects to other nations. In the United States, continuing Native American concerns over human remains and cultural objects in museums led to the 1990 passage of NAGPRA, the Native American Graves Protection and Repatriation Act. Other countries—for example, Australia—similarly began to adopt policies or laws regarding indigenous human remains and cultural objects.

But looting, thefts, and smuggling remain major problems, and further steps to control them are being considered. Simultaneously, there has been a sharp increase in the interest of many indigenous people, and their representatives in the United Nations, in seeking the voluntary repatriation of culturally sensitive objects now in museums. In other words, the conditions and concerns that led to the 1970 Convention and to NAGPRA have not disappeared; if anything, they have become more international and at the community level will continue to confront museums as major ethical and perhaps even legal issues. The ethical issue is a human rights concern and centers on the presence of human remains, and sacred, patrimonial, or illicitly obtained specimens in museum collections; the legal issue is already seen in international attempts to create new conventions and agreements on repatriation, as well as in the potential replication of special treaties and customs agreements such as those now in effect between the United States, Mexico, and other nations.

It is also clear that repatriation has sparked new interests on the part of indigenous peoples in other aspects of their traditional cultures, aspects also collected and now in museums and libraries. This currently focuses on the kinds of knowledge and lore best-known collectively as "intellectual property." The growing indigenous community movement to regain control over such property represents another, future repatriation issue that lies on the museum doorstep today.

In general, repatriation is such an important ethical and legal concept that, once underway, it is impossible to imagine that it could be stopped, deterred, reversed, or otherwise eliminated from our professional life. Instead, it is the kind of concept that is likely to lead to expanded perspectives of concern in areas that were not at all originally contemplated. Whether this process will fundamentally change the way in which museum staff and scholars conduct research, document and acquire collections, or even work autonomously all remains to be seen—but all of these are potential outcomes that we must as museum professionals consid-

er when contemplating the volatile future of repatriation.

JAMES NASON

See patrimony; intellectual property rights; museums, and the matter of ethics.

revivalism. The origin of this term seems to be American, for early nineteenth-century British travelers to the United States often commented on encountering revivals or revivalism. Revivalism refers to evangelistic enthusiasm, usually in the form of meetings held to revive or awaken religious fervor. Mrs. Trollope, in her book *Domestic Manners of the Americans* (London, 1832, I, p. 105), described encountering revivals where "they preach and pray all day, and often for a considerable portion of the night in various churches and chapels. . . . This is called a Revival."

See William W. Sweet, *Revivalism in America: Its Origin, Growth, and Decline* ([1944] Gloucester, Mass., 1965); Whitney R. Cross, *The Burned-over District: The Social and Intellectual History of Enthusiastic Religion in Western New York, 1800–1850* ([1950], N.Y., 1960).

See religion, history of.

Roman Catholic Church. See Appendix B.

Romanians. See Appendix A.

Roots. The genealogical novel *Roots* by Alex Haley (1921–1992) was published in 1976 (N.Y.) and in 1977 converted into a popular television miniseries. Its influence was significant, for the book and the film encouraged a great many people who would not previously have thought that they could engage in genealogy to research their family background.

Roots, a mostly fictional account of Haley's search for his family, carries the strong message that "unless we know our ancestors, we cannot know who we are." Historian James A. Hijiya observes that Haley asserted that "who you are is not determined by what you do, but where you come from" ("Roots: Family and Ethnicity in the 1970s," *American Quarterly* 30, no. 4 [fall 1978]: pp. 548–56). Through his research into his family, Haley discovered a sense of ethnicity. Other works, too, asserted that family and ethnic values determined character and action. For some, this has been a positive experience.

But some writers, such as Maxine Hong Kingston (*The Woman Warrior: Memoirs of a Girlhood among Ghosts* [N.Y., 1977]), found ethnic background a burden, which places her, according to Hijiya, in the tradition of those who "claim that there is relatively little influence of the family or ethnic group on the character of an individual." As Hijiya notes, "At stake in this intellectual combat is the idea of the self-made man."

See Nathan Glazer and Daniel P. Moynihan, eds., *Ethnicity: Theory and Experience* (Cambridge, Mass., 1975).

See also ethnicity; genealogy; genealogy, African American; genealogy, Jewish.

Russians. See Appendix A.

S

Sabbatarian. A Sabbatarian is one who keeps the seventh day of the week as holy, as directed by the fourth commandment.

salting the archive. According to the dictionary, salting is the devious practice of placing in a mine a small amount of gold dust or other high-grade ore, in order to make the mine appear valuable. In the case of local history, when we talk about salting, we are not out to deceive; but salting an archive is something to consider if we think of it as finding ways to increase our archival

collections by soliciting letters from people about their lives, encouraging people to keep annotated scrapbooks of community events, suggesting topics about contemporary life about which people might write, or assigning to a photographic group the task of documenting aspects of the community for the society's archives. In these cases, salting refers to a conscious effort made on behalf of collecting materials from our own time in order to represent our era to the future.

See photography.

Sanborn fire insurance maps. Sanborn fire insurance maps are useful but often overlooked tools for local historians. Using these maps, historians can chart the growth and changes of commercial, residential, and industrial areas; they can also refer to the Sanborn maps for valuable architectural and historical information in the preparation of National Register nominations. Many details about the buildings on these fire insurance maps are not available in other sources.

Fire insurance maps first appeared in the United States around 1785. Although maps from these and later companies are available at archives, Sanborn fire insurance maps grew to dominate the business and became the standard fire map in the United States after the founding of the D. A. Sanborn Fire Insurance Company in 1867 (located at 629 Fifth Avenue, Pelham, N.Y. 10803; [914] 738-1649; e-mail <www.sanbornmap.com>). Between 1867 and 1967, Sanborn developed maps for about 12,000 U.S. cities and towns.

The maps are important not only because they featured a standard key of symbols over the years, but also because they were updated on a regular basis, making it possible to trace buildings over time and to identify new or lost construction. Through a complex series of symbols, the Sanborn maps provided information on different types of buildings, including their size and shape, roof type, occupancy, and addresses. The maps were also color-coded to indicate construction materials. The maps were drawn to a scale of one inch to 50 or 100 feet.

The information to be gleaned from the symbols and coding of Sanborn maps is especially useful in the study of urban U.S. development in the nineteenth and twentieth centuries. Local historians can use Sanborn maps to chart the growth of towns and cities, including the changes to individual blocks and neighborhoods. The information from the maps can be combined with *census information, *photographs, *city directories, deed records, and other research material to develop the history of an urban area.

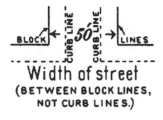

Detail from the Key to Sanborn maps.

The most extensive collection of Sanborn maps is housed at the *Library of Congress (LOC) in Washington, D.C. The LOC collection consists of approximately 700,000 sheets in bound and unbound volumes. Many university and state archives also have collections of Sanborn maps of their local area. The *Union Lists of Sanborn Fire Insurance Maps Held by Institutions in the United States and Canada* provides a listing of such depositories, and many libraries have guides available to aid in understanding the maps. Microfilm copies of the maps can also be purchased from the LOC Photoduplication Service, Chadwyck-Healey, Inc. (800-752-0515), and

Sanborn Mapping (914-738-1649). In 1998 the LOC announced a new program to digitize the Sanborn collection and place the maps on the Internet.

Historians face a few problems when using Sanborn maps. First, microfilm copies of the maps have lost much of the color-coded information of the original maps. Second, many of the maps were updated with paste-on corrections, and the microfilm copies typically do not provide information on the exact date of these corrections. Third, many of the maps are still protected by copyrights, so reproduction for publication requires permission from the Sanborn company. Finally, the company mapped only urban areas; rural areas have little or no documentation in the Sanborn maps.

Information about the maps can be found at <www.lib.berkeley.edu/EART/snb-intr.html> and <lcweb.loc.gov/spcoll/215.html>. See also *Catalogue of Insurance Maps Published by Sanborn Map Company 1950* (N.Y., Chicago, and San Francisco [1949]), in which all the maps issued by the company are listed with guidance to their use.

ED SALO

Schomburg Center for Research in Black Culture. The Schomburg is a national research library devoted to sources documenting people of African descent. The collection was begun in 1926 when the personal collection of Puerto Rican–born Arturo Alfonso Schomburg was added to the Division of Negro Literature, History, and Prints at the 135th Street Branch of the New York Public Library. For six years thereafter, Schomburg served as curator of the collection.

The collection houses arts and artifacts; an archive of manuscripts, archives, and rare books; moving image and sound recordings; and photographs and prints. The library features exhibits and programs, and sponsors a number of conferences throughout the year.

The Schomburg Library is a branch of the New York Public Library. It is located at 515 Malcolm X Boulevard, New York, N.Y. 10037-1801; (212) 491-2200; <www.nypl.org/research/sc/history.html>.

Scots. See Appendix A.

Scots-Irish. See Appendix A.

Scottish local history. Scottish local history is necessarily separate and different from English local history. Until three centuries ago, Scotland was a separate nation. Since the Act of Union (1707) the system of law, the established church and much administrative procedure have been distinct. The new Scottish Parliament, elected in 1999, will only accentuate these differences. The primary sources and the archive depositories run on separate lines.

This has not necessarily worked in Scotland's favor. The Stewart kingdom was lightly administered, with much law enforcement and administration in the hands of the local aristocracy, and of the "heritors" (owners of land). Many of these records have disappeared haphazardly. There is no Scottish equivalent of the Doomsday Book, with its Norman recording efficiency. The demographic records are poor, depending on the luck of surviving parish records. The land records are good, with the institution in

1617 of the Register of Sasines, which recorded all land transactions. Land was the basis of all power in Scotland.

Very often the first good records of a place will be the poll taxes and hearth taxes of the late 1690s. Then in the late-eighteenth century, Sir John Sinclair organized the unique *Statistical Account of Scotland* (*OSA*, or *Old Statistical Account*) of all the parishes of Scotland, which presents a picture, locality by locality, of the basic facts: demography, landowning, economic activity. This is a treasure of Scottish local and national history.

The church records are very important. From the Reformation in 1560 onwards, the Scottish Presbyterian Church ran much of local life: the ministers and kirk sessions kept registers of baptisms, marriages, and—more rarely—funerals. They regulated local morals, keeping notes of local sins and punishments, children in school, ran public announcements, and generally provided the backbone of local life. The survival of these records is patchy, especially in the Highlands where clerical rule came late. For the period before the advent of compulsory registration of births, deaths, and marriages in 1855, the parish records are invaluable.

The main archive center in Scotland is the Scottish Record Office, a splendid eighteenth-century building at the end of Princes Street in Edinburgh. There has been much effort recently to decentralize archive records, back to the archive centers run by the local councils. Local authorities in Scotland, much reorganized in the recent decades, have yet to settle a permanent structure of local archives, and service can be patchy, with both centers of excellence, and dearth of provision.

Local history is left largely in the hands of archivists and librarians on the one hand, and *amateurs on the other. One of the great failings of the academic history community of Scotland has been its lack of interest, and research, in local history; but there are honorable exceptions. Perhaps they have to recover first from the long neglect of Scottish history as a subject—patchily taught in schools—before embarking with confidence into local avenues along continental lines.

There are hundreds of local history and family history societies in Scotland, a few actively engaged in research. Little is coordinated, although the Scottish Local History Forum, a charity run entirely by volunteers, acts as the umbrella organization and publishes *Scottish Local History*.

CHANTAL HAMILL

scrapbooks. Most archives have scrapbooks. Some are valuable sources for research, while others are frustrating collections of pictures or newspaper articles or even mementos from dances and parties that are pasted in, sometimes on top of the book's original contents. These scrapbooks are often difficult to use, although many contain interesting items. What these books do not usually contain are commentaries, explaining the items entered, or the situations in which the mementos were collected.

Yet, scrapbooks are interesting. More than that, they are also a model of what people today might consider as an appropriate way of documenting their own lives. For historical societies that might want to encourage members to keep scrapbooks, a lesson about the necessity of providing context would be appropriate so that modern scrapbooks contain commentary as well as artifacts. A community scrapbook might also be considered, with society members contributing at will to a scrapbook that reflects many people and many different points of view. This might be most appropriate during a centennial season or at a special time, such as at high school reunions and family picnics.

In the 1990s, "scrapbooking" appeared as a hobby, combining an interest in family mementos and their artful design and display. The materials for scrapbooking can be found at craft stores, and include stencils, die cuts, picture frames, theme pages, and other detailing materials to create "memory pages."

See photography; salting the archive.

Sephardic Jews. Jews who originated from Spain and Portugal before the Inquisition; they were the first Jews to come to the New World.

See Appendices A and B, Jews.

Serbs. See Appendix A.

Seventh-Day Adventists. See Appendix B.

sixties (the 1960s and local historians). In dealing with particular periods of history, and especially *recent history, there is always a danger that we will find what we are looking for rather than seeing what actually happened. As an example of the opportunities and

pitfalls open to those who are interested in researching a particular period of time, the 1960s offer a number of pertinent lessons.

In the history of the 1960s there are two kinds of places: those where it is widely known that something important happened, and those where it isn't. The first includes locales like Selma, Alabama, or Chicago; the latter includes the great majority of U.S. communities. Each offers particular chances and challenges for local historians.

An example of the first type is Berkeley, California. Home of the Free Speech Movement of 1964, Berkeley is associated in the popular mind with student radicalism, protest, liberation, and disorder. A history of Berkeley in the 1960s, such as W. J. Rorabaugh's *Berkeley at War* (N.Y., 1989), is bound to focus on the happenings that made the city famous (or notorious, depending on one's point of view). However, Rorabaugh looks beneath the colorful events and carefully explains the social conditions that made those events possible. Remembering that "Berkeley" is a city as well as a university, he examines such crucial matters as racial demographics and municipal government, often presenting his data in maps and statistical tables.

Not every history of a community is so scholarly—or needs to be. Across the bay from Berkeley is a neighborhood that got its fifteen minutes of fame during the 1960s. Not burdened by footnotes or a bibliography, Charles Perry's *The Haight-Ashbury* (N.Y., 1984) vividly describes a district in San Francisco: the hippies, the drugs, the visions, the music, the sex, the underground press, the tourists, the crime, the end. Like *Berkeley at War*, *The Haight-Ashbury* is not a general history of a community in all its aspects but a narrowed study of what gave that community its historical distinction.

Walt Crowley faced a different problem. His city of choice, Seattle, was a vibrant metropolis but not particularly noteworthy in the 1960s. Consequently, his book, *Rites of Passage: A Memoir of the Sixties in Seattle* (Seattle, 1995), is about the sixties in Seattle rather than about Seattle in the sixties. Therefore, much of the book is devoted to events in Washington the city, instead of Washington the state, to Vietnam and the rest of the world instead of to Seattle. What happens in that city seems merely a replication of or reaction to what happens in the famous places like Berkeley and the Haight, and maybe it was. But maybe not.

Maybe the sixties were different in each particular place. Rorabaugh suggests as much. Noting that historians have written few local studies and that, preoccupied with the national scene, they have interpreted society as "unraveling" in the 1960s, he says that his study of Berkeley shows that actually it was only centralized authority, the power of the nation-state, that unraveled. Rorabaugh argues that at the local level "community spirit and individual liberty" actually grew during that decade and continued to do so. Charles Perry challenges conventional periodization in a different way, recording the ceremonial "death of hippie" in the Haight in 1967, a year before *Hair* appeared on Broadway. Thus he shows how the truly hip moved on (and, often,

out of Haight-Ashbury). As one sign at the Wake for Hippie said, "Nebraska Needs You More."

What might be useful now would be histories of communities that were relatively obscure in the 1960s, but histories that make those communities the true center of attention, examining their peculiar internal dynamics and not just using them to supply examples of what presumably was going on everywhere in the country. Instead of striving to ferret out local instances of racial unrest, antiwar protest, and sexual liberation, studies such as these would seek to describe whatever was happening in that community, however hip or unhip those happenings might be. Such histories might confirm existing interpretations of the decade. They might modify the current periodization, showing that "the sixties" did not actually happen in the 1960s. They might even show that in much of the country "the sixties" never happened at all. Did the Haight actually rematerialize in Nebraska?

Because the 1960s are close to the present in time if not in spirit, historical source materials for local history are readily available. It is easy to round up the usual documents: municipal archives, daily *newspapers, etc. In addition, however, there are materials harder to obtain for earlier eras: school newspapers and yearbooks; personal diaries, letters, and *scrapbooks; and, of course, the oral histories of people old enough to remember the decade and willing to talk about it. Here, too, though, the historian must be careful not to restrict attention to the people and documents most likely to illustrate the supposedly typical aspects of the 1960s, but instead should try to discover the actual community, whether it seems like a sixties phenomenon or not.

See Dominick Cavallo, *A Fiction of the Past: The Sixties in American History* (N.Y., 1999); and Allen J. Matusow, *The Unraveling of America: A History of Liberalism in the 1960s* (N.Y., 1984).

JAMES A. HIJIYA

slang. Slang consists of those nonstandard words used in informal speech to mark social or regional identity or identity within a particular interest group. In this way, slang is related to jargon, which consists of the technical terms used by a particular group. Slang focuses instead on words basically used for fun, words used to show the difference between the speaker and the general population. What slang does is set the stage for the level of discourse in a conversation; it declares that the conversation will be very informal. Slang also marks group solidarity. People do not use slang terms to hide information from outsiders, but people outside a group will be less likely to use slang terms from outside their own group. Thus, teenagers would use teenage slang, either within or without their group, to exhibit solidarity with their peers. Although often the province of youth, many other types of groups use slang in this way: the military, sports players and aficionados, sailors, college students, doctors, cowboys, urban blacks, computer users, actors and others in the theater, people living in particular cities, narcotics users, prisoners, etc.

Within some of these groups it is important to distinguish technical jargon from slang. Unlike jargon, slang is not the technical vocabulary of a group or profession, but is jocular, informal vocabulary. For instance, baseball has a large specialized vocabulary, many of whose words are technical terms of some kind ("hit," "error," "shortstop"), but many of which are actually slang ("bases drunk" to mean "bases loaded," "dinger" for "home run," "hot corner" for "third base," and "tools of ignorance" for "catcher's gear"). Note that each slang term is a synonym for an apparently adequate term previously in use. For the most part, slang consists of inventive synonyms for standard words, and some slang terms are little more than manipulated versions of current words ("binocs" for "binoculars" or "spazz" for "a pathetic person, a spastic").

Though sometimes restricted to one region, slang usually escapes the province of one area and moves by slang-railroad across broad speech communities. In New York state, there is a definite movement of youth slang from New York City to the cities of upstate New York. A slang term that is restricted regionally would be considered a *regionalism, but there remain significant differences between the terms. Whereas slang is a language of fun and abuse and invention, a regional dialect develops more slowly, remains longer, and is used for all colloquial conversations. Slang and regionalisms can both separate groups of people, but slang is not necessarily regional. Many slang terms used by the medical profession or teenagers are virtually as popular in all corners of the country.

Slang has long been thought to include nothing but ephemeral terms, but the *Random House Historical Dictionary of American Slang* has proved that some slang terms actually have had lifetimes that have lasted centuries, often without experiencing significant changes in meaning. The term "cool" meaning "suave" has been current slang since at least the early 1920s. The nautical word "barnacleback" for a seasoned seaman remained in circulation at least from 1846 to 1967, quite a long time for an ephemeral term. Jazz musicians of the 1930s invented the term "groovy," which we now generally associate exclusively with the psychedelic 1960s. Most people probably believe that the term "bad" (counterintuitively meaning "good") originated as a slang term in the 1980s, but they would be off by a century.

Most slang terms, however, are quickly replaced in the marketplace of words as the old slang loses its novelty and effect, becoming (in the now-defunct mid-1990 term of North American teenage slang) "played." Few people now would recognize the mid-1850s term "ipsydinxy," meaning whiskey, or the Civil War term "blenker," meaning "to plunder civilian possessions." The teenage term "dope" (meaning "cool") arrived on the scene in the 1980s and is already disappearing. Because of the well-known rapid obsolescence of many slang terms, Hollywood has occasionally taken the protective steps of developing a panoply of slang especially for a particular movie, so that the slang within it would not be outdated by the time the movie was released (see 1989's *Heathers* and 1995's *Clueless*). Although slang words often become archaic, many never quite become obsolete. We

still understand them, though we rarely use them. The real problem with the history of slang is that many terms truly are fleeting, so many are never collected or remembered in any way.

Slang terms can also transform into standard words in the language, especially where the language has no other word to describe the idea. Examples include the very common words, "blizzard," "hijack," "jazz," and "quiz." More commonly, slang terms become the jargon of the professions or avocations that use such slang, just as sports slang occasionally becomes technical terms in the field.

Many slang terms function as terms of opprobrium, the mechanisms for heaping contempt upon others. Many of these terms are vulgar and avoided in polite conversation, but even a modest term like "bootlicker" is full of strong negative connotations. People often fear that this offensiveness is the only use of slang, and they consider this its defining element. Since slang is generally a collection of anti-establishment terms, such words are common, but vulgarity and contempt are not the major function of slang. Principally, slang serves as an important social marker, separating one group from others as it brings that group more closely together.

In local terms, slang is interesting for two reasons. First, there may be regional slang that is interesting to study. Many localities, for instance, have at least developed slang terms for geographical features, well-known buildings, and transportation systems in their area. One of the richest examples of this is Boontling, a slanguage used exclusively in the Anderson Valley of

Mendocino County, California. Originally and consciously designed as a secret lingo—probably for the adults of the valley to speak of sensitive matters without their children understanding—Boontling eventually became a second language of the valley as people learned the language from context. This language probably began in the 1880s and persisted until the teens of the twentieth century, with its zenith occurring in the 1890s. Second, though much more difficult to track adequately, people can study the geographical sources and dates of appearance of slang terms used in a region. For instance, looking at cities in the state of New Jersey, which slang terms common there originated in New York City, which originated in Philadelphia, and which are indigenous to the Garden State? In California, is there a separate development of slang in San Francisco versus Los Angeles?

GEOF HUTH

Slovaks. See Appendix A.

Slovenes. See Appendix A.

smallpox. Smallpox is a highly contagious viral infectious disease, controlled by inoculations. See Ethel L. N. Thorpe, *The Social Histories of Smallpox and Tuberculosis in Canada* (Winnipeg, 1989).

social class. When Americans speak colloquially of "the wrong side of the tracks," they acknowledge the salience of social-class differences in the histories and on the townscapes of ordinary American communities. What has so

long been inscribed in popular speech did not, however, find its way into the earliest written chronicles of town life. The nineteenth-century founders of American local history generally did not examine class differences, even while they established the distinctiveness of local elites through extended discussions of the "leading families," or the "bench and bar" of their towns, or by publishing separate biographical volumes devoted to sketches of wealthy and influential men.

Social class emerged as a significant theme of local history only much later, and then most frequently in scholarly analyses of community life rather than in town chronicles. Pointing the way were several notable sociological studies, the first and most influential being Robert S. and Helen Merrell Lynd's thorough study of Muncie, Indiana, published in 1929 as *Middletown: A Study in Modern American Culture. This book, along with the *"Yankee City" series of studies published by W. Lloyd Warner and his associates (between 1941 and 1959), August Hollingshead's *Elmtown's Youth* (N.Y., 1975), and others, searched for methods through which the residents of a community, their living patterns and institutions, and even their belongings, could be made to speak of meaningful social divisions. All of these were contemporary studies that provided ideas about social class but few methodological insights for historians who necessarily rely on a written record, and on artifacts no longer in daily use. The historians who would eventually inject a class dimension into local history were, for the most part, those interested above all in the formation of a U.S. working class, and who, inspired by work in England by E. P. *Thompson and in America by Herbert Gutman, sought to explore the totality of working-class experience by examining the lives of working men and women in specific industrial and communal settings. Their studies of industrial towns in turn inspired historians interested in middle and upper classes as distinct social formations to turn their attention to local communities. By the 1980s the exploration of social class in specific local settings was an established and well-recognized practice of American academic historians.

Examining class in any community requires an understanding both of conceptual issues and of the relevance and use of specific sources. Concepts of social class are generally of two types: those that interpret class as a derivation of prevailing (in modern society, capitalist) "modes of production," and that, for the most part, stress the binary opposition of employers and employees in a categorically defined two-class society, or those that interpret class as a set of status clusters, or even as a continuum of status differences, as these manifest themselves in the living standards and styles, and in the perceptions and terminology, of any community or larger population. The first, Marxian type of class theory has had its greatest impact on historical studies of working-class formation in industrial communities; it is the organizing principle, for example, of Paul Faler's *Mechanics and Manufacturers in the Early Industrial Revolution: Lynn, Massachusetts, 1780–1860* (Albany, N.Y., 1981). The latter type has informed most sociological studies of American communities, and even where sociologists have stressed the divide between business proprietors and workers (as in *Middletown*, where the authors found "the outstanding cleavage" in the community to be the "division into working class and business class"), they have insisted on a more comprehensive empirical validation of social differences of this sort in the day-to-day lives, the social perceptions, and the sensibilities and ambitions, of those who lived on both "sides of the tracks."

Apart from (but also deriving from) the question of what class means, is the further question of how to examine social differences through surviving and available historical sources. These may be plentiful or scarce in any given community, and the significance of the variation from one place to another is magnified by the fact that there are few national or state sources relevant to the study of local social structures. The most obvious and significant extra-local documents are the manuscript schedules of various national (and in some cases, state) population schedules, which identify the occupation, age, place of birth, race, and in a few censuses the (self-reported) value of real and personal property of each local inhabitant. For some American communities there is also an unusually informative tax register created in pursuance of a national direct tax levied in the year 1798. The types and quality of information recorded on these extracommunity records vary, however, and are available only for specific years. The local historian must examine, for the most part, local records, of which the most useful are official tax, land, and probate records (the latter are especially important where they include detailed *inventories of decedents' goods), local newspapers, records of churches and other local organizations, *maps and *photographs of the physical town and its inhabitants, and, perhaps above all, personal records such as diaries and correspondence, particularly those that name friends and associates, discuss social affinities and divisions, and express social assumptions in an identifiable language of status or class. Few communities, and few archives beyond the community's borders, can be expected to contain collections of sources that yield a comprehensive view of local social divisions and relations; in particular, documents written about and by the poorest and most transient inhabitants are few and far between. But in most if not all, there are the materials for exploring at least some dimensions of inequality, some aspects of social status, and some of those local inhabitants of "the wrong side of the tracks" who were so frequently excluded from the first local histories.

STUART M. BLUMIN

See local government records; mug books.

social history. Once upon a time, early in the twentieth century, most historical writing emphasized political, institutional, military, and diplomatic matters. When the realization dawned that many aspects of history were thereby being neglected, social history came to be defined as "history with the politics left out." In other words, social history was *everything else*. During the middle third of the twentieth century, therefore, social history tended to emphasize *material culture and the ways people lived in times past. (Note the concurrent appeal of museum "period rooms.") Consequently, social history paid considerable attention to such matters as urban transportation, firefighting, bathtubs, department stores, home appliances, and sanitation.

During the later 1960s, professional historians began to develop what is referred to as the "new social history," new because it stressed the history of society in a holistic way: the history of social structure and class, the history of mobility (social and physical), the history of intergroup relations, ethnicity, race, gender, and religion. For two pioneering works that proved to be especially influential, see Stephan Thernstrom, *Poverty and Progress: Social Mobility in a Nineteenth-Century City* (1964), a study of Newburyport, Massachusetts, in the later nineteenth century that used *census data in an innovative manner, and Thernstrom and Richard Sennett, eds., *Nineteenth-Century Cities: Essays in the New Urban History* (New Haven, Conn., 1969).

Two developments in historical scholarship in Europe were particularly seminal in stimulating the new social history. British historians, along with Scandinavian and French to a lesser degree at first, pioneered in using such demographic sources as tax lists; records of births, baptisms, marriages, and deaths; wills, parish and census records—all in an effort to investigate such matters as the distribution of wealth and the transmission of property, average age of marriage for males and females, premarital pregnancy, life expectancy, fluid versus static populations in communities, and so forth.

Second, the French and then others began to use the in-depth case study of particular communities or provinces as a way of testing broad generalizations that had been asserted without adequate attention to regional differences and variations. Influential French local studies tended to focus upon periods and places when conflict was especially prominent. They did so because the records can be very rich for times of crisis (such as the Inquisition or the French Revolution), and because an emphasis upon contestation tended to highlight unequal distributions of wealth and power. Therefore, even though these case studies concentrated on temporal "moments" such as a year, a decade, or a generation, they often illuminated long-standing resentments and related issues within a community.

Critics of the new social history became increasingly vocal from the mid- and later 1980s onward. They acknowledged that the new social history provided a much greater degree of precision, and opened whole new areas for investigation (especially what was called "history from the bottom up," meaning the history of ordinary people), yet offered very little of a qualitative nature concerning the history and role of human values. Therefore these critics pleaded for a closer alliance of social and cultural history, a marriage of quantitative with qualitative information and interpretive insight. For a striking comparison between a breakthrough book in relatively "pure" (i.e., quantitative) social history and a social/

cultural study of the same locality, see Merle Curti, *The Making of an American Community: Democracy in a Frontier County* [*Trempeleau County, Wisc.] (Stanford, Calif., 1959), and Jane Marie Pederson, *Between Memory and Reality: Family and Community in Rural Wisconsin, 1870–1970* (Madison, Wisc., 1992).

The implications of these developments for local historians should be self-evident. For too long, historians have neglected nonliterary source materials that are abundant though frustratingly incomplete at times (and occasionally inaccurate), materials that make us realize that for centuries we perceived only the tip of the iceberg of the human past. Used with care, and especially in the context of case studies, such neglected data enable us to test the conventional wisdom about such significant subjects as the New England town as the seedbed of American democracy. (An important cluster of case studies in 1970–1971 helped us realize that we really needed a *typology* of the New England town, because it mattered a great deal whether the town was coastal and commercial or inland and agricultural, or who the initial settlers were and what expectations they had concerning optimal farm size or apprenticeship for artisanal training.)

The new social history has now spawned a very rich body of literature on such ethnic enclaves as Chinatown in San Francisco or Poles and parish life in Detroit. Combined with mobility studies, it has told us a great deal about the African American migration northward to Chicago, ca. 1915–1945. Combined with biography it has illuminated life in a small town like Emporia, Kansas, home of William Allen White, who became famous as editor of the *Emporia Gazette*. And combined with ethnicity and the particularities of economic change, it has shaped our understanding of intergenerational change in a place like Whiting, Indiana.

See John Bodnar, "Moral Patriotism and Collective Memory in Whiting, Indiana, 1920–1992," in Bodnar, ed., *Bonds of Affection: Americans Define Their Patriotism* (Princeton, N.J., 1996), pp. 290–304.

MICHAEL KAMMEN

social purity. The American social-purity movement began as a response to two developments in the late eighteenth and early nineteenth centuries. One was a growing concern about the tendency of immigrants and native-born Americans to crowd together in impersonal cities where immoral enticements abounded but where community standards and social disapproval had little influence on behavior. The other was the growing belief, given birth by waves of evangelical enthusiasm that swept westward in the early nineteenth century, that moral suasion could help to perfect society. Throughout the century, various theories about how to control urban temptations and how to monitor the experiences and behaviors of the morally vulnerable attracted reform-minded middle-class Americans.

It became clear early that institutional religion alone did not have the power in cities that it did in small, intimate communities. Increasing numbers of Irish and German immigrants, most of whom were either Catholic or had no formal religious beliefs, could not be reached by sermons preached in Protestant churches. The social and cultural segregation imposed in ghettos isolated these people from the moral influence engendered in smaller, more socially diverse settlements. Nor could the law be relied on to control vice and to punish those who engaged in immoral but highly attractive activities. Ordinances to control behavior that did not appear to harm anyone were not popular in a country where the individual freedoms of its male electorate were considered inviolate. To change attitudes and behaviors the reformers had to become active in the community at large. Reform groups used two approaches, subtle coercion and militancy.

Many of the earliest and more subtle efforts at establishing moral purity were variations of activities already practiced formally in Protestant churches. The Bible Society movement presented immigrants with gifts of Testaments, simultaneously engendering a sense of welcome and a feeling of indebtedness to the giver. The Tract Society movement freely distributed other publications that told stories centering around moral choices: heroes and heroines who chose rightly prospered or were comforted, and those who made immoral choices suffered. The Sunday School movement in its early years focused on the formation of moral attitudes in young, impressionable minds, and church members attempted to attract immigrant children to these classes. However, their goal of blending social classes so that the morality and social

413

responsibility of middle-class children would become a model for poor street urchins was short-lived, and in many churches Sunday school attendance eventually became an exclusively middle-class experience.

During the latter half of the nineteenth century, many reform movements focused on controlling the environment in which people lived and worked. Changing environments was a more expensive proposition than publishing, preaching, and psalm singing, and social-purity organizations adopted businesslike practices. Wealthy patrons supplied funding for paid staffs and facilities where middle-class values could be inculcated in selected groups. The YMCA movement, for example, was established in 1851 to give young clerks, salesmen, and banktellers places where they could develop wholesome interests and participate in healthful activities. As industrialization grew, women's industrial unions sprang up, offering single-female factory workers safe and temptation-free accommodations, and monitoring their experiences. Some industries even chose remote locations, establishing communities where the lives of workers and their families might be observed and controlled. And the City Mission movement figuratively held derelict children captive by offering meals, beds, baths, and clothing and at the same time immersing them in sermons and hymn singing. In some extreme cases, children were literally kidnapped and sent to live with families in small towns in the nation's interior, where they would hopefully learn responsibility and adopt middle-American values.

On the other hand, groups like the Female Reform Society, founded in 1834, took militant stands against the vices prevalent in cities. The Society not only led public protests against houses of prostitution, but it also published the *Advocate of Moral Reform*. Hoping to shame the evil-doers, this periodical published clients' names for all to see. Similar reformers saw alcohol as the major factor in poverty, abuse, and indolence. The American Temperance Union, Washington Temperance Society, and Sons of Temperance conducted parades against alcohol consumption. Hoping perhaps to force innkeepers and other purveyors of spirituous liquors out of business, they signed volunteer pledges and pressured others to join their abstinence campaigns.

Toward the end of the century, the Anti-Saloon League became even more aggressive, raiding taverns and pubs, frightening customers, and destroying property. Activities of groups like the Anti-Saloon Crusade culminated in the passage of the 18th amendment, which ushered in Prohibition in 1919. Reports about the exploits of groups of axe-wielding matrons led by Carrie Nation appear in turn-of-the-century newspapers. Televised documentaries have incorporated early motion pictures to capture the fervor and fanaticism of these late reformers, and to recount their activities.

See in particular, *The Dry Crusade: The Prohibition Era*, produced by the British Broadcasting Corporation, 1997. During the late 1800s, popular social-purity movements became professionalized. In the twentieth century, specially trained social workers and probation officers apply theories of urban sociologists and psychologists in their work with those judged socially impure. And ironically, the middle class seems to have removed itself to the suburbs, a place where it tries to control its own environment rather than the environment of others.

See Paul Boyer, *Purity in Print* (N.Y., 1968), and *Urban Masses and Moral Order in America* (Cambridge, Mass., 1978).

TERESA LEHR

Society of American Archivists.

The Society of American Archivists was organized in 1936, shortly after the establishment in 1934 of the National Archives. It is the principal professional organization for archivists in the United States and has a worldwide membership of 3,500 individuals and institutions. Fourteen "Sections" and twenty-three "Roundtables" provide members opportunities for exchange of more specialized professional information relevant either to their type of institution (museums, religious collections, college and university archives) or to the kind of work an archivist does (preservation, visual materials, description).

The Society publishes a semiannual professional scholarly journal, *American Archivist*, and a monthly newsletter. Its other publications include an *Archival Fundamental* series as well as more specialized scholarly and technical monographs. Its annual meetings, held in late August or early September, offer workshops for advanced as well as fundamental training in professional archival skills. Workshops are also available regionally throughout the year, and the Society publishes a *Guide to Graduate Archival Programs*. Under its auspices, an independent organization, the Academy of Certified Archivists (<www.uwm.cdu/Dept/Library/arch/aca/index.html>) was created in 1989 to administer a professional certification program. The Society of American Archivists is located at 527 S. Wells Street, Chicago, Ill. 60607; (312) 922-0140; <www. archivists.org> and <info @archivists.org>.

CONSTANCE SCHULTZ

Society of Friends. See Appendix B.

Soundex.
To use the Soundex Indexing System to locate census information about a person, you must know his or her full name and the state or territory in which he or she lived at the time of the census. It is also helpful to know the full name of the head of the household in which the person lived, because census takers recorded information under that name.

The Soundex is a coded surname (last name) index based on the way a surname sounds rather than the way it is spelled. Surnames that sound the same, but are spelled differently, such as "Smith" and "Smyth," have the same code and are filed together. The Soundex coding system was developed so that a surname can be found even though it may have been recorded under various spellings.

To search for a particular surname, you must first work out its code. NARA's on-line Soundex Machine (<www.nara.gov/genealogy/soundex/soundex.html>) can code surnames automatically. The instructions below will help you code a name yourself and understand the Soundex process.

Basic Soundex Coding Rule: Every Soundex code consists of a letter and three numbers, such as W252. The letter is always the first letter of the surname. The numbers are assigned to the remaining letters of the surname according to the Soundex guide shown below. Zeroes are added at the end if necessary to produce a four-character code. Additional letters are disregarded. For example: Washington is coded W252 (W, 2 for the S, 5 for the N, 2 for the G, remaining letters disregarded). Lee is coded L000 (L, 000 added).

The Soundex Coding Guide:

Number	Represents the Letters*
1	B, F, P, V
2	C, G, J, K, Q, S, X, Z
3	D, T
4	L
5	M, N
6	R

---

*Disregard the letters A, E, I, O, U, H, W, and Y.

Additional Soundex Coding Rules:

1. Names with double letters: If the surname has any double letters, they should be treated as one letter. For example, Gutierrez is coded G362 (G, 3 for the T, 6 for the first R, second R ignored, 2 for the Z).

2. Names with letters side-by-side that have the same Soundex code number: If the surname has different letters side-by-side that have the same number in the soundex coding guide, they should be treated as one letter. For example: Pfister is coded as P236 (P, F ignored, 2 for the S, 3 for the T, 6 for the R). Jackson is coded as J250 (J, 2 for the

C, K ignored, 5 ignored, 5 for the N, 0 added).

3. Names with prefixes: If a surname has a prefix, such as Van, Con, De, Di, La, or Le, code both with and without the prefix because the surname might be listed under either code. For example: Van Deusen might be coded two ways: V532 (V, 5 for N, 3 for D, 2 for S) or D250 (D, 2 for the S, 5 for the N, 0 added). (Note: *Mc* and *Mac* are not considered prefixes.)

This article is based on *Using the Census Soundex, General Information Leaflet 55* (Washington, D.C., National Archives and Records Administration, 1995), a free brochure available from the National Archives and Records Administration. You may also request it via e-mail: <inquire@nara.gov> (include your name, postal address, and "GIL 55 please").

MARY RYAN

South Asians. See Appendix A.

South East Asians. See Appendix A.

Southwest region. Typically defined, the Southwest consists of modern-day Arizona, New Mexico, southern Utah, Nevada, Colorado, and northern Mexico. There were three major actors in the Southwest: Indian, Anglo, and Hispanic. Although treated as separate, "unified" categories, each broad group varied in terms of settlement pattern, religion, class, occupation, etc.

One of the most unifying themes of this region is the search for water. Water was an issue to the prehistoric Indians. Pueblo Indians developed both a rich mythology and ceremonial cycle in order to bring rain clouds. Hispanics established acequia communities and codified a whole series of legislation so that they could preserve and protect *water rights. Anglos fought Indians and Hispanics over water by using their own legal traditions; litigation still continues unabated today.

The Southwest is home to three major archaeological traditions: Hohokam, Mogollon, and Anasazi. Roots of these great prehistoric cultures can be traced back almost 2,000 years when these groups began settling down and experimenting with farming and long-distance trade. The Hohokam principally occupied the Salt and Gila River drainages from northern Mexico to north-central Arizona. They built extensive irrigation networks, ball courts, and platform mounds and lived in wattle-and-daub housing (Stephen Plog, *Ancient Peoples of the American Southwest* [London, 1997]). The Mogollon lived in southeastern Arizona and southwestern New Mexico. They, along with the Anasazi to the north, were known for their adobe-clay apartment-style villages known as "pueblos." Some of the Anasazi sites, like Chaco Canyon and Mesa Verde, were quite spectacular cliff palaces that were linked by a series of roads.

Beginning about A.D. 1140, many of the great prehistoric Indian societies underwent a series of major transformations. Many sites were abandoned; the great Chaco road system collapsed; warfare became more endemic; and eventually, a long-standing drought spread over parts of the region (see George Gummerman, ed., *Themes in Southwest Prehistory* [Santa Fe, 1994]).

The prehistoric groups were thought to have "disappeared," much like the enigmatic water. We now know, however, that the prehistoric populations grew too large for the carrying capacity of their lands. When the large villages could no longer be sustained by traditional farming, prehistoric groups picked up and moved away to found new, smaller settlements. These new settlements survived to become the ancestors of contemporary Indian societies, like the Pima and O'odham (related to the Hohokam) and Pueblos (related to the Anasazi and Mogollon).

Modern-day Indians have distinctive languages and cultures. They are represented by several language families: Uto-Aztecan (e.g., Hopi, Pima, Tohono O'odham), Zuni (Zuni), Keresan (e.g., Acoma), Tanoan (e.g., Picuris, Sandia, Isleta, San Juan, Tesuque, Jemez), Athapaskan (Navajo and Apache), and Yuman (e.g., Havasupi, Walapai, Yavapai, Maricopa, Mohave, among others); and two broad settlement patterns: the nucleated apartment-style pueblos and the dispersed settlement rancherias (Plog, 1997: 22–23; Kehoe, 1992: 127). There are "significant differences in group organization and religion" between the Pueblos and rancherias:

Typically, a Pueblo ritual leader is a prominent person within his social group and village; ritual, political and social leadership are closely intertwined. Among the rancheria peoples ordinary men, rather than priests, perform ritual songs and speeches in a cycle of communal ceremonies focusing on rain and fertility. The well-defined hierarchy of offices found in the Pueblos is lacking here. Kivas and Kachinas are also absent.

When the Spanish began their explorations of the Southwest in the sixteenth century, they were both intrigued and repelled by the native peoples they encountered. The Spanish quickly wore out their welcome among the Pueblos by taxing Indian farmers with continued demands for food and water. In some cases, the Spanish simply took over the Pueblos and forced the occupants to move. Cabeza de Vaca (1530s) was one of the first who came in search of emeralds and other riches. He was followed by Coronado in the 1540s, who led one of Spain's greatest expeditions into the Southwest. Coronado was outfitted with cattle, soldiers, Mexican Indians, and priests. Coronado's legacy became the legacy of exploitation. When pueblos along the Rio Grande could no longer feed Coronado's huge appetite, the Spaniard fought back and burned Indians at the stake (Weber, 1992: 24, 46–49).

Juan de Onate was probably even less well liked than Coronado by the Indians. Imagine his entrance into the pueblo he named "Santa Domingo" in 1598. He brought everyone together, read them a Spanish document that said that they were all now vassals of the Crown and must therefore embrace the King and the Catholic Church. Although the Pueblos may not have fully understood this new Spaniard's strange document at the time, they quickly began to experience its implications. The pueblos were expected to feed and house Onate's huge entourage. Acoma became tired of extending so much hospitality and rebelled, but not before Onate could punish the offenders by ordering the amputation of each adult male's right foot. While many Hispanics in the Southwest celebrate the bicentennial of Onate's great exploration and settlement today, the Pueblos remember the severe punishment meted out to Acoma (see David Weber, *The Spanish Frontier in North America* [New Haven, Conn., 1992]).

In 1680 the Pueblos joined together and revolted against the Spanish. It was not until the 1690s that the Spanish could renew their toehold in the Southwest. When they returned, they remembered the lessons of the past. This second reconquest was not as exacting, and a new set of laws, known as the *Recopilacion de las Indies*, guided Spanish and Indian relations (C. Briggs and R. Van Ness, eds., *Land, Water and Culture: New Perspectives on Hispanic Land Grants* [Albuquerque, 1987]). Indians and Spanish found common grounds. They began to work together to create irrigation networks, to afford mutual protection against Apache raids, and to meet the demands of a new conquistador—the Anglos.

Anglos had been trickling west for some time, but with the cession of much of the northern areas to Mexico in 1821, more and more Anglos headed west to find their fame and fortune. The Santa Fe trail system opened commerce between Mexicans, Americans, and Indians. Trade, however, became a source of contention. Anglos from the newly created Republic of Texas attempted to divert commerce to themselves, and in 1846, war was declared between the United States and Mexico (D. W. Meinig, *Southwest: Three Peoples in Geographical Change, 1600–1970* [N.Y., 1971]). U.S. General Stephen Kearny conquered New Mexico and established Fort Marcy in Santa Fe, thereby establishing Santa Fe as one of the most important new outposts of the United States (James Byrkit, "Land, Sky and People: The Southwest Defined," in *Journal of the Southwest* 3:3 [1992]). The Treaty of Guadalupe Hidalgo followed by the Gadsden Purchase conferred American status to most of what we now know as the American Southwest. With the transfer of the region to U.S. hands, Anglos established a regional railroad system that linked the Southwest to the rest of the United States. The gold rush in California as well as cattle ranching and mining also enticed Anglos westward across the Southwest. The floodgates opened and Anglos poured in.

The new Anglo invasion created a plethora of problems for both the Indians and the Hispanics. Spanish land grants that had been honored by the Mexican government were no longer protected under U.S. law. "Instead of attempting to learn how New Mexican authorities dealt with land grants, the United States imposed its own view of Spanish and Mexican law on the adjudication process—a view that was colored by the bias of a different legal system." In addition to the land-grant confusion were the continuing raids upon Pueblos and Hispanics by marauding Navaho, Ute, and Apache raiders who seized horses, cattle, and whatever else they could take. The Anglo presence merely provided another target for these Indian raids, and the Anglos fought back, and quite often, indiscriminately. They retaliated against any Indians, even those with demonstrated friendship to Anglos (Richard White, *A New History of the American West* [Norman, Okla., 1991]).

By the end of the twentieth century, Indian tribes throughout North America had been conquered in a series of brutal wars and forced evacuations from their homelands. Each Native American group and each Hispanic community has a unique story to tell about the problems they faced as outsiders in a land where they were once insiders. Their communities were engulfed by the larger Anglo society. Today, the Southwest has become a mecca for retirees, New Agers, holistic healers, and a whole variety of other seekers who are looking for a healthier and more relaxed lifestyle. As these new populations press into the Southwest, more and more water from the aquifers, the Colorado, Gila, Rio Grande and Pecos Rivers is being tapped using modern technologies that have all but sucked the waters dry.

Some of the excellent regional histories of the Southwest include Byrkit (1992) and Meinig (1971). These authors summarize the previous regional histories of the area and examine the Southwest from numerous perspectives, including geographical (boundaries), cultural (prehistory and history of the peoples), economic (trade, railroads, industry), and climatic and environmental considerations (temperatures, watersheds, specific environments). Byrkit also includes a great deal of information about how the Southwest is portrayed in academic writing and in popular culture (fiction, art, cultural imagery).

LAURIE WEINSTEIN

See regionalism.

Spaniards. See Appendix A.

state historical journals. East of the Mississippi many journals date their founding from the nineteenth or early twentieth century. The 1920s were a particularly fertile time for establishment of these periodicals in the Midwest and Plains states. *Colorado Heritage* (founded 1981), *Nevada Historical Quarterly* (1957), and *The California Historian* (1954) carried such enterprises across the continent. The nation's youngest states established the *Hawaiian Journal of History* and *Alaska History* in 1967 and 1984, respectively.

State history journals publish original researched articles and other materials about the history of the state and the surrounding region. Some editors take a broad view of this general purpose. Typical is *West Virginia History*, which calls itself a "journal of history, biography, genealogy, and bibliography" and offers to publish "articles, documents, book reviews, and notes" as well as manuscripts that focus on the state, the region, and the *Appalachians. At the other end of the continuum, some journals limit themselves to articles and book reviews with a state focus.

In between, one finds a variety of content. Some publish one or more of the following: primary documents; programs and transactions of state and historical societies; historic *photographs; book excerpts; *obituaries and memorials, especially of persons prominent in state historical work; descriptions of recently processed manuscripts in state archives; queries seeking research help; editorials; and letters to the editor. Some journals reject in advance material of an *antiquarian or genealogical nature. Others reflect in the queries they print the recent popularity of family studies. The most common type of article found in state history journals is the case study. The heyday of a defunct institution, the settlement of a geographic tract of the state, a wink of time in a city—all find their chroniclers. Another popular subject is the neglected life of a minor figure. Rare is the interpretive framework; a synthesizing article or survey is seldom seen. Journal writers often borrow a convention from scholarly publishing generally and impose an inflated or sensational title over a narrow subject. A recent survey of journals notes two examples: "To Perpetuate Holy Memory," about baseball in a state's cities during a seven-year period, or "Negroes and All Other Animals," on slavery in an antebellum county.

Some contents pages display articles devoted to traditional categories, such as economic, political, or military history. Other journals' editors print articles with social and ethnic themes, cultural history and race, class, and gender studies.

State history journals carry material submitted by academic historians, graduate students, public historians, archivists and librarians, civil servants, professional people outside the history field, journalists, and *independent historians and writers. Candidates for tenure in the universities earn publication credits, and the journals provide an outlet for excerpts from theses and dissertations. Yet names of senior faculty can occasionally be found on the contents page.

State history journals are typically state-owned or state-subsidized enterprises. Tax dollars appropriated by the legislatures cover printing costs. Editors' salaries come from the same source. These personnel often work at the state library and archives, the state historical commission, a state university press, or teach in the department of history at the state university, sometimes managing the publication in connection with other duties. The journal's administrative costs—supplies, telephone, postage—come from those institutional budgets.

These arrangements in turn underwrite and sustain the membership in state historical societies. The journal is often the chief benefit for joining the society.

Most state history journals have editorial boards, variously called. They range in size from only a few persons to dozens. A sampling of boards indicates that they comprise a mix of academic and laypersons. In many cases, boards reflect the mixture that may be found among contributors, although in some cases, state history institutions have established seats on the board.

Journal editors utilize these boards as they see fit. Board members may be called upon to read articles submitted for publication; they may be asked to recruit articles or prospective articles; they may be ignored. "I make the final decision about which manuscripts are accepted for publication," writes an editor for a journal in a Midwestern state, a prerogative generally enjoyed by his counterparts.

State history journals range in circulation from fewer than a thousand to more than 5,000 copies. Content analysis discloses little about subscribers to these journals. "About one-half library, one-quarter academics, one-quarter people generally interested in history," estimates the editor of a journal in the East having a circulation of about 1,000. "Mostly academics and members of the historical society," says a colleague in the Midwest.

The identity of readers is an even more elusive question. Some categories of historical-society membership are suggestive, especially "institutional" and "corporate." "Institutional" means mainly libraries, which are often the bulk of some journals' business. Libraries at graduate institutions feel compelled to carry state history journals from their region, fewer from places more distant. The state history journals of New Jersey, Pennsylvania, Virginia, and North and South Carolina enjoy corporate support, but they are among the minority.

Publishers' characterizations of their readers fall into broad, abstract categories: "Those who are historically minded" says one masthead of a Mid-Atlantic state's journal. "A medium of publication and discussion of history," intones a Southern periodical. "Designed for professional historians and lay readers interested in Western and Great Plains history," says the masthead of one from that region.

In one way or another, the overwhelming number declare that their purpose is to publish. One editor of a Southern journal remarked at the state historical society's annual meeting that the journal "continue[s] to serve as a quality publication for the *authors* of articles pertaining to state and local history" (emphasis added). Being sustained by their state's taxpayers, publishers have little incentive to ask questions about their audiences or whether the journal serves its needs.

There are other history publications:

- In some states, popular magazines of history far outstrip the scholarly state history journal in numbers of subscribers: *Alabama Heritage, Colorado History Now, Iowa Heritage Illustrated, Michigan History Magazine, Montana, The Magazine of Western History, Timeline* (Ohio), and *Virginia Cavalcade*. Most of these have made their appearance in the years since World War II. With larger trim sizes, reader-friendly type and graphics, and copious illustrations, they have influenced many traditional state historical journals to adopt similar elements.
- Regional history journals provide still another outlet for scholarly publishing resembling the state journals in content and format. Some, such as *East Tennessee History* and *Southern California Quarterly*, focus on a distinctive cultural and geographic place within a state's bounds. Others, like *Pacific Northwest Quarterly* and *Southwestern Historical Quarterly*, elude political borders.
- The publisher of the state historical journal often produces a newsletter as well. Its content is usually ephemeral: calendars of history events, meetings of the state historical society and of local societies, new acquisitions to collections and the like. The price of the newsletter is usually included in the membership dues for the historical society, and is a lagniappe for joining.

Some journal editors are putting abstracts of articles on websites or posting tables of contents to newsgroups. Internet publishing seems destined to have more in common with visual documentaries than annotated scholarship, but it is also less capable of definition. The rich investigation, the subtle argument, qualifications, or copious footnotes will remain the province of print.

A rising generation whose members will sit in legislative assemblies has received little classroom work in rigorous history of any kind. No one knows the consequences of folding state and local history into "social studies" and attenuating them in rigor and content, but one possible consequence is the attenuation of a long-standing commitment by state governments for the publication of history journals.

JAMES SUMMERVILLE

state historical organizations. For a list, including name, address, phone, and Internet address, see Appendix C.

state historical societies. America's state historical societies are the country's oldest historical institutions. The first, the Massachusetts Historical Society (1791), New-York Historical Society (1804), and American Antiquarian Society (1812), were products of the Age of Enlightenment. A fervor for learning and the zeal of patriotism motivated their founders, who had great faith in the power of reason and knowledge. They were also determined to preserve the memory of the glories of the American Revolution and the creation of the infant American nation.

In the next three decades several other state societies were created, including the first in the South, the Virginia Historical Society (1831), and the first in the Midwest, in Ohio that same year. These early societies were totally private both in financial management and governance. But in the 1850s, historical societies in Wisconsin and other states in the Midwest began to receive significant state appropriations to support operations and programs. This model holds true today. The majority of the state historical societies on the eastern seaboard and the South are private institutions, while most in the Midwest and west of the Mississippi River are supported substantially by public funds.

These institutions vary in size and the functions they perform. On one end of the spectrum are the dozen or so large central agencies such as the State Historical Society of Wisconsin and the Minnesota Historical Society. Almost fully funded by public dollars and staffed in some cases by hundreds of employees, each serves as the state library and archives, the state history museum, the state historic preservation office, the overseer of numerous historic sites, and providers of extensive field-service programs. On the other end of the spectrum are small, private institutions like the Tennessee and South Carolina historical societies that receive little public funding, have small but rich collections, and are often overshadowed by larger, publicly funded history museums, libraries and archives, and historic-preservation offices that operate as separate state agencies.

Initially, most early state historical societies built their collections eclecti-cally. In addition to acquiring documents, books, paintings, and objects relating to their state's history, they often collected animal, vegetable, and mineral specimens; Egyptian rarities, including mummies; and artifacts of indigenous Indian tribes. Many of these institutions actively collected historical materials representing other regions of the country. In the nineteenth century, the State Historical Society of Wisconsin, for example, acquired significant manuscript collections from the American South. The Massachusetts Historical Society built a large collection of materials from the American Revolution and early national period from several of the original states, especially Virginia. Eventually these institutions narrowed their fields of collecting to their own state.

Well into the twentieth century, the functions of most state historical societies revolved around their archive, library, and publications departments, which were often staffed by scholars and librarians. But in the last quarter of the century, with but few exceptions, these institutions have significantly broadened the scale and scope of their activities to include major museum exhibitions and extensive educational programs. This increase in the size and scope of activities at state historical societies has resulted in significant expansions in staff and buildings. In the last twenty-five years, they have invested more than a billion dollars in building facilities to carry out their expanded missions. The result is that today, as a group, our state historical societies are well armed to inform Americans of their past. They have gone from serving the few to reaching the many. And they have often set the standards for professionalism and scholarship for other historical institutions in their states to follow.

CHARLES F. BRYAN JR.

See Appendix C; local history in the U.S.; repatriation; state historical organizations; state involvement with history.

state humanities councils. In 1965, Congress enacted legislation creating the National Foundation for the Arts and Humanities composed of the *National Endowment for the Humanities and the *National Endowment for the Arts. The humanities councils trace their origin to the 1970 legislation that authorized both agencies for an additional five years and called for exploration of a structure for "state programs" as part of the National Endowment for the Humanities. In 1971, NEH organized the first volunteer "state committees" in a handful of states and granted funds to these quasi-autonomous boards for local re-granting. Widely viewed as an experiment, these earliest programs flourished and found a niche in the mix of local programming and educational support. In rapid manner, NEH facilitated the establishment of additional state committees. In 1976, with the intent of ensuring that the U.S. public enjoyed the benefits of the humanities, Congress set aside a designated amount of funds appropriated to NEH for the exclusive use of the new state-based programs. In operation today are 56 autonomous state humanities councils, one in each state and in American Samoa, the District of Columbia, Guam, the Northern Mariana Islands, Puerto Rico, and the U.S. Virgin Islands.

The mission and statutory rules governing humanities councils have evolved since the earliest legislation. Congress initially limited councils to making grants in support of thematic humanities and public-policy programs. In 1976 these restrictions were lifted, enabling councils to make grants in all areas of humanities education such as NEH itself.

The legislation also requires that councils be governed by elected boards made up of a broad representation of scholars and the public in each state. These boards rotate regularly and are self-perpetuating, though each council must publicly solicit new members. The governor of each state appoints six board members.

Humanities councils apply to NEH for a portion, or in some cases, most of their funding. Prior to 1996, councils followed a procedure not unlike any other applicant to NEH. Each council submitted a proposal that was evaluated by a review panel with the chairman making the final funding decision. Only one designated entity in each state is eligible to receive funds. In 1996, the chairman of NEH replaced this grantor–grantee model with a certification process.

The councils operate with an autonomy and flexibility unusual in federal–state partnerships. This is attributable to several factors. By incorporating as private, nonprofit organizations, councils avoid the bureaucratic impediments of public agencies. Careful management by NEH, council boards and staff in the earliest years of the state program avoided embarrassments that might have triggered greater Washington control. The stipulation by Congress and the Office of Management and Budget of wise guidelines for the expenditure of funds (e.g., federal funds may not be used for lobbying), combined with requirements for annual audits and reports, has helped establish a rigorous standard of accountability. Finally, and not least important, the effective advocacy and mediation of the Federation of State Humanities Councils, the councils' membership organization founded in 1977, has helped define the appropriate balance between national oversight and local control.

As partners, the NEH and state humanities councils help carry out the congressional mandate of strengthening scholarship and equitably disseminating the results to the American people. Not surprising, there is inevitable competing state-based and national perspectives that grow out of this unique relationship that are both challenging and fruitful. In the mid-1990s, strong Congressional support for the kinds of grass-roots programs that humanities councils favor helped shore up support for NEH at a time when NEH's existence was challenged by new forces in Congress. There have also been times when strong support for NEH benefited the states. Moreover, NEH has imported into its thinking and priorities some of the innovative concepts of council programming, such as library-based discussion programs. Likewise, "blockbuster" NEH programs—and strong, popular NEH chairs—have helped reinforce council initiatives at the state level. What is clear is that the NEH and the councils are not simply mirror images of each other operating at different planes. While that is probably healthy pluralism, there is still an unrealized potential in this partnership. It is worth remembering that the councils, and NEH too, are relatively young organizations that have no precedent in U.S. history.

While each state receives federal funds through a complicated formula that balances equal distribution with population, every year more states councils add "outside" funds to their basic federal grant. Councils now receive support from state government, private foundations, corporate foundations, and individual donors. The long-term trend is toward budgets that reflect a healthy and proportionate mix of public and private funding sources.

Related to new funding priorities is the growing level of activism toward agencies of government and legislatures. Unlike their sister organizations, arts agencies, all of which are agencies of government, humanities councils enjoy wide latitude with regard to advocacy provided no federal funds are used for this purpose. Volunteers serving on council boards are not restricted in their political activism as private citizens—nor are the grant recipients of council funds or the audiences who benefit directly from council-funded programs. These groups make up a powerful grass-roots constituency that is one of the keys to public support for humanities funding at the state and national levels. The big question facing councils is whether this growing base of constituent support can be converted into larger state and federal appropriations for the humanities. At the state level, the trend is positive, as most state councils now receive some form of state support.

Another important trend is in types of programs that councils fund and conduct. From the beginning, humanities councils made grants to community, civic, and cultural organizations, including colleges and universities, in order to promote greater public involvement in the humanities. Scholars usually are involved in council-funded programs as project directors, presenters, or consultants. As a rule, councils avoid funding projects that are intended exclusively for strictly student audiences, though programs for teacher enrichment are commonly funded. Some councils fund scholarship; the majority do not. A typical council grant might range from several hundred dollars to $20,000 or more. Examples of projects are media programs (television and radio), the development of museum exhibitions, library-based programs, workshops for school teachers, speakers' bureaus, community symposia, conferences, and interpretation of archeological and historic sites. In most states, the councils have been the major source of grant support (often, the only source) for local history programs for the public.

Increasingly, states are pursuing council-conducted opportunities that follow newer kinds of strategic thinking aimed at gaining greater public and private funding support, building audiences and constituencies, and deepening their impact. A byproduct is diminishing funds for grant-making, in part a reflection of near-stagnant federal support upon which the grant-making program depends. But grants will never be eliminated entirely because so many councils recognize that grants offer the ideal mechanism for responding to initiatives that bubble up from the community and not infrequently become a basis for new council initiatives.

Some of these new council initiatives in fact represent new models of programming for the future. In Virginia, the council has created a center and fellowship program that is attracting scholars and students of Virginia history and culture from around the world for a period of residency that entails research, writing, and public programs. Connecticut's council is partnering with the state legislature in helping to make local history the state's major cultural tourism industry. Louisiana's council is publishing *Cultural Vistas*, a statewide magazine that connects the state's citizens with their local history, folkways, culture, and history. The Tennessee council's *Southern Festival of Books* is pioneering a connection between writers and the public that typically features stories of a particular place. The Alaska, Washington, Kansas, and Florida councils are developing an entrepreneurial approach to programming that suggests an entirely new way of thinking about and carrying out programs on local history and culture as well as other topics. The Minnesota council has created a nationally unique center for teachers. The North Carolina council is engaged in a nationally significant literacy program that is helping to instill nurturing values in new readers, families, and children. The Georgia council has developed and published a

New Georgia Guide that highlights local culture and history and is linked with a travel guide. These experiments can be multiplied around the states and suggest a new surge of creativity at work.

As the missions of councils become more focused and pragmatic, so too does their programming. In the mid-1990s we are witnessing a move away from the academic definition of the humanities and the reliance on traditional models of programming (the university-centered outreach approach that emphasizes humanities disciplines) toward a more dynamic definition that grows, as it were, from the needs and wants of communities. This trend is more gradual than sudden. It owes something to a more generalized change in *philanthropy that looks at systemic problems. It also reflects a natural process of maturation whereby councils set new goals for themselves in response to opportunities as well as obstacles.

The priorities of scholars and scholarship remain important in council programs, but the influence of each is waning as newer types of leaders appear on council boards and staff, recruited precisely because of the "real-world" expertise they bring (corporate, organizational, philanthropic, political, fundraising). Inventive or "relevant" programs that in former years would have been seen as outside the domain of the humanities disciplines are developing around new, local priorities. These include battling adult illiteracy, encouraging family-reading programs, promoting community dialogues that clarify values and strengthen mutual respect, serving rural communities, forming partnerships with schools and teachers to strengthen humanities instruction, and reaching poor and underserved youth. Councils are also developing signature projects with a wide public appeal, such as traveling Chautauqua shows, book and humanities festivals, popular magazines, state encyclopedias, and cultural tourism.

The majority of the programs supported by councils involve history and heritage; in many states, humanities councils have been the single-most important source of program support (sometimes the sole source) for museums, historical societies, and libraries. The success of almost 30 years of funding efforts can perhaps best be measured by the geometric increase in public humanities and history programs that now take place in hundreds of communities on a weekly or even daily basis.

Paradoxically, as more of the public enjoys the humanities, within our institutions of higher education, the domain of the humanities is shrinking in the competition with more "practical" fields of study. Though it has not always been so obvious, the fact remains that the long-term health of history and the humanities, whether in the community, the classroom, or in scholarship, are entwined. The hope is that all three can grow together.

JAMIL S. ZAINALDIN

state involvement with history. Three periods in American history were especially fecund for state engagement with historical concerns. The first, in the late nineteenth and early twentieth centuries, can be understood as part of the great associational movement of the time. *State historical societies blossomed (sometimes being new growth on an older shoot), and some of these were adopted by legislatures as state agencies.

In 1949 the formation of the *National Trust for Historic Preservation was followed by a rise of mainly private groups dedicated to acquisition and protection of venerable homesites of famous names in a state's history. Civic leaders involved with this movement sometimes championed a state role in the process. Finally, in 1966, the National Historic Preservation Act drew every state and territory into the history business.

State agencies for history are created or formally recognized in statutory law. Each state also designates a State Historic Preservation Officer (SHPO), as required by the National Historic Preservation Act and usually employs a staff to carry out its provisions. Sometimes the SHPO holds another appointment, such as an office in the gubernatorial cabinet, and discharges these duties through a deputy. In a few states, the SHPO and the historic-preservation office are an independent agency.

Most state agencies for history have statewide responsibilities, which means public outreach programs of one kind or another. The state library maintains collections, offers reference services and the like, but it also implements federal programs related to local library services and public records. The museum displays and interprets artifacts, but depends on goodwill of legislators from outside the capital city, and so may sponsor traveling exhibits. Statutory existence, federal compliance, and the necessity of public relations are the few common elements in states' history work.

State agencies for history range widely in their formal responsibilities. The single-purpose agency is rare, although Louisiana's historic-preservation office limits its work to sites, structures, and districts. In some states, the historic preservation office manages sites as well as carrying out NHPA mandates. Sometimes preservation and archaeology are under the same agency, perhaps because many early state-historical societies had a strong antiquarian focus.

Idaho, Mississippi, North Dakota, Ohio, Pennsylvania, and South Carolina exemplify states that have organized history work into comprehensive political entities. Each history agency in these states has sprawling responsibilities: the SHPO and the historic-preservation office, the state library and archives, the state museum, and records management, and in some cases, archaeology.

Such comprehensive agencies, besides carrying out the functions of the NHPA, manage historic sites; provide teacher services and other education programs; give grants; and publish books, scholarly journals, popular-history magazines, and other periodicals. They may also sponsor public celebrations; undertake joint endeavors with ethnic groups and tribal governments; have an awards program; and conduct meetings, conferences, and workshops.

Unified history programs are exceptional. More often, history functions are scattered among departments of state government. The library may be under the secretary of state. The museum is often an independent agency or a division of a subcabinet office for the arts. *Archaeology is found in environment and conservation departments, cultural-resources divisions, or elsewhere. In most states, history and *historic preservation are assigned to a subdivision of a cabinet-level department. This means that managers report to bureaucrats and ultimately to the governor or the legislature.

State parks and recreation departments run the historic preservation programs in some states, including Missouri, New York, and Wyoming. New Hampshire organizes history together with *tourism, arts, and cultural affairs, including folklife. In other states, cabinet departments of environment and conservation, commerce, cultural affairs, and education, among others, oversee the historic-preservation office. Cooperative activities are not uncommon. Neither is conflict and overlap, as where, for example, one state department owns and manages historical resources that the official agency for history has no authority over.

Some states present an amalgam of mixed governance for history programming. A council, bureau, board, or commission comprising professional people in history, civic leaders, and business executives, sometimes serves as the state review board under the NHPA and advises the history agency or sets policy for its staff to carry out. This whirligig world of civil-service history is illustrated in one Southern state, where the executive director of the historical commission nominally reports to an assistant head of a cabinet department. At the same time he is employed by the commission, which is appointed by the governor, and funded by the legislature—while the staff devotes the greatest part of its time to federal mandates!

The history agency is called the state historical society in several states. The State Historical Society of Wisconsin, which manages a comprehensive program, is governed by a board of curators, some of whom are elected by the society's dues-paying members and the rest of whom are appointed by the governor, or serve ex officio. A similar form of organization "makes the South Dakota State Historical Society appear to be a private organization when it is actually a state agency," says an official publication.

State agencies for history thus vary considerably in their purposes, structures, powers, and span of responsibilities. It is hardly surprising that one state, Oregon, recently saw the need for a "heritage commission" to coordinate an array of public and private history programs. Other cultural forces and trends may encourage a greater degree of centralization and organization in years to come: a need for better statewide planning on such issues as urban sprawl; the growth of heritage tourism; and the need for liaison and cooperation between state and local preservation activities.

JAMES SUMMERVILLE

See local history in the U.S.; state historical organizations; state historical societies.

Swedes. See Appendix A.

Swiss. See Appendix A.

syphilis. This sexually transmitted disease was known in the United States as the pox or the french pox. See Claude Quetel, *History of Syphilis* (Baltimore, 1990).

T

---

tax records. See Civil War Federal Tax Records.

technology. It is quite natural for those of us who live in wealthy and developed Western nations to take technology and its place in our lives for granted. Historians are not immune to this tendency. While we all recognize the importance of certain momentous events—the invention of the printing press or the steam engine or the completion of the first transcontinental railway—we often fail to examine the more mundane but no less important story of how technology has shaped and changed our communities and our individual lives. The evidence of technology's pervasiveness is all around us—from the buildings we live and work in to the cars we drive and the roads we drive on—yet it seems as if most of us seldom notice it until it breaks down. Only then, when we are confronted by the reality of our dependence on machines, do we take an interest in the systems and devices that permeate every aspect of our lives. During the ice storm of January 1998 in northeastern North America, people suddenly discovered that gas furnaces and water heaters needed electricity to work, that the dairy industry was totally dependent on electrical power not only to heat barns and operate milking equipment but also to process the raw milk, that the average home fireplace could not heat even a small house effectively in below-freezing temperatures.

The history of technology may seem difficult or remote, but it needn't be. You don't have to understand every minute detail of how a machine works or grasp all the intricacies of the inventive process in order to write about technology. What you do need is a few basic principles, a good chronology of events, and some advice on where to look for reliable information on the technology you want to explore.

Broadly speaking, there are three basic principles that you should keep in mind when researching the history of any technology. First, people create technology. Scientists, inventors, and engineers create tools to solve problems and to enhance our ability to do work. At the same time, though, their work is shaped by wider social, political, and economic forces. Thus, if a society decides it doesn't need or want a certain technology—nuclear-power reactors are one example—that technology will not succeed no matter how useful or practical it is.

Second, technology is a tool; it is neither inherently good nor inherently bad. In North America we have tended to stress the positive attributes and accomplishments of technology, associating it with progress and prosperity. Yet every invention has costs as well as benefits.

Finally, there is much more to the history of technology than invention. It is only one stage in the long, complex, cumulative process by which people transform experience, ideas, and abstract scientific principles into working technologies. A patent record will tell you who holds the legal claim to an invention, but it will not tell you how many other people contributed to the process of invention or how much effort it took to turn a patentable device into a usable appliance. Nor does it tell us anything about the application and adaptation of technology that may be every bit as important as invention, particularly in a local history context.

There are many different ways to approach the history of technology. The most familiar is probably that which focuses on the history of a particular machine and explores its local use or impact. This is a straightforward method that allows researchers to look at any number of technologies from the telegraph to the washing machine. For residents of industrial towns it is also possible to research a local factory, mine, or other worksite by looking at the machines the workers used or the products they were making. This approach can highlight the ways in which business has applied technology to improve productivity and how this has changed many people's working lives, not always for the better. There are also more abstract ways to look at the influence of technology, such as by studying how it has changed our perceptions of time, speed, distance, and efficiency, or what impact electronic communication systems have had on our sense of local and regional identity and on our ability to preserve them.

There is also a wide variety of sources available to researchers. For general-reference purposes, there is a number of books, guides, dictionaries, and encyclopedias that list and describe important inventions. Most cover a wide range of devices and developments, from the everyday to the exotic—one even has an entry for gas-chamber execution—and are popular in style and format. *Eureka! How and When the Greatest Inventions Were Made* (London, Eng., 1974) edited by Edward de Bono, is large-format book with plenty of images to support the text. Divided into sections by broad themes, it provides a fairly comprehensive survey of developments up to the 1970s, with entries that are at least three paragraphs long and yet manage to convey the main points as well as some of the complexity of technological change. This book also has a chronological table placing technological breakthroughs in the context of other important events. Gerald Messadié's *Great Modern Inventions* is a handbook guide with shorter entries that begin with a brief description of how the process or device works and then provide a brief sketch of its development. Other quick reference guides include *Science and Technology Desk Reference* compiled by James E. Bobick and Magery Peffer, which has a 15-page chronology and an extensive bibliography, and the *Biographical Dictionary of the History of Technology*, edited by Lance Day and Ian McNeil.

For more detailed information and analysis, researchers can turn to *A History of Technology* (Oxford, 1979), a seven-volume compilation of essays on the development of technology from ancient times until about 1950. These volumes are especially strong in "big"

SOME IMPORTANT DATES IN THE HISTORY OF TECHNOLOGY

1800   Alessandro Volta invents the voltaic pile, the first source of continuous electrical current.

1814   George Stephenson introduces the first practical steam locomotive.

1834   Cyrus Hall patents his reaping machine.

1837   Charles Wheatstone and William Cooke patent and demonstrate the first practical electromagnetic telegraph.

1844   Friedrich Gottlob Keller invents wood-pulp paper.

1856   William H. Perkin prepares the first aniline dye.

1857   E.G. Otis installs the first safety elevator.

1866   Britain and North America linked by the first viable trans-Atlantic submarine telegraph cable. (First attempts made in 1857–1858 and 1865.)

1872   Brooklyn Bridge opened but not to traffic until 1883.

1874   H. Solomon introduces pressure-cooking methods for canning foods, which begin to appear in stores around 1880.

1876   A.G. Bell registers his telephone patent just hours ahead of fellow inventor Elisha Gray.

1880   Swan and Edison independently develop the first practical electric lights.

1885   Karl Benz builds a single-cylinder engine for motor cars.

1906   R.A. Fessenden broadcasts the human voice via radio waves to ships at sea.

1908   L.H. Baekeland introduces Bakelite. With its commercial manufacture the following year, the "Age of Plastic" begins.

1909   Charles Saunders distributes Marquis wheat, a revolutionary early-ripening hard spring wheat, to farmers on the northern Great Plains.

1913   Ford introduces assemblyline techniques that revolutionize automobile production.

1920   First scheduled radio broadcasts take place in North America. By 1924 there are 2.5 million radio receiving sets in use in the U.S., and by 1925 there are 1.65 million in Great Britain.

1928   John Logie Baird demonstrates color television, while George Eastman exhibits the first color motion pictures. The following year Kodak introduces 16mm color movie film.

1931   The Empire State building, started in 1929, is completed.

continued

1936 The Boulder (Hoover) Dam is completed, creating the largest reservoir in the world.

1938 Lajos Biró invents the ballpoint pen.

1940 Howard Florcy develops penicillin as a practical antibiotic. It is used successfully to treat chronic diseases in 1943.

1942 Magnetic recording tape is invented. The first magnetic recording of sound had been accomplished in 1899.

1947 Researchers at Bell Laboratories in the U.S. invent the transistor. Its first widespread commercial use is in transistor radios introduced in 1954. By the 1970s, engineers have developed a method of putting multiple circuits on one piece of semiconductor material and the integrated circuit or microchip is born.

1955 Nuclear-generated power is used in the U.S. for the first time. Other Western countries join the nuclear club soon after.

1956 The first trans-Atlantic telephone cable is laid, making direct telephone contact between Europe and North America possible. Until this time all overseas conversations were carried by short-wave radio systems set up in the late 1920s and early 1930s.

1962 Rachel Carson's environmental exposé *Silent Spring* and revelations about the effects of Thalidomide begin to undermine society's confidence in science and technology. Seven years later, the U.S. government takes steps to ban DDT and removes cyclamates from the market.

1966 Color television, introduced to U.S. viewers in 1951, is finally becoming more popular.

1971 The largest ship built to date, the 372,400-ton tanker Nisseki Maru, is launched in Japan. With the dramatic rise in oil prices after 1973, builders begin to construct even larger super-tankers that put increasing stress on port facilities and pose huge risks for the environment.

1975 The CN (Canadian National) tower, begun in 1973, is completed. At just over 1,815 feet (553 meters) it is the tallest free-standing structure in the world.

1977 The Apple II personal computer is introduced. IBM introduces its own DOS-based system in 1981. By the late 1980s, the computer has become a fixture in most of our lives.

1982 Barney Clark lives 112 days after receiving an artificial heart to replace his own failing heart.

1986 The first module of the *Mir* space station is launched. The space shuttle *Challenger* explodes shortly after takeoff; and the largest nuclear accident in the world takes place at the Chernobyl power reactor spreading radioactive fallout across much of Europe.

technologies such as power generation and distribution; industrial processes and machinery; *mining; building and construction, including bridges, railways and roads; and water supply and treatment systems. Essays average about 20 pages and each is followed by a list of references that will guide the truly tireless researcher to even more specialized works on the topic. As with all works that try to cover a lot of historical and technological ground, these books do not always get the details right. The popular books seldom reflect the latest specialist research, and they all tend to concentrate on the achievements of great world powers and major international companies, often neglecting the contributions of the less well known. Also, most overviews seem to celebrate technological change and only rarely point out its negative consequences, consequences that we sometimes see all too vividly in our local communities when local rail lines are abandoned or jobs are lost to automation, rationalization, and globalization.

Those researchers who want more critical and current analysis of technological developments can also search by subject, and in most fields they will find at least a few useful sources. This is especially true in the United States, where the history of technology is a large and well-developed academic and public-history field. Though some of these works may be a little complex or theoretical, they do offer a more detailed and subtle picture of technology and society and can lead readers to a wealth of other sources on the subject, including archival collections and other documentary records.

At the local level, historians have to use their instincts and their imagination in tracking down sources relating to technology. *City directories and newspaper ads can provide some basic information about what types of businesses existed at different times and where they were located. Old catalogues, trade magazines, and car or appliance manuals contain valuable technical and production information as well as the names of local dealers. Large construction projects such as the installation of street lighting, power and water service, and public transit systems were often topics of heated debate in towns and cities and are thus likely to be recorded in municipal government records and local newspaper articles.

Business records can be harder to track down and, where they have survived, are usually devoted to administrative and financial matters rather than manufacturing processes and machinery. Larger companies with national networks—telephone and railway companies are obvious examples—that kept detailed records over time, will sometimes have information relating to local infrastructure and the most historically conscious may even have photo and artifact collections. Researchers can also fill some of the gaps in local business records by locating and interviewing former employees who can sometimes provide personal accounts of how a factory evolved over time and what impact retooling and automation had on the conditions and quality of work there. All of these sources, though, should be used carefully and corroborated wherever possible.

*Photographs can also be a valuable

and interesting source of information. Streetscapes are especially useful since they often depict everything from modes of transportation, road surfaces and buildings to public lighting and signage to trolley, telegraph, telephone, or electrical wiring. The alert researcher may also notice parking meters, gas stations, broadcast antennas and countless other technological details that might normally escape our notice. Interior images can also reveal a great deal about the technological past. Does the room have a fireplace? Is it fueled by wood, coal, or gas? Or is the room heated by a radiator? Are there any electrical outlets or appliances visible? What kind of lamps are in use?

Once you start thinking about technology, you will begin to see it everywhere. Its history is as varied and complex as the history of the people who for centuries have created and used it. And thinking about the history of technology not only helps us to understand the central role it has played in the evolution of our communities, it also enhances our ability to understand and make decisions about the role of technology in our lives today and in the future.

SHARON BABAIAN

See automobile; virtual shopping.

tenement. A tenement is a dwelling house or building, generally associated with the poor, that is divided into separate apartments and rented to different families. These buildings usually feature shared facilities, such as bathrooms. The first tenement houses were said to have been built in New York City about 1835.

Thompson, E. P. E. P. Thompson (1924–1993), whose work inspired new directions for research in *social history in England and the United States because of its fresh approach and deep passion, has been much lauded but seldom really emulated. It is not an exaggeration to suggest that E. P. Thompson's profound explorations in history still present the best opportunity to develop a richer, more meaningful field of local history. Indeed, that opportunity is a fundamental responsibility.

Thompson is perhaps best known for his 1963 classic, *The Making of the English Working Class* (N.Y., 1963), and some powerful articles on time and work-discipline and on the English crowd, although his interest, research, and range of writing proved far broader. At the heart of his scholarship he focused on the ways in which people deal with the circumstances of their existence in a society that tends by its organization and purpose to reduce them to economic definitions instead of regarding them as human beings. Thus his history looked at people historians had usually neglected, people who did not leave diaries and documents, people at the middle and bottom of society, people who sometimes lived outside the law, people who were often regarded with condescension and contempt by the authorities. He studied popular behavior and sentiments and evolving social movements—parts of history that had been generally overlooked—and he put them all together into a coherent whole, and he revealed people who formed, over time, a common identity in opposition to the prevailing social order. He thereby gained a clearer picture of the whole community by looking at those who seldom received its blessings.

His perception that the lives of average people are worthy of the attention of the historian and that that attention must be focused on where they live their lives—not in the halls of power, but in their own communities and neighborhoods—helped shift the focus so that more groups outside the prevailing system are now included in academic and public history examinations of life at the local level. As productive as subsequent scholarship has been, however, shining the welcome light of inquiry in the darkened corners of history, those studies tended to show mainly that different cultures *existed* among the American people. They rarely demonstrated, beyond a vague notion of being outside the mainstream, a pattern of cultural growth in which people developed a common consciousness and connected at some level with others. Thus the new scholarship often even *narrowed* the focus to particular groups that had been ignored instead of broadening it to include the complex of social and class relations over time—which is what Thompson above all provided.

What have often been missed by those emulating Thompson's work, in the rush to adopt his social judgments and cultural sensitivity, are his creative insights into social processes. Probing the issues of everyday life, Thompson engaged in "an examination of repeated patterns emerging over time," which revealed people who make choices, people who "act, experience, think, and act again." Indeed this formulation of what he called "agency" caused him to

break with rigid Marxist models of analysis and also to reject the prevailing Western historical orthodoxies that, like society itself, reduce people to manageable economic categories. Not surprisingly, that historical agency can be seen clearest in the local arena because there the inquiry allows a deeper familiarity with the webs of relationships and provides an opportunity for even the most conventional sources to reveal far more than their creators intended. The community, the neighborhood, the village—that is where the whole of a society can be seen, in all its colors and textures, and is where a sense of historical context can emerge.

That notion of a historical context other than progress—or the alter-ego of progress, economic and institutional growth—is at the core of Thompson's work but has usually been the first part jettisoned. By context, Thompson meant a conceptual framework in which the subtle elements—patterns of behavior, institutions, traditions, work, play, values, and more—of a community's history could be brought together in a meaningful whole that is greater than the sum of its parts. Context is not just a matter of placing the political and economic and cultural realms side-by-side, but engaging in an analysis that tries to figure out the way each is connected with the others, the way they shed light on each other. As Thompson said, "The discipline of history is, above all, the discipline of context; each fact can be given meaning only within an ensemble of other meanings...." In emphasizing the importance of historical context, of the "agency of the people," and of a microcosmic view of life and history, E. P. Thompson showed how large issues could be explored with powerful results at the local level.

Yet most studies of local history remain isolated, devoid of context beyond finite geographic boundaries. Very few community histories explore the impact of economic change on the way people live, and then how those people respond to it over time and how that relates to what is happening elsewhere. Academic historians tend to gravitate toward the centers of power where "real" issues can be studied and *public historians tend to ignore the broader picture of which their subjects form a crucial part.

Yet, if this kind of study can not be done at the local level, where can it be done? The alternative really is not to look elsewhere but to abandon the search completely and rest satisfied with the construction of compartments into which we neatly pigeonhole our subjects, whether they are towns, villages, or people. To do so, however, does an injustice to those people we study and also misses an important opportunity and evades a crucial responsibility of historians. We need always to ask, as E. P. Thompson urged, "those questions of satisfaction, of the direction of social change, which the historian ought to ponder if history is to claim a position among the significant humanities."

MICHAEL CASSITY

See economic history; work, history of.

Tocqueville, Alexis de. Alexis de Tocqueville (1805–1859) and his companion Gustave de Beaumont traveled in the United States in 1832 to study the U.S. prison system. Upon returning to France, Beaumont wrote a novel about slavery while Tocqueville wrote two volumes about his experiences, *Du système penitentiaire aux États-Unis, et de son application en France* (published in France in 1833; an English translation followed that same year). Tocqueville's most important work, *De la démocratie en Amérique,* or *Democracy in America,* first appeared in English in a London edition in 1836; then in New York 1843–1845. This book offers insights about localities and about American culture, especially concerning *voluntary societies, *politics in America, slavery, and the status of *labor and *women.

See travel literature.

tourism. "Heritage tourism," often interchangeable with "cultural tourism," is a term that refers to the promotion and marketing of the history of a particular locality, region, nation, or cultural and ethnic heritage in order to attract visitors and tourists. There is nothing new about the fusion of history pilgrimage and commerce. The earliest religious pilgrimages to sacred landscapes and ancestral homelands were a form of heritage tourism. And vendors, moneychangers, and mendicants have always existed at those sites.

In the United States, the tourism that developed with the rise of a middle *class in the nineteenth century featured sites important to the evolving national story of European, especially English, settlement and the founding of the American republic. George Washington's home, Mount Vernon, was a desti-

take primacy over economic planning, and the community must do comprehensive and accurate research and data collection. Issues of cultural resources and site integrity must be negotiated and mediated. The community should be an informed and discerning "first tourist."

Heritage tourism is essentially commmercial and seeks to both entertain and inform its audience. It will indeed produce revenue for some areas, but will fail to meet expectations in others. If local historians have been part of the process of cultural inventory and have made their research methods known and accepted, there will be community benefits beyond tourism revenue.

Several recent books review the process by which U.S. towns and cities have become sites for heritage tourism. Among the best is Dennis R. Judd and Susan S. Fainstein, eds., *The Tourist City* (New Haven, Conn., 1999). A book of essays by scholars, it describes the evolution of towns and cities from centers of trade and production through eras of abandonment to current efforts to market them as centers of historical landscapes, structures, and services. They divide these efforts into three categories: (1) the resort city, such as Las Vegas; (2) the traditionally historic city, such as Boston; and (3) the converted city that has purposely developed a tourist section, such as Seattle. The latter may be the most problematic for local historians because it is often set apart from the "real" city, depends on a Disneyesque version of the American past, and succeeds in driving out whatever was unique in an area. Yet the authors understand the importance of tourism in a postindustrial world with a global economy. Good chronicles of the recent woes of cities, towns, and even suburbs are Richard Moe and Carter Wilkie, *Changing Places: Rebuilding Community in the Age of Sprawl* (N.Y., 1997), and Jon C. Teaford, *The Rough Road to Renaissance* (Baltimore, 1990). A theoretical but very useful account of changes in U.S. neighborhoods and cities is Michael Sorkin, ed., *Variations on a Theme Park: The New American City and the End of Public Space* (N.Y., 1994).

A brief article in *History News* by Roy C. Turnbaugh, "Myths and Realities: The Uses and Misuses of History" (54/1 [winter 1999], pp. 18–21), succinctly notes the origins of much local legend in popular culture, citing the need such fictions fill, and notes the power of "toxic historical myths" in an age of mass communication. Another brief article, with a good bibliography, is Michelle J. Dorgan's, "Why Heritage Is Not a Bad Word: The Role of Historians in the Heritage Industry," *Public History News* 18/1 (fall 1997). The article focuses primarily on the development of heritage areas. In 1996, a presidential commission on the arts and humanities published *Exploring America Through Its Culture*, projecting the increased economic importance of cultural tourism. The commission, in conjunction with *AASLH and the National Trust for Historic Preservation, published *Heritage Tourism: Partnerships and Possibilities* (Nashville, Tenn., 1994).

For a general background to the subject of heritage tourism, start with Eric Hobsbawn and Terence Ranger, *The Invention of Tradition* (Cambridge, Eng.,

1974), one of the first books to examine the origins of traditions. David Whisnant's *All That Is Native and Fine* (Chapel Hill, N.C., 1981) is an excellent chronicle of how well-meaning outsiders "helped" *Appalachians, in the early years of the twentieth century, to rediscover and market their past. For the origins of tourism, see John F. Sears, *Sacred Places: American Tourist Attractions in the Nineteenth Century* (N.Y., 1989).

National context for local issues may be found in John Bodnar, *Remaking America: Public Memory, Commemoration, and Patriotism in the Twentieth Century* (Princeton, N.J., 1992); Michael Kammen, *Mystic Chords of Memory: The Transformation of Tradition in American Culture* (Ithaca, N.Y., 1991); Edward Linenthal, *Sacred Ground: Americans and Their Battlefields* (Urbana, Ill., 1991). International (primarily European and North American) context may be found in David Lowenthall, *Possessed by the Past: The Heritage Crusade and the Spoils of History* (N.Y., 1996).

A useful survey of Americans' approach to history is David Thelen and Roy Rosenszweig, *The Presence of the Past: Popular Uses of History in American Life* (N.Y., 1998).

MARIE TYLER McGRAW

See heritage; travel literature.

town. A town is bigger than a village or hamlet, but smaller than a city. In New England, a town is a unit of local government, a political subdivision of the state — such as a county or city government. It may also be called a township.

toys. Most historical museums have children's toys exhibited as curious or collectable or even as quaint and attractive objects. The history of toys, however, is worth considering in a somewhat broader manner. The word "toy" itself is interesting. Today it is used to denote a plaything exclusively for children, but previous to the eighteenth century, "toy" described anything from a bauble of little value, to a small dog, or a costly miniature.

While children have always played, their toys were often objects that came to hand. The earliest manufactured doll dates to 1413 in Germany. Toys were brought to the New World in 1585 with the Roanoke Colony as gifts for the Indians. Through the eighteenth century, children of wealthy parents were likely to have toys, mostly of European manufacture. Children's portraits, in Europe and in the New World, often show a boy or girl holding a prized plaything.

The earliest American manufacture of toys dates to the 1830s, although before that toys were handmade for individual children. There are also early advertisements for imported toys and toy stores that appear in some urban newspapers.

There has been continuity in the types of toys produced, as well as changes in what people have thought appropriate for children. There are safety issues, the dilemma of war play for children to be considered, gender issues, and the social aspects of toys and play. The literature of the history of toys begins in the 1930s with an emphasis upon the manufacture of toys.

See, in particular, James S. Tippett, *Toys and Toy Makers* (N.Y., 1931); recent books address collecting antique toys or the manufacture of toys by specific companies. Richard O'Brien provides an overview in *The History of American Toys: From the Puritans to the Present* (N.Y., 1990), which has a useful bibliography. Marshall and Inez McClintock, *Toys in America* (Washington, D.C., 1961) is also helpful. Thomas W. Holland published *Boys' Toys of the Fifties and Sixties: Memorable Catalog Pages from the Legendary Sears Christmas Wishbooks, 1950–1969* (Sherman Oaks, Calif., 1997), along with a companion book for girls. An important book to see is Gary Cross, *Kids' Stuff: Toys and the Changing World of American Childhood* (Cambridge, Mass., 1997).

There are various museums of toys and some museums have collections of toys on display. Notable among those that exhibit children's playthings is the Margaret Woodbury Strong Museum in Rochester, New York.

See children's history.

transcript. A modern rendering of a document; a copy or representation.

travel literature. The genre of travel writing poses a particular dilemma for local historians. By definition, the traveler is alien, the consummate outsider; the travel narrative itself is, it seems, inevitably a form of colonialism, an effort by that traveler to filter the local story through his own sense of necessary order and structure. Travel writing thus becomes something for the local historian to challenge, to resist, to correct. Aside from the occasional collaborator, no self-respecting Canaanite would turn to the Book of Genesis to learn the

history of her people and place. Likewise, those living in the cedar forests outside of the Sumerian city of Uruk would have resented their characterization as howling beasts by the hero of the *Epic of Gilgamesh*. From the earliest entries in the field, travel writing serves as a record of what *they* think of *us* (or what *we* think of *them*), a record that is tarnished by all the sins for which such colonial ventures have become known.

Yet historians know that they can ill afford to discard any available source. If the accounts of even sympathetic outsiders can be faulted for their narrowly selective vision (think of Margaret Mead in New Guinea, or Carl Van Vechten in Harlem), then the record produced by loyal insiders might be equally tainted by parochialism and a kind of xenophobic *boosterism. Mark Twain's biting skepticism went a long way toward deflating the pretensions of self-styled local aristocrats, both in the American South and in Europe. By his own account, Richard Wright might never have escaped the South had he not encountered H. L. Mencken's sustained assault on Southern manners and mores. If the mirror the traveler holds up is always a bit distorted, it is also true that such distortion is often informed by a kind of truth that might otherwise be missed.

Travel writing is thus both a bane and a boon for the local historian. Nowhere, I think, has this duality been more obvious than in the United States. Americans have long received the views of outsiders with both wary skepticism and an almost indiscriminate enthusiasm. Glance at any nineteenth-century newspaper and chances are good that you will find a report of some visiting dignitary's observations upon the local scene. Of course, the tactful visitor was always prepared with, well, some tactful observations, for many a traveler has learned the hard way that hell hath no fury like local pride scorned. Those same American citizens who yearned to hear such worldly authorities as Matthew Arnold, Charles Dickens, or Mrs. Trollope praise their local institutions and manners were quick to dismiss those observers as ignorant if they were unduly judgmental of those institutions and manners. Indeed, so obsessed were these Americans with the views of the outsider that they granted alien status to one of their own: Henry James might well be said to have made his career as an insider on the outside looking back in at the American scene.

Of course, historians have been generally cautious in using such accounts. James's pose as an almost disembodied outsider is particularly easy to dismantle, and while his account does tell us a good deal about the manners and customs of the America he visits, it ultimately tells us more about Henry James than it does about Boston or New York in 1904. A notable and significant exception to this legacy of benign skepticism involves the mother of all travel books, Alexis de *Tocqueville's *Democracy in America.* Over 150 years after the travels it depicts, Tocqueville's text exercises a hold on the American imagination that often exceeds that of such secondary documents as the Constitution and the Declaration of Independence. In some circles—academic, congressional, cultural—Tocqueville's observations about the essence of the United States are revered with a kind of fundamentalism that would impress William Jennings Bryan. Indeed, Tocqueville has so thoroughly influenced the study of U.S. culture and politics that debate over his legacy has focused less on whether or not he got it right than on whether or not the United States *should* be the kind of country he described.

If the mark of a successful travel book is its thorough absorption into the culture it purports to describe, then Tocqueville's two-volume opus is peerless in its achievement. The exhaustive detail with which the Frenchman regales his audience seems to crush any instinct to treat his account with a skeptical eye. The sheer weight of his work lends it an authority that has proven difficult to resist. Among the many lessons his book and its legacy offer is one about the perils of relying too heavily on the outsider to tell us who we are. This is a different but no less serious peril than rejecting that outsider as having nothing to tell us that we need to hear. While the learned outsider's account might provide an antidote to parochialism, it also might erase those features that are distinctively local and vulnerable to assimilation.

Much of the older tradition of travel writing sought to locate a sense of national identity at the local level. Nineteenth- and early twentieth-century observers of the American scene generally aimed to uncover a cohesiveness and unity within the myriad parts that made up the United States. Such accounts neatly served the purposes of those working to keep the Union from fraying in the years before the Civil War, and those working to swiftly heal old wounds and get back to business in the years after. This emphasis on what different American places held in common persisted through the middle of the twentieth century, when increasing mobility put millions of Americans on the road in search of the comforts of home. Popular travel writing mixed just enough of the exotic with a healthy dose of the familiar, allowing the mobile consumer to enjoy an authentic experience with minimal risk. Not coincidentally this brought great joy to chambers of commerce around the country, where efforts to accommodate local conditions to the expectations of the traveler mirrored the efforts of those who sought to bring American history into agreement with Tocqueville's observations. The epitome of this trend is the authentic adobe McDonald's restaurant in Taos, New Mexico.

While this trend is far from played out, the homogenization of the local in service to the traveler has spawned a counter-tradition in travel writing. In academic, cultural, and tourism circles, Americans have rediscovered "sense of place," that amorphous quality that distinguishes Portsmouth, New Hampshire from Portsmouth, Virginia. Whether in the *New York Times*'s "Sophisticated Traveler" column, the "Local Scene" section of the ubiquitous Frommer's guide, or one of the hundreds of recently published books celebrating the uniqueness of America's places, the goal is the same: to articulate what makes this place special, worth visiting or living in, worth learning about. And central to achieving this goal is allowing the place to speak for itself, a conscious if always imperfect commitment to resisting the colonial impulse.

Of course, even the best of this new travel writing reveals the contradictions at the heart of this endeavor. Defining "sense of place" makes nailing Jello to the wall seem easy. Moreover, an obsessive search for the unique and idiosyncratic—the *sine qua non* of the genre—can too easily lead to caricature. Can you be a true resident of Seattle without having tasted a latte? At a fundamental level, the effort to define a place for visitors, that is, for tourists, for consumers, inevitably leads to the transformation of that place: how long will locals continue to go to a place to which the tourists are now flocking to see where the locals go? How much observation can unique local traditions and rituals endure before they cease being truly local? Listen to old-timers talk about the gentrification of the Missoula, Montana, Farmer's Market and you will understand how transient a sense of place can be. For the local historian, travel writing is as notable for the way in which it alters its subject as for the way in which it reflects it. But that is simply the meat of modern historiography. I recently led a group of students on a study tour of the Southwest. While in Santa Fe, we visited several places that had been identified in our reading as true local hangouts, places where we could learn from authentic Santa Feans what the place was "really about." What we found, at bar, coffee shop, and hot spring, was mostly other visitors who had read the same books and were on a similar quest for the "authentic Santa Fe." And what our group came to understand, as we moved from place to place, was that however much we wanted to learn about those places we visited, the real risk was that we would wind up learning something about ourselves. That may be the ultimate lesson travel writing has to teach, whether we are the visitor or the visited.

CHARLES MITCHELL

traveler's accounts and tourism. See cultural tourism; travel literature.

Trempealeau County. Trempealeau County, Wisconsin, is the locale of Merle Curti's *The Making of an American Community: A Case Study of Democracy in a Frontier County* (Stanford, Calif., 1959). Curti, the distinguished student of Frederick Jackson Turner, published this classic study of a frontier community in 1959. Curti's inspired work tested Turner's *"frontier thesis." Turner had traced U.S. democratic institutions and character to frontier opportunities. Anticipating later trends in social history, Turner and Curti focused upon the experience of ordinary people. In Turner's poetic and imaginative view of the frontier, democratic institutions and distinctly American ways and values such as self-reliance, individualism, egalitarianism, generosity, and neighborliness emerged from the many frontier communities and shaped the American character and an American mind. Following Turner's lead, Curti suggested that the very task of forging a community on the frontier created not only a local culture but also a uniquely American one.

Between 1850 and 1880 a generation of pioneers transformed a rugged wilderness into a settled rural community. New Englanders who traced their families back to the first Pilgrims at Plymouth Plantation and to the settlers of the Massachusetts Bay Colony reenacted again the drama of building a community in the wilderness. Relying heavily on quantitative data, Curti interrogated the relationship between economic opportunities and political democracy. As Curti explained, "We have not tried to test the [Turner thesis] but rather our interpretation of Turner's theory that the ready accessibility of free or almost free land promoted economic equality and that this was followed by political equality."

While Curti claimed that he had a limited goal, in fact he left few aspects of rural culture unexamined. Everything from public education to popular entertainment was scrutinized in relationship to Turner's thesis. As Curti probed the creation of communities in Trempealeau County, he grappled with the difficult task of making "explicit the values implicit in social behavior in the family, the school, the lyceum, the town meeting, the church, the fraternal organization," and with discerning the "social creed" of the community as it was expressed "on the lecture platform, at the literary society, and in the newspaper, letters, and memoirs." The social creed embraced by Trempealeau's pioneers bore close resemblance to those American values that Turner concluded were nurtured on the frontier. Thus the frontier by 1880 was, as the title of his book suggests, creating "American Communities."

The frontier became a powerful force for the "Americanization" of the immi-

445

grant, effectively assimilating a mixture of ethnic groups. Norwegian and Polish immigrants, both of whom arrived impoverished and unschooled in democratic ways, rapidly caught up with their Yankee neighbors economically and by 1880 made themselves a political presence to be reckoned with. The frontier worked as a melting pot, transforming even poor immigrants. Diverse cultural groups came to share common attitudes and outlooks on life. In Turner's and Curti's analyses, the process of assimilation of immigrants and the frontier experience were profoundly interconnected and Curti concluded Americanization was well underway by 1880.

Curti looked back to Turner for his questions, but pioneered the new *social history of the 1960s and 1970s in his choice of sources and methods. As a historian working in the 1950s, Curti challenged the historical profession by his questions, methods, and conclusions. By that time Turner's work had faced three decades of debunking; the agrarian republican traditions valorized by Turner had been denigrated as backward-looking pathology. Curti countered with the intensive research in local sources and the hardest of data. His innovative use of early computer technology and quantitative analysis was a model for a generation of social historians attending to the lives of ordinary people ranging from blacks in slavery to workers in Massachusetts.

The Making of an American Community still stands as the outstanding historical study of a Midwestern frontier community. Curti's work on Trempealeau County has informed the work

of historians of the *Midwest and of the new rural history and provided a foundation for the work of a more recent study of rural Wisconsin. In *Between Memory and Reality: Family and Community in Rural Wisconsin, 1870–1970* (1992), Jane Pederson returned to Trempealeau County to study rural America in the postsettlement period. While relying upon Curti's work as a base, Pederson considered the subsequent story of a rural community and the culture of Trempealeau after the frontier. Typical of the new rural history, *Between Memory and Reality* engaged key issues of concern to contemporary historians including ethnicity, gender, sociability, class, and market relations. She asked what happened to rural families and communities in the twentieth century as the nation became increasingly urban. What was the impact of the expansive market economy, new technologies of farm production, transformations in communication, transportation, and education on rural life? How did ethnicity shape rural communities, and how did ethnicity influence rural strategies in contending with the challenges of modernity?

Pederson argued that American migrants from New York and New England, and European immigrants from Norway, Poland, and Germany often moved to rural Wisconsin for conservative reasons. The frontier and rural Midwest provided a context in which traditional cultures that valued landownership, kinship, religion, and sociability could sustain themselves. The "memory" of the homeland culture structured the rural ethnic communities, and the "reality" of the American environment presented opportunities and challenges. The local work culture, religious rituals and institutions, cooperative economic organization, and kinship bound people together in strong ethnic communities and provided a potent basis for resisting and managing the "reality" of market capitalism and urbanization.

Pederson identified three stages in the communities' history: the frontier or settlement stage from 1850 to 1880, the period studied by Curti; a postfrontier stage between 1880 and 1945 in which ethnic rural cultures flowered; and a final stage extending from World War II to 1970. The postfrontier period brought some surprises unanticipated by Curti. In the 1870s, large numbers of immigrants, particularly from Norway and Poland, arrived. Between 1880 and 1945, rather than rapidly being Americanized, rural ethnic neighborhoods flowered and claimed local hegemony in the townships of Trempealeau. Politically the immigrants brought their own brand of democratic politics that had a direct impact on Wisconsin progressivism. They also had their own ideas about how to organize the work and economy of their households and communities. Valuing kinship and persistence on the land, they adapted cooperative strategies of Scandinavian and European peasants to modern technologies and market opportunities to sustain their family farms.

Ethnic groups redirected local politics, economic organization, and culture. Rural residents of Trempealeau depended on extended kin and community networks as they negotiated the opportunities and necessities of geographic and social mobility. Analysis of gender constructions indicate immigrants adapted their own traditions and values. Courtship and marriage patterns reveal conflicting constructions of ethnicity, gender, and class.

JANE PEDERSON

Turks. See Appendix A.

twentieth-century topics for local historians. Now that we are at the end of it, the twentieth century should become an important topic for local historians. As with any era, there are local issues unique to a community, and there are topics that come from or reflect regional or national history. Some of those larger topics, for the twentieth century would be World Wars I and II; suffrage and the Nineteenth Amendment; Prohibition and the Eighteenth and Twenty-First Amendments; the Depression of the 1930s; civil rights; technological change and its economic and political influence on local life. These provide a broad background against which the locality might be seen. Numerous questions arise: how did local voters respond to Al Smith, for example; what was the local response to the abortion question in the 1980s and 1990s; the local reaction to population change as new ethnic groups appeared? How has the community coped with the loss of manufacturing jobs and the women's movement? There will, of course, not be a uniform local response to any of these issues, but seeing just how a particular community mirrors a regional or national pattern, and how that locality veers away from any general pattern allows us to know more about the places and people we study.

447

For a comment upon the diversity of community opinion, see Richard Wohl and A. Theodore Brown, "The Usable Past: A Study of Historical Traditions in Kansas City," *Huntington Library Quarterly* 23 (May 1960), reprinted in *Pursuit of Local History* (Walnut Creek, Calif., 1997).

See sixties (the 1960s and local historians); technology; topics in recent history.

typhoid. An infectious bacterial disease caused by contact with fecal material from an infected person. Typhoid causes inflammation of the intestines, high fever, and prostration. See Judith Walzer Leavitt, *Typhoid Mary: Captive to the Public's Health* (Boston, 1996).

typhus. A disease caused by a particular class of microorganisms and transmitted to humans by a vector, such as rat, fleas, or body lice. Typhus is characterized by a rash, prostration, and delirium.

U

Ukrainians. See Appendix A,

underground railroad. There is probably no subject more troublesome to local historians than that of the underground railroad. Conceived in secrecy, conducted in silence, there are few records to tell its story—and possibly, far too many places credited as having associations with it.

Sources are the main problem—the lack of them and the responsible use of those that do exist. "I had a diary giving the names, dates, and circumstances of all the slaves I had helped run away," wrote John P. Parker, himself an escaped slave and thereafter an aide to runaways who came through Ripley, Ohio. Parker explains, however, that as a family man, a property owner, and the proprietor of a business, he had a great deal to lose if his record book were discovered. So "as a matter of safety I threw this diary into the iron furnace, for fear it might fall into other hands" (see *His Promised Land*, edited by Stuart Seely Sprague [New York, 1996], pp. 99–100).

This caution was shared. Parker explains that after passage of the Fugitive Slave Act in 1850, "everyone engaged in the work destroyed all existing evidence of his connection with it." The work of aiding fugitives, however, continued apace; "in fact," he writes, it was pursued "more aggressively than ever which speaks well for the conscience and courage" of those involved.

Under these circumstances it is easy to see that the sources for study of the underground railroad are difficult to come by, and why those that have survived are especially to be treasured. It is also easy to understand why local enthusiasts, eager to find evidence of abolition activity, have expanded upon those sources with folklore and fiction, suspending critical analysis at the very time when they need to take the most care.

The interesting question to ask is why so much interest in underground railroad history should be erupting now, at the end of the twentieth century. There are a number of possible answers. The Sanctuary movement conducted by some Americans to aid and shelter Central Americans who fled to this country for refuge might have spurred interest in the older activity. Certainly the current interest in the actions of those who aided Jews during the Holocaust is another reason. In addition, underground railroad activities have been featured on television shows, and the underground railroad is an active destination on the Internet. Newspapers too, have cited underground railroad sites as tourist attractions.

Most importantly, local historians have also turned to the subject in their search to understand and illuminate African American local history, which until recently has been long neglected in the local canon and difficult to research because of the lack of many of the traditional sorts of records.

These are manifestations of current interest in the subject. The most overriding reason for a revival of history of underground activity is surely that in this nation where race has been a pressing national concern, tales of the underground railroad soothe misgivings about the nature of that conflict. They stress interracial cooperation, give some people a way of asserting moral correctness about the position they think they would have—or that their communities did take. This is because actions of those involved in the underground railroad can be divided today into the just and unjust—for there were people who did a right thing, and people who did wrong or bad things. Thus, underground railroad activity becomes a symbol of positive behavior in our long national history of racial anguish. It is a way of saying that all white people were not guilty, that black and white and Native American aided the fugitive to escape an unjust situation.

Local historians tend to be careful about this topic. In the face of casual disregard of the facts, especially by journalists and local promoters, it is the local historians who are doing their best to document the claims they make for their communities. The problem, however, is that school teachers, in particular, and others in general, are so avid for any information that whatever is available—especially in print—is likely to be believed and used.

The story of the underground railroad is more complicated and interesting than one of escaped slaves and those who aided their progress north. The story is really one of community conflict, of moral decisionmaking, of the law abiding—who therefore were those, after 1850, who did *not* aid fugitives, even if they might have wanted to—and of those courageous people who took risks in order to lend a needed hand. The story is also of communities known as safe and those that were decidedly unsafe, and it is the story of a shifting network of routes that changed with times and local attitudes, one particular route used on one day, a different way the only sure path on another. It is the story of churches that split apart over this issue and of ministers finding ways to justify the return of slaves because they were under the aegis of the laws of Caesar, not the laws of God.

All this makes the underground railroad even more interesting and important because *in context* it becomes an episode in courage and moral character.

See two pamphlets produced by the National Park System to aid in underground railroad research: *Exploring a Common Past: Researching and Interpreting the Underground Railroad* (Washington, D.C., 1998), and *Underground Railroad: Official National Park Handbook* (Washington, D.C., 1998) are valuable to anyone interested in this research. See also Larry Gara, *The Liberty Line: The Legend of the Underground Railroad* ([1961] Lexington, Ky., 1996).

unions. See labor history and the history of communities.

Unitarian Universalist Christian Fellowship. See Appendix B.

United Church of Christ. See Appendix B.

United States government records. See archives and local history; Bureau of Reclamation; Library of Congress; National Archives and Records Administration, The.

urban history. Historian Richard Hofstadter, commenting upon the metamorphosis of the agrarian American republic, wrote that: "The United States was born in the country and has moved to the city." He referred to the great population movements that had characterized the course of American history, especially those that had produced concentrated settlements and had dramatically transformed the landscape. In 1790, the nation's first census found that approximately 5 percent of the U.S. population lived in "urban" communities, defined as places possessing at least 2,500 inhabitants. Within a few short decades, America's urban population was growing faster than its rural counterpart. While 15 percent of Americans lived in cities by 1850, the subsequent decades were characterized by increased industrialization, new modes of public transportation, expanding residential areas towards the city's perimeter, and the development of business districts in the central city. The nation experienced such tremendous growth during these decades that by 1920, 51 percent of the American people resided in cities. The ensuing years witnessed more dramatic increases so that according to the 1990 census, over 75 percent of Americans lived in an urban area.

The specialized field of urban history arose in the twentieth century as professional historians sought answers to questions about the nature of our changing society by examining issues and themes associated with population concentration, industrialization, and cultural developments in America's cities. Simply defined, urban history pertains to the historical analysis of the spatial distribution of people, the diverse institutions and activities that occur within the context of cities and their immediate suburban surroundings, and the cultural identity of each place. Decades after the formalization of urban-history studies, historians continue to debate the exact focus of the field, questioning whether urban-history centers on issues limited to a specific local community or whether it deals with larger issues and processes common to urban areas, such as industrialization and suburbanization.

The writing of urban history has evolved dramatically over the generations. The earliest attention given to the development of America's cities surfaced in the 1870s amidst the nation's centennial observance. Written by lay historians or gentleman-scholars, these histories chronicled the evolution of a local community over the course of the century. They focused on the transformation of pioneer settlers to modern city dwellers and referred nostalgically to a "simpler past," though celebrating the progress made by merchants and businessmen and the advance of cultural developments. Generally, these enthusiastic works exuded a spirit of local *"boosterism" and self-promotion rather than offering any serious analysis of the community's history.

In the late nineteenth century, cities encountered new problems and challenges, brought about by rapid industrialization, in-migration of foreigners and rural residents, and continuing urbanization. About the same time, the historical profession emerged, which led academic historians, many of whom were influenced by Progressive and reformist tendencies, to begin examining cities' problems with a more critical eye. Urban histories of the period, however, continued to be what many called "urban biography," simply a narrative of a city or a specific issue related to an urban location.

The roots of a more serious and analytical urban history can be found in the Chicago School of Sociology of the 1920s and 1930s. Sociologists viewed the city as a social laboratory in which to explore elements of the changing society. Robert E. Park and Ernest Burgess of the University of Chicago, in exploring the internal structures and dynamics of neighborhoods and the meaning of community in America's cities, pioneered new explanations of population movements and behavior in urban environments, thereby providing a deeper understanding of people's responses to the evolving urban society.

Any consideration of the origins of urban history must include Arthur M. Schlesinger Sr. and his works *The Rise of the City, 1878–1898* (N.Y., 1933) and "The City in American History" (*Mississippi Valley Historical Review*, June 1940). Like historian Frederick Jackson Turner (*frontier thesis), who in 1893 argued the "significance of the frontier in American history," Schlesinger acknowledged the city as the "new" frontier where ideas and innovation for the modern age originated, people learned to adapt to new experiences, and American life was reshaped. Recognizing the importance and vibrancy of cities, Schlesinger called upon historians to investigate the economic and social aspects of urban areas, claiming that their efforts would provide a better insight into the emergence of contemporary American society.

Over the ensuing decades, the field of urban history crystallized as professional historians began writing analytical case studies of U.S. cities, the first ones focusing on Holyoke, Massachusetts; Memphis, Tennessee; New York City; and Chicago. New methodologies, inspired by influences from the social sciences, encouraged historians to utilize previously neglected sources in studying cities more thoroughly. Oscar Handlin relied upon nineteenth century census and immigration records in writing *Boston's Immigrants* (Cambridge, Mass., 1941); R. Richard Wohl used an interdisciplinary approach in exploring the culture, formation of communities, and institutionalization of Kansas City.

While Schlesinger's thesis of the centrality of cities in history continued to predominate, two key developments arose within the field. Both built upon traditional historical analysis, but encouraged deeper inquiries into the urban experience. First, historians who proclaimed the significance of the American city and its contribution to American life extended their investigations beyond the city's corporate boundaries to explore the relationship between the city and its "hinterland," or the region surrounding the city. Richard C. Wade's *The Urban Frontier: The Rise of Western Cities* (Chicago, 1959) was among the first to examine this connection. Second, Eric Lampard, in his article "American Historians and the Study of Urbanization" (*American Historical Review*, October 1961), concluded that urban history should not simply focus on the history of cities and their problems, but should study "urbanization as a societal process." Consequently, both approaches led to broader examinations of cities within American society.

As a result of the social changes of the 1960s and the emerging ethnic/racial/gender awareness of groups previously excluded from the historical narrative, urban historians embarked upon new scholarly inquiries that became known as the "new urban history." Heavily influenced by the social sciences, this innovative, multidisciplinary approach attempted to examine the complexities of urban life and to investigate new subjects, especially those pertaining to ordinary people. Of particular note was the emergence of computers and quantitative methods, which allowed researchers to use large quantities of social data found in *censuses, *city directories, and other serial records in their analysis of populations. The "new urban history" was characterized by studies in geographical, social, and economic mobility; migration; acculturation and community life; and demographic patterns, among other topics. Noteworthy studies in the field include Stephan Thernstrom's *Poverty and Progress* (Cambridge, Mass., 1964), a case study of social mobility in nineteenth-century Newburyport, Massachusetts; Peter Knights's *The Plain People of Boston* (N.Y., 1971); and Kathleen Neils Conzen's *Immigrant Milwaukee* (Cambridge, Mass., 1979), an analysis of Germans in this nineteenth-century Wisconsin city. Two influential studies on suburban development include Sam Bass Warner Jr.'s *Streetcar Suburbs: The Process of Growth in Boston, 1870–1900* (Cambridge, Mass., 1962), and Kenneth T. Jackson's *Crabgrass Frontier: The Suburbanization of the United States* (N.Y., 1985).

With the use of new methodologies

and an interdisciplinary approach, the study of urban history has expanded well beyond the urban biographies of earlier decades. Historians have begun to examine the history of individual cities within the larger historical and cultural context of the regions in which they exist. David Goldfield's *Cotton Fields and Skyscrapers* (Baton Rouge, La., 1982) explored Southern urbanization in relation to Southern history and culture. William Cronon, in *Nature's Metropolis: Chicago and the Great West* (N.Y., 1991), blended local history and regional analysis in a study of Chicago as the center of a regional network of settlements. Such studies enhance our understanding of urban locations by allowing us to examine the relationship between places and to realize that cities and their surroundings do not exist separate from each other.

Since the late 1980s, interest in urban history and culture has produced two other outlets for scholarly research and public dissemination. Urban *encyclopedias, such as those produced for Cleveland (1987), Indianapolis (1994), and New York City (1995), provide fairly comprehensive histories of their cities, serve as reference volumes, and point researchers toward new realms of investigation. Research centers devoted to the study of urban areas also have arisen. The Center for *Middletown Studies (1980) at Ball State University continues the research agenda begun by sociologists Robert S. and Helen Merrell Lynd in the 1920s. The Polis Center at Indiana University–Purdue University at Indianapolis (1989) employs interdisciplinary methods in studying issues affecting the Indianapolis metropolitan area.

Urban history remains an active field of study. *The Journal of Urban History* began publication in 1974, and historians founded the Urban History Association in 1989. Many colleges and universities offer courses in the subject. Ancillary fields, such as urban planning, have led to the formation of specialized professional organizations, such as the Society for American City and Regional Planning History, thereby widening the scope of urban analysis.

The developments within the field of urban history in recent decades have laid a strong foundation for the continued study of America's cities and the urban phenomenon. For the field to remain vibrant in the coming decades, urban historians must broaden their investigations to study the processes of urbanization, compare the urban experiences of cities, examine the impact of suburbanization, and investigate the roles that religion and other aspects of culture play in urban life. As a result, we will, as historian Samuel P. Hays concluded, begin to explore the evolution of our urbanized society in order to develop a more effective understanding and context for the history of our cities.

DAVID VANDERSTEL

utopianism. The term "utopianism" is based on Sir Thomas More's book of 1516 *Utopia* and refers to a visionary scheme for a perfect social order.

North American utopianism has taken many forms, ranging from the Adonoi Shomo Corporation, a Millerite Adventist group, to the Society of Separatists of Zoar in Ohio, and Zodiac, a Mormon community of the late 1840s in Gillespie County, Texas. There have been Hutterites, the Doukhobors from the Transcaucausus who settled in Manitoba, the Fourierists, Owenites, the Transdentialists of Brook Farm, and the various religious communialists such as Benedictine and Cistercian monastic communities. In addition, there have been ethnic utopias such as the Swedish Janssonists at Bishop Hill. There have been Shakers and vegetarians, Theosophists, and spiritualists. There were, in addition, the socialist, communist, anarchist, and free-love experiments, as well as the communes of the 1960s. Some of these groups separated from the rest of society; others lived in the midst of our cities; some had charismatic or dictatorial leaders; some practiced group leadership. In many cases their dress and their architecture have been distinctive.

These utopian experiments were frequently observed in the *travel literature of Canada and the United States. They have also been the object of study by academic scholars who have sought to find what is American or New World about them, seeking also what they brought from the Old World and looking, too, at the relationship of these communities to society at large. *Backwoods Utopias: The Sectarian Origins and the Owenite Phase of Communitarian Socialism in America, 1663–1829* (Philadelphia, 1970), by Arthur E. Bestor Jr., is one of the starting places for anyone interested in this subject; he lists 130 communities. In addition, see the *Dictionary of American Communal and Utopian History*, edited by Robert Fogarty (Westport, Conn., 1980), and his *All Things New: American Communes and Utopian Movements, 1860–*

1914 (Chicago, 1990). See also J. Gordon Melton's *Biographical Dictionary of American Cult and Sect Leaders* (N.Y., 1986), and his *Encyclopedia of American Religions* (Detroit, 1978–1994).

New and particularly helpful is Donald E. Pitzer, ed., *America's Communal Utopias* (Chapel Hill, N.C., 1997), which contains very useful essays, including one by Lawrence J. McCrank on "Religious Orders and Monastic Communalism in America," that pulls together information about Roman Catholic communal groups. Pitzer's book also contains chronologies of a number of communal orders and an extensive and useful list of all communal experiments, including those still underway. The book also contains a long bibliographical essay that will be very useful for any researcher.

There are many specialized studies that are important. Robert V. Hine's classic work *California's Utopian Colonies* (N.Y., 1966) is a model of a book that looks at one state's contribution to social experimentation. Dolores Hayden has written about the architecture of utopias in *Seven American Utopias: The Architecture of Communitarian Socialism, 1790–1975* (Cambridge, Mass., 1976). See also Uri D. Herscher, *Jewish Agricultural Utopias in America, 1880–1910* (Detroit, 1981); William H. Pease and Jane H. Pease, *Black Utopia: Negro Communal Experiments in America* (Madison, Wisc., 1963); and the Syracuse University Press series on utopianism and communalism that includes several important books, including Spencer Klaw, *Without Sin: The Life and Death of the Oneida Community* (Syracuse, 1993), and Wendy E. Chmielewski,

Louis J. Kern, and Marlyn Klee-Hartzell eds., *Women in Spiritual and Communitarian Society in the United States* (Syracuse, N.Y., 1993), with its interesting essay by Carol Kolmerten on women's experiences in Owenite communites.

$\mathcal{V}$

vernacular. "Vernacular" implies belonging to, or characteristic of a place. Associated primarily with architecture, it can also be used with writings of a local nature, of paintings, words, or other creations that stem from a locality and help define that place. When used with architecture it often refers to buildings created without an architect.

See pattern books.

veterans records. See pension records.

Victoria History of the Counties of England. Called the *VCH*. The writing of English county history began in 1899 as a private enterprise, supported by subscribers, one of whom was Queen Victoria. One hundred sixty volumes were projected, to be completed in six years; at present there are over 200 volumes, but the project is far from complete. The books were to be a "scholarly and comprehensive encyclopaedia of English local history in all periods, a repository of essential information and the starting point for further research." The project is currently based at the Institute of Historical Research at the University of London.

village. From the Latin *villaticus*, meaning a collection of dwellings, a village is larger than a hamlet but smaller than a town. It is not an urban area and usually has a population of 2,500 inhabitants or fewer.

Virginia Antiquities, Association for the Protection of. Founded in 1889 to protect from decay the Jamestown site, this is the earliest association of its type in the United States. Today the Association oversees 34 historic properties and encourages research. The headquarters is located at 204 W. Franklin St., Richmond, Va. 23220; <www.apva.org>.

virtual shopping. What happens when the local goes global, when the global tries to avail itself of the local? An organization that promotes place-based, community-minded education has, for the last two years, maintained a website to facilitate the sharing of information among its widely dispersed audience of educators, activists, and organizers. Recently, it has expanded this website to include a partnership with an on-line company whose work involves the high-volume, discount selling of books. The reason for this partnership was rather simple: to make available to this widely dispersed audience a collection of books that deal with issues of concern at the local level. Of course, the organization also earns a commission for each book the company sells through this partnership, thereby soothing the troubled consciences of its members who might otherwise be expected to buy their books locally.

A visit to this virtual downtown can be instructive. For discounts ranging from 10–30 percent off cover prices, one can purchase such volumes as George C. Benello's *Building Sustainable Communities: Tools and Concepts for Self-Reliant Economic Change* (Ward Morehouse, ed. [1989] N.Y., 1997) or Lucy Lippard's *The Lure of the Local: Senses of Place in a Multi-Centered Society* (N.Y., 1997). As might be gleaned from the titles, these books decry the very phenomenon of virtual commerce through which they can be acquired. Indeed, the entire genre of publication ventures, think tanks, and community organizations dedicated to "the local" that has flowered over the past 15 years (including the organization that has established the partnership with the online bookstore) recognizes Internet shopping as the latest and most sophisticated threat to the values it holds most dear. It is enough, one editorialist quipped, to make one nostalgic for the mom-and-pop atmosphere of Wal-Mart and fast-food chains. Clearly, the rise of "the local" to a kind of trendy prominence has not escaped the twisted reach of irony. The major scholarly organizations, which once considered local historical societies second only to

school teachers in irrelevance, increasingly look for ways to incorporate such societies into their programs and institutional structures. Graduate programs and undergraduate specializations in local history have achieved a kind of glamour among academics disaffected by the humanities' descent into theory. In my own community, the monster chain bookstore has a wider collection of books on local history, and books by local authors, than the older, locally owned stores. The economics and institutional politics of this phenomenon are obvious. What interests me is how this burgeoning attention to, and accessibility of all things local affects the way local identity is understood.

So, what can you learn about where you are, or where you might be going, through a visit to Amazon.com? I have often used this website as a database, availing myself of its relatively speedy and reliable search engine to check on the availability, price, and ISBN numbers of books I will be ordering for my classes. It also serves as a convenient, if sometimes quirky bibliography, generating extensive lists of both in- and out-of-print books for thousands of subject areas. Working on a reading list for a course on the American Southwest, I was able to browse, from my office chair, hundreds of promising titles, including a healthy smattering of cookbooks. This search offered me such fruitful subject areas as "New Mexico—local history"; "New Mexico—art and literature"; "Santa Fe"; and "New Southwest States." Could it get any better than this?

Well, perhaps. As with any classification system, Amazon.com's is only as good as the classifier and the database.

For those of us wedded to the Library of Congress system, a visit to Amazon.com, or even to an actual Barnes and Noble or Border's store, can be perplexing. In one store, I found Walker Percy's *Lost in the Cosmos* shelved with "Essays and Memoirs," Barbara Kingsolver's *High Tide in Tucson* featured in the "Travel Writing" section, and Marilyn Robinson's *The Death of Adam* tucked away under "Religion—General." For my money, each of these books belongs on the same shelf, though I must confess that I am unsure which shelf that should be. Making comparisons between different outlets of the same store is also instructive. Depending upon which city you live in, John Brincker-hoff Jackson's *A Sense of Place, a Sense of Time* may be found under "Architecture," "Cultural Studies," "Philosophy—General," or "Travel Writing." What shape do such commercially-driven categories give to the material of local history?

Well, let's start with my own neighborhood and radiate outward. A subject search for "Elmira" turns up exactly one title, William Reed Gordon's *Elmira and Chemung Valley Trolleys in the Southern Tier*, an out-of-print volume that Amazon.com will search for through its network of used bookstores. This is also the only volume under the subject "Chemung River Valley." There are no listings pertaining to Elmira's notorious Civil War prison camp, to the valley's important place in Revolutionary War history, or to the area's rich, nineteenth-century religious and cultural history, even though each of these subjects is well-covered in both in- and out-of-print books. Indeed, a little

searching suggests that Gordon's book on trolleys is included in the database primarily for the benefit of railroad buffs, since a click on the "Search for related books about: railroads" button yields hundreds of entries.

This, in fact, is one of the most useful, and most intriguing, features of an Amazon.com search. The initial subject-area search generates a list ranging from one to thousands of titles. A single click brings the user to a page of information about the selected title—availability, price, a synopsis, and a selection of brief reviews. Here, one can also consult a convenient list of "related subjects" offering one-click access to all books classified under that subject. In addition to "railroads," "Elmira," and "Chemung River Valley," Gordon's book on trolleys allows me to jump to a wider search under "New York (State)." With no regional intermediaries—no "Chemung County," "Southern Tier," or even "Finger Lakes Region" categories to move onto—it appears that my search will not be radiating outward all that neatly after all. So, I click on "New York (State)" and await the results.

Within seconds I am rewarded with a list of 6,471 entries, arranged in alphabetical order. Had I the patience to scroll through 130 screens of 50 items each (there are, I notice, several double entries), I would no doubt discover a remarkably idiosyncratic range of titles somehow yoked by a shared attention to things New York. I must admit that I do not have this patience, and stop scrolling after noting such gems as *60-Minute Museum Visits, Book 1: New York City*; *The Amityville Horror Conspiracy*; Bill Bonanno's *Bound by Hon-*

or: A Mafioso's Story; and William Kennedy's *Ironweed*, which, I am informed, can also be purchased in its movie version.

To think that someone could capture the essence of New York (State) so easily, without ever leaving home, is strangely comforting. One other entry catches my eye, however, and renews my hope for a more gradual geographical progression from city to state: *30 Bicycle Tours in the Finger Lakes Region*. A quick click brings me to the full page for this entry, and I am delighted to learn that this volume is part of the "25 Bicycle Tours Series." I knew it was tough to contain this region within conventional categories, and here was the proof. Scrolling down the page to the "related subjects" box, I hit the mother lode: in addition to "New York (State)" I can explore such subjects as "Finger Lakes Region," "Finger Lakes (N.Y.)," "United States–Mid-Atlantic–New York," and "United States–Northeast–Middle Atlantic (General)." From this one spot, perhaps, I could piece together my region's identity.

I am disappointed, however, when "Finger Lakes (N.Y.)" returns only two titles, both, it appears, "pictorial histories." A move to "Finger Lakes Region" is more rewarding, with 17 entries, including two geological histories, a folk-art catalog, a pricey picture book of gorges and waterfalls, Deborah Tall's problematic *From Where We Stand*, and a gift-shop history of Seneca Falls and the Women's Rights Movement. While this list would provide the visitor with a good introduction to the major features of the region, there are striking and significant absences. Nothing at all

on the Iroquois, the *burned-over dis-trict, Joseph Smith's encounter with the angel Moroni; no social, cultural, or political history of any kind. The same condition prevails at the next subject category, "United States–Mid-Atlantic–New York," which offers 132 entries, 131 of which are travel or adventure guides.

The unique entry under this subject is a novel, *Moon, Moon, Tell Me True*, written by Ellen Tifft, a "lifelong resident of Elmira." This is also the single work of fiction among the 17 titles located under "Finger Lakes Region." I am intrigued by this solitary representative of the world of literature, and wonder how it came to be singled out as an exemplar of both regional and state identity. Nothing in the synopsis suggests an answer to this question. Indeed, it is not at all clear that the book is even set in New York State, let alone the Finger Lakes. Its subject is carnival life after World War II, so there may well be some local color in it. Still, what merits its exclusive position? Where are the other novels, plays, or volumes of poetry written by local authors or set in the region? Where is A. R. Ammons' *Lake Effect Country*? What about Kurt Vonnegut's *Hocus Pocus*, which told me more about life teaching at a small college in the Finger Lakes than I ever thought I would need to know? The folks at Amazon.com are too busy to answer such specific questions, and unless my grant proposal is approved, I have neither the time nor the resources to research them in any great depth. The privileged inclusion of *Moon, Moon, Tell Me True* may simply reflect the more aggressive marketing tactics of the book's small publisher, since Amazon.com does permit publishers to comment on their books and, perhaps, suggest subject categories. What is clear is that no objective criteria can explain this phenomenon of categorization. And that may be the ultimate lesson of this exercise. The purpose of Amazon.com's search engine, after all, is to facilitate impulse buying. Shoppers expressing interest in a region through a subject-area search are more than likely looking for guidance in consuming that region. They want to know where to eat, sleep, and shop, they want to know what to look at, and they want a succinctly narrated context for what they are looking at. Amazon.com thus defines a region as a place of recreation, photogenic scenery, and interesting rock strata. One can hike and bike there, and maybe squeeze in sixty minutes studying quaint legends and lore. As for history, well, that is a different subject.

CHARLES MITCHELL

vital statistics. Prior to the twentieth century, the compilation of birth and death records in the United States was sporadic and differed greatly from place to place. Churches were initially keepers of vital records; ministers in many colonies were required by law to report christenings and burials to civil authorities. In some areas, consequently, these events are recorded in both civil and church records. Given the transient, rural population, however, only stable, tightly-knit parishes had accurate statistics.

Vital statistics of the population on a national level first appeared in the 1850 decennial census. Broken down by state and territory, they included births, marriages, and deaths reported to have happened during the year ending June 1, 1850. The notes at the beginning of the tables, however, cast doubt on the figures. "The tables of the census which undertake to give the total number of births, marriages, and deaths in the year preceding the first of June, 1850, can be said to have but very little value. . . . Against all reasonings, the facts have proved that people will not, or cannot, remember and report to the census taker the number of such events, and the particulars of them. . . . The table of births . . . includes only those who were born within the year, and were surviving at the end of it: in other words, it comprises the . . . population under one year of age. . . . Upon the subject of the deaths no one can be deceived by the figures of the census, since any attempt to reason from them would demonstrate a degree of vitality and healthfulness in the United States unparalleled in the annals of mankind. . . . The truth is, but a part of the deaths have been recorded. . . ."

The main sources of information about births and deaths in the United States in the twentieth century are the annual reports of deaths since 1900, *Mortality Statistics* (U.S. Bureau of the Census, 1900–1936), and births since 1915 in *Birth, Still Birth, and Infant Mortality Statistics for the United States* (U.S. Bureau of the Census, 1915–1936). In 1937 the information was combined in an annual set of volumes called *Vital Statistics of the United States* (Rockville, Md., U.S. Dept. of Health, Education, and Welfare, Public Health

459

Service, National Center for Health Statistics, 1937–).

In a recent volume of *Vital Statistics*, you can find statistics on, for example, "Live births, birth rates, and fertility rates, by race: U.S. 1909–92"; "Birth rates by age of father and race: U.S., 1940, 1950, and 1960–92"; "Live births by birth weight and race of mother: U.S. and each state, 1992." There are 175 such tables in the 1992 *Birth* volume. The *Mortality* volume has 47 tables, such as, "Deaths from 282 selected causes, by race: U.S. and each state, 1992." Data with greater geographic detail is given in the second part of this volume.

A two-volume compendium, *Historical Statistics of the United States: Colonial Times to 1970* (Washington, D.C.: U.S. Dept. of Commerce, Bureau of the Census, 1975), compresses the tables to give data over time. Examples: "Birth rate: total and for women 15–44 years old, by race: 1800–1970"; "Death rates for selected causes, 1900–1970"; "Infant mortality rate, for Massachusetts, 1851–1970." It is helpful to look at the explanations of the data in these and other tables. Some early statistics are based on estimates, or on samples of the population, and definitions changed over time.

States have their own statistical compilations and registries of vital statistics. For information about individual vital records maintained only on file in state and local offices, some of them from the nineteenth century, see *Where to Write for Vital Records* (Hyattsville, Md., U.S. Dept. of Health and Human Services, Public Health Service, Office of Health Research, Statistics, and Tech-

nology, National Center for Health Statistics; Washington, D.C., 1982–).

In Canada, vital statistics have been collected on a national basis since 1921 except for the Province of Quebec, which entered the system in 1926, and Newfoundland, which entered in 1949 when it joined the Confederation. The principal source for vital statistics in Canada is *Vital Statistics* (annual, 1921–). See also *Historical Statistics of Canada* (2d ed., F. H. Leacy, ed., Ottawa, Canada, 1983).

See U.S. Bureau of the Census, *The Statistical History of the United States from Colonial Times to the Present* (Stamford, Conn., 1965); James H. Cassedy, *Demography in Early America; Beginnings of the Statistical Mind, 1600–1800* (Cambridge, Mass., 1969); and John Cerny, "Research in Birth, Death, and Cemetery Records," in *The Source: A Guidebook of American Genealogy*, Loretto Dennis Szucs and Sandra Hargreaves Luebking, eds. (Salt Lake City, 1997).

MARTHA R. HSU

volunteers. A seemingly limitless supply of eager but disparately motivated would-be helpers began lining up almost immediately after the first public announcement of our new program, which was inspired by the European local history movement and by cooperative social history initiatives operating in American cities from Philadelphia to Phoenix. We took on student interns, retirees, returning mothers, and local history enthusiasts—asking them to help retrieve and record some already-identified information on members of the defined study. Energy immediately bred anarchy as eager helpers "turned loose" in local repositories brought home a strange and wonderful array of historical prizes that they wanted to drop inside before returning to the hunting grounds. Some had photocopied the actual documents. Others had made notes on what they had seen (often without specifying sources). Others had enlisted friends to help—interpreting the project's mission with great imagination.

After a short period of innocent floundering amid a sea of misconceptions and wild expectations, I realized that everyone (the worker bees, sponsors, the public, and myself) needed a more comprehensive understanding of the program, more clearly defined goals, and much more guidance. By 1984, I had developed the first version of a printed primer. This guide defined the project's vision, purposes, and scope. It introduced the human, historical, and institutional resources to be used. It presented the research design, data collection and analysis plans, and described the new resources that would be created—an open-ended biographical file for every community member, a graphics archive of visual representations, and a supplementary library of copies of contemporary and modern resources. A large middle section addressed programming (how findings could be interpreted and presented to diverse audiences). A final part described how project resources would be shared to serve external initiatives and the needs of other organizations, groups, and individuals. Appendices recognized staff members, associates, sponsors and benefactors, and chronicled organizations served. The *Guide* became required

reading for interns and volunteers and for anyone else really interested in learning about what we were doing.

Frequently revised, the *Guide* has become an indispensable part of our practice. It defines terms, answers questions, and provides a basic common denominator for project members. Newcomers are ready to join in the fun when they can pass a short quiz on the program as described in the *Guide*.

To date, more than 200 individuals have graduated from our training program. They have been senior-year history majors, volunteers (a more diverse group), and a few individuals who were considering similar efforts in other communities.

Volunteers must complete our basic training program. Each receives an intake evaluation to determine expectations and levels of interest and commitment. Recruits are asked to read the *Guide* and a selection of published articles on the people of colonial Albany. After passing a readiness quiz, each newcomer imagines the historic community on a guided, street-level tour of the city today. And finally, recruits attend several public presentations that are essentially visual, provide links between the research and programming, and get recruits thinking about engaging diverse audiences. The recruit is then ready to begin.

The training experience is practical and is motivated by essentially different yet happily compatible purposes. First, even the most innocent and unprepared individual needs to appreciate and understand the issues in conducting historical research on a preindustrial topic. The other motivating factor stems from

461

the project's need to mobilize a large and diverse workforce to mine historical information from literally mountains of records, documents, and other resources, and to have the data recorded comprehensively and interpreted in consistent or "project-useful" ways.

The first exercise brings the trainee face to face with raw information recovered and recorded by previous interns. They begin by organizing existing material so that it can be applied to individual case histories. The trainee learns names, grapples with eighteenth-century spelling and reference quirks, and confronts modern recording inconsistencies. After ten hours of alphabetizing—looking for improperly filed material—and much encouragement, the trainee begins to appreciate the need for precision in recording and consistency in filing. The trainee is becoming an intern and begins to recover information from new historical resources—the central part of the basic training experience. Constant monitoring reveals readiness to move on to more complex and challenging sources. Some interns process several sets of church, government, court, real property, and business records. Others are not able to progress beyond the most simple collection procedures. It matters not, as a seemingly limitless supply of copies of all of those primary sources awaits processing and almost all trainees are able to take pride in adding hundreds of bits of "good" information to larger data files. At that point, the most arduous and least glamorous part of the internship has passed. Each intern is assessed and managers reach consensus on how they will spend the rest of the program.

Staples of the second half of the internship are family reconstitution, neighborhood mapping, construction of individual group biographies. Another set of choices involves the most gifted and ambitious interns in developing the graphics archive, articulating the real-property database, and in preparing simple programming items such as maps, guides, and reading lists. In these activities, interns are able to apply the bits of information gleaned and organized into subfiles to developing the in-progress biographies of individuals, their families, and other identity groups. They comprehend the elements of biographical study, the life course as an analytical tool, and how historic individuals functioned as parts of larger social units within the preindustrial community. In the absence of literary resources, they are encouraged to make judgments about historic lives based on recorded or inferred actions. By the end of their program, more than half of the interns have become disciples of the "New Social History" approach.

The young graduates go on to law school, public service, and to the private sector. Most of those who pursue graduate study in history return to us for a second internship, which provides them with personal research topics, a grounding in historiography, and an academic framework for producing an informational publication, lecture, or teaching packet. They also learn to conduct more advanced research and to act as information managers working with new recruits. The older (ranging in age from 25 to 75), nonaffiliated graduates generally remain with us, taking on many of the above roles and sometimes completing another 150 hours of advanced training to earn the status of "Research Associate." The latter group (more than twenty people covering all age groups) has made huge contributions to all parts of our program.

Born out of necessity, the program has optimized the substantial contributions made by a diverse and largely volunteer workforce. At the same time, it has instilled in its graduates a unique perspective on historical study and the humanities. Treating each trainee's time and effort as precious, the program continues to evolve to take better advantage of their contributions.

STEFAN BIELINSKI

$\mathcal{W}$

wages. It is often helpful for historians to have a general idea of the average wage for workers in a particular time period. To accurately determine the value of wages paid, one must ask who earned the wages, for what kind of work, in what region of the country, and at what period in history. The era prior to the Civil War is marked by a great deal of uncertainty because the data is sparse, and it is extremely difficult to agree what "average" market wages were. However, recent scholarship by Robert Margo ("Regional Wage Gaps and the Settlement of the Midwest," *Explorations in Economic History* 36, [1999], 128–43) suggests that markets were more integrated than previously thought.

After the Civil War, the picture becomes clearer: price indices become more reliable and more economic evidence is available. The figure of one dollar a day for the average worker is often cited as a general rule of thumb for this period. However, the figure should be used with great caution, since there are many exceptions, and wages varied across regions and through time.

See especially Stanley Lebergott, *The American Economy: Income, Wealth, and Want* (Princeton, N.J., 1976), and <www.orst.edu/Dept/polsci/sahr>, which gives consumer price information based upon historical statistics.

To calculate the worth of money in the past, try <www.westegg.com/inflation>. This site allows you to translate the value of money at one time to any other time as long as the dates are between the years 1800 and 1998. For example: a dollar in 1937 would be worth $11.51 in 1998, and goods bought for a dollar today would have cost $0.09 in 1937.

NORMA PRENDERGAST

walking tours. For many years, visitors to Boston hiked about the city on the Freedom Trail. Walking a city is the way to see neighborhoods, an activity long used by preservationists as a means of public education and appreciation. In Seattle, the Underground Tour blossomed into popularity in the 1980s, and shortly after that, in New York City there appeared a variety of walking tours available for resident and visitor alike. On June 28, 1999, for example, the *New York Times* (p. E36) carried advertisements for tours offered by Joyce Gold History Tours, Big Onion Walking Tours, Food of New York Tours, the Municipal Art Society, Dr. Phil New York Talks and Walks, Tours by Oscar Israelowitz, Century Walking Tours, the Outdoors Club, Historic New York Tours, Village Alliance, Adventure on a Shoestring, Gotham Walk, Central Park Conservancy, NYC Discovery Tours, 92nd Street Y, Tours by Elliot Rabner, the American Museum of Natural History, Radical Walking Tours, Street Smarts N.Y., Harlem Heritage Tours, Battery Park City Parks, New York City Cultural Walking Tours, Mainly Manhattan Tours, and New York Curmudgeon Tours—surely a testimony to the popularity and availability of walking tours. Some are free, others range in price between $10 and $20. These are generally well focused and led by knowledgeable tour guides.

In evaluating or creating tours it is a good idea to keep in mind the following points:

- The best walking tours encourage users to slow down and take the time to look, to enjoy and to appreciate the *built environment as both a visual treat and as a window to the past.
- Tours do more than communicate easily forgotten facts; they place information into context and suggest ways that the past is relevant to the present.
- Many tours encourage self-discovery. They challenge users to think, to consider history from different perspectives, and to draw new conclusions. Some walking-tour guides are written so that parents and children (or teachers and students) can explore a route together, rather like a treasure hunt. These tours are liberally sprinkled with questions. They say "find" and "look."
- The language of the best walking tours is lively. Active verbs and descriptive details create images in the mind. The brain is engaged. Imagination is unleashed. Each of the senses is employed. Users are asked to visualize, to smell, and to hear the past.
- Walking tours should be personalized with stories of real people. How do their experiences compare to our own? Are there letters, diaries, or news reports that reveal thoughts, impressions, and emotions from another era? If so, use these recorded words to allow the past to speak for itself.
- Finally, successful tours often have a theme, a story that is easily followed, remembered, and retold. Rather than attempt to cover everything, they focus our attention. The same topic connects the stops along the route. Each entry builds upon the others. Inevitably, a thematic tour requires research, organization, and ultimately discipline.

Many cities have guidebooks that plot walks. One of the best is Hope Cooke's, *Seeing New York: History Walks for Armchair and Footloose Travelers* (Philadelphia, 1995), in which the author presents fourteen discrete ways of looking at that city. An older book with a great deal to offer is Walter Muir Whitehill's *Boston: A Topographical History* ([1959] Cambridge, Mass., 1968).

RON THOMSON

water rights in the West. A clear line of demarcation separates the nation into the east and west at the 98th meridian. East of the line, rainfall averages 20 inches or more per year and agriculture is practiced with ease. West of the boundary, rainfall averages less than 20 inches per year, with isolated exceptions, and agriculture can only be managed with the aid of artificial irrigation. New legal requirements, new technology, and new ways of living were required to practice agriculture in the arid West. The most important of these from a local history aspect is the doctrine of prior appropriation, which established rights to water in the West.

The prior appropriation doctrine is summarized simply as "first come, first served." The first person or group to put water to beneficial use has the first right to it. The concept of first in time, first in right is traced back to Spanish-era legal doctrines and mining law as applied in the West. Today, the doctrine of prior appropriation became the keystone of Western water law. In addition to a system of appropriation based on priority of use, the doctrine requires that water be used "beneficially"—not wasted or misused.

There are other systems of water rights in use in the West as well, including the federal reserved-rights system and the riparian system. Federal re-

served rights imply that the federal government reserves sufficient water to fulfill the purposes of land set aside in the West, such as Indian reservations. Riparian water rights, originating from English law and followed in the East, give owners of property adjacent to watercourses the right to use a portion of the flow. Some Western states incorporate riparian provisions into their water-law statutes while all Western states recognize federal reserved rights to some degree.

The prior appropriation doctrine is a boon for local historians because water rights had to be documented, resulting in a treasure trove of filings in state and local government offices. Water users frequently were required to file applications to use water or proof of beneficial water use with county recorders or state engineers' offices. Even when not required by law to file, many water users filed anyway to protect their beneficial use of water from subsequent users. The information contained in these documents provides a valuable record to local historians, consisting of a record of the people and places associated with early development in the West.

Today, many critics of prior appropriation have emerged. Conflicts have developed between early water users, who have a documented right to beneficial use, with federal reserved-water-right-holders. Many federal reserved-water-rights have never been quantified or put to use, resulting in potential claims against prior appropriators. Some water uses, such as instream flows for wildlife and fish habitat, have only recently been recognized as being in need of protection. These challenges to the prior appropriation system, originating in the civil rights and environmental movements since World War II, have led to a need for compromise between many water users.

Where compromise and negotiation fail, disputes over water in the West often end up as legal disputes. An old saying in the West is "whiskey is for drinking, and water is for fighting." The voluminous litigation over water rights provide another valuable source for local historians. County and Federal courts have records of water rights disputes that provide considerable information on early water projects and uses.

DOUG KUPEL

websites for local historians. The following websites indicate how local historians can find the Internet an extremely useful and indispensable tool. Still more sites are being added on a daily basis. Rather than rely only on search engines to keep current with the Web, local historians should become familiar with Internet portals. These are subject directories to Internet sites that are periodically reviewed by experts for usefulness and accuracy. One of the best portals for local historians is the Librarians' Index to the Internet, especially its history and government subdirectories. Its URL is <http://sunsite. berkeley.edu/InternetIndex>.

American and British History Resources on the Internet <www.libraries.rutgers. edu/rulib/socsci/hist/amhist.html>.

This inclusive gateway to history links connects with timelines, archives, reference resources, listservs, and to more specialized history gateways.

*American Association of Local and State History <www.aaslh.org>.

The AALSH's comprehensive site includes an introduction to the association, schedules of workshops and continuing education programs and other useful information. The Resource Center Page links to other organizations and sites of interest to local historians.

American Civil War Homepage <sunsite.utk.edu/civil-war/warweb.html>.

This excellent site incorporates hundreds of links to material about the American Civil War. Local historians will appreciate its special subdirectory to local and state studies of the American Civil War.

American Memory <memory.loc.gov>.

Maintained by the Library of Congress, this searchable multimedia database contains primary documents, photographs, recordings, and motion pictures.

American Studies Web <www.georgetown.edu/crossroads/asw>.

The American Studies Association maintains this multidisciplinary gateway to numerous sites. Its Historical and Archival Resources subcategory should be particularly useful to local historians.

*Balch Online Resources <www.balch institute.org>.

The Balch Institute of Philadelphia emphasizes the study of immigrant and ethnic history. Its website contains on-line versions of primary documents such as emigrant handbooks and steamship advertisements.

Civil War Soldiers & Sailors System <www.itd.nps.gov/cwss>.

This computerized database contains basic facts about the individual soldiers and sailors enlisted in both the Union and Confederate armies and navies.

Civil War Women <http://scriptorium. lib.duke.edu/collections/civil-war-women.html>.

This electronic repository of primary scanned images includes transcripts of letters and diaries from women who witnessed the American Civil War.

Documenting the American South <http://metalab.unc.edu/docsouth/ dasmain.html>.

Sponsored by the University of North Carolina, this site incorporates over 300 books and manuscripts on Southern history, including slave narratives and other personal accounts.

Flite: Federal Legal Information through Electronics <www.fedworld.gov/sup-court/index.html).

This searchable site contains the complete text of more than 7,000 U.S. Supreme Court decisions from 1937 to 1975.

H-Local <www.h-net.msu.edu/~local>.

H-Local is a group that encourages on-line discussion of local and state history. Its moderated discussion list provides an excellent vehicle for the interchange of ideas and information.

*Historic American Buildings Survey <www.cr.nps.gov/habshaer/coll>.

This is the on-line guide to the Library of Congress's collection of drawings, photographs, and written accounts of more than 32,000 historic structures and sites.

*National Archives and Records Administration <www.nara.gov/>.

This site serves as a guide and introduction to the National Archives and includes access to NAIL, the NARA Archival Information Locator, the invaluable guide to material in the National Archives.

*National Park Service Links to the Past <www.cr.nps.gov>.

The National Park Service is responsible for maintaining several historically significant sites, including many significant battlefields. This website contains much relevant materials for local historians.

Oh California! <http://home.pacbell. net/theyer/california.html>.

This comprehensive gateway focuses upon California. It is representative of dozens of similar websites that concentrate upon a particular state or region.

*Library of Congress Local History & Genealogy Reading Room <http://lcweb. loc.gov/rr/genealogy/lhg.html>.

This is the on-line guide to the world's most comprehensive collection of United States and international genealogical and local history holdings. The collection is not digitized, but the website offers a comprehensive introduction of the Library's holdings in this area.

*Local History Magazine <www.local-history.co.uk>.

This site links to 100 websites useful to individuals interested in local history in the United Kingdom.

National Register Information System <www.nr.nps.gov/nrishome.html>.

This is the official database of the National Registrar of Historical Places. It contains an easily searchable database of sites of historical interest organized by state or county.

*Schomburg Center for Research in Black Culture <www.nypl.org/research/sc/sc. html>.

The research branch of the New York Public Library contains two rich digital collections; "African American Women Writers of the Nineteenth Century" and "Images of

African Americans from the Nineteenth Century."

ANN SULLIVAN

Welsh immigrants. See Appendix A.

West Indian immigrants. See Appendix A.

Western history and local historians. As a graduate student, eager to find some undiscovered treasure with which to craft my dissertation on the urban development of the American West, I was frustrated by the seeming lack of original sources. My advisor encouraged me to tap into the abundance of local historical societies scattered throughout southern California. His advice seemed logical, but rarely, if ever, did I see references to such institutions in the books I had read throughout my undergraduate and graduate career. I was skeptical, but thought I would give it a try. The next afternoon I called the Torrance Historical Society, steward of a small local history museum twelve miles south of Los Angeles, and spoke with a wonderful woman named Grace. She informed me that the society possessed assorted primary materials dealing with the history of the town from its earliest days. Heartened, I decided to brave the Riverside and Harbor Freeways and have a look for myself.

The museum was a fine example of the intersection of local and public history. On display were clothing, furniture, and photographs spanning almost a century, goods produced by factories long since closed, the man-drawn hose cart used by the city's first volunteer fire department. The society's archives held the correspondence and corporate records regarding the city's development, subdivision maps, deed restrictions, advertisements, and even a few oral-history transcripts, everything I could possibly want in order to conduct a good part of my research. It was among these materials that I became familiar with the history of one small community in the American West. Unfortunately, I also found that there were some troubling aspects to Torrance.

Torrance was originally the home of the Chumash Indians, hunter-gatherers who built their economy on the rich plain that is today's Los Angeles Basin. Victims of the Spanish conquest, the Chumash were gathered into the Mission San Gabriel, and their lands became part of the Dominguez Rancho, a massive land grant awarded to Sergeant Juan Jose Dominguez in gratitude for his service to the Spanish crown. Following California's incorporation as a territory of newly independent Mexico, the rancho passed down to the good sergeant's descendants. Torrance's Spanish population now called themselves "Californio," and the Chumash and their fellow Gabrielenos served as the labor force in Alta California's semifeudal social structure. After U.S. forces conquered southern California in 1847, the Dominguez family was one of the few Mexican landholders who managed to legitimate their property holdings in the U.S. courts. The rancho passed to the six daughters of Manual Dominguez, and the women continued to manage the estate, selling parcels of the former home of the Chumash as they saw fit.

In the fall of 1911, Los Angeles businessman Jared Sydney Torrance purchased a 3,000-acre tract from the Dominguez estate. He hoped to build a model factory town in order to lure industrialists shaken by the bombing of the anti-union *Los Angeles Times* and the near election of Socialist Job Harriman to the Los Angeles mayoral office earlier that year. Torrance incorporated the Dominguez Land Company to develop the site bearing his name, and hired landscape architect Frederick Law Olmsted Jr., to design the town. The Dominguez Land Company built model housing, planted trees, and provided parkways in the expectation that an ideal living environment would preempt any inclination by Torrance workers to unionize. Within two years of Torrance's founding however, a major recession impaired the town's development, a strike crippled the local shoe factory, and Los Angeles workers refused to relocate to the open-shop paradise. Torrance would grow, not because of the Olmstedian landscape, but because oil was discovered on Maria de los Reyes Dominguez Francis's parcel in 1922. The oil industry soon overtook the town, and during the first half of the decade Maria Dominguez Francis paid more income tax than any woman in the United States had paid up to that time. Today, the trolley station once used by Torrance workers is now a restaurant, serving executives of the Honda Motor Car Company of America, a striking example of the contemporary links between California and its Pacific Rim Trading partners (see Dennis F. Shanahan and Charles Elliot Jr., *Historic Torrance: A Pictorial History of Torrance, California* [Redondo Beach, Calif., 1984]).

After familiarizing myself with the history of Torrance, I concluded that, despite its idiosyncrasies, Torrance was in many ways a typical western locality. This typicality, this representative quality, might surprise most Americans. That, in a nutshell, is the trouble with Torrance.

When most Americans hear the term "the West," they think of a land inhabited by cowboys, pioneers, gunfighters, and "wild Indians," images crafted by a complex but curious blend of Jeffersonian agrarianism, Free Soil ideology, John Wayne, the Marlboro Man, and *Dances with Wolves*. For historians, this image is associated with the historical model crafted by Frederick Jackson Turner. Arguably the most influential U.S. historian in the twentieth century, Turner intellectualized the link between a place loosely defined as "the West" and an equally vague concept known as "the frontier" (see *frontier thesis). Presenting his theory at the World's Columbian Exposition in Chicago in 1893, Turner held that the key to understanding the history of the United States was the frontier experience. For him, the frontier was a constantly moving line of demarcation where "savagery" met "civilization," and successive waves of European infiltration drove civilization's advance irresistibly forward. Trappers and traders heralded the decline of wilderness barbarism. Permanent settlers soon followed, bringing with them increasingly intensive modes of agricultural production. Finally, the appearance of "manufacturing organization with city and factory system" represented the ultimate triumph of American nationalism (see Frederick Jackson

Turner, "The Significance of the Frontier in American History," reprinted in *History, Frontier, and Section: Three Essays by Frederick Jackson Turner* [Albuquerque, 1993], 59–91).

A native of Wisconsin, Turner was determined to make the West the focal point of United States history. When Turner wrote the frontier thesis, the "germ theory" then prevalent in scholarly circles established the roots of American culture within the tribal antecedents of medieval Teutonic civilization. Such a view suggested that the American experience was a mere footnote to historical processes long since past. The implication of Turner's hypothesis was the complete reverse. The frontier was the cradle of American values. The distance of the wilderness from established institutions and, hence, European origins produced a spirit of individualism, spurred the growth of democratic traditions, and "Americanized, liberated, and fused" a diverse stock of immigrants "into a mixed race, English in neither nationality nor characteristics." (Turner, *History, Frontier, and Section*, pp. 1–7, 75–76). The taming of the frontier then represented a process, a mechanism by which Europeans could craft a new, homogenous, and democratic culture. The "West" was merely the incidental direction people headed in the course of becoming American.

Whatever the merits of the frontier thesis, it should be readily apparent that the trouble with the frontier thesis is that Turner's story is not Torrance's story. Torrance's history does not appear to comply with the popular myths of Western history. Turner never talked about land grants, or Mexicans, or Californios, or women like Maria Dominguez. The Turner thesis assumed, if not celebrated, the destruction of the Indians, not the possibility that Native Americans might have adapted and even survived with much of their cultures intact. Turner spent little time on the influence of the federal government on frontier development, although Maria Dominguez was certainly aware of the long arm of the Internal Revenue Service. He gave a nod to the rise of the city, but only as an end point in his historical process, not as a concurrent method of conquest and settlement. There is a passing note to the development of the factory system, but the egalitarian qualities of the frontier supposedly suppressed any aspect of class. There is no open-shop Los Angeles, no shoe-worker's strikes, no plebeian bombers. Turner's developed West was a region full of farmers, not of oil derricks busily extracting irreplaceable resources from the land.

Many of these omissions were understandable in so short an essay. Some of Turner's exclusions stem from his nineteenth-century convictions. Turner himself moved on to refine his view of history. Many in the profession did not. Whatever the difficulties inherent in the frontier thesis, now so apparent in hindsight, much of the unwillingness of historians to challenge Turner came from the fact that the frontier thesis in so many ways spoke to them. Turner's America looked much like the small towns from which numerous historians originated. The frontier thesis meant that America was special, that it was energetic, triumphant, and democratic. It also gave them a benchmark from which to view their own rapidly changing world, filled with anxiety about the "closing of the frontier" and the nation's rapid industrialization and urbanization, a sense of loss that Turner himself seems to have felt. Professionally, local historians could now weave their provincial subjects into a wider historical narrative (Turner, *History, Frontier, and Section*, pp. 1–26).

Although the frontier thesis dominated historians' view of the West for more than a half century, challenges to its basic assumptions sporadically appeared, only to reach a torrent in the past two decades. These new approaches to the history of the West, gathered today under the general banner of the "New Western History," suggest the range of lenses through which local historians can view their subjects as examples or products of Western localities. Patricia Nelson Limerick's *The Legacy of Conquest: The Unbroken Past of the American West* (N.Y., 1987) is rightly seen as one of the most important attempts to give the New Western History a broad conceptual framework. Limerick openly rejected Turner's concept of the frontier as a social process. Beyond such ethnocentric demarcations as "civilization" and "savagery," one of the problems with the Turnerian view is that it really says little about the West. The frontier moves over time, from Puritan New England to the Dominguez Rancho, so to speak. The frontier therefore is as much the domain of an historian of Colonial Williamsburg as an historian of Albuquerque. Contrasting social structures, technologies, cultures, and environmental conditions

make little difference it seems, as long as the localities sit somewhere on the frontier.

Instead of seeing the West as a process, New Western Historians see the West as a place. Now just where the West is has been open to debate. Limerick equivocated on the subject, but I like Donald Worster's assertion that it is the region of diminishing rainfall west of the 100th meridian. (See Limerick, *The Legacy of Conquest*, p. 26. For Worster's opinion on just where the West is, see Donald Worster, *Under Western Skies: Nature and History in the American West* [N.Y., 1992], p. 25.) Yes, it is arbitrary, but you have to start somewhere. If your locality happens to be on the 99th meridian and you consider it to be a western place, feel free to move the West, but only just a little.

In regards to the particulars of that place, New Western Historians generally accept the notion that the West is a region that has undergone conquest. Unfortunately for the pioneers, when they arrived in the West, people were already living there. All of North America is such a place, but the West's position as a global crossroads between indigenous America, Anglo-European America, Spanish America, and Asian America made it more extreme. Once the pioneers settled their farms, they may have been surprised that the Indians and Mexicans did not go away. In fact, they may have been surprised that other groups kept coming. The West may not have had the teeming immigrant neighborhoods of Brooklyn, but the region did and does have its Chinatowns, its Japan Towns, its Little Saigons, and its South Central Los Angeles.

As a cultural crossroads, scholars now focus on those left out of Turner's story. Women are now major players in the history of the West. The "pioneer woman" challenges old myths about the "minimal" role of frontier women and the ability of the "democratic frontier" to subsume traditional gender roles. More recent studies highlight women's role as cultural intermediaries between the men in their lives, an insight that fits nicely into the theme of the West as global crossroads. The decade of the 1960s likewise saw an increase in interest in the history of the Spanish-speaking peoples of the West, reminding historians of the region that when they speak of the "frontier," they must address the question of just whose frontier they are talking about. Native Americans were not simply on the anterior side of those multiple frontiers, but they continued to dwell within those lines long after their passage. Rather than portraying native peoples as passive victims, historians in the post-Turnerian era point to Indians as engaged historical actors, and emphasize indigenous societal structures and cultural forms as well as postcontact resistance, adaptation, and survival. And when we address aspects of "European contact," we must be careful of old generalizations. If one chanced upon a clash between Native Americans and U.S. Army units in the West, there was a good chance that the latter were also composed of men of African descent, and even natives of other tribes.

As problematic was the fact that western people inhabited a region that was rich in natural resources but less than hospitable to human occupation. What-ever the accomplishments of the rugged individualists of Western lore, they could not have conquered and settled the region without the help of large institutions. Not only did the U.S. Army and the state militias fight a series of wars against native bands, but they secured original access to those lands by engaging in a major war against Mexico. The federal government divided the land and distributed it to homesteaders, railroads, and miners. Federal and state water projects brought water to the desert, and nurtured agricultural and industrial development in many ways. Land companies subdivided the towns, and corporate mining quickly replaced the forty-niners of lore. This conquest of nature may have appeared to Turner's generation as the triumph of civilization, but New Western Historians recognize that such changes in the land brought a heavy price in environmental damage.

Through such conceptualizations local historians can cast their subjects as definitively "Western." However, local historians, like Western historians in general, should not lose sight of the qualities their topics share, no matter how nearby and personal they may appear, with wider aspects of national, or even global history (Limerick, *The Legacy of Conquest*, p. 26). However, I do not mean to suggest that local historians completely abandon traditional conceptions of the frontier. The rugged pioneer and the lonely cowboy were very real parts of the Western experience, and should be examined where they are pertinent. Historians will be hard pressed to expunge John Wayne from the American consciousness, even if they wanted to. In a symposium on the teaching of the history of the American West held at the annual conference of the Western History Association January 1999, William Cronon presented what I think is a suitable place for the frontier of tradition:

The frontier is such a powerful mythic force in American culture that it's usually best not to act as if one can assault it frontally in the classroom and thereby expunge its influence on the minds of students. The myth is in fact more powerful than we are, and usually wins. The better course of action is teach as if one were practicing Judo, using the weight and energy of the myth to move the students forward by first engaging them with it and then shifting its momentum in the more historical directions we hope to carry them. Better to try to shift and reshape the myth, acknowledging its partial truths while denying its distortions, than to claim that it has no reality whatsoever.

(William Cronon to the author, January 28, 1999)

For in-depth discussions of these themes, see William Cronon, George Miles, and Jay Gitlin, eds., *Under an Open Sky: Rethinking America's Western Past* (N.Y., 1992); Patricia Limerick, Clyde A. Milner III, and Charles E. Rankin, eds., *Trails: Towards a New Western History* (Lawrence, Kan., 1991); Gerald D. Nash, *Creating the West: Historical Interpretations, 1890–1990* (Albuquerque, 1991); Gerald D. Nash and Richard Etulain, *The Twentieth Century West: Historical Interpretations* (Albuquerque, 1989); and Patricia Nelson Limerick, *The Legacy of Conquest: The Unbroken Past of the American West* (N.Y., 1987), 26.

ROBERT PHELPS

See frontier thesis.

Western Reserve Historical Society. Founded in 1867, the Western Reserve Historical Society (WRHS) is the largest privately supported regional historical society in the United States. WRHS operates seven historical properties in northeast Ohio. The History Museum, the Crawford Auto-Aviation Museum, and the Archives/Library are housed within Cleveland's University Circle complex. Other properties include: James A. Garfield National Historic Site, Hale Farm and Village, Loghurst, and Shandy Hall.

The WRHS Archives/Library is the largest American history research center in northern Ohio. It is the principal repository for histories, records, *newspapers, prints, and *photographs relating to the growth and development of Cleveland and that portion of northeastern Ohio once known as the "Western Reserve of Connecticut." Archival programs emphasize urban and Ohio labor history, business, philanthropic, ethnic, African American, Jewish, Irish American, and lesbian/gay history.

One of the first institutions in the United States to collect genealogical materials, the Archives/Library is one of the largest *genealogy research centers in the nation with collections that cover the United States. Other notable collections include: Shaker literature and manuscripts; Civil War books, manuscripts, official records, and photographs concerning Union and Confederate forces; and one of the nations largest auto-aviation collections including books, shop manuals, sales literature, periodicals, and photographs.

WRHS catalog is available on-line and includes references to museum and library collections. There is an admission charge. The WRHS is located at 10825 East Boulevard, Cleveland, Ohio 44106; (216) 721-5722; <www.wrhs.org>.

BARBARA WAITKUS BILLINGS

wills. People dispose of their property after their death by means of a will. Those people who do not have a will are said to die *intestate, allowing the laws of the state to determine the distribution of their goods. This personal property includes all those items that would have been owned by an individual; real property is real estate, that is, land. Wills are useful documents that can reveal a good deal about the wealth of an individual, his or her relationship to family, and how an individual's wealth is to be distributed. Often there is an *inventory of goods that follows a death and this inventory can reveal information about the composition of households. Collectively, wills from an area can be used to document the introduction of foreign goods, the culture of reading, family size, information about *philanthropy as opposed to keeping goods and wealth within a family, and even patterns of family geographic distribution.

woman's sphere. This concept was defined by Barbara Welter in an important essay, entitled, "The Cult of True Womanhood, 1820–1860," that appeared first in *American Quarterly* (18 [1966]: 151–74) and has been widely reprinted. "Woman's sphere" refers to the segment of life to which women were believed to be naturally inclined. It also defines the attributes nineteenth-century women expected of themselves and by which they were judged by others. Those attributes were submission, chastity, religious sensibility, and an interest in all things associated with home and family. Woman's sphere is also called the domestic sphere. Woman's role was to minister to the physical and emotional needs of her family.

women's history. The past 30 years have seen major research and new scholarship in the field of women's history. This scholarship, embodied in hundreds of dissertations, articles, monographs, and specialized books, has spawned many new general publications, community cultural-preservation and oral-history projects, exhibitions, interpretive programs at *living history museums and historic houses, and the identification and official civic recognition of landmarks and other meaningful places in the history of American women. This increased interest corresponded with the 1976 celebration of the Bicentennial, the women's movement, and the focus on *social history in museums and historical organizations.

Early works of women's history emphasized finding new role models, new heroes, and new places of power. Major early works included Gerda Lerner's *The Grimké Sisters of South Carolina* ([1967] N.Y., 1998); Kathryn Kish Sklar's *Catharine Beecher* (New Haven, Conn., 1973); and Nancy Cott's *Bonds of Womanhood* ([1977] New Haven, Conn., 1997). Scholars also explored women and social movements, including suffrage and education, women and the *built environment, and women and *work. A useful basic text on women's history in America is *Born for*

Liberty: A History of Women in America (N.Y., 1989), by Sara M. Evans. Marion Tinling's *Women Remembered: A Guide to Landmarks of Women's History in the United States* (N.Y., 1986) is another pioneering study.

The *National Trust for Historic Preservation, the *National Park Service, and many major museums have turned their attention to women's history, although often in sporadic and episodic ways. Many individual museums have mounted exhibitions on individual women of note, women of a particular ethnic group, women in domestic situations, the labor force, the professions, and politics. Often these exhibits have served as springboards or catalysts for new collecting efforts.

The interpretation of women's history for the public in museums and historical societies has taken a variety of forms. Generally, it began with a "hall of fame" focus on major, iconic figures in American history, such as Amelia Earhart, Susan B. Anthony, Willa Cather, and Harriet Tubman. In addition, previously lesser-known women, such as Paiute activist Sarah Winnemucca, California architect Julia Morgan, and ex-slave Biddy Mason, have become part of an ever-expanding roster of better-known women historical figures. Finally, the collective role of women in labor, community social networks, education, politics, and religion has received attention and informed museum presentations, as have studies of women in specific ethnic groups (Jewish women, Chinese American women, African American women). Recent studies have also explored women throughout the twentieth century.

Nonetheless, few museums deal with relationships among women of different classes, races, or ethnic groups, and some subjects, including sexuality and reproduction, have had little attention. Other emerging themes include women and spirituality, women and the environment, the study of gender, and the relationships among women and between women and men. As Ellen Carol Du Bois and Vicki Ruiz note in *Unequal Sisters* (N.Y., 1990): "The journey into women's history itself has to be remapped. From many quarters comes the call for a more complex approach to women's experiences, one that explores not only the conflicts between women and men but also the conflicts among women; not only the bonds among women but also the bonds between women and men."

Much of the new scholarship remains unknown to the general public and in the schools. The *National Women's History Project, in Windsor, California, publishes a catalog of materials available for school use. Yet much needs to be done. In many local historical societies and museums, women's history remains on the margins. Even when some notable women are recognized, there is seldom an effort to situate them in the larger context of their community. The relationships among women in households, workplaces, farms and ranches, industry, and recreation are rarely treated; similarly the relationships between women and men in public and private arenas usually get short shrift.

An emerging trend is museums devoted solely to women's history. Existing sites include the Women's National

Rights Historic Park in Seneca Falls; the National Women's Hall of Fame; the Cowgirl Museum and Hall of Fame; the National Women Soldiers' Memorial at Arlington Cemetery; the Women of the West Museum in Denver; the International Museum of Women in San Francisco, and the National Women's Museum that hopes to be located in Washington, D.C. The work of Page Putnam Miller, Gail DuBrow, Polly Welts Kaufman, Heather Huyck, and others has also led to increased recognition of women's landmarks and historic buildings.

In July 1998, on the occasion of the 150th anniversary of the Women's Rights Convention in Seneca Falls, New York, President Bill Clinton established a presidential Commission for the Celebration of Women in American History, thus becoming the first president to recognize the importance of women's historical contributions to the creation and development of our country. The commission was charged with making recommendations to the president "on ways to best acknowledge and celebrate the roles and accomplishments of women in American history." The report was issued in March 1999.

The challenges posed by presenting women's history are not unlike those posed by the interpretation of any ethnic or religious group. Women must be assessed in their own right as well as part of the dominant culture. Ultimately, the goal is to incorporate the new research into a revised, more inclusive history of the United States that fully acknowledges the complex and significant roles of women in the national story.

The challenges that face professionals in the presentation of women's history also parallel those of any local history project. Members of the community should be involved in the creation, interpretation, and preservation of local stories, documents, artifacts, and monuments of women's history, but care must be taken to avoid *nostalgia and oversimplification. Effective presentations also must use a variety of programmatic and interpretive strategies to engage a broad audience, especially an audience increasingly accustomed to visual, experiential (hands-on), or electronic learning.

The new research on women's history is rich material for local history museums, especially when combined with community participation in creating new exhibitions, curricular and interpretive materials. A new generation of traveling exhibitions can take the work of the previous decades, update it in content and presentation, and reach new audiences throughout the country in ways that connect individuals, families, and communities to a changed and more inclusive understanding of the overall story of American history.

See The President's Commission on the Celebration of Women in American History, *Celebrating Women's History: Recommendations to President William Jefferson Clinton* (Washington, D.C.: March 1, 1999); Dolores Hayden, *The Power of Place: Urban Landscapes as Public History* (Cambridge, Mass., 1997); Katharine Martinez and Kenneth L. Ames, *The Material Culture of Gender. The Gender of Material Culture* (Winterthur, Del., 1997); National Park Service, *Exploring a Common Past: Interpreting Women's History in the Na-*

tional Park Service (1996); Linda K. Kerber and Jane Sherron De Hart, *Women's America: Refocusing the Past* (N.Y., 1995); Linda K. Kerber, Alice Kessler-Harris, Kathryn Kish Sklar, *U.S. History as Women's History: New Feminist Essays* (Chapel Hill, N.C., 1995); U.S. Department of the Interior, National Park Service, "Placing Women in the Past," *Cultural Resource Management*, vol. 20, no.3, 1997; Lynn Sherr and Jurate Kazickas, *Susan B. Anthony Slept Here: A Guide to American Women's Landmarks* (N.Y., 1994); Ruth Barnes Moynihan, Cynthia Russett, and Laurie Crumpacker, *Second to None: A Documentary History of American Women*, vol. I: *From the Sixteenth Century to 1865*; vol. II: *From 1865 to the Present* (Lincoln, Neb., 1993); Page Putnam Miller, ed., *Reclaiming the Past: Landmarks of Women's History* (Bloomington, Ind., 1992); Ellen Carol DuBois and Vicki L.Ruiz, *Unequal Sisters: A Multicultural Reader in U.S. Women's History* (N.Y., 1990); Sara M. Evans, *Born for Liberty: A History of Women in America* (N.Y., 1989); Warren Leon and Roy Rosenzweig, *History Museums in the United States: A Critical Assessment* (Urbana, Ill., 1989); and Marion Tinling, *Women Remembered: A Guide to Landmarks of Women's History in the United States* (N.Y., 1986). See <www.nwhp.org/links.html>.

MARSHA SEMMEL

See National Women's History Project.

women's legal status. Until quite recently in the United States, the primary determinant of a woman's legal status was her standing as married or unmarried. Under definitions of the English common law, which were incorporated into the laws of American states after independence, a single woman (or "feme sole") had all the legal rights and obligations of a man, with the exception of voting and such male-only responsibilities as jury or militia service. A married woman (or "feme covert"), by contrast, was civilly dead. In general, she could not make a will, inherit or own property, make contracts, or sue or be sued in court without the consent and participation of her husband.

When a woman wed, any personal property she possessed immediately became her husband's (thus he owned her clothes, jewelry, and so forth), and her real estate was her husband's to manage until the time of her death, at which point it passed automatically to their legitimate offspring. A few women, primarily wealthy widows, reached prenuptial agreements with their future spouses, voiding some or all of these adverse consequences of marriage, but on the whole married women found themselves greatly constricted in legal terms.

In return, the law provided widows with dower rights in the property of which their husbands died possessed. Such rights—which varied from colony to colony and later from state to state— usually provided that a widow would receive a one-third life interest in her husband's real property (which she could manage and live on, but not sell, at least not without a court's permission) and a proportion (commonly ranging from one-third to one-half) of

477

her husband's personal property, which usually meant that she thereby "inherited" what she regarded as her own possessions. With respect to criminal proceedings, the law's assumption that a wife always operated under her husband's direction freed her from responsibility for crimes committed in his presence. He, not she, was liable for such conduct.

The first changes in this system were introduced in the 1830s and 1840s, when various states adopted Married Women's Property Acts, allowing wives to hold in their own names any property acquired before marriage or inherited during marriage. At first, however, such laws did not give wives the right to retain current earnings nor did they affect wives' capacity to sue or be sued independently of their husbands. Such reforms took many years to accomplish; in some states, for example, only in the 1970s could married women finally establish credit in their own names or not be required to have their husbands countersign certain documents.

An excellent introduction to the intricacies of women's legal status in the colonial and early national periods is Marylynn Salmon, *Women and the Law of Property in Early America* (Chapel Hill, N.C., 1986).

MARY BETH NORTON

work, history of. The subject of work, that most basic of social activities, in American life and history has preoccupied historians in the last few decades. In the past, historians, influenced by ties to the trade-union movement, were primarily concerned with the effects of industrial capitalism from the antebellum period on and focused chiefly on skilled craftsmen. Today, studies of myriad trades abound, and historians have widened their compass to include female workers, blacks, Hispanics, Asians, and diverse status's such as indentured servants, enslaved peoples, casual laborers, and illegal immigrants. If there has been an effort to connect labor history with the baseline narrative of politics and the triumph of liberal capitalism, an equally powerful response has sharpened understanding of life on the shop floor, whether in a factory or a field. As a result, the study of work in America now incorporates many of the concerns previously comprehended as *social history. This essay looks at significant trends within a chronological framework and at the same time reflects how variables of class, race, and gender impact upon individual and collective workers.

The Colonial Period: Once dismissed as merely a prelude to the era of industrial capitalism, the colonial period is now a battleground for competing visions of early American work. Formerly, scholars, heavily influenced by Louis Hartz, believed all European-American males became capitalists as soon as they jumped off the boat on New World shores. Enslaved black experience was a separate and seldom-considered topic while women's work and Native American labor were barely noticed. Today, Native American work is regarded as a key measure of Indian acculturation to Western mores. Virtually all western (and biased) observers commented on the gendered separation of work in Native American societies. Women performed household and agricultural duties while men hunted and fished and relaxed when at home. Daniel Richter's study of the Iroquois, James Merrill's work on the Catawba, Daniel Usner's book on the Lower Mississippi Valley, Richard White's mammoth analysis of the Middle Ground, and Ramon Gutierrez's study of the House Pueblo employ this paradigm. In each, European demands for such trade materials as animal skins, precious metals, and food, pushed male workers further into the frontiers, often taking with them, devastating diseases. Gutierrez has shown how European adventurers in New Mexico transformed female sexuality into prostitution as House Pueblo society struggled to survive. In all cases, the demographic holocaust and trade demands chiefly revolutionized Native American work patterns.

Though some were caught in the web of slavery, Native Americans did not make good chattel. Much of the history of work in the seventeenth and early eighteenth century is about how one person controls another person's labor to make a fortune. Thus, Virginia tobacco planters, as Edmund Morgan has powerfully demonstrated, purchased white indentured servants in the first half of the century. Then, when Bacon's Rebellion in 1676 showed how unruly former servants had become, planters turned to enslaved blacks as the principal workforce. David Galenson and Alan Kulikoff have altered this thesis slightly by showing that fewer English servants were available after 1660, but Morgan's fundamental thesis is that the contract between elite and yeoman whites to guarantee land for the latter produced a series of racist Indian wars,

and the acquisition of generations of African slaves created the paradox of American Slavery/American Freedom. Kathleen Brown's expert expansion of this thesis defines its effects on the growing division between white and black females.

Similar to Morgan's argument is Peter Wood's masterful study of slavery in South Carolina. Margaret Washington has demonstrated how Gullah religion enabled slaves in the low-country rice plantation to resist acculturation while performing exhausting labor. Philip Morgan's encyclopedic study of low-country agriculture is ultimately unsatisfying because it lacks a central thesis and often skirts opposing views, such as Wood's and Washington's. In all, however, scholars of slavery in the South have shown how discovery of a staple crop, and the acquisitive, ruthless drives of planters secured a massive enslaved population. As Washington's and Wood's work shows, these patterns did not occur without resistance. Themes of worker struggle, often borrowed from older labor histories, are constant refrains. The latest study of black work in the North can be found in my study of Monmouth County blacks or in my larger work on black workers in and around New York City (*Root & Branch: African Americans in New York and East Jersey, 1613–1863*). Key to understanding northern slavery are its small-scale ownership patterns, frequent contact between free and enslaved peoples, occupational and personal mobility, and the eventual transfer into free wage labor.

New England experimented with slavery, but eventually chose another path of bondage. As Daniel Vickers has demonstrated, family bondage, in which social patterns of inheritance bound sons to fathers for decades, dominated labor relations in the northeast. Vickers expertly compared fishermen, whom he regards as entering into capitalist relations early in the colonial period, with farm workers who usually were related to or knew their employers well and who expected eventually to own farms, or the means of production. Laurel Ulrich in her study of female roles and later, in a book on midwives, has examined how women's work formed a separate sphere. Her work is critical for moving into the period of industrial capitalism. There, Thomas Dublin's several works on the transformation of farm girls into factory workers tell the story. New England is also the arena where historians argue about when capitalism defined labor relations and human expectations. Vickers, joined by Stephen Innes and Winnifred Rothenberg, contend that among farmers it happened early, while Michael Merrill has countered by insisting that a moral economy governed relations and behavior well into the eighteenth century. At this point, neither side has gained preeminence.

Laborers in colonial cities have received scant attention. The continued importance of Richard B. Morris's *Government and Labor in Early America* (N.Y., 1946) after a half century is indicative. An excellent updating of Morris and earlier work by Carl Bridenbaugh is Gary Nash's *Urban Crucible* (Cambridge, Mass., 1979), itself 20-years old. Also important are Howard Rock's *Artisans of the New Republic* (Baltimore, 1995) about semiskilled craftsmen in New York, and my own study of cartmen or one-horse teamsters, both of which, following Morris, uncover the ties between government and unskilled workers. David Roediger has used this connection to push his thesis about "wages of whiteness" for European-American workers who take racial privilege to secure economic status.

From Revolution to Civil War: Eric Foner's book on Tom Paine encapsulates what most scholars accept: whatever unevenness occurred before, the American Revolution marked the change to captialism in virtually all of American society. If industrialism did not happen for five more decades, the expansive nature of revolutionary republicanism—with its emphasis on patriotism, egalitarianism, abandonment of mercantile regulations, and demographic explosion into the interior of the continent—created a new person: the acquisitive individual. Whether in city or countryside, Americans had a collective political consciousness with individual goals. Nowhere was this better demonstrated than in politics. Shrugging off colonial patterns of deference, American artisans and farmers demanded their own representation, contending that they were as capable as the elite to govern the new nation. That goal of political equity had to wait until the decline of the Federalist party in 1800, but the shift toward full white-male citizenship made it inexorable.

In the meantime, a fundamental conflict between two founding fathers, Thomas Jefferson and Alexander Hamilton, forecast social differences about work. Jefferson in his *Notes on the State of Virginia* (first published in

Philadelphia in 1788) heralded a nation of small farmers, with workshops and cities left to Europe. Hamilton, by contrast, planned a new industrial community in Paterson, New Jersey. At first, Jefferson was correct, but in the long run, Hamilton's vision prevailed.

Hamilton's ideas won because of a parallel development in the crafts. United in the famous Federalist processions celebrating the new Constitution in 1788, the skilled trades rapidly changed. Centuries of traditional development of the individual worker from apprentice to journeyman to master craftsman gave way to entrepreneurial masters who employed dozens of apprentices and, eventually, unskilled females. The difficulty of establishing a shop now meant that journeymen might never make the final ascent into independence. This happened in textiles, cabinetmaking, and gunnery first, but by 1820, the trend was inescapable. Few trades remained unindustralized by 1850, and factory conditions that horrified Jefferson appeared in Lowell, Massachusetts, and in New York and Philadelphia. Masters became employers while skilled journeymen and apprentices gave way to casual laborers and immigrant families. Labor relations worsened as workers attempted to protect gains made since the Revolution, while masters increasingly embraced a laissez-faire philosophy that abhorred unionism and government regulation.

The Revolution's insistence on equality convinced many northerners to abandon slavery. By 1804, every state north of Delaware had gradual emancipation laws that meant that slaves would eventually have some freedom while "compensating" their masters with the most productive years of their lives. As Gary Nash, Shane White, and I have shown, gradual emancipation was accompanied by a dismal rise in racism, as Northern elites and workers determined that blacks could not be equal citizens. For example, Hamilton's plan for Paterson, New Jersey, included no blacks, even though he was a charter member of the New York Society for the Abolition of Slavery. Similarly, the 1821 constitution, which finally created universal white-male suffrage, levied a $250 bond on prospective black workers. As newly freed African Americans flooded into the cities, they found little acceptance in the white trades and were forced to work in shadow occupations as the sole blacksmith, cabinetmaker, or butcher for the black community. By the 1830s, severe racism sent black urban residency and job opportunities into a tailspin.

Whatever misgivings Southerners had about slavery after the Revolution were dispelled by the emergence of cotton as a cash crop, the invention of the cotton gin by Eli Whitney, and increased sectionalism in American society. By 1820, spurred by South Carolina, the South depended almost entirely on enslaved black labor and was determined to push its vision into the newly conquered western regions, setting up the great division that would create the Civil War. As southern economies matured, blacks held a huge variety of positions from highly skilled artisans and domestics to field workers. Completing Morgan's argument, incoming European immigrants to southern cities toiled as artisans for a while, then purchased land and slaves and headed west. There they encountered the remnants of once-proud Native American nations, now demoralized as marginal workers. White Americans pushed them out of the way, either by deceit and fraud, as in the Trail of Tears, or by military conquest, as in the Seminole Wars of the late 1820s.

White Americans' way west was enabled by transportation improvements, first in shipping, next in canals, and finally in railroads. Financed by government and speculation, these vast enterprises employed tens of thousands of workers, often Irish immigrants, to build and then operate them. By the late 1840s, America's demographic landscape was altered by the arrival of over a million Irish and German workers who coexisted uneasily in cities with each other and earlier immigrants. Irish women often worked as domestics, taking over this occupation from black women. As Elizabeth Blackmar has shown, significant class divisions occurred in the antebellum period between women of the bourgeoisie and the poor who labored for them, though often with great resentment. Many young women, discouraged by factory and domestic work, preferred prostitution, especially given the relaxed mores in the cities. They often serviced young male clerks, a new breed commonly known as Young America, who were more assertive, temperate, and acquisitive than their revolutionary fathers. Fully imbibing the myth of upward mobility (a concept heavily debated by scholars), these aspirants to the Good Life became a bulwark against working-class consciousness in America. Still other young men and some not-so-young African Americans took to the sea as American shipping advances meant far more employment than in the previous century.

From the Civil War to the Great Depression: As it did in every aspect of American life, the Civil War clearly demarcated change. Foremost, the Union victory over the rebellious Confederacy insured the freedom of 2.5 million African American slaves. Second, it advanced industrialism everywhere, even in traditional trades such as meat-cutting, which, using advanced refrigeration methods and transport improvements made during the war, propelled a local occupation into giant corporate entities. Militarization also created a huge new government bureaucracy, rationalized civic work including police, fire, and sanitation, and enhanced corporate control over recalcitrant workers. Tragically, the war cost the lives of a generation of young men, necessitating enticements to prospective European immigrants.

The radicalization of society, started before the war, now more bitter after the cost of lives, North and South, insured the near-destruction of the Native American in a series of vicious wars. It also cast profound doubts about the place of Asians, especially Chinese, who, welcome before the conflict and considered a model minority, were now regarded by white labor as dangerous aliens. The Chinese, who literally built the western portion of the transcontinental railroad, were rewarded by dismissal from jobs. These dismissals were reinforced by the Chinese Exclusion Acts of the 1870s and 1880s, the only immigration laws aimed at excluding laborers of a specific minority. African Americans, after a brief, heady taste of real political and occupational equity during Reconstruction, faced harsh repression at work and home. They were pressed into sharecropping, which was barely above slavery and at times as bad. For minority people, race amplified class as African Americans, Asians, and Mexicans were cast into narrow, agriculturally-based work or service jobs in the cities, accounting for the emergence of Chinese laundries and restaurants. For Native Americans, wars of extirpation denied any entrance into the world of American labor.

The Civil War advanced the cause of unionism among white, industrial workers. The Knights of Labor appeared in the 1870s; the American Federation of Labor (A.F.L.) under the leadership of Samuel Gompers formed soon after. The A.F.L. in particular survived by concentrating on specific craft organization by shop, conservative social policies, and restrictive political activities. Nor could it be said to satisfy laborers. An incredible 24,000 strikes occurred between 1876 and 1900. Several, including the Homestead Strike of 1877, were brutally repressed by a combination of government troops and private armies.

In addition to preserving wages, workers also fought for a shorter work day, achieving a ten-hour day in the 1880s, and eight hours in the early twentieth century. Personal-injury compensation came in small doses after the turn of the century.

Labor's gains were hardly universal and rarely extended beyond skilled whites. By the onset of the twentieth century, a militant group of unskilled workers known as the Industrial Workers of the World (I.W.W.) organized the only general strike in U.S. history, shutting down the city of Seattle in 1917. Harsh government repression, including forcible deportation, eventually doomed the I.W.W. Meanwhile, industrialization marched on, and as the U.S. economy neared parity with Europe, millions more immigrants including Italians, Poles, Eastern European Jews, and Greeks flooded into the nation's cities. While they found ready employment, it would take until the 1920s before they would gain political power and even later for social acceptance. At the same time, Northern blacks faced exclusion and slow rates of economic growth. White terrorism and the mechanization of agriculture in the South sent tens of thousands of black workers into Northern cities. For women, the rise of corporations in urban America brought some new opportunities. Young women, known as typewriters, and skilled in the new office machinery, replaced the traditional male scrivener. Communications improvements brought a new class of telephone operators, many of whom knew an incredible array of languages and family names. Other young women combined work as prostitutes with new jobs as waitresses, servicing the vast number of hotels that sprang up after the Civil War.

At the turn of the twentieth century, the urban future of America was apparent. As Robert Wiebe has shown, the majority of Americans lived in cities after 1876, and in the new century, the vast wealth of the United States had in proved workers' conditions in some ways, but wages remained depressed.

World War I temporarily renewed government regulation of the economy, spurred job growth in war-related industries, and further regimented society via the draft. Even the prosperous 1920s barely lifted working conditions. A 1929 survey of wages by the U.S. Department of Labor showed scarce growth since 1840. For some groups, particularly African Americans, this period was the nadir, with no political representation, stultifying segregation, and terrorism keeping the black worker down. While women, as noted, earned new places in the world of work, much of it was still related to the domestic sphere and upward mobility was limited by glass ceilings.

The Depression to the Present: The effects of the Wall Street Crash of 1929 rocked American society for the next decade. With President Herbert Hoover unwilling to jumpstart the economy and conservative laissez-faire policies ruling business, by 1932 fully one-fourth of while male adults were unemployed. Jobs vanished. A generation of "Depression virtuosos"—educated men—drove cabs vainly around cities in search of elusive fares. Farmers lost homesteads, many abandoning home places for promised land in California.

The election of Franklin Delano Roosevelt in 1932 meant the federal government turned to intervening in the economy. Most important was Roosevelt's creation of a social security system to help workers through hard times and retirement. A huge, enforced savings plan, Social Security saved untold amounts of money for corporations, who avoided pension plans for decades. Massive public works projects—building post offices, city halls, and libraries—employed tens of thousands of Americans producing some of the most distinguished public architecture ever seen in the nation. Artists and writers working for the Works Progress Administration churned out massive but excellent state histories and specialized volumes on cities, the survivors of slavery, and on America's greatest sites. Cities also managed jobs more closely, as exemplified in Fiorella LaGuardia's organization of taxi drivers in a medallion system in 1937. La Guardia was also concerned about communist activity in the fledgling Taxi Workers Union, later the Transport Workers. Labor generally acted against the perceived red menace. In 1933, the A.F.L. acted with the Congress of Industrial Organizations (C.I.O) to squeeze out communist sympathizers.

Positive government intervention eventually saved the U.S. economy and prepared it for further struggles in World War II. With several million men in uniform, women entered factory jobs in large numbers for the first time in almost a century. Blacks gained jobs in the arms industry. Newer industries such as rubber, aerospace, and plastics created vast new jobs, and the slightly older industries of automaking and oil exploded into huge amounts of production just after the war.

Prepared for a bigger role in the economy, workers in postwar America acted quickly, with a wave of strikes right after the war rivaling in numbers those of the late nineteenth century. As American politics became conservative, the government passed the Taft-Hartley Act in

1946 to curtail union powers. Ostensibly seeking to curb union abuses, government and business were in fact alarmed over union power. The spike upwards in the U.S. economy generally meant higher wages, an intensification of male power in the family (and the subsequent dismissal of women from work outside the home), and the very gradual liberalization of civil rights, exemplified by the entrance of Jackie Robinson, the first black major league baseball player in the century. Gender relations remained conservative and paradoxical until the 1970s. While most Americans regarded the domestic sphere as woman's place, middle-class families increasingly required two incomes. Women's share of the workforce rose from about a quarter to a half in the single generation after World War II, paving the way for feminist gains in the last quarter of the century.

By the 1960s, the election of John F. Kennedy as a middle-of-the-road Democrat did not insure better labor relations. Kennedy's younger brother, Robert, demonized the Teamsters Union, by far the largest single union, and kept its officials under constant supervision. At the same time, public unionism gained power with Robert F. Wagner's recognition of collective bargaining by New York City workers in 1959 and President Kennedy's Executive Order 10988 in 1962. During the next decade public workers were among the most militant as strikes broke out among doctors, nurses, hospital workers, police, firefighters, air traffic controllers, and postal employees. Typifying militant labor leadership was Albert Shanker, head of the teachers' union. Public unions were in the forefront of organizing low-wage workers, particularly blacks, Mexican Americans, and Puerto Ricans.

America's workforce changed dramatically with the Hart-Celler Immigration Act of 1965, which removed national quotas and opened the door to hundreds of thousands of immigrants from the Far East, the West Indies, Africa (for the first time since 1800), and the Indian subcontinent. As the U.S. economy sustained fairly constant growth, immigrants moved into low-paying jobs at wages far above any available in their home lands. Some accumulated enough capital to return home. Others, particularly Koreans and Soviet Jews, used family labor to staff small-scale groceries and, while working for low wages, pool resources to gain security.

Other new immigrants were not so lucky. Chinese immigrants, many of them smuggled into the United States by "snakeheads," worked in virtual enslavement in sweatshops in cities. Immigrant women, along with historic minorities such as blacks, worked as keypunch operators in the booming computer sector, with monotonous jobs and repetitive motion injuries. Others lost via politics. For decades, the Texas and California economies depended on migrant workers from Mexico. Under the conservative presidency of Ronald Reagan, Mexicans often were maligned as illegal immigrants, despite their essential participation in the workforce. For the first time since the abolition of slavery in 1865, a group of workers were denied the potential benefits of U.S. citizenship. Reagan as well attempted to control public unions by peremptorily firing the nation's air-traffic controllers in a dispute in 1982. Unionism also faced declines as younger workers in service and emerging technological industries preferred the dream of individual mobility to collective organization.

Each American worker's status became complicated by the nation's leadership in globalization after the fall of communism in Russia in 1989 and the choice by China's rulers to opt for a market economy. The North American Free Trade Agreement in 1994 further weakened unions. Free global flow of capital and rapid transport meant that employers, especially in textiles and shoes, could send out work to any state or local government prepared to offer the best deal, or, increasingly, to countries in the Far East with virtually no protection of wages. Clothing, once a proud American product, was made cheaply in tiny nations few Americans could even identify. This model threatened traditional industrial workers all over the nation and led to increased militancy in the late 1990s. As politicians moved closer to the center or were distracted by divisive "moral" causes such as abortion, workers at the close of the century worried about the stability of the nation's prosperity and moved to protect hard-earned social benefits. At the dawn of the millennium, workers in the United States were infinitely more complex, diverse, and threatened than any time since World War II.

For general studies of American work see Jacqueline Jones, *American Work: Four Centuries of Black and White Labor* (N.Y., 1998), and Richard B. Morris, *The American Worker* (1976). For excellent overviews of black work and status in early America, see Ira Berlin, *Many Thousands Gone: The First Two Centuries of Slavery in North America* (Cambridge, Mass., 1998); and Edmund Morgan, *American Slavery/American Freedom* (N.Y., 1975).

On blacks in the North, see Graham Russell Hodges, *Root & Branch: African Americans in New York and East Jersey, 1613–1863* (Chapel Hill, N.C., 1999).

Regarding women, see Kathleen Brown, *Good Wives, Nasty Wenches and Anxious Patriarchs* (Chapel Hill, N.C., 1997), and Laurel Ulrich, *Good Wives* (N.Y., 1984).

For early nineteenth-century industrialism, see R. Sean Wilentz, *Chants Democratic: New York City & the Rise of the American Working Class, 1788–1850* (N.Y., 1984).

For work and politics after the Civil War see David Montgomery, *The Fall of the House of Labor* (Cambridge, Eng., and N.Y., 1987). An excellent text covering the twentieth century is also available on CD-Rom, *Who Built America?*, by Bruce Levine et al. (N.Y., 1992).

GRAHAM RUSSELL HODGES

writ. A writ is an order from a court that either requires an act be carried out or gives the authority to someone to have the thing done. There are many kinds of writs.

Y

Yankee. The origin of this word is murky. In 1683, according to the *Oxford English Dictionary,* Yankee was in use in England as a surname, possibly of Dutch origin. British soldiers in the New World colonies used it as a term of contempt, and thereafter it came to mean a New Englander. After the Battle of Lexington, New Englanders began to use the word themselves, even making up a mythical band of Indians, the Yankos (meaning *Invincibles*), from which they claimed the word came. The word was often used by Southerners about those north of the Mason-Dixon line, often with negative overtones. Yankee was often preceded by epithets, especially "damned." In addition, during the two world wars the term "Yanks" was used by Europeans to describe all Americans. For a more detailed discussion of the word, see "Yankee" in Stephen Thernstrom, ed., *Harvard Encyclopedia of American Ethnic Groups* (Cambridge, Mass., 1980).

Yankee City Series. The Yankee City Series consists of five volumes published by social anthropologist W(illiam) Lloyd Warner between 1941 and 1959 describing Newburyport, Massachusetts in the mid-1930s. Warner employed numerous assistants, three of whom—Paul Lunt, Leo Srole, and Josiah Low—appeared as coauthors on individual books in the series. The researchers conducted thousands of hours of interviews, profiled each of the roughly 17,000 Newburyport residents, examined in detail virtually every social institution in the city, and in general collected data so aggressively that Warner's project probably still stands as the most extensive study of a mid-sized American community ever undertaken. An abridgment of all five volumes came out as a single volume in 1963.

Conventional intellectual concerns of academic social scientists working in the Depression years helped shaped the contents of the Yankee City series. These concerns reflected the Marxian beliefs that individual humans should be identified as members of a class, that class antagonism provided a central dynamic of human interaction, and that industrialization had created a new form of antagonism pitting workers against management and owners. Today the word "Progressive" is used to describe historians (Charles Beard, for example) who wrote during and after the Progressive era in American politics. They thought of themselves as social scientists and cast their works in terms of group or class conflict. Interest in "stratification" or "stratification theory" was the social anthropologist's equivalent of the progressive historian's interest in class. The first two volumes of the Yankee City series divided Newburyport residents into six distinct class groupings and described the status system operating in the overall community. The idea of class conflict informs volume four, published in 1947, which has as its full title, *The Social System of the Modern Factory. The Strike: A Social Analysis*, and includes a good deal of antimechanization and anti-industrialization commentary. Volume three places heavy emphasis on linkages between ethnicity and class. By the time the final volume appeared in 1959, academic fashion had begun to change. Warner, writing without a coauthor, published *The Living and the Dead: A Study of the Symbolic Life of Americans*. Many consider it the most thoughtful and imaginative of the five Yankee City publications.

Chapter 8 and the appendix of Stephan Thernstrom's *Poverty and Progress: Social Mobility in a Nineteenth Century City* (N.Y., 1964) provide a detailed critique of Warner's methodology and conclusions.

JERE DANIELL

YIVO: Institute for Jewish Research. See Appendix A, Jews.

youth culture. The concept of a youth culture has undergone interesting transformations during the past century. Although the concept has existed almost continuously throughout the twentieth century, it has meant different things at different times, and even meant different things to diverse people at the same time. Early in the century, for example, a journal such as *Youth's Companion* was respectable and nationalistic, but simultaneously so-called Muckrakers caused concern about "street arabs," children who appeared to be homeless, antisocial, and a threat to decent communities.

During the 1920s the phrase "youth culture" invoked young people of college age and slightly older, partying extravagantly in raccoon coats and swallowing goldfish. A decade later, when swing bands enjoyed immense popularity, youth culture usually referred to intensely active dancers, jitterbugging wildly to boisterous music and perhaps, because of body contact, stimulating lascivious behavior. By the early 1940s, "crooners" like Frank Sinatra created hysterical adoration from young fans, mainly female, and set a pattern that persisted through the eras of Elvis Presley, rock and roll, and the Beatles.

The most important phase in the history of youth culture, however, occurred after World War II, and especially during the early and mid-1950s when a variety of authorities decided that comic books, films, and television were inciting juvenile delinquency, primarily in the form of violence and premature sexuality. Senator Estes Kefauver held televised hearings that caused a national stir as one expert after another testified that a "generation gap" existed and that young people felt misunderstood and responded with rebellion, aimed at society in general but family in particular. It was common to hear that family values were in jeopardy.

Less familiar but more important because it was more enduring, advertising began to target young people as a separate market that had disposable income and needed to be attracted with different kinds of ads than the ones that appealed to adults. Eugene Gilbert was the immensely influential pioneer who became a pied piper of marketing techniques for a distinct youth culture. His syndicated columns, books, journal articles and speeches paved the way for a permanent revolution in the promotion of goods directed to teenagers and eventually even preteens. By the end of the 1950s, for example, blue jeans had become the universal mode of dress for young people—and eventually for those not so young. But while disputes raged over wearing jeans to school (1950s and 1960s), jeans became a prime symbol of the newly entrenched youth culture.

During the later 1960s and 1970s, the concept of youth culture became intensely politicized because of bitter opposition to the war in Vietnam, because of young people experimenting with drugs and openly acknowledged sexual activity, burning draft cards, and rejecting the lifestyle and values of people over the age of 30. Free speech and the desire for a less authoritarian, more democratic society also moved many young people to activism—much of it constructive, some of it destructive and even self-destructive.

By the 1980s many of those "young people" had re-entered the mainstream of American society, but a recurrence persisted of concern about the impact of television and film upon the antisocial behavior of youth. In addition, a diminution of job opportunities during the 1980s and early 1990s caused a sense of despair among many young people—a feeling that they would not have the same opportunities in life that their parents had enjoyed.

See James Gilbert, *A Cycle of Outrage: America's Reaction to the Juvenile Delinquent in the 1950s* (N.Y., 1986); Paula Fass, *The Beautiful and the Dammed: American Youth in the 1920's* (N.Y., 1977); and Joseph F. Kett, *Rites of Passage: Adolescence in America, 1790 to the Present* (N.Y., 1977).

MICHAEL KAMMEN

Z

zoos and animal collections. Since the eighteenth century, Americans have been instructed and entertained by collections of captive animals. The earliest exhibitions typically featured single creatures—a lion, an elephant, a "Pig of Knowledge"—hauled from one place to another on foot or in rolling cages. With the development of canals and railroads in the early nineteenth century, enterprising showmen began touring entire menageries to small towns and rural areas. Yet traveling menageries also cultivated an oddly metropolitan aura, often advertising their connections to more permanent collections in New York or Philadelphia. This paradoxical association of exotic animals with urban sophistication may help to explain the growth and appeal of American zoos.

By the mid-nineteenth century, promoters in several major cities were indeed calling for the development of full-fledged zoological gardens, modeled on the more formal animal collections of European capitals. The Zoological Society of Philadelphia (the nation's first) was established in 1859, with its garden opening in 1874. A year later, the Cincinnati Zoo welcomed its first visitors, and by the 1890s, even larger zoological parks had opened in Washington, D.C., and the Bronx. Unlike menageries, dime museums, circuses, and other animal amusements, zoological gardens presented their wild creatures in commodious quarters with scientific labels, all arranged within pleasant, pastoral settings. Furthermore, many urban boosters saw zoos as elite cultural institutions, intellectually allied with museums, libraries, and concert halls—those civilized attractions of any self-respecting metropolis.

Almost immediately, American zoos achieved an overwhelming popularity, as a wide-ranging public responded to the strange allure of exotic creatures in a familiar landscape. Yet that same allure, and that same popularity, also guaranteed that zoological gardens would never attain the social cachet of more "highbrow" institutions. Most visitors came to the zoo for entertainment, not edification, viewing the captive animals as amusing personalities rather than scientific specimens. Moreover, in many smaller cities—from Baltimore and Buffalo to Dallas and Denver—zoos were developed not as grand cultural enterprises but as modest ventures of local parks departments. While few of these municipal zoos could offer visitors even the rudiments of a natural-history education, such parks clearly answered a perceived need, and perhaps even fulfilled a civic responsibility by providing convenient, respectable recreation to city-dwellers hungry for cheap amusements.

By the interwar years, the older, typically Northeastern view of zoos as highbrow institutions had largely disappeared as newer parks in the Midwest and West—particularly those in St. Louis and San Diego—rose to prominence on the proudly populist ideal of "showmanship." A new crop of enthusiastic directors promoted their collections through trained-animal shows, celebrity creatures, and professional publicity, trumpeting the zoo as a site for family entertainment. At the same time, zoos maintained their hold on the public purse, as millions of dollars in New Deal relief funds revived declining parks and inaugurated new ones, reinforcing the image of zoos as valuable community resources. Postwar prosperity would only accelerate these trends, facilitating a construction boom at the nation's zoos and providing a huge new generation of eager young visitors.

In recent decades, though, American zoos have become less local and more global, promoting wildlife conservation around the world while merging into the international culture of theme parks and the mass media. In addition, their long-standing ties to urban life have gradually disintegrated. Sprawling new "megazoos" have forsaken loyal neighborhood visitors for automobile-driven suburbanites and tourists; municipal governments have transferred control of public zoos to private nonprofit corporations. Such developments have led some observers to wonder what a zoo is really *worth* to a community, what edu-

cational or entertainment value it retains in an age of the Discovery Channel and the Internet. Nevertheless, the city zoo is hardly an endangered species. As long as children want to see an elephant up close, the traditional local functions of zoological gardens—as cultural attractions and as recreational spaces—will likely keep these urban jungles alive and growing.

See Elizabeth Anne Hanson, "Nature Civilized: A Cultural History of American Zoos, 1870–1940" (Ph.D. diss., University of Pennsylvania, 1996); R.J. Hoage and William A. Deiss, eds., *New Worlds, New Animals: From Menagerie to Zoological Park in the Nineteenth Century* (Baltimore, 1996); Bob Mullan and Garry Marvin, *Zoo Culture* (London, 1987); and Richard W. Flint, "Entrepreneurial and Cultural Aspects of the Early Nineteenth-Century Circus and Menagerie Business," in *Itinerancy in New England and New York*, Peter Benes, ed. (Boston, 1986), pp. 131–49.

JEFFREY HYSON

Zouaves. A special unit of the French army, made up of Algerian soldiers, was known as Zouaves. The regiment wore a brilliantly colored uniform with baggy trousers, gaiters, a short open jacket, and a turban or fez. They were popularized in the United States by Elmer Ellsworth (1837–1861) who, before the Civil War, organized the Chicago Zouaves into a spectacular drill team that he toured about the country giving exhibitions. At the outbreak of war, Ellsworth raised a company called the Fire Zouaves (the 11th New York Volunteer Infantry). In Alexandria, Virginia while removing a Confederate flag fro▮

the roof of a tavern, Ellswoth was killed by the inn's proprietor. The tavern owner, in turn, was shot by a member of the regiment. The incident received a great deal of publicity, and the Zouaves became widely known and admired.

APPENDIX A

Ethnic Groups

For research concerning ethnic groups, we suggest consulting any of the recent guides to ethnicity. Two very useful titles are *American Immigrant Cultures: Builders of a Nation*, edited by David Levinson and Melvin Ember (N.Y., 1997); and the *Harvard Encyclopedia of American Ethnic Groups*, edited by Stephan Thernstrom (Cambridge, Mass., 1980). These books include detailed essays on most ethnic and many religious groups with ethnic backgrounds. Articles relate history, origins, periods of greatest emigration, social composition, settlement patterns, occupations, churches and schools, organizations, politics and culture, folk customs, ties with the homeland, and assimilation patterns. There are useful bibliographies. These books also contain exceedingly informative essays that deal with questions of American identity, folklore, intermarriage, labor, prejudice, and religion.

In addition, the *AASLH *Directory of Historical Organizations in the United States and Canada* directs the researcher to libraries, archives, museums, ethnic foundations, and associations. The last *Directory* was issued in 1990, and another is in preparation.

What appears below, by ethnic group, is the most recent scholarship. Not every national group is included—only those with a substantial representation in the 1990 census. Periodical literature, for the most part, is also not included. The recent literature will lead to that which is older and the encyclopedias, noted above, will give a fuller list. The Internet is another source of information, full in some cases, spotty in others. The major study centers concerning immigration and ethnicity should be consulted; each has a presence on the Web. See also entries above for the *Balch Institute and *Immigration History Research Center.

African immigrants. The *Balch Institute is conducting research on the immigration of Africans to the United States. See Marilyn Halter, *Between Race and Ethnicity: Cape Verdean American Immigrants, 1860–1965* (Chicago, 1993), especially the useful bibliography. Also see J. Rollings, ed., *Hidden Minorities* (Washington, D.C.,1981).

Albanians. The major archive for Albanian Americans is the Fan S. Noli Library at St. George Albanian Orthodox Cathedral in Boston. See *The Albanian Struggle in the Old World and New* (Boston, 1939), a WPA project, and Constantine A. Demo, *The Albanians in America: The First Arrivals* (Boston, 1960).

Arabs. The Arab American Ethnic Studies Foundation was founded in 1972. It is located at 4367 Beverly Blvd., Los Angeles, CA 90004; (213) 666-1212. Arab Americans appear in the archives of the *Immigration History Research Center at the University of Minnesota. See Mohammed Sawaie, *Arabic-Speaking Immigrants in the United States and Canada: A Bibliographical Guide* (Lexington, Ky., 1985).

Armenians. The Armenian Library and Museum of America is located at 380 Concord Ave., Belmont, MA 02478-3032; (617) 489-2284. See Robert Mirak, *Torn Between Two Lands: Armenians in America, 1890 to World War I* (Cambridge, Mass., 1983); Michael J. Arlen, *Passage to Ararat* ˙N.Y., 1975); Aram Serkis Yeretzian, *A ˙istory of Armenian Immigration to ˙erica with Special Reference to Conditions in Los Angeles* (San Francisco, 1974); and M. Vartan Malcom's *Armenians in America* ([1919] San Francisco, 1969).

Austrians. See Franz A.J. Szabo, *Austrian Immigration to Canada* (Ottawa, 1996); E. Wilder Spaulding, *The Quiet Invaders: The Story of the Austrian Impact upon America* (Vienna, 1968); and Wilhelm Schlag, "A Survey of Austrian Emigration to the United States," in *Ostreich und die angelsächsische Welt*, Otto von Hietsch, ed. (2 vols; Vienna and Stuttgart, 1961).

Basques. There is a Basque Studies Program at the University of Nevada in Reno, with some additional Basque materials at the University of Idaho in Moscow; at the *Newberry Library; and the New York Public Library. The Basque Memorial Museum is located at 301 S. Ave Q, Bosque, TX 76634; (817) 675-3845. There was a Basque-language newspaper, published in Los Angeles in 1885, another that lasted from 1893 to 1898, and none until 1974 when *Voice of the Basques* was issued in English from Boise, Idaho. See Grant Edwin McCall, *Basque-Americans and a Sequential Theory of Migration and Adaptation* (San Francisco, 1973); Flavia M. McCullough, *The Basques in the Northwest* (San Francisco, 1974); and the writings of Robert Laxalt, including "Lonely Sentinels of the American West: Basque Sheepherders," *National Geographic Magazine* 129 (1966): 870–88.

Belgians. There is a Belgian American Resource Collection at the Cofren

Library, University of Wisconsin at Green Bay for which there is a printed guide. The Web address is <www.uwgb.edu/~library/dept/spc/spc/belgian_amer.html>. See Luc Sante, *The Factory of Facts* (N.Y., 1998); Henry Verslype, *The Belgians of Indiana . . .* (Mishawak, Ind., 1987); and Henry Lucas, *Netherlanders in America* (Ann Arbor, Mich., 1955); and Henry G. Bayer, *The Belgians: First Settlers in New York* (N.Y., 1925).

Bosnian Muslims. There is a Slavic American Collection at the Louisa H. Bowen University Archives and Special Collections, Lovejoy Library, Southern Illinois University at Edwardsville, Edwardsville, IL, 62026-1063; (618) 650-2665; fax (618) 650-2717; <www.siue.edu/~skerber> and <skerber@siue.edu>. See George J. Prpic, *The Croatian Immigrants in America* (N.Y., 1971); and Gerald G. Govorchin, *Americans from Yugoslavia* (Gainesville, Fla., 1961).

Bulgarians. There is a Slavic American Collection at the Louisa H. Bowen University Archives and Special Collections, Lovejoy Library, Southern Illinois University at Edwardsville, Edwardsville, IL, 62026-1063; (618) 650-2665; fax (618) 650-2717; <www.siue.edu/~skerber> and <skerber@siue.edu>. See Nikolay Altankov, *The Bulgarian Americans* (San Carlos, Calif., 1979).

Caribbeans. See Miguel Gonzalez-Pando, *The Cuban Americans* (Westport, Conn., 1998); Catherine A. Sunchine and Keith Q. Warner, *Caribbean*

Connections: Moving North (Washington, D.C., 1998); Roy Bryce-Laporte and Delores Mortimer, *Caribbean Immigration to the United States* (Washington, D.C., 1976); Richard S. Dunn, *Sugar and Slaves* (Chapel Hill, N.C., 1972); Gilbert S. Osofsky, *Harlem: The Making of a Ghetto* (N.Y., 1971).

Central and South Americans. See A. J. Jaffee et al., *Spanish Americans in the United States: Changing Demographic Characteristics* (N.Y., 1976). For a local study, see Carlos U. Lopez, *Chileños in California: A Study of the 1850, 1852, and 1860 Censuses* (San Francisco, 1973).

Chinese. The Chinese and Chinese American History Association is located at 1355 Arlington Blvd., El Cerrito, CA 94530; (415) 233-9322 and the Southern California Chinese Historical Society at 969 N. Broadway, Los Angeles, CA 90012; (213) 621-3171. There is a Museum of Chinese in the Americas at 70 Mulberry Street, on the second floor, New York, NY 10013; (212) 619-4785; <MoCa-org@juno.com>. See the Hawaii Chinese History Center at 111 N. King St., Suite 410, Honolulu, HI 96817; (808) 521-5948. See Arthur Bonner, *Alas! What Brought Thee Hither: The Chinese in New York, 1800–1950* (Madison, N.J., 1997).

See also Asian American history.

Croats. Consult the *Immigration History Research Center, University of Minnesota; the Croatian Ethnic Institute in Chicago, and the archives of the Croatian Fraternal Union in Pittsburgh.

The Slavic American Collection is located at the Louisa H. Bowen University Archives and Special Collections, Lovejoy Library, Southern Illinois University at Edwardsville, Edwardsville, IL 62026-1063; (618) 650-2665; fax (618) 650-2717; <www.siue.edu/~skerber> and <skerber@siue.edu>. See Frances Kraljic, *Croatian Migration to and from the United States, 1900–1914* (Palo Alto, Calif., 1978); Vladimir Markotic, ed., *Biographical Directory of Americans and Canadians of Croatian Descent* (Calgary, Alberta, 1973); Geroge J. Prpic, *The Croatian Immigrants in America* (N.Y., 1971); and Gerald G. Govorchin, *Americans from Yugoslavia* (Gainesville, Fla., 1961).

Cubans. *Cuban Studies* is published by the Center for Latin American Studies at the University of Pittsburgh. See Felix Roberto Masud-Pilato, *From Welcomed Exiles to Illegal Immigrants: Cuban Migration to the United States, 1959–1995* (Lanham, Md., 1996); Maria Cristina Garcia, *Havana USA: Cuban Exiles and Cuban Americans in South Florida* (Berkeley, 1996); Eleanor Meyer Rogg, *The Assimilation of Cuban Exiles: The Role of Community and Class* (N.Y., 1974); and Richard R. Fagen, Richard A. Brody, and Thomas J. O'Leary, *Cubans in Exile: Disaffection and the Revolution* (Stanford, Calif., 1968).

Czechs and Slovaks. Materials can be consulted at the Archives of Czechs and Slovaks Abroad at the University of Chicago, 1100 E. 57th St., Chicago, IL 60637; (312) 753-2856, and at the *Immigration History Research Cen-

ter. See also the Czech Heritage Collection at the University of Nebraska, in Lincoln. There is a Czechoslovak Heritage Museum and Library at 2701 South Harlem Ave., Berwyn, IL 60402; (312) 795-5800. For Slovaks, see the collection of materials at the Jankola Library in Danville, Penna. See also the Immigration History Research Center of the University of Minnesota. See Esther Jerabek, *Czechs and Slovaks in North America* (N.Y., 1977); Vera Laska's chronology, *The Czechs in America, 1633–1977* (Dobbs Ferry, N.Y., 1977); Emily Greene Balch, *Our Slovic Fellow-Citizens* ([1910], N.Y., 1969), and R. W. Seton-Watson, *A History of the Czechs and Slovaks* ([1943] Hamden, Conn., 1965).

Danes. The Danish American Heritage Society, organized in 1977, is located at 29672 Dane Lane, Junction City, Ore. 97448; (503) 998-6725. See Henning Bender and Birgit Flemming Larsen, eds., *Danish Emigration to the U.S.A.* (Aalborg, Denmark, 1992), and *Danish Emigration to Canada* (Aalborg, Denmark, 1991); Peter L. Petersen, *The Danes in America* (Minneapolis, 1987); Frederick Hale, *Danes in North America* (Seattle, 1984); *Danes Go West: A Book about the Emigration to America* (Copenhagen, 1976); Kristian Hvidt, *Flight to America: The Social Background of 300,000 Danish Emigrants* (N.Y., 1975); and John H. Bille, *A History of the Danes in America* (San Francisco, 1971).

Dutch. The Association for the Advancement of Dutch American Studies, founded in 1979, is at 3207 Burton SE,

Grand Rapids, MI 49506; (616) 957-6310. The Holland Society of New York Library is located at 122 E. 58th St., New York, NY 10022; (212) 758-1675. There is a Netherlands Museum at 8 E. 12th St., Holland, MI 49423; (616) 392-3129. See Henry S. Lucas, *Dutch Immigrant Memoirs and Related Writings* (Grand Rapids, Mich., 1997); Rob Kroes and Henk-Otto Neuschafer, *The Dutch in North-America: Their Immigration and Cultural Continuity* (Amsterdam, 1991); Gerald F. De Jong, *The Dutch in America, 1609–1974* (Boston, 1975); and Henry S. Lucas, *Netherlanders in America: Dutch Immigration to the United States and Canada, 1789–1950* (Ann Arbor, Mich., 1955).

East Asians. See Katy Gardner, *Global Migrants/Local Lives: Travel and Transformation in Rural Bangladesh* (Oxford, Eng., 1995); Johanna Lessinger, *From the Ganges to the Hudson: Indian Immigrants in New York City* (Boston, 1995); Niaz Zaman and Kamal Uddin Ahmed, *Migration, Migrants and the United States* (Dhaka, Bangladesh, 1992); Hugh Tinker, *The Banyan Tree: Overseas Emigrants from India, Pakistan and Bangladesh* (Oxford, Eng., 1977); Norris Hundley, ed., *The Asian Americans* (Santa Barbara, Calif. 1976); Leona B. Bagai, *The East Indians and the Pakistanis in America* (Minneapolis, 1972). See *Division of Hearts*, a video recording by Salli Khanna and Peter Chappel (N.Y.: First Run Icarus Films, 1987). See also "Mehndi Party" posted at <www.balchinstitute.org>.

English. See Charlotte J. Erickson, *Invisible Immigrants* (London, 1972);

Stanley C. Johnson, *A History of Emigration from the United Kingdom to North America, 1762–1912* (N.Y., 1966); Wilbur S. Shepperson, *British Emigration to North America* (Oxford, Eng., 1957); and Bernard Bailyn, *Voyagers to the West: A Passage in the Peopling of America on the Eve of the Revolution* (N.Y., 1986).

Estonians. There is Estonian material at the *Immigration History Research Center at the University of Minnesota; a collection of materials at Estonian House in New York City; and at Kent State University in Ohio. See Jaan Pennar, *The Estonians in America, 1627–1975: A Chronology and Fact Book* (Dobbs Ferry, N.Y., 1975).

Filipinos. See Joyce Yukawa, *Migration from the Philippines, 1975–1995: An Annotated Bibliography* (Quezon City, Philippines, 1996); and Frank H. Winter, *The Filipinos in America* (Minneapolis, 1988).

Finns. The Finnish American Historical Library is located at Suomi College, 601 Quincy St., Hancock, MI 49930; (800) 682-7604; <www.suomi.edu/index/html>. A second collection of materials about Finns in America is located at the *Immigration History Research Center of the University of Minnesota. See Philip J. Anderson, Dag Blanck, and Peter Kivisto, eds., *Scandinavian Immigrants and Education in North America* (Chicago, 1995); Reino Kero, *The Finns in North America: Destinations and Composition of Immigrant Societies in North America before World War I* (Turku, Finland, 1980);

John I. Kolehmainen's *Finns in America: A Bibliographical Guide to Their History* (Hancock, Mich., 1947) is the standard guide to source material; A. William Hoglund's, *Finnish Immigrants in America, 1880–1920* (Madison, Wis., 1960), provides an overall view.

French. See Jean-Louis Houde, *French Migration to North America, 1600–1900* (Chicago, 1994); Hubert Charbonneau, *The First French Canadians: Pioneers in the St. Lawrence Valley* (Newark, Del., 1993); James S. Pula, *The French in America, 1488–1974: A Chronology and Factbook* (Dobbs Ferry, N.Y., 1975). See also Mason Wade, *The French Canadians, 1760–1976* (N.Y., 1968); and Robert Rumilly, *Histoire des Franco Américans* (Montreal, 1972).

Germans. The major archives include the German Society of Pennsylvania located at 611 Spring Garden St., Philadelphia, PA 19123; (215) 627-4365; fax (215) 627-5297; <www.libertynet.org/gencap/germanpa.html>. There is material also at the *Balch Institute in Philadelphia and the Max Kade German American Research and Document Center at the University of Kansas. See <www.cc.uKans.edu/~german/kadedec.html> for the newsletter published there. See Andreas Lehmann, *Go West! Ostdeutsche in Amerika* (Berlin, 1998); *People in Transit: German Migrations in Comparative Perspective, 1820–1930*, Dirk Hoerder and Jöeg Nagler, eds. (Washington, D.C., 1995); and Timothy Walch, *Immigrant America: European Ethnicity in the United States* (N.Y., 1994).

Greeks. There is an archive devoted to Greeks in this country at the University of Utah. The Web address is <www.utah.edu>. There are also materials about Greek immigration at the New York Public Library. See Thomas Burgess, *Greeks in America* (N.Y. 1970); Michael N. Cutsumbis, *A Bibliographic Guide to Materials on Greeks in the United States, 1890–1960* (N.Y., 1970); and Theodore Saloutos, *Greeks in the United States* (Cambridge, Mass., 1964).

Gypsies. There is a Gypsy Lore Society at the Victor Weybright Archives of Gypsy Studies, Cheverly, MD 20785; (301) 341-1261; <http://rtracy.addr.com/gls>. See Marlene Sway, *Familiar Strangers: Gypsy Life in America* (Urbana, Ill., 1988); Gabrielle Tyrnauer, *The Gypsy in Northwest America* (Olympia, Wash., 1977); and Rena C. Gropper, *Gypsies in the City: Culture, Patterns and Survival* (Princeton, N.J., 1975).

Haitians. See Michel S. Laguerre, *Ethnicity as Dependence: The Haitian Community in New York City* (N.Y., 1978); Roy Bryce-Laporte and Dolores Mortimer, eds., *Caribbean Immigration to the United States* (Washington, D.C., 1976); and Jervis Anderson, "The Haitians of New York," *The New Yorker* (March 31, 1975).

Hungarians. The *Immigration History Research Center of the University of Minnesota has a significant collection of material. In addition, there is the Hungarian Research Center at the American Hungarian Foundation, 177

Somerset St., New Brunswick, NJ 08903; (201).846-5777. See Joseph D. Dwyer, ed., *Hungarians in the United States and Canada: A Bibliography: Holdings of the Immigration Research Center* (Minneapolis, 1977); and Joseph Széplaki, ed., *The Hungarians in America, 1583–1974: A Chronology and Fact Book* (Dobbs Ferry, N.Y., 1975).

Indians, East. See East Asians.

Indochinese. There is a Vietnamese Immigration Collection at the State University of New York at Buffalo. See Darrel Moutero and Marsha I. Weber, *Vietnamese Americans: Patterns of Resettlement and Socioeconomic Adaptation in the United States* (Boulder, Colo., 1979); and Gail B. Kelly, *From Vietnam to America: A Chronicle of Vietnamese Immigration to the United States* (Boulder, Colo., 1977).

Irish. The American Irish Historical Society is located at 991 Fifth Avenue, New York, NY 10029; (212) 288-2263. The library contains more than 10,000 volumes, chronicles, and histories of the Irish in America. The archives include newspapers, records of Irish-American organizations, and letters and documents of important Irish Americans. There is, in addition, a popular-culture collection containing playbills, sheet music, flyers, photographs, programs, and other ephemera. Consult: <www.aihs.org/aihslib.html>. See Frank D' Arcy, *The Story of Irish Emigration* (Cork, Ireland, 1999); Arthur Gribben, ed., *The Great Famine and the Irish Diaspora in America* (Amherst, Mass., 1999); Edward Laxton,

The Famine Ships: The Irish Exodus to America (N.Y., 1997); Noel Ignatiev, *How the Irish Became White* (N.Y., 1995); John Duffy Ibson, *Will the World Break Your Heart? Dimensions and Consequences of Irish American Assimilation* (N.Y., 1990); Carl Wittke, *The Irish in America* ([1956] N.Y., 1970); and William V. Shannon, *The American Irish* (N.Y., 1966).

Italians. The Italian Historical Association is located at 209 Flagg Ave., Staten Island, NY 10304. There is a Center for Migration Studies, Staten Island, N.Y. with materials on Italians in America. In addition, there is the Urban History Collection at the University of Illinois at Chicago Circle, and the *Immigration History Research Center, University of Minnesota. See S. M. Tomasi and M. H. Engel, *The Italian Americans* (N.Y., 1971); and Joseph Lopreato, *Italian Americans* (N.Y., 1970). In addition, there are many regional studies about Italian Americans.

Japanese. The Japanese American National Museum is located at 369 East First Street, Los Angeles, CA 90012; (213) 625-0414; fax (213) 625-1770; <www.lausd.k12.ca.us.janm>. The National Japanese American Historical Society is located at 1885 Folsom St., San Francisco, CA 94103; (415) 431-5007; fax (415) 431-0311; <www.nike.heritage.org>. See Ronald Takaki, *Issei and Nisei: The Settling of Japanese America* (N.Y., 1994); Roger Daniels, *Asian America: Chinese and Japanese in the United States since 1850* (Seattle, 1988); H. Brett Melendy, *Chinese and*

Japanese Americans (N.Y., 1984); and Robert A. Wilson and Bill Hosokawa, *East to America: A History of the Japanese in the United States* (N.Y., 1980).

See also Asian American history.

Jews. The American Jewish Historical Society has headquarters at 2 Thornton Road, Waltham, MA 02453-7711; (716) 891-8110; <www.ajhs.org>. The most important archives are at the Jacob Rader Marcus Center of the American Jewish Archives, 3101 Clifton Ave., Cincinnati, OH 45220; (513) 221-1875; <huc.edu/aia> and YIVO: The Institute for Jewish Research, located at 15 West 16th Street, New York, NY 10019; (212) 246-6080; fax (212) 292-1891; <www.centerforjewishhistory.com/yivo.html> or <yivomail@yivo.cjh.org>. See Roberta Rosenberg Farber and Chaim I. Waxman, *Jews in America: A Contemporary Reader* (Hanover, N.H., 1999); Jeffrey S. Gurock, *American Jewish History* (N.Y., 1998); J. Gordon Melton, *Encyclopedia of American Religion* (Detroit, 1993); Howard M. Sachar, *A History of Jews in America* (N.Y., 1992); Abraham J. Karp, *Haven and Home: A History of Jews in America* (N.Y., 1985); Irving Howe, *World of Our Fathers* (N.Y., 1976); Henry Feingold, *Zion in America* (N.Y., 1974); and Nathan Glazer, *American Judaism*, rev. ed. (Chicago, 1972).

See also Appendix B, Jews.

Koreans. The Korean American Historical Society is located at 10303 Meridian Ave. N., Suite 20, Seattle, WA 98133-9483; (206) 528-5784, fax (206) 523-4340; <www.kahs.org>; the e-mail contact is <kahs@arkay-intl.com>. There is a Center for Korean Studies at the University of Hawaii, located at 1882 East-West Road, Honolulu, HI 96822; (808) 956-7041; <www2.hawaii.edu/korea>. See Elaine H. Kim, *East to America: Korean-American Life Stories* (N.Y., 1996); Pyong Gap Min, *Caught in the Middle: Korean Merchants in America's Multiethnic Cities* (Berkeley, Calif., 1996); Ronald Takaki, *From the Land of Morning Calm: The Koreans in America* (N.Y., 1994); Hyung-chan Kim and Wayne Patterson, eds., *The Koreans in America* (Minneapolis, 1977). For Hawaii, see Arthur L. Gardner, *The Koreans in Hawaii: An Annotated Bibliography* (Honolulu, 1970).

Latvians. The best collection of materials can be found at the Latvian Association in Washington, D.C.; the Latvian Research Institute in New York; the *Immigration History Research Center at the University of Minnesota; at Kent State University in Ohio; and the Hoover Institution on War, Revolution, and Peace, Stanford University, Stanford, California. See Maruta Kārklis, *The Latvians in America, 1640–1973: A Chronology and Fact Book* (Dobbs Ferry, N.Y., 1974).

Lithuanians. Archival collections can be found at the World Lithuanian Archives, 5620 S. Claremont Ave., Chicago, IL 60636; the American Lithuanian Cultural Archives are on Thurber Road, Putnam, CT 06206; (203) 928-9317. There is also material in the University of Pennsylvania Library in Philadelphia, and in the New York

Public Library. See David Fainhauz, *Lithuanians in the USA: Aspects of Ethnic Identity* (Chicago, 1990); Antanas J. van Reerian, *Lithuanian Diaspora: Königsberg to Chicago* (Lanham, Md., 1990); Milda Danys, *DP, Lithuanian Immigration to Canada after the Second World War* (Toronto, 1986); Leo Alilunas, *Lithuanians in the United States* (San Francisco, Calif., 1978); and Algirdas M. Budreckis, *The Lithuanians in America, 1651–1975: A Chronology and Fact Book* (Dobbs Ferry, N.Y., 1976).

Macedonians. See George J. Prpic, *South Slavic Immigration in America* (Boston, 1978); Stoyan Christowe, *My American Pilgrimage* (Boston, 1947), and *This Is My Country* (N.Y., 1938).

Mexicans. See *Chicano history and see "Mexican Day of the Dead" posted at <www.balchinstitute.org>. See Carlos M. Fernández-Shaw, *The Hispanic Presence in North America from 1492 to Today* (N.Y., 1999); A. J. Jaffe, Ruth M. Cullen, and Thomas D. Boswell, *Spanish Americans in the United States: Changing Demographic Characteristics* (N.Y., 1976); and Leo Grebler, Joan Moore, and Ralph Guzman, *The Mexican American People* (Los Angeles, 1970).

Norwegians. The Norwegian American Historical Association, established in 1925, is located at 1520 St. Olaf Ave., Northfield, MN 55057; (507) 646-2222; <www.STOLAF.edu>. It publishes works about the Norwegian-American experience. There is a Scandinavian Studies program at Luther College, Decorah, IA, where Westerheim, a museum devoted to Norwegians in the United States, is located. The address is 502 West Water Street, Dakorah, Iowa 52101; (309) 382-9681. There is additional material at the Sons of Norway in Minneapolis (<www.sofn.com>) and at the historical societies in Wisconsin and Minnesota. There is a Nordic Heritage Museum at 3014 NW 67th St., Seattle, WA 98117; (206) 789-5707. See David C. Mauk, *The Colony That Rose from the Sea: Norwegian Maritime Migration and Community in Brooklyn 1850–1910* (Northfield, Minn., 1997); John E. Bodnar, *Collective Memory and Ethnic Groups: The Case of Swedes, Mennonites, and Norwegians* (Rock Island, Ill., 1991); Ingrid Semmingsen, *Norway to America: A History of the Migration* (Minneapolis, 1978); Arlow W. Anderson, *The Norwegian Americans* (Boston, 1974); Theodore C. Blegan, *Norwegian Migration to America, 1825–1860* ([1931] N.Y., 1969); and Carlton C. Qualey, *Norwegian Settlement in the United States* (Northfield, Minn., 1968).

Pakistanis. See East Asians.

Poles. There is an archive at the Polish Museum of America, 984 N. Milwaukee Ave., Chicago, IL 60622; (773) 384-3352; <member.aol.com/pgsamerica/pma.html> and also at the *Immigration History Research Center at the University of Minnesota. The Central Council of Polish Organizations, established in 1930 by the Polish Historical Society, is located at 4291 Stanton Ave., Pittsburgh, PA

15201; (412) 782-2166. The Polish American Historical Society is located at 984 N. Milwaukee Ave., Chicago, IL 60622; (312) 384-3352. See also the information about Poles in the United States in "Presenting Polonia in America" at <www.balchinstitute. org>. See James S. Pula, *Polish Americans: An Ethnic Community* (N.Y., 1995); Waclaw Kruszka, *A History of the Poles in America to 1908* (Washington, D.C., 1993); John J. Bukowczyk, *And My Children Did Not Know Me: A History of the Polish Americans* (Bloomington, Ind., 1987); Frank Renkiewicz, ed., *The Polish Presence in Canada and America* (Toronto, 1982); Joseph Anthony Wytrwal, *Behold! The Polish-Americans* (Detroit, 1977); Caroline Golab, *Immigrant Destinations* (Philadelphia, 1977); Helena Z. Lopata, *Polish Americans: Status Competition in an Ethnic Community* (Englewood Cliffs, N.J., 1976); and Victor Greene, *For God and Country: The Rise of Polish and Lithuanian Ethnic Consciousness in America, 1860–1910* (Madison, Wis., 1975).

Portuguese. See David J. Viera, *The Portuguese in the United States: A Bibliography* (Durham, N.H., 1989); Frederic A. Silva, *"All Our Yesterdays . . .": The Sons of Macao—Their History and Heritage* (San Francisco, 1979); Carlos Almeida, *Portuguese Immigrants: The Centennial Story of the Portuguese Union of the State of California* (San Leandro, Calif., 1978); Leo Pap, *The Portuguese in the United States: A Bibliography* (Staten Island, N.Y., 1976); Manoel da Silveria Cardozo, ed., *The Portuguese in America, 590 B.C.–1974: A Chronology and Fact Book* (Dobbs Ferry, N.Y., 1976). See also, Maria José Lagos Trindade, "Portuguese Emigration from the Azores to the United States during the 19th Century," in *Portugal and America: Studies in Honor of the Bicentennial of American Independence* (Lisbon, 1976).

Puerto Ricans. El Museo del Barrio is located at 1945 Third Ave., New York, NY 10029; (212) 831-7272. See The United States Commission on Human Rights Report, *Puerto Ricans in the Continental United States: An Uncertain Future* (Washington, D.C., 1976); and Francesco Cordasco and Eugene Bucchioni, eds., *The Puerto Rican Experience: A Sociological Sourcebook* (Totowa, N.J., 1973); and Oscar Lewis, *La Vida: A Puerto Rican Family in the Culture of Poverty—San Juan and New York* (N.Y., 1972).

Romanians. The Romanian Library is located at 200 E 38th St., New York, NY 10016; (212) 687-0181. See Gerald Bobango, *The Roumanian Orthodox Episcopate of America: The First Half-Century, 1929–1979* (Jackson, Mich., 1979); Mary Leuca and Peter Georgeoff, *Romanian Americans in Lake Country, Indiana: Resource Guide* (Lafayette, Ind., 1977); Joseph J. Barton, *Peasants and Strangers: Italians, Rumanians, and Slovaks in an American City, 1890–1950* (Cambridge, Mass., 1975); and Christine A. Galitzi, *A Study of Assimilation among the Roumanians of the United States* ([1929] N.Y., 1968).

Russians. There is material about Russian Americans in the Bakhmeteff

Archive of Russian and Eastern European History and Civilization at Columbia University: (212) 854-3986; <www.columbia.edu/cu/libraries/indiv/area/slav>. Others materials can be found at the History of Russia/Commonwealth of Independent States Collection, Hoover Institution Library and Archives at Stanford University. The address is H. Hoover Memorial Building, Courtyard, Stanford, CA 94305; (650) 723-3563; fax (650) 725-3445; <www-hoover.stanford.edu>. The Museum of Russian Culture, which contains a library and archive, is located at 2450 Sutter St., San Francisco, CA 94115; (415) 751-1572. There are additional materials at the *Library of Congress and a large and useful bibliography of Internet resources at the University of Pittsburgh. See Ira A. Glazer, ed., *Migration from the Russian Empire: Lists of Passengers Arriving at the Port of New York* (Baltimore, 1995); Susan Wiley Hardwick, *Russian Refuge: Religion, Migration, and Settlement on the North American Pacific Rim* (Chicago, 1993); and Vladimir Wertsman, *The Russians in America: A Chronology and Fact Book* (Dobbs Ferry, N.Y., 1977)

Scandinavians. The American Scandinavian Foundation is located at 127 E. 73rd St., New York, NY 10021; (212) 879-9779. The Foundation issues *Scandinavian Review* (1913–).

See also Danes; Finns; Norwegians; Swedes.

Scots. Archival records can be found at the Presbyterian Historical Society and the Historical Society of Pennsylvania, in Philadelphia; at the New-York Historical Society; the North Carolina State Department of Archives and History in Raleigh; the University of North Carolina Library in Chapel Hill; and the *Library of Congress. There is, in addition, a Scotch-Irish Society Library (P.O. Box 181) in Bryn Mawr, PA 19010. See Ian Adams, *Cargoes of Despair and Hope: Scottish Emigration to North America, 1603–1803* (Edinburgh, 1993); Donald Whyte, *Dictionary of Scottish Emigrants to the U.S.A.* (Baltimore, 1972); Rowland R. Berthoff, *British Immigrants in Industrial America* ([1953] N.Y., 1968); George F. Black, *Scotland's Mark on America* ([1921] San Francisco, 1972); and Gordon Donaldson, *The Scots Overseas* (London, 1966).

Scots-Irish. See Edward R. R. Greed, ed., *Essays in Scotch-Irish History* (London, 1969); and James G. Leyburn, *The Scotch-Irish: A Social History* (Chapel Hill, N.C., 1962).

Serbs. The Slavic American Collection at the Louisa H. Bowen University Archives and Special Collections, Lovejoy Library, Southern Illinois University at Edwardsville, Edwardsville, IL 62026-1063; (618) 650-2665; fax (618) 650-2717; <www.siue.edu/~skerber> and <skerber@siue.edu>. See Robert P. Gakovich and Milan M. Radovich, eds., *Serbs in the United States and Canada: A Comprehensive Bibliography* (Minneapolis, 1976). In addition, see Adam S. Eterovich, *Croations from Dalmatia and Montenegrin Serbs in the West and South 1800–1900* (San Francisco, 1971).

Slavs. The Slavic-American Society headquarters is at 3616 Grand Ave., Oakland, CA 94610; (415) 526-0151; the Slavic Museum is at 203 Plaza Building, Pittsburgh, PA 19219; (412) 391-8470. There is also the Slavic American Collection at the Louisa H. Bowen University Archives and Special Collections, Lovejoy Library, Southern Illinois University at Edwardsville, Edwardsville, IL 62026-1063; (618) 650-2665; fax (618) 650-2717; <www. siue.edu/~skerber> and <skerber@siue.edu>.

Slovaks. See Czechs.

Slovenes. The largest collection of materials on the Slovenes is at the *Immigration History Research Center, University of Minnesota, Minneapolis. See George J. Prpic, *South Slavic Immigration in America* (Boston, 1978); Marie Prisland, *From Slovenia —to America: Recollections and Collections* (Chicago, 1968); and Gerald Gilbert Govorchin, *Americans from Yugoslavia* (Gainesville, Fla., 1961).

Spaniards. See Carlos M. Fernández-Shaw, *The Hispanic Presence in North America from 1492 to Today* (N.Y., 1999); and A. J. Jaffe, Ruth M. Cullen, and Thomas D. Boswell, *Spanish Americans in the United States: Changing Demographic Characteristics* (N.Y., 1976).
See Basques.

South Asians. See East Indians.

Southeast Asians. See Norma Murphy, *A Hmong Family* (Minneapolis, 1997); Kalsuyo Howard, *Passages: An Anthology of the Southeast Asian Refugee Experience* (Fresno, Calif., 1990); James H. Jafner, Jeannine Muldoon, and Elizabeth Bower, *Southeast Asian Refugees in Western Massachusetts* (Amherst, 1989); and Franklin Ng, *The History and Immigration of Asian Americans* (N.Y., 1985).
See also Indochinese.

Swedes. The Swedish-American Historical Museum, founded in 1926, is at 190 Patterson Ave., Philo, PA 19145; (215) 389-1776. There is a Swedish American Historical Society, at 5125 N. Spaulding St., Chicago, IL 60626; (773) 583-5722. There is a collection of books and archival materials at the Augustana College Library, Rock Island, IL 61201; (309) 794-7266. The American Swedish Institute is located at 2600 Park Ave., Minneapolis 55407; (612) 871-9907; <www.americanswedishinst.org>. See Axel Friman, George M. Stephenson, and H. Arnold Barton, eds., *America, Reality & Dream: The Freeman Letters from America & Sweden, 1841–1862* (Rock Island, Ill., 1996); Rhipip J. Anderson, Dag Blanck, and Peter Kivisto, eds., *Scandinavian Immigrants and Education in North America* (Chicago, 1995); H. Arnold Barton, *A Folk Divided: Homeland Swedes and Swedish Americans, 1840–1940* (Carbondale, Ill., 1994); and Ulf Beijbom, *Swedes in America: Intercultural and Interethnic Perspectives on Contemporary Research* (Vaaje, Sweden, 1993).

Swiss. There is a Swiss American Historical Society located at Old Dominion University, Norfolk, VA 23508.

See, Heinz K. Meier, *The Swiss American Historical Society, 1927–1977* (Norfolk, Va., 1977). See Konrad Basler, *The Dorlikon Emigrants: Swiss Settlers and Cultural Founders in the United States* (N.Y., 1996); Leo Schelbert, *America Experienced: Eighteenth and Nineteenth Century Accounts of Swiss Emigrants to the United States* (Camden, Maine, 1996); Leo Schelbert, *Swiss in North America* (Philadelphia, 1974), and *New Glaus, 1845–1970: The Making of a Swiss American Town* (Glaus, Switzerland, 1970).

Turks. See Barbara C. Aswad and Barbara Bilgé, eds., *Family and Gender among American Muslims: Issues Facing Middle Eastern Immigrants and their Descendants* (Philadelphia, 1996); and "Turks" in Stephan Thernstrom, *Encyclopedia of American Ethnic Groups* (Cambridge, Mass., 1980).

Ukranians. There are several Ukranian cultural centers in the United States and Canada. The Ukranian Museum, founded in 1978, located at 203 Second Ave., New York, NY 10003; (212) 228-0110, contains primarily ethnographic and photographic materials. The Ukranian American Archive and Library is at 11756 Charest St., Detroit, MI 48212; (313) 366-9764. See

Myron Kuropas, *The Ukrainian Americans: Roots and Aspirations 1884–1954* (Toronto and Buffalo, 1991), *To Preserve a Heritage: The Story of the Ukrainian Immigration to the United States* (N.Y., 1984), and *The Ukrainians in America* (Minneapolis, 1972); and Vasly Markus, "Ukrainians in the United States," in *Ukraine: A Concise Encyclopedia,* Volodymyr Kubijovič, ed. (Toronto, 1971).

Welsh. See William D. Jones, *Wales in America: Scranton and the Welsh, 1860–1920* (Cardiff, Wales, and Scranton, Penna., 1993); Rowland Berthoff, *British Immigrants in Industrial America 1790–1950* (N.Y., 1968); Alan Conway, ed., *The Welsh in America* (Minneapolis, 1961); and Arthur H. Dodd, *The Character of Early Welsh Emigration to the United States* (Cardiff, Wales, 1957).

West Indians. See Roy Bryce-Laporte and Delores Mortimer, *Caribbean Immigration to the United States* (Washington, D.C., 1976); and Richard S. Dunn, *Sugar and Slaves* (Chapel Hill, N.C., 1972). See also Gilbert Osofsky, *Harlem: The Making of a Ghetto,* 2d ed. (N.Y., 1971); and Ira Reid, *The Negro Immigrant* ([1939] N.Y., 1970).

See also Caribbeans.

APPENDIX B

Religious Groups

J. Gordon Melton has written and edited a number of very useful books for the study of religion. See in particular his *Encyclopedia of American Religion* (Detroit, 1993), which is updated with some frequency.

Adventists. See Gary Land, ed., *Adventism in America: A History* (Grand Rapids, Mich., 1986); J. F. C. Harrison, *The Second Coming: Popular Millennarianism, 1780–1850* (London, 1979).

African Methodist Episcopal Church. The headquarters of the African Methodist Episcopal Church is at 500 8th Street Street, Nashville, TN 37203. See J. Gordon Melton's *Encyclopedia of American Religion* (Detroit, 1993); Howard D. Gregg, *History of the A.M.E. Church* (Nashville, 1980); and Carol V. R. George, *Segregated Sabbaths* (N.Y., 1973).

African Methodist Episcopal Zion Church. The church headquarters can be reached by writing to Box 23843, Charlotte, NC 28232. See J. Gordon Melton's *Encyclopedia of American Religion* (Detroit, 1993); and William J. Walls, *The African Methodist Episcopal Zion Church* (Charlotte, N.C., 1974).

Amish. See J. Gordon Melton, *Encyclopedia of American Religion* (Detroit, 1993); Steven M. Holt, *A History of the Amish* (Intercourse, Penna., 1992); Stephan Thernstrom, *Harvard Encyclopedia of American Ethnic Groups* (Cambridge, Mass., 1980); and John A. Hostetler, *Amish Society* (Baltimore, 1968).

Askhenazi Jews. See Irving Howe, *World of Our Fathers* (N.Y., 1976) Henry Feingold, *Zion in America* (N.Y.

1974); and Nathan Glazer, *American Judiasm* (Chicago, 1972).

See also Sephardic Jews; Jews.

Bahai. The Bahai Faith Library and Archives is located at 5209 N. University Ave., Peoria, IL 61614; (309) 691-9311. It contains books, pamphlets, and copies of the journal *Star of the West.* The world headquarters is in Haifa, Israel. See Peter Smith, *A Short History of the Bahai Faith* (Oxford, Eng., 1996); and J. Gordon Melton, *Encyclopedia of American Religion* (Detroit, 1993).

Baptists. Local materials will be of greatest importance to historians, but major archives include: Baptist General Conference Archives, 3949 Bethel Drive, St. Paul, MN 55112; American Baptist Historical Society Library, 1106 S. Goodman Street, Rochester, NY 14620; and American Baptist Archives, Box 851, Valley Forge, PA 19482. Canadian materials are located at the Canadian Baptist Archives, McMaster Divinity College, Hamilton Ontario, Canada L85 4K1 or <colwellj@mcmail. CIS.McMaster.ca>. See Timothy and Denise George, eds., *Treasures from the Baptist Heritage* (Nashville, Tenn., 1996); Ellen MacGilvra Rosenberg, *The Southern Baptists: A Subculture in Transition* (Knoxville, Tenn., 1989); William H. Brackney, *The Baptists* (N.Y., 1988); Leon McBeth, *The Baptist Heritage* (Nashville, Tenn., 1987); Henry C. Vedder, *A Short History of the Baptists* ([1907] Valley Forge, Pa., 1978); James E. Wood, *Baptists and the American Experience* (Valley Forge, Pa., 1976); William W. Sweet, *The Baptists: A Collection of Source Material* (N.Y.,

1964); and Robert G. Torbet, *A History of the Baptists* (Philadelphia, 1950).

Christian Science. The Christian Science headquarters is at the Christian Science Center, Boston, MA 02115; <www.tfccs.com/GV/TMC/TMCmain. html>. See Gill Gillian, *Mary Baker Eddy* (Reading, Mass., 1998); Stuart E. Knee, *Christian Science in the Age of Mary Baker Eddy* (Westport, Conn., 1994); and Robert David Thomas, *"With bleeding footsteps": Mary Baker Eddy's Path to Religious Leadership* (N.Y., 1994). The works of Robert Peel are also important. See his *Health and Medicine in the Christian Science Tradition: Principle, Practice, and Challenge* (N.Y., 1988), *Mary Baker Eddy: The Years of Authority* (N.Y., 1977), *Mary Baker Eddy: The Years of Trial* (N.Y., 1971), and *Christian Science: Its Encounter with American Culture* (N.Y., 1958).

Church of England. See Episcopal Church.

Congregational Church. See J. Gordon Melton, *Encyclopedia of American Religion* (Detroit, 1993); John Van Rohr, *The Shaping of American Congregationalism 1620–1927* (Cleveland, 1992); J. William T. Youngs, *The Congregationalists* (N.Y., 1990); Alan Heimert and Andrew Delbanco, eds., *The Puritans in America* (Cambridge, Mass, 1985); Donald F. Wells, *Reformed Theology in America* (Grand Rapids, Mich., 1985); and William W. Sweet, *The Congregationalists, A Collection of Source Material* ([1939] N.Y., 1964).

See United Church of Christ.

Ethical Culture. See Horace Leland Friess, *Felix Adler and Ethical Culture* (N.Y., 1981).

Fundamentalism. See David O. Beale, *In Pursuit of Purity: American Fundamentalism since 1820* (Greenville, S.C., 1986).

Greek Orthodox Church. The Greek Orthodox Church headquarters is located at 8-10 East 79th Street, New York, NY 10021. See Demetrios Constantelos, *The Greek Orthodox Church* (N.Y., 1967).

Hutterites. There are several headquarters, each associated with a particular leader. See the listings in Melton. The last group to arrive is the Bruderhof, who came to Rifton, N.Y., in 1954. It is known as the Hutterian Brethren of New York (P.O. Woodcrest, Route 213, Rifton, NY 12471. See J. Gordon Melton, *Encyclopedia of American Religion* (Detroit, 1993); Merrill Mow, *Torches Rekindled: The Bruderhof's Struggle for Renewal* (Ulster Park, N.Y., 1989); John Horst, *The Hutterian Brethran 1528–1931* (Cayley, Alberta, 1977); David Flint, *The Hutterites* (Toronto, 1975); and Victor Peters, *All Things Common* (N.Y., 1971).

Jehovah's Witnesses. The headquarters of the denomination is 25 Columbia Heights, Brooklyn, NY, 11201. See Jerry Bergman, ed., *Jehovah's Witnesses: A Comprehensive and Selectively Annotated Bibliography* (Westport, Conn., 1999); M. James Penton, *Apocalypse Delayed: The Story of Jehovah's Witnesses* (Toronto, 1997); and J. Gordon Melton's *Encyclopedia of American Religion* (Detroit, 1993).

Jews. The American Jewish Historical Society is located at 2 Thornton Road, Waltham, MA 02453-7711; (716) 891-8110; <www.ajhs.org>. Important archives are the American Jewish Archives at the Jacob Rader Marcus Center of the American Jewish Archives, 3101 Clifton Avenue, Cincinnati, OH 45220; (513) 221-1875; <huc.edu/aia>; and at *YIVO. See Roberta Rosenberg Farber and Chaim I. Waxman, *Jews in America: A Contemporary Reader* (Hanover, N.H., 1999); Jeffrey S. Gurock, *American Jewish History* (N.Y., 1998); Howard M. Sachar, *A History of Jews in America* (N.Y., 1992); Abraham J. Karp, *Haven and Home: A History of Jews in America* (N.Y., 1985); Stephan Thernstrom, *Harvard Encyclopedia of American Ethnic Groups* (Cambridge, Mass., 1980); Irving Howe, *World of Our Fathers* (N.Y., 1976); Henry Feingold, *Zion in America* (N.Y., 1974); and Nathan Glazer, *American Judaism*, rev. ed. (Chicago, 1972).

Latter Day Saints. See Mormons.

Lutherans. The Lutheran Theological Seminary and Historical Archive are located at 7301 Germantown Avenue, Philadelphia, PA 19119-1794; <lutthelib@ltsp.edu>. The church headquarters is located at 8765 West Higgins Road, Chicago, IL 60631. See David A. Gustafson, *Lutherans in Crisis: The Question of Identity in the American Republic* (Minneapolis, 1993); Todd W. Nichol, *All These Luth-*

erans (Minneapolis, 1986); Clifford Nelson, ed., *The Lutherans in North America* (Philadelphia, 1980); Johannes Knudsen, *Formation of the Lutheran Church in America* (Philadelphia, 1978); and Carl R. Cronmiller, *History of the Lutheran Church in Canada* (Toronto, 1961).

Mennonites. The Mennonite Historical Library and Archive at the Mennonite Heritage Center, Box 82, 565 Yoder, Harleysville, PA 19438; (215) 256-3020; fax (215) 256-3023; <info@mhep.org>. The Historical Library is at Goshen College, Goshen, IN 46526; (219) 535-7418; fax (219) 535-7438; <joeas@goshen.edu>. See Harry Loewen, *Through Fire & Water: An Overview of Mennonite History* (Scottsdale, Pa., 1996); Katie Funk Wiebe, *Who Are the Mennonite Brethren?* (Hillsboro, Kan., 1984); and Cornelius J. Dyck, *An Introduction to Mennonite History: A Popular History of the Anabaptists and the Mennonites* (Scottsdale, Pa., 1981).

Methodists. See Barrie W. Tabraham, *The Making of Methodism* (London, Eng., 1995); Russell E. Richey, Kenneth E. Rowe, and Jean Miller Schmidt, *Perspectives of American Methodism: Interpretive Essays* (Nashville, Tenn., 1993); A. Gregory Schneider, *The Way of the Cross Leads Home: The Domestication of American Methodism* (Bloomington, Ind., 1993); Russell E. Ritchey, *Early American Methodism* (Bloomington, Ind., 1991); John G. McEllhenney, ed., *Proclaiming Grace & Freedom: The Story of United Methodism in America* (Nashville, Tenn., 1982); Emory Stevens Burke, ed., *The*

History of American Methodism (N.Y., 1965); and William W. Sweet, *Methodists: A Collection of Source Materials* (N.Y., 1964).

See African Methodist Episcopal Church; African Methodist Episcopal Zion Church.

Moravians. The headquarters of the Moravian Church of America is 1021 Center Street, Box 1245, Bethlehem, PA 18026-1245. Moravian Archives are divided. The Northern Archives is located at 211 W. Locust Street, Bethlehem, PA 18078; (610) 866-3255, and the Southern Archives at 4 East Bank Street, Winston-Salem, NC 27101-5307; (336) 722-1742. See J. Taylor Hamilton and Kenneth G. Hamilton, *History of the Moravian Church* (Bethlehem, Pa., 1983); and Allen W. Schattschneider, *Through Five Hundred Years* (Bethlehem, Pa., 1956).

Mormons. The major archive of the Church of the Latter Day Saints is the *Family History Center in Salt Lake City. See Leonard J. Arrington, *The Mormon Experience: A History of the Latter Day Saints* (Urbana, 1992); Richard Bushman, *Joseph Smith and the Beginnings of Mormonism* (Urbana, Ill., 1984); Stephan Thernstrom, *Harvard Encyclopedia of American Ethnic Groups* (Cambridge, Mass., 1980); and Wallace Stegner, *Gathering of Zion: The Story of the Mormon Trail* (N.Y., 1964).

See International Genealogical Index.

Presbyterians. The Presbyterian Church Historical Society, founded in 1852, is located at 425 Lombard Street,

Philadelphia, PA 19147; (215) 627-1852; <ushistory.org/tour/-PhS.html>. The Presbyterian Church in Canada is located at 50 Wynford Drive, North York, Ontario, Canada M5C 1S7; (416) 441-1111; (800) 619-7301; fax (416) 441-2825; <www.presbyterian.ca/more about/incanada.html>. See James H. Smylie, *A Brief History of the Presbyterians* (Louisville, Ky., 1996); J. Gordon Melton, *Encyclopedia of American Religion* (Detroit, 1993); William W. Sweet, *Presbyterians: A Collection of Source Materials* ([1936] N.Y., 1964); and Lefferts Augustine Loetscher, *A Brief History of the Presbyterians* (Philadelphia, 1958).

Protestant Episcopal Church. The headquarters of the Protestant Episcopal Church is 815 Second Avenue, New York, NY 10017. See J. Gordon Melton, *Encyclopedia of American Religion* (Detroit, 1993); David Lynn Holmes, *A Brief History of the Episcopal Church: With a Chapter on the Anglican Reformation and an Appendix on the Annulment of Henry VIII* (Valley Forge, Pa., 1993); Robert W. Prichard, *A History of the Episcopal Church* (Harrisburg, Pa., 1991); and William Snyder, *Looking at the Episcopal Church* (Wilton, Conn., 1980).

Quakers. There are important archival collections at the Friends Historical Library at Swarthmore College, Swarthmore, Pennsylvania; in the Quaker Collection at Haverford College, Haverford; and at Earlham College in Richmond, Indiana. The Friends United Meeting, the largest Friends group, is located at 101 Quaker Hill Drive, Richmond, IN 47374. The Society of Friends Library is at 1515 Cherry Street, Philadelphia, PA 19102; (215) 241-7220; fax (215) 567-2096. The Friends General Conference headquarters, of the Quakers who followed Elias Hicks, is located at 1216 Arch Street, 2B, Philadelphia, PA 19107. See J. Gordon Melton, *Encyclopedia of American Religion* (Detroit, 1993); Hugh Barbour, *The Quakers* (N.Y., 1988); Richard S. Dunn and Mary Maples Dunn, *The World of William Penn* (Philadelphia, 1986); and Francis B. Hall, *Friends in the Americas* (Philadelphia, 1976). For a history of the Hicksite Quakers, see Robert W. Doherty, *The Hicksite Separation* (New Brunswick, N.J., 1967).

Roman Catholics. Roman Catholic archives are contained in regional sites. There are some 4,000 parish histories in the Catholic University Library Archives, 620 Michigan Avenue NE, Washington, DC 20064; (202) 319-5000; <www.cau.edu>. See James Hennesey, *American Catholics* (Oxford, 1981); Stephan Thernstrom, *Harvard Encyclopedia of American Ethnic Groups* (Cambridge, Mass., 1980); and John Tracy Ellis, *American Catholicism* (Garden City, N.Y., 1965).

Russian Orthodox Church. Headquarters of the Russian Orthodox Church is at St. Nicholas Patriarchal Cathedral, 15 East 79th Street, New York, NY 10029. See J. Gordon Melton, *Encyclopedia of American Religion* (Detroit, 1993); and M. Pokrovsky, *S Nicholas Cathedral of New York: Hist and Legend* (N.Y., 1968).

Seventh-Day Adventists. The headquarters of the church and the archive is located at 12501 Old Columbia Pike, Silver Spring, MD 20904; (301) 680-5022; fax (301) 680-6090; <cashew@gc. adventist.org>. See J. Gordon Melton's *Encyclopedia of American Religion* (Detroit, 1993); Joel Bjorling, *The Churches of God, Seventh Day: A Bibliography* (N.Y., 1987); and [Ellen G. White] *A Critique of Prophetess of Health* (Washington, D.C., 1976).

Unitarian Universalist Christian Fellowship. The library of the Harvard Divinity School (at 45 Francis Avenue, Cambridge, MA 02138) serves as the repository of documents relating to both Universalist and Unitarian history. The Unitarian Universalist Alliance headquarters is located at 25 Beacon Street, Boston, MA 02108; (612) 742-2100; <www.uua.org>. The Unitarian Universalist Historical Society publishes biennially the *Journal of Unitarian Universalist History*. See J. Gordon Melton, *Encyclopedia of American Religion* (Detroit, 1993); Conrad Wright, *A Stream of Light: A Short History of American Unitarianism* (Boston, 1982); George Huntson Williams, *American Universalism* (Boston, 1971); David B. Parke, *The Epic of Unitarianism* (Boston, 1957); and Clinton Lee Scott, *The Universalist Church of America: A Short History* (Boston, 1957).

United Church of Christ. The headquarters of the United Church of Christ is 700 Prospect Avenue E, Cleveland, OH 44115-1100. The Evangelical and Reformed Historical Society, founded in 1925, is located at 475 E. Lockwood Avenue, Webster Groves, MO 63119-3192; (314) 961-3627; fax (314) 961-5738; <zuckl@library2.websteruniv.edu>. The Evangelical and Reformed Society–United Church of Christ Archives, which dates from 1863, is at the Lancaster Theological Seminary, 555 W. James Street, Lancaster, PA 17603; (717) 290-8734. See J. Gordon Melton, *Encyclopedia of American Religion* (Detroit, 1993); and David Dunn et al., *A History of the Evangelical and Reformed Church* (Philadelphia, 1961).

State Historical Organizations

The following is a list of state historical organizations, state archives, or libraries. Included for each organization, where available, are its mailing address, telephone and fax numbers, internet and e-mail addresses. Heads of these organizations are not listed, although in some cases the e-mail address is to an individual, sometimes the director. We have included those web addresses that are available. Also included at the top of the list, is the address for *AASLH.

AASLH
1717 Church Street
Nashville, TN 30203
(615) 320-3203; fax (615) 327-9013
<history@aaslh.org>

Alabama Department of History and Archives
P.O. Box 300100
Montgomery, AL 36130-0100
(334) 242-4441; fax (334) 240-3433
<www.asc.edu/archives/agis.html>

State archives and history museum

Alabama Historical Commission
725 Monroe Street
Montgomery, AL 36130

(205) 261-3184

State historic-preservation agency

Alaska Historical Society
P.O. Box 100299
Anchorage, AK 99510-0299
(907) 276-1596
<www.alaska.net~ahs>

Private historical society

Arizona Historical Society
949 E. Second Avenue
Tucson, AZ 85719
(628) 577-4520; fax (628) 577-5695
<www.axstarnet.com>

State historical society

Appendix C

Arizona State Museum
P.O. Box 210026
University of Arizona
Tucson, AZ 85721-0026
(520) 621-6302; fax (520) 621-2976
<www.statemuseum.arizona.edu>

State museum

Arkansas History Commission and State Archives
One Capitol Mall
Little Rock, AR 72201
(501) 682-6900
<www.state.ar.us/ahc/index.html>

State archives

California Historical Society
678 Mission Street
San Francisco, CA 94105
(415) 357-1848; fax (415) 357-1850
<info@calhist.org>

State historical society

California State Archives
1020 O Street
Sacramento, CA 95814
(916) 445-4293
<www.ss.ca.gov/archives>

State archives

California State Library
Box 942837
Sacramento, CA 94237-0001
(916) 654-0174; fax (916) 654-0064
<csl-adm@library.ca.gov>

State library

Colorado Historical Society
1300 Broadway
Denver, CO 80203

(303) 866-3682

State historical society and museum

Connecticut Historical Society
1 Elizabeth Street
Hartford, CT 06105
(203) 236-5621
<www.chs.org>

Private historical society

Connecticut Historical Commission
59 S. Prospect Street
Hartford, CT 06106
(203) 566-3005
<http://archnet.uconn.edu/topical/
crm/conn/ctshpo.html>

Delaware Division of Historical and Cultural Affairs
Hall of Records
P.O. Box 1401
Dover, DE 19901
(302) 736-5314; fax (302) 739-6711

State preservation agency, archives and museum

Delaware State Museum
P.O. Box 1401102
S. State Street
Dover, DE 19903
(302) 739-9316; fax (302/)739-6712
<www.hsd.org>

State museum

Historical Society of Delaware
505 Market Street
Wilmington, DE 19801
(302) 655-7161; fax (302) 655-7844
<hsd@dca.net>

Private historical society and museum

Historical Society of Washington, D.C.
1307 New Hampshire Avenue NW
Washington, DC 20036
(202) 785-2068; fax (202) 887-5785
<www.hswdc.org> and
<heurich@ibm.net>

District historical society

Florida Historical Society
1320 Highland Avenue
Melbourne, FL 32935
(407) 259-0694; fax (407) 259-0847
<www.florida-historical-soc.org>

Private state historical society

Museum of Florida History
500 South Bronough Street
Tallahassee, FL 32399-0250
(904) 488-1484
<dhr.dos.state.fl.us>

State museum

Georgia Department of Archives and History
330 Capitol Avenue SE
Atlanta, GA 30334
(404) 656-2393; fax (404) 657-8427
<www.sos.state.ga.us/archives> and
<reference@sos.state.ga.us>

State historical society and archives

Georgia Historical Society
501 Whitaker Street
Savannah, GA 31499-2001
(912) 651-2128; fax (912) 651-2831
<www.georgiahistory.org>

Private historical society

Bishop Museum
1525 Bernice Street
Honoluli, HI 96817-0916
(808) 848-4142; fax (808)841-4575
<pato@bishopmuseum.org>

Hawaiian Historical Society
580 Kawaiaho Street
Honolulu, HI 96813
(808) 537-6271; fax (808)537-6271

Private historical society

Idaho State Historical Society
1109 Main Suite 250
Boise, ID 83702-5642
(208) 334-2682; fax (208) 334-2774
<www2.state.id.us/ishs>

State historical society

Illinois State Historical Society
Old State Capitol Plaza
Springfield, IL 62701-1507
(217) 782-2635; fax (217) 524-8042
<www.prairienet.org/ishs>

Private historical society

Illinois State Museum
Spring and Edwards Streets
Springfield, IL 62706
(217) 782-7387
<webmaster@museum.state.il.us>

State museum

Indiana Historical Bureau
140 North Senate Avenue
Indianapolis, IN 46204
(317) 232-6277; fax (317) 232-3728
<Ihb@statelib.lib.in.us>

State historical commission

Indiana Historical Society
450 West Ohio Street
Indianapolis, IN 46202-3269
<www2.indianahistory.org> and
<pharstad@indianahistory>

Private historical society

Indiana State Museum
202 North Alabama Street
Indianapolis, IN 46204
(317) 232-1637
<www.ai.org>

State museum

State Historical Society of Iowa
600 East Locust
Des Moines IA 50319
<www.state.ia.us/government/
dca/shsi>

State historical society

Kansas State Historical Society
6425 SW Sixth Avenue
Topeka, KS 66615
(785) 272-8681; fax (785) 272-8682
<www.kshs.org>

State historical society and museum

The Filson Club Historical Society
1310 S. Third Street
Louisville, KY 40208
(502) 635-5083; fax (502) 635-5086
<Filson@filsonclub.org>

Private historical society

Kentucky Historical Society
100 W. Broadway
Frankfort, KY 40601-1931
(502) 564-1792; fax (502) 564-4701

<www.kshs.org>
State historical society and museum

Louisiana State Museum
751 Chartres Street
New Orleans, LA 701161
(800) 568-6968
<lsm@crt.state.la.us>

State historical society and museum

**Maine Historical Society/
Center for Maine History**
485 Congress Street
Portland, ME 04101
(207) 774-1822; fax (207) 775-4301
<www.mainehistory.org>

Private historical society

Maine State Museum
83 State House Station
Augusta, ME 04333-0083
(207) 287-2301; fax (207) 287-6633

State museum

State Archivist Maine
State Archives
84 State House Station
Augusta, ME 04333-0084
(207) 287-5788; fax (207) 287-5739
<www.state.me.us/sos/arc>

State archives

Maryland Historical Society
201 W. Monument Street
Baltimore, MD 21201
(410) 685-3750, ext. 341; fax (410) 385-2105
<www.mdhs.org>

Private historical society

Massachusetts Historical Society
1154 Boylston Street
Boston, MA 02215
(617) 536-1608; fax (617) 859-0074
<library@masshist.org>

Private historical society

Historical Society of Michigan
2117 Washtenaw Avenue
Ann Arbor, MI 48104
(313) 769-1828; fax (313) 769-4267

Private historical society

Michigan Historical Center
717 W. Allegany
Lansing, MI 48918
(517) 373-6362; fax (517) 3737-0851
<sos.state.mi.us/history/history.html>
and <www.sos.state.mi.us/history/
archive/referenc.html>

*State historical agency (museums,
archives, historic preservation,
archaeology)*

Minnesota Historical Society
345 Kellogg Boulevard West
St. Paul, MN 55102-1906
(651) 297-7913; fax (651) 296-1004
<www.mnhs.org>

State historical society and museum

**Mississippi Department of
Archives and History**
P.O. Box 571
Jackson, MS 39205-0571
(601) 359-6850; fax (601) 359-6975
<www.mdah.state.ms.us>

*State archives, museum, historic prop-
erties and SHPO*

Missouri Historical Society
P.O. Box 11940
St. Louis, MO 63112-0040
(314) 746-4599; fax (314) 454-3162
<www.mohistory.org>

*Private history museum and library
and research center*

**State Historical Society of
Missouri**
1020 Lowry
Columbia, MO 65201
(573) 882-7083; fax (573) 884-4950
<www.system.missouri.edu/shs>

State historical society

Montana Historical Society
225 N. Roberts Street
Helena, MT 59620
(406) 444-4706; fax (406) 444-2696
<www.his.mt.gov>

State historical society

Nebraska State Historical Society
1500 R Street
P.O. Box 82554
Lincoln, NE 68501-2554
(402) 471-3270; fax (402) 471-3100
<www.nebraskahistory.org>

State historical society and museum

Nevada Historical Society
1650 N. Virginia Street
Reno, NV 89503
(702) 688-1191; fax (702) 688-2917
<Plbandur@lahontan.clan.lib.nv.us>

State historical society

New Hampshire Historical Society
30 Park Street
Concord, NH 03301
(603) 225-3381; fax (603) 224-0463
<www.nhhistory.org>

Private historical society

New Jersey Historical Commission
P.O. Box 305
Trenton, NJ 08625-0305
<www.state.nj.us/state/history/hisidx.
html>

New Jersey Historical Society
52 Park Place
Newark, NJ 07102
(973) 596-8500; fax (973) 596-6957

Private historical society

New Jersey State Museum
205 West State Street CN530
Trenton, NJ 08625-0530
<www.prodworks.com/trenton/njs-
mus.html>

State museum

Museum of New Mexico
P.O. Box 2087
Santa Fe, NM 87504
(505) 827-6451; fax (505) 827-6427
<www.nmsu.edu/~museum>

State museum

New-York Historical Society
170 Central Park West
New York, NY 10024-5194

Private historical society

New York State Historical Association/The Farmer's Museum/ Fenimore House Museum
P.O. Box 800, Lake Road
Cooperstown, NY 13326
(607) 547-1400; fax (607) 547-1404
<www.nysha.org>

Private historical society

New York State Museum
Empire State Plaza
Albany, NY 12230
<www.nysm.nysed.gov>

State museum

North Carolina Division of Archives and History
109 E. Jones Street
Raleigh, NC 27601-2807
(919) 733-7305; fax (919) 733-8807
<jcrow@ncsl.dcr.state.nc.us>

State historical society and archives

North Carolina Museum of History
5 E. Edenton
Raleigh, NC 27601-1011
(919) 715-0200
<jcw@moh.dcr.state.nc.us>

State history museum division

State Historical Society of North Dakota
North Dakota Heritage Center
612 E. Boulevard Avenue
Bismarck, ND 58505
<Histsoc@state.nd.us>

State historical society

Ohio Historical Society
1982 Velma Avenue
Columbus, OH 43211-2497
(614) 297-2300
<ohiohistory.org>

Private historical society

Oklahoma Historical Society
2100 N. Lincoln Boulevard
Oklahoma City, OK 73105
(405) 522-5202; fax (405) 521-2492
<www.ok-history.mus>

State historical society

Oregon Historical Society
1230 SW Park Avenue
Portland, OR 97205
<www.ohs.org> and
<cheto@ohs.org>

Private historical society

Pennsylvania Heritage Society
P.O. 11466
Harrisburg, PA 17108-1466
(717) 787-2407
<www.paheritage.org>

Pennsylvania Historical and Museum Commission
P.O. Box 1026
Harrisburg, PA 17108-1026
(717) 787-3034; fax (717) 787-4822
<www.pbmc.state.pa.us>

State historical society

Historical Society of Pennsylvania
1300 Locust Street
Philadelphia, PA 19107-5699
(215) 732-6200, ext. 213;

fax (215) 732-2680

Private historical society

Rhode Island Historical Society
110 Benevolent Street
Providence, RI 02906
(401) 331-8575; fax (401) 351-0127
<www.rihs.org>

Private historical society

South Carolina Archives and History Center
8301 Parklane Road
Columbia, SC 29223-4905
(803) 896-6187; fax (803) 896-6186
<www.state.sc.us/scdah> and
<stroup@scdah.state.sc.us>

State SHPO and archives

South Carolina Historical Society
100 Meeting Street
Charleston, SC 29401
(803) 723-3225; fax (803) 723-8584
<www.schistory.org>

Private historical society

South Carolina State Museum
P.O. Box 100107
Columbia, SC 29202-3107
(803) 737-4921; fax (803) 737-4969
<www.museum.state.sc.us>

State museum

South Dakota State Historical Society
900 Governors Drive
Pierre, SD 57501
<www.state.sd.us/deca/cultural> and
<marye@chc.state.sd.us>

State historical society

Tennessee Historical Commission
2941 Lebanon Road
Nashville, TN 37243-0442
(615) 532-1550; fax (615) 532-1549
<www.state.tn.us/environment/hist>

State historical commission

Tennessee Historical Society
War Memorial Building
Nashville, TN 37243-0084

Private historical society

Tennessee State Museum
505 Deaderick Street
Nashville, TN 37219
(615) 741-2692; fax (615) 741-7231
<tnstmuseum@aol.com>

State museum

Texas Historical Commission
P.O. Box 12276
Austin, TX 78711-2276
(512) 463-5853

Texas State Historical Association
2/306 Richardson Hall
University Station
Austin, TX 78712
(512) 471-1525; fax (512) 471-1551
<comments@www.tsha.utexas.edu>

State historical society

Utah State Historical Society
300 Rio Grande
Salt Lake City, UT 84101

State historical society

Vermont Historical Society
109 State Street
Pavilion Building
Montpelier, VT 05609-0901

(802) 828-2291; fax (802) 828-3638

Private historical society

Library of Virginia
800 East Broad Street
Richmond, VA 23219-1905
(804) 692-3554; fax (804) 692-3556

State library

Virginia Historical Society
428 N. Boulevard
P.O. Box 7311
Richmond, VA 23221-0311
(804) 342-9656; fax (804) 355-2399
<charles@vahistorical.org>

Private historical society and museum

Washington State Historical Society
1911 Pacific Avenue
Tacoma, WA 98402-3109
(206) 798-5900; fax (206) 272-9518
<www.wshs.org>

State historical society

West Virginia State Museum
1900 Kanawha Boulevard
East Charleston, WV 25303
(304) 558-0220; fax (304) 558-2779

State museum

State Historical Society of Wisconsin
816 State Street
Madison, WI 53706-1488
<www.shsw.wisc.edu>

State historical society, museum and archives

Wyoming State Historical Society
1740 Del Range
Cheyenne, WY 82009
(307) 635-4881

State historical society

Wyoming State Museum
6101 Yellowstone Road
Cheyenne, WY 82002
(307) 777-7022; fax (307) 777-3543

State museum

$\mathcal{NARA}$ Facilities

The addresses of the National Archives and Records Administration (NARA) regional facilities are listed below. The hours are as follows: The National Archives Building and the National Archives at College Park are open for research Monday and Wednesday, 8:45 A.M. to 5 P.M.; Tuesday, Thursday, and Friday, 8:45 A.M. to 9 P.M.; Saturday, 8:45 A.M. to 4:45 P.M. Closed federal holidays. Regional records-services facilities and presidential libraries are open Monday through Friday; some locations have evening or Saturday hours. Call for specific hours. Closed federal holidays.

National Archives Building
700 Pennsylvania Avenue, NW
Washington, DC 20408-0001
(202) 501-5400

National Archives at College Park
8601 Adelphi Road
College Park, MD 20740-6701
(301) 713-6800

Washington National Records Center
4205 Suitland Road
Suitland, MD 20746-8001
(301) 457-7000

Anchorage: NARA's Pacific Alaska Region
654 West Third Avenue
Anchorage, AK 99501-2145
(907) 271-2441

Microfilm holdings.
Archival and records-center holdings: Alaska

Atlanta: NARA's Southeast Region
1557 St. Joseph Avenue
East Point, GA 30344-2593
(404) 763-7474

Microfilm holdings.

Appendix D

Archival and records-center holdings:
Alabama, Florida, Georgia, Kentucky,
Mississippi, North Carolina, South
Carolina, and Tennessee

Boston: NARA's Northeast Region
380 Trapelo Road
Waltham, MA 02452-6399
(781) 647-8104

Microfilm holdings.
Archival and records-center holdings:
Connecticut, Maine, Massachusetts,
New Hampshire, Rhode Island, and
Vermont

Chicago: NARA's Great Lakes Region
7358 South Pulaski Road
Chicago, IL 60629-5898
(773) 581-7816

Microfilm holdings.
Archival and records-center holdings:
Illinois, Indiana, Michigan, Minnesota,
Ohio, and Wisconsin

Dayton: NARA's Great Lakes Region
3150 Springboro Road
Dayton, OH 45439-1883
(513) 225-2852

Records-center holdings: Indiana, Ohio,
Michigan, and selected sites nationwide

Denver: NARA's Rocky Mountain Region
Denver Federal Center, Building 48
West 6th Avenue and Kipling Street
P.O. Box 25307
Denver, CO 80225-0307
(303) 236-0817

Microfilm holdings.
Archival and records-center holdings:
Colorado, Montana, New Mexico,
North Dakota, South Dakota, Utah,
and Wyoming

Fort Worth: NARA's Southwest Region
501 West Felix Street, Building 1
P.O. Box 6216
Fort Worth, TX 76115-0216
(817) 334-5525

Microfilm holdings.
Archival and records-center holdings:
Arkansas, Louisiana, Oklahoma, and
Texas

Kansas City: NARA's Central Plains Region
2312 East Bannister Road
Kansas City, MO 64131-3011
(816) 926-6272

Microfilm holdings.
Archival and records-center holdings:
Iowa, Kansas, Missouri, and Nebraska

Laguna Niguel: NARA's Pacific Region
24000 Avila Road
P.O. Box 6719
Laguna Niguel, CA 92607-6719
(949) 360-2641

Microfilm holdings.
Archival and records-center holdings:
Arizona, Southern California, and
Clark County, Nevada

Lee's Summit: NARA's Central Plains Region
200 Space Center Drive
Lee's Summit, MO 64064-1182

(816) 478-7625

Records-center holdings: New Jersey, New York, Puerto Rico, and the U.S. Virgin Islands

New York City: NARA's Northeast Region
201 Varick Street, 12th Floor
New York, NY 10014-4811
(212) 337-1300

Microfilm holdings.
Archival holdings: New Jersey, New York, Puerto Rico, and the U.S. Virgin Islands

Philadelphia (two locations): NARA's Mid-Atlantic Region
900 Market Street
Philadelphia, PA 19107-4292
(215) 597-3000

Microfilm holdings.
Archival holdings: Delaware, Maryland, Pennsylvania, Virginia, and West Virginia

NARA's Mid-Atlantic Region
14700 Townsend Avenue
Philadelphia, PA 19154-1096
(215) 617-9027

Records-center holdings: Delaware, Maryland, Pennsylvania, Virginia, and West Virginia

Pittsfield: NARA's Northeast Region
10 Conte Drive
Pittsfield, MA 01201-8230
(413) 445-6885

Microfilm holdings.
Records-center holdings: selected sites nationwide.

St. Louis (two locations): NARA's National Personnel Records Center
(Civilian Personnel Records)
111 Winnebago Street
St. Louis, MO 63118-4199
(314) 425-5722

NARA's National Personnel Records Center
(Military Personnel Records)
9700 Page Avenue
St. Louis, MO 63132-5100
(314) 538-4247

San Francisco: NARA's Pacific Region
1000 Commodore Drive
San Bruno, CA 94066-2350
(650) 876-9009

Microfilm holdings.
Archival and records-center holdings: Northern California, Hawaii, Nevada (except Clark County), the Pacific Trust Territories, and American Samoa

Seattle: NARA's Pacific Alaska Region
6125 Sand Point Way, NE
Seattle, WA 98115-7999
(206) 526-6501

Microfilm holdings.
Archival and records-center holdings: Idaho, Oregon, and Washington.

ABOUT THE CONTRIBUTORS

PETER AGREE worked as an acquisitions editor for books in American history at Cornell University Press for over fifteen years.

KENNETH G. AITKEN is the Prairie History Librarian at Regina Public Library, in Regina, Saskatchewan, Canada. He is a professional genealogist, and writes and lectures on local history and family history research.

ROBERT W. ARNOLD III is Chief of Government Records Services, New York State Archives and Records Administration. He was Director of Public Records, City of Albany, New York, and Executive Director of the Albany County Hall of Records.

STEPHEN C. AVERILL received his Ph.D from Cornell University, and is currently an associate professor in the history department at Michigan State University, where he teaches courses on modern China and modern East Asia.

SHARON BABAIAN is a historian at the National Museum of Science and Technology, Ottawa, Canada. In that capacity she has researched and written a number of reports on the history of technology in Canada. Her most recent works deal with marine navigation and nuclear energy.

M. TERESA BAER is editorial assistant for the microfilm edition, *The Papers of William Henry Harrison, 1800–1815*, at the Indiana Historical Society. She can be contacted through the Publications Division at (317) 233-6073. The address is 450 West Ohio Street, Indianapolis, IN 46202.

GEORGE W. BAIN is Head of Archives and Special Collections, Ohio University Libraries in Athens, Ohio.

BARBARA C. BATSON is exhibitions coordinator at the Library of Virginia, Richmond. She has worked at Old Salem, Inc., in Winston-Salem, N.C., Historic De field in Massachusetts, and the Valentine Museum in Richmond.

about the contributors

LAUREN E. BATTE is Director of Programs for the American Association for State and Local History. Ms. Batte has spent eight years in public and educational programming for history and preservation audiences.

STEFAN BIELINSKI is the founder and director of the Colonial Albany Social History Project, a community history program sponsored by the New York State Museum.

BARBARA WAITKUS BILLINGS is head of Reference Services, at the Western Reserve Historical Society, Cleveland.

GEROGE S. BOBINSKI has completed 29 years at the University at Buffalo as dean of the School of Information and Library and has returned to the faculty as professor, with primary research activity in the field of library history.

JOHN BODNAR is professor and chair, Department of History, Indiana University, and author of *The Transplanted: A History of Immigrants in Urban America* (1985).

BETH M. BOLAND has been a historian for the National Register of Historic Places for more than 25 years. Currently she directs the office's Teaching with Historic Places program in addition to reviewing nominations.

JERRY BRISCO is the president of Arizona Public Historians, Inc., a history consulting firm based in Tempe, Arizona. He has degrees from Princeton and Harvard. His specialties are business history and Arizona Mormon history.

SIMON J. BRONNER is Distinguished Professor of Folklore and American Studies and Director of the Center for Pennsylvania Culture Studies at The Pennsylvania State University, Harrisburg. He is the author of a dozen books and over 100 articles on American history and culture.

G. DAVID BRUMBERG was the director of the New York Historical Resources Center, and is currently history bibliographer with the task of building the local history collection in Cornell's graduate library.

CHARLES F. BRYAN JR. has served as director of the Virginia Historical Society since 1988. Previously, he was executive director of the East Tennessee Historical Society and the St. Louis Mercantile Library Association, respectively.

JOHN A. BURNS, FAIA is an architect with the National Park Service, Historic American Buildings Survey/Historic American Engineering Record, editor of the book *Recording Historic Structures*, and co-author of the book *Yesterday's Houses of Tomorrow*.

R. H. CALDWELL is a part-time military historian at the Directorate of History and eritage, Department of National Defense, National Defense Headquarters, awa, Canada. He is a contributing author to the operational history of the l Canadian Navy in World War II.

GAVIN JAMES CAMPBELL received his Ph.D. in history from the University of North Carolina at Chapel Hill. He has published in the *Journal of American Folklore*, and is the music editor for *Southern Cultures*.

MARK C. CARNES is professor of history at Barnard College and served in 1982 as county historian of Orange County, New York. He has published *Secret Ritual and Manhood in Victorian America* and *Meanings for Manhood: The Construction of Masculinity in Victorian America*.

MICHAEL CASSITY is an independent professional historian. He has taught social history at the University of Georgia and the University of Wyoming. He makes his home in Laramie, Wyoming, and Mount Prospect, Illinois.

JEFFREY S. COLE wrote his dissertation on "The Impact of the Great Depression and New Deal on the Urban South: Lynchburg, Virginia as a Case Study, 1929–1941." He is a member of the history faculty and chairs the American Studies Program at King College in Bristol, Tennessee.

GOULD COLMAN is a historian of rural life and agriculture. For many years he was the archivist of Cornell University. He is now retired and serves on the Board of Education for the Ithaca [N.Y.] City School District.

REBECCA CONARD is associate professor of history at Middle Tennessee State University. She is the author of *Places of Quiet Beauty: Parks, Reserves, and Environmentalism*, as well as several articles on state parks, interpreting the built environment, and the integral nature of physical and cultural landscapes.

TERRY COOK is visiting professor, archival studies, Department of History, University of Manitoba, after a 23-year career at the National Archives of Canada. He has edited three national journals in archives or history, published extensively on archival issues, and lectured on every continent.

JAMES CORSARO is associate librarian of Manuscripts and Special Collections, New York State Library, Albany. As part of his responsibilities in the position, he has worked in all aspects of map librarianship.

TOM COSTA is associate professor of history at the University of Virginia's College at Wise, where in addition to local history, he teaches early American and pre-colonial African history.

JERE DANIELL is a professor of history at Dartmouth College, where he teaches a course on "The New England Town." He lectures frequently on local history topics, usually in the states of Maine, New Hampshire, and Vermont.

RONALD R. DAVIDSON is a student in the public history program at Kent State University. He received the master of library science degree from SUNY-Buffalo in 1995.

about the contributors

TERRY L. DAVIS is the executive director and CEO of AASLH, to which she came from the Indiana Humanities Council.

ROBERT DAWIDOFF is the Maguire Distinguished Chair and Professor of History at the Claremont Graduate University, and co-author with Michael Nava of *Created Equal: Why Gay Rights Matter to America* and *Making History Matter*.

CHRISTOPHER DENSMORE is university archivist at SUNY-Buffalo. He has written on archival administration, is co-editor of *Quaker Crosscurrents: Three Hundred Years of the New York Yearly Meetings*, and author of *Red Jacket: Seneca Orator and Diplomat*.

JOHN R. DICHTL is the assistant executive director of the Organization of American Historians. He is completing a doctoral dissertation at Indiana University on the subject of Catholic–Protestant interaction on the Midwestern frontier in the early republic.

DAVID A. DONATH is president of the Woodstock Foundation, Inc., which oversees the Billings Farm & Museum in Woodstock, Vermont, where he has been director of the museum since 1985. He is vice-chair of the Vermont State Advisory Council for Historic Preservation.

PETER EISENSTADT is editor of *The Encyclopedia of New York State* (forthcoming); he was managing editor of *The Encyclopedia of New York City* and author of *Affirming The Covenant: A History of Temple B'rith Kodesh, Rochester, N.Y., 1848–1998*.

BRUCE ELLIOTT teaches at Carleton University, Ottawa, Canada. He is the author of *Irish Migrants in the Canadas* and *The City Beyond*, which won the 1993 Fred Landon Award for the best book on Ontario local or regional history. In 1992 he received a certificate of commendation from the AASLH.

DAVID M. EMMONS is professor of history at the University of Montana. He is the author of *The Butte Irish: Class and Ethnicity in an American Mining Town, 1875–1925*.

TOYIN FALOLA is professor of history at the University of Texas at Austin. He is editor of the University of Rochester series on African History and the Diaspora. His most recent book is *Yoruba Gurus: Indigenous Production of Knowledge in Africa* (1999).

BARBARA FLEISCHMAN is president of the Board of Trustees of the Archives of American Art, which was founded by her late husband.

JAMES FOLTS is a historian with the New York State Department of Archives.

JOHN FOUSEK is currently associate director of the Center for Global Change and

Governance at Rutgers University, Newark, New Jersey. He is author of *To Lead the Free World: American Nationalism and the Cultural Roots of the Cold War Consensus*.

RHONDA HUBER FREVERT is curator of Local and Family History for the Newberry Library. She holds degrees in history and library and information science from the University of Wisconsin-Milwaukee.

MICHAEL FRISCH teaches history and American studies at SUNY-Buffalo. He is the author, with photographer Milton Rogovin, of the prize-winning oral history of deindustrialization, *Portraits in Steel*, as well as *A Shared Authority: Essays on the Craft and Meaning of Oral and Public History*.

DAVID GLASSBERG is professor of history and director of the public history program at the University of Massachusetts at Amherst. He is the author of *American Historical Pageantry* and other works exploring the place of the past in American life.

SUSAN GREENE is the principal of *American Costume Studies*, a consultation service and resource/study collection of nineteenth-century costume (<www.costumestudies.com>). She is based in Alfred Station, New York.

SUSAN GRIFFITHS was curator of the Mansfield Museum in Nottinghamshire, England, for nine years. She has a certificate in local history from Nottingham University, and since 1984 has been co-editor of *Local History Magazine*.

PETER DOBKIN HALL has been director of Yale's program on Non-Profit Organizations and lecturer in the university's economics department. He has recently been appointed Hauser Lecturer in Nonprofit Organizations at the Kennedy School of Government at Harvard.

CHANTAL HAMILL is a French law librarian. She has lived in Scotland for a quarter of a century and is engaged on a social study of the seventeenth-century West Lothian parish of Livingston. She edited *Scottish Local History* for several years, and is now the secretary of the Scottish Local History Forum.

JAMES L. HANSEN, F.A.S.G. is reference librarian and genealogical specialist, State Historical Society of Wisconsin. In 1994–1995 he was president of the Association of Professional Genealogists and is a fellow of the American Society of Genealogists.

BEATRIZ B. HARDY joined the staff of National History Day after teaching for five years. She earned her Ph.D. in colonial American history at the University of Maryland.

DEAN HERRIN is a historian with the Historic American Engineering Record, National Park Service, and co-founder of the Catoctin Center for Regional Studies Frederick, Maryland.

about the contributors

JAMES A. HIJIYA is professor of history at the University of Massachusetts-Dartmouth. He spent the 1960s in Spokane, Washington, and Providence, Rhode Island.

GRAHAM HODGES is professor of history at Colgate University. His most recent book is *Root & Branch: African Americans in New York and East Jersey, 1613–1863*.

ROBERT HOWARD came to local history via his activities as a local politician. In 1982 he co-founded the first Nottinghamshire (England) oral history project. Since 1984 he has been co-editor of *Local History Magazine*.

BARBARA J. HOWE is director of the public history program at West Virginia University and has worked with numerous local and community history projects. She has been a member of the AASLH council and an officer of the National Council on Public History.

MARTHA RUSSELL HSU moved, after many years in the reference department, to collection development at Olin Library, Cornell University, where she is responsible for selecting material in German literature and history.

CARTER HUDGINS is executive director of Historic Charleston Foundation. Prior to moving to Charleston, he was a member of the faculty of the department of historic preservation at Mary Washington College.

GEOF HUTH is the regional advisory officer of the New York State Archives and Records Administration, in the Region 4 Office, Queensbury.

JEFFREY HYSON is revising his dissertation, entitled "Urban Jungles: Zoos and American Society." He is an assistant professor of history at St. Joseph's University in Philadelphia.

MITCHELL A. KACHUN is currently visiting professor of history at Grand Valley State University in Allendale, Michigan, and is completing a book on African American emancipation celebrations.

CAROL KAMMEN writes editorials for *History News* and is the author of *On Doing Local History: Reflections on What Local Historians Do, and Why*, and *Pursuit of Local History: Readings on Theory and Practice*, and of twelve plays. She teaches history at Cornell University and is the appointed Tompkins County Historian.

MICHAEL KAMMEN teaches history at Cornell University and is the author of *American Culture, American Tastes: Social Change and the Twentieth Century*, in addition to *Mystic Chords of Memory: The Transformation of Tradition in American Culture* and a number of other books.

THEODORE J. KARAMANSKI is professor of history at Loyola University-Chicago. He s been a consultant with the National Park Service and other public agencies and private groups, is the author of four books of Midwestern history, and is the past president of the National Council on Public History.

DESMOND KENNARD was deputy director of Sydney's Powerhouse Museum and was the director of the Australian Bicentennial (Travelling) Exhibition. He is now principal consultant of *Museums in the Making.*

ROBERT J. KIBBEE is a reference librarian at Cornell University's Olin Library. He specializes in statistical resources, humanities bibliography, and electronic resources and services.

CHRISTINE KLEINEGGER is senior historian at the New York State Museum, Albany. Her research interests include women's history and social history. She is currently researching a social history of sleep.

SHEILA KOLLASCH is curator and registrar at the Desert Caballeros Western Museum in Wickenburg, Arizona. She is a professional-development workshop trainer for Presenting History on Stage.

DOUG KUPEL is a water-rights historian for the City of Phoenix.

DAVID E. KYVIG is professor of history at Northern Illinois University. In addition to co-authoring *Nearby History*, he wrote *Explicit and Authentic Acts: Amending the U.S. Constitution, 1776–1995* and edited *Unintended Consequences of Constitutional Amendment.*

LEO E. LANDIS is a curator at Henry Ford Museum & Greenfield Village. He received an M.A. degree in historical administration from Eastern Illinois University, and is completing his doctorate in agricultural history and rural studies from Iowa State University

GABRIELLE M. LANIER teaches historic preservation and public history at James Madison University. She is co-author, with Bernard L. Herman, of *Everyday Architecture of the Mid-Atlantic: Looking at Buildings and Landscapes.*

HERBERT I. LAZEROW is professor of law and director of the Institute on International and Comparative Law at the University of San Diego. His genealogical research includes major east-coast cities in the twentieth century, and the nineteenth-century Russian empire.

TERESA K. LEHR has written on the history of health care, and is co-author of *To Serve the Community: A Pictorial History of Rochester General Hospital, 1847–1997,* and author of *Let the Art of Medicine Flourish: The Centennial History of the Rochester Academy of Medicine.*

HARTMAN H. LOMAWAIMA is associate director of the Arizona State Museum, University of Arizona, curator of ethnology, and a member of the faculty in the

American Indian Studies Program. He serves as a council member of AASLH. Mr. Lomawaima is a Hopi from the village of Sipaulovi, Second Mesa, Arizona.

PHILIP LORD JR. is on the staff of the New York State Museum, with responsibility for the management of the Cultural Resource Survey Program, the state historic-marker program. He is currently researching travel in the 1790s.

BARRY MACKINTOSH is National Park Service bureau historian. He researches and writes on the history of the National Park Service, its parks, and its programs.

MARY K. MANNIX is the library director of the Howard County Historical Society and the Maryland Room manager of the C. Burr Artz Library, Frederick County Public Libraries. She is a co-moderator of H-Local, the H-Net listserv.

PHIL MAPLES is curator of the Baker-Ceberberg Museum and Archives of Rochester General Hospital and co-author of *To Serve the Community: A Pictorial History of Rochester General Hospital, 1847–1997.*

HARRY BRADSHAW MATTHEWS is associate dean of the Sondhi Limthongkul Center for Interdependence and president of the United States Colored Troops Institute at Hartwick College. He is the author of *Honoring New York's Forgotten Soldiers: African Americans of the Civil War.*

LAURIS MCKEE received her Ph.D. degree from Cornell University and is associate professor emerita of Franklin and Marshall College. Her field research sites are in the Andean region of Ecuador.

DAVID R. MCMAHON is a doctoral student in history at the University of Iowa in Iowa City. His dissertation explores the origins and impact of heritage tourism in Iowa. He contributed a chapter on sports for a forthcoming book on African-American history in Iowa.

PAGE PUTNAM MILLER received her Ph.D. degree in American history from the University of Maryland. Since 1980 she has served in Washington, D.C., as the executive director of the National Coordinating Committee for the Promotion of History.

VINCENT MILLIOT is maitre de conferences at University of Orléans and associate-scholar at the Institute of Modern and Contemporary History in France. He is a specialist in urban social history and contributred to the *Guide Pour l'histoire locale en France.*

R. LAURENCE MOORE has written widely on the subject of American religion and culture. He received his degree from Yale University and joined the Cornell faculty in 1972. He is the Howard A. Newman Professor of American Studies.

N. BROWN MORTON holds the Prince B. Woodard Chair of Historic Preservation at Mary Washington College. An international architectural conservator, he is co-author of *The Secretary of the Interior's Standards for Rehabilitation*.

JAMES D. NASON is a member of the Comanche tribe and is professor of anthropology and director of the graduate museology program at the University of Washington and curator of ethnology at the Thomas Burke Memorial Washington State Museum.

HAROLD R. NESTLER is a dealer of rare and out-of-print books. Compiler of *A Bibliography of New York State Communities* and *Encyclopedia of New York State Ephemera and Americana*, which contains over 20,000 entries (on three diskettes).

ALAN S. NEWELL is president and a co-founder of Historical Research Associates, Inc., a public history consulting firm. He has been active in the National Council on Public History and the board of editors for *The Public Historian*. Mr. Newell was elected president of NCPH for the term 2000–2001.

MARY BETH NORTON is a professor of early American history at Cornell University, where she has taught since 1971. She has published works discussing women's legal status in both the seventeenth and eighteenth centuries.

TYLER T. OCHOA is an associate professor at Whittier Law School. He received his A.B. and J.D. degrees from Stanford University. Before becoming a professor, he was in private practice and was a judicial clerk at the U.S. Court of Appeals for the Ninth Circuit.

CYNTHIA OGOREK is a historian and director of the Matteson Historical Museum, Matteson, Illinois. She is also one of the founders of the Calumet City Historical Society Museum, Calumet City.

TAMARA OHR-CAMPBELL is a freelance cartoonist from Chapel Hill, N.C.

GARY Y. OKIHIRO teaches at Columbia University. He is author of *Margins and Mainstreams: Asians in American History and Culture*, and is a past president of the Association for Asian American Studies.

SUSAN OUELLETTE has a degree from the University of Massachusetts at Amherst. Her special interests are in colonial America, and family and gender history. She teaches at Saint Michael's College in Colchester, Vermont.

KATHLEEN PAPARCHONTIS is a graduate student in public history. She is also a freelance indexer and copyeditor of scholarly books.

LESLIE PARIS is currently completing a dissertation at the University of Michigan, in the program in American culture, concerning interwar children's summer camps.

about the contributors

JAN PARTRIDGE is a lecturer in the Department of Information Studies, Curtin University of Technology, Perth, Western Australia. She is the president, Local Studies National Section, Australian Library and Information Association.

RANDALL L. PATTON is associate professor of history, Kennesaw State University. His publications include *Carpet Capital: The Rise of a New South Industry*, as well as articles in *Labor History, Georgia Historical Quarterly*, and *Atlanta History*.

PHILLIP PAYNE is a professor at St. Bonaventure University, where he teaches public and American history. His research interests are in local, industrial, and political history. Previously, he worked as the site manager of President Warren G. Harding's Home and Museum in Marion, Ohio.

JOHN PEARCE is director of the James Monroe Museum and Memorial Library and of the James Monroe Presidential Center. He is based at Mary Washington College in Fredericksburg, Virginia.

ROBERT PHELPS is currently an assistant professor at California State University, Hayward, where he specializes in the history of California and the American West. His current research focuses on the urban development of California.

JOSH PIKER received his Ph.D. degree in history from Cornell University, and is in the history department at the University of Oklahoma. He is currently working on a study of the eighteenth-century Creek Indian town of Oakfuskee.

RICHARD POLENBERG is Goldwin Smith Professor of American History at Cornell University, where he has taught since 1966. His most recent book is *The World of Benjamin Cardozo*.

NORMA PRENDERGAST received her Ph.D. degree in art history from Cornell University and is co-editor of this volume.

LAURA J. QUACKENBUSH is curator/administrator of the Leelanau Historical Museum, Leland, Michigan.

WILLIAM REEVES is an independent scholar in New Orleans.

PATRICIA REYNOLDS is museums development officer for Surrey, England, and a degree candidate at the University of York. She has a special interest in the study and interpretation of vernacular architecture.

GEOFFREY W. RICE is associate professor of history at the University of Canterbury, Christchurch, New Zealand. He was general editor for the revised second edition of the *Oxford History of New Zealand*.

ALAN ROGERS is with the University of Nottingham and is a scholar engaged in local-community history teaching and research. He is the author of several standard works including *Approaches to Local History* and *Group Projects in Local History*, as well as detailed local studies.

ED SALO is working on his doctorate degree in historic preservation at Middle Tennessee State University. He is focusing on the preservation of the United States's industrial heritage.

PHILIP SCARPINO teaches at Indiana University–Purdue University, Indianapolis. He is a specialist in public and environmental history, with publications and museum consulting experience that reflect those interests. He is presently at work on an environmental history of the Great Lakes that compares Canada and the United States.

CONSTANCE B. SCHULZ is professor of history and co-director of the public history program at the University of South Carolina, where she teaches archives administration. Her publications include editions of photographs from the Farm Security Administration, a videodisc of images for teaching U.S. history, and state history slide collections for Maryland and South Carolina.

MARSHA L. SEMMEL is president and CEO of the Women of the West Museum in Boulder, Colorado. She was previously president of Conner Prairie, a living history museum in Fishers, Indiana, and director of public programs at the National Endowment for the Humanities.

CAROL D. SHULL has worked in historic preservation for over 25 years and is keeper of the National Register of Historic Places and chief of the National Historic Landmarks Survey for the National Park Service.

JOEL SILBEY is a professor of history at Cornell University and a specialist in American political history. His most recent book is *American Party Battle: Election Campaign Pamphlets 1828–1876*.

PATRIZIA SIONE is a reference archivist in labor history at the Kheel Center for Labor–Management Documentation and Archives at Cornell University.

RAYMOND STARR is professor emeritus of history at San Diego State University where he taught and wrote about local history. His publications include *San Diego: A Pictorial History* and *San Diego State University: A History in Word and Image*.

BRIT ALLAN STOREY has taught at Auburn University; was deputy state historian, acting state historian, and research historian at the State Historical Society of Colorado, and was a historian on the staff of the Advisory Council on Historic Preservation. He is now senior historian of the Bureau of Reclamation.

RICHARD STRASSBERG is a historian of American labor and serves as the director of the Kheel Documentation Center at Cornell University, and as associate director of the Industrial and Labor Relations Library.

about the contributors

JAMES SUMMERVILLE edits and publishes the newsletter *Tennessee History*. His books include *Southern Epic* and *Nashville Through 200 Years*. He serves as the governor's representative on the Tennessee Historical Commission.

ROBERT P. TABAK is director of programs at the Balch Institute. He received his Ph.D. degree from Temple University, where his dissertation topic was "The Transformation of Jewish Identity: The Philadelphia Experience, 1919–1945." He is interested in the roles of myth, symbol, and public expression as aspects of ethnic identity.

JOHN TAYLOR is an associate professor of history at Carleton University in Ottawa, Canada. He is author of *Ottawa: An Illustrated History* and co-editor of *Capital Cities/Les Capitales*. He was a founding member of the Canadian Urban History Association and of the *Urban History Review/Revue d'histoire urbaine*.

RON THOMSON was trained in American history. He worked as an interpretive specialist for the National Park Service for 21 years. Now he operates Compass, a small business that provides interpretive planning and writing.

BRYANT F. TOLLES JR. is director of the museum studies program and associate professor of history and art history at the University of Delaware. He is the author of *The Grand Resort Hotels of the White Mountains* and *Summer Cottages in the White Mountains*. He teaches a course on the history of tourism in America.

WERNER TROßBACH studied in Berlin (West) and Bochum. He is a rural historian at the University of Kassel, Department of Agriculture (Witzenhausen).

MARIE TYLER-MCGRAW is a historian and education specialist with the National Park Service and an American studies Ph.D. recepient. She has worked in museums, public schools, and universities.

DAVID G. VANDERSTEL is the executive director of the National Council on Public History. He also serves as senior research associate in the Polis Center and as adjunct assistant professor of history at Indiana University–Purdue University, Indianapolis.

REN VASILIEV is a member of the department of geography at the State University of New York, Geneseo. One of her current research projects is a book about New York state placenames.

LAURIE WEINSTEIN is associate professor of anthropology at Western Connecticut State University. She is general editor for *Native Peoples of the Americas* series; her forthcoming edited volume is *Negotiating Land, Water and Ethnicities: Native Peoples of the Southwest*.

MARY L. WHITE is a graduate learner with the Union Institute who lives and works in Ithaca, New York. She has spent several years gathering information for a book on health-care providers of the Civil War era.

JAMIL ZAINALDIN has worked at the American Historical Association and the Federation of State Humanities Councils, and is a specialist in the fields of American legal history and the public humanities. He is president of the Georgia Humanities Council and adjunct professor at Emory University.